PACIFIC
PINOT NOIR

PACIFIC PINOT NOIR

A COMPREHENSIVE WINERY GUIDE
FOR CONSUMERS AND CONNOISSEURS

JOHN WINTHROP HAEGER

UNIVERSITY OF CALIFORNIA PRESS | BERKELEY LOS ANGELES LONDON

University of California Press
Berkeley and Los Angeles, California

University of California Press, Ltd.
London, England

Library of Congress Cataloging-in-Publication Data

John Winthrop Haeger,   1944-
Pacific pinot noir : a comprehensive winery guide for
consumers and connoisseurs / John Winthrop Haeger.
     p.   cm.
  Includes index.
  ISBN 978-0-520-25317-9 (pbk : alk. paper)
  1. Pinot noir (Wine)—California.   2. Pinot noir
(Wine)—Oregon.   3. Wine and wine making—
California.   4. Wine and wine making—Oregon.
I. Title.

TP557.H343   2008
641.2'223—dc22   2008013577

Manufactured in the United States of America
13 12 11 10 09 08 07 06 05 04
10 9 8 7 6 5 4 3 2 1
The paper used in this publication meets the minimum
requirements of ansi/niso z39.48-1992 (r 1997)
(Permanence of Paper).

Cover photograph: Sea Smoke Vineyards, Santa Rita
Hills, California. Photo courtesy Kirk Irwin.

To our memories of

Bryce Bagnall
Michael Bonaccorsi
Jimi Brooks
Duane Cronin
Reginald Oliver
and
Don Talley

Passionate growers and crafters of American pinot
noir who recently passed from the scene

CONTENTS

Acknowledgments

Like most wine books, *Pacific Pinot Noir* owes a huge debt of gratitude to the hundreds of men and women who grow and vinify pinot noir in California and Oregon. Time and again, these individuals have responded generously to requests for information and samples, made themselves available for long conversations, walked me through vineyards, explained the logic of their choices in both vineyard and cellar, tolerated endless and sometimes naïve questions, and raided their wine libraries for a few remaining bottles of old vintages. Their generosity has vastly outstripped self-interest and can be explained only by their genuine and serious commitment to getting the story of pinot noir in the Americas told as completely, accurately, and engagingly as possible. This book would not have been possible without them, and I am deeply grateful for their help throughout.

I am also grateful to colleagues and wine merchants throughout the country and overseas, and to organizations and events dedicated to wine appreciation and enjoyment for their friendly interest in *North American Pinot Noir* and for contriving opportunities to make it visible. Their interest was an indispensable prerequisite to *Pacific Pinot Noir*. Special thanks are due to Debbie Zachareas, Peter Granoff, and Ferry Plaza Wine Merchant in San Francisco; Nancy Girard and Half Moon Bay Wine and Cheese Shop in Half Moon Bay, California; Patrick Bouculat and Wine Cellars of Annapolis in Annapolis, Maryland; Tom Stephenson and Crush Wine & Spirits in New York City; Brian Duncan and Bin 36 in Chicago; James Handford MW and Handford Wines in London, England; Siobhan Turner and the Institute of Masters of Wine; Fred Dame and the Court of Master Sommeliers; Naoya Iki and Maruzen Company in Tokyo, Japan; Peter Palmer, Farallon Restaurant, and PinotFest in San Francisco; Amy Wesselman and the International Pinot Noir Celebration in McMinnville, Oregon; Felicia Montemayor and the World of Pinot Noir in Arroyo

Grande, California; Bill Knight and The Wine House in Los Angeles; Paul Smith and Woodland Hills Wine Company in Woodland Hills, California; Karen Cathey and the National Capital Chapter of the American Institute of Wine and Food; and Hanna Lee and the New York Chapter of Women for Wine Sense.

For special hospitality over the course of my research for *Pacific Pinot Noir*, I thank Milla Handley and Handley Cellars; Jean Sessions and Hanzell Vineyards; Greg La Follette, Cyndicy Coudray, and De Loach Winery; Richard Sanford and Alma Rosa Vineyards and Winery; and Bill Stoller and Stoller Vineyards.

A few individuals went to special lengths, provided exceptional data or private tutorials, or chased missing information on my behalf. Allen Meadows (the world famous *Burghound*) shared reflections on American and Burgundian editions of pinot noir. Cole Danehower (*Oregon Wine Report*) kindly provided a list of the Oregon producers *Oregon Wine Report* had covered. Ginny Lambrix (then De Loach Vineyards, now Truett Hurst Winery) took me on an uncommonly educational tour of vineyards in western Sonoma and provided numerous tutorials on viticultural issues. Roy Cloud (Vintage '59 Imports) joined forces to educate consumers about red Burgundies and American pinots. And the text would never have met its schedule without the talented and indispensable work of Gilian Handelman (then *Wine & Spirits*, now Kendall-Jackson Estates) who contacted scores of producers on my behalf, arranged dozens of appointments, and kept oceans of information under control as this book was going to press.

On the home front, the book depended absolutely on the patience and unflagging support of Julianne Frizzell, who tolerated endless tasting and spitting at dinner, a kitchen endlessly full of unconsumed bottles, and my all-too-frequent late nights at the computer.

As always, the responsibility for errors, omissions, and other shortcomings is mine alone.

When I wrote *North American Pinot Noir* between 1999 and 2003, wine publications and consumers had just begun to rediscover American editions of pinot noir after a long, cold winter of discontent. That book's seven main chapters covered pinot noir's European origins, what is known about its genetics, the history of its transplantation to North America, the regions where it is grown, its clones, the winegrowing and winemaking processes, and the delicate matter of how Burgundies and American pinots compare. Seventy-two American producers were then profiled, in an effort to tell part of the story through histories, descriptions, and assessments of individuals and businesses who had played or were then playing important roles in establishing the legitimacy of pinot as an object of viticultural and enological attention, and whose wines illustrated, more or less, the state of the art.

Four years after publication, the book's main chapters are still largely current, but the profiles have aged prematurely. Specific information about proprietors, winemakers, plantings, fruit sources, cellar treatments, and wine programs has changed, of course. A few iconic labels have changed hands entirely, and some veterans are now in business under new names. Furthermore, as I explain in the Introduction, the number of players has exploded. Some of this growth can be attributed to a vanity effect—a me-too scramble that may not be durable over the long run—but many of the new entrants are impressively serious and are at least as dedicated to pushing the envelope with American pinot as any of their predecessors were a quarter century earlier. Taken together, the seventy-two profiles in *North American Pinot Noir* now paint a much less satisfactory picture of the state of play than they did at the beginning of 2004. To set things right, an entirely new and much expanded family of profiles seemed well warranted, and for this updated collection I have chosen a new title, *Pacific Pinot Noir.*

With producer profiles identified as the new book's core content, it seemed important to establish a consistent and defensibly objective methodology for determining which producers to report. In *North American Pinot Noir*, I focused on producers with a substantial *stake* in pinot noir and with a *track record* consisting of at least four vintages made and released by press time. I also allowed my selection to be biased in favor of producers whose personal or corporate stories contributed disproportionately to the overall story of pinot in North America, because they were pioneers or early-adopters, or because they set benchmarks, made exemplary wines, or attracted special respect and attention from their peers. In the end, however, the criteria were soft and very imperfectly objective. Conversely, however, using totally objective criteria—such as "largest-selling brands" or "largest-selling restaurant brands"—would have been plainly incompatible with sensitivity to outstanding quality and sympathetic attention to small and often benchmark producers. Critic ratings, the meat and potatoes of the American wine industry, are nonobjective by definition, even when they are aggregated or averaged.

For this book, I wanted an approach capable of identifying producers who are more than routinely visible in the national marketplace for very good wines and who attract the attention of people serious about fine wine. This segment of the wine market can be defined as the channels and venues where wines are selected by knowledgeable and often passionate staff who usually have a tolerance for a variety of wine styles offered at a range of price points, who are not put off by wines that are available only in tiny quantities, and who taste constantly and quasi-comprehensively. Thus, it made sense to give special attention to producers who repeatedly figure on the lists of restaurants with very serious and intelligent wine programs or on the shelves of retailers with similar discipline. It also made sense to afford attention to the coverage of a few widely read and trusted critics—although not to their wine ratings—and to the participant lists of some of North America's largest consumer-and-trade events focused on pinot noir, where participation is filtered directly or indirectly by peer review. Because there is no way to derive from industry or regulatory sources a comprehensive list of wineries, producers, brands, or labels that make one or more editions of American pinot noir, nor is there a variety-based trade group, the producer list featured in this volume had to be built incrementally from the bottom up, not winnowed from the top down. In the end, I collated information from serious wine retailers and wine-friendly restaurants in major markets throughout the country, along with lists of winery participants (over the last five years) from the two largest consumer-and-trade events devoted to pinot noir, reviews from trusted critics, and the entire list of pinot producers known to *Wine & Spirits* magazine, regardless of whether or how favorably their wines were reviewed. This aggregation generated a base list that appeared to reflect producers' visibility in the *hand-chosen* marketplace. However, since simply collating the three dozen source lists produced more than 800 producer names, it was necessary to sift it. The inclusive list was reduced to 238 by eliminating producers whose names appeared fewer than three times in the combination of sources. Something in this range seemed a reasonable target: large enough to represent, more or less reasonably, the seriousness of purpose associated with pinot and the current state of play, but small enough to be managed in the time available.

The methodology is, of course, not unimpeachable. Its most obvious flaw is that only three dozen information sources were used—a very small sample of the nation's serious wine shops and restaurants with important wine lists. The small size of the sample means that some producers covered here would not have been covered if the list of selected retailers and restaurants had been compiled only slightly differently. Another limitation is that wine lists from my chosen sources also reflected, of necessity, producers whose wines were available at the time the lists were provided; such lists must be understood as snapshots, not as comprehensive histories of all pinot producers represented in the retailers' stocks or on the restaurants' lists over the course of the preceding or ensuing months or years. Overall, however, the list of 238 produced few serious anomalies. If skewed, it is biased in favor of qualitative superiority adjusted for price performance, which seems a reasonable outcome. Consumers can thus expect to find here information about *most* of the wines they will find on lists in good, pinot-friendly restaurants and on retail shelves where wines are carefully selected by knowledgeable staff.

Inevitably, a small number of the producers I sought to cover opted out, were unresponsive, or could not provide essential information. In a very few cases, it was simply impossible to make mutually convenient appointments. This reduced the final tally to the 216 producers featured in the Table of Contents. Once this final group was composed, my personal favorites and qualitative judgments were not a selection criterion, although personal favorites have been flagged.

One consequence of my selection methodology is that no producer outside what, in *North American Pinot Noir*, I called the Pacific Pinot Zone, survived into the final list. With utmost apologies to the intrepid pinot-makers working in British Columbia, Ontario, New York, Ohio, Michigan, Virginia, New Mexico, Texas, and other states, sometimes with impressive results, the entries in this book are ultimately confined to producers working in California and Oregon. Simply put, the Pacific Pinot Zone, which stretches from the mouth of the Columbia River to the Santa Barbara Channel and extends no farther inland than about 25 miles from the Pacific coast, accounts for more than 95 percent of North American pinot activity and for virtually all of the activity visible in interstate commerce.

Each profile contains a bit of history and background, either personal or corporate, as appropriate; a summary of wines produced now and in back vintages, including the vineyard sources for each; notes about winegrowing and winemaking protocols; an overall assessment of the producer's style with pinot; and tasting notes. This information cross-references the discussions of regions, plant material, winegrowing, and winemaking that were presented in *North American Pinot Noir,* but these discussions are not repeated in this book. Full-color regional maps that locate individual vineyards can also be found in *North American Pinot Noir*; only simplified, larger-scale black-and-white maps that locate American viticultural areas but not individual vineyards are included in this book. Readers unfamiliar with winegrowing terminology may wish to consult the main chapters of *North American Pinot Noir,* its glossary, or other reliable sources of general information like *The Oxford Companion to Wine* for help. With the exception of a few who are no longer in business or who no longer make pinot noir, most California and Oregon producers profiled in *North American Pinot Noir* are reprofiled here. Where stories or circumstances have changed since 2004, the profiles have been substantially revised, but some information has also been slightly condensed for reasons of space.

At the head of each profile, a series of small icons appears, which conveys information about that producer. The icons denote whether public tasting is available and whether it occurs regularly or by appointment; whether the producer's wines are based on estate-grown grapes, purchased grapes, or both; how much wine is produced; how extensively the producer's wines are distributed; and how the wines are priced. A key to the icons appears on page *xli*. Web sites and telephone numbers appear on page 411. Readers are advised to consult Web sites, or to contact wineries by telephone, for completely current information about visits, tours, and tasting. Producers themselves are also the best source of information about the availability of their products. The icons that represent total production and producers' distribution strategies, taken together, are a measure of how hard or easy the product may be to find, but nearly all producers are happy to provide specific details if asked, and most producers can and will ship to customers in most states.

In order to shorten the descriptions of winemaking that appeared in *North American Pinot Noir,* the present book assumes, in general, that most producers follow a common, consensus-derived protocol. Most begin by separating individual berries from their stems, and then discarding the stems. They then allow the fruit to macerate cool or cold before fermentation starts, to extract some color, flavor, and related "stuff" in a nonalcoholic environment. This step is called cold-soaking or prefermentation maceration. The fermentation vessels used for pinot noir—typically plastic bins, wooden cone sections, or stainless steel tanks—are usually topless, so that cellar workers have easy access to the fermenting fruit and juice and can manipulate them with their hands or feet, or with plungers. Most makers add an active, dried form of one or more cultured yeasts to each fermentation vessel to kick-start the fermentation process. New wine is generally drained or pressed off the skins, seeds, and other detritus when all the grapes' sugar has been converted to alcohol, although some makers prefer to press the must before full conversion or to extend skin contact after active fermentation ends. At this point the new wine goes into barrels where it is "raised" for at least ten months, directly or after a short period of settling in tanks. Blends—essentially decisions regarding which lots of wine will go into which final bottlings—are made during or at the end of *élevage*, and the finished wines are bottled, with treatments designed to ensure clarity and microbiological stability. In this book, most of the winemaking notes are confined to *departures* from this "consensus protocol," to interesting adaptations, or to the explanations individual winemakers give for particular choices. The most common of such, and perhaps also the most consequential, are elimination or truncation of cold-soaking, fermentation at very hot or very cool temperatures, full reliance on resident or ambient yeast populations for primary fermentation, long postfermentation maceration, and *élevage* that extends until after the following vintage.

Readers should be aware, when digesting these notes, that no artisan winemaker treats all grapes the same way, or the same way every year, since the properties of the fruit vary from year to year as a function of weather and other factors. Cellar conditions may also fluctuate. These descriptions reflect general approaches and

---

A WORD ABOUT BARRELS

Most red wines spend some period of time in oak barrels after fermentation and before bottling. This phase in the life of a wine is usually called by its French name, *élevage*, and wines so treated are often described in English as "barrel-raised." (Wines raised without time in barrels are usually called "tank-raised.") Winemakers' barrel choices are aesthetic and subjective, but they have a huge impact on wine style. In these pages, I try to capture the main elements of choice. These are, first, how long the wines spend in barrels; second, what percentage of the barrel stock is newly purchased for each vintage, versus the percentage that is being reused a second, third, or fourth time; third, from which manufacturers the barrels are purchased; fourth, whether the winemaker has a preference regarding where the stave wood for the barrels was sourced; and fifth, whether any idiosyncratic choices have been made about the dimensions of the barrels, the manner of their manufacture, or pre-use treatments after the barrels have been delivered. Most American pinot producers rely entirely on barrels coopered from French oak, on the theory that its flavors are subtler than Hungarian or American oak and more flattering to pinot. Wood from trees grown in the Allier, in central France, is said to be especially tight-grained, which means (in theory) that "oaky" and "vanilla" flavors leach slowly into the wine. Wood from trees grown in the Vosges, the mountain spine between Lorraine and Alsace, are usually described as imparting "sweet" or "meaty" flavors. Among widely used coopers, François Frères, well-known for intense flavors of chocolate and vanilla, is often chosen by winemakers who like barrels to leave a strong imprint on their wines; Remond, Sirugue, and Gillet are more frequently chosen by makers who place primary emphasis on subtlety, finesse, and bright fruit flavors. Many winemakers describe the signature of Rousseau barrels as exotic, imparting spicy, mocha, or earthy flavors. More information about barrels is found in Chapter 6 of *North American Pinot Noir*.

sensitivities, but these practices are not invariable or industrial formulae. It is also appropriate to bear in mind that when vintners pick grapes very ripe, for whatever reason, a variety of interventions and adjustments may be required in the cellar, including but not limited to additions of water, acid, or both, and additions of yeast nutrients to keep the active yeasts working even as the amount of alcohol rises during the course of fermentation. In some cases makers resort to industrial processes to reduce the percentage of alcohol in the finished wine or to stabilize wines that contain both unfermented sugar and yeasts or bacteria, using additives that deactivate microorganisms. Some makers are reluctant to talk about these matters openly, so their descriptions of winemaking may be elliptical. Generally, my notes reflect only what a winemaker has been willing to tell me.

Most profiles also report information about the vineyards from which the producer sources grapes. Some of these are so-called estate vineyards, which the vintner owns and farms; others are independently owned and sell grapes to one or several producers. When several producers source fruit from the same vineyard and use the vineyard name on the label, I flag this fact for easy cross-reference. As far as possible, I provide information about the location, geology, and mesoclimate of each site and describe when and how each vineyard was planted. Most winegrowers believe that various properties of site—soil, mesoclimate, aspect, exposure, and air circulation—are critical determinants of wine character and quality, especially when wine is made unblended, from grapes grown in a single site. They summarize these properties as "site-specificity" or use the French word *terroir*. How a vineyard is laid out, and when it was planted, can also be significant. Metrics like row orientation and vine spacing are much debated by viticulturists and winemakers, although it is generally (if not universally) accepted that older vineyards, where vine plants are fully established and deeply rooted, show site-specificity better than vineyards that have only recently begun to produce. It complicates the picture, however, that mature vineyards in California and Oregon (though not in France) almost always display wide vine spacing, whereas vineyards planted in the last decade and a half reflect a "modern" view that more vines per acre and less fruit per vine is associated with better wine. This view is deservedly controversial. Beyond the facts of planting, abundant evidence suggests that special viticultural practices, including dry, organic, and biodynamic farming, are not only good for the planet in general, but correlate well with better flavors in finished wine and better expression of site-specificity. Because these matters are all arguably consequential for finished wine, they are called out in many vineyard descriptions.

In addition, a major topic of discussion among winegrowers and winemakers is the identity of the plant material used in each vineyard. Although all the world's pinot noir has a common origin, mutation over time has created hundreds of distinctly different instances of the variety, among which growers choose today when they set out to plant or replant a vineyard. These instances of pinot, called selections or clones, are known by a jumble of overlapping alphanumeric designations and "common" names that are actually far from common and are sometimes also imprecise. A full discussion of clones and selections is found in Chapter 5 of *North American Pinot Noir*, but a few essentials are summarized in the box below.

Most insiders agree that clones are different and that they result in wines with distinctly different flavors and structural properties, but the fingerprint of clones is generally less distinctive than the stamp of the wine's *terroir*.

CLONES AND SELECTIONS OF PINOT NOIR

Most selections of pinot noir discussed in these pages fall into one of four groups:

- Selections made in France since about 1950 identified by three-digit numbers assigned by the Comité technique permanent de la sélection (CTPS). The most important subset consists of selections made in Burgundy that are commonly called "Dijon clones." Selections identified in these pages as "Dijon 113" and so forth fall into this group. These selections were not available in North America until the 1980s and 1990s, but now account for a majority of new plantings. Their common characteristics are low yields and early ripening. Many exhibit black-fruit rather than red-fruit flavors. Dijon 828 is an especially muddled story; see the Archery Summit Estate profile for details.
- Selections made in several European sites by persons affiliated with Foundation Plant Services at the University of California Davis between the late 1940s and the 1960s, and then quarantined, tested, and certified disease-free at Davis and distributed officially since about 1955. These selections are known by one- or two-digit numbers preceded with the "UCD" label, for example "UCD 4," but they also have common names. For example, UCD 4 is commonly known as the "Pommard clone." Selections in this category account for an overwhelming percentage of the pinot noir planted in California and Oregon before 1990.
- Selections made from California vineyards, then tested and certified at the University of California Davis. The earliest examples were distributed in the 1950s, but new selections are still made and released after testing and treatment, nearly every year. The most important selections in this category are the Martini clones, also known as UCD 13 and 15, which were widely planted in Carneros, in Monterey, and along the Southern Central Coast in the 1960s and 1970s.
- Undocumented selections taken directly from European vineyards, which have existed since the middle of the nineteenth century. Unlike other selections, undocumented selections often originated with cuttings taken from multiple vines, which makes them heterogenous "mass" selections rather than homogeneous "clonal" selections. Sometimes informally identified with the name of the European vineyard from which they were allegedly culled (e.g., the "La Tâche clone"), they are more commonly known by the name of an American vineyard where they were planted on this side of the water (e.g., "Mount Eden selection"). Because it has been illegal to import plant material without appropriate quarantine since 1948, many undocumented selections are dubbed "suitcase" or "Samsonite" clones in the trade.

As in *North American Pinot Noir*, the tasting notes at the end of each profile are intended to give readers a good picture of my recent experience with the producer's wines and a fair picture of what to expect from that producer, pinot-wise, overall. Most wines described in these pages were tasted at home, unblind, twice: once with food and once in clean-palate circumstances, using Riedel Vinum Burgundy glasses or their equivalent. In some cases, however, wines were tasted with producers, on their premises, or even at wine events, where some aspects of the tasting experience were beyond my control. Most of the individual wines described herein will have disappeared from the market before the book is published, however, so readers will be disappointed if they attempt to use *Pacific Pinot Noir* as a buying guide. Readers are also cautioned that all wine tasting is existential. Even the same wine will taste different to the same taster at different moments in time. All fine wines evolve constantly, and there is inevitable bottle-to-bottle variation. And pinot noir has a well-documented tendency to go through "tight" or "dumb" phases after it has been bottled, sometimes repeatedly. During such phases, the wine can seem aromatically mute or unexpressive, or flavor challenged.

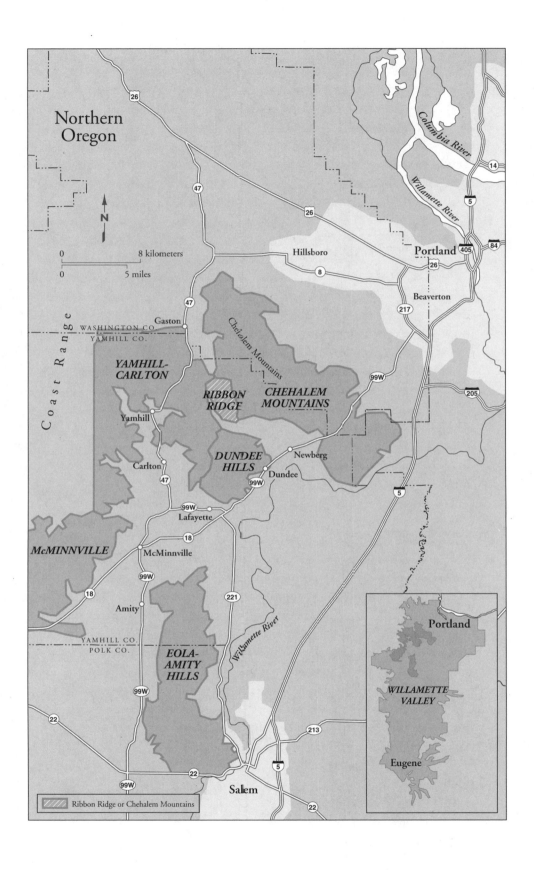

Northern
Oregon

0   8 kilometers
0   5 miles

N

Coast Range

Columbia River

Willamette River

Portland

Hillsboro

Beaverton

WASHINGTON CO.
YAMHILL CO.

Gaston

YAMHILL-
CARLTON

Chehalem Mountains

RIBBON
RIDGE

CHEHALEM
MOUNTAINS

Yamhill

Carlton

DUNDEE
HILLS

Newberg

Dundee

McMINNVILLE

Lafayette

McMinnville

Amity

YAMHILL CO.
POLK CO.

EOLA-
AMITY
HILLS

Willamette River

Salem

Portland

WILLAMETTE
VALLEY

Eugene

Ribbon Ridge or Chehalem Mountains

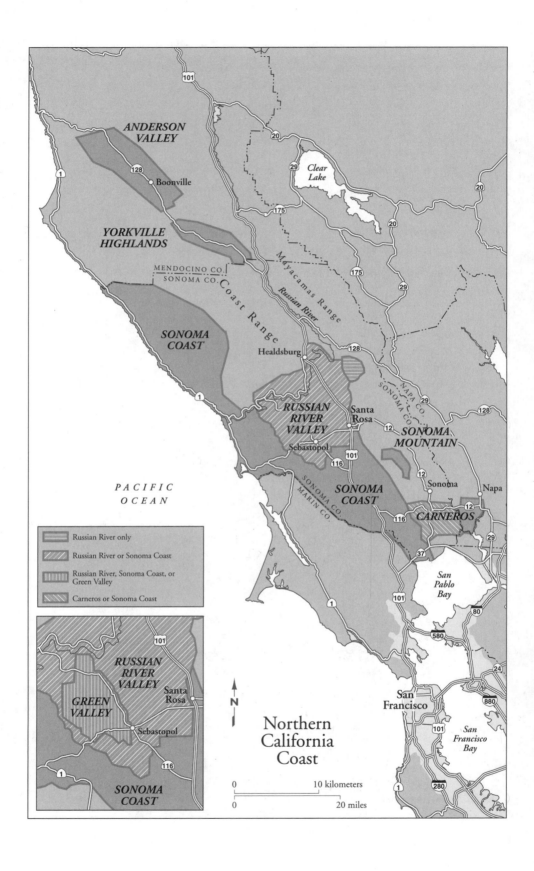

ANDERSON
VALLEY

YORKVILLE
HIGHLANDS

MENDOCINO CO.
SONOMA CO.

SONOMA
COAST

Boonville

Clear
Lake

Coast Range

Mayacamas Range

Russian River

Healdsburg

RUSSIAN
RIVER
VALLEY

Santa
Rosa

Sebastopol

SONOMA
COAST

SONOMA CO.
MARIN CO.

NAPA CO.
SONOMA CO.

SONOMA
MOUNTAIN

Sonoma

Napa

CARNEROS

PACIFIC
OCEAN

San
Pablo
Bay

San
Francisco

San
Francisco
Bay

Russian River only

Russian River or Sonoma Coast

Russian River, Sonoma Coast, or
Green Valley

Carneros or Sonoma Coast

RUSSIAN
RIVER
VALLEY

GREEN
VALLEY

Santa
Rosa

Sebastopol

SONOMA
COAST

N

Northern
California
Coast

0   10 kilometers

0   20 miles

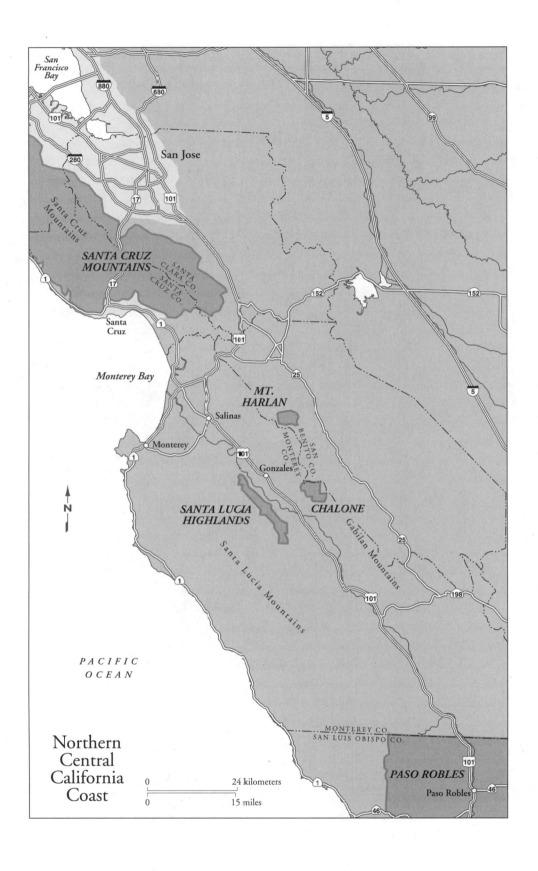

San
Francisco
Bay

880

680

101

280

5

99

San Jose

17

101

Santa Cruz Mountains

**SANTA CRUZ
MOUNTAINS**

SANTA
CLARA CO.
SANTA
CRUZ CO.

17

1

152

152

Santa
Cruz

1

101

Monterey Bay

25

5

**MT.
HARLAN**

Salinas

SAN
BENITO CO.
MONTEREY
CO.

SAN
BENITO CO.
MONTEREY CO.

1

Monterey

101

Gonzales

CHALONE

25

**SANTA LUCIA
HIGHLANDS**

Gabilan Mountains

1

Santa Lucia Mountains

198

101

PACIFIC
OCEAN

MONTEREY CO.
SAN LUIS OBISPO CO.

101

Northern
Central
California
Coast

0   24 kilometers

0   15 miles

PASO ROBLES

Paso Robles

46

1

46

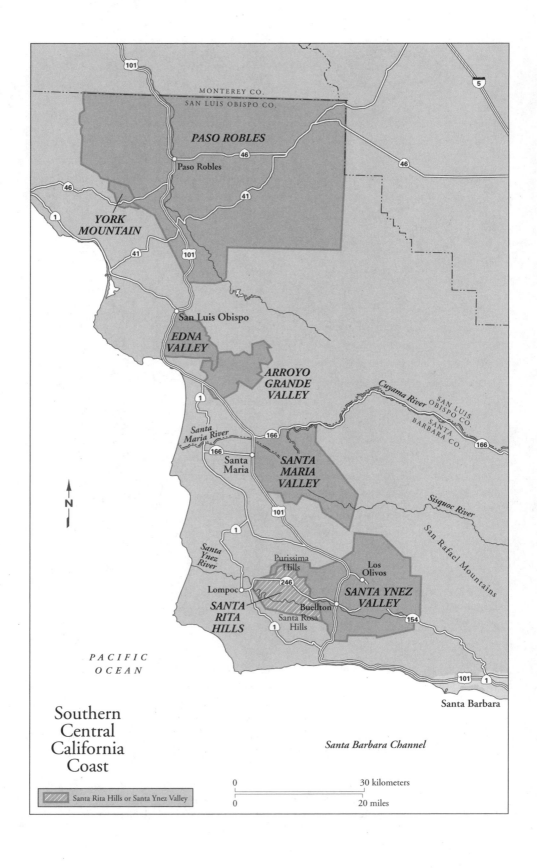

MONTEREY CO.
SAN LUIS OBISPO CO.

PASO ROBLES

Paso Robles

**YORK
MOUNTAIN**

San Luis Obispo

**EDNA
VALLEY**

**ARROYO
GRANDE
VALLEY**

Cuyama River

SAN LUIS
OBISPO CO.
SANTA
BARBARA CO.

Santa
Maria River

Santa
Maria

**SANTA
MARIA
VALLEY**

Sisquoc River

San Rafael Mountains

Santa
Ynez
River

Purissima
Hills

Los
Olivos

Lompoc

**SANTA
RITA
HILLS**

Buellton
Santa Rosa
Hills

**SANTA YNEZ
VALLEY**

*PACIFIC
OCEAN*

Southern
Central
California
Coast

Santa Barbara

Santa Barbara Channel

| Santa Rita Hills or Santa Ynez Valley |

N

0   30 kilometers
0   20 miles

THE STATE OF NORTH AMERICAN PINOT NOIR

It seems inevitable that any assessment of North American pinot noir in 2008 should begin with The Movie. *Sideways*, released in November 2004 by Twentieth Century Fox Film Corporation, is the story of two college buddies approaching middle age: one bitter, maladjusted, clinically depressed, and divorced; the other a failing actor, philistine, and lunk about to marry. The duo opt for a week of male bonding in Santa Barbara's wine country before the impending marriage. By Hollywood standards, it was a low-budget film, costing only about $17 million to make, and based on a novel for which the author had, at the time, been unable to find a publisher. It was generously reviewed; was nominated for four Academy Awards, one of which it won; and was a box office triumph, promptly earning its studio more than nine times the cost of its production. But the movie's greatest impact was on wine. As one critic observed, "*Sideways* is drunk on wine." Wine-talk metaphors suffuse its dialog. Wines, grape varieties, *terroirs*, and vintages are the stuff of the main characters' conversations. Cabernet, usually accepted as the king of red wines, is dismissed as a "survivor" grape that can "withstand neglect." Merlot is cast as the villain variety, produced for mass consumption. Pinot noir emerges as the main metaphor for the film's only legitimate romance: "thin-skinned and temperamental," it "can only grow in specific little tucked away corners of the world"; it "has achingly beautiful qualities," but "can be coaxed into its fullest expression" only when "someone has taken the time to truly understand its potential."

Almost overnight, millions of Americans who had previously lived insular wine-drinking lives in bubbles of cabernet, merlot, and chardonnay—who had often been barely aware that a variety called pinot noir existed—began asking for it by the glass in bars and restaurants, and scrabbling it up from the shelves of wine shops. The business of restaurants and winery tasting rooms in Santa Barbara County exploded.

Buellton's Hitching Post II restaurant, where the character played by *Sideways*'s female lead waitressed, tore through its remaining stock of Highliner, the prestige cuvée of its eponymous brand of pinot. At the Los Olivos Café, where the movie's lead characters dined together in an early scene, the telephone rang off the hook with requests for lunch and dinner reservations—specifically for the exact table where the scene had been filmed—and with requests for pinot by the glass and bottle when the guests arrived. Wineries throughout California and Oregon specializing in pinot found themselves overwhelmed by demand and scrambled to increase their production.

To understand how a movie with this kind of relationship to wine was made and how pinot noir, among varietal wines, came to play in its starring role, it is necessary to flash back, very briefly, to the very beginnings of American interest in European wine grape varieties, in the 1850s. Before then, the California wine "industry" was not interested in grape varieties for the simple reason that the entire landscape consisted of a *single* European variety, known in California as "mission." (We know now that mission was actually a Spanish variety also known as listan prieto and palomino negro, but at the time, no one knew or cared.) East of the Mississippi, American winegrowing depended almost exclusively on the grapes of American vine species and on hybrids bred from American and European species. Vulnerable to phylloxera, a small, root-feeding aphid native to eastern North America, European varieties perished whenever they were planted in the country's eastern third.

Beginning around 1850, in the wake of revolutions across Europe after 1848, the lure of the California Gold Rush, and a population shift from southern to northern California, the American wine scene changed fundamentally. Much of California's North Coast was settled by European immigrants. More than a few of these set themselves up as farmers and nursery operators. They imported a range of alimentary and ornamental plants from their homelands, including a large assortment of European wine grape varieties. Although zinfandel, whose European pedigree was very imperfectly understood and sometimes denied, quickly emerged as the most popular of the "new" European grape varieties by far, many of the varieties we know today—grenache, cabernet, riesling, and pinot noir, among others—gained significant toeholds. And in the second half of the century, European varieties became the basis for the first signal successes in American wine.

By the time the Columbian Exposition was held at Chicago in 1893, varietal American riesling, semillon, cabernet, malbec, and barbera were all on display, along with a so-called Chambertin produced by J. Gundlach and Company, a Sonoma- and San Francisco–based wine business, which was probably pinot noir, in whole or in part. Phylloxera, which moved west in the 1870s, and Prohibition, which began in 1919 with the adoption of the Eighteenth Amendment to the Constitution, set the industry back, but these events did not entirely disrupt its interest in dry table wines based on European varieties. After the amendment's repeal in 1933, business picked up more or less where it had left off, gradually laying the foundation for the dry, blend-averse, variety-based, ultra-premium business that dominates the entirety of the New World today. Pinot noir was an unhandicapped object of attention in this evolution, attracting notice from all the key players, including BEAULIEU VINEYARD, Inglenook, Paul Masson, Louis M. Martini, and Wente Brothers, as well as some of the state's first boutique vintners. Pinot noir made by Beaulieu and Fountaingrove, a Sonoma producer that disappeared in 1953, was served at Wine and Food Society tastings in New York immediately after World War II. Tom Marvel and Frank Schoonmaker, writing their post-Prohibition assessment of American wines in 1941, called pinot "the one serious rival to cabernet sauvignon in Napa, Sonoma, and the Santa Cruz Mountains," where it yielded "as good wines as it yields in general in France."

So far, so good—and not really the stuff of which movies are made. But late in the 1960s, quite suddenly and within the space of less than a decade, pinot's good reputation as a fine European variety, capable of being made into wines that could rival European benchmarks, disintegrated. Pinot began to disappoint seriously, repeatedly, and systematically. No longer a rival to cabernet sauvignon, which got steadily better, pinot became a combination of wayward child and black sheep: a persistent underperformer that drove producers crazy. It was termed "hard to grow and hard to make," was viewed as "temperamental" in the cellar, and was said to give plainly flawed wines. There were frequent reports of browning colors, "thin edges," "volatile off-odors," and "dirty" flavors.

This abrupt reversal of pinot's fortunes was a mystery to all concerned. Winemakers who had just "made it" a decade earlier, now debated *how* to make it and how to "solve its problems." Ferment the grapes with stems attached, perhaps, or without any stems at all, or ferment it very cold or very hot, or blend in some zinfandel or petite sirah at the end to replace the color that mysteriously disappeared? Confusion reigned. Even André Tchelistcheff, the Russian immigrant who was Beaulieu Vineyard's longtime winemaker and the godfather of the "modern" California wine industry, who had made perfectly good pinots himself in the 1950s, gave his fellow winemakers terrible advice. Some winemakers rushed off to Europe seeking a silver bullet for their troubles in Burgundy's hallowed cellars, but found none. Burgundy's winemakers were just plugging away as usual, although the state of their vineyards was deplorable following two decades' use of chemical fertilizers and herbicides.

In retrospect, the problem was clear enough: American winemaking had changed in the 1960s as new technology, processes, and equipment were adopted without much reflection simply because they were new, available, and affordable. The classic recipe for red wine had been replaced with an entirely new one that relied on industrial processes, heavy-handed intervention, risk minimization, and fault correction. It involved pumps, destemmer-crushers, harsh presses, and heavily toasted French oak barrels. Cabernet, zinfandel, and various red field blends tolerated these treatments fairly well; but pinot, possessed of much lesser concentrations of tannins and antho-cyanins, and differently structured chemically, was almost destroyed. When vintners tried to rescue their hollow shells of browning pinot by blending in substantial per-centages of other sturdier, deeper-colored varieties, they simply compounded one error with another and ended up with wines that had no varietal character at all. Before this catastrophe could be understood or rectified, a long list of benchmark producers, including Louis Martini, Sterling, Caymus, Freemark Abbey, and Heitz Cellars, had abandoned pinot to its fate and formed a chorus of nay-sayers who intoned, over and over, that pinot noir could not be made well in the New World. They forgot that it *had been made well* a generation earlier.

Pinot's renaissance after this debacle is the prologue to *Sideways* and to the real-life wine-world story behind its script. For the most part, the actors in the real renaissance were small producers who turned to pinot or persevered with it when industry stalwarts abandoned it, who turned their backs on the new universal red wine recipe introduced in the 1960s, and who applied considerable energy and dedication to succeeding where others had failed. Most of the names are with us still: HANZELL VINEYARDS near Sonoma, purpose-focused on pinot from the outset; CHALONE, near Pinnacles National Monument, where pinot noir had been planted (quite unaccountably) on the eve of Prohibition; MOUNT EDEN in the hills overlook-ing Saratoga, which assumed the mantle of Paul Masson and Martin Ray; Carneros Creek, where Francis Mahoney tried to sort out the special mysteries associated with pinot's subtypes, called clones; JOSEPH SWAN VINEYARDS, where a commer-cial airline pilot fascinated with wine planted pinot in 1970 near Forestville in the heart of what is now the Russian River Valley AVA; and CALERA, where Josh Jensen, who had discovered the charms of fine Burgundy when he read anthropology at Oxford found his grail for California pinot on a remote and unlikely hilltop in San Benito County. There were also Coury, Lett, Erath, and Ponzi, who studied climate data, concluded that all of California was too warm for pinot, and moved north to Oregon's Willamette Valley.

Since none of the pioneers save Hanzell founder James Zellerbach had significant financial resources, they kept their winemaking simple and low tech by necessity, which miraculously eliminated the technology-related problems that had ruined pinot's reputation a decade earlier. It also helped (though it was not crucial) that many of the new environments staked out by the pioneers were, in fact, cooler than mid-valley Napa. The pioneers' story as they planted vines in sometimes inhospitable sites and crushed grapes by hand in repurposed dairy tanks was a counterpoint of epic strife and operatic drama. Many of them self-described as members of a luna-tic fringe. Many admitted to pursuing a holy grail of wine. And pinot, the object of their attention, because it had behaved so badly before they began to tame it, was pronounced quixotic, capricious, petulant, and tantalizing. It was the stuff of epics, or opera, or something, just waiting for the right artist. And it could certainly become metaphor for a gentle, timid romance.

First, however, pinot's good name had to be partially redeemed. Some remarkably good wines were made in the 1970s: Joseph Swan's 1973, THE EYRIE VINEYARDS'S 1975 South Block Reserve, and the inaugural vintage from Sanford & Benedict in 1976. But pinot's reputation took time to reestablish among the cognoscenti, as well as among disappointed consumers, who had fled when it underperformed at the end of the 1960s. Many observers argue that the consumer tide did not begin to turn until the end of the 1980s. One milestone was set when WILLIAMS SELYEM'S 1985 Rochioli Vineyard Pinot Noir was named sweepstakes winner among *all* wines judged at the 1987 California State Fair, and Williams Selyem, hitherto unknown and operating from a garage like any good *garagiste*, was chosen as winery of the year. Larry Brooks, who had been making pinot at ACACIA since 1979, remembers 1988 as the first vintage "of low supply and great demand," and the first to create a "feeding frenzy" when it hit the market in 1990. During the 1990s, vineyard acres dedicated to pinot noir quintupled in Oregon, exploding from about 1,000 to more than 5,000; in California pinot acreage more than doubled. The price charged and paid per ton of grapes rose too, soaring (in California) from $804 a ton in 1991 to $1,849 in 2001. Cabernet specialists like W. H. SMITH (of La Jota Vineyard on Howell Mountain), Joseph Phelps, and Steve Girard birthed pinot noir projects, and producers like Louis Martini and Caymus, who had abandoned pinot in the 1970s, sought reentry paths. There had been only a few dozen pinot producers in California and Oregon combined in 1990; there were several hundred by the turn of the new millennium.

In the same sense that social revolutions arise not from starvation and repression but from rising expectations, *Sideways* would have been written differently—and might not have featured pinot at all—if it were not for the quantum leap in enthusiasm about pinot that swept across the American wine scene in the 1990s. Cloaked in the imagery of David-sized producers growing pinot outside of mainstream wine regions like Napa Valley and succeeding where Goliaths had failed, and wrapped in a producer vocabulary of gentle treatment and minimalist winemaking suffused with requirements for consumer sensitivity as the prerequisite for vinous epiphanies, pinot became a perfect metaphor for the fragile, unlikely love story *Sideways*'s author wanted to tell and wanted his audiences to remember, in spite of the comic debauchery with which he surrounded it. In the end, *Sideways* owes its charm and coherence to pinot's special story; just as pinot owes *Sideways* for its spurt of double-digit growth.

In the movie's wake, people who care about wine trends and about pinot tend to ask four questions: first, is the so-called "*Sideways* effect" real; second, is it durable; third, has the boom, such as it is, been good *qualitatively* for the variety; and fourth, is pinot noir disproportionately affected by the general industry tension, involving producers, critics, and consumers, between elegant wines on the one hand and massive wines on the other. The short answers to these questions are, respectively, yes; probably; it-is-much-too-soon-to-tell; and it-depends-on-whom-you-ask. The somewhat longer answers go like this:

The *Sideways* effect is a statistical reality as far as wine sales are concerned. The A. C. Nielsen Company, the same firm that produces the audience share ratings for television programs, compiles data that tracks so-called "supermarket sales" of all products identified with "universal" bar codes. For the thirteen-week period ending in early June of 2005, compared with the same period a year earlier, Nielsen found that "supermarket" sales of pinot noir had risen 83 percent in dollar terms and 77 percent by volume—one of the largest year-on-year increases in the history of wine-sales data. Double-digit increases persisted, year-on-year, from 2005 to 2006 and from 2006 to 2007, although the slope of the curve flattened. Given that a large percentage of high-priced wine is not sold through outlets tracked in supermarket-scan data, Nielsen's calculations probably *understate* the real increase, especially in dollar terms. Industry sources report that 93 percent of online wine sales involve wines priced higher than $20 per bottle. In restaurants, wine sales are tracked by *Wine & Spirits* magazine's annual poll, which gathers data from about 300 restaurants in major markets throughout the country and specifically documents sales in the last calendar quarter of each year. *Wine & Spirits* found that pinot, as a percentage of top selling wines overall, increased from 10 to more than 13 percent from 2004 to 2005—a more than 30 percent increase—and by almost another 2 percent from 2005 to 2006, with almost 90 percent of the action having been associated with American pinot—not with red Burgundy or other imports. Sommeliers told *Wine & Spirits* early in 2007 than pinot noir was "still hot," with sales so intense that maintaining inventory was a growing struggle. One Los Angeles restaurant reported a decline in the number of pinots on offer from four pages on the restaurant's list to three, only because the wines sold out faster than they could be replaced. Prices rose, too. A number of producers who had compensated for the overall market downturn after 9/11 by introducing "entry-level" pinots priced to sell for around $15 a bottle, raised the price point for these wines to $18, $20, or even $22 without encountering any resistance from the market. Increases of 10 or 15 percent in the prices asked for high-end bottlings were also typical. On restaurant lists, these hikes were reflected in a 21 percent average increase, from $53.66 to $64.20, between 2004 and 2006. At the same time—and offering an interesting commentary on wine price behaviors, especially in restaurants—the average price for merlot, *Sideways*'s villain, also rose from 2004 to 2006, though by only 12 percent.

Unhappily for producers, the vintage on offer when the movie appeared—2003—was based on a very small crop in California's pinot-friendly regions. In Sonoma, the state's largest pinot-producing county, the crop was the smallest in seven years. Oregon had been plagued with pathological heat, which gave rise to many wines that were no one's favorites. The 2004 vintage was not much better. The crop was once again smaller than average, and hot weather was again problematic, although this time in many parts of California, and especially along the southern Central Coast, rather than in Oregon. In 2005, the first growing season in which the industry could truly react to *Sideways*, yield (expressed as tons per acre) still lagged behind historical averages, but a very large increase in the amount of bearing acreage (the result of new plantings coming into production) more than compensated, resulting in bumper quantities when the 2005 vintage was released to the market late in 2006. In 2005 California crushed almost 25,000 more tons of pinot than it had in 2004, an increase of almost 36 percent; Oregon producers crushed almost 3,000 additional tons, for an increase of 30 percent. Existing producers bought as much fruit as they could find, and the number of producers exploded.

Although there is no reliable data on the number of wineries making pinot noir, I estimate that the number of commercially visible producers grew from between 400 and 450 in 2003 to between 950 and 1,000 by the end of 2006—an approximation which includes neither the dozens, perhaps hundreds, of vanity brands made in tiny quantities, nor the hundreds of home winemakers operating without a bond. With more producers scrambling for more fruit, the overall grape surplus that began in 2001 and touched pinot noir briefly in 2003 was completely absorbed before the 2005 crop was picked. The buyer's market for pinot grapes that had existed briefly in 2003 was turned upside down, and the average price per ton set a new record in 2006. Non-estate producers without firm, long-term contracts reported stiff competition for fruit, and many saw coveted sources disappear. In Oregon, one independent vineyard with a stellar reputation for good pinot placed its entire crop under contract to a restaurant consortium for fifteen years, beginning with the 2007 harvest, thus shutting out a large number of small producers who had been regular fruit clients for two decades or more.

The longer answer to the second question—whether the *Sideways*-induced boom and the renaissance of consumer interest that followed it can persist—is necessarily speculative. There are many reasons to predict that continuing double-digit increases beyond 2008 are unlikely. The American wine consumer, aided and abetted by wine publications' appetite for new news, has always displayed a persistent affinity for novelty, and today's novelty is tomorrow's boredom. In New World wine, because of varietal labeling, the sensations of novelty and boredom are easily attached to grape varieties. Sales of chardonnay, once so much the darling of the California wine industry that it was proclaimed synonymous with white wine, have plummeted by half in the last twelve years, as consumers say they will drink "any white wine but chardonnay." Now riesling, which had almost been displaced entirely by chardonnay when the latter boomed in the 1970s, shows signs of revival. Merlot, the fastest-growing variety in the 1980s, has lost ground steadily since 2000 and has plunged in popularity since being reviled in *Sideways*. In Oregon, one very good pinot-maker told his customers in 2007 that "those fickle American wine consumers will eventually latch on to 'the next big thing.'" He is almost certainly right to assume that pinot's current popularity will have no greater staying power than other varieties had commanded before it. In fact, it may have less for two reasons: First, it is intrinsically expensive. Supply and demand aside, pinot is expensive to produce simply because it is a shy-bearing variety. The corollary of this proposition is that it is hard to be successful economically with inexpensive pinot, so the large brands that sustain profitability in the wine business are difficult to build. Second, pinot makes a wine, as Dorothy Gaiter and John Brecher explained in the *Wall Street Journal* (September 8, 2006), "that you have to go to, because it won't come to you." As the *Sideways* script expresses the same observation, pinot is not "bold" or "proud," but "nuanced" and "restrained." Since this portrait, like Rembrandt drawings and art-house movies, demands effort and investment from the consumer, pinot seems an unlikely candidate for universal appeal, except perhaps in Burgundy, where everyone grows up with it. Many palates accustomed to lustier reds will find pinot insufficiently expressive or just plain lightweight, thin, and underwhelming. However, pinot's slim chance for continued double-digit growth does not mean it cannot grow a bit more, slowly, for at least the immediate future, or that the gains of the last three years will disappear as consumers flee to "the next big thing." It is reasonable to argue that pinot is at least a bit insulated from downturn by the sheer smallness of its total market share even after three years of double-digit growth. American consumers may have spent $132 million on pinot noir in 2005, and this may have represented a 60 percent increase over the previous year, but it is still only about half of what was spent on pinot grigio, a quarter of what was spent on merlot, and 13 percent of what was spent on chardonnay. Unless the current perception that pinot noir actually represents good value plus hedonistic pleasure, despite its relatively high price point, is undone, it is reasonable to imagine that pinot could hold onto its slightly improved share of the total wine market for a considerable time. It is in fact possible to argue that pinot's truly minuscule market share in absolute terms (it accounts for only about 2 percent of worldwide wine-grape acreage and barely more than 1 percent of worldwide wine production) makes the recent mini-boom more of a correction than an unsustainable advance, bringing actual consumption rates closer to the levels reasonably associated with its international reputation for excellence.

On the production side of the ledger, there is little reason to foresee an excess of supply in the immediate future, although a glut is not impossible to imagine over the longer term. Despite a more than threefold increase in planted acreage devoted to pinot noir in both California and Oregon since 1990, planted but non-bearing acreage, which is usually taken as an excellent predictor of future production since grapevines must be planted at least two years before they produce a commercially viable crop, is near an all-time low. In Oregon only 14 percent of planted pinot acreage was non-bearing in 2005, down from a high of 30 percent in 2000. California's circumstances were similar, with 8 percent of planted pinot acreage being non-bearing in 2005, down from almost 20 percent in 2000.

The longer answer to the third question—whether the spotlight, booming sales, increased production, and lengthening list of players has been genuinely good for the product—is almost impossible to address objectively or conclusively. Everyone asks whether there are better pinots now—or perhaps individual wines that are more consistently successful from year to year—or whether there are simply more of them. Or, conversely, they wonder whether pinot has actually suffered a qualitative decline as more wines from more producers and more young vineyards have come to market. A proper answer would require consistent diachronic data, adjusted to eliminate the idiosyncrasies associated with individual palates and tastes, compiled across multiyear period before *Sideways* and after with each period long enough to eliminate the potentially skewing effect of better and lesser vintages. But the growing list of players and increasing number of wines produced has had such a dramatic impact on the number of wines critics are reviewing that two samples taken, say, from 1998 to 2003 and 2005 to 2010 might lack comparability based simply on sample size.

But here is what we can say, based on data that we do have: First, snapshots of American pinot noir taken by various observers since *Sideways* are generally consistent with standard bell-shaped-curve distributions of wine quality: a few top-quality wines are produced, a much larger number of "good" wines stack up beside them, quite a few average efforts occur, and a small number of underperformers trail down the other end of the curve. Evaluating North American pinots in April of 2006 with a Master-of-Wine–studded panel of professionals, Britain's much-respected *Decanter* magazine tasted through 197 wines, rated 2 as "outstanding," 13 as "very good to excellent," 106 as "good," and 14 as "poor," suggesting to the editors that the scene was characterized by a "preponderance of very attractive, well-made and competent wines," and "relatively few duds." *Wine & Spirits*'s screening panels, composed of sommeliers, retailers, winemakers, and other wine professionals, picked 50 recommendable pinots from a field of 167 tasted early in 2007, and awarded 90 or more points to 28 of the 50. The world's largest-circulation wine magazine, *Wine Spectator*, awarded 90 or more points to 18 percent of the 472 California pinots it reviewed during 2005 (results reported in 2006), and another 42 percent scored between 85 and 89 points. Such distributions are quite similar to those seen for other varieties. For example, *Wine Spectator*'s 2005 results for pinot were mirrored almost perfectly by its analogous results for syrah.

Second, it may be significant that new producers do not seem to operate at any disadvantage. Indeed, producers entirely new to the wine scene since 2000 took some of the top honors for pinot when the 2005 and 2006 vintages were reviewed in the *Wine Advocate* and the *Wine Spectator*, with first, second, or third releases often outshining wines made by producers with much longer track records. Although this data is not statistically significant, it does not suggest any *prima facie* correlation, or inverse correlation, between length of track record (aka "experience") and quality of wine. It must be observed, however, that newly-minted producers are not always novice winemakers. In some instances, very experienced winemakers create new brands; in other cases, experienced and talented viticulturists and winemakers provide back-up for new labels, sometimes serving as contracted winemakers or consultants, or as winemakers-in-fact at custom-crush operations. It is probably also relevant that a growing number of producers means the arrival of a critical mass of human talent in most pinot-friendly regions—a raft of informal advisors freely available and close at hand—and the development of institutionalized information- and experience-sharing venues like the Steamboat Conference held annually in Oregon. Indeed this bit of sociology may turn out to explain how growing interest and an increasing population of players, far from threatening wine quality, actually improves it across the board, as the proverbial rising tide lifts all boats.

In addition, both experienced producers and new producers seem to do well with fruit from young vineyards, challenging the conventional wisdom that the best wines come from old vines in great sites. Here the offset probably has to do with critical and consumer acceptance of wine styles that are ripe and fruit-forward, and therefore tend not to discriminate between young vines and old. But it is probably also relevant that expensive precision farming, once reserved for fine, proven, and mature vineyards, is now lavished on young vineyards as well, as new winery business plans require that expensive wines be made from young vines virtually from the outset. It is also the case that new plantings tend to be concentrated cheek-by-jowl with vineyards that have already proven their potential, tempering the risk of failure or irretrievable mediocrity. Consider the venerable Sanford & Benedict Vineyard at the west end of the Santa Ynez Valley, now surrounded by an entire appellation of young pinot plantings. Consider Joseph Rochioli's and Charles Bacigalupi's first efforts with pinot in the Russian River Valley, which have been stretched into a virtual carpet of vines extending almost 10 miles along Westside Road between Healdsburg and Guerneville. Note the first plantings in Oregon's Dundee Hills, which have been transformed into the state's densest concentration of pinot noir. Even David Hirsch's near-pioneer planting on the True Sonoma Coast north of the Russian River has attracted neighbors.

The longer answer to the fourth question is long indeed. Debate has swirled for some years about the tendency of New World wines to be made generally "bigger," with higher finished alcohol and from fruit picked when it has accumulated more sugar—than "classically proportioned" wines from Bordeaux, Burgundy, Barolo, and elsewhere in Europe. Sometimes this debate is restated not as a contrast between the New World and the Old, but as an evolution within both worlds, between wines made thirty years ago and those being made today. Insofar as this issue concerns pinot, I explored many of its parameters in *North American Pinot Noir*. I add here that the debate demands restatement as an inquiry into the permissible boundaries of wine style.

In its simplest form, as it affects pinot, the question regards the aromatic, flavor, and textural bandwidth in which pinot can be expressed without losing its quality or essence: how full-bodied, rich, warm, lush, dense, or dark can a pinot be before it has become caricatured, untrue to variety, or qualitatively flawed? Or, conversely, how much subtlety and understatement can it embrace before it underperforms and disappoints? Is an utterly transparent, lightly tinted pinot with intense floral and spice flavors a triumph, or (as one American winemaker has argued publicly) is it a marketplace liability? All other things being equal, is a pinot that looks and tastes like a syrah, or that leaves a burning sensation on the consumer's lips after the wine is swallowed, still qualitatively praiseworthy as a pinot?

If these hypothetical situations are extreme, there are a host of slightly less extreme formulations encountered constantly, by professionals and ordinary consumer alike, at tastings held in wine shops and at pinot-centric events around the country, month in and month out. If there are overriding differences in shape, weight, flavor, and structure between two wines made from the same variety, is that difference rooted in fundamental differences between sites (i.e., is it a matter of *terroir*), or is it deliberately and specifically stylistic? Finally, and perhaps most important, are there properties of pinot noir, compared to other red grape varieties, that argue for defining the bandwidth of permissible style more broadly, or more narrowly, than the analogous ideal bandwidth for other varieties?

Understanding style, and its legitimate limits, means first unscrambling *terroir* and winemaking. In its simplest form (although the matter is anything but simple), *terroir* is the idea that site makes and marks wine, or at least that this is the case with unblended wines made from grapes grown in a single, specific place. Dedicated *terroir*ists believe that, as long as the grapes are well farmed, various properties of site, most of them physical, will be expressed in well-made wines. This is the perspective behind assertions like "wine is made in the vineyard," "winemakers are intermediaries between *terroir* and wine," and "winemakers are passive actors in the transformation of grapes into wine." There is huge truth behind this perspective, which now has considerable currency on both sides of the Atlantic, as tastings of different wines from the same or almost the same site often attest. It is not the whole picture, however. Despite periodic assertions to the contrary, fine wine does *not* make itself. Each instance of fine wine is the product of an enormous matrix of individual artisan choices, some philosophical; some environmental; some truly independent; and some conditioned heavily by the circumstances of farming, weather, fermentation chemistries, and cellar logistics. Winemakers differ, even when they are using essentially the same grapes from the same place, in their tolerance for risk and in their image of the wine they want to make. Even two dedicated *terroir*ists may differ in their judgments about the various properties of site that should be expressed in its wines. This space is the province of wine style, and the territory is vast. As Remington Norman makes clear in *The Great Domaines of Burgundy* (New York, 1992) the debate over *terroir* and style, midwifery and cooking, passive winemaking and style-driven intervention, is alive and well even among Burgundian *vignerons*, who are often seen as the purest *terroir*ists anywhere, and stylistic variations among Burgundians are ubiquitous. Anyone who has compared Clos de la Roche made by Hubert Lignier with Clos de la Roche made by Pierre Amiot, to cite just one example, has seen style at work.

But in Burgundy the province of style is often constrained by the marginality of the mesoclimates, except in pathological vintages like 2003. On this side of the Atlantic, wine style is a vaster territory, simply because, in many vintages, choices are possible in pinot-friendly regions of North America—including Oregon—that are usually impossible in the higher-latitude regions where pinot is grown in Europe. We often say the difference is about very ripe flavors and elevated alcohol levels, but we could better say that it is about the balance between primary flavors and aromas such as fruit, flowers, and earth, and secondary properties, which can include a wide array of animal, vegetal, bacterial, and process-derived indicators. Many winemakers profess "zero tolerance" for brettanomyces, a yeast associated with volatile phenols that tend to smell either like animal skins or like cloves; others think small concentrations of "*brett*" improve the complexity of pinot. Style is involved when winemakers decide how hot to ferment and how much to manipulate the cap of skins and seeds that fermentation pushes to the top of each fermentor. It is involved when they decide whether to press new wine off the skins before all the grapes' sugar has been converted into alcohol, or to keep the new wine in contact with the exhausted skins for a week longer, or for two or three. It continues through the choice of barrels, which have a huge impact on the aromatic properties of young wines, and the decision of how long the wine is kept in barrels before being bottled, which impacts the color and how "primary" the wine tastes when it is released. Quite a few of these choices also impact texture, palate length, and the taste of the wine after five, ten, or twenty years of bottle age.

A good case can be made that all stylistic choices are more consequential with pinot than with other red varieties because pinot is typically less generously endowed with the customary stuff of red wines—especially tannins and anthocyanins. Just as it is uncommonly transparent to *terroir*, it also shows more vividly (for better or worse) the marks of stylistic choices and interventions. For two generations at least, this has translated into a sizeable bandwidth for style-driven variations among pinots, Old World and New, as well as to more disagreement (or perhaps just more confusion) about the properties of good pinot than we see with any other variety. As early as the 1980s, when veteran wine writer Norm Roby convened variety-specific tasting panels for *Vintage* magazine, he cited major intra-panel rifts over acceptable tannin levels, body style, and volatility in pinot noir, with some panelists preferring light and delicate styles and others privileging intensity of flavor. "For many pinots," Roby wrote, "two tasters loved it, two hated it, and two felt it was just average in quality."

This sort of disagreement is still with us a quarter century later. I taste often with winemakers who comment critically if a given wine seems substantially marked (with smoky and vanilla-based flavors) by the barrels in which it was raised. Diametrically opposite comments on the same wines can be found in some mainstream critical reviews. Very fruit-forward wines can seem underwhelmingly simple to some tasters, whereas to others, making wines in this style can seem a totally apposite choice. DAVID BRUCE, the Santa Cruz Mountains producer who has now made forty-seven vintages of American pinot noir, wrote to me recently that he has "learned to exaggerate fruit-forwardness" because "this is our palate." Others are far less accepting. The concentration of ripe-picked, high-alcohol wines among the wines scored highest by national publications and nationally influential critics has led to criticism that critics are driving a perceived trend to bigger wines. Bigger wines do appeal to critics and consumers alike for reasons of lushness, voluptuousness, substantial mouthweight, and dark, impressive flavors. Opposers of this style accuse winemakers of crafting wines that are cynically designed to grab points. When winemakers respond, they often refuse to admit that their style was the consequence of choice—in the vineyard and in the winery—alleging instead that they were constrained by circumstance. Relatively warm climates, young vines, clean clones, and other viticultural circumstances, they say, caused sugars to accumulate faster than the grapes could ripen physiologically. To get physiologically ripe grapes, they claim, they were forced to accept very ripe flavors and alcohol levels that were not seen any place in the wine world until relatively recently.

In truth, as far as pinot noir is concerned, it probably has not helped that most new plantings in California and Oregon have been done with clonal material from France selected specifically to privilege early ripening; or that a large percentage of American vineyards are still planted, as they have been for more than a century, in sites where the soils are too high in nitrogen to favor fruit development over canes and leaves; or that there is now enough money in the wine industry to use vine-by-vine farming, which ensures that the slightly underripe clusters that used to be picked and fermented along with the ripe ones are now eliminated before harvest. There is also growing evidence to suggest that various cultivation practices, sometimes including irrigation, may be exacerbating the disconnect between sugar ripeness and physiological ripeness, making long "hang times" self-defeating. But it is time to admit that, nine times out of ten, *very ripe picking is a matter of choice and not of necessity.* Grapes are being picked very ripe because, in the Indian summer conditions that prevail in most California regions for early-ripening varieties like pinot noir, and in most recent Oregon vintages, there is no compelling reason to pick earlier, so winegrowers are free to *choose* riper picking. Since it is almost always equally possible to pick earlier—the proof of which is that some vintners do and are able to make excellent wines—it is fair to conclude that most of the time, very ripe picking is a stylistic choice. The question for American pinot is this: when the choice to pick very ripe is exercised, and winemaking is adapted to deal with all the consequences of very ripe picking, and when the wine emerges with saturated color, a lush mouthfeel, a huge structure, great density, and finished alcohol somewhere between 15 and 16 percent—or when at least some of these stylistic parameters prevail, or the wine is de-alcoholized before it is finished to "fix" the alcoholic excess but leave the rest in place—is pinot any more affected than other varieties?

This is a fair question, and it deserves thoughtful reflection. On one hand, our time and place is not the first to impose a new style on pinot noir. It happened at the end of the nineteenth century, when Burgundians routinely blended headier reds from the French south into their pinots to make the results attractive to export markets in northern Europe whose buyers had developed a taste for bigger wines. On the other hand, it is impossible not to wonder, if beefy style is the goal, whether pinot noir is the best place to start, and whether a very broad spectrum of styles for pinot noir plays to the special strengths and accounts for the particular liabilities of this old variety.

With allowance made for the unfinished debate over style, the state of North American pinot noir in 2008, overall, seems good. There are more varietally correct and appealing pinots, made by more talented and motivated winemakers, from more well-farmed vineyards, in more pinot-friendly regions (including quite a few outside California and Oregon) than ever before. The best of the bunch, some of which it has been my privilege and pleasure to taste for this book, compare without handicap with the best pinots grown and made anywhere. On the other hand, it remains true, as I wrote in *North American Pinot Noir*, that too much American wine, pinot included, is being grown in soils that are too deep and too high in nitrogen to produce really good wine without extensive intervention in the form of aggressive crop-thinning or canopy management or both, and that the huge investments now required to plant a vineyard make it difficult to abandon choices that prove suboptimal after the initial fact. And nothing differentiates North American from European wine lands, and from Burgundy in particular, more than the average age of vines today and the elapsed time since vines were first grown in particular sites. In the end, despite the good wines from young vineyards and from newly-minted producers, there is no substitute for experience and track record. American winegrowers like to say that they have "dialed in" a site and learned how to make its wine within a few years after planting it. The claim will be more credible, however, when we can point to more than a handful of sites, farmed and vinified by two or even three generations of the same family, replanted once or twice, with deep wine libraries to document experience. The game is still young.

Icon Key

Historic interest		Producers with especially long track records, old vineyards, or other claim to historic interest; or those new since 2000
New producer		

Tasting room — Producers with tasting rooms open on a regular schedule and those willing to arrange visits by prior appointment

By appointment

Estate producer — All-estate producers; and those that depend entirely (for pinot noir) on purchased fruit.

No estate-grown grapes

Fewer than 2,500 cases — Annual production (of all varietals)

2,500–10,000 cases

10,000–35,000 cases

More than 35,000 cases

Mostly winery-direct — Distribution strategies, ranging from least to most distributed

Selected domestic markets

Most domestic markets

Domestic and international

Under $23 — Suggested average retail prices for pinot noir, weighted by volume (the street prices for widely available wines are typically lower)

$23–35

$35–50

Over $50

A personal favorite

A TO Z WINEWORKS
Dundee, Oregon

Established in 2001, A to Z is a partnership of Cheryl Francis, Sam Tannahill, Bill Hatcher, and Debra Hatcher. Separately, Francis and Tannahill own the FRANCIS TANNAHILL brand, and the Hatchers own the WILLIAM HATCHER brand. Together, the foursome has experience with more than a dozen Oregon pinot projects and some of the state's most respected names, including DOMAINE DROUHIN OREGON, ARCHERY SUMMIT ESTATE, THE EYRIE VINEYARDS, CHEHALEM, and SHEA WINE CELLARS. From 2001 to 2003, A to Z operated entirely as a *négociant* operation, purchasing already-made wines from producers with surplus product, and then crafting a single pinot noir and a single pinot gris from each vintage (plus a pinot blanc and a red blend from southern Oregon in 2003) from their chosen components. In 2004, partially because the volume of good, available bulk wine began to shrink and partially because vinifying some lots gave them more control over quality, the partners began sourcing fruit in addition to purchasing partially finished wines. In 2005 A to Z further diversified varietally—into sangiovese and unoaked chardonnay—and the proportion of made wine to bulk wine shifted substantially toward the former. By 2006 the label had expanded to more than 90,000 cases, including 6,000 cases of pinot noir sold to Costco. Two thirds of the total volume was made from grapes handled entirely by A to Z staff in two Willamette Valley locations, while the balance came from custom-crush agreements with third parties. Late in 2006, the wunderkind brand took another huge leap forward by acquiring the venerable REX HILL WINERY, which it had used as a production facility since 2003. With this acquisition, A to Z became Oregon's largest winery. The brand has established an enviable reputation for good value wines from all of Oregon, and its pinot noir is a fine example of well-made, tasty, varietally correct pinot for about $20 a bottle.

TASTING NOTE
2005 Oregon (tasted in 2007):
Transparent medium garnet; dried walnut and hickory shells, then herbal and slightly resinated with a strong presence of raspberries; medium-weight, nicely crafted, and varietally correct; much better than most Bourgogne Rouge.

ACACIA WINERY
Napa, California

The creation of Acacia was the second seminal event of the 1970s in Los Carneros, after the debut of Carneros Creek Winery. A large group of investors underwrote the early years of the project, which was dedicated exclusively to pinot noir and chardonnay. Michael Richmond was Acacia's evangelist, and Larry Brooks was its founding winemaker. The 1979 and 1980 vintages were made at Kenwood in Sonoma, but a large, barnlike winery was built on Las Amigas Road in time for the 1981 harvest. Within a few years, however, amid rumors of mismanagement and misappropriation of funds, and with some cabernet sauvignon and merlot having been bottled under the Acacia name without the knowledge or consent of key partners, the winery was put up for sale. In

July 1986 it was acquired by Chalone, Inc. Although their titles and responsibilities changed several times, Richmond and Brooks remained close to Acacia for most of the next decade. After tours elsewhere on Chalone's behalf, Richmond returned to Acacia as general manager from 1998 to 2002. Brooks's fingerprints are on every Acacia pinot noir made between 1979 and 1996, when he left to work as a consultant and to launch his own label. Michael Terrien, an enologist trained at the University of California Davis, who had joined Acacia as a harvest worker, succeeded Brooks from 1997 to 2005, at which time the reins were passed to Anthony King for two harvests, and then to Matthew Glynn, previously with Gallo of Sonoma, who joined the Acacia team in 2005. These last changes followed the sale of Chalone Wine Group to Diageo Chateau and Estate Wines late in 2004.

Acacia was the first California winery to establish a reputation for vineyard-designated pinot noir based on purchased fruit. Three of these wines were made in Acacia's inaugural vintage, from the Iund Vineyard, east of the winery; the St. Clair Vineyard, across Las Amigas Road to the south; and Ira Lee's vineyard, less than a mile away, near Saintsbury. Vineyard-designated wines from the Madonna and Winery Lake vineyards debuted in 1980. Of these five, only St. Clair has remained an uninterrupted source of vineyard-designated wine to the present day. Winery Lake and Lee were made until 1983, Madonna until 1987, and Iund until 1992. Worries about phylloxera-induced interruptions of supply then drove Acacia to curtail its vineyard-designate program in favor of producing a reserve wine, which was made from 1993 to 1996. (Even the St. Clair vineyard-designate carried the word *reserve* on its label—in addition to the vineyard designation—for

several years in the early 1990s.) But later in the decade, after Lee's vineyard and parts of the Iund Vineyard were replanted on resistant rootstock, vineyard-designation was revived. An SVS (for Single Vineyard Selection) wine was made from Las Amigas Vineyard—Beckstoffer, in 1995. Lee's vineyard was replanted in 1992, in east–west-oriented, 11-foot rows with 5 feet between vines. The scion material is primarily Swan selection and Dijon 115. An SVS edition of Lee was resumed in 1997; DeSoto yielded its first SVS wine in 1998. Vineyard-designated pinot was once again made from the Iund Vineyard in and after 1999. St. Clair, Acacia's heirloom non-estate vineyard, was planted in 1973 to a field selection from Las Amigas Vineyard. Now substantially virused but lovingly dry farmed by Jim St. Clair, the vineyard's wide, 12-foot rows with 6-foot intervine spacing now yield barely 1 ton to the acre but generate the most elegant and least flamboyant of Acacia's SVS bottlings, generally picked at a lower Brix than the others. Beckstoffer-Las Amigas was originally planted by Louis P. Martini in 1963 and is the only part of Martini's pioneer Carneros plantings still in production. Beckstoffer is dry farmed like St. Clair and yields parsimoniously at about 1.3 tons per acre. The Winery Lake Vineyard, which has belonged to Sterling Vineyards since the mid-1980s and was recently replanted to Dijon clones, was added to the SVS program in 2004.

In addition to the vineyard-designated wines and the short-lived reserve program, Acacia made and released a Carneros blend every year except from 1980 to 1983. The Carneros wine, like the vineyard-designates, relied almost entirely on purchased fruit until very recently. The sources—in addition to parcels that are also used, or have been used, in the single-vineyard program—are CVI (Carneros

Valley Investors purchased the Stanly ranch about 1980), Truchard, Hudson, and Ahollinger. A second blend of non-estate fruit, called "A from Acacia," built on fruit from the Central Coast, Sonoma County, and Carneros, debuted in 2005. "A" is competitively priced.

In the second half of the 1990s, Acacia took several steps to anchor its pinot program with estate vineyards and to reduce its dependence on purchased fruit. In addition to 15 acres of mature pinot just east of the winery that were acquired from Andy Beckstoffer's Napa Vineyard Company in 1994, new vines were set out to replace older, failing vines on the remainder of the former Beckstoffer land in 1997 and on a contiguous 20-acre parcel acquired in 1993. In 2000 and 2001, more pinot noir was planted on a 50-acre parcel at the corner of Las Amigas and Duhig roads that was purchased in 1999. More or less simultaneously, the chardonnay vineyard planted around the winery building in 1979 was ripped out and has been replanted mostly to pinot noir. The aforementioned parcels, all contiguous and now collectively called either Acacia Estate or Lone Tree Vineyard, cover the eroded foothills at the extreme southern end of the Mayacamas Range, near the east–west midpoint of the Carneros appellation. An estate pinot was made in 2001 and 2002, and the 2002 edition of Acacia's Carneros wine was so dependent on estate fruit that its label carried an estate bottled designation for the first time in the history of the brand. A Lone Tree Vineyard wine debuted in 2005. In recent vintages, the single-vineyard wines have been ripe-picked, rich, and high in tannin, with considerable aging potential.

WINEMAKING NOTES

Winemaking at Acacia has changed rather dramatically over the years. Vintages (made by Brooks) before 1996 typically relied on a significant percentage of whole clusters and some postfermentation maceration. It is also obvious from tank records that grapes were picked at substantially lower Brix than they are today. Since 1996, grapes have been destemmed completely, and some of the fruit is crushed. (Crushed fruit, because it releases sugar quickly into the must, ferments at a higher temperature than do whole berries, thus extracting more tannin, so crushing is minimized if the tannins are perceived to be strong.) Fermentors are jacketed stainless steel cylinders 7 feet in diameter with 3-foot top openings. There is no cold soak. Instead, a "fast and furious" fermentation is started with "a hefty punch" of cultured yeast, and peak fermentation temperatures reach about 90°F. Acacia employs a combination of pumpovers and punchdowns (pneumatic devices installed before harvest in 2006 facilitate punchdowns in the large tanks), and pressing (since 1996) is done before the must is dry. For the Carneros blend, 40 percent new barrels are used; the ratio for the SVS wines ranges from 40 percent to 60 percent. François Frères is the predominant cooper. Barrel lots destined for the SVS program are selected in March following each vintage, at which time the first blend for the Carneros wine is also done. The wines stay in barrel eight to nine months, are racked once, and are cartridge filtered (but not fined) before bottling.

TASTING NOTES

2005 *Lone Tree Vineyard (tasted in* 2007): Transparent, bright medium crimson; red cherry and fresh flowers on the nose; intense and almost sharp on the palate; cassis and black pepper flavors; texture of polished cotton; some bite at the end.

2005 *Winery Lake Vineyard (tasted in* 2007): Transparent, medium black-red;

ACACIA WINERY: A VERTICAL TASTING OF IUND VINEYARD WINES

Acacia made single-vineyard wines from the Iund Vineyard from 1979 to 1992 and again after 1999. Anthony King, Acacia's winemaker in 2005 and 2006, organized this tasting on August 3, 2005, at the winery. Although the Iund retrospective was less impressive overall than a similar tasting of single-vineyard wines from the St. Clair Vineyard (reported in *North American Pinot Noir*, pp. 199–200), virtually all the wines were still sound, and several were excellent. The winery's tank records appear to show a major evolution. The 1979 to 1981 vintages (and some later vintages) were picked at about 22.5 Brix with as much as ten grams of acidity; vintages as recent as 1992 were picked at 23; more recent vintages such as 1999 and 2000 were picked much riper.

2000: Dark black-red; volatile aromatics, candle wax, and sage aromas; very ripe on the palate with some black fruit and black licorice; sweet and extracted with an almost viscous and chewy texture.

1999: Dark, almost opaque; black fruit, cola, and rose petal on the nose, plus barrel-derived vanilla and cedar; more black fruit and black pepper on the palate; sweet, full-bodied, and quite grippy in the mouth but near satiny on the finish.

1992: Transparent, medium-dark garnet with a terra cotta rim; potpourri nose but also very barrel marked; sweet, ripe plum and cherry fruit on the palate, with hints of Tootsie Roll, earth, cinnamon, clove, and charcoal; very full and slightly chewy at mid-palate; long. A preferred wine in this tasting.

1990: Slightly hazy, medium black-red verging on terra cotta; floral, nutty, and cotton-candy aromas; cola, resin, and briary brush in the mouth; slightly exotic; suede-like overall but grippy at the end.

1989: Medium terra cotta color but still red at the center; aromas of camphor and tar; sweet, cherry-berry fruit in the mouth; velvety and medium-long; finishes a little hard.

1988: Transparent terra cotta; very floral nose with some leathery highlights; interesting Oriental sweet-sour properties on the palate, plus tart apple, anise, black pepper, and clove; sweet, silky, and medium-long. Very attractive.

1986: Medium-dark and barely transparent; dried flower and herb aromas, plus tar; dried cherries in the mouth with a hint of exotic nuts, pepper, and clove; medium-weight and long; silky through mid-palate, then grippy at the end.

1984: Terra cotta core; orange at the rim; very distinctive pungent-nutty nose suggestive of fig, honey, and candied fruit (the grapes may have been botrytis-affected); tobacco, licorice, clove, cinnamon, and briar in the mouth; slightly sweet, long, and elegant; very attractive.

1982: Transparent, medium terra cotta with a vibrant, red core; menthol, eucalyptus, other volatile oils, and a hint of balsamic condiment on the nose; tart cherry, tar, toffee, and earth on the palate with hints of merbromin, cedar, and clove; very intense and satiny; a favorite in this tasting.

1980: Transparent, medium-dark terra cotta; mostly dried leaves on the nose; fading raspberry with a bit of strawberry jam in the mouth with earth and cinnamon, but also slightly bitter; still grippy with very fine-grained tannin and considerable length. Another favorite in this tasting.

1979: Browning terra cotta; sautéed peppers, dried fig, menthol, mint, and tobacco on the nose; minty in the mouth with some white pepper and clove; lightweight, slightly grippy and bright, with an overall satiny texture.

toasted nut shell aromas; slightly sweet, rich, round, and creamy with notes of dark fruit, vanilla, and expresso; grippy from mid-palate to finish with a sensation of black pepper and persimmon peel at the end.

2005 *Beckstoffer/Las Amigas Vineyard (tasted in 2007):* Medium-dark garnet; very distinctive nose of spring daphne overlaying mulled wine; dense, viscous, and intensely flavored; deep black cherry, toffee, and spearmint; briary, clove-infused, and almost pungent; long.

2005 *St. Clair Vineyard (tasted in 2007):* Very transparent, medium rosy-ruby color; engaging, exotic nose of faded flowers, red cherry, and sandalwood; lovely soft red-fruit flavors in the mouth; tends to unfold in layers, sometimes showing peppery spice; considerable grip but still silky and elegant overall; fine.

ADEA WINE COMPANY
Gaston, Oregon

Early in the 1980s, Dean Fisher, who had been a jet mechanic in the waning days of the Vietnam War, reinvented himself as a fabricator of metal equipment for the electric power industry. Based in Yamhill County, southwest of Portland, Oregon, he found himself surrounded by an emerging cottage industry with a quite separate appetite for metal fabrication, at which point he began custom building tanks, hoppers, and sorting tables for Oregon wineries. In the winter months, when the vineyards were dormant, Michael Etzel (see BEAUX FRÈRES), who was then absorbing winemaking expertise as a cellar rat for PONZI VINEYARDS, worked for Fisher, learning welding and other skills.

When Etzel's own vineyard, planted on Ribbon Ridge in 1988, began to bear, he and Fisher conceived a home winemaking project, making three barrels of pinot between them in 1990, and seven in 1991. Beaux Frères was born in 1992, when Etzel (after some effort) persuaded his brother-in-law (Robert M. Parker Jr.) to expand their vineyard project to include the production of finished wine. (It is said that the home wine Etzel and Fisher had made from Beaux Frères grapes was material to this persuasion.) Fisher and his wife were given an opportunity to become co-investors in Beaux Frères, but declined, at which point Etzel and Parker invited Robert Roy, a Canadian wine lover and investor to join them instead. Fisher, however, provided some of the labor and a lot of the construction savvy that transformed Etzel's pig barn into a viable winery, and he used the new facility to make his own "home" wines, alongside the first vintages of Beaux Frères, in 1992, 1993, and 1994.

In 1995 Fisher was ready to make wine into a second small family business, alongside his continuing work in metal fabrication, and Fisher Wine Company's commercial debut was made with a few barrels of Willamette Valley pinot sourced from Beaux Frères's upslope neighbor, Whistling Ridge (see PATRICIA GREEN CELLARS and KEN WRIGHT CELLARS). The first three commercial vintages were made at Hal Medici's winery—after Fisher had repeated his pig-barn wizardry by transforming Medici's dairy barn into a winery. Production moved to the new and substantially grander LEMELSON WINERY in 2001, and then to a dedicated facility on Fisher's own ranch near Gaston in 2002. Meanwhile, following the 1998 vintage, Fisher's brand and corporate name were changed to ADEA (the first initials of the given names of each member of Fisher's nuclear family) to resolve an intellectual property dispute with (no surprise!) Fisher Vineyards, a Sonoma-based producer of cabernet sauvignon and chardonnay. Officially divested of the metal fabrication business after 2002, and nominally henceforth a full-time vintner, Fisher remains in huge demand from winemaking neighbors who need a bit of help with tanks and related equipment.

DISTINCTIVE, SERIOUS NONMAINSTREAM PINOTS THOUGHTFULLY MARKED BY VARIATIONS ON A COMMON METHODOLOGICAL THEME

WINES AND WINEMAKING NOTES
Since the name change in 1998, Fisher has made the following pinots in each vintage: in 1998, a Willamette Valley blend and a reserve wine; in 1999 a Willamette Valley wine only; in 2000 the Willamette Valley and reserve wine duo again; in 2001 and 2002, a barrel-selected reserve called Dean-O's Pinot, the Willamette Valley wine, and vineyard-designated wines from YAMHILL VALLEY VINEYARDS and from the Coleman Vineyard in the McMinnville AVA; in 2003 the Reserve, along with vineyard-designates from Demarest and Hawk's View, plus the Willamette Valley and Dean-O's wines; in 2004 only Dean-O's, Hawk's View, and a new vineyard-designate from Momtazi in the Coast Range; and in 2005 the Willamette Valley cuvée, proprietarily renamed "Ann Sigrid," plus the Dean-O's and reserve blends.

Grapes are about 90 percent destemmed, but some are retained as whole clusters as long as the stems and seeds are both brown. Fermentors are 2.5-ton jacketed stainless steel open-tops, and the fruit from each source vineyard is fermented separately. After a five-to-seven day cold soak, each fermentor is slowly warmed. Older-vine vineyards are usually left to ferment with resident yeast; commercial yeast strains are used to inoculate fruit from younger vineyards. Fisher extends the vatting until the cap is nearly ready to fall, buckets juice into his press, presses very lightly, and barrels the wine in a stock that consists of about 30 percent new French *pièces*, 30 percent *pièces* that are one-year old, a few *pièces* coopered from Oregon oak and previously used for a single vintage of chardonnay, and some slightly older French *pièces*. Fisher reports that he has recently begun using some light-toast barrels made by Tonnellerie Ermitage, and may use more. Wines stay in barrel from eleven to sixteen months. Very interesting, distinctive, serious, non-mainstream pinots, marked by intelligent methodological variation and commendable insistence on good acidity, are made here.

TASTING NOTES
2005 *Reserve (tasted in* 2007*)*: Medium rosy-magenta; rose petal, ripe cherry, and a hint of furniture polish on the nose; cherry-raspberry with a hint of citrus on the palate; bright, slightly tangy, and nicely structured, with the texture of polished cotton; medium weight and length.

2005 *Dean-O's Pinot (tasted in* 2007*)*: Brilliant ruby, shy, mineral-dominated nose with some nutty undertones, but with bright, lifted flavors and attractive acidity on the palate; silky and persistent and a bit rounder than the Reserve, with some smoky notes.

2005 *Ann Sigrid (tasted in* 2007*)*: Transparent, medium ruby-garnet; floral and red-berry nose; slightly spicy and peppery palate, most black-fruit flavors; some barrel marking, almost creamy at mid-palate; verges on richness with an elegant structure.

2004 *Hawks View Vineyard (tasted in 2007):* Transparent light-to-medium garnet; savory nose touched with green olive and briar; just a hint of green character on the palate too, but still fruit-sweet at mid-palate; some hints of cola and barrel char; noticeable grip from mid-palate to finish. Very seriously made and distinctive wine that displays an interesting juxtaposition of savory-green and ripe-fruit elements.

ADELAIDA CELLARS
Paso Robles, California

As far a pinot noir is concerned, the story of Adelaida Cellars is the most recent chapter in the story of Hoffman Mountain Ranch. This story began in 1964 when Stanley Hoffman, a Beverly Hills cardiologist, wine connoisseur, and amateur winemaker, planted 60 acres of vines in an enormous walnut orchard northwest of Paso Robles, including the first (and for some time the only) pinot noir in the area. It is not clear whether Hoffman was looking for limestone soils, or whether he got them by happenstance, but this is one of the few spots on the Pacific coast where limestone-based subsoils are omnipresent. The initial planting was 32 acres of pinot laid out in 12-foot rows with 6 feet between vines, on a mostly southwest facing slope, using scion material that was probably taken from what is now known as MOUNT EDEN VINEYARDS, then owned by Martin Ray.

Nine years later, Hoffman moved his primary residence to Paso, hoping to reinvent himself as a country doctor but, as the only cardiologist for tens of miles, he ended up with no more time to pursue his hobby than he had enjoyed in Beverly Hills. His sons stepped in and made several vintages of wine (including pinot noir) in the early and mid-1970s, apparently coached personally by André Tchelistcheff, whom Hoffman had engaged as a consultant. At least the 1975 edition of Hoffman's pinot gained considerable notoriety; it is said to have bested Domaine de la Romanée-Conti and other luminary red Burgundies at tastings in France. It is true that the Hoffman wine was entered in two famous tastings held in Paris and Beaune in 1979 and 1980, respectively. The first, a comparative tasting of 330 wines from 33 countries, sponsored by the French food and wine magazine *Gault Millau*, and rather grandly styled "Olympiades des Vins du Monde," was judged by an international jury. The second was hosted by Maison Joseph Drouhin. In the first, the Hoffman wine competed against a mostly motley assortment of pinot noirs from Australia, France, Switzerland, Romania, Greece, and America, in which the French wines were three *négociant* bottlings of Clos de Vougeot, Côtes-de-Beaune Villages and Mercurey, created for the Nicolas chain of French wine shops. Here it came in third, after the 1976 vintage of Tyrell's Pinot Noir from Hunter River and the 1969 Clos de Vougeot made for Nicolas. In the Drouhin tasting the following year, as one of the six highest-placing non-French pinots from the first tasting, it was paired with six pinots made by Joseph Drouhin; here it finished ninth in a field of twelve, besting only two wines from Switzerland's Valais, and one from Greece.

In 1976, Hoffman built a proper winery on his ranch to replace the very basic facilities he had used for the first vintages, but despite a considerable investment of energy from his sons and some cheerleading from Tchelistcheff, the wines seem not to have succeeded very well in the marketplace, and both winery and vineyard were largely abandoned in the 1980s. Quite recently, the winery was sold to a Wisconsin couple that has plans to revive it as a production facility and wine destination. The vineyard, dry farmed and deeply rooted, traveled a different path. Having survived more than a decade of neglect, all of it (including the 32 acres of pinot, plus some chardonnay, cabernet sauvignon and gamay noir) was purchased in 1994 by Adelaida Winery, a neighboring cabernet-based enterprise established in 1981 by winemaker John Munch. Four successive winemakers at Adelaida—Munch until 1998, Steve Glossner from 1999 to 2001, Jon Priest (see ETUDE WINES) in 2002, and Terry Culton since 2003—have worked to restore the historic vineyard, and Adelaida has made "HMR Estate" pinot noir, based almost entirely on the revived original vines, since 1996. One 8-acre block of Hoffman's pinot was replanted in 1995 without changing the original vine spacing, using cuttings painstakingly taken and nursery-propagated from the original plants; the fruit from this block is generally not included in the HMR bottlings, but is instead directed to Adelaida's second label, which is called Schoolhouse. Among Adelaida's winemakers, Culton has especially rich experience with pinot, accumulated at WILD HORSE, Edmeades, WILLAMETTE VALLEY VINEYARDS, and CALERA. The HMR pinots (there is sometimes a reserve wine as well as an estate release, made from the vineyard's high end where the topsoil is shallowest) are created with a large proportion of whole-cluster fruit, some *saignée*, resident yeast fermentation, and hand-plunging in open-top tanks, followed by between fifteen and eighteen months' *élevage* in lightly toasted barrels coopered by François Frères and Claude Gillet, of which about 25 percent are new for the estate wine, and 70 percent are new for the

reserve. (Munch worked with American oak cooperage, searching to produce a distinctively "American" pinot noir.) Both wines are distinctive and elegant editions of pinot noir and are well worth the effort invested in reviving the historic vineyard.

TASTING NOTES

2003 *HMR Estate Vineyard (tasted in 2006):* Medium rosy brick red; expressive, open nose of dried leaves, leather, and raspberry; racy and elegant on the palate with bright red fruit, a hint of tangerine peel, an undertone of hard spice, and a slight grip of tannin on the finish; slightly austere, with a texture somewhere between silk and polished cotton; medium-long and very attractive.

2003 *HMR Estate Vineyard Reserve (tasted in 2006):* Transparent medium garnet with rosy highlights; powerful nose of cherries and black pepper; grippy and intense on the mid-palate with a hint of orange peel and noticeable barrel char; slightly tart, long, and austere.

ADELSHEIM VINEYARD
Newburg, Oregon

David Adelsheim's role in shaping Oregon's wine industry, and its focus on the cool climate grape varieties of northeastern France, is so intuitively and circumstantially obvious to his peers that they often take his record for granted. Initially more interested in country living than in grapes or winemaking, Adelsheim drifted into wine incrementally, eventually playing a catalytic role in the creation of the Willamette Valley and Umpqua AVAs, and the smaller AVAs later carved out of the Willamette Valley; the state's wine-labeling regulations; and many of its key institutions, including the Oregon Wine Board and the world-famous International Pinot Noir Celebration. Armed with a bachelor's degree in German literature, a two-month *stage* at Beaune's Lycée Viticole, and several years' experience as a sommelier in Portland restaurants, Adelsheim helped organize the first international symposium on cool-climate viticulture; advocated for American trials of pinot and chardonnay clones isolated during postwar work in Burgundy and Champagne; and helped orchestrate the establishment of a grapevine importation and quarantine program at Oregon State University, eliminating the state's erstwhile dependence on facilities at the University of California Davis. He was an early ambassador-at-large, knitting technical relationships between Oregon and Europe, and a friendly broker for the deal that brought Maison Joseph Drouhin to the Dundee Hills. He was also the only Oregon pinot pioneer to focus personal attention on the south face of the Chehalem Mountains, several miles from the industry's consensus cradle in the Dundee Hills. In fact, Adelsheim argues that the Dundee Hills were no more a "cradle" than several other areas, considering Chuck Coury's planting in the Coast Range, Dick ERATH's planting in the Chehalem Mountains, and the PONZIS' investment in the Tualatin Valley.

In 1972, he planted Adelsheim's first estate vineyard in very old, balsaltic clay-loam soils on Quarter Mile Lane, about 5 miles northwest of Newberg; six years later, the Quarter Mile Lane vineyard birthed Adelsheim Vineyards's first wine, a 1978 vineyard-designated pinot noir, appropriately labeled "First Harvest," plus small amounts of chardonnay and riesling. Additional commitments to the Chehalem Mountains were made in 1988, when 52 acres were acquired on lower-elevation benchland along Calkins Lane, on which 40 acres of vineyard were eventually planted; in 1989, when Adelsheim planted a vineyard on 19 acres of south- and southwest-facing property owned by Jess and Joy Howell called Bryan Creek, adjacent to Quarter Mile Lane; in 1993, when the present winery buildings were started at the Calkins Lane site; and in 1996, when plantings began on steep property owned by Lynn and Jack Loacker in the Chehalem Mountains subdistrict called Ribbon Ridge, with the vineyard itself called Ribbon Springs.

ADELSHEIM PINOTS ARE AN INTERESTING REFLECTION OF OREGON VITICULTURE'S TWO MAIN SOIL TYPES

(The Loackers joined the Adelsheims as owners of Adelsheim Vineyards in 1994.) Ribbon Springs and Calkins Lane are both sedimentary-soil sites, quite different from the higher-altitude vineyards at Bryan Creek and Quarter Mile Lane, and they gave Adelsheim perceptible heartburn until he and his staff learned how to manage the potential for drought stress and high tannin that derive from the sedimentary soils.

From 1978 to 1985, David Adelsheim was his own hands-on winemaker—despite his self-confessed "lack of formal training in viticulture and enology"—as the winery focused on Quarter Mile Lane and a few other "bits and pieces." Adelsheim remembers "Burgundy-attentive" winemaking in this period, with (for example) considerable interest in whole-cluster fermentations. From 1986 to 1998, under the winemaking leadership of Don Kautzner and in order to increase production, the brand began to rely on fruit purchased from several Polk County vineyards, while the new plantings at Bryan Creek and Calkins Lane were brought on stream. After an "interregnum" from 1999 to 2000, Dave Paige (a Davis graduate who worked previously at Cloninger Cellars in the Santa Lucia Highlands) took the winemaking reins in 2001, presiding over a mostly estate-based program split between the blended Willamette Valley and Elizabeth's Reserve bottlings, and single-vineyard pinots culled from the aforementioned estate vineyards in the Chehalem Mountain and Ribbon Ridge AVAs. In the 1980s, riesling and chardonnay competed almost equally with pinot noir for the winery's attention, but both were overtaken in the 1990s by pinot gris, which is now Adelsheim's flagship white. At the same time, Adelsheim has become an active dabbler in lesser-planted varieties like tocai friulano and auxerrois.

WINES AND WINEMAKING NOTES

Among Adelsheim pinot noirs, the most persistent bottlings have come from Quarter Mile Lane, made as a vineyard-designate in 1978 and from 1988 to 2005, except in 1997 and 2004. Although the winery's main blend—called Yamhill County from 1979 to 1984, Oregon from 1985 to 2004, and Willamette Valley since 2004—was also anchored with Quarter Mile Lane fruit in many vintages, notably from 1981 to 1985 (the main exception came in 1986, when it was labeled Polk County and derived mainly from Bethel Heights and Seven Springs fruit). A reserve program, under the name Elizabeth's Reserve, was begun in 1986 and 1987, incorporating lots from Quarter Mile Lane and lots from vineyards in the Dundee Hills. Abandoned in 1988 and

1989, the Reserve was resumed in 2000, based largely on fruit from the Chehalem Mountains estate vineyards. Vineyard-designated wines from purchased fruit were made at the end of the 1980s and throughout the 1990s: a Seven Springs bottling was made from 1988 to 1998, except for 1997; a Bethel Heights wine was made exceptionally in 1989; Harry Peterson-Nedry's Ridgecrest vineyard was used for a vineyard-designated wine in 1993, 1996, and 1997; and the Goldschmidt Vineyard (see DUSKY GOOSE) was made in 1998, 1999, and from 2001 to 2005. Vineyard-designated wines based on Adelsheim's estate vineyards (apart from Quarter Mile Lane) debuted in 1998 with a Bryan Creek bottling, and in 2001 with Calkins Lane and Ribbon Springs bottlings. Second wines have also been made since 1988 under the Wallace Brook and Southern Slopes labels.

Dave Paige describes winemaking since 2001 as "open minded" and "the opposite of recipe driven." Paige generally picks around 23 Brix if possible, insisting that high Brix is "the enemy of balance," and that "you have waited too long if you wait for all the flavors to appear in the unpicked grapes." Almost all fruit is destemmed, cold-soaked for (usually) four days, inoculated, and fermented on the cool side. Most settling occurs in barrel, and malolactic fermentations are unleashed by a combination of resident bacteria and inocula. Paige relies on a large assortment of coopers, including Damy, Sirugue, Seguin Moreau, Cadus, and François Frères, using about 25 percent new barrels overall, and filters most lots as insurance against subsequent yeast infections. Fining decisions are made on a lot-to-lot basis. Many of the lots destined for the Willamette Valley bottling are identified early in *élevage*, but the final selection of barrels for the single-vineyard and Elizabeth's Reserve wines must be made before the final Willamette Valley blend is constructed.

Adelsheim pinots are an interesting reflection of Oregon's two main viticultural soil types. In recent vintages, buoyed by warm and dry growing seasons, the wines have been made a bit richer than they were historically, but they remain nicely balanced editions of Oregon pinot, without excessive alcohol. Nonetheless, the vineyard-designated wines all benefit from bottle age, which opens them aromatically.

TASTING NOTES

2005 *Elizabeth's Reserve (tasted in 2007):* Medium black-red; slightly smoky berry fruit with some high-register citrus notes; well-behaved cherry and raspberry with some white pepper and considerable minerality on the mid-palate; very slightly sweet, nicely structured, and attractive.

2004 *Bryan Creek (tasted in 2006):* Brilliant, medium-dark magenta; tar and black-fruit aromas with hints of tobacco; brambly raspberry flavors; full-bodied and slightly creamy; texture of heavy velvet and considerable length. A large wine that needs time to open and soften.

2004 *Calkins Lane (tasted in 2006):* Dark black-red color; slightly exotic nose redolent of sandalwood and Indonesian spice plus wet slate; red fruit and earth on the palate; full bodied and slightly sweet.

2003 *Quarter Mile Lane (tasted in 2006):* Transparent, light-to-medium rosy-garnet color; earth, pepper, mace, and cardamom aromas; cherry, raspberry, and red licorice on the palate with a hint of nuts; intense flavors, medium weight, concentrated, slightly grippy, and very slightly bitter at the end.

2003 *Ribbon Springs Vineyard (tasted in 2006):* Transparent, medium black-red; aromas of wet slate and granite; infused violets, pepper, dark cherry, and plum in the mouth, with overtones of smoke and

tree bark; concentrated and grippy, with the texture of rough silk.

1994 *Elizabeth's Reserve (tasted in 2007):* Deep opaque mahogany; cinnamon, clove, tobacco, and leather aromas; lovely on the palate with a silky but substantial feel; notes of citrus and tobacco-tinged red fruit; very fine-grained tannins; long and fine.

ALMA ROSA WINERY AND VINEYARDS
Buellton, California

Alma Rosa is the third act in Richard and Thekla Sanford's long and distinguished career growing cool-climate wines (and especially pinot noir) on California's southern Central Coast. The story begins with Sanford's wartime service in Vietnam, which drove him to seek a civilian career "working close to the earth and caring for the landscape." Travels in France also birthed a passion for viticulture and for fine Burgundies. Act One was the venerated Sanford & Benedict Vineyard, which eventually comprised 130 acres of cabernet, merlot, riesling, chardonnay, and pinot noir near the west end of what is now the Sta. Rita Hills AVA. (Although "Santa Rita Hills" is the conventional form of the name for this area, "Sta. Rita Hills" is used on wine labels and in all formal references to the AVA to satisfy a settlement made between local vintners and Viña Santa Rita of Chile. For simplicity, "Sta. Rita Hills" is used throughout this book.) This vineyard, first planted in 1971, now belongs to the SANFORD WINERY and Terlato Wine Group. Estate grown Sanford & Benedict pinots were made at the vineyard from 1976 to 1980. It was a bootstrap operation then. The winery was a repurposed rustic barn that relied on portable electric power and gas lamps.

In Act Two, the SANFORD WINERY (*sans* Benedict) consumed Sanford's energies from 1981 until 2005, at which time he exchanged his remaining interest in the brand and its new winery at La Rinconada for El Jabali Ranch (the site of Sanford's celebrated old-West *rancho*-style tasting room and his personal residence) and La Encantada, its newest vineyard, on Santa Rosa Road about 1 mile west of Sanford & Benedict. In this transaction Anthony J. Terlato's family, who also own the Chicago-based Terlato (formerly Paterno) Wine Group, became the majority owners of Sanford, while Alma Rosa, which involves just Richard and Thekla Sanford, established a new wine portfolio based on El Jabali and La Encantada.

La Encantada, while still young, seems an exceptionally promising site. Like Sanford & Benedict, much of it is north-facing, its soil is rock-strewn and marly, and its hilly topography creates a diversity of microclimates even within single vineyard blocks. It is planted in 10-foot rows with 5 feet between vines, has been farmed organically from the outset, and has been certified organic since 2004. The first vintage of Alma Rosa pinot was made in 2004, at Sanford, with Sanford's then winemaker, Bruno d'Alfonso, in charge, but the project moved to Orcutt Road Cellars in the Edna Valley before the 2005 harvest, where BAILEYANA winemaker Christian Roguenant assumed the hands-on winemaking responsibilities, following Richard Sanford's winemaking protocols. In both vintages, two pinots were made: a vineyard-designated La Encantada cuvée, and a Sta. Rita Hills bottling, also crafted from La Encantada fruit but not vineyard-designated. The Sta. Rita Hills wine is built from all of the selections of pinot grown at La Encantada—Dijon 114, 115, 667, 777, Swan, and UCD 4—while the vineyard-designated wine relies mostly on the blocks planted to Swan and 667. While Alma Rosa's production grows to its final target of 25,000 cases, some of the La Encantada pinot noir grapes are sold to other producers, including ROESSLER CELLARS, HITCHING POST WINES, FOLEY ESTATES and Casa Baranca, as well as to Bruno d'Alfonso, who created his own labels after leaving Sanford in 2006. There is also a bit of Alma Rosa pinot noir rosé, dubbed Pinot Noir Vin Gris, made from pinot vines at El Jabali. Eventually, according to Sanford, El Jabali fruit may also be used in the Sta. Rita Hills cuvée.

WINES AND WINEMAKING NOTES
The 2004 and 2005 wines are quite different, reflecting the distinct signatures of the hands-on winemakers as well as Richard Sanford's decision, in 2005, to pick fruit less ripe and to reduce the percentage of new barrels used to raise the wines. The new protocol avoids the need to add water during fermentation by picking between 24 and 25 Brix, destemming all fruit, cold-soaking briefly, and kick-starting fermentations with yeast additions. Fermentations peak above 90°F; the new wines are pressed before they are dry, settled for twenty-four hours, and then finished in barrel on their gross lees. The first racking is done after the malolactic fermentation has finished. Natural acidity at La Encantada keeps the wines bright without acidification, and enzymes are added during fermentation. The wines are bottled after nine to eleven months in barrel. The 2005 wines are aromatically expressive and display good mid-palate length. The vineyard-designated cuvée is the silkier and more elegant of the two wines, whereas the Sta. Rita Hills wine tends toward blacker flavors, a plusher texture, and more brawn.

TASTING NOTES

2005 *Sta. Rita Hills (tasted in 2007)*:
Dark, intense black-red color; very forward
nose redolent of black licorice and lavender
pastilles; assertive flavor expressing very
dark fruit; mouth coating and long with a
very slightly bitter finish.

2005 *La Encantada Vineyard (tasted in
2007)*: Medium rosy-magenta; aromas of
black cherry, bay laurel, and sage; fine and
silky in the mouth with a hint of expresso;
bright and higher-toned fruit than the Sta.
Rita Hills; capable of developing elegance
with more time in bottle.

AMITY VINEYARDS
Amity, Oregon

Myron Redford, who purchased Amity
Vineyards from its first owners in 1974,
just three years after it had been planted, is
appreciated as something of a counterculture
figure in the Oregon wine scene. He is said
to have discovered wine while hitchhiking
from Ankara, where he spent a year in
a collegiate study abroad program, to
London, via (among other spots) the
Mosel Valley. Eating and drinking along
the Mosel, he learned the essential truth
of *terroir*: that each riesling from each
vineyard in each village was distinctive—
the individual site marked each wine.

Redford's first job in the wine business
was at Associated Vintners in the Seattle
suburb of Kirkland, the pioneering
Washington State enterprise that grew
from the home-winemaking exploits of
several University of Washington faculty.
At Amity a few years later, Redford
sold the vineyard's 1974 and 1975 crops,
and part of the 1976 crop, to home

winemakers while he, a carpenter-friend,
and two high school students built a
tiny winery. The vineyard consisted of 10
planted acres, of which 4 acres were pinot
noir: 1.5 were UCD 2A, and 2.5 were the
"upright clone" of pinot, erroneously
alleged to be gamay, that was distributed
as UCD 18. Redford made one barrel
of "proper" pinot noir from the 1976
vintage, but generated some instant cash
by making some pinot noir nouveau as
well, which he released on the timetable
of Beaujolais nouveau, when the new wine
was still fizzy from the just-completed
primary fermentation. Both wines were
commercially successful, and production
of both continued until the nouveau
cuvée was discontinued in 1994.

Vintages from 1977 to 2002 were built
primarily from purchased fruit with a
minority percentage of estate grapes. By 1982
the pinot program consisted of three wines:
an Oregon cuvée, a Willamette Valley cuvée,
and a barrel selection called "Winemaker's
Reserve." Barrels thought to have "world
class" potential—if any—were tapped
first for the reserve wine; the balance were
divided between lots "with more depth and
complexity" and "lighter" lots, the former
being directed into the Willamette Valley
wine, and the latter being earmarked for
the Oregon cuvée. After 1984, to keep the
Oregon wine affordable, an effort was made
to find vineyards whose grapes could be
purchased at an acceptable price point. An
estate cuvée was also made "occasionally," if
any of it met the twin tests of high quality
and distinctive character. Total pinot noir
production rose to 4,600 cases.

In 2002 the Oregon wine was
discontinued, and the program was scaled
back to less than 400 cases of single
vineyard wines. By 2006 the program,
minus the Oregon cuvée, was back up to
3,900 cases. Redford was his own hand-on
winemaker until 2007, when he handed

the baton to Darcy Pendergrass, a 1999 graduate of the University of Montana in microbiology who had worked at Amity Vineyards in various capacities since 2001. The winery also makes significant amounts of pinot blanc, gamay noir, gewürztraminer, and riesling, among other things.

WINES AND WINEMAKING NOTES
The Willamette Valley blend has been made in all recent vintages and relies primarily on fruit purchased from a number of mostly well-known vineyards, including Anden (the lower part of Seven Springs Vineyard), Croft in the foothills of the Coast Range, Sunnyside Vineyard south of Salem adjacent to Highway 5, and Hyland in the McMinnville AVA. Non-estate single-vineyard wines have been made annually since 1998 from the Schouten Vineyard, set in sedimentary Peavine-series soils in the McMinnville AVA, and since 2002 from Crannell Farms, from whence Redford sources Dijon 115, grafted on chardonnay or riesling roots, or grown on its own roots, and UCD 4 grown on its own roots. A single-vineyard estate wine has been made many times since its debut in 1981.

Redford's sometimes contrarian approach to pinot has led to several significant departures from the consensus protocol often mentioned in these pages. Convinced that it is possible to make fine pinot entirely from cool sites that are normally harvested at less than 24 Brix, Redford has become a low-Brix picker by habit and conviction, and says he has added tartaric acid to the fermenting must only "once or twice" in his Oregon winemaking career. He has also concluded that pruning protocols aimed at a single cluster of fruit per vine shoot are "too radical," and may actually contribute to the proliferation of highly extracted and super-concentrated wines. He targets the estate and other vineyards

where he controls the farming to produce about a half-ton more than the regional average—2.5 tons per acre rather than 2.0—and then relies on green harvesting to reduce the final crop. In another departure from the mainstream, Redford has used no new barrels since 1988, to "protest" what he saw as the "march toward an international style of heavily oaked fruit bombs." He did, however, at the request of his new winemaker, purchase four new barrels in 2006, as an "experiment." He returned to his "no-new-oak regime" in 2007, and no more new barrels have been purchased. Since 2005 Redford has also used a EuroSelect destemmer (made by Scharfenberger Maschinenbau in Bad Durkheim, Germany), whose technology enables separation of each berry from its stem so perfectly that only about 5 gallons of juice are released by a ton of grapes, as well as a cross-flow filtration system. New wines are settled for two days after being pressed and before being barreled. For many years Redford also bottle aged pinots for two or three years before release, but after the volume of production was reduced in 2003, his "backlog" was eliminated, so since 2003 wines have been released with a year or less of bottle age.

The Amity pinots I have tasted are brightly acidic, finely structured wines with very modest finished alcohols. When I suggested to Redford they might be reminiscent of good red Sancerre, he disagreed strongly, observing that his wines have "a long history of being considered comparable. . .to Burgundy." In truth, they have a checkered reputation, sometimes eliciting high praise from respected critics, but sometimes attracting criticism for excessive tannin, herbaceousness, and thin, edgy structures. Almost without exception, the wines show better with bottle age and some exposure to air after uncorking.

TASTING NOTES

2006 *Willamette Valley (tasted in 2007, finished and bottled but before its release):* Pretty, luminous, light-to-medium ruby; attractive, vibrant red berry nose; slight sweet attack with racy, flower-infused red berry flavors and hints of red licorice, spice, and earth; very nicely built; some grip on the finish.

2005 *Winemaker's Reserve (tasted in 2007):* Bright, rosy-ruby; dusty floral notes over red berry fruit; bright red berry flavors with hints of brown spice and white pepper; light-weight, medium-length, and fruit-driven throughout.

2005 *Schouten Vineyard (tasted in 2007):* Brilliant, medium ruby; cherry and violets on the nose; sweet red cherry also dominates the palate; notes of earth, tarragon, and bay laurel; silky and elegant with a bit of mid-palate weight; tea and some grip; also a hint of spritz.

ANCIEN WINES
Napa, California

Ken Bernards grew up in what is now the heart of the Oregon wine country, surrounded by cellar rats and pinotphiles. Armed with a degree in flavor chemistry from Oregon State University, he began his winemaking career at Domaine Chandon in 1987, working first as a research enologist and later as associate winemaker. In 1989 a trip to Burgundy solidified his enthusiasm for pinot noir, and a road sign near Dijon, pointing the way to an archaeological site, provided the name he was to use a few years later for wines of his own. Ancien Wines was created in 1992 as a personal side

project, and when Bernards left Domaine Chandon to become winemaker at Truchard Vineyard in 1994, he took the Ancien project with him. Then, in 1997, Ancien moved to a tiny shared-space winery on the eastern edge of Napa, where it blossomed into a nearly full-time passion, subsidized by Bernards's consulting work at sites as close as Carneros and as far away as the coastal valleys of Chile.

In 1992 Ancien's Carneros pinot noir was produced entirely from a single knoll in the first of Domaine Chandon's Los Carneros vineyards: an especially well-drained, low-vigor site planted in 1973 to UCD 13 on St. George rootstock. The fruit from this site was deemed too intense for Chandon's sparkling program and was therefore made available for Bernards's personal project. The Ancien Carneros pinot became a blend in 1998, when Bernards added fruit from Ferguson Ranch—also a well-drained knoll, virtually identical in vine age and planting density, and also planted to UCD 13. In 2000, Bernards began sourcing fruit from a third Carneros site: a small parcel of the Donum Estate, then part of BUENA VISTA's holdings, not far from the Ferguson Ranch parcel. The surface soil in this block is black clay—not usually promising for pinot noir—but on this site, the subsoil is well-drained gravel, which seems to compensate for the liabilities of the topsoil. Although Bernards originally intended to blend the Donum fruit into his Carneros bottling, he subsequently decided to release it separately. In 2001, it was the source for a small release of so-called Diablo Cuvée.

At the end of the 1990s, the object of Bernard's Carneros-oriented attention began to shift toward the Toyon Farm Vineyard, a parcel overlooking Larry Hyde's well-known property on the north side of the Carneros Highway, where Bernards had been involved in the layout and choice of plant material. The latter is a combination of Swan selection (from Carneros Creek via CASA CARNEROS) and Dijon 115, planted quite densely in 7-foot rows with 5-foot intervine spacing. The first Toyon Farm fruit came online in 2002, and was used in a vineyard-designated bottling from 2004, when it became Ancien's sole source of Carneros

---

MEDIUM-WEIGHT, DISTINCTIVE WINES FROM SITES CHOSEN BECAUSE THEY ARE ATYPICAL

---

pinot. Meanwhile, in 1996, the Ancien pinot program was expanded to include a non-Carneros wine "as different as you can get" from the Carneros bottling. The source, from 1996 through 2003, was Dave Steiner's Sonoma Mountain vineyard, a cool site on the northwestern side of the mountain overlooking Bennett Valley that was cursed with late budbreak and poor set, although these factors also helped to limit yields and to produce wines of great intensity. In 2004 the Sonoma Mountain source shifted to the Red Dog Vineyard, not far from Steiner, which was custom-planted in 2000 to Ancien specifications, using 80 percent Swan selection from the Mink Vineyard and 20 percent Dijon 777. Fruit from Red Dog is shared with TALISMAN WINES.

In 1999 Bernards added a Napa Valley wine to the Ancien portfolio, using fruit from the aforementioned Mink Vineyard, adjacent to the production facility he now shares with Whitford Cellars off of Coombesville Road in East Napa. Mink is 2.5 acres of Dijon 115 and Swan selection

from Casa Carneros planted in a topsoil of cobbly alluvium underlaid with white volcanic ash, and the site has turned out to be exceptionally cool—so cool in fact that September overnight temperatures frequently fall into the low 40s, helping to retain acidity. It was so genuinely cold in 2001 that the crop was completely wiped out by April overnight temperatures in the low 20s. (Bernards argues that Mink's layer of volcanic ash operates like the limestone in Burgundy: it is a wick for deep moisture.) A Russian River Valley pinot was also added in 1999. From 1999 through 2003, it relied on Kent Ritchie's Poplar Vineyard at the intersection of Eastside Road and the Trenton–Healdsburg Road, a 1973 planting of UCD 13 on a well-drained hillside where the surface soil is powdery loam, and the subsoil consists mostly of volcanic ash; beginning in 2004, the Russian River wine was a vineyard-designate from the Perez Vineyard, a parcel of Dijon 115 southwest of Sebastopol near Bloomfield Road custom-planted for Ancien in 2000. In 2004 Ancien also produced its first southern central coast pinot, from the Fiddlestix Vineyard in the Sta. Rita Hills (see FIDDLEHEAD CELLARS).

WINES AND WINEMAKING NOTES
Ancien pinots are medium-weight, distinctive wines from sites chosen because they are somehow special, sometimes even atypical of their region, and they are explicitly crafted to be quite different from one another. Bernards says he "enjoys blending" but prefers "interesting, eccentric wines" to "necessarily complete" wines. The Carneros wines, fairly true to type, have a tendency to display primarily red-toned fruit and to be fruit forward, whereas the Mink Vineyard wine shows the special promise of this relatively neglected corner

of the Napa Valley AVA. Ancien's Sonoma Mountain wines are exotically aromatic and slow to evolve. Although Bernards varies his winemaking practices to suit each vineyard and vintage, he does not diverge far from what he describes as his "default mode." Very small lots are fermented in one-ton fruit bins. He likes the surface-to-volume ratio and cap depth of these bins, which enable good extraction. The clusters are destemmed directly into the bins, and the stems are entirely discarded in "nine vintages out of ten." A four-day cold soak at 55 to 58°F is followed by seven to nine days of hot (94 to 95°F) fermentation, which is jump-started with RC 212 and Assmannshausen yeasts. Punchdowns are performed throughout the cold soak and fermentation processes. The must is lightly pressed with a bladder press; press fraction and free-run juice are combined, and the wine goes into barrel dirty. Bernards inoculates about half of his barrels to induce malolactic fermentation but is happy to wait until May or June of the year following the vintage for this process to spread to the balance of lots and to be completed.

Barrel regimes are tailored to each wine. One hundred percent Remond barrels, of which about 55 percent are new, are used for the Sonoma Mountain wine. (Bernards likes the marriage of the Remond wood with the Sonoma Mountain fruit for its "seamless" support of the wine's palate from attack through finish, and for its "respect" for the floral and sage perfumes that characterize this fruit.) The Russian River wine takes all François Frères. Mink Vineyard seems to work well with Cadus barrels, and the Carneros blend gets a combination of François Frères and Billon, of which about 25 percent is new. Bernards is reluctant to stir the lees in barrel, citing research that plenty of autolysis occurs without manipulation

and arguing that stirring "can strip a wine of lively fruit and 'muddy' it." The Mink Vineyard wine spends the least time in barrel (about ten months), followed by the Carneros (eleven months), the Russian River (eleven to twelve months), and the Sonoma Mountain (sixteen months). All the wines are normally racked once in the spring and are generally not fined. Pinots may be pad filtered before bottling if Bernards has any reason to be concerned about stability in bottle.

TASTING NOTES

2004 *Toyon Farms Vineyard (tasted in* 2007*):* Brilliant, deep magenta; huge nose of earth, fresh flowers, black raspberry, and barrel-derived vanilla; explosive palate of bright earth, strawberry, cherry, and plum; mouth coating, serious, and hedonistic but still elegant; very fine. A personal favorite.

2004 *Mink Vineyard (tasted in* 2007*):* Deep, almost saturated black-red; cherry pie and barrel char on the nose; sweet, rich, and very ripe black fruit in the mouth with considerable grip and slightly ferric minerality; highlights of citrus peel, milk chocolate, and hard spice; expressive and exuberant but also serious and distinctive; long.

2004 *Perez Vineyard (tasted in* 2007*):* Brilliant, deep magenta; fruit-driven nose of Bing cherry with high notes of cranberry and flowers; very sweet attack that is often characteristic of young vines; rich, exuberant mid-palate with a hint of mocha; mouth coating, long, and grippy on the finish.

2002 *Sonoma Mountain Steiner Vineyard (tasted in* 2005*):* Very limpid, medium-garnet, with rosy highlights; aromatic overlay of floral elements with charcuterie; elegant, silky, and very complex on the palate, with tar, black licorice, white pepper, and a hint of clove; nice, gentle grip; very minerally, pretty, and hugely successful. A personal favorite.

ANDREW RICH WINES
Carlton, Oregon

Andrew Rich explains that the first "really good" wines he remembers came from a friend of his parents who was "into wine." Later, having become an avowed Francophile armed with a degree in French literature from the University of Massachusetts at Amherst, Rich took an entry-level job at *Travel & Leisure* in New York, where one of his responsibilities was to edit the magazine's front-of-the-book wine department. This assignment brought an avalanche of invitations to the endless succession of tastings and wine lunches with which the industry courts the New York–based wine press, and led to a personal preoccupation with syrah. When the glamour of living as a young professional in New York City wore off, Rich was well enough hooked to decide that his calling was to do *something* in the wine business. He consulted the best importers of European wines—luminaries like Robert Chadderdon, Neal Rosenthal, and Robert Haas—but concluded in the end that he wanted to make wine hands-on.

In the summer of 1987, Rich took off for Burgundy, where he befriended the legendary Becky Wasserman, made arrangements to work the harvest with no less than Gérard Chave in Hermitage, and enrolled in the well-known Centre de formation professionnelle et de promotion agricole (CFPPA) course at Beaune's Lycée Agricole. A fellow student at the Lycée, John Elaisson (who later founded La Bête), would eventually become his introduction to Oregon, but meanwhile, still preoccupied with Rhône varieties, Rich worked for six years in California with Randall Graham at Bonny Doon. In 1995 he moved to Oregon, where he founded Andrew Rich wines with a few hundred cases of grenache rosé vinted from grapes grown in Washington state.

Rich's pinot noir program—always a second fiddle to his Rhône varieties—was launched the following year with grapes from a Dundee Hills vineyard that was later sold to DOMAINE SERENE; in 1998 his fruit source shifted to CHEHALEM'S Corral Creek Vineyard. In 1999 he made his "main" pinot (labeled Willamette Valley) from a combination of Corral Creek and Meredith Mitchell Vineyard fruit, concluded that a blend-based program worked best for his style, and began searching for a palette of vineyards that, taken together, could exemplify pinot from the northern Willamette Valley. He also created the first edition of a lighter, less age-worthy, entry-level pinot (which he called Cuvée B) crafted from barrels declassified from the main blend. By 2006 the Willamette Valley program was being crafted from eight vineyards in four AVAs, among which the structural anchor is Hyland Vineyard in the McMinnville AVA, whereas Cuvée B, made in every vintage except 2002, is typically anchored with Corral Creek fruit. Pinot accounts for about one third of Rich's total production, the lion's share of which is faithful to his original preoccupation with Rhône varieties, plus a bit of sauvignon blanc and late harvest gewürztraminer. Since 2002, Andrew Rich Wines has been an anchor tenant in the Carlton Winemakers Studio.

WINEMAKING NOTES

For pinot, most winemaking protocols follow the consensus protocol, relying on "completely ripe" fruit, all of which is destemmed and given four to five days of cold-soaking before the resident yeast become active, small inoculations to move the process along smartly thereafter, a combination of double-height fruit bins and small (3- and 4-ton) stainless open-tops, and a vatting that lasts a total of two to three weeks. The must is pressed when it goes dry. The new wine is then settled for twenty-four hours before being barreled in a roughly even mix of new, once-used, and twice-used *pièces*, most of which were coopered by Sirugue or Cadus. This regime, according to Rich, avoids excessive smokiness, which he does not like. Lighter-weight lots come out of barrel about thirteen months after the vintage, but the balance stay in wood until January two years after the vintage. My experience with Andrew Rich pinots is limited to the 2005 vintage, with Cuvée B showing nicely as a bright, red-fruit-and-flowers wine, while the Willamette Valley bottling, tasted prerelease, was seriously earthy with deeper color and a combination of blue and black fruit.

TASTING NOTES

2005 *Cuvée B (tasted in 2007):* Transparent, medium black-red; berry fruit and potpourri dominate the nose, with a whiff of white pepper; cranberry, cassis, and raspberry on the palate; polished tannins with some grip at the end.

2005 *Willamette Valley (tasted prerelease in 2007):* Medium-dark black-red; wet earth with blue and black fruits plus some raspberry on the nose; more fruit with hints of clove, mocha, merbromin, and tree bark on the palate; medium-weight and long; satiny on the mid-palate and grippy at the end.

ANNE AMIE VINEYARDS
Carlton, Oregon

Anne Amie is the new name, since 2001, of Château Benoit, a property located between Carlton and Lafayette that was first planted to wine grapes in 1979. Twenty years later, it was acquired by Robert Pamplin Jr., a somewhat larger-than-life Oregon businessman, farmer, minister, author, entrepreneur, and founder of the *Portland Tribune*, a twice-weekly, controlled-circulation newspaper. It was then so completely refocused qualitatively that it was renamed, though the Château Benoit moniker has been retained to designate a second label. Thirteen acres of pinot noir (UCD 4 and Dijon 115) were planted on the winery site between 1999 and 2004, on an east-southeast facing slope. Ten additional acres were planted on land Pamplin owns separately on the south face of the Chehalem Mountains west of Newburg, in sites dubbed Boisseau (between the 600- and 800-foot contours) and Louise (between the 470- and 520-foot contours), in 2000 and 2003, respectively. Both sites feature Laurelwood-series soils. The first scion material at Boisseau was entirely Dijon 114; at Louise it was entirely Dijon 777. Vines in both are planted densely at 2,000 per acre, and both sites are farmed sustainably. Forty more acres of pinot were planted in 2006 on these sites, of which 60 percent were dedicated to UCD 4 and 20 percent were dedicated to Dijon 777. In addition to these estate vineyards, Anne Amie sources pinot noir from several respected non-estate vineyards in the Yamhill-Carlton, Dundee Hills, Chehalem Mountains, and Eola-Amity Hills AVAs. These include Hawk's View, a 100-acre, south- and southeast-facing site near Sherwood that is sourced by numerous makers; Rainbow Ridge, in the foothills of the Coast Range northwest of McMinnville; La Colina, where Anne Amie gets about 4.3 acres of UCD 2A and 4 and three Dijon clones, located in the southwest corner of the Dundee Hills; and Deux Vert Vineyard near Yamhill. Scott Huffman, a local product who learned winemaking on the job at REX HILL and at Château Benoit before its acquisition by Pamplin, was the founding winemaker, serving from 2000 through 2006. He was succeeded in 2007 by Thomas Housman, a one-time professional dancer and home brewer later trained in viticulture and enology at California State University, Fresno, who worked at PONZI VINEYARDS from 2002 to 2006.

WINES AND WINEMAKING NOTES

The first pinots to appear under the Anne Amie label were vineyard-designated wines from non-estate vineyards, made in 2001. This list consisted of Hawk's View, Yamhill Springs, Laurel, Rainbow Ridge, and Doe Ridge, of which the last was made in 2001 and 2002 only. La Colina and Deux Vert wines were added to the portfolio in 2002. A high-end blended wine called Willamette Valley Winemaker's Selection, designed for depth, complexity, and agreeability, was introduced in 2004. Its complete opposite, a blend crafted from the cellar's more "fruit-forward" lots, was added the following year, and dubbed Cuvée A. Some fruit is sourced specifically for Cuvée A. Most recently, a reserve

cuvée debuted in 2006. The Château Benoit label was reintroduced in 2007 to designate an entry-level pinot, raised entirely in tanks. For the moment, all the estate fruit is being used in the Winemaker's Selection, the Reserve, or Cuvée A wines, although some single-vineyard wines should appear as the vines in these sites mature.

Anne Amie destems all fruit unless some of the stems are "fully lignified," in which case up to 20 percent may be used in whole-cluster form. From 2007, fermentations have relied entirely on resident yeasts. The percentage of new oak is low. In all other respects, Anne Amie follows the consensus protocol for pinot noir. Overall, these are attractive wines with light-to-medium weight and elegance.

TASTING NOTES

2005 *Cuvée A (tasted in 2007):* Bright, transparent, ruby; strawberry, raspberry, and cosmetic-case aromas; silky and very slightly peppery on the palate with an abundance of bright berry fruit; tasty, easy-drinking pinot noir.

2005 *Willamette Valley (tasted in 2007):* Brilliant, medium ruby; black-and-red-fruit nose with hints of earth; bright raspberry and cherry on the palate with notes of pepper and orange peel; nicely built without much weight and with just a hint of grip; long and silky overall with some spicy complexity at the end; attractive.

2005 *Deux Vert (tasted in 2007):* Brilliant medium-dark magenta; earthy nose with some conifer and cola; earth, hard spice, candied orange peel, and dark cherry in a bright, elegant package with a soft texture, medium weight, and considerable length; very attractive.

ARCADIAN WINERY
Santa Ynez, California

Joseph Davis, the eldest son of a Monterey, California, fishing family, financed his college education at the University of Puget Sound through the combination of an athletic scholarship and work in Tacoma's Vinoteque wine shop. The latter was seminal. For Christmas in 1982, one of the shop's loyal customers gave Davis a bottle of 1978 Domaine Dujac Clos de la Roche. Davis remembers that the wine was so impressive that it dictated his choice of career. Following graduate extension work in enology at UC Davis, ten vintages at MORGAN WINERY in Salinas, and a year's stint as acting president of Bernardus Winery in the Carmel Highlands, Davis launched Arcadian, an operation dedicated primarily to Burgundian varieties.

Arcadian's first wine was a chardonnay from the 1996 vintage; the first pinot noirs were made in 1997, and since 1999 there has also been a bit of syrah. Drawing on his experience at Morgan, where he began work in 1984 and made pinot from 1986 to 1994, and on hugely important lessons derived from time spent in Burgundy between assignments at Morgan and Bernardus, Davis chose to operate Arcadian, in his words, as a "traditional *domaine*." "I recognized," he says, "the distinction between being a winemaker and a winegrower. Burgundy also teaches us that a proactive approach to working the land helps to see the bigger picture and make better decisions for both the wine and the land." For Davis this meant complete control over farming decisions and their execution; working his rows of vineyard with his own crews; pruning and

trellising to his own specifications; and even planting, replanting, and (in some cases) interplanting by his own lights; not to mention paying for the grapes not by the ton of picked fruit but by the acre of farmed land. Davis believes yield is preeminently important to wine quality, and he prefers to measure yield as pounds per vine plant rather than as tons per acre. The ideal spacing in California, he finds, is 5-foot rows with about 5 feet between vines, which translates to around 1,850 vines to the acre. Davis believes such spacing is best farmed to produce between 2 and 2.5 tons of fruit per acre, or approximately 2.2 pounds per vine.

Arcadian's pinot program is now anchored with fruit from three regions: the Santa Lucia Highlands AVA in Monterey County, and the Sta. Rita Hills and Santa Maria Valley AVAs in Santa Barbara County. In the Santa Lucia Highlands, Robert Talbott's Sleepy Hollow Vineyard and Gary PISONI'S eponymous vineyard have been used continuously from the outset. At Sleepy Hollow, Davis farms six well-drained acres of sandy loam and Monterey shale at the top end of the vineyard in Block A, which is planted to a combination of UCD 13 and an unidentified upright clone. At Pisoni, Davis's parcel is another ridgetop site, this time 7 acres large, in Big Block. Since 1999 he has also sourced fruit from a 5-acre parcel in the Pisoni-Franscioni joint venture called Garys' Vineyard. In the Santa Maria Valley, Davis sourced Bien Nacido fruit from 1997 to 2001, at which point his attention shifted to the Dierberg Vineyard on the Santa Maria mesa, where he uses 6 acres split between two soil types—one primarily sandy loam, and the other mostly clay loam. The first Bien Nacido fruit came from Block T; in 1999 the source shifted to Block 2; in 2001 the sources were

Blocks N and Q. The first Dierberg (in 2002) was made almost entirely from UCD 31 with a dribble of Dijon 115; in 2003 Dijon 667 and UCD 13 were added to the mix. Gradually Davis shifted his southern Central Coast attention from the Santa Maria Valley to the Sta. Rita Hills, sourcing fruit from the Rio Vista

---

TRULY STUNNING WINES WITH GREAT AROMATIC COMPLEXITY THAT ARE GENUINE BENCHMARKS IN AMERICAN PINOT NOIR

---

and Fiddlestix vineyards in the Santa Ynez River valley. At Fiddlestix, an alternate-vintage protocol observed by the co-owners, FIDDLEHEAD CELLARS and Fosters Wine Estates, means that Arcadian cannot obtain fruit from exactly the same rows each year: the 2001 fruit was a combination of UCD 4, Dijon 113, and Dijon 115; in 2002 UCD 5 replaced the UCD 4, and Dijon 667 complemented the 113 and 115.

WINES AND WINEMAKING NOTES
Most Arcadian pinots are made as vineyard-designated wines, but regional blends are made occasionally, to accommodate wine lots that underexpress their site, or to accommodate the fruit of young vines. The Sleepy Hollow and Pisoni vineyard-designates have been made every year since 1997, and the Garys' has been made since 1999. Vineyard-designated wine from Bien Nacido was made from 1997 through 2001; in 1997, 1999, 2000, and 2001 it carried the submoniker "Jill's *Cuvée*." (In 2000 there were two Bien Nacido bottlings, one with the Jill's moniker, and one called

simply Bien Nacido.) Since 2001, there has also been a bottling from the Gold Coast Vineyard sold for an exceptionally reasonable price, though mostly to restaurants for by-the-glass programs. A blend of Garys' and Sleepy Hollow, labeled Santa Lucia Highlands, was made in 2000 and 2001. In 2001 Davis also made a special cuvée to celebrate the birth of his daughter. This cuvée, dubbed Francesca, was a blend of the four best barrels in the Arcadian cellar—all with exceedingly low pH. With half the production reserved for Francesca herself, and a quarter donated to children's charities, only a few cases of this exceptional wine were released commercially.

Davis is unusual in picking early by California standards and typically picks between 22.5 and 23 Brix. Flavors are well developed even at these low levels of sugar accumulation, he explains, as long as the winegrower manages yields to roughly the same levels demanded for *premier* and *grand cru* wines in Burgundy, which is between 2.0 and 2.5 tons per acre. (Ideally, this also equates to about 2.2 pounds per vine.) Stems and seeds will also be ripe, according to Davis, if irrigation, especially after veraison, has been minimized. Arcadian fruit is rigorously sorted on a long triage table to eliminate leaves, bunch rot, and mold. Fermentors are small wooden open-tops holding 1.5 to 1.75 tons each. A two-day cold soak enforced with dry ice precedes inoculation with RC212 yeast. Most lots are whole-cluster fermentations, which are foot-treaded to ensure very gentle extraction. The must is pressed just prior to going dry and is transferred, without much settling, to barrels, where the wine then spends as much as twenty-two months generally undisturbed and still on its gross lees. The press fraction is kept separate, used as topping wine, and sometimes reintegrated when the final blends are made.

For pinot noir, Davis prefers François Frères barrels, made from staves that have been air dried for three years and coopered entirely from Allier forests, but when he downsized his chardonnay program in 2001, quite a few of his favorite chardonnay barrels, coopered by Sirugue, were repurposed for pinot noir. A large percentage of new barrels is used to raise the pinot noir, but the impact of this is still subtle because Arcadian's early-picking protocol generates low-alcohol wines, which are slow to absorb tannins and flavors from their wooden environment. The long *élevage* and relatively high-acid, low-pH profile of the wines also ensure that they clarify naturally, so Arcadian pinots are finished without fining or filtration. Davis says plainly that he is trying to make wines that are "reminiscent of the Old World," and he favors protocols that would be considered "traditional" even in Burgundy. Owing to early picking, the finished wines are typically low in alcohol by American standards—normally less than 14 percent—and high in total acidity. (The Sleepy Hollow wines tend toward slightly lower acidities and higher pH levels than do the other Arcadian wines; these wines can therefore exhibit a slight haziness in their youth.) Arcadian pinots need their long barrel times to integrate, but in my experience the bottled wines are resolutely elegant and exceptionally food friendly. The combination of whole-cluster fermentations and long barrel times also seems conducive to aromatic complexities rarely found in California pinots and to an unusually delicate balance between primary, fruit-based flavors and focused, spicy-herbal aromatics. Many observers describe Arcadian pinots as "Burgundian," which is fair to the extent that non-fruit aromatics take up more of the wines' organoleptic space than is the case with many American pinots. As a group, they are truly stunning wines by any standard and genuine benchmarks in American pinot.

TASTING NOTES

2003 *Fiddlestix Vineyard (tasted in 2007):* Brilliant, rosy-magenta; walnut shells, potpourri, and merbromin on the nose; very bright red berry fruit with a hint of custard on the palate; finishes long with notes of garam masala; silky, serious, seductive, and impressive.

2003 *Gold Coast Vineyard (tasted in 2007):* Very transparent, medium black-red; aromas of black tea, dried seaweed (nori), potpourri, and raspberry; sweet raspberry, and black and white pepper on the palate; slightly lactic character; a very attractive, high-toned wine that finishes with barely a hint of grip.

2003 *Sleepy Hollow Vineyard (tasted in 2007):* Transparent medium black-red; earthy nose that is redolent of leather and tree bark; bright red fruit, red-hot candy, and coffee on the palate; rich, almost creamy, savory, rewarding, and distinctive.

2003 *Rio Vista Vineyard (tasted in 2007):* Transparent medium black-red; strongly floral nose with some conifer and hickory shell notes; nutty, savory, and spicy in the mouth; abundant high-toned red fruit and a surprising hint of sambuca; smooth, almost chamois-like texture; overall impression of serious elegance; very fine.

2002 *Pisoni Vineyard (tasted in 2007):* Stunning medium-dark rosy-magenta; explosive nose of white pepper and flowers with some raspberry and tangerine peel; tight and slow-to-open on the palate, but finally shows some creamy black custard and a bit of charcuterie; may soften with more time in bottle.

2001 *Santa Lucia Highlands (tasted in 2004):* Light-to-medium garnet and very slightly hazy; smoke, briar, cocoa powder, and black pepper on the nose; cinnamon and clove on the palate; medium weight and concentration; linen texture with just a hint of emery on the finish.

2001 *Sleepy Hollow Vineyard (tasted in 2004):* Light-to-medium crimson-garnet; again slightly hazy; rose petals, dried leaves and wild strawberry aromas; then briar and clove in the mouth; medium weight but quite intense.

2001 *Garys' Vineyard (tasted in 2004):* Brilliant, medium-dark ruby; aromas of dried flowers and wild strawberries; rich and complex palate of ripe cherries and raspberries, with tar, tree bark, black licorice, and black pepper; huge concentration on a medium-weight frame; long and satiny.

2001 *Central Coast "Francesca's Cuvée" (tasted in 2004):* Transparent, medium-dark black-red; aromas of cassis and potpourri; a feast on the palate, with wet earth, tar, licorice, and a hint of bay laurel; slightly minty at the end; chewy and grippy but still elegant; suede-textured; medium in weight and very long. Fine.

2000 *Pisoni Vineyard (tasted in 2004):* Transparent, medium-dark garnet; nose dominated by cocoa and charcuterie; cherry, cassis, licorice, and resin on the palate, with undertones of clove and cinnamon; a briary wine that is simultaneously rich, structured, serious, full-bodied, elegant, concentrated, and long; very fine.

1999 *Pisoni Vineyard (tasted in 2007):* Very transparent dark ruby; on the nose, Vosne-like earth, black pepper, exotic nuts, and a very appealing dried sweet ancho pepper character; rich, structured, and serious on the palate with more dried sweet red peppers, smoky earth, and hints of *salumi*; opens up progressively with time in the glass and then persists. Majestic, serious, and elegant; more than any other wine I have tasted, this shows the true power of the Pisoni site.

ARCHERY SUMMIT ESTATE
Dundee, Oregon

Archery Summit was Gary Andrus's first Oregon-centered and pinot-oriented wine venture, begun in 1992. Andrus had discovered wine during travels related to his first career as an Olympian and professional skier. He worked harvests in Bordeaux when it was too warm to ski in the northern hemisphere, studied enology at Montpellier in France, and used the proceeds from his share in the Copper Mountain, Colorado, ski resort to finance the purchase of Pine Ridge Winery in Napa Valley, which was his inaugural wine project. Eventually drawn by the challenge of pinot noir, finding that he liked Oregon pinots best in comparative tastings, and emboldened by Robert Drouhin's investment in Oregon, Andrus bought property immediately adjacent to DOMAINE DROUHIN in 1992 and also acquired the Fuqua vineyard on Red Hills Road. The first Archery Summit pinots were then "prototyped" at Pine Ridge in 1993 and 1994, an exercise which informed the design for the no-expense-spared, state-of-the-art, gravity-fed production facility subsequently built on Archery Summit Road in 1995—an establishment that includes an extensive network of barrel cellars dug into the hillside. In 1991 Andrus and his wife sold 90 percent of Pine Ridge LLC, which included both the California and the Oregon properties, to Leucadia National, a New York–based investment house whose other holdings span lumber, plastics, telecommunications, and health care; in 2002 Leucadia acquired the Andruses' remaining share.

Archery Summit owns four pinot vineyards in the Dundee Hills, and leases a fifth on Ribbon Ridge. The easternmost of the Red Hills sites—the former Fuqua vineyard, now renamed Red Hills Estate—anchored Archery Summit's pinot program during the 1990s. The oldest plantings here are currently out of production until 2009 for replanting. Just west of Red Hills Estate is Archery's Arcus Vineyard, a steep, bow-shaped parcel (hence the name), formed from the fusion of parts of two adjacent vineyards that had been purchased simultaneously in 1993. Andrus cannily redeveloped Arcus. Only the east-, south-, and southeast-facing blocks were retained for pinot. An old six-foot by nine-foot block of UCD 4 was interplanted and intraplanted so that the vines are now spaced three feet by four and a half, close to the meter-by-meter density favored in Burgundy. The third estate vineyard, on Archery Summit Road, is a steep, south-facing slope spanning elevation contours from about 230 to 520 feet that Andrus planted from scratch. Touching the edge of this vineyard in its highest northeastern corner is a separate, ridge-top vineyard called Renegade Ridge.

Most of the vines in all four vineyards are now Dijon clones on various rootstocks, although significant acreage is devoted to the Oregon workhorse selections, UCD 2A and 4. A great deal of attention, and some mythology, has been focused on cuttings Andrus claims to have imported from La Tâche, La Romanée-Conti, and Le Musigny, which he says he planted on Renegade Ridge. And indeed, Renegade Ridge appears (based on visual inspection) to have been planted, at least in part, to vines that display idiosyncratic properties quite unlike commercially available selections. Something said to have come from La Romanée Conti was subsequently designated ASW1; something said to have come from La Tâche was designated ASW2; something said to have come from Le Musigny was designated ASW3. Between 1997 and 2001, other wineries and growers obtained cuttings of one or more of these from Andrus. Some of these went, interalia, to neighboring Argyle, and to the Cerise Vineyard in Anderson Valley and other California sites; from Cerise and elsewhere, but not from Argyle, the plant material was further distributed. It seems that ASW1 and ASW3 showed visible signs of virus early on, and that most vines propagated from these cuttings (along with the parent vines or Renegade Ridge) were destroyed. ASW2 seems to have been a different matter, however. First grown in a demonstration block adjacent to the Archery Summit winery building, then in Block 1 at Renegade Ridge, and later in Block 21 at Red Hills and Looney (see below), ASW2 presented far fewer viral issues, an unusual and decidedly upright growth habit and, at Archery Summit and elsewhere, especially in marginal growing conditions, gave intensely flavored fruit with good color. For reasons that are not entirely clear, but apparently stem from conversations Andrus allegedly had with some of the vintners and growers who obtained cuttings, some ASW2, propagated in other vineyards, and redistributed by nurseries, has come to be known as Dijon (or CTPS) 828, even though it almost certainly is not. As this incorrect identity has become clear, some growers have begun to call it "faux-828" instead. (Meanwhile, the trademarked instance of 828 is not available in North America. Having tested positive for Redglobe virus in France and at FPS, it remains in quarantine at the University of California Davis, and will not be distributed by ENTAV in North America until a sanitized instance is available.)

Archery Summit's fourth estate vineyard, called Looney, is a leased site on Ribbon

Ridge between BRICK HOUSE and BEAUX FRÈRES, is a 17-acre parcel on a southeast-facing slope planted to eleven selections of pinot between 2000 and 2004.

Andrus was his own executive winemaker until his departure in 2001, but most day-to-day winemaking at Archery Summit was done by Sam Tannahill (see FRANCIS TANNAHILL) from 1995 until 2002. Anna Matzinger, who had come to Archery Summit in 1999, was named to succeed Tannahill in 2002. She is a graduate of Washington State's Evergreen State College with a background in environmental and Soviet studies whose wine training was gained, more or less, on the job. She previously worked at Beringer and Preston (of Dry Creek) in California, and in New Zealand and Australia. Leigh Bartholomew joined the staff as vineyard manager in 2000. She has been responsible for the transition of all the vineyards to essentially organic (though not certified organic) farming, and to the introduction of biodynamic protocols in the Renegade Ridge Vineyard from 2004.

WINES AND WINEMAKING NOTES
Archery Summit's wine portfolio was a bit complicated during the 1990s, partially because the fruit from young vines was segregated into two special bottlings (called Jeunesse and Archer's Edge) and partially because, until 2001, Archery Summit purchased fruit and made vineyard-designated wines from non-estate vineyards, including Brick House, SHEA, and two blocks at CRISTOM. Since 2001 the program has been a good deal simpler. There is a vineyard-designated wine from each of the four estate vineyards and (since 2003) from Looney, and one blend, called Premier [sic] Cuvée. Premier Cuvée uses fruit from all five vineyards and is the property's main release, accounting for the equivalent of about 6,000 cases.

Winemaking has not changed enormously since Andrus's day, although Matzinger likes wooden fermentors and has purchased enough to handle about one third of a typical vintage. Whole-cluster utilization averages around 20 percent. A five-to-ten day cold soak (tanks chilled by their jackets and wooden fermentors dry-iced) is followed by resident yeast fermentations that seem to peak naturally around 90°F in the wooden tanks and are held (via jackets) to about the same maximum temperature in the stainless open-tops. Conveniently, the thick siding and conical shape of the wooden tanks seems to hold the fermentation warmth for some time after the primary fermentation has finished, assuring a warm postfermentation maceration. The stainless tanks are allowed to cool after primary fermentation, to between 70 and 75°F. Matzinger explains, however, that vintages are different. In 2005, she reports, "fruit was quite happy to ferment between 65 and 75 degrees without enzyme additions." Total vatting times range from fifteen to thirty days. Archery Summit often finds that it drains or presses off the new wine several days after each fermentor tests dry, "at the sweet spot where tannin and mouth-feel coalesce."

The barrel stock is now quite different from the heavy-toast François Frères and Rousseau pièces to which Andrus was partial. Only about 50 percent of the barrel stock is now François Frères; Damy, Rousseau, Sylvain, and Sirugue barrels make up the balance. The Damy barrels usually figure prominently in the Arcus cuvée, as do Rousseau and François Frères in the Red Hills Estate wine. Archery Summit Estate is raised mostly in François Frères barrels; Renegade Ridge sees primarily Sirugue and Sylvain. Looney "is a bit of a collage." Wines are usually racked and blended at the beginning of June following the vintage. Red Hills Estate and Archery Summit Estate are blended first, returned to barrel for six or seven additional months, and bottled fifteen to seventeen months after the vintage. The rackings and bottlings of the Arcus, Renegade Ridge, and Looney lots vary by vintage. Overall, Archery Summit pinots display more black fruit and other dark flavors than red, and are extracted, serious, and fairly tannin-laden wines. They can be aromatically shy when they are young and almost always benefit from long breathing or decanting before being served.

TASTING NOTES

2005 *Red Hills Estate (tasted in 2007):* Dark, slightly purplish black-red; black fruit, charcoal, brown spice, and dark Belgian beer on the nose; blackberry with strong minerality and hints of molasses on the palate; good acidity but a substantial load of persistent tannin; dry from mid-palate to finish.

2004 *Archery Summit Estate (tasted in 2007):* Medium black-red; potpourri, vanilla, and cosmetic-case aromas; slightly sweet red fruit and a slightly spicy cherry-vanilla custard impression; very fine-grained tannins; sober and attractive; takes time to open aromatically after the cork is pulled.

2004 *Red Hills Estate (tasted in 2007):* Transparent, medium-dark magenta; slightly exotic nose of nut meats; expressive and attractive red fruit core; then rich, earthy minerality on the finish; mouth filling but leanly built and silky; very attractive.

2004 *Renegade Ridge (tasted in 2007):* Barely transparent dark black-red; smoky, slightly resin-y nose; very slight fruit-sweet attack; then almost austere with a silky mid-palate and some grip at the end; slight suggestive of good Gevrey-Chambertin.

2000 *Red Hills Estate (tasted in 2007):* Dark brick red; clove, soy, barrel char, and very ripe fruit on the nose; dominantly tannic and minerally with some very strong black tea; very masculine, concentrated, stalwart, and solid; tannins now soft on the front palate, but the wine is still serious and grippy from mid-palate to finish, with only a hint of fruit sweetness left.

ARGYLE WINERY
Dundee, Oregon

Argyle, on Dundee's main drag, occupying a combination of a former filbert processing plant and centenary frame house that served for a time as the town hall, is the creation of Rollin Soles, its founder and winemaker, and Brian Croser, one of the most important figures in Australian wine. Soles is a born and raised Texan (he talks the talk and looks the part) who discovered wine in college, worked as a cellar rat in Switzerland, earned a master's degree in enology at the University of California Davis, and worked in California for both Wente and Chateau Montelena—all before heading for South Australia's Petaluma Winery, where he joined the ranks of talented young winemakers mentored by Petaluma's founder, the aforementioned Croser. Somehow Soles and Croser cooked up an appealingly "crazy" idea: they would join forces to make sparkling wine in Oregon. Soles found the disused hazelnut processing facility, bought it bit by bit, identified hillside vineyards from which he could source fruit and, with some investment from Petaluma Winery Australia and Cal Knudsen, a partner with Dick Erath in Knudsen-Erath until 1990, created Argyle as Oregon's first dedicated producer of bottle-fermented, Champagne-method sparkling wine. Knudsen's 120-acre Dundee Hills vineyard, an object of continuing investment as new plant material became available and new viticultural practices were understood, was the foundation of Argyle's success with sparkling wines, which were sourced from its highest elevation blocks.

Finding that Oregon was warm enough to ripen red grapes for still wine as well as sparkling, and to ensure consistent quality from year to year, Argyle diversified into still pinot noir in 1992. This program, like its sparkling sibling, was anchored with Knudsen grapes, sourced from blocks just below the ones used for the sparkling wine, and supplemented with purchased fruit, from 1992 to 1997. In 1997 the STOLLER VINEYARD (q.v.), which Argyle farms for the Stollers, began to produce, and Stoller grapes entered the program. In 1999, Argyle's wholly owned estate vineyard came online and now anchors Argyle's still pinot program. The estate vineyard, called Lone Star, is 116 acres of vines planted in 1997 in the northeast corner of the Eola-Amity Hills AVA. All of the fruit for Argyle's high-end pinots is sourced today from tightly-spaced, grafted vines that represent a range of clonal material. Soles explains that the idea is to "derive pinot noir fruit from a range of elevations divided into lower, mid-, and high that allow us to move with Mother Nature vintage to vintage."

WINES AND WINEMAKING NOTES
Since 1999, in most vintages, Argyle has made five pinots. The largest volume, about 5,000 cases, is associated with the Willamette Valley blend. A Reserve, crafted for "subtlety," was originally anchored with fruit from the original planting at Knudsen—UCD 4 planted in 1972—but now derives most of its fruit from various Dundee Hills vineyards planted to high densities and featuring mostly Dijon clones. Argyle also makes small amounts of three wines with proprietary names: "Nuthouse," a big, inky wine that depends mainly on fruit

sourced from densely-planted, low-elevation vineyards and from blocks planted after 1995; "Spirithouse," which is based mainly on hillside vines including the 1993 high-density Dijon-clone plantings at Knudsen, plus UCD 4 from Knudsen and "a bit" of Stoller; and "Clubhouse," a barrel selection of Lone Star lots that is composed mostly of Dijon 667 and 777 for now, but may use fruit from the newest replantings at Knudsen in the future.

Soles finds the picking window for "good flavor" in still pinot to be wide, certainly by comparison with the analogous window for sparkling wine, and he usually uses a small percentage of whole clusters. Winemaking begins with grapes that are chilled overnight to 35°F and cold-soaked for five to seven days. Inoculations are based on strains of yeast selected privately from European cellars and grown at Argyle. Cap management relies entirely on hand-plunging, which Soles characterizes (to the amusement of his staff) as "team building," and there is a postfermentation maceration "for complexity and tannin management," whose length varies from vintage to vintage. After pressing, the new wines are sometimes settled for a day and sometimes sent directly to barrel. Unusually, most lots go into "fairly neutral" barrels first, where they remain until after the malolactic fermentation has finished in the February or March following the vintage. At this point Soles believes he can identify the style of each lot, match styles to coopers, and get better value for the new barrels which are then moved into the program. Most of the barrel stock is from Dargaud & Jaeglé, although some others are used "for spice." The duration of *élevage* has been increased in recent vintages to about seventeen months for all but the Willamette Valley pinots, and all are bottled without filtration. The Reserve and the "house" cuvées regularly attract high scores from *Wine Spectator*. I have a personal preference for the Reserve, which tastes a bit brighter and livelier to me than the "-house" wines. The latter display riper picking and warmer structures.

TASTING NOTES

2005 *Reserve (tasted in* 2007*):* Transparent, medium garnet; expressive nose of flowers and red berry fruit; slightly sweet and fruit-forward attack but then sober, smoky, and barrel-marked on the palate; nicely built and almost silky on the finish; medium-length.

2005 *Spirithouse (tasted in* 2007*):* Medium garnet; aromas of ripe black fruit; sweet on the palate with blackberry and boysenberry flavors and some infused flowers; some grip and barrel marking; tightly-knit and mouth coating; suede-like texture; warm finish.

2005 *Nuthouse (tasted in* 2007*):* Transparent, medium black-red; floral and nutty on the nose with some cabinet-shop aromatics; intense on the palate with very black fruit, smoke and a substantial load of very fine-grained tannin; warm and serious.

1999 *Spirithouse (tasted in* 2003*):* Transparent, medium black-red; exotic spices, *lapsang souchong* tea, and a hint of dried leaves; on the palate, more dried leaves over a moderately sweet core of cherry-berry fruit, toasted Indonesian spice, and white pepper; medium weight, long and seductive.

AU BON CLIMAT
Los Olivos, California

Jim Clendenen is one of the authentic pioneers of fine pinot noir in North America. Famous for his substantial physical stature, wild coiffure, occasionally outlandish dress, and outspoken opinions about winemaking and connoisseurship,

he could more justifiably be appreciated for his fundamental enological and viticultural curiosity, his encyclopedic familiarity with the best makers in Burgundy and elsewhere (built on a gregarious personality and fluent French), and his uncompromising craftsmanship. Born in Ohio to (by his own description) "gastronomically impoverished parents during the culinary Dark Ages of the American 1950s," Clendenen studied prelaw at the University of California Santa Barbara, played third-division basketball in Bordeaux, more or less memorized Edmund Penning-Rowsell's *Wines of Bordeaux* before graduating from college, and visited Burgundy and Champagne during the 1977 vintage. Having thereafter abandoned his remaining enthusiasm for legal studies, he made his first pinot noir as assistant winemaker for Zaca Mesa Winery in 1979, returned to Burgundy to work for Domaine Duc de Magenta in 1981, and founded Au Bon Climat (with fellow Zaca Mesa alumnus Adam Tolmach and a paltry $50,000 in capital) in 1982. The project was named for a hill just in front of the dairy barn at Los Alamos Vineyards, where Clendenen and Tolmach made their first vintages of pinot noir and chardonnay. The hill looked to Clendenen like a good Burgundian *mi-côte climat*.

The 1982 through 1986 vintages of Au Bon Climat pinot were made exclusively from Los Alamos Vineyards fruit, which was entirely UCD 5 clone, except for one lot of fruit trucked down from Oregon in 1985 and crafted as a separate bottling. But pinot noir was a hard sell in the early 1980s, and by 1986 Au Bon Climat had reduced its production to a mere 300 cases—against 3,000 cases of chardonnay. In 1987, however, Clendenen was able to purchase pinot noir grapes from the Sanford & Benedict vineyard, which then became a staple in his portfolio and served initially as the high-end anchor of Au Bon Climat's revived and expanded pinot program. In

1988, with the "home" Los Alamos vineyard up for sale, Clendenen made a deal with the Millers of Bien Nacido. The Millers built Clendenen a no-nonsense metal warehouse of a winery on the northwestern corner of the Bien Nacido ranch, and Au Bon Climat began to purchase Bien Nacido grapes. Fruit from Brian Talley's Rincon and Rosemary's vineyards debuted in Clendenen's pinot program in 1991. Ever since, Au Bon Climat's pinot program has been anchored with fruit from this trio of sources, spanning the Santa Ynez, Santa Maria, and Arroyo Grande valleys.

In addition, pinots have been made under two related labels: Ici/Là Bas and Cold Heaven. The former is a new company that Clendenen and the François Frères cooperage established in 1992. Ici/Là Bas pinots were initially made entirely from Oregon's Montinore vineyard, raised in 100 percent new heavy-toast François Frères barrels, explicitly designed to demonstrate that such cooperage was not—as many Oregon winemakers alleged at the time— "too strong" for Oregon fruit. Ici/La

---

A TRIUMPH OF THOUGHT OVER METHOD: INFINITE ATTENTION TO THE OPPORTUNITIES EACH VINTAGE AND VINEYARD PRESENTS

Bas's Oregonian orientation continued until 2002, but the project was gradually refocused on California grapes after 1997, beginning with a California-Oregon blend in 1997, and Anderson Valley pinot noirs after 1998. Cold Heaven, a brand that belongs to Clendenen's now ex-wife, Morgan, otherwise devoted to viognier, has also made pinot noir and was the first of the Clendenen brands to use grapes from

his first estate vineyard, Le Bon Climat. Planted in 1998, Le Bon Climat is 44 acres due south of Bien Nacido and due west of Byron on Palmer Road, and relies on Dijon 113, 115, and 667; UCD 5; Swan selection; Mount Eden selection from Sanford & Benedict; and UCD 2A from TALLEY. The array of pinots under the three labels is dizzying, but the common characteristics are varietal character (which Clendenen calls "pinocity") and a high tolerance for the foresty flavors that are sometimes described as "Burgundian funk."

WINES AND WINEMAKING NOTES
In Au Bon Climat's lineup, the main volume until 2001 was associated with two blended wines: a Santa Barbara County bottling (a blend of pinot noir and up to 18 percent mondeuse) and a Santa Maria Valley cuvée. Owing to inexorable increases in the price of grapes, the Santa Maria Valley wine was not made in 2002 or 2003, and was offered only for export after 2004. For the domestic market, a "basic" wine made entirely from estate fruit ("Le Bon Climat") debuted in 2002. Among the high-end Au Bon Climat pinots, the Sanford & Benedict is a genuine vineyard-designate, made in every vintage since 1987. The fruit Clendenen purchases from Brian Talley's Arroyo Grande vineyards travels various paths. Sometimes lots of Talley pinot are made as single-vineyard-designates, labeled either Rincon or Rosemary's. In 1996 and 1998, Rincon fruit was blended with fruit from Laetitia, also in the Arroyo Grande valley, to create a Laetitia and Rincon bottling. In 1994, 1997, 1999, and 2000, lots of Rincon and Rosemary's were blended with each other, appearing as Rincon and Rosemary's. In most years, Talley fruit also goes into the Isabelle bottling (see below).

The Talley vineyards are planted entirely to UCD 2A, but in this site UCD 2A gives a deeply colored, lush wine, quite different from its performance in Los Carneros, the Russian River valley, and Oregon. Clendenen's vineyard-designated pinot from Bien Nacido is called La Bauge au Dessus. The name is vintage Clendenen. *Bauge* is French for a pigsty. By extension it denotes filthy accommodations, sordid spots, and brothels. When Clendenen determined, in 1990, that the upper portion of Bien Nacido's Block Q (23 acres of UCD 4 planted in 1973) produced a wine with strong barnyard aromas and intense flavors, he appealed to French slang for its moniker. La Bauge au Dessus has been made every year since 1990, but fruit from Block 2 (a 1994 planting just above Q on Bien Nacido's main south-facing bench) and Block 11C, a small hillside parcel custom-planted in 1997, has now entered the Bauge blend. As if this array of wines were not enough, Clendenen decided to celebrate the conception of his daughter in 1994 and his son in 1998 by creating two additional Au Bon Climat pinots, eponymously designated Isabelle and Knox Alexander, respectively. Both are barrel selections. Isabelle consists of "the best barrels from the best sites" available to Clendenen, generally including some Rosemary's and some Sanford & Benedict, but often extending to barrels from as many as eight or nine sites. The first vintage of Isabelle, in 1994, was anchored with grapes from John Dyson's Vista Verde vineyard in Monterey County. From 1995 through 2003, Isabelle relied mainly on the Talley vineyards in Arroyo Grande. Since 2004, its anchor has been the new plantings at Sanford & Benedict. Knox Alexander, which debuted in 1998, was an even blend of the best lots of wine from Dijon clone plantings at Bien Nacido with the best non-Dijon lots until 2004. Since 2004 it has been made from custom plantings undertaken at Bien Nacido for Au Bon Climat and from fruit from Le Bon Climat.

Clendenen is first and foremost a champion of natural winemaking with few interventions or additives. He also insists that pinot should be picked "early" and "not too ripe." For him, La Tâche 1962 is an example of great wine from ripe fruit, whereas La Tâche 1971 is a great wine from less-ripe fruit. "Early" means 23 to 24.5 Brix. "Fruit at 25 Brix is nothing but a problem for us," he asserts. "The fermentation tends to get too warm and to stick, and the wine then ends up sweet and unstable." Au Bon Climat picks early in the morning so the fruit is guaranteed cold, and a "natural" cold soak follows. Primary fermentation is allowed to begin spontaneously with resident yeast, but the must is then inoculated "as a security blanket." Clendenen likes to build slowly to "a lot of heat"—peak temperatures reach 95 to 99°F—and advocates pumpovers rather than punchdowns on the front end "to keep seeds inside the grapes," to hold the pH down, and to preserve balance. By day six, he moves to a combination of punchdowns and pumpovers, or entirely to punchdowns. Although he began his career making pinot using 100 percent whole clusters, he has now backed off to zero on stem retention, but about one quarter of the fruit is retained as whole berries. Fermentors are 5-ton, 6-foot by 6-foot open-top stainless steel cylinders that are not temperature controlled. The must is generally pressed when dry, consolidated in tank, and then barreled in 35 percent to 100 percent new François Frères cooperage.

Until about 2002, Clendenen practiced an interesting variation of this theme, bleeding a small fraction of highly pigmented juice from each fermentor on day four of the vatting, which was then fermented separately in barrel and reassembled, either at first racking or in the consolidation tank after pressing. Clendenen found that these barrel fermentations favored the development of special aromatic properties, notably chocolate, coffee, and mocha. In recent vintages, however, these *saignée* operations have been largely discontinued, except when they have been deemed useful to achieve "balance." Once barreled, Au Bon Climat pinots spend twelve to twenty months in wood. Fining is routine, but only about one pinot in twenty is filtered. Observers often claim that Burgundy is "intellectual" wine. I have never been entirely sure what this is supposed to mean, but Clendenen's pinots do give the impression of thought prevailing over method. Each of the wines described below, and many others I have tasted closer to their maturity, testify to site, and sometimes also to blends, expressed with infinite sensitivity and attention to the opportunities each vintage and each vineyard presents.

TASTING NOTES

2005 *Bien Nacido Vineyard (tasted in 2007):* Transparent rosy-magenta color; aromas of moss, earth and sweet fruit; rich, nuanced, and layered on the palate, featuring apple peel, cranberry, strawberry, dark cherry, and Santa Rosa plum; bright and nicely built with a satiny mid-palate and a bit of signature Bien Nacido black pepper at the end; very attractive.

2005 *Los Alamos Vineyard (tasted in 2007):* Light-to-medium rosy-red color; aromatically unusual, offering both herbs and salt; bright and almost delicately structured on the palate, but richly flavored; mostly red berry fruit but also earthy; silky to mid-palate, then austere from mid-palate to finish; attractive and distinctive.

2005 *Sanford & Benedict Vineyard (tasted in 2007):* Transparent medium rosy-garnet color; exotic spice, licorice, gum camphor, and flowers on the nose; red currants and mesquite on the palate; first slightly sweet

and silky, then grippy, stalwart, solid, and Gevrey-like from mid-palate to finish; a beautiful, leanly built, mysteriously elegant wine meant for the ages.

2005 *Le Bon Climat (tasted in 2007):* Medium rosy-ruby color; intense, slightly smoky, dark-fruited nose; the sweetest of the single vineyard wines in this vintage; quite black with rich flavors including mocha and black licorice; a tightly knit, seamless wine; grippy from mid-palate to the end; impressive.

2005 *Isabelle (tasted in 2007):* Transparent medium-dark ruby color; red fruit with hints of orange peel and cabinet-shop aromas; elegant, voluptuous, nicely knit fruit and mineral flavors; some cherry-clove properties and an impression of cinnamon-spiked plum *clafouti*; very serious and fine.

AUGUST WEST WINE
Sebastopol, California

August West is a partnership of Howard Graham, a retired Silicon Valley financial executive who was most recently the CFO for Siebel Systems; Gary Franscioni, a Salinas Valley farmer involved with wine grapes since 1996 (see ROAR WINES); and Ed Kurtzman, the winemaker at TESTAROSSA VINEYARDS from 1999 to 2002. Graham was an early investor in Testarossa, and remains a member of its board of directors. Kurtzman is an alumnus of Bernardus (in Carmel Valley) and CHALONE, where he worked from 1995 to 1998; he is also the winemaker for FREEMAN VINEYARD AND WINERY. Founded in 2002, August West is dedicated entirely to pinot noir, syrah, and chardonnay made from the partners' vineyards: Franscioni's Rosella's Vineyard in the Santa Lucia Highlands and the Graham Family Vineyard in the Green Valley corner of the Russian River Valley AVA. Rosella's is 50 acres of vine planted between 1996 and 2003, of which 37 are pinot noir. It is sandy loam benchland located about 4 miles southwest of Gonzales. Graham Family consists of 8.5 planted acres, all pinot noir, on a 12.5-acre site off Ross Station Road, adjacent to HARTFORD COURT's Arrendell Vineyard, overlooking IRON HORSE. It is a southwest-facing plateau of chalky Goldridge soil sloping very slightly northeast and is irrigated so conservatively that it could almost pass for being dry farmed. The plant material is mostly Swan selection and Dijon 667 and 777, with smaller amounts of Dijon 828 and Calera selection. The first crop off the Graham Family Vineyard was harvested in 2004 and divided between Testarossa and August West, with a bit also earmarked for SIDURI WINES. In 2005 the very small crop was divided between Testarossa and August West. In 2006 some pinot was also sold to LORING WINE COMPANY and to KOSTA BROWNE.

WINES AND WINEMAKING NOTES

In 2002 and 2003, August West produced only one wine, a vineyard-designated pinot noir from Rosella's. In 2004 and 2005, a vineyard-designated wine from the Graham Family Vineyard joined the portfolio. Additional vineyard-designated wines from Graham's second vineyard, a joint project with vineyard manager Charlie Chenoweth in the Sebastopol Hills; and from Franscioni's new vineyard 5 miles south of Rosella's, are expected to enter the lineup in 2009. Kurtzman picks pinot at approximately 26.5 Brix, destems completely, cold-soaks for three to five days, allows

fermentations to start with resident yeast but then inoculates to ensure unimpeded completion, and presses lightly when the must is dry. Wines usually spend nine to ten months in a combination of Cadus and François Frères barrels, about 40 percent of which are new in each vintage. This regime produces wines that are ripe, soft, and mouth filling, but which still showcase both vintage and *terroir*. They also display a broad palette of flavors but can finish warm.

TASTING NOTES

2005 *Graham Family Vineyard (tasted in 2007):* Darkish blue-black hue; earthy nose with hints of black pepper and dried cherries; sweet and ingratiating in the mouth, with a slight flavor of molasses; a fine-grained, mouth-filling, and long wine.

2005 *Rosella's Vineyard (tasted in 2007):* Brilliant and a tad paler than the 2002 and 2003 vintages; gum camphor aromas; spicy, rich, dark, and slightly sweet on the palate; noticeably, if softly, grippy and long.

2002 *Rosella's Vineyard (tasted in 2007):* Deep, almost saturated black-red color; spicy, rosy-floral nose marked with gum camphor; slightly sweet, soft, and elegant in the mouth with notes of black cherry and orange peel; an impression of glycerin, a round mouth-feel, and medium weight. Drinking well in 2007.

B. KOSUGE WINES
Napa, California

Byron Kosuge, a Davis-trained enologist who began college as an English major, worked for a decade at SAINTSBURY, then amassed intercontinental experience making mostly pinot noir and syrah in California (see the MIURA profile for additional information) and Chile, where he is the winemaker for Kingston Family Vineyards in the Casablanca Valley. He launched his own wine brand in 2004.

EXCEPTIONALLY PRETTY, STRUCTURALLY ELEGANT, AND UNCOMPROMISINGLY SITE-SPECIFIC WINES

The B. Kosuge portfolio is focused on coastal California north of San Francisco, and primarily on pinot noir, with syrah cast in a supporting role.

In 2004, there were three pinots, one called "The Shop," crafted from a three-acre vineyard on the north side of the Carneros Highway just east of its junction with Old Sonoma Road that serves primarily as a shop site for a local vineyard management firm; a vineyard-designated wine from the much-respected HIRSCH VINEYARDS near Cazadero in the True Sonoma Coast; and a second true-coastal, vineyard-designated wine from the Manchester Ridge Vineyard in Mendocino County. Manchester Ridge was planted in 2001, at the 2,000-foot contour of the mountain ridge closest to the Pacific coast, north of Point Arena. The Carneros vineyard is planted to Dijon 115, 777, and (unusually) UCD 38, an especially aromatic selection of pinot noir taken from a vineyard in the Jura *département*. Because of rainy spring weather that interfered with fruit set, there was no Manchester Ridge bottling in 2005, but otherwise the three cuvées with which Kosuge launched the brand have persisted.

Kosuge is an exceptionally reflective winemaker, who thinks deeply about the assets and liabilities of each of the sites

he uses, as well as related experience, and adapts his protocols accordingly. Concerned, for example, that Carneros pinots can be deficient in aromatic expression, Kosuge ferments The Shop lots with up to one-third whole-cluster fruit and relies primarily on barrels (such as those from Taransaud) that have an "understated" impact on aromatics. Overall, he is a believer in relatively early picking, resident-yeast fermentations, carefully managed extractions, and bottling before the next vintage. The incidence of new barrels used for any single wine rarely exceeds 30 percent. The wines are exceptionally pretty, structurally elegant, and uncompromisingly site specific.

TASTING NOTES

2005 *The Shop (tasted in 2007):* Brilliant, medium rosy-ruby; earthy and floral nose; rich, soft, sweet black cherry with some black pepper on the palate; medium-long and very attractive.

2005 *Hirsch Vineyard (tasted in 2007):* Transparent, dark black-red; very expressive nose of herbs, flowers, and orange flower water; spicy and intense on the palate, with some dark fruit, slate-y minerality, grip, and bright acidity. Still young, but very promising.

BABCOCK WINERY AND VINEYARDS
Lompoc, California

In 1978, the same year that Bryan Babcock entered Occidental College in Los Angeles, his parents purchased 110 acres of ranchland on Highway 246 between Buellton and Lompoc as a retreat from careers in dentistry and restaurants. Two years later, having observed the preoccupations of their new neighbors, the Babcocks converted 25 acres of their ranch to vineyard. When Bryan graduated from college in 1982, the lure of the vineyard was strong enough to overcome his fascination with "ideas, goods, services, and the marketplace." He abandoned the idea of earning an MBA and enrolled instead at the University of California Davis to study food science and enology. In 1984 he stayed home for the first crush at the family's new, small winery, and "forgot about school altogether." The once-small winery now turns out 25,000 cases annually, and the vineyard surface on the ranch has grown to 75 acres.

Although the ranch was originally planted entirely to white varieties, and the brand was best known for fine sauvignon blanc until late in the 1990s, Babcock has been involved with pinot noir from the outset. Early vintages of pinot noir were made from grapes purchased from the Sierra Madre Vineyard; later on, and until 1997, fruit was also purchased from Bien Nacido's Block G. In 1986 the first vines of pinot noir were set out in the estate vineyard, and the first commercial release of estate pinot followed in 1989. Over the years, as phylloxera forced Babcock to replant blocks of own-rooted white varieties, and as the vocation of the Sta. Rita Hills turned unambiguously toward Burgundian varieties, the estate commitment to pinot noir increased.

By 2007, 32 acres had been dedicated to pinot, and Babcock had begun a major "reengineering" of the entire vineyard. Babcock explains that he spent his first decade on the ranch "learning how to make wines," and the second "learning how to be a business person." Part of the reengineering involves tightening vine spacing from the 11-foot rows with 3 feet between vines, used historically at Babcock, to 6- or 7-foot rows with 3 or 3.5 feet between vines, with the exact "geometry" of planting tailored to the variety and microtopography. The balance is based on dismantling and reassembling secondhand tractors in the ranch's machine shop, slicing these (using a huge rock drill manufactured by Ingersoll Rand) in half, and then rebuilding them as behemoth tractors that can span, spray, and cultivate simultaneously across *two* 6-foot rows.

Babcock is committed to identifying and respecting what he calls "the sweet spots that affect wine quality," but also to searching for ways to improve grape-farming efficiency, to replace labor with machines, and to increase the surface area a single laborer can cover in a working day. Babcock argues persuasively that the American wine market will be unable to absorb the volume of pinot noir that expensive farming will produce in the coming decade. His mission, in this timeframe, is to be sure that Babcock can produce "a really good bottle of Sta. Rita Hills pinot" for around $20 a bottle—alongside boutique quantities of ultrapremium pinot where no corner is cut.

WINES AND WINEMAKING NOTES
From 1984 through 1988, Babcock's only pinot noir was a Santa Barbara County bottling, made initially from Sierra Madre fruit and then from Bien Nacido. Beginning in 1989, when the first estate fruit came on stream, the best lots of estate grapes were used to make a pinot labeled Estate Grown, whereas the balance was blended into the Santa Barbara County wine. Occasionally, when the Bien Nacido fruit was "extraordinary," it was made as a vineyard-designate.

After the 1997 harvest, Babcock decided to concentrate on the estate vineyard and its immediate neighbors in the Sta. Rita Hills, so he discontinued the purchase of

Santa Maria Valley grapes and changed the composition of the Santa Barbara County wine. The estate pinot, called Grand Cuvée from 1998 through 2001, when the name was repurposed (see below), was joined by the first of several vineyard-designated wines from neighboring non-estate vineyards. A Mount Carmel vineyard-designate was made from 1997 through 2004, except in 1999, when the harvest was tiny, and in 2002, when hungry deer ate the entire crop. A second vineyard-designate from Peter Cargasacchi's 1999 planting of Dijon 115 was made from 2001 through 2005. Meanwhile, a blended wine called Tri-Counties Cuvée, which combined estate fruit, other Santa Barbara fruit, and grapes from Sonoma and Mendocino counties, was created as a response to the short harvest in 1999. It proved so popular with consumers and distributors that it was revived from 2001 through 2005, during which time it served to confirm Babcock's view that modestly-priced pinot was essential to his portfolio.

Beginning in 2006, the modest-priced "blended wine" segment of the pinot program, rechristened Rita's Earth, was made to rely entirely on grapes from the Sta. Rita Hills AVA. The estate wine (Grand Cuvée until 2001) was renamed Ocean's Ghost in 2004. And, in the background, Babcock rediscovered a Templeton Gap vineyard, planted in limestone soils and owned by Rabbit Ridge, that he had admired when he thought—erroneously—that it was planted to syrah. He called this block Déjà Vu, and used it as the basis for a block-designated pinot from the Paso Robles AVA beginning in 2005.

Overall, Babcock's winemaking is organized to ensure that the wines are "the natural product of their fruit." "You can predict the wine from the fruit," Babcock asserts. "Pinot noir that starts off nice and rich and dark in cluster samples will usually make a great wine." Sta. Rita Hills pinot is usually picked between 24 and 26 Brix, which corresponds to pH levels around 3.25 in the berries, or 3.6 to 3.7 in the finished wine. Lower pH levels, he believes, make the wine "too sharp." Grapes are picked cool, are completely destemmed, and are inoculated within twenty-four hours. Fermentors are 1.5-ton stainless steel open-tops. Fermentations move quickly and usually finish in eight or nine days, with once-daily punchdowns. Babcock prefers juice temperatures between 85 and 95°F, which he thinks produce "silky" wines; higher temperatures are rare anyway since small fermentors lack the mass to generate high heat. Pressing can occur at or just before dryness, but malolactic cultures are not introduced until each cuvée tests dry. Gentle press fractions are often reunified with the free-run juice. Harder press fractions are evaluated. If they pass a taste test, they go into the Rita's Earth cuvée; otherwise, they are bulked out. Postfermentation, the Rita's Earth wine is treated quite differently from the better cuvées. Essentially, it is tank raised, with some assist from wood chips and/or powders, while the other pinots are barreled for ten to sixteen months. In the latter program, Remond and Marsannay are the favored coopers, and tighter grain wood (e.g., wood from the Tronçais and other Allier forests) is preferred.

In recent years, Babcock has come to favor medium-to-heavy toasts, whereas lighter toast had previously been his main choice. One third to two thirds of the barrel stock is new at any time. Wines are rarely fined but are filtered as necessary "for stability"—although the better cuvées are handled so that filtration is almost never required. After bottling, Babcock pinots are generally held for three to six months before release. In general, Babcock pinots are fruit-driven wines with plush textures, although some older vintages also show strong minerality.

2005 Ocean's Ghost (tasted in 2007):
Very ripe, red fruit suggestive of fruit
pie; camphor-y, spicy, and intense on the
palate, with some noticeable grip at the
end; sweet vanilla on the finish.

2005 Déjà Vu (tasted in 2007): Very
transparent, light-to-medium garnet;
preponderance of floral aromatics on a
background of strawberry and raspberry;
intense and slightly sweet in the mouth;
raspberry and cherry fruit, with a hint of
hard spice and herbs; peppery and slightly
warm at the end; lingering; linen-textured;
attractive.

BAILEYANA WINERY
San Luis Obispo, California

For most of the twentieth century, the Niven
family operated a chain of retail grocery
stores covering most of northern California,
from Fort Bragg to Fresno. Under increasing
pressure from larger chains in the 1960s,
Purity Stores was first downsized, and then
liquidated, as the family turned its sights
to new opportunities. Agriculture appealed
generally; viticulture appealed in particular.
Advisers from the University of California
Davis and California State University
Fresno, hired by the family in 1969 to survey
viticultural opportunities up and down the
California coast, were especially bullish about
the Edna Valley's potential for ultrapremium
wine grapes. On this basis, Jack Niven
planted Edna Valley's first large commercial
vineyard, which he called Paragon, in 1972
and 1973.

Although Paragon was planted to a bit of
many grape varieties, in the shotgun fashion
of the day, pinot noir and chardonnay

proved most successful and attracted the
attention of CHALONE founders, Dick
Graff and Philip Woodward. This led to the
creation of EDNA VALLEY VINEYARD as
a Chalone-Niven partnership, and finally
spawned the Baileyana brand. Baileyana
itself began as Catharine Niven's very
personal, pint-size, front-yard foil to her
husband's giant Paragon project. The first
wines, chardonnay from a 3-acre vineyard on
Tiffany Ranch Road, were made in 1984 and
sold under the Tiffany Hill name; Tiffany
& Co. sued, and the name was changed to
Baileyana in 1991.

In the second half of the 1990s, Catharine
and her husband both passed away, leaving a
second generation responsible for the family's
constellation of wine-related businesses.
The first pinot bottled under the Baileyana
label was made in this period and was
sourced from the Paragon Vineyard, while a
second large, commercial vineyard, dubbed
Firepeak, was planted about 2 miles away,
at the foot of an extinct volcano called Islay
Mountain. The family engaged Christian
Roguenant, a native of Burgundy and the
founding winemaker at nearby Maison
Deutz, as the winemaker for Baileyana and

BRIGHT, INTENSE WINES
BUILT ON A BACKGROUND
OF BLACK PEPPER, SAGE,
AND BAY LAUREL

---

chief designer for Orcutt Road Cellars, a new
winemaking facility built on the Firepeak site
to serve Baileyana and a large custom-crush
business, optimized for pinot noir.

The Firepeak Vineyard is an unusual
combination of marine sedimentary soils and
volcanic remnants. It consists of 192 planted
acres, of which 82 are pinot noir, in thirteen
different blocks. The scion material is

UCD 2A, 4, and 23, and Dijon clones 115, 667, and 777 on various rootstocks, planted in 10-foot rows with 4- and 6-foot intervine spacings. Roguenant explains that the "big insights" he derived from earlier experiences with pinot noir in the southern Central Coast were the importance of clonal selection, the fundamentality of north–south row orientation in coastal vineyards, and the necessity of ensuring that grape clusters are not shaded from the sun.

WINES AND WINEMAKING NOTES

An Edna Valley estate pinot was made in every vintage from 1996 to 2001. From 1996 to 1998, its exclusive source was the Paragon Vineyard, although a second pinot, from the La Colline Vineyard (originally planted by Maison Deutz and now farmed by Laetitia, its successor) in Arroyo Grande, was made in 1997, and a pinot composed of both Edna Valley and Arroyo Grande fruit was made in 1998. In 1999 and 2000, the Edna Valley estate wine was made from a mix of Firepeak and Paragon fruit, while a second "estate" wine joined the lineup, made only from Firepeak grapes. In 2001 Baileyana's nationally distributed prestige cuvée, called Grand Firepeak Cuvée (GFC), a selection of the best "clones, blocks, and barrels," debuted. By 2002 Baileyana's entire pinot program was based on Firepeak grapes, and a trio of block- and clone-specific wines had joined the "plain" estate wine and the GFC in the portfolio.

Roguenant performs detailed analysis of grape phenolics before harvest; measures anthocyanins, polyphenols, glucosides, and glycosides inter alia; and tailors several parameters of winemaking to account for phenolic variations from vintage to vintage. In the vineyard he is a fairly aggressive leaf puller and a relatively early picker—although his idea of early picking usually equates to about 25 Brix. In recent vintages he has developed a preference for relatively cool fermentations—around 82°F—to maximize perfume, and he hot washes new barrels before using them for pinot to minimize wood-derived flavors in the finished wines. Baileyana pinots are bright, intense wines, with elegant structures, medium weight, and nuanced aromatic profiles, whose background consists of black pepper, sage, and bay laurel.

TASTING NOTES

2003 *GFC (tasted in* 2006*):* Medium-dark black-red color; rose petal aromas; cherry and cassis on the palate, with hints of mocha, tar, and white pepper; denser color and more glycerin than the older vintages; sweet and savory; velvety and medium-long.

2002 *GFC (tasted in* 2006*):* Brilliant, medium black-red; intense camphory nose with some black pepper; cherry, cassis, and blackberry on the palate, with infused violets; simultaneously savory and fruit-sweet, but elegant; suede-textured; soft and medium-long.

2001 *GFC (tasted in* 2006*):* Brilliant, medium rosy-garnet; very bright, nicely lifted aromatics; intense red fruit flavors in the mouth; hints of herbs, clove, and pepper; texture of rough silk; medium-long; very attractive.

BEAULIEU VINEYARD
Rutherford, California

Beaulieu, the iconic wine estate founded by Georges de Latour at the turn of the last century, has been involved albeit peripherally in the story of American pinot noir ever since. A good deal of folklore has grown up around the record, however, and certain key information is not known for sure. What is known is described in Chapters Three and Four of *North American Pinot Noir* and summarized here for convenience.

First, although pinot noir was planted and bearing in Beaulieu's Rutherford vineyards before Prohibition, the origin of the plant material is not documented. De Latour's early interest in pinot seems to have turned on its use in sparkling wine, however, and there is no record of still varietal pinot noir at Beaulieu until the 1940s. Second, although it is true that Beaulieu's legendary winemaker from 1938 until 1973, the Russian-born chemist André Tchelistcheff, had great affection for pinot noir and was an early champion of Carneros as a site for cool-climate varieties, Beaulieu pinots made in the 1940s and 1950s were *not* made from Carneros-grown grapes, but instead from pinot grown in the estate vineyards known internally as BV1 and BV2, located on the west side of Highway 29 in Rutherford. The pinot vines currently in BV1 and BV2 may have been survivors from de Latour's initial plantings ca. 1900 and 1907, respectively, but are more likely to have been propagated when these vineyards, like many others in Napa, were replanted, in whole or in part, following the repeal of Prohibition in 1934. Beaulieu's first Carneros vineyard was not planted until 1965, and the brand's pinot program was not anchored there until the end of the 1960s. Third, although the winery cites the 1946 vintage as its first for pinot noir, varietal pinot had been made there at least as early as 1943; 1943 Beaulieu Pinot Noir was on offer in San Francisco's Bohemian Club in 1949. Fourth, despite Tchelistcheff's great expertise, Beaulieu was an active player in the confusion over what was, and was not, authentic pinot noir in the 1960s and 1970s. Beaulieu's

"Beaumont" bottling, made throughout this period, was indeed vinified from 100 percent pinot noir; however, so was its apparently varietal Gamay Beaujolais, which was not made from gamay noir.

Relatively contemporary developments at Beaulieu are, of course, much better documented. The family sold the brand, winery, and business to Heublein Inc. in 1969, and various successors to Heublein, currently Diageo Chateau & Estate wines, have owned it since. Beaulieu owns or leases 1,100 acres in Napa and Carneros and produces more than 400,000 cases. Three bottlings of pinot noir are now made: BV Coastal, introduced in 1998 as a reformulation of the value-priced line that had been "Beaumont"; Carneros Pinot Noir; and Reserve Pinot Noir. All of these are built from fruit grown in Beaulieu's three Carneros vineyards: the BV5 vineyard Tchelistcheff first planted in 1965, and two newer sites called BV8 and BV9.

Beaulieu's most senior winemaker and now vice president for winemaking is the much-respected Joel Aiken, a University of California Davis-trained enologist who has been at Beaulieu since finishing his graduate work at Davis in 1982; hands-on responsibility for pinot noir (along with sangiovese, grenache, and some white varieties) has belonged since 2004 to Domenica Totty. Most fermentors are bled to increase concentration, and the *saignée* is used to make a pinot noir rosé. Although a relatively large volume is produced, I have had limited experience with recent vintages of Beaulieu pinot noir.

TASTING NOTE

2004 *Reserve (tasted in* 2007*):* Medium-dark black-red: on the nose, smoke, cherry-raspberry fruit, menthol, and eucalyptus; remarkably persistent juxtaposition of sweet fruit and strong graphite-and-barrel-char character; from mid-palate to finish, the wine is dry and chalky.

BEAUX FRÈRES
Newburg, Oregon

Beaux Frères is a well-known, all-pinot-noir project owned by Michael Etzel; his world-famous (in wine circles) brother-in-law, Robert M. Parker Jr.; and a Canadian wine lover and investor named Robert Roy. It is in the newly minted Ribbon Ridge AVA of Oregon's Willamette Valley. Etzel and his wife found the property, which was then an 88-acre pig and dairy farm, in 1986. The first 5 acres of vines were planted in 1988, and the first fruit, harvested two years later, was sold to KEN WRIGHT and PONZI VINEYARDS. Etzel, who was then working for Ponzi as a cellar rat, was impressed with the Ponzi wine made from Beaux Frères's fruit. At the same time, Parker, according to Etzel, grew "tired of dumping money" into the unprofitable grape-growing venture. The brothers-in-law sold a one-third share in the property to Roy, whose investment was sufficient to transform the farm's pig barn into a winery and launch the Beaux Frères brand (see ADEA WINE COMPANY for additional background). Three barrels of Beaux Frères pinot noir were made in 1991; the year 1992 was the first serious commercial release. As a matter of policy, Parker does not review Beaux Frères wines.

The Beaux Frères estate vineyard is laid out on south- and southeast-facing hillsides above the pig barn turned winery, between the 400- and 500-foot contours. The rows—which are oriented 19 degrees east of north–south to accommodate the prevailing slope—are spaced 6 feet apart with 1 meter between vines, which yields a very dense 2,200 vines per acre. The scion material for the 1988 planting was own-rooted UCD 2A and 4 sourced from a nursery; for the 1989 and 1990 plantings, it was budwood from nearby vineyards. Beginning in 1992, 8 more acres were planted to nursery-sourced Dijon clones, for a total of 24 acres. Some of the early own-rooted plantings have since been replaced, owing to phylloxera.

The first Dijon-clone fruit appeared in Beaux Frères wines in the 1997 vintage. A separate, higher-elevation vineyard called Beaux Frères—The Upper Terrace, an 11-acre, southeast-facing hilltop parcel, was planted at the end of the 1990s, entirely to Dijon 113, 114, 115, 667, and 777; it produced its first crop in 2002. (For variety, there are also fifteen rows of grenache on the Upper Terrace. Upper Terrace pinot has been vinified and finished as a wine of its own from the outset.)

Viticultural practices are fastidious, with spring pruning to a single cluster per shoot, vertical shoot positioning, leaf pulling on the east side of each row, and green harvesting before veraison to achieve a target yield of approximately 2 tons per acre. No synthetic treatments except for fungicides are used; farming has been essentially organic, although not so certified for several years, and fully biodynamic (although again, not so certified) since 2006. Cover crops, including nitrogen-fixing legumes, such as Australian pea, help control the vines' tendency to vigor. The Willakenzie soils are relatively deep at Beaux Frères but are very well drained. Fruit sales to other wineries were terminated after the 1992 harvest.

WINES AND WINEMAKING NOTES
Picking is done in quarter-ton bins, and the fruit is hand sorted at the winery. Following

a five-day cold soak in 2- and 4-ton jacketed stainless steel fermentors, heat is used to kick-start the alcoholic fermentation, which relies primarily on resident yeast. Tank jackets are used to flatten the fermentation's naturally bell-shaped curve and keep the maximum juice temperature around 85°F.

A RIPE-PICKED, WELL-EXTRACTED BLACK-FRUIT STYLE

Punchdowns are done twice daily, until the must is approximately dry; extended maceration continues until the entire vatting has lasted for nineteen to twenty-one days. After pressing, the wine is barreled without settling.

With the exception of the 1993 and 1995 vintages, every vintage of Beaux Frères until 1999 was raised in 100 percent new, heavy-toast François Frères barrels. Beginning with the 1999 vintage, the norm became 80 percent new wood, medium to medium-plus toast, and barrels made from three-year-air-dried staves. Malolactic fermentation is left to begin spontaneously, and often does not finish until the spring after the vintage. The wines are not racked until just before bottling, which is done in the autumn or winter after the vintage. There is no fining or filtration.

From 1991 to 1995, Beaux Frères made only one wine each year, entirely from estate fruit. In 1996—confronted with a demand from some customers for a lighter-weight, less-extracted wine, "less like a zinfandel or a syrah," in Etzel's phrase—Parker and Etzel launched Belles Soeurs. This was, as it sounds, wine of a different style, built from barrels of Beaux Frères estate wine exhibiting lighter color, lower alcohol, and less black fruit character.

From 1998 through 2004, non-estate fruit was purchased expressly for Belles Soeurs. In 1998 this fruit came entirely from the Shea Vineyard, and that year's edition of Belles Soeurs was vineyard-designated. In 1999 fruit was acquired from both Shea and ARCHERY SUMMIT, and two Belles Soeurs wines were made: a vineyard-designated Shea bottling, and a Yamhill County Cuvée, which contained some Shea, some Beaux Frères, and all of the Archery Summit fruit. In 2000 fruit was purchased from Temperance Hill and Muirfield as well as from Shea, and four vineyard-designated Belles Soeurs wines were made, including a Belles Soeurs Beaux Frères Vineyard. By 2004, however, Etzel grew weary of explaining that Belles Soeurs was simply a "different wine" and not a second label, so Belles Soeurs was replaced in 2005 by a Beaux Frères Willamette Valley bottling.

The reputation of Beaux Frères has been predicated on a ripe-picked, well-extracted, black-fruit style, and serious wine that is ageworthy. It is, in fact, nothing less.

TASTING NOTES

2005 *Willamette Valley (tasted in 2007):* Transparent, very dark black-red; intense, slightly mentholated nose with black cherry, incense, and fir balsam; inky, ripe, rich, and sweet on the palate, but also racy; good tannin and acidity, and with a texture of polished cotton. Texturally impressive and seamless; quite grippy at the end (and this is Beaux Frères's "feminine" wine!).

2005 *Beaux Frères Vineyard (tasted in 2007):* Transparent, medium garnet; intense nose of high-toned, red fruit tinged with gum camphor and vanilla; sweet, minerally, and gritty, with cured meat flavors; huge intensity on the palate and considerable grip, but also silky, long, serious, and fine. This wine will reward a decade's patience.

2003 *Beaux Frères Vineyard (tasted in 2005)*: Medium-dark magenta; wet stones and reticent fruit on the nose; opens impressively in the mouth, with fruit tea and very intense blackberry flavors; silky mid-palate; rich, mouth coating, and possessed of considerable weight; alcohol and tannins dry the finish.

BELLE GLOS
Rutherford, California

Charles F. Wagner's family has farmed in the Napa Valley for more than a century. The family planted riesling, pinot noir, and cabernet sauvignon on a ranch east of Rutherford in the 1960s, sold grapes to neighboring wineries, and founded Caymus Vineyards in 1972. Caymus's reputation for distinctive, concentrated, and ageworthy wines was built on the cabernet—especially a bottling called Special Selection that debuted in 1975. The Wagners abandoned their riesling in 1987, and their pinot noir (which gave relatively large-framed, low-acid wines on the Rutherford site) in 1990. The family's enthusiasm for pinot persisted, however, perhaps in honor of their Alsatian roots. Following a search for California sites capable of yielding pinot is good as their Rutherford cabernet, Wagner and his son Chuck leased (and later purchased) a parcel in the True Sonoma Coast in 1994, on the ridge between Occidental and Bodega Bay, near the Summa Vineyard, where Scott Zeller was already obtaining impressive results. The new site was less forgiving than the Wagners had expected, however, and did not produce a financially viable or qualitatively satisfactory crop until 2002.

In 1999, hedging their bets in another region altogether, the family leased part of the venerable Santa Maria Hills Vineyard, which had been planted between 1972 and 1973 on the mesa southeast of Santa Maria, and named this parcel Clark and Telephone for the roads that bound it. Although the Sonoma Coast site, called Taylor Lane, was planted in a "modern," tight-spaced style, entirely to Dijon 113, 114, and 115, Clark and Telephone was its polar opposite: widely-spaced rows of ungrafted UCD 13. Not content with these two sites, but drawing inspiration from their Mer Soleil chardonnay project in the Santa Lucia Highlands, the family made a third investment in pinot noir in 2001, planting 15 benchland acres 6 miles south of Mer Soleil and just north of Paraiso Springs, called Las Alturas.

On the basis of these anchors, set in some of the most promising pinot regions of the state, the family launched a new pinot noir program called Belle Glos. (Glos was Charles F. Wagner's wife's maiden name.) The viticulturist and winemaker is Wagner's grandson Joseph. The first vintage was a Santa Maria Valley wine made from a combination of Clark and Telephone grapes and fruit purchased from Clark and Telephone's next-door neighbor, Casa Torres. In 2002 the program expanded to three bottlings: vineyard-designated wines from Clark and Telephone and Taylor Lane, plus a Sonoma Coast wine made from Taylor Lane grapes and fruit purchased from other growers in various corners of the sprawling Sonoma Coast appellation. In 2004 the Las Alturas Vineyard debuted in the Belle Glos portfolio, bringing the program to four wines in each vintage. With the 2005 vintage, further adjustments were made to the lineup. First, the Sonoma Coast bottling was given a proprietary name, Meiomi. Second, a vineyard designated wine was made, on a one-time-only basis, from the Weir Vineyard in the Yorkville

Highlands AVA. Third, Joseph Wagner made the first wines in what he calls his "Gambit Series." There are described as unfined, unfiltered, and unsulfured. Wagner explains that Gambit wines will not be made every year, or necessarily from the same vineyards in successive years. The point, according to Wagner, is "big, sweet wines with intense flavors" made from "very ripe fruit" with "fully lignified seeds" and very extended malolactic fermentations. Two such wines have been made thus far, one from Garys' Vineyard and one from Griffin's Lair in the Sonoma Coast appellation. Wagner says "high risk" and "high production costs" make these wines expensive; he sells them for about four times the price of his vineyard designates and eight times the price asked for the Sonoma Coast appellation wine. The Gambit bottlings were not released at the time this book went to press, and I have not tasted them.

Joseph Wagner argues in favor of picking pinot relatively ripe (over 26 Brix) to avoid "acidity that is too evident" and asserts that "soft, full-flavored pinot noir" requires special attention to managing its seeds. Cold soaks can be as short as five days or as long as six weeks; the fermentors are a combination of fruit bins and 5- to 10-ton stainless steel open-tops; no acid or enzymes are added, and the new wines are pressed when the must goes dry. The barrel regime (which relies on about 60 percent new oak from Dargaud & Jaeglé, Boutes, and Jean-Paul Treuil) is a short nine months, and the wines are bottled unfined and unfiltered. The resulting wines are very deeply colored, almost opaque, sweet, often a bit grippy or chalky, and they display flavors that emphasize very ripe black fruit.

TASTING NOTES

2005 *Sonoma Coast (tasted in 2007):* Nearly opaque black-red; redolent of plum, spice, and violets; very intense flavors of black fruit, cinnamon, and orange peel; a substantial load of fine-grained tannin that finishes between velvety and chewy.

2005 *Taylor Lane Vineyard (tasted in 2007):* Barely transparent, dark black-red; deep, earthy nose of very ripe fruit; bright fruit with some *charcuterie*, licorice, and lemon-drop flavors; sweet, medium-weight, and slightly chalky.

2005 *Clark and Telephone Vineyard (tasted in 2007):* Highly perfumed with mint and eucalyptus; sweet attack of racy, ripe, black fruit; long finish with earthy and bay-leaf notes; texture of rough silk.

2005 *Las Alturas Vineyard (tasted in 2007):* Opaque, dark black-red; clove and tobacco on the nose; dark berry character on the palate, with some flavors of root beer and cola; creamy, rich texture with fine-grained grip at the end.

BELLE PENTE VINEYARD AND WINERY
Carlton, Oregon

Brian O'Donnell's first career, in the late 1970s and 1980s, involved product marketing for some of the companies— including Intel and Xerox—that built the global reputation of Silicon Valley and birthed the personal computing revolution. Some evenings and weekends, however, O'Donnell took courses about wine, and he made wine and beer in his San Jose garage. Through the local home wine- and beer-making crowd, he met Rick Moshin, a grape grower in the Russian River Valley; an early batch of O'Donnell's home wine was vinted from Moshin's 1987 harvest of pinot noir. (Commercially, Moshin's grapes were sold to DAVIS BYNUM, among others.) In 1989, the Loma Prieta earthquake made O'Donnell and his wife, Jill, reconsider their commitment to Silicon Valley, and in 1992 the couple relocated to a 70-acre parcel in the rolling (but geologically stable!) hills 2 miles northwest of Carlton, Oregon, which was being farmed as pasture and which harbored a defunct prune orchard. Two years later, they set out their first grape vines: 2 acres of several varieties in north–south oriented, 8-foot rows with (variously) 3 and 5 feet between vines, facing mostly southwest. The topsoil is 18 to 30 inches of silty clay-loam over bedrock sandstone; the first block of vines, like others that have followed, is situated between the 240- and 500-foot contours.

In 1998 the O'Donnells planted another 6 acres of vines in three steep, mostly south- and southwest-facing blocks that were vine spaced slightly tighter than the first, and another 4 acres were set out in

---

BRIGHT, SHYLY-COLORED
WINES WITH ADMIRABLE
FRUIT- AND FLOWER-BASED
COMPLEXITY

1999. Meanwhile, most of the 1994 block was grafted to pinot noir, giving Belle Pente, at the turn of the millennium, a total of 15 vineyard acres, of which all but 4 are pinot noir. The scion material is a half UCD 4 and 2A, and half a combination of Dijon clones.

From the outset the vineyard has been entirely dry farmed, and has been "informally organic" since 2000. A small gravity-flow winery was built downhill from the vineyard in 1996, and a barrel cellar was added next door to it in 2001. The balance of the parcel is still pasture, and highland cows, sheep, and goats

survey visitors on their way up a long gravel driveway from Rowland Road. The inaugural vintage was made in 1996.

WINES AND WINEMAKING NOTES
Belle Pente now makes five pinots in each vintage, three of which are based on estate fruit, and two on purchased grapes. The estate-based wines are a Belle Pente Vineyard bottling that relies primarily on the 1998 plantings; an estate reserve that is nominally a combination of lot and individual barrel selections, but is mostly fruit from the 1994 plantings and UCD 2A from the 1998 plantings; and a Yamhill-Carlton bottling that derives mostly from the estate's 1999 plantings. Since 2006, Belle Pente's Willamette Valley cuvée has depended primarily on fruit from 6- and 7-year old plantings at the Bella Vida Vineyard in the Dundee Hills. There is also a vineyard-designated wine from a 6-acre block of the Dundee Hills' Murto Vineyard, for which Belle Pente has contracted since 1996.

O'Donnell reports that, when the Belle Pente project started, he studied Remington Norman's *The Great Domaines of Burgundy* (New York, 1992), in which he saw a virtual "recipe book" of documentation for Burgundian winemaking practices, and selected from it techniques that corresponded to wines he liked. Belle Pente wines are all made with a relatively long cold-soak of entirely destemmed fruit, followed by two days' "transition," and four to six days of active primary fermentation. The musts are adjusted as necessary with water, acid, and sugar, but there is no addition of enzymes or oenotannins. Fermentors are fruit bins and 3-ton stainless steel open-tops. When the must tests dry, each lot is pressed directly to barrel without settling, and the barrels are kept in an unheated cellar; as a result, malolactic fermentations progress slowly and frequently do not finish until the summer after the vintage. At this point the wines are racked, and the Yamhill-Carlton and Willamette Valley cuvées are bottled after twelve months in barrel. The remaining wines spend another six months in wood. The barrel stock is a mix of Sirugue, François Frères, and Remond barrels, with a few coopered locally at Oregon Barrel Works from Oregon white oak, of which 25 to 33 percent are new in each vintage. The 2004s, which are my only experience with Belle Pente, are bright, shyly-colored wines, with admirable fruit- and flower-based complexity, pretty textures, and attractive structures.

TASTING NOTES

2004 *Willamette Valley (tasted in 2007)*: Light-to-medium garnet; raspberry and potpourri aromas; of medium-weight, and moderately intense on the palate, with considerable minerality and a hint of pepper.

2004 *Yamhill-Carlton (tasted in 2007)*: Transparent, rosy-garnet color; crushed raspberries with hints of custard and rose petal on the nose; marginally richer mouth-feel and with more structure than the Willamette Valley wine; hint of white pepper.

2004 *Murto Vineyard (tasted in 2007)*: Rosy-garnet color; distinctive nose of gingerbread, Christmas pudding, and cinnamon; intense raspberry-cherry flavors on the palate, with infused flowers and more spice; attractive length.

2004 *Belle Pente Vineyard (tasted in 2007)*: Herbs and flowers dominate the nose; then creamy on the palate, like raspberry crème brûlée; infused flowers; of medium-weight, long, and very attractive, with bright acidity and good grip at the end.

2004 *Estate Reserve (tasted in 2007)*: Medium rosy-garnet color; wild black cherries with herbal-floral notes; impression of rich and serious wine with great length on a medium-weight frame. Fine.

BELLE VALLÉE CELLARS
Corvallis, Oregon

Joe Wright moved from high school in Southern California to the wine business in Oregon via work in a Glenwood Springs, Colorado, wine shop, where he absorbed wine information voraciously. After attending a seminar presented by Kevin Chambers, then president of the Oregon Wine Board, at the Little Nell Restaurant in nearby Aspen, Wright was so firmly hooked that he packed his bags for the Willamette Valley, landed a cellar rat job at WILLAMETTE VALLEY VINEYARDS, and continued his vinous education on what the trade calls "the production side of the house." In the course of six years at Willamette Valley Vineyards, he worked successively as the brand's barrel room manager, bottling line manager, and (finally) cellarmaster. Then, at a consumer tasting of Bordeaux and Rhône varieties from southern Oregon in 2002, Wright met two native Oregonians, Steve Allen and Mike Magee, the former a lawyer, the latter a veteran of high technology. Allen and Magee became his partners straightaway, and Belle Vallée Cellars was launched less than three months later. Magee, his wife, and his son have all taken active roles in the new enterprise, developing its business plan, weaving its network of distributors in key markets across the country, and designing its colorful and unconventional labels; Wright has made the wines.

The brand is devoted 70 percent to pinot noir; the balance of its production is mostly pinot gris and (to honor the tasting where the partners met) a bit of red wine from southern Oregon. The offices and production facility are found in an unglamorous cement warehouse in Corvallis. Belle Vallée's growth rate is impressive: production has soared to more than 20,000 cases barely four years after the partners cut their formative deal.

WINES AND WINEMAKING NOTES
Belle Vallée makes four pinots, all blends, all sourced from Willamette Valley vineyards. The main source and the anchor for the two best wines is the Alpine Vineyard on Green Peak Road west of Monroe, which was first planted in 1976 and was once used by BROADLEY VINEYARDS, among others. Other sources are the Whybra Vineyard near Elmira, Temperance Hill and Elton in the Eola Hills, Freedom Hill in the Coast Range, Stermer (owned by LEMELSON) near Carlton, and the Momtazi and Hyland vineyards in the Coast Range west of McMinnville. The top-end wine, called Grand [sic] Cuvée, is blended first. In 2006 all lots for Grand Cuvée were sourced from UCD 4 blocks in the Alpine Vineyard. A reserve is blended next. The balance of the fruit is used for a Willamette Valley bottling. There is also an "entry-level" wine, said to taste like a Beaujolais and made entirely by carbonic maceration, which Belle Vallée calls "Whole Cluster Pinot Noir." While the rubric is technically appropriate, consumers should not confuse whole-cluster carbonic maceration with whole-cluster, open-top fermentation, which produces entirely different results.

Except for the carbonic maceration wine, winemaking by and large follows the consensus protocol for pinot noir. Cold soaks (which can be as long as ten days) and fermentations occur in 6.5-ton jacketed stainless steel open-tops that are plunged with pneumatic *piges*. New wines are settled for two to five days between pressing and barreling, and spend eleven months in a relatively high percentage of new wood, ranging from about 45 percent for the Willamette Valley wine to 65 percent for the Grand Cuvée. The wines are neither fined nor filtered. On the basis of the 2005 vintage, which is my only experience with Belle Vallée, the pinots show as deeply colored, approachable, barrel-marked, fruit-sweet wines.

TASTING NOTES
2005 *Willamette Valley (tasted in 2007)*: Transparent, medium garnet; ripe, plummy nose marked with vanilla, mocha, and hard spice; fruit-sweet with plum and cherry on the palate, some black licorice; attractive acidity, smooth texture, and some grip from mid-palate to finish.

2005 *Reserve (tasted in 2007)*: Medium-deep ruby; aromatically closed at this tasting but suggestive of dark fruit and earth; rich on the palate with blackberry, marionberry, and infused violets; some espresso; seamless and mouth coating with considerable grip; needs time to open and soften.

2005 *Grand Cuvée (tasted in 2007)*: Transparent, medium-dark crimson-ruby; dark fruit and barrel-derived vanilla, plus a slightly exotic note suggestive of juniper berry on the nose; rich and sweet on the palate; intensely fruity and vaguely spicy; extracted, round, and grippy at the end.

BENTON-LANE WINERY
Monroe, Oregon

In the 1980s Steve Girard owned a winery and vineyard his father had planted at the corner of the Oakville Cross Road and the Silverado Trail in the Napa Valley. Enamored of pinot but unable to grow it well in mid-valley Napa, Girard studied the alternatives. His assessment of climates, exposures, and soils led him to settle on the southern Willamette Valley, between Eugene and Corvallis, which he considered to be the "ideal" spot. In 1988 he purchased several hundred acres of southeast-facing sheep ranch in the lee of a mountain, known locally as Old Baldy, near the town of Monroe; in 1989 he planted the first of 126 acres to UCD 4 and 2A, the Oregon workhorse selections, and to Dijon 113, 114, 115, 667, and 777. His partner in the enterprise was Carl Doumani, then the owner of Napa's "other" Stags' Leap winery—the one in which stag is plural, and the apostrophe follows rather than precedes the final "s." The plan was clear from the outset: estate pinot of excellent quality would be grown and made under family control, no more than 30,000 cases would be produced, and the wines would be sold for reasonable prices. The vineyard is farmed sustainably, yield is managed to less than 3 tons per acre even in years when a larger crop could be ripened, and a production facility was built onsite in 1998. (Meanwhile, Girard has divested his property in Napa, selling it to Leslie Rudd, the founder of Dean & DeLuca, who reinvented it as Rudd Estate before selling the Girard name to Pat Roney, a member of the Dean & DeLuca board,

who repurposed the trademark as a new identity for the former Harrison Winery on Pritchard Hill. Who said the wine business was simple?)

Benton-Lane's first winemaker was Gary Horner, a BETHEL HEIGHTS alumnus who went on to ERATH VINEYARDS WINERY in 2002; Damien North, an Australian, covered the 2003 and 2004 vintages; since 2005 the winemaker has been Tim Wilson, previously assistant winemaker at EDNA VALLEY VINEYARD.

WINES AND WINEMAKING NOTES
Benton-Lane produces two pinots in most vintages. The main release is labeled Willamette Valley; the other, not made in every vintage, carries the designation "First Class." (The winery's label is a riff on an old postage stamp, which explains the logic behind the name.) The Willamette Valley wine is made entirely from estate-grown fruit in most vintages, although some purchased fruit was also used in 2005 and 2006; it also includes a large number of lots that have been closed-tank fermented with *pneumatage* (see below). First Class is an all-estate block-and-clone selection, and then a selection of the best barrels from among those blocks and clones. Wilson says he looks for the twenty or so barrels that are "best in the house," which are disproportionately Dijon 667 and 777.

Both wines are fermented in a combination of small 1.25-ton fruit bins and 16-ton, closed-top stainless steel tanks, although there is a preference for fermenting lots that are likely candidates for First Class in the fruit bins. A short cool soak precedes inoculation with Assmannshausen or RC212 yeast; dry ice is not used because Wilson finds it "too extractive." To manage the cap in its tanks, Benton-Lane asserts a "revolutionary technique" it calls *pneumatage*. This involves "pulsing" air into the bottom of each tank in a way that forms large bubbles about the size of basketballs, at the rate of about sixty beats per minute. The bubbles are said to be large enough "to roil the cap in liquid at the top of the tank," keeping it moist. Visually, according to Wilson, "it is almost like watching a landslide into the sea." Although the process is potentially oxidative, the wine actually picks up little oxygen because the must is enveloped with carbon dioxide during active fermentation. Conversely, in fact, Wilson indicates that *pneumatage*, with some nutrients added, "is a great way to manage reduction."

The new wines are pressed at dryness and barreled. The barrel stock involves "eight or ten" coopers and emphasizes oak from Allier forests, with a lesser proportion of wood from the Vosges mountains, and less yet from the Nevers. About 10 percent of the barrels used to raise the Willamette Valley cuvée are new; 35 percent new barrels are used for the First Class wine. The Willamette Valley wine is bottled before the following harvest; First Class spends sixteen months in wood. Neither wine is fined or filtered, and both are bottled under screw caps. Both wines are attractive, varietally correct editions of American pinot, with an emphasis on red rather than black fruit. The Willamette Valley wine represents exceptionally good value, and First Class is an attractive, medium-weight wine that drinks nicely.

TASTING NOTES

2005 Willamette Valley (tasted in 2007): Light-to-medium rosy-ruby; fresh-crushed strawberries and raspberries with a hint of smoke; smoky raspberry-cherry on the palate with a hint of citrus; light-to-medium weight; short-to-medium length; very drinkable and varietally correct.

2005 First Class (tasted in 2007): Slightly deeper, darker, and blacker than the Willamette Valley wine; smoky and slightly tar-y cherry aromas; fruit-driven, smooth, and almost silky attack; a bit of grip on the mid-palate and on the finish; lightweight but flavorful; nicely structured; fruit persists to the end.

BERAN VINEYARDS
Hillsboro, Oregon

In the 1970s Bill Beran was a physicist at Tektronix Inc., a Beaverton, Oregon, firm best known for test and measurement equipment, and a home winemaker. In 1979 Beran and his wife, Sharon, moved to a farm 8 miles south of Hillsboro, Oregon, where they planted a small vineyard. About 3 acres were dedicated to own-rooted pinot noir, 1.5 acres to riesling, and 1.5 to chardonnay, all acquired from ERATH VINEYARDS'S nursery. Sometime later, they discovered that their farm was also home to another acre of pinot, subsequently identified ampelographically as UCD 2A, planted in 1972, that had been abandoned and had become overgrown, and this they painstakingly revived. In 1999 they field grafted the riesling and chardonnay to Dijon 115. At the turn of the new millennium, Beran Vineyards then consisted of 7 acres, all pinot noir, on vinifera roots between twenty and thirty years old.

Although Beran and his wife had initially intended to make wine commercially as soon as the 1979 planting began to bear, this plan was postponed until 1997. Home winemaking continued in the interim, however, at the rate of one or two barrels annually, while the balance of the crop was sold, first to ERATH and then to Oak Knoll. Once the commercial project was finally launched in an historic converted dairy barn onsite, the Beran label consumed all the vineyard's fruit until 2005, when Beran leased 1 acre of the UCD 4 and 1 of the grafted Dijon 115 to his vineyard manager in return for tractor work (which Beran had done himself prior to that point); the vineyard manager sold the fruit from those 2 acres to SIDURI WINES in 2006 and 2007, where it was used in a Chehalem Ridge bottling.

WINES AND WINEMAKING NOTES
In most vintages, Beran Vineyards has made a single cuvée of estate grown pinot noir. Fruit is carefully sorted, completely destemmed but barely crushed, cold-soaked for "a few days," and warmed and inoculated to start the primary fermentation. The new wine is pressed off at dryness and settled briefly before being barreled for eleven months. Malolactic fermentation happens naturally in barrel during the winter following the vintage, after which all barrels are racked once. The blend is made at the time of bottling, and there is no fining or filtration. The wines are extremely distinctive, bright, transparent, savory, and marked with aromas and flavors of pine needles and mint.

TASTING NOTES
2004 *Estate (tasted in* 2007): Light-to-medium mahogany; aromas of potpourri with hints of mint; savory on the palate with notes of sage, tarragon, and citrus peel on a background of raspberry; silky with a hint of bitterness on the finish; elegant and very distinctive, although some tasters will find it to be "green."
2003 *Estate (tasted in* 2007): Vibrant, medium brick-red; conifer, ripe fruit, and

dried currants on the nose; ripe black fruit with some raisins on the palate; significant grip; serious structure; considerable bay laurel; long.

BERGSTRÖM WINES
Newburg, Oregon

Josh Bergström was an undergraduate at the University of Oregon in 1996, majoring in business, when his parents decided to leave Portland, where Josh had been raised, to retire in, of all places, Dundee. Bergstrom describes his parents as "professional amateurs" in vinous matters, suddenly taken with the idea of a vineyard as a retirement project. As for himself, Bergström confesses to having an underlying "artistic temperament" that attracted him to such things as photography and probably contraindicated

DEEPLY-COLORED, SWEET, EXTRACTED, AND GRIPPY WINES WITH INTENSE CONCENTRATION

his planned-for career in business. Simultaneously, it seems, father and son applied themselves to wine. They made overnight driving trips to the University of California Davis for extension classes in viticulture and winemaking. They prepared to plant vines on the newly-purchased "retirement" estate on Worden Hill Road.

Bergström *fils* worked the 1997 harvest at REX HILL and the 1998 harvest at PONZI, absorbing experience from Lynn Penner-Ash and Luisa Ponzi. In 1998 and 1999, irretrievably bitten by the wine bug, he enrolled in a certificate program at the Centre de formation professionnelle et de promotion agricole (CFPPA) in Beaune—fortuitously armed with fluent French, stemming from years at Portland's French-American International School. By 1999, and now married to a fellow alumna of the CFPPA, he was back in Oregon working for Eric Hamacher and crafting the first vintage of Bergström wine from 3 tons of fruit supplied by none other than the legendary Gary Andrus (see ARCHERY SUMMIT ESTATE)—fruit which had been culled from his esteemed Arcus, Red Hills, and Archery Summit Estate vineyards.

The family's Worden Hill Road vineyard (dubbed Bergström Estate), came into production in 2001. A second estate vineyard—an 8-acre parcel on Calkins Lane northwest of Newberg called De Lancellotti and owned by Bergström's brother-in-law—followed in 2003. Winemaking moved from Lemelson, where it had begun in 1999, to Flynn in Rickreal in 2000, and then to a new custom-built facility on Calkins Lane in 2001.

WINES AND WINEMAKING NOTES

Bergström made a single pinot in 1999 and 2000, labeled Willamette Valley, anchored with grapes from the Archery Summit parcels in 1999, and with fruit from the Hyland Vineyard west of McMinnville in 2000. In 2001 the portfolio expanded: the Willamette Valley wine was based on the first year's harvest from the Bergström Estate Vineyard, the Reserve bottling was made primarily from Hyland fruit, and a vineyard-designated wine was made from Arcus grapes. Beginning in 2002, the percentage of Hyland fruit in the reserve wine (henceforth renamed Cumberland

Reserve in honor of the street in Portland where Bergstrom grew up) gradually decreased, and the wine evolved toward a widely sourced blend, featuring fruit from (variously) the Nysa, Shea, Anderson Family, Palmer Creek, Bishop's Creek and Maresh vineyards. A vineyard-designated Bergström Estate wine also debuted in 2002. In 2003 vineyard-designated wines from Shea and Broadley (the latter derived from a fruit-exchange agreement between Bergstrom and BROADLEY VINEYARDS) were added to the portfolio, along with a whole-cluster selection from the Bergström Estate. To date, the whole-cluster wine has been made only in 2003 and 2005, and the Broadley cuvée was not made in 2005.

Bergström describes the following evolution in his picking protocol: "In the early years we strove for the highest possible Brix as early as possible; now we strive for the lowest possible Brix with the longest possible hang time." When the Brix level is high regardless, he adds acid to adjust the pH. A long, ten-to-twelve day cold soak is normal (except in the case of the Shea fruit), followed by a short, hot alcoholic fermentation. Enzymes are added if the natural level of pectolytic enzymes is low, and water is often added to moderate high levels of alcohol. According to Bergström, brettanomyces is the "ugliest thing in the wine world"; as a result, he has abandoned reliance on native yeasts to induce the malolactic fermentation, and systematically filters his wines to "keep the library safe."

The Willamette Valley wine is raised entirely in barrels already used for one or two wines; the reserve wine sees about 50 percent new wood; the vineyard-designates see 90 to 100 percent. Almost without exception, Bergstrom pinots are deeply-colored, sweet, extracted, and grippy wines, with intense concentration that can be tough going when they are young.

2005 *Bergström Vineyard Whole-Cluster Selection (tasted in 2006):* Aromas of ripe olives and cured meat; intense signature of whole-cluster fermentation represented as camphor and stems; tar, tobacco, earth, anise, and black pepper on the palate, plus a hint of dark chocolate; medium-to-heavy weight, chewy, and concentrated with a grippy finish and an emery-like texture.

2005 *Bergström Winery Estate (tasted in 2006):* Saturated black-red; bay leaf and rosemary aromas; herbal on the palate with black tea, black pepper, and mesquite; very grippy and tannic overall and very concentrated.

2005 *Cumberland Reserve (tasted in 2006):* Barely transparent deep garnet; herbs and licorice on the nose; intense, juicy, and inky on the palate with huge extraction and a hint of bitter chocolate; rustic overall, and very grippy at the end.

2005 *Willamette Valley (tasted in 2006):* Transparent, dark black-red; aromas of black fruits, tar, and resin; bright and citrus-scented on the palate but simultaneously mouth-coating and intense; satiny texture notwithstanding some grip; long.

1999 *Willamette Valley (tasted in 2006):* Hazy, deep, brick-red color; leathery nose with aromas of exotic woods and herb-infused beets; then, pretty wild strawberry flavors, seemingly wrapped in incense; very attractive and medium-long.

BETHEL HEIGHTS VINEYARD
Salem, Oregon

Bethel Heights is a 75-acre site on the west slope of the Eola Hills, just north of Bethel Road and south of the Temperance Hill Vineyard. It represents one of the earliest vineyard plantings in the Eola Hills (the first 14 acres of vines were set out in 1977), and a durable hands-on partnership of five individuals variously related by blood and marriage. It is a pioneer in sensible and sustainable viticulture and is one of the most respected producers of pinot noir in the state. The estate vineyard is just shy of 50 planted acres—an undulating rectangle roughly bisected by a wooded ravine and oriented north–south—of which 37 are pinot noir. The whole rectangle is a south-facing slope between the 480- and 620-foot contours. Six of the 37 acres called West Block are UCD 2A and 23, planted on their own roots in 1977; 16.3 acres (called Flat Block, South Block, and Southeast Block) are UCD 4 planted on its own roots in 1979; 5.5 acres are Dijon 114 and 115 planted on rootstock in 1994 and 1996; 2.2 acres (Shed Block) are Dijon 777 grafted to 20-year old chardonnay roots in 2000; and 6.5 acres are Dijon 115, 777, and UCD 4 planted on rootstock in the vineyard's northeast quadrant in 2002. All vines are pruned to one cluster per shoot, or to one cluster per two shoots, and the yield is managed to about 2 tons per acre.

Although Bethel Heights operated first as a vineyard, selling grapes to other makers, a winery was built, and estate production began in 1984, and no estate fruit has been sold since 1992. On the contrary, since 1995 Bethel Heights has been a net purchaser of grapes from other Willamette Valley vineyards, notably Seven Springs, which has recently been leased to a New York consortium, making its fruit unavailable to most of its prior clients; Elton, in the northeast corner of the Eola Hills; Freedom Hill, a Coast Range site northwest of Monmouth; Nysa in the Dundee Hills; and (beginning in 2007) the Jessie James Vineyard, in the

Walnut Hill corner of the Eola Hills. Some of the principals in Bethel Heights have also developed a vineyard on the property just south of the main estate that is called Justice, and most Justice fruit is used in the Bethel Heights Estate wine (see below), but some is sold to other producers. Two twin brothers, Terry and Ted Casteel, both graduates of Whitworth University in Spokane, Washington, are Bethel Heights's vineyard manager and winemaker, respectively. In his life-before-wine, Ted taught European history at the University of Michigan Dearborn;

CAREFUL, SUSTAINABLE GRAPE GROWING AND WELL-CRAFTED WINES

Terry was a clinical psychologist with a practice in Seattle. Ted spent some time doing coursework at the University of California Davis after the Casteels bought the property in 1978, in order to learn at least the basics of winegrowing; Terry apprenticed himself to another local winemaker when he was not tending Bethel's vineyards, to "learn the ins and outs of commercial winemaking."

WINES AND WINEMAKING NOTES
Bethel Heights's "core" pinot is an estate or estate grown bottling, made every year since 1984. Since 2001 it has been a "broad blend" of the estate blocks and the blocks at Justice. A reserve program was begun in 1985, based on the principle of barrel selection. In 1991, increasingly fascinated with the differences among the wines from the estate's various blocks, Bethel Heights chose to make a multiplicity of

block-designated wines in lieu of a single barrel-selected reserve. Objections from distributors, who wanted to offer only two Bethel pinots in each vintage, forced restoration of the reserve program in 2002, but the winery has continued to make small quantities of the block-designated wines for direct and tasting room sales. When the reserve program was revived, the reserve wine was renamed Casteel Reserve, and it has sometimes included lots from non-estate sources. An Eola–Amity Hills blend, from a combination of estate and non-estate fruit, has been made since 2004. Vineyard-designated wines from non-estate sources have been made irregularly since 1997, notably from the Seven Springs, Freedom Hill, Nysa, and (most recently) Jessie James vineyards. In addition, some of the Justice fruit has been vineyard-designated since 2004, although Justice is best understood as a separate estate vineyard with overlapping but slightly different ownership from Bethel Heights itself.

Terry Casteel says he would like to pick pinot "fully ripe at 23.5 Brix" but ends up picking "later than most." In ripe years, 25 to 30 percent of the fruit is retained as whole clusters. Fermentors are a combination of 4- and 5-ton stainless open-tops and 1.5-ton fruit bins; there is a five- to six-day prefermentation maceration; primary fermentations are started using one third of the total inoculum; and enzymes are added for color extraction. No effort is made to mix the initial inoculum into the must for two days; the rest of the inoculum is then added, and punchdowns or pumpovers are begun. The new wine is pressed when it tastes dry, which is generally less than zero Brix, settled overnight, and then barreled in "99 percent" French oak, of which about 30 percent is new in each vintage. Favored coopers include François Frères, Cadus, Rousseau, and Remond, with Cadus being preferred for wine from the estate's Southeast Block. Malolactic starter is added in barrel, the wines are not racked unless they develop substantial reduction, and *élevage* lasts for thirteen to fourteen months. Egg-white fining is done to increase clarity and to polish tannins, but the wines are "almost never" filtered.

Bethel Heights enjoys great respect for its careful, sustainable grape growing and its well-crafted wines. Bethel's blended pinots are subtle and nicely made, and West Block and Flat Block excel (in my opinion) among the block designates. Of these, West is the more powerful and flashier wine, while Flat features sturdy elegance. The 2005 edition of Seven Springs is beautiful and is in a class of its own.

2006 *Eola-Amity Hills Cuvée (tasted in 2007):* Transparent, light-to-medium rosy-garnet color; dusty floral and red berry nose; bright raspberry-strawberry fruit with subtle spiciness; silky, light-to-medium weight, and of medium length; attractive.

2005 *Estate (tasted in 2007):* Medium garnet; earth and pine tar aromas with a fresh floral underlay; slightly sweet red berry flavors on the palate; silky attack with just a bit of soft grip after mid-palate; elegant, slightly understated, and attractive; medium-length.

2005 *Seven Springs Vineyard (tasted in 2007):* Brilliant medium garnet; slightly earthy, slightly resinous, dark-fruited nose; exceptionally pretty dark cherry fruit and wet earth on the palate; layers of soft spice and pepper; nicely built wine with elegance, depth, and a mostly silky mouth-feel. Fine.

2005 *Casteel Reserve (tasted in 2007):* Transparent, medium ruby; notes of vanilla, nutshells, potpourri, and raspberry on the nose; open, slightly sweet, red-fruit driven, and satiny; then turns serious with abundant black licorice and some grip; very nicely built, attractive, and long.

2005 *West Block Reserve (tasted in 2007):* Transparent, medium-dark black-red; resin, linseed oil, vanilla, and red fruit aromas; sweet, powerful cherry-raspberry fruit and some earthiness on the front palate; briefly satiny and almost creamy, then structured and a bit grippy; huge concentration with modest alcohol; very attractive.

2005 *Flat Block Reserve (tasted in 2007):* Transparent, medium magenta; smoke, cherry, conifer foliage, and forest floor on the nose; a bit sweet but also ferrous on the palate; a nicely built, serious, medium-weight wine with rounded edges and sturdy elegance. Fine.

BOUCHAINE VINEYARDS
Napa, California

Bouchaine Vineyards occupies an historic structure on Buchli Station Road in Los Carneros that was built in 1899 as the Garetto Winery. The building has been operated continuously as a winery ever since, even during Prohibition, when it was used to produce sacramental wine. Beringer Brothers used the premises as a racking and blending facility between 1951 and 1980, but sold it to a Delaware-based partnership headed by Gerret and Tatiana Copeland in 1981. Known first as Château Bouchaine, it was rechristened Bouchaine Vineyards shortly after the Copelands became sole owners in 1991. The couple are serious Francophiles who have been active in the Confrérie des

Chevaliers du Tastevin for many years. The old winery building was extensively remodeled and expanded in 1995, at which time the winery's massive redwood tanks were creatively recycled into exterior siding and interior paneling. Eighty-five acres of estate vineyards surround the winery and stretch south of it; the acreage encompasses two dramatic 200-foot knolls commanding panoramic views of surrounding Carneros and San Pablo Bay. Forty of the 85 acres are dedicated to twenty blocks of pinot noir planted (or replanted) between 1998 and 2004. Virtually all of this, except for two terraced blocks on the knolls, is planted in 8-foot rows with 5 feet between vines and is a combination of UCD 4, 5, 12, and 23, and Dijon 114, 115, 667, and 777. Bouchaine's winemaker and general manager since 2002 has been Michael Richmond, a key player when nearby ACACIA WINERY was established in 1979; the architect of Carmenet Winery's dynamite brand of cabernet; and a co-organizer of the Steamboat Conference, where an entire generation of pinot-makers has shared wines, passions, curiosities, and frustrations since 1980. At Bouchaine, Richmond has had responsibility for completing the replanting program begun at the end of the 1990s, and for redeveloping the brand, which was, by most assessments, underperforming its potential when he arrived.

WINES AND WINEMAKING NOTES
For most of the 1980s and 1990s, the main release of pinot was a blend of estate and non-estate wine lots labeled "Carneros–Napa Valley." Until 1997 a small amount of reserve pinot was also made in most vintages, from barrels that displayed a bit more concentration and complexity than those used in the main bottling. Beginning in 1999, Bouchaine replaced the reserve wine with a revolving vineyard-designate program, making only one or two vineyard-designated wines each year, but allowing the choice of vineyards to shift from year to year. An estate wine was introduced with the 2004 vintage.

Since Richmond's arrival, the quality of the estate fruit has substantially improved as new and replanted blocks have come into production, and as the purchased fruit has come to rely primarily on three trusted sources. The Gee Vineyard, across Buchli Station Road from Bouchaine, is 16 acres of dry-farmed UCD 13 that result in grapes with deep black fruit flavors reminiscent of the fruit from Jim St. Clair's vineyard about a mile away; CASA CARNEROS is Melissa Moravec's impeccably farmed site on Bayview Avenue, long a respected source of budwood for other vineyards; and Las Brisas is a 95-acre site on Ramel Road planted and farmed by Francis Mahoney, the founder of Carneros Creek Winery and the father of clonal trials that reshaped the way winegrowers look at pinot noir in California. The revolving vineyard-designate program has continued, but it has been made part of what the winery calls its "Bacchus Collection," sold primarily at the winery and to mailing-list customers. A vineyard-designated wine from Paul Gee's vineyard was made in 1999, 2004, and 2006, and a "Mariafeld" wine, built entirely from UCD 23 vines in Mahoney's Las Brisas Vineyard, was made in 2005.

Richmond likes to harvest grapes "across a range of ripeness" that still avoids extremes of "greenness" and "raisining." On the crushpad, the fruit is completely destemmed, partially crushed, and cold-soaked for several days. Once active fermentations begin, the cap is managed with a combination of punchdowns and pumpovers. A combination of 3- and 10-ton tanks has recently replaced the set of stainless-lined, concrete open-tops used in an earlier era at the winery and retained through the remodeling in 1995. The new wines are pressed as soon as the fermentations go dry, settled briefly, and barreled in a combination of French and Hungarian oak, plus a "smidgen" of 60-gallon American oak barrels. Barrels are retired each year at a rate that allows each wine to be raised in somewhere between 20 to 50 percent new wood. Coopers of choice for the French barrels are Roberts and Mercurey; the Hungarian and American oak barrels are purchased from Trust Cooperage in Hungary. The Carneros and Estate wines are bottled before the following vintage; the vineyard-designated or clone-specific wines may stay in barrel a bit longer.

Richmond, who believes that microbial populations accumulate in an 80-year-old facility, insists that all the wines be filtered to assure stability. Richmond observes that he has begun to worry about the state of American pinot overall, finding more and more wines offered to market with elevated levels of alcohol or "amped up" with oak or oak alternatives. However, he recognizes what he calls "a new paradigm for pinot noir," deriving from new "viticultural practices and new clonal material," that drives alcohol levels closer to 14 percent than to the 12.5 to 13 percent range that prevailed in past decades. In 2004 and 2005, Bouchaine made very attractive Estate and Carneros blend wines.

TASTING NOTES

2005 *Carneros (tasted in* 2007*):* Rosy, medium black-red; sweet black cherry aromas, with some licorice; slightly tannic, dark, and slate-y on the palate; sweeter and blacker than the 2004; velvety and mouth coating with noticeable grip; some sweet oak and citrus peel; cherry and lingonberry linger into the finish. Extremely attractive.

2005 *Estate (tasted in* 2007*):* Transparent, medium-dark black-red; earthy and minerally with mostly black fruit on the nose; fruit-driven and mineral-supported attack with an initial impression of sweetness; some peppery-cinnamon spice on the palate; clean, of medium-weight, nicely built, and noticeably barrel marked.

2004 *Carneros (tasted in* 2007*):* Medium-dark black-red; nose of grilled nut meats and charcoal; slightly sweet with very black fruit and infused rose petals on the palate, with fine-grained tannins; significant grip; nice structure and good balance.

BRANDBORG VINEYARD AND WINERY
Elkton, Oregon

Terry Brandborg, a San Francisco warehouseman and longshoreman, began winemaking as a hobby in 1975 and founded Brandborg Cellars, duly bonded, in 1986, in a Marin County, California, garage. That year, he produced 300 cases of riesling, chardonnay, zinfandel, and pinot noir from Anderson Valley fruit. Production increased gradually to 1,000 cases by 1990—at which point production outgrew the garage—and then to 2,500 cases made in leased space near Point Richmond in 1991. The pinot produced in this period was sourced from the Bien Nacido Vineyard in Santa Maria, and from several Russian River Valley sites. In 2001 Brandborg and his wife participated in the Steamboat Conference held annually in the Umpqua River Valley east of Roseburg. They took a few extra days to explore potential vineyard sites nearby because they thought the landscape was "reminiscent" of Mendocino County's Anderson Valley; ultimately, they acquired land and transported their brand to Oregon in the spring of 2002, where they re-launched Brandborg Cellars as Brandborg Vineyard and Winery. The property covers 145 acres near Elkton in the coastal hills, between the 750- and 1,150-foot contours, in sandstone-based sedimentary soils. The first 5 acres of vines were planted in 2002: Dijon clones 113,

---

NICELY STRUCTURED EARTH-AND-SPICE FLAVORED WINES FROM RIPE FRUIT PICKED WITH GOOD ACIDITY

115, and 777 on 101-14 and 3309 rootstocks, oriented north–south, on steep south-facing slopes with 8 feet between rows and 5-foot intervine spacing. A reference vineyard research project begun in 2005 found the site cooler than most Willamette Valley spots, probably owing to its high elevation.

The Brandborgs have since become huge proponents of the Umpqua Valley for pinot noir, following the tradition initiated by Richard Sommer in the 1950s and continued in the last two decades by several neighboring vineyards, including Bradley and Melrose. The Brandborgs' entire wine program is now based exclusively on Umpqua Valley fruit. The pinots are nicely structured, earth-and-spice flavored wines from ripe fruit that has been picked with good acidity.

TASTING NOTES

2005 *Northern Reach (tasted in 2007):* Transparent, medium black-red; rich aromas of earth and wet clay; ripe but still bright red fruit with flavors of sarsaparilla,

sage, and bay laurel; slightly sweet, nicely structured, and serious, with a noticeable load of very fine-grained tannins at mid-palate; a bit of barrel char on the finish; texture of heavy silk.

2005 *Bench Lands (tasted in 2007):* Very transparent, light-to-medium ruby; soft spice and dusty fruit on the nose; soft and round on the palate with hints of infused flowers, pepper, and orange peel; silky, attractive, and elegantly built.

2005 *Ferris Wheel Vineyard (tasted in 2007):* Brilliant, light-to-medium magenta with a pinkish-orange rim; aromas of clove, spice, and resin; intensely spicy palate with almost overpowering ripe plum and berry fruit flavors; satiny mid-palate and some grip on the finish; nice structure throughout; a hint of Angostura bitters at the end.

2002 *Barrel Select (tasted in 2007):* Brilliant, slightly orange-rimmed medium ruby; leather, resin, and raspberry on the nose; very slightly sweet on the palate with hints of camphor, mint, Tootsie Roll, clove and orange peel; bright and elegant, grippy at the end, and a little warm. Attractive.

1992 *Bien Nacido Vineyard (tasted in 2007):* Transparent, medium mahogany; leather, raisins, pine needles, and dark chocolate; then, slightly sweet with raspberry and rosewater on the palate; silky and beautifully mature with good grip at the end.

BREGGO CELLARS
Boonville, California

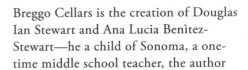

Breggo Cellars is the creation of Douglas Ian Stewart and Ana Lucia Benìtez-Stewart—he a child of Sonoma, a one-time middle school teacher, the author of a book about small-scale farming in the Brazilian Amazon, and a proprietor of an ice creamery in San Francisco; she an Equadorian who once worked as a park ranger in the Galapagos and as a fundraiser for Galapagos-based research and protection. In 2000, having searched across northern California for affordable land well suited for a vineyard, Stewart purchased a 200-acre sheep ranch in the Anderson Valley between Boonville and Philo, where he and Ana Lucia were subsequently married. The reluctance of banks to loan money for new vineyard projects in the wake of the economic downturn that followed 9/11 forced postponement of Stewart's plan to plant the vineyard immediately; instead, the couple converted ranch buildings into a winery and tasting room, and launched a wine brand with purchased fruit. Pinot noir, which accounts for less than half of Breggo's production, is sourced from the nearby Savoy, Ferrington, and Donnelly Creek vineyards and made by Ryan Hodgins, an Oberlin College graduate with a master's degree in viticulture and enology from the University of California Davis, who was also the assistant winemaker at HANZELL VINEYARDS in Sonoma until 2008.

The first wines, vineyard-designates from Ferrington and Savoy, and an Anderson Valley appellation wine, were made in 2005. A vineyard-designated wine from the Donnelly Creek Vineyard was added in 2006. In 2007, fruit sources expanded beyond Anderson Valley to the Alder Springs vineyard (see PATZ & HALL). The new winery boasts two bits of brand new, state-of-the-art equipment: a EuroSelect destemmer (see AMITY VINEYARDS) and a bucket press from Coquard. The beauty of the destemmer is complete separation of stems and berries with barely a bruised grape and almost no released juice, which is ideal for long cold-soaking. Most fermentations rely on resident yeast, although reluctant lots are inoculated, and Hodgins favors peak fermentation temperatures into the 90s. Punchdowns are stopped before all the grapes' sugar has been converted, and the open-top tanks are covered, so the fermentations finish without cap manipulation but are protected with a blanket of carbon dioxide. The net result of these protocols is long cavaisons lasting from 17–24 days. Free-run juice goes to barrel after settling overnight, while the pumice is transferred to the Coquard press, whose design—with perforations on the bottom of the press pan only—ensures that "the more you press, the fewer the solids that pass through." Stewart says Breggo is "a big fan" of Gillet barrels, although some Sirugue and François Frères are also used. The inaugural vintage of Breggo pinots suggests relatively ripe-picked, deeply colored, fruit-driven wines, with characteristically velvety textures (resulting in part from the preponderance of UCD 4 in all the sourced fruit) and moderate but noticeable tannins.

TASTING NOTES

2005 *Ferrington Vineyard (tasted in 2007)*: Medium-dark, rosy black-red; briar, mesquite, and wild berries on the nose; moderately fruit-sweet over the entire length of the palate; ripe cherry and plum; smoky, velvety, mouth coating, and long; considerable grip from mid-palate to finish.

2005 *Anderson Valley (tasted in 2007)*: Transparent, deep magenta; aromas of dark cherry fruit, smoke, and boot polish; warm and smoky on the palate with dark cherry and cassis flavors, some hard spice, and considerable barrel char; velvety but not plush; tendency to dry at mid-palate and beyond.

2005 *Savoy Vineyard (tasted in 2007)*: Transparent, medium brick-red color;

attractive nose of vanilla, flowers, and sandalwood; fruit-sweet attack, with black fruit, pepper, and some blueberry on the mid-palate; very dry thereafter with considerable grip on the finish; warm.

BREWER-CLIFTON
Lompoc, California

Brewer-Clifton is a micro-producer dedicated to a simple, pure protocol. It crafts single-vineyard wines from Santa Barbara sources (now almost entirely Sta. Rita Hills) that are farmed identically, and it employs identical methods and treatments on all its wines. At least in theory this protocol eliminates all factors that could obscure each vineyard's unique fingerprint. Furthermore, a key feature of the protocol is 100 percent whole-cluster fermentations, which are now greatly out of favor almost everywhere, except among hardcore traditionalists in Burgundy.

Greg Brewer is a former French instructor at the University of California Santa Barbara, who reinvented himself as a winemaker before his thirtieth birthday. His day job is to make the wines at MELVILLE VINEYARD. Steve Clifton is a onetime musician and restaurateur who similarly retooled, learning winemaking on the job at Rancho Sisquoc. In 1996 Brewer was the assistant winemaker at Santa Barbara Winery, and Clifton was at Beckman Vineyards—both blend-oriented houses—when they resolved to launch a label dedicated entirely to small lots of vineyard-designated chardonnay and pinot noir. The project was itinerant until 1999, when the partners

acquired dedicated space in the Lompoc "wine ghetto."

Although Brewer-Clifton made vineyard-designated pinots from several Santa Maria Valley sites between 1996 and 2000, including CAMBRIA WINERY'S Julia's Vineyard, and from the Santa Maria Hills Vineyard, the partners decided to focus exclusively on vineyard sites in the new Sta. Rita Hills appellation in 2001. In addition to two blocks at Melville (a 1-acre block of Dijon 114 and 115, and a 0.4-acre planting of Dijon 777 vinified separately as Kimberley's) and all of the 13 acres at Mount Carmel on the spine of the appellation, Brewer-Clifton also sources pinot from 3.5 acres of Dijon 667 and 777 at Rio Vista; 1.5 acres of Dijon 667 at Rancho Santa Rosa (see FOLEY ESTATES VINEYARD); 4 acres of Dijon 114 and 155, and UCD 4 at Ashley's Vineyard (subsequently Gaia, following an ownership change, and now Lindsay's, following its acquisition by LINCOURT); 1 acre of UCD 4 at Clos Pepe; 2 acres of Dijon 115 at Peter Cargasacchi's vineyard near Fe Ciega; 5 acres of Dijon 113, 114, and 115 at Zotovich; and 5 acres of Dijon 115 at Huber. Twenty additional acres in four additional sites will come into production between 2007 and 2010.

WINEMAKING NOTES
Even though it is not an estate producer, Brewer-Clifton has become extremely prescriptive in the management of all the vineyards from which it sources fruit. In particular it has become locally famous for very aggressive leaf pulling, designed to be sure virtually all clusters receive direct sunlight and to promote very ripe flavors. Picking decisions are focused on what Clifton calls "the human perception of physiological ripeness," by which he means, *inter alia*, slight puckering of the grape skins

and no pulp sticking to the seeds. Among the numeric indicators, the winemakers want to see a pH of at least 3.1 before picking, and they will allow sugars to rise as high as 27 Brix if necessary. Rigorous sorting is done to remove damaged clusters, leaves, and miscellaneous detritus, first on the tractors during the pick and subsequently on a sorting table at the winery.

Fermentations take place in stainless steel open-tops. The fruit is kept entirely in the form of whole clusters, and no enzymes are added. A five- to seven-day prefermentation maceration occurs in a 36°F refrigerated room. The fermentors are then removed from the cold room, allowed to warm up for twenty-four hours, and inoculated with yeast. (Consistent use of a single laboratory yeast is one more way to eliminate any possible variations in winemaking technique. In the beginning, the winemakers used Assmannshausen yeast, but they decided it had a tendency to generate too much spice. Beginning with the 2000 vintage, they switched to RC 212, which seems, they say, to heighten the wines' fruit profiles and to generate more color—an obvious advantage in the whole-cluster environment.) Fermentations are long and cool, peaking in the high 70s or low 80s, and postfermentation maceration can last up to two weeks, making for total vattings of twenty-eight to thirty-five days. (Again, to minimize winery-related variables, Brewer-Clifton tries, in each vintage, to impose exactly the same length of vatting on all its pinots.) The new wine is then pressed directly to barrel.

Sirugue custom makes Brewer-Clifton's barrels, using a mix of Chatillon, Allier, and Vosges wood in *each* barrel, so that even a one-barrel lot can be seasoned with a mixture of wood from the three forests, eliminating any differences in barrel treatment from wine to wine. One quarter of the barrels are new each year. The wines are bottled in August after the vintage. There is no fining or filtration. The wines are released either the October after the vintage or during the following calendar year.

I have tasted most vintages of Brewer-Clifton since 2000, most recently the 2005s described below. I confess to a love-hate relationship. I loved the Rozak Ranch wines from 2000 and 2001, which were the lightest of the Brewer-Cliftons; these were discontinued after 2002. Some wines from the drought vintages in 2002, 2003, and 2004 were so strongly marked by their history of whole-cluster fermentation that I found them unpleasant and caricatured. The 2005s are unmercifully high in alcohol, deriving from the twinned practices of aggressive leaf pulling and crop-load limitation, plus an insistence on picking very ripe. This does show on the palate, but the wines are not overly extracted. Sometimes they are even light in color; always they are distinctive and interesting, and the different *terroirs* do show through the very ripe-picked raw material.

TASTING NOTES

2005 *Rio Vista (tasted in 2007):* Light, transparent garnet, barely darker than many rosés; raspberry, rose petal, white pepper, and savory herbs on the nose; bright berry fruit with a hint of citrus-skin bitterness combined with some very peppery, macerated apple peel in the mouth; some grip; long and warm. Utterly distinctive.

2005 *Mount Carmel (tasted in 2007):* Light, salmony-garnet; incense, toasted coriander, and dill seed aromas; slightly fruit-sweet raspberry, cherry, and plum skin; almost satiny texture; impressive juxtaposition of textural richness with light-footed flavors; definite marking of whole cluster fermentation; very warm and long.

2005 *Clos Pepe (tasted in 2007):* Brilliant, medium rosy-garnet; some mesquite and bay laurel on the nose; tar, juniper berry, and plum skin on the palate; some tar-y and almost bitter properties alongside the fruit; hints of cherry *eau-de-vie*; creamy, then slightly grippy; utterly serious but also very, very warm.

2001 *Melville (tasted in 2007):* Transparent, brilliant, deep garnet verging on brick-red; cigar-box nose plus a bit of tar; still slightly fruit-sweet, with dark cherry, plums, and rosewater; silky to mid-palate and a bit beyond, then grippy toward the end; serious elegance that derives from whole-cluster fermentation and grip; but high alcohol also makes the wine spirity.

BRICK HOUSE WINE COMPANY
Newburg, Oregon

Doug Tunnell's first career, in television news, involved postings in Bonn and Paris, among other places, in the 1980s. In an hour on the autobahn, he could get from Bonn to vineyards in the Ahr, Mosel, and Rheingau; an hour by high-speed train took him from Paris to Burgundy. He grew passionate about wine. When he learned that Burgundy *négociant* Robert Drouhin had purchased land in Oregon, a stone's throw from Tunnell's grandfather's farm outside McMinnville, Tunnell resolved to forsake television news, to return to his Oregon roots, and to reinvent himself as a grape grower. In 1989 he purchased 40 acres of declining hazelnut orchard on Ribbon Ridge, overlooking the Chehalem Valley. The property included a pleasant brick house, built in the 1920s by the engineer who had dredged the port of Portland, and

a barn used to accommodate goats, ponies, and (unintentionally) barn owls.

In 1990 Tunnell ripped out 16 acres of hazelnut trees and planted 10.5 acres of pinot noir. The brick house gave its name to the vineyard. In 1993, realizing that plain grape growing was not financially viable, he converted the barn into a low-tech winery (carefully retaining its farm barn ambience, however, down to bales of hay used for seating) and engaged Steve Doerner, of CRISTOM VINEYARDS, to custom crush the first vintage of Brick House pinot. Gradually, Tunnell learned to make the wines, absorbing insights informally from Doerner and from other neighbors, including BEAUX FRÈRES'S Michael Etzel, CAMERON'S John Paul, John Thomas, and Mark Vlossak.

Vineyard consultant Joel Meyers, EYRIE'S onetime vineyard manager, guided the 1990 planting at Brick House: unusually dense (for the time) 8-foot rows with 1 meter between vines, and 100 percent nursery-sourced UCD 4. The first crop, in 1992, was sold to AMITY VINEYARDS. From 1993 to 2002, Tunnell shared the crop, variously, with Cameron, ST. INNOCENT, and ARCHERY SUMMIT, all of which made Brick House vineyard-designates from time to time during the 1990s. St. Innocent's last Brick House fruit was supplied in 2000; Cameron continued to buy fruit until 2002, and both used it to make vineyard-designated wines. Cristom also received small quantities of Brick House fruit during the 1990s, but used it in blends.

In 1995 Tunnell planted three additional blocks of pinot, just slightly more widely spaced than the first blocks, north and east of the barn *cum* winery. These blocks, which cumulate in 9 acres of Dijon 113, 114, and 115, produced their first crop in 1998. The soils throughout the estate are thin Willakenzie clay-loam, and farming practices have been resolutely organic from the outset. The topsoil in the Dijon blocks is even thinner than in the UCD 4 blocks—hence the decision to reduce the density from 1 meter to 4.5 feet between vines. Yields are derisory. The Dijon blocks produce barely 1 ton to the acre in a miserly vintage like that of 2004, and about 2 tons in a generous vintage; the UCD 4 blocks outperform the Dijon blocks very slightly in generous years.

SUCCULENT, INTENSE, CONIFER-MARKED WINES WITH DEEP COLOR, GOOD LENGTH, AND SUBSTANTIAL TANNIN

WINES AND WINEMAKING NOTES

From 1993 through 1997, Brick House produced a single pinot noir called Cuvée du Tonnelier. (*Tunnell* is in fact an anglicization of *tonnelier*, French for "cooper," so the name translates both as the cooper's cuvée and as Tunnell's cuvée.) In 1998, when the Dijon clones began to bear, Tunnell began production of a second pinot called Les Dijonnais. A third "core" wine debuted in 2003, dubbed Eveyln's. This was sourced from one block of the old UCD 4 plantings known informally as Boulder Block for the round, water-washed basaltic rocks, ranging in size from golf balls to basketballs, strewn throughout the topsoil. In addition to these core wines, or sometimes as replacements, other cuvées were made in 1999 and 2001, and after 2003. The variation in 1999 was six barrels of 100 percent UCD 4, chosen for their special texture and richness but coincidentally from a lot made with 50 percent whole clusters, which was separately bottled as Cinquante. (At the same time, some Dijon clone fruit was blended into the Cuvée du Tonnelier, primarily clones 113 and 115, leaving the

114 to anchor the 1999 edition of Les Dijonnais.)

In 2001, because Tunnell was slightly disenchanted with the lots that normally comprise Les Dijonnais, these and some UCD 4 lots were combined to make a Willamette Valley cuvée, offered to the market at a lower price than the Tonnelier and Dijonnais wines. This bottling continued in most subsequent vintages until it was replaced, in 2005, with a similarly priced cuvée, assembled from individual barrels unsuited for any of the three core wines, called Select. (In 2005 there was no Cuvée du Tonnelier, however.)

Although Tunnel ferments up to half his fruit as whole clusters in long, cool vintages like that of 1999, he finds that the average whole-cluster usage has dropped in recent years to between 15 and 25 percent. His fermentors are 5.5 by 5–foot cylindrical open-tops, ingeniously mounted on waist-high wheeled platforms designed in such a way that Tunnell can move the containers rather than the wine. Thus, gravity can be used to transfer wine to barrels, and one person with a forklift can, if necessary, perform all winery operations. Fermentations are allowed to begin naturally with resident yeast. In cool harvests, a natural cold soak can last as long as seven or eight days, while chillers are used to compensate for high ambient temperatures at harvest. Thereafter, Tunnell likes the fermentation to peak at quite a warm temperature, and he will even warm his fermentors to maintain temperature as the fermentation subsides. But the generous use of stems also extends the fermentation time, so that the total vatting can last as long as eighteen days. Acid is added as necessary to combat the natural tendency of the pH to creep upward toward the end of the fermentation.

When the must is dry, and sometimes even a bit before, Tunnell presses and racks to barrel. The press fraction is kept separate but is blended back whenever possible. Since 2003, the barrel regime has relied almost entirely on wood from Vosges and Nevers forests, coopered by Cadus and toasted medium. Generally, the pinots are not racked until bottling time, unless extreme funkiness develops. The Cuvée du Tonnelier and Select are bottled after fourteen months in barrel; Les Dijonnais gets sixteen months. Egg-white fining is sometimes done to take the edge off harsh tannins, but the wines are not filtered. Brick House pinots are all succulent, intense, evergreen wines with deep colors, moderate extraction, and good length; however, the dry-farmed, "mottled," and sedimentary soils make for substantial tannins. From warmer vintages, all bear and deserve aging.

TASTING NOTES

2005 *Select (tasted in 2007):* Medium brick-red; spirity nose with gum camphor and licorice; intense, dark fruit flavors with minerality; very rich, muscular wine, but nicely structured; tannins and acid both very perceptible; long.

2003 *Les Dijonnais (tasted in 2007):* Rich, slightly earthy nose suggesting orange peel and red fruit; bright on the palate with white pepper, herbs, and a hint of hard spice and cardamom; simultaneously hard and elegant like a good Gevrey; considerable load of very fine-grain tannin; fine.

2003 *Evelyn's (tasted in 2007):* Transparent, deep ruby; conifer and raspberry aromas with a suggestion of evolution; very intense, rich, and mouth-coating mocha-tinged cherry and raspberry; impressive tannins; still young and partially unresolved.

2000 *Les Dijonnais (tasted in 2007):* Dark mahogany; intense conifer nose

with dried currants; slightly sweet attack resolves quickly to fading raspberry and omnipresent, very fine-grained tannins; some leather; a chamois-like texture that is very mouth coating and long; still young structurally.

BROADLEY VINEYARDS AND WINERY
Monroe, Oregon

Craig Broadley's conversion from a career in book publishing and distribution to serious, small-scale winemaking began in the early 1970s and revolved around an unlikely trio of institutions: Berkeley's legendary Chez Panisse restaurant, San Francisco's City Lights bookstore and publishers, and Kermit Lynch Wine Merchant. At Chez Panisse, just a block from home, the Broadleys developed a taste for food and wine. Kermit Lynch's Burgundies, from makers who were just beginning to break with *négociants* and bottle their own wines, became favorites. And City Lights, Broadley's employer, was amenable to a book-distribution scheme based not in San Francisco but in rural Oregon. Broadley completed the first year of coursework in the University of California Davis's viticulture and enology program. He and his wife then sought out Oregon's pinot pioneers and looked for property in the Willamette Valley. In 1977 they moved from Berkeley to Eugene, and in 1982 they planted their first 5 acres of vineyard on a northeast-facing slope near Monroe, a farm town with one main street and ceaseless truck traffic, northwest of Eugene.

Broadley's estate vineyard has now grown to 35 acres, wrapped around the northern end of an 850-foot hill. The first planting in 1982 was followed by a second 12-acre installment in 1983, several subsequent small additions, and about 7 acres planted since 1996. The 1980s plantings were roughly three quarters UCD 5 and one quarter UCD 2A on their own roots; the most recent increments (as recently as 2001) have been done with Dijon 113, 114, 115, and 777, on 3309. There is also an ongoing replanting program to replace the own-rooted vines. (Interestingly, the Broadleys have observed that the grafted vines are less vigorous than the own-rooted ones.) Spacing is mostly 11-foot rows with 4 feet between vines, and the trellising, atypically, is lyre shaped. Although the site is primarily a northeast-facing slope, the planted parcels are mostly oriented east or southeast. This southern end of the Willamette Valley is warmer than the northwestern quadrant, where most pinot vineyards are now concentrated, so the Broadleys deliberately chose northern and eastern exposures, to capture the proverbial cooler sites in a warmer climate. The vineyard is farmed and harvested in blocks that correspond to the speed of fruit ripening. The first blocks to be harvested are those facing north and northeast; the last to be picked are those that face southeast.

During the 1990s, the "main" Broadley bottling made use of grapes purchased from a few neighbors and from the Walnut Ridge Vineyard in Lane County, in addition to their estate fruit, but the wine has been all-estate since 2003. There are, however, a few vineyard-designated non-estate pinots: from SHEA, from STOLLER VINEYARDS, and (since 2007) from Sunny Mountain Vineyard, a 10-acre site 4 miles south of Monroe. The "winery" is a converted Pontiac dealership on Monroe's main drag. Morgan Broadley now shares the winegrowing duties with his father, and Morgan's wife, Jessica, is the lead figure on the sales and marketing side, but both generations are active. Broadley remains what is has been from the beginning: a hands-on, all-in-the-family enterprise.

WINES AND WINEMAKING NOTES

The 1980s pinot noir program at Broadley was based primarily on estate fruit, although small quantities of grapes were also purchased. The best barrels went into a Reserve; the next best went into a vintage-dated Oregon pinot noir, and a nonvintage blend was occasionally made with leftovers. The current program was born in the early 1990s. Claudia's Choice, the Broadleys' flagship wine and their "objective" throughout the 1980s, debuted in 1994, when the owners believed they had enough volume of top-quality wine to justify a separate bottling. Ostensibly a selection of the darkest and most intense barrels, Claudia's Choice has turned out to be almost a block-designate, made from the mid-slope and lower-slope portions of the original 1982 and 1983 plantings. Marcile Lorraine is another block-designate, made from 2 acres at the top of the old vineyard, plus some adjacent younger vines; it was first made in 1996. Once only, in 2000, a *single* barrel, chosen from among those set aside for the combination of Claudia's and Marcile Lorraine, was bottled separately as Olivia. Everything else is used to make the Willamette Valley cuvée, which accounts for most of the Broadleys' production. The Broadleys find that they are now picking grapes a bit riper than they did when the project began, now generally around 26 Brix; however, relatively long hang times also give them ripe stems and seeds, so they have no trouble retaining a large fraction of the crop in whole-cluster form. (Whole-cluster fermentations have been a Broadley hallmark since the beginning.)

A walk-in cooler is employed to chill the picked fruit. Fermentors are a combination of small, stainless steel and wooden open-tops that hold 2 to 3 tons each. After being transferred from the cooler to the fermentors, the fruit is allowed to warm up slowly. When the grapes are healthy, indigenous fermentations are tolerated, but the Broadleys do not hesitate to use one or more of several laboratory yeasts on hand if there is a reason to get the fermentation going quickly. The must is first pumped over, then "walked down" by foot, and finally punched down by hand; even so, Morgan Broadley reports that they have replaced some instances of punchdown with pumpovers in recent years, in response to the slightly riper fruit. The stainless steel tanks are usually dry in about eighteen days, but the whole-cluster lots in wooden fermentors, which never go completely dry, are pressed after about three and a half weeks, on the basis of taste. The new wine may go directly to barrel or may first settle overnight in tank. Whenever possible, the press fraction is immediately reunified with the free-run juice from the same fermentor, but the press fraction from tannic lots may be segregated.

Since 2004, the entire barrel stock has been from Tonnellerie Claude Gillet in St. Romain. For the Claudia's Choice and Marcile Lorraine bottlings (see below), 100 percent new wood is used, and for the Reserve, anywhere between 25 percent and 100 percent. Malolactic fermentation usually happens spontaneously, but often is not complete until April or May. The wines are racked once thereafter, at which point barrels provisionally earmarked for the Claudia's Choice and Marcile Lorraine bottlings are culled, and some are redirected to the Reserve; some lots raised to this point in new barrels are moved to older wood. The Reserve is bottled in November after the vintage; Claudia's Choice and Marcile Lorraine stay in barrel until the following spring. There is no fining or filtration. Broadley pinots are broad-shouldered, concentrated, intensely flavored wines that are not fruit-flavored despite being picked ripe. The signature of whole cluster fermentation is usually strong, but the wines are also nicely layered and medium-weight, and the tannins are well behaved and fine-grained.

TASTING NOTES

2005 *Willamette Valley Estate (tasted in 2007)*: Transparent, dark, rosy black-red; juniper berry, resin, and dark fruit on the nose; rich, round, peppery, and slightly minty on the palate with a bittersweet hint of red vermouth; cherry is the dominant fruit; good acidity and length.

2005 *Shea Vineyard (tasted in 2007)*: Transparent, medium-dark black-red; rose petal, violets, spice, and resin on the nose; red fruit on the palate with citrus peel accents and a hint of green apple; silky and very elegant with some of fruit-and-flower properties of Beaune *premier cru*; attractive and long.

2004 *Claudia's Choice (tasted in 2007)*: Barely transparent, saturated dark red; very expressive nose of juniper berries, savory and ripe fruit; bright but very intense attack featuring resinous red fruit and black pepper; satiny to mid-palate, then grippy with very fine-grained tannins; an attractive edition of Claudia's; long.

2003 *Claudia's Choice (tasted in 2007)*: Saturated dark brick-red color; aromas of bayberry, juniper berry and candle wax; huge, rich, ripe palate featuring dark chocolate, marionberry and slate; tannic throughout, with a dry, grippy finish.

2003 *Lemelson [Johnson and Stermer Vineyards] (tasted in 2005)*: Brilliant, medium-dark magenta; spice, resin and other indicators of whole-cluster fermentation dominate the nose; resin, licorice, black tea, roasted coffee beans, and some dark chocolate on the palate; rich at mid-palate, then grippy; needs time.

2002 *Claudia's Choice (tasted in 2006):* Transparent, dark black-red, showing a touch of terra cotta; herbal, juniper-berry nose; creosote and tar; allspice, cinnamon, and glög flavors; nicely structured with a silky mid-palate and some grip; medium-long and just beginning to mature; serious and attractive wine.

 ## BROGAN CELLARS
Healdsburg, California

Margi Williams Wierenga is the daughter of WILLIAMS SELYEM's co-founder Burt Williams. She was a teenager when her father and Ed Selyem launched their *garagiste* project, and she was working for Williams Selyem as a salaried employee when it was sold in 1998. Rather than take a position "within the corporate environment," she launched her own brand, named for her paternal grandmother. The first vintage, in 1998, consisted of zinfandel, chardonnay, and pinot noir from Lone Redwood Ranch on Laughlin Road at the south edge of the Sonoma County Airport, and some semillon sourced from the northern part of Sonoma County. The winery was a makeshift facility, cobbled together from repurposed dairy tanks and secondhand equipment, in a leased Dry Creek Valley garage. The garage is still used for barrel fermentations and storage, but in 2006 all production was moved to a facility

on property Williams Wierenga and her husband own in Hopland, California.

WINES AND WINEMAKING NOTES
Brogan Cellars produces only a little over 2,000 cases of pinot noir, plus even smaller quantities of chardonnay, zinfandel, and sauvignon blanc, but the portfolio of separate bottlings has grown from one in 1998 to ten in 2006. In 1999, a Reserve and an appellation bottling were added to the lineup, followed by an Olivet Lane bottling in 2000 (but for one year only) and a Helio Doro wine in 2001. Helio Doro is a 24-row block in the Buena Tierra Vineyard on the east side of the Russian River's Middle Reach that was previously used by other wineries entirely for sparkling wine.

In 2002 Williams Wierenga added wines from the Summa Vineyard on Taylor Lane east of Occidental; in 2003 she began sourcing fruit from Mark Lingenfelder's Russian River Valley vineyard; in 2004 sources expanded to include her father's new vineyard in Anderson Valley and the Benovia Vineyard, an old, 6.5-acre planting in very rocky soil almost on the north edge of the Russian River Valley appellation formerly known as Cohn Vineyard. This list understates the complexity of things, however, since two cuvées (one labeled Young Vines) have sometimes been made in the same vintage from Summa, and Burt Williams's vineyard, properly called Morning Dew Ranch, was used to make three separate block-designated wines in 2006. Several reserve bottlings, carrying both Russian River Valley and Sonoma Coast designations, have been made intermittently; an Anderson Valley appellation wine was made in 2004; and the fruit sourced from Lingenfelder switched from a block planted to UCD 13 that was used in 2003 to a block planted to UCD 4, used since 2004. Along the way,

Lone Redwood Ranch was discontinued after 2003, and Summa was discontinued after 2004.

Williams Wierenga says she likes to harvest pinot between 23 and 24 Brix, but says this can sometimes be hard to manage. A combination of whole clusters and destemmed, whole berries is co-fermented, but the ratio varies as a function of stem condition, tank capacity, and other factors. The fermentors (repurposed dairy tanks, see above) are walked down at the beginning of each fermentation, and are hand plunged thereafter. All fermentations rely entirely on resident yeasts; tartaric acid is "sometimes" required, but sulfur dioxide is rarely added to any lot unless "mold exceeds our limits." New wines are pressed off at dryness. The barrel stock is all from François Frères. Wines spend eleven months in approximately 50 percent new barrels, with the other 50 percent having been used previously for one, two, or three wines. Wines are not filtered. Each Brogan Cellars wine is distinctive and quite different from the others, and none is shyly made. Some wines are nearly elegant; others are quite bold and brash. In every case, the wine benefits from having time to breathe after being opened, with decanting as an alternative.

TASTING NOTES

2005 *My Father's Vineyard (aka Morning Dew Ranch, tasted in 2007):* Deep, nearly opaque black-red; expressive nose of resinous, sappy fruit; intense cherry on the palate, like cherry *eau-de-vie*; bright cranberry highlights; rich structure and a silky texture; notes of briar, chaparral, spice, and pepper; very young but attractive.

2002 *Buena Tierra Vineyard Helio Doro Block (tasted in 2007):* Pretty, transparent, medium mahogany with something of an orange edge; earthy, resinated wood with pine needles on the nose; elegant on the palate with a bit of leather, strong merbromin, and some red berry sweetness; secondary aromatics and flavors overall; satiny, rich, long, and very attractive.

2000 *Olivet Lane Vineyard (tasted in 2007):* Medium garnet with some terra cotta; pot pourri, underbrush, and wild berry aromas; sweet, red berry attack, then strong notes of cinnamon, allspice, and pepper on the mid-palate; of medium length and elegantly structured; a nice testament to old UCD 13 (Martini) vines in Russian River.

BUENA VISTA CARNEROS
Sonoma, California

Buena Vista is one of the oldest names in California wine, having been created in 1857, when the famous—and also infamous—Colonel Agoston Haraszthy abandoned his effort to grow vines at Crystal Springs on the San Francisco peninsula; he established himself and his project in Sonoma instead, where it attracted considerable attention. The vineyards, which were then northeast of Sonoma in the foothills of the Mayacamas Range, succumbed thereafter to phylloxera, and the brand lapsed until it was acquired in 1941 by Frank Bartholomew, a San Francisco newspaperman.

In 1968 Bartholomew sold the historic stone winery and the Buena Vista name to Vernon Underwood of Young's Market Company, a wine and spirits distributor in Southern California, but retained title to Haraszthy's original vineyards, at which point the "new" Buena Vista began to invest seriously in Los Carneros, where it eventually came to be the largest single landowner. Buena Vista was sold again at the end of the 1970s, this time to A. Racke GmbH & Co. of Bingen, Germany, a producer of still wines and *sekt*; yet again to Allied Domecq in 2002; and finally to Beam Wine Estates Inc., a division of Fortune Brands, in 2005. The estate vineyard now consists of two adjacent parcels totaling 1,000 acres near the center of the Carneros appellation, south of the Carneros Highway, overlooking San Pablo Bay. Here, 800 acres are planted to vines laid out in more than 167 blocks, of which 70 blocks and 335 acres are dedicated to pinot noir. Following extensive replanting since 1998, the oldest pinot vines are now ten years old, while the youngest, in 2007, were not yet bearing. By 2005, however, for the first time in the brand's history, *all* Buena Vista wines were Carneros grown.

WINES AND WINEMAKING NOTES

Since 2003 Buena Vista has made Carneros appellation wines built from estate fruit under the Carneros and Ramal Vineyard designations. In addition to a straight Ramal Vineyard bottling of pinot—a blend of UCD 5 and UCD 13; Dijon 115, 667, and 777; and Swan selection—two clone-specific wines were made in 2005: Ramal Vineyard Clone 828 and Ramal Vineyard Clone 5 Pommard. All fruit for the Ramal Vineyard wines is destemmed; about 70 percent is retained as whole berries. Fermentations take place in 5-, 7-, and 10-ton stainless steel, open-top fermentors. Acid is added as necessary, but there is no use of enzymes. A five-to-eight day cold soak is followed by six to nine days of primary fermentation, which relies about 40 percent on resident yeasts and 60 percent on inoculations with Assmanshausen, RC 212 and Wädenswil isolates. The new wine goes to barrel after

settling overnight and spends nine months in oak before being bottled without fining or filtration. The barrel stock is about 35 percent new and comes from Francois Frères, Rousseau, Remond, Mercurey, Demptos, and Dargaud & Jaeglé. Many barrels are used through four wines. Buena Vista's winemaker since 2004 has been Jeff Stewart, who previously accumulated valuable experience making relatively large volumes of pinot using the consensus protocol at LA CREMA. The clone-specific bottlings are attractive wines, distinctly different one from another, with good varietal character and aromatic interest.

TASTING NOTES

2005 *Ramal Vineyard Clone* 828 *(tasted in* 2007*):* Brilliant medium garnet color; dusty floral fragrance with raspberry and strawberry aromas; substantially fruit-driven palate with rosewater; then, smoky with a bit of peppery and gingery bite; generally delicate finish with a modest load of very fine-grained tannin.

2005 *Ramal Vineyard Clone* 5 *Pommard (tasted in* 2007*):* Brilliant medium black-red; earth on the nose with a hint of tar; brewed black tea with red berries and cherries; soft, dusty mid-palate; then, some grip toward the end; silky overall, lightly mouth coating, and long.

BYRON VINEYARD
AND WINERY
Santa Maria, California

Byron is an exceptionally complicated piece of California's recent wine business history. It began life in 1984 when a partnership driven by Byron Kent Brown (see KEN BROWN WINES) and several partners purchased a small, 10-acre parcel adjacent to the historic Tepusquet Vineyard, built a barn-like, wood-shingle winery in time for that year's harvest, and planted a few acres of chardonnay. Although Brown and his partners focused on both major

AN EXCEPTIONALLY COMPLICATED PIECE OF CALIFORNIA'S RECENT WINE BUSINESS HISTORY

Burgundian varieties, they did not grow pinot noir until much later. Instead, from 1984 through 1989, they purchased their pinot grapes from neighboring Tepusquet, from Sierra Madre (about 7 miles west of the winery on the Santa Maria Mesa), and from Sanford & Benedict.

Between 1988 and 1990, three interlocking business transactions rearranged the game board. First, in 1988, ROBERT MONDAVI WINERY purchased part of the Tepusquet Vineyard from Jess Jackson and Barbara Banke, who had acquired it a few months before from its developers, Louis and George Lucas. (Jackson's and Banke's retained portion of Tepusquet became CAMBRIA WINERY AND VINEYARD.) Second, in 1989, Brown successfully negotiated the purchase of Uriel Nielson's vineyard, the very first vineyard to have been planted on the bench back in 1964, located just upslope from Tepusquet and adjacent to Brown's 10-acre parcel. Third, in 1990, Mondavi purchased Byron. With access to fruit from Nielson assured, Byron discontinued its use of Sanford & Benedict and applied the Byron name to the Nielson vineyard.

Another succession of changes occurred in the mid 1990s. In 1996 Mondavi purchased the Sierra Madre Vineyard. The following year, Byron abandoned use of Byron as a *vineyard* name, reviving Nielson; but Nielson was used, beginning in 1998, to denote the (now) Mondavi-owned parts of the old Tepusquet Vineyard, which Uriel Nielson never owned, as well as Nielson proper. These already complicated circumstances prevailed, more or less, until 1993, when Mondavi directors, preparing to offer the company for sale, began to divest assets and sold Sierra Madre inter alia. With this handwriting on the wall, Brown, Byron's founder and namesake, stepped away from the winery he had created to establish his own brand. At more or less the same time, Ken Volk, who had just sold WILD HORSE in Templeton, purchased the *original* Byron parcel and winery from Mondavi, making it the home for Volk's new brand, Kenneth Volk Vineyards.

In 2004 the Robert Mondavi Company was sold to Constellation Brands, which immediately divested Byron (along with the Arrowood Winery and Vineyards in Sonoma), selling both to a newbie player called Legacy Estates Group LLC. Legacy already owned Napa's Freemark Abbey Winery, but to finance its new acquisitions, Legacy borrowed from a hedge fund. When it was unable to service its debt and declared bankruptcy eight months later, Legacy (including Byron and Arrowood) was sold, from bankruptcy, to Jackson Family Wines, which already owned CAMBRIA WINERY AND VINEYARD.

Unsurprsingly, Byron's pinot program reflects the aforementioned phases and benchmarks in its complex business history. Fruit for the 1984, 1865, and 1986 vintages was purchased from Tepusquet and Sierra Madre. The main release, variously labeled as Central Coast, Santa Barbara County, and Santa Maria Valley, was a blend from the two sites. A Reserve was also made exclusively from Sierra Madre fruit, but was not vineyard-designated. In 1987 and 1988, the "main" release was a blend of lots from Sierra Madre and Sanford & Benedict, while the Reserve evolved into a barrel selection from the same sources.

After the trio of late 1980s transactions, Byron's main source of pinot shifted to the former Nielson Vineyard, and use of Sanford & Benedict grapes was discontinued. When a major replanting program pulled large parts of ex-Nielson out of production after 1991, the pinot program lived for several years on a combination of fruit purchased from neighboring Tepusquet and from Sierra Madre. The year 1996 saw the first vineyard-designated wine from the replanted ex-Nielson property (called Byron Vineyard at this point; see above) and from Mondavi's purchase of Sierra Madre. On the strength of the latter, Byron launched a vineyard-designated Sierra Madre cuvée in 1997 and abandoned its reserve program. In 1996, Byron also recanted its use of the Byron name to denote a *vineyard*, reviving Nielson, but (see above, once again) treated Mondavi-owned parts of Tepusquet as part of Nielson, even though Nielson had never owned or farmed them. All of the Nielson part of the Nielson Vineyard was replanted at some point in the 1990s to a combination of Dijon clones, UCD 1A, 2A, 9, 16, and 23, and a field selection from Sanford & Benedict; there was also at least one experimental use of scion material imported directly from France. Multiple planting densities were used experimentally, but none was less than 1,200 vines per acre; row orientation, which had run across the slope parallel to the river, was changed to north–south. Nielsen fruit not used by Byron was redirected, until Mondavi sold Byron, to the Mondavi Coastal program.

At the present time, Bonaccorsi Wines, Kenneth Volk Wines, and AU BON CLIMAT are fruit clients. Use of Sierra Madre fruit was discontinued between 2002 and 2005, but resumed in 2006 and became vineyard-designated. Since 2002 Byron has also purchased pinot noir grapes from Blocks 1 and T at Bien Nacido, mostly for use in the Santa Maria Valley blend, but some of it was vineyard-designated in 2005 and 2006. In 2005, in addition to the appellation wine and the Bien Nacido cuvée, there was a vineyard-designated wine from the Nielson Vineyard, and a small volume of the "best lots" from Nielson labeled as Monument Hill. To this list, in 2006, Byron added the aforementioned Sierra Madre wine, a single vineyard wine from Cambria's Julia's Vineyard, next door, and a bottling called Historic Nielson.

Among Santa Maria Valley pinots, Byron's are uncommonly elegant and rewarding. The Sierra Madre bottlings seemed especially silken and softly spicy in their day; the Nielson bottlings are often more richly fruity and earthen. Brown was the winemaker for Byron until 2003, at which point he was succeeded by Jonathan Nagy, a chemistry graduate of the University of California Davis, who worked for Mondavi in Napa and at Cambria before joining the Byron staff as assistant winemaker in 2001.

WINEMAKING NOTES
Byron picks pinot ripe enough to avoid hard tannins and what Brown called "simple strawberry flavors," when a good percentage of the seeds are dark, and when the vine's basal leaves just begin to yellow. In general, the grapes at this point have a sugar level between not much less than 24 Brix and not much more than 25. Fruit is sorted rigorously—in the vineyard before harvest, in the vineyard again during the

pick itself, and (using custom-designed tables) on the crushpad—to eliminate second-crop clusters, botrytis, and leaves. Stems are generally discarded. The largest fermentors are 6-ton, stainless steel open-tops, but some lots are fermented in small plastic bins. To make sure the small bins develop sufficient heat, they are placed in a warm room. Native yeast fermentations usually start after about four to five days of cold soak, and about half of the pinot fermentations rely entirely on native yeast. Brown argued that native-yeast fermentations "promote less fruit expression, but tend to produce wines of greater complexity," making native yeast, therefore, the protocol of choice with old-vines fruit, which has "more complexity potential." Nagy reports increasing use of drain-and-return as a cap management method in recent vintages, based on a discovery that pinot tolerates exposure to oxygen quite well as long as there is unconverted sugar in the must.

The new wines are pressed off at dryness, or the maceration is extended for as much as seven additional days, depending on the vintage. Extended maceration is generally permitted only in warm years, when there are few green seeds. The basket press's natural tendency to filter the juice sometimes makes tank settling unnecessary, in which case the wine can go directly from press to barrel. Malolactic inoculation occurs during pressing. Barrels are 60 percent to 70 percent François Frères; the balance are mostly Remond or Boutes. (Boutes is a Bordeaux-based cooper not often used with pinot.) The percentage of new wood varies from about 25 percent for the Santa Maria Valley wine to 40 percent for Nielson. The Santa Maria Valley wine spends ten months in barrel; Nielson spends closer to sixteen. About 80 percent of lots are egg-white fined for tannin management, but most lots are not filtered.

TASTING NOTES

2004 *Santa Maria Valley (tasted in* 2007*):* Transparent, medium ruby; savory, herbal nose; slightly sweet, mixed-berry fruit on the palate; mouth coating at mid-palate; very soft, fine tannins give an impression of linen; moderate length; attractive.

2003 *Nielson Vineyard (tasted in* 2007*):* Transparent, medium ruby; earth and pepper on the nose; intense blackberry, briar, and black pepper on the palate; tightly knit, persistent, and long, with some grip and warmth at the end.

CALERA WINE COMPANY
Hollister, California

Josh Jensen, a Bay Area dentist's son who discovered good Burgundy while reading for a master's degree in anthropology at Oxford, is one of the authentic pioneers of pinot noir in North America. Convinced from the outset that "dirt, low yield, and barrels" were the keys to great pinot, and passionately dedicated to the proposition that the right dirt was the same limestone-rich soil that underlies the slopes of the Côte d'Or, Jensen chose the loneliest course of any North American pioneer. Because there is very little limestone in California, his Calera Wine Company was, until very recently, many miles from any other winery on a site originally developed to house a rock-crushing plant. His vineyards—a half-hour's crawl uphill from the winery via miles of steep, sinuous dirt track across cattle guards and through farm gates—occupy an appellation of their own. The only earlier enterprise in these parts, 90 miles south of San Francisco in San Benito County, was the lime kiln, abandoned but still standing, that has given its name to Calera, and which figures on its label. To this day, the vineyard is shared by deer, wild boar, rattlesnakes, rabbits, skunks, and tarantulas.

Jensen's search for California's limestone soil began in the early 1970s. After discovering Mount Harlan, battling for ownership, and prevailing over water-grasping neighbors, Jensen planted his first three vineyards—all to pinot noir—in 1975. These were two 5-acre parcels facing each other north and south across Indian Creek—Selleck (south- and southwest-facing, and named for the dentist colleague of Jensen's father whose connoisseurship had first introduced Jensen to the pleasures of wine) and Reed (north- and northeast-facing, and named for Jensen's first and only nonfamily partner in the Calera venture)—and a 14-acre parcel laid out in four differently exposed and variously oriented blocks, named "Jensen" in honor of Jensen *père*. Nine years later, in 1984, a fourth parcel of pinot noir was planted overlooking Harlan Creek, a stone's throw from the first three. This was named for Everett Mills, a colorful local character instrumental in helping Jensen find his limestone soil and winery site.

Jensen testifies that he was deeply influenced by Chalone Vineyard's founder, Dick Graff, "a stickler for the highest quality and for traditional Burgundian methods." Jensen liked Graff's Chalone pinot noirs so much that he used field-selected Chalone budwood for all of the 1975 plantings except two thirds of Jensen, which was planted to an unknown nursery clone. (Stories persist in the industry that Jensen was one of the importers behind the so-called new plantings at Chalone, so that his supposed Chalone selection was in fact none other than a second-generation import from Burgundy; but these stories cannot be confirmed.) Cleaving to natural

practices, Jensen chose St. George for rootstock. In 1984, believing that there was no reason to tamper with success, he took budwood from Selleck to plant Mills, but the Mills vines were own-rooted. Additional pinot was planted in a block bridging the rise between Jensen and Mills in 1997; a new block, named "Ryan" after Jim Ryan, Calera's vineyard manager since 1979, was planted in 1998 north of the

---

DARK, COMPLEX, SERIOUS WINES THAT MAINTAIN THE INHERENT ELEGANCE OF PINOT NOIR

---

lime kiln in rocky soil overlooking the headwaters of Harlan Creek. The first fruit from the 1997 field was harvested in 2000; the 1998 planting yielded a tiny first crop in 2002. The planting density of the first four vineyards is 6 feet between vines in 10-foot rows, and the historic yield (1982–1997) is barely 1.5 tons to the acre. The 1997 and Ryan fields are twice as dense—mostly 4 feet between vines in 7.5-foot rows—but some steeper sections are 5 feet between vines in 8-foot rows.

When the brand was established in 1975, Calera made zinfandel from purchased grapes. This practice continued through the 1985 harvest. The year 1978 marked the first, albeit small, harvest from the three small original vineyards on Mount Harlan; in 1980 Jensen reaped his first commercially significant crop, enough for about 370 cases. The breakthrough vintage, according to Jensen's memory, was 1982, from which vintage the Selleck Vineyard pinot won a platinum medal in the American Wine Competition, and the Jensen Vineyard was named Best American Pinot Noir in a competition sponsored by the American

Restaurant Association. In retrospect, Jensen thinks the 1978 through 1981 vintages were hampered by his view at the time, shaped by Burgundian advice, that pinot noir should be harvested at about 22 degrees Brix, to yield finished wine with approximately 12 percent alcohol. "We were trying so hard," he recalls, "to be sure the wines were not pruny." In "a major winemaking shift," Calera began picking riper in 1982, which allowed the wines to finish at about 13 percent to 13.5 percent alcohol—which in Jensen's view improved them dramatically.

Steve Doerner, a biochemist without formal training in enology, was Calera's winemaker from 1979 to 1991, at which point he moved to CRISTOM in Oregon, but Jensen and Doerner collaborated on all key decisions throughout his tenure. Diana Vita, a Cornell graduate in enology, joined the Calera team in 1987, beginning an era Jensen calls "major-winemaking-decisions-by-committee-of-three," which continues to this day. Vita is now the winery manager, with responsibility for "institutional memory" and the "maintenance of house style." After Doerner's departure, the winemaker title was held by Sara Steiner from 1992 to 1995 and by New Zealander Belinda Gould for the 1997, 1998, and 1999 harvests. In 2000 Jensen reclaimed the winemaker title for himself but engaged Terry Culton, a veteran of WILD HORSE, Edmeades, and WILLAMETTE VALLEY VINEYARDS, as his assistant for the 2000, 2001, and 2002 harvest years, at which point Culton moved on to ADELAIDA CELLARS. Corneliu Dane, originally of Romania, was the assistant winemaker for the 2003, 2004, and 2005 vintages.

WINES AND WINEMAKING NOTES
Calera's single-vineyard wines are generally dark, complex, and saturated.

They are also very structured—in a way that is common among wines from mountain vineyards—and angular. But they are not heavyweight wines; the inherent elegance of pinot is maintained. Jensen says plainly that these flagship wines are usually "backward" and "really don't taste that great" until they are three or four years old. The Selleck and Mills bottlings are not even released until three-and-a-half or four years after the vintage, and the Reed, Ryan, and Jensen are typically held for three; the winery recommends drinking them six to twelve years after the vintage. The Central Coast blend, by contrast, is designed to be ready young. With only a handful of exceptions, all the Mount Harlan fruit goes into the single-vineyard bottlings, and the Central Coast wine is made almost entirely from purchased fruit. In 1993 some lots from three of the four estate vineyards were declassified into a Central Coast Reserve wine, and in 1997, another high-yield year, 2,042 cases of Calera Mélange Mount Harlan were made from declassified, lighter lots. Starting with the 2002 vintage, this wine concept has now been renamed Mt. Harlan Cuvée Pinot Noir and is now a regular, annual wine composed of the smoother, softer batches from the various single-vineyard plantings. So far, it varies in quantity from 292 cases (in 2003) to as many as 998 cases (in 2004). It is priced considerably lower than each of the five single-vineyard wines. Until 2006 most of the fruit for the Central Coast blend came from four vineyards: the San Ysidro vineyard outside Gilroy in Santa Clara County, Laetitia in Arroyo Grande, Wente in Arroyo Seco, and Gimelli, less than a mile from Calera's winery in San Benito County. 2007 was sourced differently. The main sources in 2007 were the Los Alamos Vineyard,

Doctor's Vineyard in the Santa Lucia Highlands, Flint Vineyard in the Cienega Valley, and several vineyards on the floor of the Salinas Valley near Chualar and Greenfield. Pinot noir accounts for about 60 percent of Calera's total production, which also includes chardonnay and viognier; the percentage will increase slightly when the 1997 and 1998 blocks are in full production.

Unsurprisingly, Jensen follows a classical, almost old-fashioned Burgundian winemaking protocol. Fermentations take place in 2,000-gallon open-top tanks, and (very uncharacteristically for the New World) all the stems are used. In fact, Calera does not own a destemmer-crusher, which Jensen describes as a "doomsday machine." Grape clusters are tipped from picking bins directly into the fermentors. There is no cold soak save for the couple of days it takes the resident yeast to build up their population to the point where they can begin fermentation naturally. Calera "almost always" adds acid and never bleeds the must. The vatting normally lasts about fourteen days at a maximum temperature of about 86°F. The pomace is bladder pressed when the must is dry; the press fraction is immediately reunited with the free-run juice, and the Mount Harlan wines go into about 30 percent new oak. (Only 10 percent new oak is used for the Central Coast blend.) Eighty-five percent of the cooperage is François Frères CF (for Central France) barrels, but a small amount of other cooperage is used "for curiosity value." The Central Coast blend is kept in barrel for eleven to twelve months, but the vineyard-designated wines spend fifteen to sixteen months in wood. The wines are not racked until bottling, nor are they filtered; however, each barrel is usually fined with one egg white "for clarity or to help manage tannin."

TASTING NOTES

2005 *Thirtieth Anniversary Vintage Central Coast (tasted in 2007):* Light-to-medium garnet; smoky, slightly spicy nose; bright, slightly resinous berry fruit with layers of spice, minerality, and black pepper; a moderately intense wine with a bantam-weight frame; attractive.

2005 *Mt. Harlan Cuvee (tasted in 2007):* Transparent, medium-dark brick-red with a rosy edge; allspice and juniper berry on the nose; simultaneously slightly sweet, savory, and intense; brewed Darjeeling tea with red currants and a bit of infused rose petal; light-to-medium in weight, and silky at mid-palate; noticeable grip, and dry on the finish; very attractive.

2003 *Mills Vineyard (tasted from a half-bottle in 2007):* Transparent, light-to-medium garnet; dusty nose featuring cosmetic-case aromas, talc, and potpourri; slightly sweet with bright fruit and raspberry on the palate; hints of resin; medium in length.

2003 *Reed Vineyard (tasted from a half-bottle in 2007):* Light-to-medium terra cotta; earthy, almost feral nose with pine needles; briary juniper berry flavors on the palate; verges toward tar; deep and very ripe fruit; medium in weight, and nicely elegant.

2003 *Selleck Vineyard (tasted from a half-bottle in 2007):* Medium brick-red; intriguing nose of beeswax, boot polish, nuts, and vanilla with floral overtones; softly spicy and tobacco-y in the mouth; elegantly structured, exotic, and very attractive; good length and some grip at the end.

2003 *Jensen Vineyard (tasted from a half-bottle in 2007):* Transparent medium-dark terra cotta; intense nose of dried fruit and flowers with a hint of mocha; vibrant, rich palate with deep cherry, brewed Darjeeling tea, and lots of very fine-grained tannins; richly structured, long, and rewarding, but needs more time.

CAMBRIA WINERY
AND VINEYARD
Santa Maria, California

The Tepusquet Bench, the farmable benchland at the base of the San Rafael Mountains overlooking the Sisquoc River, has been the pounding heart of Santa Barbara wine country since the 1960s. The first vines were planted at the southeast end of the bench, in 1964, by Uriel Nielson and Bill DeMattei, two friends and former viticulture majors from the University of California Davis. A second and much larger investment was made in 1972 by Louis and George Lucas, table grape farmers from the Central Valley, who developed more than 1,000 acres of vineyards in the central portion of the bench, buoyed by assurances from Napa-based wineries that the fruit, when it came, could be sold easily and for good prices. As long as the American wine market thrived, the Lucases sold grapes to North Coast wineries such as ZD, Chateau Montelena, and Kendall-Jackson. In 1973 the northwest end of the bench was purchased and planted by Bob and Steve Miller, whose family had various farming interests in Santa Barbara and Ventura counties. Nielson and DeMattei's original vineyard was acquired at the end of the 1980s by BYRON VINEYARD AND WINERY to complement a tiny parcel Byron's Ken Brown had purchased next door five years earlier. The Millers' land is still owned by the family and is farmed as Bien Nacido Vineyards. The central section, for which the Lucas brothers seized the Tepusquet name, was the hardest hit of the Santa Maria vineyard developments

when the wine market softened in the late 1970s and early 1980s; it was sold in 1987 to San Francisco attorney Jess Jackson and his wife Barbara Banke. Jackson and Banke subsequently sold two parcels of the Tepusquet property to Mondavi, but the balance was transformed into what is now Cambria Estate Winery. (What the Mondavis did with the so-called Paso Robles and East Mesa parcels is related in the Byron profile.) A decade later, Cambria had become one of the most successful of Jackson's many wine properties and the flagship of Jackson's presence on the southern Central Coast.

Although the Lucases' original plantings had included, in addition to pinot noir, varieties like cabernet sauvignon, riesling, chenin blanc, and pinot blanc, most of the vineyard was grafted or replanted between 1979 and 1989 and is now overwhelmingly chardonnay, pinot noir, and syrah. Two blocks of the original pinot noir, B6 and B7, amounting to about 50 acres, remain in production, both on their own roots. Another 400 acres of pinot is new plantings or replants; Cambria now farms more pinot noir than anyone on the Tepusquet Bench. Much of it sits in the southwestern quadrant of the property between Bien Nacido's westernmost blocks and the Sisquoc River in sandy-loam topsoils strewn with quartz-rich fractured shale overlaying a cobble-y subsoil. Quite a bit is UCD 4, but there are also UCD 2A, 5, 23, and several Dijon clones. Pinot is also planted in the northwest corner of the estate in an area where the topsoil is especially thin, that is known internally as Block A 13, and as the Bench Break Vineyard on wine labels.

Cambria makes two pinots: a Julia's Vineyard bottling and a Bench Break Vineyard bottling. The Bench Break does in fact come almost entirely from the northwest blocks described above, and the majority of the fruit for Julia's comes from the southwest blocks, but the Julias Vineyard moniker is also used to denote *any* pinot grown on the estate, so the Julia's bottling can best be understood as an estate blend. There are also experimental and clone-specific bottlings sold primarily in the winery's tasting room. Since 2003 the winemaker has been Denise Shurtleff, a graduate of the dietetics and food administration program at California State Polytechnic University at San Luis Obispo who was Cambria's assistant winemaker from 1999 to 2003. Cambria also sells pinot grapes to a short list of small producers in Santa Barbara County, who make "Julia's Vineyard" bottlings under their own labels. LANE TANNER, HITCHING POST WINES, FOXEN, Bonaccorsi, Kenneth Volk Vineyards, and BYRON are the current participants. Although any of the participants could, if they chose, use pinot grapes from any block on the estate and still call their Cambria-sourced wine "Julia's Vineyard," the current participants are all happy with their separate rows in Block B 4, which is UCD 4 planted in 1974.

WINES AND WINEMAKING NOTES

Although some fermentations at Cambria are done in small, closed-top tanks that are pumped over, most are done in 10- and 20-ton open tops that are punched down in the consensus protocol style. There is not much choice, actually, considering that Cambria aims for 60,000 cases of pinot annually and sells most of it for a suggested retail price of $20. All fruit is destemmed, cold macerated for five to seven days, and then inoculated. The new wines are pressed when the must is dry, but the press juice is excluded from the final blends. There is a brief period of settling in tank, where malolactic starter is also introduced, before the wines are barreled. Principal coopers are Seguin-Moreau, Damy, François Frères, and Remond; about 30 percent of those used to raise lots destined for Julia's are new in each vintage; the percentage of new wood used for the Bench Break bottling is around 60 percent. Both pinots are bottled before the following vintage, and both are filtered. I have not tasted the Bench Break wine since the 1999 vintage, when it seemed very black-fruit dominated, spicy, and minerally, but also hard with a significant tannic load. Julia's is not usually a shy wine either, and it represents good value in the marketplace.

TASTING NOTE

2004 *Julia's Vineyard (tasted twice in 2006 and 2007):* Brilliant, medium black-red; beetroot with mentholated notes, white pepper, barrel toast, and candied orange peel; Bing cherry, raspberry, and earth on the palate, plus barrel-derived vanilla; soft and of medium length, with a slightly alcoholic bite at the end.

CAMERON WINERY
Dundee, Oregon

John Paul began his professional life with a doctorate in oceanography and a staff research job in plant biochemistry. His winemaking career commenced, a bit later, with the 1978 crush at SOKOL BLOSSER WINERY, followed by four years at Carneros Creek, some time "kicking around" in Burgundy, and six months in New Zealand. If he had not been completely preoccupied with pinot noir at the outset, there was a conclusive epiphany in 1979, when Paul was invited to a tasting of the 1976 wines from Domaine de la Romanée-Conti. He remembers that "the wines were so gorgeous that I couldn't drink them . . . I just wanted to smell them . . . that was my epiphany that pinot is the greatest grape variety in the world . . . I fell in love." On a more practical level, Paul took several lessons from his early winemaking experience: first, that Los

---

WINES OF CONSIDERABLE COMPLEXITY AND ELEGANCE THAT AGE EXCEPTIONALLY WELL

Carneros was too warm for his "kind of pinot"; second, that his kind of winery had to start and stay small—3,500 to 5,000 cases—and compensate for its small size by self-distributing; and third, that New Zealand's domestic wine market, in the early 1980s, was too weak to support self-distribution. So in 1984, Paul moved his family to Portland, Oregon, purchased land near Dundee, and made Cameron's first vintage. The fruit for this vintage was purchased from Bill and Julia Wayne's Abbey Ridge Vineyard in exchange for shares in Cameron, birthing a partnership now in its twenty-fourth year.

Abbey Ridge is one of the oldest vineyards in the Dundee Hills. The first block was planted in 1976; subsequent plantings were done in 1984 and 1990, but Cameron uses only the fruit from the 1976 and 1984 plantings in its Abbey Ridge vineyard-designated wine. There are 22 planted acres total. The site is a southwest-facing slope at the northwestern end of the hills, high and

cool at 650 feet. The 1977 and 1984 plantings were own-rooted UCD 2A and 4, plus a field selection from Charles Coury's vineyard, set in 9-foot rows with 6 feet between vines. In 1990, a 1.5-acre section, now called Arley's Leap, was planted with budwood from Cameron's "estate" parcel (see below); Cameron designates the wine made from Arley's Leap as if it were a separate vineyard. Before 1984 Abbey Ridge pinot was sold primarily to THE EYRIE VINEYARDS and to ADELSHEIM; now about 85 percent goes into Cameron, but small quantities of fruit from the 1984 block are sold to KEN WRIGHT CELLARS and to WESTREY WINE COMPANY, both of which also make vineyard-designated wines from Abbey Ridge.

Cameron's estate vineyard, on Worden Hill Road above the town of Dundee, is a former filbert orchard now called Clos Electrique for its electrified peripheral fence. Paul cleared the filberts and planted 2 acres of pinot noir immediately after purchasing the property in 1984 using "ten clones," including Dijon 113, 114, and 115. Paul will not identify the other plant material, but it can be presumed to have originated out of state, probably from several of California's heritage vineyards. Clos Electrique, like Abbey Ridge, was planted 9 feet by 6; the soil is typical of the region—iron-rich Jory. Chardonnay was planted at Clos Electrique in 1987, and small bits of Italian varieties were added in 2000. There has been some incremental planting since, as well as some replanting to replace scion selections that proved "sub-par"; these have been set out in 6-foot rows with from 3 to 6 feet between vines, "depending on the viability of particular soil subsets."

Although Cameron purchased fruit from BRICK HOUSE from 1993 to 2002 and from Croft Vineyard from 1997 to 2000, it has been entirely Dundee

Hills–based since 2003. Alongside Abbey Ridge and Clos Electrique, Cameron also used the Gehrts Vineyard, located below DOMAINE DROUHIN OREGON. It has become an important article of faith with Paul that he works entirely with fruit from dry-farmed vineyards. Pointedly, he describes irrigation as "an accountant's method of achieving quick profitability" and argues that dry farming is essential to vines deeply enough rooted that they can "accurately express *terroir*."

WINES AND WINEMAKING NOTES

Cameron generally makes four vineyard-designates: Abbey Ridge, Arley's Leap, Clos Electrique, and Gehrts. A first pick of declassified barrels is repurposed for a Dundee Hills cuvee. The remainder is blended, sometimes with wine from the next vintage, to make a nonvintage bottling sold to Portland restaurants. Paul makes the decision to pick his pinot using the usual combination of visual clues (browning seeds and yellowing basal leaves), taste, and numbers. He watches pH carefully, considering the uptick from 3.1 to 3.2 to be an indicator that the vines are beginning to shut down. He thinks the mechanism governing the uptick may be the commencing breakdown of the grapes' skin cells. He destems completely but crushes only about 20 percent of the berries. Fermentors are 6.5-foot-diameter stainless steel open-tops—"if you lie down on the bottom, you can just touch the sides with your hands and feet"— about 4 feet in height. These dimensions are important to Paul's program, which involves not only conventional plunging but also foot-treading of the vats. Alcoholic fermentation is preceded by a long, natural cold soak, lasting from seven to ten days, before the must warms up sufficiently to wake the native yeasts,

upon which Paul relies exclusively. Once started, the fermentation takes only five or six additional days, and the new wine is pressed off when the juice is dry. The "main" cooper is Claude Gillet, who visits Cameron annually to taste, and then custom crafts barrels to fit the profile of each wine. Some Mercurey and Cadus is also used. Clos Electrique is raised in a 50-percent share of new barrels; only a 10-percent share is used for the Abbey Ridge, and some Abbey Ridge lots from the 1976 planting are raised with no new wood at all. In July after the vintage, the wines are racked and transferred to neutral wood. Lots destined for vineyard-designated bottlings spend another full year in the neutral wood before they are racked again and bottled without fining or filtration. The long barrel aging regime creates wines of considerable complexity and elegance that age exceptionally well. The Abbey Ridge wine, in almost every vintage, is a personal favorite. In recent vintages the Abbey Ridge and Clos Electrique bottlings have begun to exhibit an explicit counterpoint: Abbey Ridge is elegant and floral, whereas the Clos is dark, earthy and brooding.

TASTING NOTES

2005 *Abbey Ridge (tasted prerelease in 2007):* Medium black-red; dusty floral nose with red berry notes; bright and red-fruited on the palate with hints of pomegranate and citrus; chalky minerality at mid-palate; then, intense, satiny, long, and very elegant.

2005 *Clos Electrique (tasted prerelease in 2007):* Almost saturated dark ruby; very intense nose of wet earth, fallen leaves, and predominantly black fruit; earthy, deep flavors on the palate brightened with a touch of orange peel; slate-y minerality from mid-palate to finish, and some grip at the end; almost a tour de force, and very attractive.

CAMPION WINES
Napa, California

Larry Brooks, a Rutgers University graduate who majored in botany, minored in art history, and continued his life sciences training in plant pathology at the University of California Davis, more or less stumbled into winemaking at the end of the 1970s when Michael Richmond, ACACIA WINERY'S founder and evangelist, hired him as a cellar rat. In the three decades since, however, few individuals have accumulated more hands-on experience with California pinot noir. His fingerprints, as Acacia's winemaker, are on at least nineteen vintages. Then, as a senior executive for Acacia's parent, the Chalone Wine Group, he invented the Echelon program in 1997. In 1999 Brooks left Chalone to make a new career in wine and vineyard consulting, and in 2000 he created his own label, working with several co-investors, including Stephen Dooley (see STEPHEN ROSS WINES) and Terry Spizer (see DOMAINE ALFRED). The new label was named for Thomas Campion (1567–1620), a gentleman-composer, poet, physician, and sometime student of the law whose Renaissance preoccupations embody Brooks's own enthusiasm for the humanistic sciences.

The Campion program, which is dedicated exclusively to pinot noir, is focused on Carneros, where Brooks accumulated much of his early experience, and on two appellations in the southern Central Coast to which his attentions turned subsequently: the Santa Lucia Highlands and the Edna Valley. In 2000 the debut wines were a Carneros bottling made primarily from Stanly Ranch (aka Carneros Valley Investors) fruit and a single-vineyard (but not vineyard-designated) Santa Lucia Highlands wine from old UCD 13 vines in Rich Smith's Paraiso Springs Vineyard. In 2001 there was a Carneros bottling blended from Stanly Ranch and Domaine Chandon's clonal block, and the Santa Lucia Highlands wine was sourced from three vineyards. Two Edna Valley wines were also made, one vineyard-designated and one not, both from Baileyana's Firepeak Vineyard. (The vineyard-designated wine was entirely UCD 2A.) The year 2002 saw a Carneros wine, but this time (and in all future years) from Block C ("Claire's") in Lee Hudson's impeccably farmed vineyard on the north side of the Carneros Highway. The Santa Lucia Highlands program was converted to rely exclusively on the Sarmento Vineyard. Sarmento, owned by the same family since the 1830s and once part of the ranchland belonging to the Mission Nuestro Senora de la Soledad, is 34 acres of UCD 4 and Dijon 115 near the center of the appellation. In 2003 Brooks made two Carneros wines and an Edna Valley bottling, but no Santa Lucia Highlands wine; in 2004 (owing to end-of-season heat spikes) just a single Carneros wine and a blend of Firepeak and Sarmento fruit came to market, the latter as a Central Coast blend. In 2005, the portfolio was tweaked once again to include a Carneros bottling from Hudson, an Edna Valley wine made entirely from the Dijon 777 fruit at Firepeak, a Santa Lucia Highlands bottling from Sarmento, and a Central Coast wine composed mainly of declassified lots from the Edna Valley.

The consistent logic behind this slightly kaleidoscopic array is that although Brooks believes firmly in *terroir* and pinot's ability to showcase site, he makes vineyard-designated wines only in years that produce a "reserve quality" product, declassifying even appellation wines when vintage circumstances compromise their ability to stand alone. Brooks himself is his wines' harshest critic. He claims (with forgivable modesty) to "truly love" only one Campion wine in ten. "I am done experimenting," he explains. "After twenty-six vintages, I know what I want." He

---

VISUALLY STUNNING
WINES THAT ARE
TRANSPARENT TO TERROIR
AND AROMATICALLY
IMPRESSIVE

---

relies almost entirely on Montrachet yeast. He uses only François Frères barrels, only wood from Allier forests, and only staves that have been air-dried for three years. (Barrels, Brooks observes with complete accuracy, are "a personal issue" and a "wine style.") He bottles everything just before the following vintage but insists that all wines except the Central Coast blends are bottle aged for two full years before release. He does allow himself to "play" with co-fermentation, however, crushing a bit of pinot gris with the pinot noir when the former is available at the right time and from the same vineyard. Several Campion pinots top my list of all-time personal favorites, including the 2001 Edna Valley bottling and the 2003 Carneros. Across the board, Campion pinots are visually stunning, modestly extracted, transparent to *terroir*, aromatically impressive, and texturally rewarding.

TASTING NOTES

2003 *Edna Valley (tasted in* 2007*):* Luminous, rosy-ruby color; floral and berry-driven nose; Bright, peppery raspberry on the attack, then smoky, like *lapsang souchong* tea; elegant mid-palate with infused rose petals; silky and medium weight; very attractive.

2003 *Carneros (tasted in* 2007*):* Transparent, medium ruby color; dusty floral nose; cherry, raspberry, and silk on the palate; a rich, almost chewy mouth-feel in an elegant, mid-weight package; very fine; a personal favorite.

2003 *Hudson Vineyard "Claire's" (tasted in* 2007*):* Deep ruby color; smoke, dark cherry fruit, and spice on the nose; richly elegant on the palate with dark, brooding fruit, orange peel, and a chamois-like texture; an ample wine that is precisely crafted; displays some raisin-like aromas after being open for several hours.

2001 *Edna Valley (tasted in* 2006*):* Brilliant medium rosy-magenta; cedar, bay laurel, and a hint of green olive on the nose; bright, high-toned red fruit with red licorice and orange peel on the palate; made from elegant, just-ripe fruit; silky, long, and very fine; a personal favorite.

CAPIAUX CELLARS
Angwin, California

The son of a French-born plasma physicist, raised in California's Silicon Valley, Sean Capiaux remembers that table wine was always a staple when the family dined. When the time came, as a high school senior, to pick a college, a major, and (ultimately) a career, Capiaux chose California State University Fresno and majored in enology, minoring in chemistry. When he graduated in 1989, he first worked at Jordan Vineyards and Winery in the Alexander Valley and then spent a harvest at Houghton Winery in West Australia, as well as two years as assistant winemaker for Gary Andrus's Pine Ridge Winery, before finding himself at Peter Michael in 1993, where Mark Aubert was in charge. Someplace along the way, he became enamored of pinot noir, and so he asked to make a bit as a side project in 1994. Capiaux Cellars, made first at Peter Michael and then on a custom-crush basis at the Napa Wine Company, was launched with 100 cases of pinot from Carneros's Iund Vineyard, known primarily by the vineyard-designated bottlings crafted over many years by ACACIA WINERY. In 1995 and 1996, Capiaux produced pinots from David Hirsch's vineyard on the True Sonoma Coast, and from the Demosthene Ranch in Alexander Valley, from which Kalin Cellars sourced its respected "DD" cuvee of pinot noir in the 1980s and 1990s. The program continued with fruit from Demosthene, Widdoes (a Green Valley site farmed by the Dutton family; see DUMOL), and the Pisoni and Garys' vineyards from 1997 through 2000, even as Capiaux moved to the East Coast, working and consulting for wineries on Long Island and making cabernet franc "using a lot of pinot-derived technique" while his wife finished a doctorate at Cornell's Graduate School of Medical Sciences. Back full time in California in 2001, he signed on as winemaker for the new O'Shaughnessy Winery on Howell Mountain and turned the attention of his pinot project increasingly to vineyards on the True Sonoma Coast. In 2000 Capiaux also made his first blended pinot, called Chimera. Production moved to O'Shaughnessy's stunning new winery (which Capiaux had helped design) in 2002.

WINES AND WINEMAKING NOTES

In addition to the aforementioned wines, Capiaux launched a vineyard-designed wine from the Freestone Hill Vineyard near Occidental in 2002 (no Freestone Hill was vineyard-designated in 2003,

however) and another from the Wilson Vineyard near Annapolis in 2003. (Wilson was not vineyard-designated in 2004.) By 2005 production had reached 2,600 cases. In 2006, the Chimera blend, which had hitherto consisted of barrels declassified from the vineyard-designate program, found its own anchor in the Hendricks Vineyard, also sourced by BOUCHAINE, in the Petaluma Gap, although declassified barrels are still used in Chimera. The wines rely on destemmed fruit, whole clusters, and stem re-addition in percentages that vary by vineyard and by vintage and are fermented (unusually) in custom-designed tanks, with caps irrigated with an integrated pumpover mechanism. An eleven-to-fourteen-day vatting is typical, with juice temperatures that peak relatively high, although some extended macerations are done occasionally. The wine is pressed directly to barrel without settling. Capiaux generally avoids adding cultured yeasts, yeast nutrients, or acid, but he does add malolactic bacteria, and he stirs the wine lees in barrel. Coopers are primarily Saury, Remond, and Rousseau, and the amount of new wood used is generally between 25 and 33 percent. Wines spend ten to fifteen months in barrel before being bottled, unfined, and unfiltered. They are fleshy, sensuous, flavorful, fruit-forward editions of pinot that display an intense gallery of spicy aromas, some of which are barrel-derived.

TASTING NOTES

2005 *Widdoes Vineyard (tasted in 2007)*: Limpid, medium ruby with pink highlights; strongly barrel-marked with vanilla, plus cherry and soft spice; fleshy and sensuous and mouth-coating with some wet slate and barrel-char flavors; a deep, brooding wine that is extracted and warm but also character filled; finishes long.

2005 *Chimera (tasted in 2007):*
Transparent medium ruby; gum camphor
and nuts on the nose; sweet candied cherry,
plums, and black licorice on the palate;
dark-flavored and mouth-coating; almost
oily on the mid-palate; extracted and long;
warm on the finish, but still nicely made.

CARABELLA VINEYARD
Wilsonville, Oregon

Mike Hallock was a petroleum engineer
working in Denver when an unusual
"urban" winery called Columbine Cellars
opened its doors there in 1992, using grapes
farmed primarily in western Colorado. The
winery failed, but not before Hallock had
volunteered to help the winemaker, taken a
few courses at the University of California
in his spare time, and made Columbine's
final (1994) vintage of cabernet,
chardonnay, and merlot by himself. In
1995 Hallock and his wife purchased a
vineyard site in Oregon, on the southeast
face of Parrett Mountain, a spur of the
Chehalem Mountains already "settled" by
a few grapegrowers and winemakers like
McKinley Vineyards. The following year,
Hallock planted grapes on the new site,
located between the 500- and 600-foot
contours in gravelly soils of mostly volcanic
origin, including 26 acres of UCD 2A,
4, and Dijon 113, 114, and 115, which he dry
farms. Dijon 115 is the largest block and
always anchors the Carabella wines. The
couple commuted between Colorado and
Oregon from 1996 to 2001 but moved to
Oregon permanently in 2002. Although
a majority of the vineyard's fruit was sold
to other makers when the vines began to
bear—and about half is still sold to a list

that includes PENNER-ASH WINES, BEAUX
FRÈRES, BERGSTRÖM WINES, A TO Z
WINEWORKS, FRANCES TANNAHILL, and
Daedalus—Hallock crushed some of it for
his own Carabella Vineyard wine from the
outset, using equipment from the defunct
Columbine operation that he drove to
Oregon on a flat-bed truck.

The first vintage, in 1998, was made
at YAMHILL VALLEY VINEYARDS; the
1999 through 2005 vintages were crushed,
fermented, and raised at Eola Hills Wine
Cellars in Rickreal; in 2006 production
moved to the 12th-and-Maple facility
in Dundee. Although the majority of
Carabella's production is pinot noir, and
another block of Dijon 115 was planted in
2007, the brand also makes chardonnay and
pinot gris, and Hallock has been quoted
as suggesting that chardonnay may be the
state's real "future." Winemaking follows
the consensus protocol except that the
wines stay in barrel for sixteen months,
and no more than one third of the barrel
stock, acquired from a mix of coopers,
is new in any vintage. The core release
is an estate blend made since 1998 that
carried a Willamette Valley designation
through 2004 and a Chehalem Mountains
appellation designation since 2005. Years
after 2002 have seen a barrel selection called
Inchinnan, which is designed, according to
Hallock, to be "darker [and] more tannic
and [to] last longer," but in my tasting
experience it seemed more elegant and a bit
lighter in color than the regular bottling.
These are very attractive wines with intense
spiciness, high-toned fruit, and all the
ripeness reasonable people could want.

TASTING NOTES
2005 *Chehalem Mountains (tasted in
2007):* Medium-deep black-red; very
distinctive nose of dried juniper berries,
brown spice, and savory notes; ripe, juicy,

fruit-driven attack; cherry-plum-blackberry fruit with an edge of citrus peel; considerable grip, and dry at and after mid-palate; serious and tightly knit on the finish.

2004 *Willamette Valley (tasted in* 2007*):* Transparent, medium rosy-ruby; tobacco and spice on the nose; lovely, spicy tobacco-infused foreground with red and black fruit in a supporting role; lively notes of brewed Constant Comment tea; soft and almost creamy overall, but structured seriously with good grip and considerable length. Very attractive.

2004 *Inchinnan (tasted in* 2007*):* Transparent medium ruby; expressive nose of dusty brown spice and licorice with a whiff of fading flowers; beautifully bright on the palate; cherry-cranberry fruit mostly; intense spiciness on the palate, too, with a hint of black pepper; nicely built, silky, and very attractive.

CASA CARNEROS
Napa, California

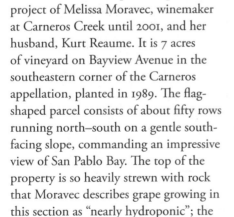

Casa Carneros is the personal pinot noir project of Melissa Moravec, winemaker at Carneros Creek until 2001, and her husband, Kurt Reaume. It is 7 acres of vineyard on Bayview Avenue in the southeastern corner of the Carneros appellation, planted in 1989. The flag-shaped parcel consists of about fifty rows running north–south on a gentle south-facing slope, commanding an impressive view of San Pablo Bay. The top of the property is so heavily strewn with rock that Moravec describes grape growing in this section as "nearly hydroponic"; the bottom of the vineyard is Haire clay-loam. Now perfectly manicured and tidily

cover-cropped, with each row's end post color-coded by clone, the vineyard bears little witness to the exhausted pastureland, rat-infested barns, and derelict cars that greeted Moravec and Reaume when they purchased the land in 1984. To undo the decades of damage, Moravec has farmed sustainably, preferring (for example) to lose a few grapes than to go to war unfairly with birds. Instead, she and Reaume were among the first to use scare eyes and metallic tape to discourage avian depredations. "We steward this land," she says pointedly; "we only own it on paper."

Although Moravec and Reaume initially intended to plant merlot and chardonnay, their affection for pinot was strong enough to overcome their business doubts. Casa Carneros became an all-pinot project right from the beginning, though a small amount of merlot was made in 1999 from purchased grapes. The choice of plant material was influenced by Moravec's invaluable hands-on experience supervising the Carneros Creek clonal trials in the mid-1980s and by her clear intention, at least for some years, to sell most of the fruit. In response to booming demand from producers of sparkling wine, she planted some UCD 18 and UCD 23 despite a personal preference for "heavier, denser, and broodier" selections. There were also healthy chunks of UCD 5 and UCD 12, plus field selections from Swan, Hanzell, Chalone, and nearby St. Clair. In many cases, Moravec took her plant material personally and directly from the clonal trial block at Carneros Creek, choosing only vines that displayed true-to-clone typicity, and then carefully handing only one selection at a time to her vineyard manager, to avoid any possibility of confusion during grafting. This great care—plus the expertise derived from six years' experience with the clonal trial block—has made Casa Carneros a favorite source of budwood when younger California vineyards have been planted. About half of each year's harvest goes into Casa's own wine, a single blend of the eight planted "clones"; the balance has been sold to ETUDE WINES, MacRostie, BOUCHAINE VINEYARDS, ACACIA, Carneros Creek, and a handful of home winemakers.

DARK, RICH, EXTRACTED
WINES THAT USUALLY
BENEFIT FROM SEVERAL
YEARS OF BOTTLE AGE

WINES AND WINEMAKING NOTES

Casa Carneros single blended pinot has been produced in every vintage since 1991. The harvest is done with consummate care: as many as seven picks are made in the tiny, 7-acre vineyard. The fruit is normally 100 percent destemmed, though a small quantity of stems is, on occasion, added back when Moravec likes the stems' smell. ("Apple pie spices" are good; "green and vegetable" smells are not.) Fermentation takes place in small, half-ton and 1-ton fruit bins, with a 2-day cold soak enforced with dry ice. Moravec normally relies on resident yeast and rarely experiences stuck fermentations but will inoculate with RC 212 if necessary. (Generally, she believes that multiple-organism fermentations produce complexity.) During fermentation, the cap is punched down three times daily; if the temperature gets too high, a fourth punchdown is added. Generally, Moravec presses at dryness, but maceration is sometimes extended for very tannic lots. The press fraction is reintegrated. About 40 percent new barrels are used each year from as many as 15 coopers—Moravec experiments constantly and tries new coopers regularly. Once the wine is in barrel, Moravec minimizes manipulation. The wine

spends twelve to fifteen months in wood and is generally racked just once before bottling unless high tannin gives reason for a second racking, as it did in 1997. The wines are typically not fined but are pad-filtered.

Production was done at Carneros Creek until 2002, when Moravec acquired her own small facility in American Canyon. Casa pinots are typically dark, rich, extracted wines, exhibiting dense fruit on a large frame; they benefit from several years of bottle ageing and are generally better suited to meat and cheese than to salmon. Since 1995 all the selections grown at Casa have been used in the estate wine; earlier vintages used a smaller palette.

TASTING NOTES

2005 *Los Carneros (tasted in 2007):* Rich, medium ruby; on the nose, an abundance of strawberry with notes of cedar and spice; bright cherry-raspberry over dominant minerality in the mouth; some slate and graphite; mouth coating but nicely acidic; some fruit persists to the end; significant grip from mid-palate on; attractive and serious.

1997 *Los Carneros (tasted in 2007):* Deep, rich mahogany, rosy-orange at the rim; leather, caramel, gum camphor, and grilled leeks (!) on the nose; rich, slightly sweet, and very minerally on the palate, with some caramel, tobacco, pepper, and alcohol; still noticeable tannins and slightly dry at the end, but quite attractive.

CASTLE ROCK WINERY
Palos Verdes Estates, California

Castle Rock is the brainchild of Greg Popovich, the head coach of the San Antonio Spurs basketball team, a reputed wine connoisseur, and a significant player in many aspects of the California wine scene. He is also a key investor in A TO Z WINEWORKS. In sales terms, Castle Rock, founded in 1994, was the twenty-ninth largest wine company in the country by 2005 and probably ranks higher now, having increased its sales by an estimated 80 percent from 2005 to 2007. Very atypically for a large-volume brand, more than half of its production is pinot noir: 206,000 cases of pinot out of a total of 330,000 cases sold in 2006, and a projected 300,000 cases out of 420,000 in 2007. The company will not be more specific about its fruit sources than "various growers in Sonoma County, Napa County, Monterey County, Mendocino County, Willamette Valley, and Columbia Valley," and it is fair to assume, given the price points at which the wines are sold, that fruit is acquired opportunistically.

Castle Rock makes an array of appellation pinots, if which the most specific is a Russian River Valley cuvée, and the most generic a California cuvée. In between, and accounting for most of the volume, are Monterey, Mendocino, and Sonoma County bottlings. The company owns no vineyards or production facilities but is reported to make most of its product at the Rombauer and Laird Family wineries in Napa and at Sebastiani in Sonoma. The winemaker is August "Joe" Briggs, a Napa-based winemaker trained at California State University Fresno, who also makes several upmarket pinots from North Coast sources for his own August Briggs label. The attractions of Castle Rock's pinots are their wide availability, very reasonable prices, and varietally correct craftsmanship. These three parameters typically have scant overlap where pinot noir is concerned, making Castle Rock a rare example of fairly good pinot for around $11 a bottle.

TASTING NOTE

2006 *Monterey County (tasted in* 2007*):* Vibrant, rosy-ruby color; cherry pie spices and vanilla on the nose; slightly sweet with substantial forward cherry and Italian plum on the palate; then soft and dry with some flesh; of medium weight, and fair in length; generic flavors but true to variety.

CHALONE VINEYARD
Soledad, California

When the son of a French homesteader planted the first wine grapes in the isolated, chaparral-covered highlands southeast of Soledad in the 1890s, his choice was no stranger than the vineyard enterprises undertaken by scores of other French, Italian, German, and even English immigrants to the Golden State. Lucien Charles Tamm's vineyard was less than 6 miles as the crow flies from Mission Nuestra Señora de la Soledad, where vines had been planted a century earlier. By 1860, as commercial winemaking replaced the original mission vineyards, more than 50,000 vines had been planted in Monterey County as a whole. But the Tamm plantings, and a neighboring vineyard planted beginning about 1920 by one Francis William Silvear—an asthmatic as much fascinated by California wildflowers as he was by wine—remained stubbornly isolated: 1,800 feet above the valley floor, a long, serpentine drive from Soledad on a road not paved until the 1980s, off the power grid until 1987, and a very long way from most stirrings in California wine. Nonetheless Silvear, who had planted a very unlikely quartet of varieties—pinot blanc, chardonnay, chenin blanc, and pinot noir—sold his grapes far afield in the 1930s. His customers included Wente, Almaden, Mirassou, and, perhaps most significantly, BEAULIEU VINEYARD, where he apparently became good friends with Georges de Latour and André Tchelistcheff. The evidence is ambiguous, but the budwood for Beaulieu's second pinot vineyard, called BV 2, may have been sourced from Silvear.

In the 1960s Silvear's vineyard, was sold and resold several times, was renamed for nearby Mount Chalone, and saw its first estate-bottled wines released under the Chalone label. Then, over a period of two decades, nearly everyone who was anyone in the California wine business filtered in and out of the Chalone story: Philip Togni, a Montpellier-trained winemaker; Rodney Strong, a retired dancer and choreographer; Berkeley restaurateur Narsai David; Sacramento food and wine merchant Daryl Corti; banker turned winemaker Dick Graff. The 1969, 1970, and 1971 vintages of Chalone pinot noir, made by Graff—who learned winemaking mostly on the job after some coursework at the University of California Davis—exploded on the California wine scene to rave reviews and established the reputation of Chalone (still an arid, isolated outpost nearly overpowered by hungry deer and pesky rattlesnakes) as one of the first makers of fine pinot noir in the New World. Eventually, Chalone Inc., the predecessor of the Chalone Wine Group, went on to spawn or acquire wine properties from Napa to San Luis Obispo, attracting investment from the Rothschilds of Bordeaux and becoming the first publicly traded wine company in America. In 2006 Chalone Wine Group was acquired by Diageo Chateau & Estates, the eighth-largest wine company in the United States.

Although it is unlikely that Chalone's original stewards knew so, the estate inhabits an almost unique geology in California. Throughout most of California, the gradual slippage of the Pacific Plate under the North American Plate has hidden deep in the earth most of the marine deposits formed when the seas retreated from the land. Limestone soils near the surface are consequently rare and widely scattered. But in the Gavilan Range on the eastern side of the Salinas Valley, an extensive tract of limestone and calcium carbonate lies near the surface, overlaid with a relatively thin coating of volcanic topsoil. What is now the Chalone AVA—8,650 acres of hilly terrain between 7 and 8 miles due east of Soledad, mostly above the 1,800-foot contour—consists of poor, low-acid soils that geologically resemble the main wine lands of Europe, except that the appellation, painfully dry, receives only about 10 inches of rainfall annually. An aerial view of the AVA suggests three slightly skewed rectangles joined along part of their long sides. The surface lies entirely within Monterey County, except for small incursions into San Benito County at three points on the appellation's irregular eastern edge.

The Chalone Vineyard's property covers about 950 acres, of which just over 100 acres are dedicated to ten separate, noncontiguous blocks of pinot noir. Chalone's oldest pinot, a 2.2-acre block planted in 1946 on the south side of the access road from Highway 146, was also the oldest block of pinot in production anywhere in North America until it was pulled out in 2003. There are also 27 acres of pinot noir in the MacWood Vineyard, a 6- by 10-foot planting laid out in 1972 and 1973 with budwood of unknown origin, and 6.4 acres in the Strip Vineyard, planted in 1985. Another 6 acres were planted in six different blocks at various times between 1990 and 2000 in the so-called Lowest, Vista, Graff, and Tower Vineyards. The upper portion of Vista has barely any topsoil at all—the surface is almost pure limestone rubble. Vine spacings in these blocks vary—the tightest is 4 feet by 8—and the plant material is a variety of Dijon clones, plus UCD 4 and Swan selection from Dehlinger. There are persistent stories that budwood brought at various times from France found a home at Chalone. In some versions, Chalone itself was the importer and gave the vines a permanent home; in other versions, Chalone was only a waystation for the imported budwood, which was subsequently ferried to other California vineyards. The waystation scenario is more likely than the former, but the facts are impossible to determine.

Philip Togni is considered Chalone's first winemaker, having made the first vintages of wine to carry the Chalone name, in 1960, 1961, and 1962. Dick Graff became a partner in the company owning Chalone in 1964; he headed immediately for Davis to study viticulture and enology, and then became Chalone's winemaker in 1966. Graff and his family were able to buy out the other owners in 1969, which was the first vintage of Chalone made under his complete control. After 1972 Dick Graff seems to have shared winemaking responsibilities with his two younger brothers, John and Peter, until Peter was officially named winemaker in 1978. In 1983 Peter was succeeded by Michael Michaud. Dan Karlsen, a marine biologist who had previously made wine at DEHLINGER WINERY, DOMAINE CARNEROS, and Estancia, served from 1998 to 2006. Robert Cook, a University of California Davis graduate and also an alumnus of Estancia, took the winemaking reins in 2007.

WINES AND WINEMAKING NOTES

Pinot was bottled under the Chalone Vineyard label from 1960 through 1962, and after 1966. In most years, there was just a single bottling, although Gavilan was sometimes used as a second label, and a reserve program was inaugurated about 1979. The reserve program, which persisted until 1996, privileged the property's oldest vines, was generally bottled unfiltered, and was supposed to have been sold primarily to the shareholders of Chalone Inc. As early as 1969, the main release attracted extravagantly positive reviews when Chalone's efforts were compared to other American pinots of the time; certainly Chalone pinots inspired several other California-based producers to work with pinot, and budwood from Chalone vines has been chosen repeatedly to plant other vineyards. In the Karlsen era, the Chalone wines were very well made, having deep colors, ripe fruit flavors, and flavor profiles suggesting mesquite, licorice, and peppery spice. But Karlsen held maverick views about pinot noir, arguing that winemaking is "not about chemistry, but hedonism," that cold soaks are "baloney," and that most California wines get not "overoaked" but "underwined." He argued there was no reason to green harvest in California, as long as the clusters ripened evenly, because there was and is "always enough heat to ripen whatever sets." He also believed (with quite a few other makers) that that pinot noir is not ripe "until there is no pulp left," which does not happen in California at less than 25 to 26 Brix. At Chalone, he compensated for a warm site by *increasing* the crop load in order to slow down the vines' maturity and to increase hang time. In the cellar, he also used a small number of puncheons to supplement the usual *pièces* and always filtered before bottling because of a self-proclaimed "zero tolerance" for brettanomyces. It remained to be seen, at the time of writing, whether Cook would make significant changes to Karlsen's farming or winemaking protocols. Consumers should note that a new line of "Chalone Vineyard Monterey County" wines debuted in 2005. Despite the name, and despite Dan Karlsen's involvement in the sourcing and blending decisions that established this label, these wines are not based on grapes grown at Chalone and are not made on the property. Instead, they are made from purchased fruit at a custom-crush facility.

TASTING NOTE

1978 *Chalone (tasted in 2007):* Deep, almost opaque mahogany; explosive nose of gum camphor, tobacco, and boot polish; rich, elegant, and evolved on the palate, but still displaying considerable primary (cassis) fruit, and still a touch grippy; considerable hard spice and some graphite; long and velvety, overall, and absolutely sound twenty-one years after the vintage. Fine.

CHATEAU ST. JEAN
Kenwood, California

Founded in 1974 by a trio of central valley table grape farmers, and entrusted from the outset to its legendary founding winemaker and first employee Dick Arrowood, Chateau St. Jean established an enviable reputation during the 1980s for a large family of intense and finely crafted single-vineyard chardonnays (and other white wines) sourced from vineyards throughout Sonoma County. Ten years

after its founding, the brand was sold to Suntory International. In 1986 Arrowood and his wife established a separate personal wine project, and in 1990 he left Chateau St. Jean to pursue his own project full time. The brand was sold again in 1996, this time to Beringer Wine Estates, which was later acquired by the Australia-based Foster's Brewing Group. Arrowood's successors were talented winemakers: Don Van Staaveren from 1990 to 1997, Steve Reeder from 1997 to 2003, and Margo Van Staaveren, Don's wife, since 2003. Margo Van Staaveren's tenure in the Chateau St. Jean cellars goes back to 1980, when she joined the staff as a laboratory technician one year after graduating from the University of California Davis with a degree in fermentation science.

WINES AND WINEMAKING NOTES

Although pinot noir has never been quantitatively significant at Chateau St. Jean—only about 5 percent of its production is pinot—the winery dabbled with pinot as early as the late 1970s, using fruit from exceptionally fine sites whose crops were also in demand from other makers. Its first pinot was produced late in the 1970s with fruit from the McCrea Vineyard on the east flank of Sonoma Mountain, and the first generation of its Sonoma County bottling, made from a combination of grapes from the Durell Vineyard (in the southwest foothills of the Sonoma Valley) and Marimar Torres's Don Miguel Vineyard (west of Graton) was made in small quantities from 1989 to 1994. Of the pinots currently produced, the first to debut was a single vineyard wine from Durell, using blocks planted after 1987, which was made beginning in 1995. The second generation of the Sonoma County bottling, widely sourced across Sonoma but anchored with fruit from Carneros, was first distributed nationally in 1997. Recent vintages have been based on grapes from Durell and the Benoist Ranch (leased, developed, and farmed by Beringer in and after 1999—see ETUDE WINES for additional information) and from Sangiacomo-owned parcels in Carneros, as well as from La Petite Etoile in the Russian River Valley, from which Chateau St. Jean also sources a vineyard-designated sauvignon blanc. Since 2000, there has also been a Sonoma County Reserve bottling, which is a barrel selection from the Durell and Benoit properties.

Winemaking generally follows the consensus protocol. Small open-top fermentors are hand plunged, and malolactic fermentation is induced after the new wine is drained, settled briefly, and barreled. All lots are assessed after ten months in wood. Lots destined for the Sonoma County bottling are selected, blended, and bottled immediately; lots deemed suitable for the reserve program or the vineyard-designated Durell bottling remain longer in wood. The Durell wine spends a total of fifteen to seventeen months in about 40 percent new barrels; the reserve is built by selecting lots a second time, after the wine has spent eighteen months in wood. Wines are not fined. Straightforward, mainstream pinots are made here, with fruit-forward, ripe flavors and reasonably managed tannins and a tendency to warmth on the back palate.

TASTING NOTES

2005 *Sonoma County (tasted in 2007):* Transparent, medium ruby; red berry nose, with some smoke; cherry, raspberry, and barrel char on the palate; considerable grip on a nicely built, medium-weight frame; medium in length and quite dry from mid-palate to finish.

2005 *Durell Vineyard (tasted in 2007):* Medium-dark black-red; barrel-derived vanilla and crushed cherries on the nose; cherry-driven attack, plus vanilla and hard spice; satiny at mid-palate, then dry and grippy with a peppery bite and some warmth.

2004 *Reserve (tasted in 2007):* Luminous medium ruby; cherry-pie nose; sweet cherry candy and boysenberry flavors in the mouth; soft and creamy like custard; warm and peppery from mid-palate to finish; ripe overall.

CHEHALEM WINES
Newberg, Oregon

Harry Peterson-Nedry, a North Carolina–born chemist whose first career was centered in high-tech manufacturing, created the Chehalem brand in 1990 to market wines made from his family's Ridgecrest estate on Ribbon Ridge. Chehalem's first wine was the 1990 vintage of Ridgecrest Pinot Noir, released in 1993. Also in 1993, Willamette Valley natives Bill and Cathy Stoller became co-owners of Chehalem, and in 1995 the partners purchased the former Veritas Winery, on Highway 99W just northeast of Newberg, for use as their production facility. Vintages before 1995 had been made in a 1,000-square-foot brick outbuilding adjacent to Peterson-Nedry's home in downtown Newberg.

Chehalem now sources pinot noir from three vineyards: Ridgecrest, now owned outright by Chehalem; Corral Creek, adjacent to the ex-Veritas winery and acquired concurrently; and Stoller, a large property near Lafayette, owned separately by the Stollers (see STOLLER VINEYARDS). Ridgecrest is the most mature of the three vineyards, having been planted in 1982 on the site of nineteenth-century walnut and prune orchards involuntarily converted into cow pasture by a legendary storm in the 1960s. Ridgecrest is now 56 acres of grapes on a 165-acre site—following the addition of an almost contiguous site called Wind Ridge that has brought the first Dijon clones and drip irrigation to Ridgecrest. The oldest vines were planted 6 feet by 10, but spacing was tightened to 4.5 feet by 10 in 1985 and to 4 feet by 8 in 1989 and 1990. The vineyard sits at altitudes ranging from 450 to 600 feet, sloping southward, on both sides of Ribbon Ridge Road. Like the rest of Ribbon Ridge, the soil series is Willakenzie clay-loam; the Ridgecrest subseries of this soil is now dubbed Wellsdale. Wind Ridge is laid out at 2,200 vines per acre, between 400 and 5,000 feet. Ridgecrest produces concentrated, black-toned pinot with overtones of wild bramble and cassis.

Corral Creek is a lower-elevation site, mostly between 200 and 450 feet, toward the base of Parrett Mountain, that was planted in

WINES WITH FORWARD FRUIT, RELATIVELY DEEP COLOR, AND GOOD LENGTH—WITHIN THE LIMITS OF EACH VINTAGE

1983 and 1984, with some replanting in 1991, when a large block of riesling was replaced with pinot noir. (Ironically, some of the vines are now being regrafted to riesling as Peterson-Nedry discovers how well it can perform in this site.) The clonal composition of the vineyard is not entirely clear, but it seems to consist primarily of own-rooted UCD 5 and UCD 2A; spacing is 5 feet by 10. The soils are shallow Laurelwood series—a brownish wild-blown silt of glacial origin. Shallower and higher-elevation parts of the

vineyard are drip-irrigated at the end of the growing season; the rest is dry farmed. Chehalem now uses about two thirds of the fruit from Corral Creek; the balance is sold to ANDREW RICH, J. K. CARRIÈRE, and Brooks Wines, inter alia. In the past, Peterson-Nedry used Corral Creek to add structure and "brightness" to blends, but since 2002 the vineyard has become the source of very consistent and balanced wines, some of which are vineyard-designated.

The youngest of the vineyards is Stoller, which produced its first crop in 1996. Stoller is a 373-acre site, of which 140 acres are now planted (about 80 percent to pinot noir), on a south-facing slope overlooking Lafayette, in the iron-rich Jory soil (here lightly laced with Nekia series) that is typical of the Dundee Hills. Before the Stollers began its transformation into vineyard, this property was dedicated to a combination of turkey farming and cereal crops. The site is exceptionally vigorous—Peterson-Nedry calls it "almost a factory for fruit"—and was tightly planted to compensate. Even with aggressive pruning, however, yields can still top 4 tons per acre. Unlike Ridgecrest and Corral Creek, Stoller is planted entirely on rootstock and is completely drip-irrigated. These properties make Stoller pinot less dense and deep than fruit from Ridgecrest, exhibiting lower acid and higher pH, and tending to emphasize the roundness, femininity, and precocity often associated with the southern half of the Côte d'Or. As the vines have gained a whiff of maturity, the wines have begun to show deeper color and finer tannins. Since 2001 the Stollers have vinified part of their crop under a wholly owned Stoller Vineyards brand.

From 1996 through 2002, winemaking duties at Chehalem were shared by Peterson-Nedry and Cheryl Francis, a Los Angeles native with a biology degree from Lewis and Clark College and on-the-job training in Oregon and New Zealand.

Francis departed before the harvest in 2003 to launch her own brand, FRANCIS TANNAHILL. In 2002, Michael Eyres, a viticulture and enology graduate of Lincoln University in New Zealand, joined the Chehalem staff and has since taken the co-winemaker position previously held by Francis. Patrice Rion, of Domaine Daniel Rion in Prémeaux-Prissey, consulted for Chehalem in the mid-1990s, and the property's top cuvée was named in his honor until he launched his own *négociant* brand in 2002.

WINES AND WINEMAKING NOTES

In 1990, 1991, and 1992, Chehalem made only one pinot, and this entirely from Ridgecrest fruit. In 1993 there were two Ridgecrest cuvées: one "regular" and one made from 100-percent UCD 2A. The property's flagship wine, a reserve (called Rion Reserve through 2002), was launched in 1994. This has most often been a barrel selection from Ridgecrest, not of the biggest and brawniest lots but of barrels displaying uncommon elegance, silkiness, and length. In 1996, following the acquisition of the Corral Creek vineyard and the first harvest from Stoller, Chehalem's 3 Vineyard blend was born, and one barrel of Stoller was used in the Reserve. Some lots of Stoller pinot were then vineyard-designated in 1997, and a Stoller Vineyard bottling has been made in all subsequent years. Selected lots of Corral Creek have been vineyard-designated since 1998 (except in 1999). Each year, barrels (of Ridgecrest) destined for the Reserve are selected first; then barrels are earmarked for the two or three vineyard-designates; remaining lots are used for the 3 Vineyard blend. Since 2002 Peterson-Nedry has reserved a few barrels of Ridgecrest for a personal brand called RR WINERY.

Within the limits of each vintage, Chehalem pinots tend toward relatively forward fruit, medium-to-deep colors, and considerable length; they have generally enjoyed a good deal of critical acclaim. The first vintages of Rion Reserve, now approaching maturity, are especially rewarding. Conveniently, Chehalem's three vineyards ripen sequentially, beginning with Stoller, which is followed closely by Corral Creek. Ridgecrest, largely because of its elevation, is always the last to ripen. Peterson-Nedry says that Chehalem is usually "late to pick," waiting until the cluster "begins to look a little sad and grapes fall off when you shake it" and until "our palates say that acids, sugars, and flavors are all in balance"—usually meaning sugars above 24 Brix and a pH around 3.2. Chehalem will tolerate low acids if that's what's needed to obtain ripe flavors, and Peterson-Nedry will add back a bit of acid if natural acidity has fallen too low.

With the exception of a few experimental vattings and most of the Ridgecrest fruit, the fruit is fully destemmed but the berries are not crushed; a prefermentation cold soak lasts for five to ten days without punchdowns. Fermentors come in 4-, 5-, and 8-ton sizes, and are mostly stainless steel and mostly jacketed. In "clean" years with no rot or botrytis, the winemakers rely on native yeasts—always in the case of Ridgecrest fruit and increasingly in the cases of Stoller and Corral Creek—or otherwise "blast" the vats with commercial yeast. Enzymes are sometimes used, on a lot-specific basis, to help manage aggressive tannins, to compensate for cold soaks that must be foreshortened, or to help "unwind fruit." Temperature manipulation begins after the fermentation is well started and is aimed at a slow build toward a juice-temperature peak around 88°F. Chehalem generally presses as soon as the must is dry, though the winemakers continue to experiment with varying lengths of prefermentation and postfermentation maceration. Peterson-Nedry does not want his wines to be cooper-marked, so the barrel regime involves six to eight coopers, wood from several French forests, and a mix of toast levels and stave ages. The property's big wines spend up to fourteen months in barrel; others are bottled after eleven to twelve months in wood. The winemakers have not liked the "fruit loss" they have perceived when they have held wine in wood longer than fourteen months. Lot-specific decisions are made as to racking, with a preference for avoiding manipulations until the final blends are made and bottled. Prior to bottling, lots are selectively fined or filtered, or both. Chehalem is one of the rare properties that selects the flagship reserve wine for its elegance and charm and not for its size; it is typically my favorite in most vintages. Ridgecrest is usually the largest-framed and most tannic of the Chehalem pinots; Stoller is the roundest and sweetest.

TASTING NOTES

2004 *Corral Creek Vineyard (tasted in 2007):* Light-to-medium garnet; tarragon and other grassy herbs, plus potpourri on the nose; bright, almost grassy flavors first, then sweet strawberry and charry; of light-to-medium weight, and a trifle warm on the finish, but nicely built with good acidity.

2004 *Ridgecrest Vineyard (tasted in 2007):* Brilliant medium-dark garnet; uncharacteristically tight on the nose; sweet, briary, and chewy in the mouth; a broad-shouldered, mouth-filling wine; a substantial load of dusty tannins; structurally slightly reminiscent of Gevrey but with less minerality and more deep fruit; good length; finishes warm; needs time.

2004 *Stoller Vineyard (tasted in 2007):* Medium-deep black-red; earth and herbs on the nose, with notes of black fruit and spearmint; sweet and round on the palate with red and black fruit; soft-textured; medium in length.

2002 *Ridgecrest Vineyard (tasted in 2007):* Transparent, medium garnet; cedar, camphor, and faded flowers on the nose; cherry and orange peel on the palate; softening tannins and considerable mid-palate minerality; bright overall and very attractive; perhaps out-of-character for Ridgecrest?

2002 *Stoller Vineyard (tasted in 2007):* Transparent, medium-dark crimson; earth, herbs, and some cabinet-shop aromas; bright and sweet in the mouth with some red and black berries; suave, velvety, and satisfyingly round; finishes soft with just a hint of grip.

2002 *Reserve (tasted in 2007):* Transparent, medium garnet; dusty floral and cosmetics-case aromas; raspberry and cherry on the palate; gently spicy with a burst of clove at the end; understated, feminine, and almost satiny with fine-grained tannins; very attractive.

1999 *Rion Reserve (tasted in 2007):* Medium-dark garnet; allspice, juniper berry, and boot polish on the nose; tar, briar, and a bit of cinnamon on the palate; slightly inky at mid-palate; intense and slightly austere overall, but long and fine.

CLOS DE LA TECH
Woodside, California

Thurman John (T. J.) Rodgers, a Dartmouth College graduate who invented benchmark technology for microchips while he was a graduate student at Stanford—and who later founded Cypress Semiconductor Corporation, a hugely successful producer of chip-based sensors, controllers, clocks, and related devices for companies ranging from Apple to Daimler-Chrysler—is also a passionate aficionado of red Burgundy and the proprietor of an all-pinot project in the Santa Cruz Mountains called, aptly if not euphonically, Clos de la Tech. Rodgers entered the pinot business in 1994 when he and his wife Valeta Massey planted a single acre at their Woodside, California, residence (dubbed Domaine du Docteur Rodgers) to Dijon 113, 115, and 777 on three rootstocks. The first "home wines" were made in 1996. The first tiny commercial release came when the 1999 vintage was ready for prime time, in 2001. The same year, Rodgers and Massey bought land for a second vineyard on the crest of the Santa Cruz Mountains (at the 2,300-foot contour) overlooking the Santa Clara Valley, where they planted 3.5 acres; the following year they embarked on a third and much larger vineyard project on the ocean side of Skyline Boulevard, overlooking the town of La Honda. The 3.5-acre vineyard was christened Domaine Valeta, and the La Honda property was named for Rodgers's mother, Lois Louise. Lois Louise currently consists of 30 acres of Dijon 115, 667, 777, and 828 on a 160-acre ridgetop that falls precipitously on three sides. There are plans to add 5 acres each year until 80 acres have been established in vine.

The configuration results in primary slopes as steep as 60 percent, extending 1,000 vertical feet from crest to base, but also sloping steeply from side to side; Rodgers worked closely with a German firm to design a joystick-operated, cable-mounted tractor that could manage these conditions. The vines are planted (as in Burgundy) in a meter-by-meter grid, in fifty-six separate blocks, without soil amendments. Rain and fog, as well as winds up to 30 miles per hour, buffet the site. It is little wonder that vines planted in 2000 did not produce a first (tiny) crop until 2004! Under the ridge crest, three caves were dug to house winery operations, barrel storage, and case goods. The fermentation cave showcases other Rodgers inventions, including a robotic cap-management device built to mimic the dynamics of foot-trodden grapes—in case Massey, who is said to tread the grapes personally at present, should eventually tire of such strenuous labor—and a modern variation on the ancient basket press that follows the basic design of a French-press coffee pot.

The investment associated with Domaine Lois Louise is nothing less than mind-boggling, but this has not reassured Rodgers's neighbors in La Honda, who live in the vineyard's shadow and raise persistent objections. Rodgers has a well-established reputation for outspoken and politically incorrect views on a variety of social and business matters, and his views about wine—including what factors differentiate great wine from mediocre—are no more closely held. Although he is very Burgundy-conscious, Rodgers says plainly that he intends to make better pinot in his Santa Cruz Mountains sites than anyone has ever made in Burgundy, and he has priced even his first releases from Domaine du Docteur Rodgers at levels designed to command universal respect.

WINES AND WINEMAKING NOTES
Clos de la Tech pinots are made by fermenting all the fruit as whole clusters in 1-ton stainless open-top fermentors, relying entirely on resident yeast. Fermentation temperatures are allowed to

rise as high as 95 degrees, and the musts are pressed when they are dry or as nearly dry as whole-cluster fermentations will ever go. After pressing, the new wine spends eighteen months in 100-percent new François Frères barrels, all coopered from stave wood air dried for three years, harvested in the Bertranges forest. There is no fining or filtration. Rodgers says he is open to experiments, eventually, involving destemmed fruit, extended maceration, or 4-year-air-dried stave wood. At press time, no finished wine was yet available from Domaine Lois Louise. Limited experience with the first vintages from Domaine du Docteur Rodgers and Domaine Valeta suggest attractive wines marked by seriousness of purpose and careful craftsmanship.

TASTING NOTES

2002 *Domaine Valeta (tasted in 2005).* Transparent, medium-dark black-red; blackberry and camphor on the nose; very black, dense, and smoky in the mouth with flavors of black pepper, clove, and tree bark; concentrated and grippy on the finish.

2001 *Domaine du Docteur Rodgers (tasted in 2005):* Transparent, medium garnet; expressive nose of ripe black cherry, smoke, and gum camphor; cherry, other black fruits, cola, and dried leaves on the palate with hints of white pepper and smoke; almost silky with just a hint of grip at the end.

2000 *Domaine du Docteur Rodgers (tasted in 2005):* Transparent, medium black-red; quite floral in comparison to the 2001, with rose petal, exotic spice, orange peel, scented candles, and soft mocha; black raspberry, earth, and white pepper on the palate; medium in weight, full bodied, and very slightly fruit-sweet, with a satiny texture. Fine.

CLOS DU VAL WINE COMPANY
Napa, California

Clos Du Val, co-founded by the son of a Bordeaux *régisseur* and dedicated from the outset to cabernet sauvignon, was nonetheless a near-pioneer in Carneros, purchasing 180 acres of bare ranchland on Old Sonoma Road in the northeast corner of the appellation as early as 1973. The property, originally called Gran Val but later renamed Carneros Vineyard, remained undeveloped for seven years; however, the first pinot noir was not planted there until 1981. A total of 11.6 acres were planted to pinot between 1981 and 1984: first to a field selection said to have come from the JOSEPH SWAN VINEYARD, and then to two plantings of UCD 4 in 1982 and 1984. The budwood seems to have included a bit of something other than UCD 4, however—possibly a field selection from MOUNT EDEN— because some of these vines have thrown exceptionally small berries. Two additional waves of plantings followed: 11.6 acres from 1997 to 1999 and 10.8 acres in 2002. The first consisted primarily of Dijon clones, and the second of UCD 2A, 4, and 5, and Dijon 828, said to have come from Archery Summit via Cuvaison. Early plantings were widely spaced, but the new plantings, mostly located on steeper parts of the site, are in 9-foot rows with 4 or 5 feet between vines. The yield from the older blocks dropped inexorably through the 1990s, a result of wide spacing, missing vines, and Eutypa, to the point that these vines became economically unsustainable. The 1980s blocks were finally removed after the 2005 harvest, and the land was planted provisionally to hay, pending replanting in 2008 and 2009. The winery's first pinot was made in the 1988 vintage and released in 1992; production rose to roughly 2,000 cases by 1999. As the newer plantings and replantings come onstream, there will be sufficient fruit to propel production to around 10,000 cases, making pinot Clos Du Val's second-largest commitment among red varieties and accounting for between 16 and 18 percent of the brand's total production.

WINES AND WINEMAKING NOTES

Clos Du Val produced a single pinot noir annually between 1984 and 2002. In 2003 a Reserve bottling was introduced alongside the Carneros cuvée. The Reserve and Carneros cuvées are made identically, except that the Reserve represents fermentation lots, identified after malolactic fermentation has finished, which exhibit a bit more structure and are held a bit longer in barrel—and much longer in bottle—before release. Equipment and winemaking choices have changed substantially in the late 1990s, and Clos Du Val's 1998 release is quite different from earlier vintages. A gentle destemmer-crusher was installed to replace earlier-generation equipment in 1998. A large milk tank was brought onstream in 1995 to enable some manual punchdowns, but pumpovers continued for most of the production until stainless, open-top fermentors were installed in the summer of 2000. In 2007 there were thirteen open-tops, together capable of handling between 110 and 140 tons of grapes.

Clos Du Val uses no stems, practices a five-day cold soak, inoculates with RC 212 yeast (its "earthy" flavors are appreciated), and ferments warm for ten to fifteen days. The must is settled after the cap falls, and the wine is barreled in one third new oak for twelve to fifteen months, depending upon whether it is Carneros or Reserve wine). A single racking is done just after malolactic fermentation completes to create the blend, and the wine is then returned to barrel. Barrels are sourced from many coopers (wood from Allier forests is preferred). The wine is not fined; a clarification filtration is sometimes done. John Clews, Clos Du Val's director for vineyard and winery operations since 1998, believes strongly that pinot noir must not be overworked and that punchdowns produce better and more thorough extraction than do any form of pumpover. Clews, a Rhodesian native who gained substantial experience with pinot chez Jed Steele, is responsible for most of the very desirable and successful winemaking changes since 1998. Vintages of Clos Du Val pinot made through 1997 failed to elicit much enthusiasm from critics; the few I have tasted are underwhelming. The 1998 vintage marks the beginning of a new era. The new wines are serious and nicely balanced with well-behaved fruit.

TASTING NOTES

2005 *Carneros (tasted in 2007):* Transparent, light-to-medium ruby with a rosy rim; flowers, citrus peel, and some dusty spice on the nose; slightly fruit-sweet on the palate with some infused flowers; mouth coating and quite serious with considerable grip at mid-palate and dry from mid-palate to the end; drinks very nicely, with good length.

2001 *Carneros (tasted in 2007):* Medium garnet with terra cotta at the rim; aromas of leather, merbromin, lacquer, and fading fruit; round and almost rich on the palate with some spicy cherry and nice minerality; good intensity without weight, attractive grip, and almost creamy length; fine.

2000 *Estate (tasted in* 2002*):* Transparent, medium ruby-red; barrel char and dark berries on the nose, with a hint of root vegetables; vanilla, black fruits, black pepper, allspice, and tree bark on the palate; of medium weight and length, with some grip; very slightly sweet; suede-textured.

CLOS LACHANCE WINERY
San Martin, California

When Bill Murphy was a senior executive with the Hewlett-Packard Corporation in California's Silicon Valley in the 1980s, he thought a few acres of vineyard would be a "swell" way to landscape part of his large backyard in the hills above Saratoga. Five years later, with some "estate" chardonnay that was "good enough to sell," Murphy and his wife established Clos LaChance (LaChance is Brenda Murphy's maiden name), moved first into rented space in the historic Novitiate Winery in Los Gatos, and then to a custom-designed and custom-built facility in the heart of the CordeValle Resort in San Martin, in the Santa Clara Valley between Morgan Hill and Watsonville, where a 60,000-case winery and visitors center, and 150 acres of vineyard, are surrounded by parts of the resort community's 18-hole golf course. The Murphys also own and operate a venture called CK Vines that helps small landowners develop and manage backyard vineyards, especially in the Santa Cruz Mountains, where large vineyards are contraindicated by rugged topography.

The Clos LaChance pinot program, now dwarfed by its investment in warmer climate varieties that grow on the San Martin site, began in 1994, but no significant production took place until 1996. Early vineyard sources were Elmer Erwin's high-altitude vineyard on the crest of the Santa Cruz Mountains; the Legan Vineyard near Corralitos; and Mount Regan Vineyard, a 5.5-acre planting of UCD 4 and 13 and Dijon 115 on Green Valley Road near Watsonville. The Erwin Vineyard remains a Clos LaChance source and has been made as a vineyard-designated wine in some vintages. Biagini is now the Corralitos site of choice; it, too, is sometimes made as a vineyard-designate, and Clos LaChance has also sourced pinot from the Split Rail Vineyard, which is also used by DAVID BRUCE. A Santa Cruz Mountains blend has been made in every vintage since 1994. The winemaker from 1997 to 2002 was Jeff Ritchey, an alumnus of GUNDLACH BUNDSCHU in Sonoma; since 2003 Stephen Tebb has been the director of winemaking operations. Tebb is a fermentation science graduate of the University of California Davis who spent twelve years at Artesa Winery in Carneros. Winemaking generally follows the consensus protocol, except that the pinots are held in barrel for sixteen months, and no fining or filtration takes place. The Elmer Erwin pinots have been successful and distinctive from the outset, and the 2005 Santa Cruz Mountains wine is attractively lean with interesting aromatics.

TASTING NOTES

2005 *Santa Cruz Mountains (tasted in* 2007*):* Deep black-red; smoky nose with blackberry and boot polish; intense and fruit-driven on the palate with some shown spice; very clean and peppery; a trifle warm on the finish; texture of polished cotton.

1997 *Elmer Erwin Vineyard (tasted in* 2000*):* Bright, transparent black-red; nose dominated by wild, brambly berries and black pepper; notes of earth, forest floor, and smoke; slightly tannic on the finish; very attractive.

COBB WINES
Occidental, California

The 1,200-foot ridge between Occidental and Bodega Bay, south of the Russian River's mouth, has been an object of interest for pinotphiles ever since Scott Zeller planted his Summa Vineyard on Taylor Lane in 1980. First Williams Selyem—and then other makers—transformed Summa grapes into fine, head-turning wines, in spite of the risks associated with harvests that often stretched into November. In 1989, David Cobb, a marine biologist with San Francisco Bay Area roots whose prior hands-on viticultural experience was a backyard vineyard in Mill Valley, planted 5 acres of pinot noir on Fitzpatrick Lane, about 1 mile from Summa as the crow flies, observing that, "when it is made well, pinot is about the best wine on earth." The scientist in Cobb was determinative, so 4 acres of the new vineyard were dedicated to an own-rooted planting of essentially every selection of pinot noir that had then been certified virus-free by Foundation Plant Services at the University of California Davis. Cobb farmed this as a nursery, selling clean budwood to other growers and vintners, until there was enough fruit *and* budwood to permit grape sales to SIDURI WINES in 1998 and 1999. Two additional acres, planted to UCD 2A, 13, and 15 in 1989 and called Old Firs in honor of the large adjacent trees, were farmed for grapes and sold to WILLIAMS SELYEM, who made a Coastlands Vineyard pinot noir beginning in 1994. (Coastlands fruit was used in Williams

Selyem's Sonoma Coast blend in 1992 and 1993, and there was a combined Summa and Coastlands bottling in 1993 as well.)

The vineyard was expanded nine years later with a 4.8-acre planting of UCD 4 and 37 called "1906" Block, 5.2 acres of UCD 2A, 15, and 23 and Dijon 115 and 777 called "Big Rock," and an acre of mixed selections on the periphery of the 1989 "nursery" planting. Cobb, who lives on the property, explains that the special genius of the Occidental ridge is that "if you get a good fruit set in May or June, you are home free." "We wake up to sunshine during most of the growing season," he continues, "and there are few insect problems thanks to a strategic position on the Pacific flyway, but we do battle the fungus family. The ocean view, meanwhile, is incredible."

Cobb's son Ross, who grew up on the vineyard, repurposed his formal education in agroecology and sustainable agriculture at the University of California Santa Cruz to

---

EXTREMELY ATTRACTIVE, SERIOUS, TERROIR-DRIVEN WINES FROM THE TRUE SONOMA COAST

---

serve as the basis for a career in winemaking. He worked first as a fermentation chemist for Ferrari-Carano Vineyards in Dry Creek Valley, and then at Bonny Doon, until (no surprise, perhaps) he was recruited at Williams Selyem in 1998. Two years later, ever loyal to the True Sonoma Coast, he moved into the head winemaking position at FLOWERS VINEYARD AND WINERY near Cazadero, and in 2001, the family created Cobb Wines, a microboutique venture based on fruit from Coastlands Vineyard and its immediate neighbors on the Ridge above Bodega Bay, made by Ross Cobb in the Flowers facility. The combination of the Cobb brand and the aforementioned 1998 plantings gradually redistributed the vineyard's fruit, with Williams Selyem shifting from Old Firs to Big Rock; and Old Firs, the former nursery block, and a bit of "1906" being dedicated to the Cobb program by 2006.

WINES AND WINEMAKING NOTES

From 2001 to 2004, Cobb Wines released just a single wine, made entirely from Coastlands Vineyard fruit. In 2005 Cobb entered into a long-term contract for grapes from the Rice-Spivak Vineyard, a neighboring 5.9-acre planting of Swan selection and Dijon 115, 667, and 777, but there was so little Coastlands fruit in 2005 (owing to wet and windy weather when the vines flowered in June) that the two wines, Coastlands and Rice-Spivak, were blended into a single cuvée that was (and is) stunningly good. In 2006 Rice-Spivak was finally made into a separate vineyard-designated wine.

Winemaking follows the consensus protocol, except that grapes can be picked at Brix levels as low as 22; as much as 30 percent of the fruit is fermented as whole clusters when "ripeness and stem lignification" allow; free-run wines are drained directly from the fermentors to barrels; and the remaining must is pressed in a small basket press. All fermentations rely on resident yeast. The barrel regime is based on barrels from a handful of coopers, the percentage of new wood is matched with vine age, and the wines stay in barrel for fourteen to sixteen months. Fining and filtration are avoided as far as possible, producing extremely attractive, serious, *terroir*-driven wines that exhibit great complexity.

TASTING NOTES

2005 Coastlands and Rice-Spivak Vineyards (tasted in 2007): Medium-deep rosy-ruby, strong herbal-cherry nose; intense flavors of cherry-raspberry fruit with strong minerality; some notes of black pepper and barrel-char; long and slightly exotic.

2004 Coastlands and Rice-Spivak Vineyards (tasted in 2007): Transparent, medium-dark, almost purplish ruby; mace, nutmeg, cardamom, and cumin on the nose; a very finely delineated concerto of flavors on the palate, with a dominant minerality and cherry-raspberry counterpoint; ripe style but nicely balanced and very elegant; herbed fruit aftertaste; extremely attractive and very fine.

2004 Coastlands Vineyard (tasted in 2007): Slightly lighter, rosier hue than the blend; nose of potpourri, dried herbs, and sage with creosote, mesquite, briar, and some strawberry-raspberry; sweet but then minerally again, notes of mesquite-grilled meat and a floral layer; slightly dry at the end with a hint of grip; very attractive.

COOPER MOUNTAIN VINEYARDS
Beaverton, Oregon

The man behind Cooper Mountain Vineyards is Robert Gross, a New Yorker educated in the South and a psychiatrist, homeopath, and acupuncturist who is said to have discovered Oregon because he was in love with pinot noir. In 1978 Gross and his wife Corinne hand-planted 20 acres of pinot noir, pinot gris, and chardonnay on the west slope of Cooper Mountain, a old volcanic cone southwest of Beaverton, in the middle (more or less) of the Tualatin Valley. For some years they sold the fruit, which was coveted by neighboring winemakers; in 1985, with Rich Cushman as their consulting winemaker, they established a production facility and crushed grapes, releasing their first vintage of pinot noir in 1987. (At the time, Cushman, who was trained in enology at the University of California Davis, provided consulting services to several Oregon wineries, and was deeply involved in the launch of Laurel Ridge and Flynn, in addition to Cooper Mountain.)

The first vineyard, located in volcanic soils with a high concentration of ferric and ferrous oxides between the 400- and 600-foot contours accessed from Grabhorn Road (and therefore known internally as the Grabhorn Site), has since shrunk to 10.6 acres (of which 4.8 are pinot noir) under pressure from Beaverton's inexorable urban sprawl. A second vineyard, called the Meadowlark Site, is located on the east slope of Cooper Mountain between the 300- and 500-foot contours in deeper and partially sedimentary soils. Some blocks at Meadowlark are medium-spaced so that around 1,700 vines are planted in each acre; others are like Grabhorn, where fewer than 500 vines share each acre. In 1998 another 8 acres of pinot noir (plus a similar quantity of pinot gris and smaller stands of pinot blanc and chardonnay) was planted on a third site, three miles west of Cooper Mountain. This site, called Farmington, features elevations generally less than 200 feet above sea level and largely alluvial soils. The most recent addition to the estate is the Johnson School Vineyard, located at the base of Bald Peak Mountain west of the aforementioned sites, in sandy sedimentary soil. Of Johnson School's 40 acres, 25 are dedicated to pinot noir. In stubborn departures from prevailing practice, all of Cooper Mountain's vineyards have been planted with entirely own-rooted vines, and none of the sites is irrigated. Gross's homeopathic orientation in medicine has also made him sympathetic to sustainable, organic, and biodynamic practices in viticulture. The Grabhorn and Meadowlark sites were certified organic in 1995. All four sites have been certified biodynamic since 1999 and are sustained with a substantial in-house compost program.

The production winemaker from 2001 to 2003 was Melissa Burr, who is now the winemaker at STOLLER VINEYARDS. Since 2004, Cooper Mountain has had a full-time, dedicated winemaker: Gilles de Domingo is a Bordelais with prior experience in Australia, New Zealand, and South Africa, and at Bridgeview Vineyards and King Estate in Oregon. De Domingo finished the 2003 wines and has made every vintage since.

WINES AND WINEMAKING NOTES
Cooper Mountain has been all-estate since its first release in 1987, but it has become increasingly *terroir*-oriented as its vineyard sites have multiplied. Since 1995 the Grabhorn Site has been used primarily to produce a wine called Old Vines, characterized by long, dark fruit with good acidity; the Meadowlark Site has produced wine with its own name since 1998. A wine called Johnson School, first made in 2007, is also a vineyard-designate but is made to be slightly more fruit-forward and oak-expressive and displays higher finished alcohol. Mountain Terroir and Reserve are multivineyard blends. A second label, called Cooper Hill, is also vineyard-designated. There is also a no-sulfite pinot made without any additions of sulfur dioxide, in order to demonstrate, according to De Domingo, that the polyphenols, which occur naturally in the grapes, "can have a higher antioxidant effect than the sulfur dioxide."

Winemaking generally follows the consensus protocol, except that grapes tend to be picked early so that finished alcohol levels are very low, and additions are avoided except in the Cooper Hill wines. Thus, all primary and malolactic fermentations rely on resident yeasts and bacteria, the wines are not acidified or chaptalized, and there is no use of enzymes. The Cooper Mountain pinots seem to me a revelation. Combining completely ripe flavors with huge intensity in bright, low-alcohol envelopes, these are stand-out examples of Oregon pinot noir. *Terroir* is certainly at work here, but sustainable (even biodynamic) viticulture probably lends a hugely helping hand.

TASTING NOTES

2005 *Reserve (tasted in 2007):* Deep, luminous ruby; nose combines bright, peppery cranberry with smoky, earthy depth; concentrated, citrus-infused tart cherry flavors with savory and peppery notes; terrific intensity in a wine that finishes at just 12.5 percent alcohol.

2005 *Mountain Terroir (tasted in 2007):* Brilliant, transparent magenta, ripe cherry-cassis fruit with savory herbs; tasty, savory and almost salty on the palate with bright cherry-cranberry fruit flavors over a base of wet earth; hints of evergreen that approach mint; of medium-length and weight, with a bit of grip and an attractive structure.

2005 *Old Vines (tasted in 2007):* Transparent magenta; aromas of earth, wet stone, and pure, clean cassis; intense on the palate with hints of tobacco; high-toned mineral driven, serious, and long, with impressive grip and acidity. Fine.

COPAIN WINE CELLARS
Santa Rosa, California

Wells Guthrie, who began his wine career as the tasting coordinator for *Wine Spectator*, lived two years in the Rhône Valley (working for Chapoutier and gleaning wisdom from Jean-Louis Chave) before launching his own California label and custom-crush service in 1999. In between, he worked for one year with Helen Turley at her brother's winery in Napa, where he learned "a lot" but discovered that his own tastes and style had little in common with

---

FABULOUS, AROMATIC, ELEGANT WINES WITH ENORMOUS PERSONALITY AND SITE-SPECIFICITY

Turley's predilection for "hot fruit" and "oak-driven wines." Guthrie admits that the Rhône Valley is his first and truest love, but Copain has also produced an assortment of stunning pinots, sourced almost exclusively from the Anderson Valley right from the outset. The first of these came from the old vines in the Dennison Vineyard just north of Boonville, in 1999.

In 2000 Guthrie added wines from the Hein Family Vineyard, located off Guntley Road near HANDLEY CELLARS; from Cerise Vineyard, in the hills above Boonville; and from Hacienda Secoya, a young 3-acre planting of Dijon 115 and UCD 4, located west of Philo. In 2003 there were two more: Wiley Vineyard (used for two years only) and Kiser, a (then) three-year-old planting of mostly Dijon clones. Both of these vineyards are sited in Anderson Valley's so-called Deep End, where the weather is substantially affected by coastal fog that climbs up the valley most evenings and mornings during the growing season.

In 2000 Guthrie also launched a second label called Les Saisons du Vin, featuring one wine for each of the four seasons. The autumn edition of Les Saisons is pinot noir, priced to work for restaurant by-the-glass programs; early vintages were based on grapes sourced from vineyards in Redwood Valley, in order to maintain a reasonable price point. Guthrie dropped Hein, Cerise, and Dennison in 2005 in favor of new Deep End sources, but all of these were too frost-damaged to salvage, so there were no Copain pinots at all in 2005. By contrast, Guthrie thinks 2006 was the best vintage he has ever seen in Anderson Valley and reports that it has "redefined Copain's pinot program." The 2006 pinots, still in barrel, have "great energy" at between 12.8 and 13.5 percent alcohol, and the least alcoholic wine is the "silkiest and most concentrated."

WINEMAKING NOTES

Through 2004 Copain's approach to pinot involved fermentations in 3-ton jacketed stainless steel open-tops with a 2:1 diameter-to-depth ratio, generous use of whole clusters, and five days of cold soaking; winemaking was conducted in as natural a way as possible. Fermentation temperatures rose to around 91°F, the musts were pressed at dryness, and the new wine went straight to barrel. Malolactic fermentations were allowed to take their natural course, which usually meant that they did not finish until April after the vintage. No sulfur dioxide was used until June, and the wines were usually bottled before the following vintage. No fining or filtration took place. Most of my tasting experience is with the 2001s, which were fabulous, aromatic, elegant wines with enormous personality, great site-specificity, and near-perfect juxtaposition of concentration with food-friendly structure.

TASTING NOTES

2002 L'Automne (tasted in 2004): Very slightly hazy light-to-medium garnet; dusty plum, cherry, and berry fruit on the nose; minerals and fruit combine on the palate; substantial texture and mid-palate weight on an elegant frame; fairly dark fruit; suede-textured; medium-long.

2001 Dennison Vineyard (tasted in 2004): Transparent, medium black-red; rose petal, dried leaves, and cherry on the nose with a hint of toasted nuts; then, an explosive palate of spring-season flavors; tar, licorice, earth, and clove in a full-bodied, nicely structured, medium-weight wrapper with a suede-like texture.

2001 Hacienda Secoya Vineyard (tasted in 2004): Medium-dark but nearly saturated brick-red; aromas of potpourri and spring earth; sweet cherry-cranberry fruit on the palate with anise, black pepper, cedar, and dark chocolate; of medium weight and slightly chewy, with a velvety mid-palate and a fine emery finish.

2001 Hein Family Vineyard (tasted in 2004): Dark, saturated black-red; dark fruit and tar on the nose; large, rich, round mid-palate that is slightly chewy and slightly warm; simultaneously sweet and minerally; needs time.

COSTA DE ORO WINERY
Santa Maria, California

    $ $

Gary Burk's family, in a durable partnership with the Espinola family, has grown greenhouse tomatoes and various field crops near Santa Maria since 1978. In 1989, while Burk was in Los Angeles pursuing his quite separate career in music performance, the family diversified into wine grapes, planting 30 acres about 6 miles east of Santa Maria, not far from the confluence of the Sisquoc, Cuyama, and Santa Maria rivers. In 1993, when Burk returned home for his sister's wedding to Rick Manson, the area's most celebrated chef (Chef Rick's restaurant is in Orcutt, just south of Santa Maria), he met winemakers at the wedding dinner and discovered the "wine side" of the area where he had grown up. A conversation with AU BON CLIMAT'S Jim Clendenen, a good friend of the groom, was apparently seminal.

A year later, Burk left Los Angeles, moved home, and worked the 1994 harvest at Au Bon Climat. The harvest job turned into eight years' employment in both cellar and marketing as Clendenen coached him through making some wine of his own. Concurrent with his first harvest at Au Bon Climat, Burk launched Costa de Oro—estate wines from the Gold Coast vineyard—with one barrel each of pinot noir and chardonnay. The initial planting at Gold Coast was 12.5 acres of UCD 13 taken from the nearby and much-respected Sierra Madre Vineyard (it turns out that one of Burk's father's golf buddies was Dale Hampton, who had planted the Sierra Madre Vineyard back in the 1970s). Four additional acres were planted at Gold Coast in 1990, once again using cuttings from Sierra Madre, and 2 acres originally planted to chardonnay were grafted to pinot noir in 2002, this time using cuttings of Dijon 115 and 777 taken from Clendenen's Au Bon Climat (located practically next door).

Gold Coast was laid out in east–west-oriented rows with 10 feet between rows and 6 feet between the vertically trellised vines. Its fruit clients include some of Santa Barbara's best pinot makers: ARCADIAN WINES and PAUL LATO WINES. Costa de Oro's pinot program consisted of a single vineyard-designated wine from 1994 through 1997; in 1998 Burk added a barrel selection called "Oro Rojo," weighted to privilege fruit that was picked slightly early. Both wines have been made in every

vintage since. A slightly less expensive Santa Maria Valley wine has recently been introduced. Costa de Oro has been Burk's full-time job since 2002, and the wines are made at Central Coast Wine Services in Santa Maria.

WINEMAKING NOTES

Burk picks fruit for his pinots in successive passes through the vineyard, deliberately picking some vines as low as 23.3 Brix and postponing others until as much as 25.8. The fruit is all destemmed, cold-soaked for three to five days in small, 1.5-ton fermentors, inoculated with Assmannshausen yeast, punched down twice a day, and pressed at dryness. The new wine goes to barrel still on its gross lees, and malolactic fermentations are left to rely on resident bacteria. The main wine spends eleven months in barrel; "Oro Rojo" is left for five months longer. The barrel stock is entirely from François Frères, entirely coopered from stave wood taken from forests in the Vosges Mountains, and entirely toasted "heavy," producing what Burk calls "sweeter tones of vanilla and crème brûlée." The main wines see 30 percent new barrels; Oro Rojo sees between 60 and 100 percent. Both wines are fined with egg whites for clarity and are also filtered if necessary. Both are elegant editions of pinot that display great visual clarity, floral aromas, considerable spice, and nice length.

TASTING NOTES

2004 *Estate (tasted in 2006):* Transparent medium black-red; licorice, flowers, and some savory green properties on the nose; high-toned red fruit, including cherry and cassis, on the palate, as well as earth, meat, cinnamon, and clove; simultaneously elegant and substantial; attractive.

2003 *Oro Rojo (tasted in* 2006): Medium black-red; rose petals dominate the nose; tar, resin, black pepper, clove, and sandalwood on the palate; concentrated, intense, and even slightly sappy in the mouth; of medium weight and length; very attractive.

CRISTOM VINEYARDS
Salem, Oregon

Cristom was created in 1992 when Pennsylvanians Paul and Eileen Gerrie purchased an abandoned vineyard and failing winery on Spring Valley Road, on the eastern side of the Eola Hills. The Gerries recruited Steve Doerner, who was then winemaker at Josh Jensen's CALERA WINE COMPANY to pursue their ambitions with Burgundian varieties. Doerner, a biochemist trained at the University of California Davis, who recalls that he was "only mildly curious about wine" when he was hired at Calera, is still Cristom's winemaker a decade and a half later.

The first wines were made entirely from purchased fruit sourced from well-known vineyards elsewhere in the Eola Hills, but the abandoned estate vineyard was also simultaneously restored and was returned to production in 1994. Additional vineyard acreage was planted on the Spring Valley Road site beginning in 1993.

The estate vineyards now contain about 42 acres of pinot noir, in four individually named parcels. The restored vineyard is about 8 acres of widely spaced vines, laid out in north–south rows on a mostly east-facing slope astride the 500-foot contour. This parcel was originally planted in the

early 1980s when the property was known as Mirassou Cellars, the Oregon wine project launched by a cousin of the San Jose–based Mirassou wine family. The plant material was UCD 2A, 5, and 13, taken presumably from Mirassou's vineyards in Monterey County, and the vines were set out on their own roots. The 2A and 5 have been retained, but the 13 was converted to a combination of Dijon 115 and 777 in 1997. Rechristened Marjorie, this parcel now yields barely 1.75 tons per acre.

The new vineyards, named Louise, Jessie, and Eileen, were planted beginning in 1993, 1994, and 1996, respectively. All are vertically trellised, tightly spaced plantings with 6 feet between rows and 3 feet between vines. All include some UCD 2A and 5 and a preponderance of Dijon 113, 114, 115, 667, and 777 on rootstock. All are pruned to a single cane of about eight buds plus a two-bud renewal spur and are green harvested to yield about 2 tons per acre. Louise, which has now grown to 11 planted acres, is downslope from Marjorie on gentle south- and southeast-facing slopes and displays both north–south

---

THE MOST ENGAGING, STUNNINGLY BALANCED, AND ALTOGETHER ENCHANTING EXAMPLES OF WHOLE-CLUSTER FERMENTED PINOTS IN NORTH AMERICA

---

and east–west row orientations. Jessie is also about 11 acres, planted in east–west rows on a steep slope south of Louise and Marjorie, its low end about 300 feet above the valley floor, but rising to 500 feet at the top. Eileen is the hilltop parcel, at between 600 and 700 feet, and consists of 16 planted acres. The soils throughout are the iron-rich, basalt-based, volcanic series typical of the Eola Hills, and the vineyards ripen from the bottom of the hill to the top, reflecting the cooler temperatures associated with higher elevation.

Cristom's main sources of purchased fruit (for pinot noir) have been Eola Hills neighbors: Seven Springs and Canary Hill, used since 1992; Temperance Hill, used from 1992 through 1999; and Amalie Robert Vineyard (next to Freedom Hill), used since 2002. Occasional bits have come from Dundee Hills and Yamhill-Carlton sites, including Shea, Brick House, Knudsen, Beaux Frères, and John Thomas; Cristom once traded estate fruit for some from Archery Summit's Arcus Vineyard.

WINES AND WINEMAKING NOTES
A Willamette Valley blend (aka Mt. Jefferson Cuvée) and a reserve wine have been made in every vintage since 1992. Since 2004 the reserve has been called "Sommers Reserve." Both have relied on a combination of estate and purchased grapes since the estate vineyard was returned to production in 1994. The first vineyard-designated Marjorie was made in 1994; Louise debuted in 1996, Jessie in 1998, and Eileen in 2000. Before 1997 Doerner sometimes picked early to avoid rain and sometimes chaptalized; in recent vintages chaptalization has been entirely unnecessary. Fermentors range in size from as small as eight tenths of a ton to as large as 7 tons; Doerner's "favorite" is a 6-foot by 6-foot, 5-ton stainless steel open-top. He uses about 50 percent whole clusters and permits a four- to five-day ambient cold soak until the primary fermentation begins naturally with resident yeast. Occasionally, Doerner has added a bit of commercial yeast after the primary fermentation has started naturally. He has also been known to add a bit of acid to some lots in some vintages to balance the wine. He finds that acid additions also have the effect of

making "the environment slightly hostile for the yeast," which extends the length of fermentations, and Doerner likes longer and slightly cooler fermentations in general for the increased complexity they can bring to the finished wine. Hand punchdowns are routine. The wine is pressed as soon as the cap begins to fall, usually after about fifteen to twenty days of vatting. The press fraction is reunified with the free-run juice, and the wine goes straight from press to barrel without settling.

About 35 percent new barrels are used overall, but the vineyard-designated and reserve wines see a disproportionate share of them. Barrels are purchased from eight coopers—François Frères, Remond, Sirugue, Mercurey, Seguin Moreau, Meyrieux, Rousseau, and Dargaud & Jaeglé—and there is also a bit of Oregon oak coopered by François Frères. Malolactic bacteria are introduced into the barrels via the topping wine. Doerner says his racking trials have convinced him that "less is more"—fewer rackings produce wine with better body *and less sediment*—so racking is confined to a minimum. The barrels destined for the vineyard-designated and reserve wines are selected in September after the vintage, and the reserve wines spend an additional six months in wood. Egg-white fining for "polish" is standard—Doerner says it can even make the wine "creamy"— but there is no filtration. Doerner is truly a master winemaker and makes the most engaging, stunningly balanced, and altogether enchanting examples I know of (mostly) whole-cluster fermented pinots in North America. The wines are universally filled with character and are elegant, transparent to both method and *terroir*, and so impressive that one cannot drink them without pausing to reflect and appreciate. Of the vineyard-designates, Marjorie tends to be the biggest wine, but Jessie displays the greatest aromatic subtlety.

2005 *Sommers Reserve (tasted in 2007):*
Medium ruby; savory aromas and orange
peel; on the palate, fruit just sweet enough
to be perceptible before it gives way to
a mid-palate reminiscent of brewed tea;
considerable grip, with some pepper,
blackberry, and juniper berry; long,
elegant, and very attractive.

2005 *Eileen Vineyard (tasted in 2007):*
Transparent, medium-dark rosy-ruby;
earthy, smoky nose with clean, dark fruit;
slightly sweet blackberry fruit on the palate
but seriously structured and dry at mid-
palate; hints of nutmeg; elegant and fine.

2004 *Mt. Jefferson Cuvée (tasted in 2007):*
Brilliant light-to-medium garnet; pretty
floral and red berry aromas with hints of
resin; silky, almost creamy texture with
vibrant and very clean fruit; lightweight,
serious, attractive, and elegant with a slight
signature of whole-cluster fermentation.

2002 *Marjorie Vineyard (tasted in 2007):*
Brilliant, very transparent medium garnet;
a rich nose of moist earth, flowers, and
juniper berries; red fruit, tangerine peel,
clove, and allspice; magnificently satiny;
resin-laden signature of whole-cluster
fermentation; captivating and very fine.

CUVAISON ESTATE WINES
Napa, California

Cuvaison, founded in 1969 by two Silicon
Valley engineers, is now in its fourth life. In
the first, under the ownership of its founders,
it produced wines from the original estate
vineyard on the Silverado Trail, south of
Calistoga. In the second, from 1974 to 1979,
its owner was New York publisher Oakleigh
Thorne, whose winemaker, Philip Togni

(see CHALONE VINEYARD) attracted
attention with "eccentric" wines. From
around 1980 to the turn of the millennium,
the brand invested seriously in Carneros
and developed a fine reputation (especially
for chardonnay) with winemaking under
the charge of John Thatcher and ownership
in the hands of Thomas Schmidheiny, a
Swiss engineer whose family amassed a
considerable fortune in various construction
materials businesses during the nineteenth
and twentieth centuries. Since 2002, with
Kendall-Jackson and Southern Wine and
Spirits alumnus Jay Schuppert as president
and Steven Rogstad (formerly at Clos Pegase,
Spring Mountain, and SAINTSBURY) as
winemaker, Cuvaison has focused almost
exclusively on its two estate vineyards—one
on Mt. Veeder (cabernet sauvignon and
syrah) and the other in Los Carneros, where
it grows pinot, chardonnay, sauvignon blanc,
and merlot—and has moved its production
to a new custom-built facility co-located
with the Carneros vineyard on Duhig Road
near ACACIA WINERY.

The pinot noir program, begun in 1987,
was entirely estate based from the outset.
The first pinot noir, planted in 1981 on
nonresistant rootstock, was redeveloped
between 1993 and 2007. Fifty-seven acres
(divided among twenty-three blocks) are
now devoted to pinot noir. The pinot
vines' average age is eleven years (as of
2007) and there are twelve selections of
scion material. Cuvaison remains primarily
a chardonnay house; pinot noir accounts
for no more than 15 percent of the brand's
total production.

WINES AND WINEMAKING NOTES
In recent vintages, the main release of
pinot noir is a Carneros Estate bottling.
There are also small quantities of two
other wines: a block-designate from Block
F5 built entirely from Dijon 115, which is

Cuvaison's "reserve quality" pinot, and a single-clone wine (not made every year) called Mariafeld, the common name for the UCD 23 selection. Rogstad ferments between 30 and 40 percent of the fruit as whole clusters, cold-soaks, relies on a combination of resident and inoculated yeasts, typically bleeds the must to increase concentration, and extends the vatting time for some lots to include periods of postfermentation maceration. The Carneros Estate and Mariafeld bottlings spend about ten months in 33 percent new barrels coopered from wood sourced in forests in "central France," mostly the Tronçais and other forests in the Nevers and Allier *départements*; the block-designated wine is typically held longer in wood—up to fifteen months.

TASTING NOTES

2006 *Carneros (tasted in 2007):* Medium rosy-ruby; nutshell, cabinet shop, and dark fruit aromas; a sweet and extremely grippy wine; intense, warm, and peppery.

2005 *Block F5 (tasted in 2007):* Dark ruby; hickory, dark cherry, and Santa Rosa plum aromas; sweet, very grippy, and intensely flavored; hints of Kahlua, espresso, and cherry-flavored Nyquil; smooth mid-palate, lots of barrel char; a tarry and chewy finish that is both long and warm.

DAVID BRUCE WINERY
Saratoga, California

David Bruce, the son of staunch teetotalers and a dermatologist by profession, has been a person of note in American pinot for more than half a century. Bruce says he discovered wine through an interest in cooking while he was a medical student at Stanford University in the 1950s. "I first tasted wine," he explained in an interview with wine historian Charles Sullivan, "to see if it really was fit to enjoy with food." Bruce then bought the relatively few trade books about wine that were available at the time. Alexis Lichine's description of Richebourg in *The Wines of France*—that it had a "noble robe"—so fascinated Bruce that he bought a bottle "to see what in the world Lichine was talking about." Tasting the Richebourg seems to have caused an epiphany, because Bruce then made wines at home, worked intermittently for the eccentric Martin Ray, and helped pick grapes at nearby Ridge Vineyards. Bruce did his medical residency in Oregon, established a practice in San Jose, and began planting a vineyard of his own on Bear Creek Road in 1962. He sited the vineyard at approximately 2,200 feet above sea level, facing south and southwest toward Monterey Bay, in poor, weathered, sandstone-based soils, where the vine vigor is uniformly low. The first four blocks were dedicated, one each, to pinot noir, cabernet sauvignon, chardonnay, and riesling. Two years later, a temporary winery was bonded on the same site, and David Bruce wines went on sale in several San Jose stores in 1967.

Almost from the outset, however, Bruce, who tried to confine his medical practice to four days a week so the balance could be devoted to winemaking, and who made the wines himself with help from family and friends, had difficulty focusing on the varieties he had planted. He purchased zinfandel grapes from Day One, crafting a "white zinfandel" before the category was formally invented. He also made some zinfandels in an ultraripe, late harvest style. His estate cabernet was abandoned in the 1970s; riesling followed it in the

1980s. He persevered with chardonnay, however, although some of his best efforts, according to contemporaneous reviewers, came from purchased fruit. Bruce's estate pinot, which had been propagated with cuttings from Martin Ray's vineyard and from Wente's increase block in Arroyo Seco, persisted until 1994, when it succumbed to a combination of phylloxera and Pierce's disease; it seems to have given mixed results in its first fifteen years, prompting Bruce to diversify his attention to this variety into fruit sourced from considerable distances. Pinot was purchased from vineyards in Monterey and San Luis Obispo counties as early as 1977, from Sonoma County from about 1990 onward, and from non-estate Santa

---

WE HAVE LEARNED TO
EXAGGERATE FRUIT
FORWARDNESS BECAUSE
THIS IS OUR PALATE
—*David Bruce*

Cruz Mountains vineyards after 1992. (This category includes the RR Ranch, a cool, fog-influenced site on the Santa Cruz side of the mountains at about 800 feet; Split Rail Vineyard, at around 1,700 feet, overlooking Watsonville; Branciforte Creek, near Scotts Valley; and the Kent Barrie vineyard on Summit Road.)

Since 2000 Bruce has also sourced pinot from Chalone, from Bien Nacido Vineyard in Santa Maria, and from several vineyards in the Santa Lucia Highlands and the Sta. Rita Hills. This palette has fed an enormous assortment of labels, including a multicounty label called Vintner's Select; a Central Coast blend; a Sonoma County bottling; appellation wines from Sonoma County, Russian River, Santa

Lucia Highlands, Sta. Rita Hills, and the Santa Cruz Mountains; and a scattering of vineyard-designates from all over. In remarks made to a symposium on *terroir* in 2002, Bruce recalled that he had found it hard to make a good pinot noir in the 1960s and had been "forced" to work with other varieties until he learned "how individual varieties work differently." In his recollection, his brand became known in the 1960s for its zinfandel, and in the 1970s for its chardonnay; he did not begin making "consistent" pinot noirs until the 1980s. According to James Laube's *California Wine* (Wine Spectator Press, 1995), the Bruce portfolio "zigzagged all over the course in his 30-year career," incorporating wines from many varieties and vineyards that ranged from "bizarre or flawed" to "brilliant and well-crafted."

By the end of the 1990s, the pinot program had bifurcated completely, with more than 30,000 cases of the Central Coast blend dwarfing all other bottlings and forcing production of that wine into a custom-crush facility in San Luis Obispo; all else remained on Bear Creek Road, including the revived estate pinot, produced after 1996 for the first time since 1992. (The replanting was done with budwood saved from the Noble Hill Vineyard on Zayante Road, which had been planted in the 1980s with cuttings taken from the old Bruce parcel, plus nursery-sourced Swan selection; a field selection from Cambria; UCD 5 and 13; and Dijon 115, 667, and 777. By 2001, 9 acres of second-generation pinot were back in production on the David Bruce estate, laid out in sixteen hillside blocks, in 8- or 10-foot rows depending on the degree of slope, with 5 feet between vines.) The Central Coast wine was discontinued after the 2006 vintage, effectively cutting the brand's production in half, but apparently refocusing it, or at least trying to refocus it, on "high-end quality pinot noir."

Observers who follow the brand closely say that the end of the Central Coast programs (there was also a Central Coast petite sirah) was only part of a larger instance of "difficult transition" in the family-owned company. Wine industry professionals hired into key positions early in the new millennium, including the company's president, have all departed. Bruce is once again president of his own business, at the age of seventy-eight, while his wife is the vice president and general manager. After a decade of stability in winemaking, Ken Foster and Anthony Craig departed in 2002 and 2004, respectively, the former to take over as the winemaker for Carneros Creek Winery, and the latter to start his own label. Mitri Faravashi, a 1998 graduate of San Jose State University in biochemistry who subsequently worked in several capacities for Mirassou Cellars, took the winemaking reins. It is not clear what will happen next.

WINES AND WINEMAKING NOTES

Bruce asserts that "winemaking is an art," and that his winery has "always been noted for its interest in experimentation." All the pinots are made in small, 2-ton open-top fermentors, just over 5 feet tall and 4 feet in diameter. Stems were gradually eliminated from fermentation regimes between 1993 and 1997, but they have recently been restored, at least for the estate pinot, where Bruce says that lignified stems and ripe seeds are assured. Through most of the 1980s, plunging was done by hand and foot; this quaint practice was replaced in 1990 with a custom-designed pneumatic *pige*, and occasional use of rack-and-return. Beyond that, Bruce claims to "vary techniques depend[ing] on the state of the must, the ripeness of the grapes, and a host of other factors." In the early 1990s, American oak was used exclusively, but French and Eastern European oak were gradually introduced in the second half of the decade. By the 1998 vintage, the Santa Cruz Mountains wines were finished entirely in French barrels. Now Bruce says simply that the winery uses "a broad palate of oaks from different countries."

A coarse pad filtration was standard in the second half of the 1990s; Bruce now says that "none of our wines is filtered or fined." Stylistically, Bruce says that the winery has "learned to exaggerate fruit forwardness" because "this is our palate [and] the new-world palate." He also asserts that the winery has learned to achieve the velvetiness of old Burgundies "from the get-go" by "managing tannin structure." I have tasted only a few Bruce pinots from vintages since 2000, but the wines generally show well in comparative tastings.

TASTING NOTE

2005 *Russian River Valley (tasted in 2007):* Medium rosy-garnet; very ripe cherry jam aromas with an abundance of spice; initially silky on the palate, with more cherry, vanilla, camphor, and licorice; then, intense with grip and black pepper; fruit forward but nicely made with noticeable alcohol on the finish.

DAVIS BYNUM WINES
Healdsburg, California

Davis Bynum Wines, the second eponymous wine project of San Francisco journalist Davis Bynum, operated as a hands-on, family-run business from its founding in 1973 until the brand and its remaining inventory were sold in 2007 to RODNEY STRONG VINEYARDS, America's twenty-third largest wine company. In 1965, Bynum, who had judged wine for the California State Fair and the Los Angeles County Fair and who had made wine at home, opened a storefront facility in Albany, California, where he made some wines from scratch, blended and bottled others, and sold a large percentage of his product in gallon and half-gallon jugs, catering to a clientele of academics and graduate students with limited budgets. Becoming more serious about production and more interested in premium quality, he purchased 26 acres of vineyard in Napa in 1971, on the site that is now Whitehall Lane Vineyards, but turned his sights to Sonoma when Napa authorities imposed a moratorium on the construction of new wineries. In 1973, in lieu of vineyard land in Napa, Bynum acquired a disused hops kiln on Westside Road, west of Healdsburg; transformed the kiln into a viable winery in time for that year's crush; and created Davis Bynum Wines.

Bynum had not intended to make a mark on the history of American pinot noir, but he did. His first vintage involved, among other things, pinot grown by his new Westside Road neighbor, Joe Rochioli Jr., whose fruit had hitherto disappeared into anonymous blends. The 1973 Davis Bynum Pinot Noir, "produced from grapes grown in the vineyard of Joe Rochioli Jr. which overlooks the Russian River," was the first wine of any kind, as far as anyone knows, to carry the words *Russian River* on its label, and (along with Joe Swan's 1973 pinot noir) the first vineyard-designated pinot from what is now the Russian River Valley AVA. The brand worked entirely with purchased fruit, for pinot and other varieties, until Bynum felt able to invest in estate vineyard seventeen years later. Its pinot was purchased from numerous

growers in what is now the Russian River Valley AVA. Its reputation for this variety depended on a combination of Rochioli, Bynum's only source from 1973 to 1975, and pinot from the Allen Vineyard, across Westside Road from Rochioli, from which vineyard fruit was purchased from 1976 through 2006, even though Bynam's estate vineyard—called Lindleys' Knoll, located on a butte above the winery—was used for some very good pinots after it began to bear in 2002. (Lindleys' Knoll includes 9 acres of pinot noir, planted in 10-foot rows with 5 feet between vines, of which about 2.75 acres are UCD 4, 2 acres are Dijon clones, and 1.75 acres are UCD 2A; the balance is divided about equally between UCD 16, UCD 13, and a field selection, said to be Mount Eden, from the Moshin Vineyard. Soils on the butte are mostly Sobrante series decomposed shale with some volcanic ash, red-black in color at the surface, of low vigor, and extremely well drained. The vineyard is farmed organically, with special attention to polyculture and insectary plantings on the vineyard's periphery.)

Bynum's reputation for good pinots also owes a great deal to the skills and dedication of its longtime winemaker Gary Farrell, who served from 1979 until 2000, when he left to work full time on his own brand. The 2007 sale of the brand, but not the winery, tasting room, or estate vineyard, to Rodney Strong surprised most observers and had immediate effects. The bottled inventory was transferred to the Rodney Strong facility on Eastside Road, across the river; the unbottled inventory (mostly from the 2006 vintage) was moved in barrels to Rodney Strong's new (2005), small-lot winery-within-a-winery for finishing; Rodney Strong's small-lot winemaker Gary Patzwald became the Davis Bynum winemaker; and it was announced that the brand would rely on fruit from vineyards owned by the Klein family, Rodney Strong's owner, beginning in 2008. At the same time, the Bynum family announced plans to transform the Westside Road facility into a custom-crush operation supporting small-scale vintners. The disposition of fruit from Lindleys' Knoll, following the 2007 harvest, is not known at the time of this writing.

WINES

Inevitably, Bynum's pinot program evolved over the thirty-four years the family owned the brand. From 1973 to 1976, there was a single wine, made entirely from Rochioli fruit. Beginning in 1977 or 1978 (the winery's records are incomplete), lots of Allen Ranch and Rochioli fruit were blended to create a Sonoma Westside Road bottling. A Reserve pinot debuted in 1980, featuring the Rochioli and Allen Ranch fruit that had made the reputation of the preceding vintages; at the same time, a Russian River Valley cuvée that depended on a much wider array of vineyard sources was created for broader distribution. Later in the 1980s, the reserve rubric was abandoned in favor of so-called Limited Release and Limited Edition wines, which were barrel selections of the most ageworthy lots available to the winery. At this point, the Russian River Valley bottling evolved into a home for Bynum's lighter lots, and was crafted for early drinking; in 1991 Le Pinot emerged as a de facto vineyard-designated wine, made entirely from grapes grown in Rochioli's East Block. At the time of this writing, it is not clear what 2006 vintage pinots will be released under the Davis Bynum label, and the program is sure to be completely re-crafted from 2007 forward.

TASTING NOTES

2005 *Russian River Valley (tasted in* 2008): Brilliant, medium magenta; classic Russian River nose of cherry with floral highlights, plus some beetroot; more cherry with some mint and pepper on the palate; forward fruit gives way to mild grip on the back palate; bright overall and attractive.

2004 *Allen Vineyard (tasted in* 2008): Brilliant light-to-medium scarlet with slightly orange highlights; earth, cherry, and barrel-derived vanilla on the nose; lovely, intense, and slightly savory on the palate with hints of black pepper, nutmeg, and cinnamon; initially silky, then more like crushed velvet; finishes slightly warm.

2004 *Rochioli (tasted prerelease in* 2008): Brilliant black-red with a pinkish rim; explosive nose of walnut shells and dark, ripe cherries; sweet, sober, and serious on the palate; considerable slatey minerality; almost rich; texture that begins as polished cotton and evolves toward emery; long and warm.

DAVIS FAMILY VINEYARDS
Healdsburg, California

Guy Davis has touched wine from almost every angle. While putting himself through college in the early 1980s, he worked evenings at a French restaurant in Seattle where, after he sent out the last meal to the dining room and cooked the after-service staff supper, he shared very good bottles, and life-altering conversation, with the restaurant's French owners. At the end of the 1980s, after a stint selling securities, Davis became a wine buyer in Sonoma County. During that time, he worked a harvest at Lore Olds's Sky Vineyards on the top of Mount Veeder, where he discovered that "nurturing grape clusters" and "turning grapes into wine" were hugely rewarding activities and "the side of the wine business" he wanted to join. Before getting there, however, Davis worked briefly as a marketing director for Kendall-Jackson and founded his own company—the Passport Wine Club—organized around regular, direct-to-consumer shipments of wine selected from California's growing stable of boutique producers, and from boutique producers in France, Spain, and Italy.

After his first taste of vineyard and winery work at Sky, Davis worked the harvest for an artisan producer somewhere on the globe for every vintage until 1995, when he launched Davis Family Vineyards with 250 cases of Russian River Valley zinfandel made from purchased grapes. The following year, touched by extraordinary luck and the fortuitous sale of his Passport Wine Club to Boston-based Geerlings & Wade, he was able to buy a very neglected 10-acre zinfandel vineyard on the west side of Laguna Road, less than a mile from Joseph Swan Winery and near the center of the Russian River Valley appellation. This spectacular site in the craw of Laguna Ridge looks out over the Laguna de Santa Rosa and features Spring Mountain on the horizon. About 2.5 acres of the old zinfandel vines, originally planted in 1896, were then rescued from impending doom, but the rest of the existing vineyard was cleared, ripped, and rededicated to a combination of syrah and a 6-acre, T-shaped planting of pinot noir, half nursery-sourced UCD 4 and half Dijon clones.

Before this estate planting began to bear, Davis launched his eponymous pinot program with a Russian River Valley cuvée (in 1997 and 1998) from grapes sourced from Warren Dutton's Thomas Road and Jewel vineyards. Gradually, between 1999 and 2002, this cuvée evolved toward an estate-fruit pedigree and became an all-estate product in 2002.

Davis now makes about 900 cases of pinot each year, which is a bit less than a quarter of his brand's total production. Endlessly creative and possessed of apparently inexhaustible energy, Davis also makes sauvignon blanc each spring in New Zealand, which he imports and sells under a sister label, Gusto. He also crafts minuscule quantities of an apple brandy (cleverly named Apple-ation) distilled from crushed and macerated whole fruit, again from Dutton Ranches. And, yes, there is also a bit of very tasty olive oil!

WINES AND WINEMAKING NOTES
Through 2005 Davis made just one pinot noir. In 2006 five barrels were set aside for a second bottling called Pinnacole—a fusion of the word "pinnacle" and his son Cole's name, destined for release in the spring of 2009. (Davis's son Cole has been the cellarmaster for Davis Family Vineyards since 2004.) From the 2007 harvest, there were also a few barrels of pinot from a Sonoma Coast vineyard, scheduled for release in the autumn of 2009. This wine, said to be showing boysenberry, spice, and earth early in 2008, was sourced from a vineyard squarely in the Petaluma Gap.

The estate pinots, meanwhile, are extremely attractive, slightly understated, nicely textured wines, which display more flowers, herbs, and spice than fruit, and which are characterized by mercifully modest alcohols. In the vineyard, Davis works to minimize the addition of nutrients, and to irrigate as little as possible after veraison so that the vines get unambiguous "end-of-season signals." This approach to vine farming, combined with a picking protocol that involves multiple passes through the vineyard over a two- to three-week period, means that he can get nearly all clusters off the vines between

23 and 24 Brix, without any shrivel or dehydration, and can avoid any suggestion of super-ripeness or any temptation to add water to the fermenting musts. Having experimented briefly with five- and six-day cold soaks, which produced noticeable upward shifts in pH, he has returned to three-day regimes, which preserve natural acidity better and which avoid any need for acid additions.

The wines are pressed at dryness and settled for two full days in an effort to avoid racking later. The fine lees are stirred in barrel "for a satiny texture." Barrels are sourced from François Frères, Sirugue, Radoux, and Mercurey; most of the stave wood comes from the Tronçais or other Allier forests; and one third of the barrel stock is new in each vintage. The pinot has not been filtered, except in 2002, when another client in his custom-crush winery developed brettanomyces and put the fear of sterilization into Davis. The pinot noir is currently fermented in Rick Moshin's winery on Westside Road and finished at Davis's own facility in Healdsburg. Davis says he aims for a "pretty, sensual wine," and he gets it.

TASTING NOTES

2004 *Russian River Valley (tasted in 2007):* Brilliant rosy-ruby; strongly floral with mostly dried petals, a hint of gingerbread and white pepper; very peppery and spicy on the palate with rosewater and raspberry flavors; lightweight and elegant, but still intense; satiny and sleek in texture.

2003 *Russian River Valley (tasted in 2007):* Light-to-medium ruby, just tiling at the rim; exotic Indonesian spice on the nose, with cardamom and dried tangerine peel; infused flowers, some raspberry, white pepper, and clove in the mouth; a very pretty wine.

DE LOACH VINEYARDS
Santa Rosa, California

Cecil De Loach, a Georgian by birth, an urban anthropologist by training, and a firefighter for most of his life by occupation, purchased a 24-acre ranch on Olivet Road northwest of Santa Rosa in 1969, primarily as a place to retire. Much of the property had been planted sixty years earlier to zinfandel vines, however. De Loach learned to farm these, relying on word-of-mouth instruction from the ranch's previous owner and on extension courses taken at the University of California Davis. Subsequently, as the "wine thing" began to consume De Loach and his wife, they purchased additional land nearby, planted more vines, became active in the Sonoma County Cooperative Winery in Windsor, and built a winery of their own. In 1975, they produced the first De Loach wine—a zinfandel—and planted their first pinot noir in two separate parcels on Olivet Road. This investment in pinot qualifies De Loach as one of the variety's early adopters in Russian River—preceded by just a handful of earlier pioneers such as Davis Bynum, Joseph Swan, Charles Bacigalupi, and Joseph Rochioli Jr. When the Russian River Valley AVA was proposed in 1981, De Loach's wife, Christine, was one of the original petitioners.

Throughout the 1980s and 1990s, De Loach Vineyards flourished, increasing acreage, production, and (perhaps ill-advisedly) the size of its wine portfolio, until the company was farming more than 1,000 acres of vineyard and selling 350,000 cases of more than forty different wines. Because the expansion was heavily leveraged with borrowed capital, the business was vulnerable to the general economic downturn that followed 9/11. Forced to declare bankruptcy in 2001, De Loach Vineyards was acquired by Boisset America in 2005. Boisset America's parent company, a Nuits-Saint-Georges–based *négociant* firm founded in the 1960s, had ventured beyond Burgundy on multiple occasions in the 1990s, often reorganizing and reviving troubled wine properties. At De Loach, Boisset immediately cut production by 80 percent, eliminated outlier products such as barrel-fermented chenin blanc and blends of sangiovese, refocused the brand on Russian River's three trademark varieties (pinot, chardonnay, and zinfandel), and appointed the much-respected Greg La Follette (see TANDEM WINERY) as winemaker.

WINES AND WINEMAKING NOTES
Initially confined to an estate bottling and reserve wine called OFS (for Our Finest Selection), based entirely on the Olivet Road plantings, which were widely-spaced blocks of (probably) UCD 13 or 15, De Loach's original pinot program had expanded in the 1990s to produce large volumes of Russian River Valley pinot. This production relied on a combination of estate and purchased fruit. Most of the product was Russian River Valley appellation wine, but there was sometimes also a blended "California" wine sold for a modest price, and (once) a vineyard-designated wine from a Sebastopol Hills site that De Loach and his "farming partner" John Balletto had planted (to a combination of Dijon clones and UCD 23) at the end of the 1990s.

Beginning in 2004, under Boisset's auspices and La Follette's direction, the pinot program was reformulated to feature a small array of vineyard-designated wines from cherry-picked, non-estate sites in Sonoma and Mendocino; a blended reserve wine with the historic OFS designation; a preponderant volume of Russian River appellation wine; and a smaller volume of value-priced "California" pinot, 60 percent of which was also sourced from Russian River. The cellar was refitted to feature small, 4-ton open-top wooden fermentors, and winemaking practices were made to rely primarily on resident yeast fermentations, hand-plunging, and small-batch pressing. The winemaking team, four of whose members had been with the brand for more than a decade, initially balked at these wholesale changes to established practice. They were eventually convinced, however, that plainly better wines justified the hard work required to make significant volume with hands-on, small-batch techniques.

In 2005 the last fruit from the original estate vineyards was used for a one-time-only 30th Anniversary Cuvée, which featured a substantial percentage of whole-cluster fruit; these vineyards were then uprooted and replanted, destined for biodynamic cultivation, under the direction of Ginny Lambrix, a onetime chemical ecologist, who came to De Loach from Lynmar in 2004 and was De Loach's director of winegrowing until 2008. The non-estate, vineyard-designation program, which is plainly producing the very best of the new De Loach wines, relies on wines from properties in the Sebastopol Hills, on Sonoma Mountain, in the Petaluma Gap, and in Mendocino County. The Sebastopol Hills vineyards, well known to La Follette and Lambrix by dint of previous experience, include Maboroshi, a 1999 planting of Dijon clones, and Swicegood. There are also two Sonoma Mountain sites (Durrell, overlooking Carneros, and Van der Kamp, on the mountain's north face, overlooking Bennett Valley), plus the Hyde family's Stage Gulch Vineyard in the Petaluma Gap, and Jacob Fetzer's biodynamically-farmed Masut Vineyard near the headwaters of the Russian River in Mendocino County. As La Follette's role shrank from hands-on winemaking to occasional consulting in 2006, the day-to-day responsibilities were passed to Julia Crosby, part of De Loach's cellar team since 1996, and to Brian Maloney, who (with Lambrix and Crosby) has been a key architect of the new pinot program.

TASTING NOTES

2005 *Durell Vineyard (tasted in 2007):* Transparent, dark black-red; sweet vanilla and juniper berry on the nose; sweet and intense on the palate with clove, allspice, cherry, orange peel, and a hint of bay laurel; the cherry-berry flavors linger through mid-palate to the finish; round and very attractive.

2005 *Van der Kamp Vineyard (tasted in 2007):* Brilliant light-to-medium black-red; aromas of sausage and related *charcuterie*; licorice on the palate; sharply spicy; the signature of whole-cluster fermentation; bright and lingering.

2005 *Maboroshi Vineyard (tasted in 2007):* Transparent, medium ruby; shy nose of dust and rose petal; intense, sweet attack but then grippy at mid-palate; rich and mouth-coating with the texture of heavy silk; notes of slate and citrus. Very attractive.

2005 *"OFS" (tasted in 2007):* Medium-dark ruby with crimson highlights; earthy nose; creamy and very sweet on the palate with notes of cola and root beer; unwinds to reveal considerable spice; plush, velvety, and long.

2004 *Van der Kamp Vineyard (tasted in 2007):* Brilliant, transparent black-red; feral nose with hints of orange peel, tar, licorice, and black pepper; cherry and slate on the palate; very slightly grippy with nice acidity.

DEHLINGER WINERY
    Sebastopol, California

When Tom Dehlinger graduated from the University of California Berkeley in 1969 with a degree in biochemistry, he and his family assumed he would follow his parents into a career in medicine. But Dehlinger was not sure about medical school and thought he might like doing a bit of lab work instead, at least until he could sort his options thoughtfully. When he approached Napa and Sonoma wineries about working at their in-house labs, he was advised to obtain a proper background in enology first. So in August 1970, he explored the graduate program offered at the university's Davis campus, was offered a fellowship on the spot, and enrolled immediately. He remembers being part of a cohort of about eight students.

With his credentials established, he easily landed jobs at Beringer Vineyards in 1971 and as a winemaker for HANZELL VINEYARDS in 1972. Thoughts of a career in medicine faded forever. The next year, Dehlinger and his parents purchased a 45-acre parcel on Vine Hill Road near the intersection of Guerneville Road and the Gravenstein Highway, in the heart of the Russian River Valley's Laguna Ridge district, where there was already a good deal of zinfandel and some new interest in chardonnay and pinot, but more apple trees than anything else. (In 1980 Dehlinger bought out his parents' share in the ranch.) Dehlinger began planting grapes in 1975:

cabernet sauvignon, chardonnay, and pinot noir. Vines were planted, in the fashion of the day, in 10-foot rows with 8 feet between vines, supported by three horizontal wires and irrigated with overhead sprinklers. The vinifera was grafted to nonresistant AxR1 rootstock, which has miraculously survived. The scion material was a combination of UCD 4 and 13, the former acquired from the certified increase block at Smith Madrone on Spring Mountain; Dehlinger ran out of this material with three rows still left to graft, at which point he "filled in" with budwood taken from Joseph Swan's nearby vineyard on Laguna Road.

DRY AND SERIOUS WINES THAT CONTRAST SHARPLY WITH FRUIT-DRIVEN, CROWD-PLEASING EDITIONS OF CALIFORNIA PINOT NOIR

Soils at Dehlinger are mostly weathered marine sandstone. The hilltops are characterized by a shallow layer of silty sand and pebbles, underlain with red clay-loam and more very permeable sand; the lower slopes (which are the soil type usually described as Goldridge) generally lack the layer of clay-loam.

In 1982 Dehlinger planted additional vines, including another 3.5 acres of pinot noir, on the slopes of Octagon Hill, which takes its name from Dehlinger's eight-sided residence on the hilltop. The scion material for these vines was taken entirely from the aforementioned three rows of Swan selection. A third expansion of the vineyard was undertaken in 1988 and 1989, partially in the northwest quadrant of the original parcel and partially on adjacent land added to the estate in 1984.

Here, 5 acres were dedicated to UCD 4, propagated from second-generation cuttings from the Smith Madrone material, and 2 acres were established with more cuttings from the three rows of Swan. An additional acre of cabernet franc, planted in 1983 on the west side of Octagon Hill, was T-budded to Dijon 777 sourced from Dehlinger's neighbor, Steve Kistler, in 1996. (This space represents the only piece of the property dedicated to Dijon clones.)

At the end of the 1980s, as resources became available to handle more of the vineyard's fruit in separate lots, Dehlinger, vineyard manager Martin Hedlund, and assistant winemaker Fred Scherrer (see SCHERRER WINES) took a close look at the differences among the estate's blocks, rows, and individual vines. To manage generally high but still-variable vigor, they converted the entire ranch from the simple, inexpensive three-wire vine training system, which had been embraced when the first vines were planted in 1975, to a substantially more expensive and labor-intensive system developed early in the 1980s in Bordeaux. In the latter system, two curtains of foliage and two fruiting zones are created for each vine, until a cross-section of each vine row looks like a lyre, for which the system is named. Arguably even more important, they mapped the entire vineyard for its intensity of vigor; color-coded *each* vine blue, green, yellow, orange, or red for its respective level; and devised farming protocols optimized for the circumstances of each color. Green-coded vines, which are more vigorous, are subjected to more vigorous leaf pulling and crop thinning, but these are still farmed to yield about 4 tons of fruit per acre; red-coded vines can be treated less aggressively, but are pruned to fewer shoots per vine and managed to yield about 2.5 tons per acre. Unsurprisingly the red- and orange-coded vines, found in the higher elevation sites, ripen earliest, are picked first, and make the property's best wine. At the other extreme, fruit from blue-coded vines is no longer used, but is instead sold to other producers. Dehlinger and Hedlund have also been forced to devote increasing attention to protecting their nonresistant rootstock from phylloxera by limiting cultivation between rows, and then managing some of the nutrition deficiencies that seem to result from leaving the soil untilled, which include patches of insufficient potassium and phosphorous.

The vineyard is "rationally" but not organically farmed—Dehlinger protects aggressively against mildew—and vines are dry farmed after they reach their fourth anniversary. Dehlinger is a thoughtful winegrower, enormously respected by his peers, with the experiential advantage of having farmed a single parcel for thirty years and having vinted four varietals from its adjacent blocks. When I asked him how he felt, after thirty years, about growing pinot noir (supposedly a cool-climate variety) and cabernet sauvignon (thought to benefit from much warmer weather) side by side, he admitted that the cabernet was problematic, but observed that different years seemed to privilege good outcomes with different varieties. Some of Dehlinger's 1999 plantings include syrah.

WINES AND WINEMAKING NOTES
Although Dehlinger bought zinfandel, cabernet sauvignon, and chardonnay grapes to launch his brand in 1975 and 1976, before his own vines were bearing, the pinot program has relied entirely on estate fruit since its debut in 1977. Dehlinger says the 1977 was "not very weighty," the 1978

was "OK," and the 1979 was "the first fully ripe and high-quality wine." A single estate bottling was made in each vintage until the mid 1980s. Dehlinger explains that no other approach made sense, because everything picked together was fermented together and then raised together in large-format casks anyway. The first differentiation among the estate's pinots came late in the 1980s with a bottling simply called Lot #2, which was a vehicle to handle the vines' tendency to throw an abundant second crop.

Then, in 1993, the winery began directing fruit from the aforementioned, relatively vigorous green-coded vines into a new bottling called Goldridge, leaving mostly hillside and hilltop fruit (the red- and orange-coded vines) for the estate and other bottlings (see below). Beginning in 1994, three additional wines filled this space: an Octagon bottling made primarily from the 1982 planting of Swan selection on Octagon Hill; a reserve made mostly from the red- and yellow-coded vines in the 1975 plantings; and an Old Vines Goldridge cuvée, made from the lower elevation vines in the 1975 blocks. A High Plains cuvée, which takes its name from the in-house designation applied to the south end of Block 15, a 1989 planting of UCD 4, was also made separately from 1999 to 2002. The multiplicity of pinots was useful commercially while Dehlinger operated an onsite tasting room, as was the case until 1996. Thereafter, the large portfolio seemed more a liability than an asset and was gradually reduced. From 2003 until the present, Dehlinger has made only the estate and Goldridge bottlings, except in 2004 and 2006, when it also made a Reserve. Octagon, Old Vines Goldridge, and High Plains all disappeared.

Having harvested the fruit by passing through the vineyard several times to pick each vine at the right time, which Dehlinger describes as "dead ripe but not overripe" or about 25.5 Brix, Dehlinger cold-soaks pinots for three to five days before inoculation and plunges the must by hand once the primary fermentation is active. Most fruit is destemmed, and the 1 acre of UCD 13 is crushed, but about 10 to 15 percent of the hillside lots are retained as whole clusters "if the stems taste good." Winemaking seeks to ensure that every lot ferments dry as quickly as possible. Fermentors are then covered, blanketed with carbon dioxide, and plunged once a day for five to eight days after dryness "to produce a smoother wine with a thicker mid-palate." After draining, the new wines are settled overnight and transferred to barrels, of which about 60 percent are medium-toast François Frères *pièces* coopered from Tronçais wood, 30 percent are Tronçais-sourced stave wood from other coopers, and 10 percent are "experiments." (A large percentage of puncheons were used in lieu of *pièces* until 2001; pinot has been raised exclusively in *pièces* since.) Press wine has been bulked out since 2002. Blends are made in June after the vintage. The Goldridge wine is bottled in February, two years after the vintage, the estate in March, and the reserve in April. There is no fining or filtration.

A succession of uncommonly talented assistant winemakers has passed through Dehlinger over the years, including Dan Karlsen, who went on to DOMAINE CARNEROS, Estancia, and CHALONE; Fred Scherrer; and Eric Sussman (see RADIO-COTEAU). Dehlinger himself handled all the winemaking after Sussman's departure in 2002 until 2005, when Tom Klassen, an alumnus of Landmark Vineyards, joined the staff as enologist.

Owing to its fastidious farming, Dehlinger's vineyard has been a favored source of budwood for plantings elsewhere, and his wines enjoy a fine reputation. The pinots display a dry and serious character that contrasts sharply with fruit-driven, crowd-pleasing editions of the variety that emanate from other makers. A large proportion of their organoleptic space is taken up with minerality, floral properties, understated spice, and herbs. The dry-farmed vines have a tendency to produce fruit that retains acidity well, resulting in wines that are nicely built. The Goldridge bottling, once conceived as a second-tier wine, has developed its own distinctive character as the vines have gotten older; Goldridge now seems a mature, elegant, treble-clef cousin to the bass-clef Estate and Reserve wines.

TASTING NOTES

2005 *Goldridge (tasted prerelease in 2007):* Pretty, medium ruby; dusty nose redolent of flowers, sage, and tar; bright red fruit on the palate, with an intense spicy flavor and a hint of orange rind; silky texture with some grip at the end.

2005 *Estate (tasted prerelease in 2007):* Visually pretty again and just a shade darker than the Goldridge; earthy nose with some gutsy, lower-register components and brown spice; earthy, dark red fruit on the palate, with minerality and hints of bay laurel; satin texture, good grip, and considerable length.

2004 *Goldridge Vineyard (tasted in 2007):* Medium black-red; slightly floral aromatically; elegant and suave on the palate, with red berry fruit, orange peel, and rosewater; bright, long, and attractive.

2004 *Estate (tasted in 2007):* Transparent, medium ruby; black aromatics featuring very ripe fruit, coffee beans, and pepper; slightly fruit-sweet on the palate, with resinous and silky properties; some allspice and dark cherry; elegant and concentrated, with grip and peppery warmth on the finish.

2004 *Reserve (tasted in 2007):* Transparent, medium, pinkish-ruby; reticent nose, but with some cherry, cassis, and oak; slightly fruit-sweet and flower-infused until mid-palate; then, concentrated and silky; finally, grippy and warm; bright overall, and long and attractive.

2003 *Estate (tasted in 2007):* Medium ruby; aromas of ripe fruit with floral highlights; bright, intense, floral-infused, and slightly citric on the palate; fruit-sweet but also smooth, serious, and slightly spicy; long and attractive.

2002 *Octagon (tasted in 2007):* Deep, almost opaque black-red; shellac and black fruit aromas; sweet cherry and blackberry flavors, with quite intense pepper and barrel char; rich, mouth filling, soft edged, and almost creamy; nicely formed, rewarding, and impressive.

1994 *Reserve (tasted in 2007):* Deep mahogany; fruit, leather, and merbromin on the nose; a slight sensation of sweetness on the palate, with flavors of mocha and dark cherry; rich, elegant, and long.

1993 *Estate (tasted in 2006):* Stunning, brilliant brick-red color; leather, licorice, fennel seed, and hazelnut on the nose; bright on the palate, with fading cherry and a hint of orange zest; substantial minerality with just a slight tannic grip at the end; very fine.

DIERBERG VINEYARD AND THREE SAINTS
Santa Ynez, California

Jim Dierberg is a Missourian, a lawyer, and banker, who credits his interest in wine (which also includes the cross- and hybrid-based Hermannhof Winery west of St. Louis in the Missouri River Valley) to his mother, who had French *vigneron* roots. Turning his sights toward true vinifera in the 1990s, Dierberg purchased a 20,000-acre ranch in Happy Canyon, in the warm east end of the Santa Ynez Valley in the 1990s, and began planting cabernet sauvignon there in 1997. That same year, he acquired a second parcel well suited for pinot noir—165 acres on the south side of Orcutt Road, not far from the historic Santa Maria Hills and Sierra Madre vineyards—and began a second project in tandem with the first.

Like most terrain on the Santa Maria Mesa, Dierberg's Santa Maria soils consist of about 2 feet of very sandy topsoil over a deeper layer of sandy clay-loam, where vines typically root about 4 feet deep. The first Santa Maria blocks, laid out in 1997, were planted to UCD 13 (the historic workhorse selection on the mesa), UCD 23, and UCD 31; the 23 showed a tendency toward "brawniness and reduction" when the first wines were made and was later grafted to Dijon 828. A second round of planting was done in 1997 and 1998, mostly to UCD 2A and 4, and to Dijon 115; a third (in 2000 and 2001) set out Dijon 667 and 777, a Mount Eden selection from HIRSCH VINEYARDS, and Swan and Calera selections from the Hyde Vineyard in Carneros. The first harvests were sold to several Santa Barbara County producers, some of which made vineyard-designated Dierberg wines; in 2006 there were still three fruit clients: ARCADIAN WINES, FLYING GOAT CELLARS, and TANTARA WINERY.

The brand was launched in 2001 with production at Orcutt Road Cellars in Edna Valley. Chuck Ortman (see ORTMAN FAMILY WINES) was the winemaker for the first two vintages;

Craig Becker made the 2003s. Nicholas de Luca, who had previously worked at Fisher Vineyards in Sonoma, WILLIAMS SELYEM, and Byington Winery in the Santa Cruz Mountains, signed on as winemaker in July of 2004. Paul Hobbs, who was de Luca's mentor at Fisher Vineyards, is a consultant. Production moved to a new, dedicated facility on the Star Lane Ranch in Happy Valley at the beginning of 2005.

WINES AND WINEMAKING NOTES

Two pinots are made each year under the Dierberg label—a "main" release and a small quantity of a higher-acid, best-block wine called Steven. The fruit of younger vines and the press juice are declassified into a second label called Three Saints. Most of the fruit used for the Dierberg wines comes from Blocks 3, 4, and 6, which represent UCD 2A, 13, and 31, and Dijon 115, but picking protocols since 2003 have tended to follow soil profiles rather than block outlines. Steven is from a small section of Dijon 115 and UCD 13 in Block 5. The grapes are mostly destemmed, although a small percentage of whole clusters was retained in 2001 and 2002, and a larger percentage in 2005. Fermentations rely on resident yeasts without the addition of nutrients. Natural peak fermentation temperatures are around 90°F, but as these begin to fall, the must is heated for three days "to extract every last bit of flavor the grapes have to offer." Primary fermentations then finish in barrel, where the malolactic fermentations also take place, without inoculation. Nearly 60 percent new oak is used for *élevage*, and the wines stay in barrel for about sixteen months. They are not fined or filtered. The result, especially in 2003 and 2004, is big pinots, with very deep color verging on opaque, which are brawny, full-bodied, warm, and long.

TASTING NOTES

2003 *Dierberg Santa Maria Valley (tasted in 2006):* Medium-dark, saturated red color; raspberry, tobacco, and sage aromas; cherry, blackberry, and earth on the palate with black pepper, cedar, and manzanita; mouth filling and very plush; not for the faint of heart.

2003 *Three Saints (tasted in 2006):* Medium-dark black-red; blueberry aromas; sweet attack; then, barrel-derived mocha and Tootsie Roll; persistently sweet, even on the finish.

DOMAINE ALFRED
San Luis Obispo, California

Domaine Alfred is Terry Spizer's restoration of Chamisal, Edna Valley's oldest vineyard, on Orcutt Road about 4 miles southeast of the San Luis Obispo city limits. In 1972 Norman Goss, a classical musician turned restaurateur, who owned the Stuffed Shirt restaurants in Pasadena and Newport Beach, had worked with Uriel Nielson (see BYRON VINEYARD AND WINERY) to plant 30,000 vines at Chamisal just weeks before the Niven family planted their first vines at Paragon Vineyard. Spizer, a veteran of the sales and marketing side of Silicon Valley's semiconductor business and founder of several electronics companies, acquired the property in 1994. Chardonnay and cabernet sauvignon had survived from the 1972 plantings, although the vineyard was largely overgrown. The original vines were removed in 1995, save for a single gnarled specimen of chardonnay and a bit of cabernet.

In 1996 Spizer and his consulting viticulturist Jim Efird (see TOLOSA WINERY) planted 30 acres each of chardonnay and pinot noir. The scion material for the pinot was UCD 4 and Dijon 113, 114, 115, 667, and 777, with a bit of CTPS 943 added subsequently. Three years later, 62.5 contiguous acres were purchased next door, 8 of which were planted to UCD 2A and Dijon 828. From this palette, Domaine Alfred has used an onsite facility to make two or three pinots in each vintage since 1998. Spizer was his own winemaker for the first three vintages and took substantial advice from Steve Dooley (see STEPHEN ROSS WINES). Mike Sinor, previously assistant winemaker at Byron Vineyard and Winery, took the winemaking reins in 2000. When Sinor left in 2005 to launch his own label, he was succeeded by Fintan du Fresne, a New Zealander trained in geology, geomorphology, viticulture, and enology at Lincoln University, who was previously the winemaker at Thunderbolt Junction Winery in nearby Paso Robles.

WINES AND WINEMAKING NOTES

Since the first vintage in 1998, Domaine Alfred has made a plain estate pinot noir (aka a domaine bottling) and a pinot cuvée called Califa. The estate is built from all six clonal selections grown on the property, as well as from a combination of free-run and press juice; Califa excludes the Dijon 113 and 115 fruit, and relies exclusively on free-run juice. The estate is intended as an easy-drinking wine. The Califa is bolder and displays higher levels of tannin and oak. In 2003, a third pinot, dubbed Morrito, was added to the list. Morrito is a block-designated wine from the vineyard's hill.

Winemaking generally follows the consensus protocol, although there is usually some minority use of whole clusters, and fermentations rely on combinations of resident yeasts and inocula. The fermentors are 4- and 7-ton stainless steel open-tops. A basket press is used to press the new wine directly from tank to barrel; the barrel stock is purchased primarily from François Frères, Radoux, Sirugue, and Marsannay, with a preference for oak from Allier and Nevers forests. In the first vintages, 70 to 75 percent of the barrels were new each year; Spizer says this percentage is now being reduced because the wines "seem to need less new wood" as the vines age. Overall, the pinots emphasize primary flavors and ripe fruit, and are made with considerable extraction. *Élevage* also marks these wines very plainly. Consumers who respond favorably to strong, sometimes rich, and very forward wines will appreciate the house style.

TASTING NOTES

2005 *Estate (tasted in 2007):* Medium-deep purplish-ruby; floral and red berry nose, plus barrel-derived smoke; bright, intense, vinous, and grippy on the palate; texture of polished cotton; medium weight.

2005 *Califa (tasted in 2007):* Almost opaque, dark garnet; ripe fruit nose with notes of cabinet shop; very barrel marked on the palate with strong vanilla flavor; spirity; some tartness, some grip, and some bitterness on the finish.

2003 *Califa (tasted in 2007):* Barely transparent, deep black-red; barrel marked on the nose; sweet cherry, blackberry, and vanilla flavors, plus prune, dried currants, pepper, and mocha; noticeable grip from mid-palate to finish; fleshy, almost chewy, and long.

2003 *Morrito (tasted in 2007):* Almost opaque mahogany; aromas of furniture and shoe polish, licorice, and caramel; creamy, rich, and intense on the palate; vanilla and caramel again; bright at mid-palate; grippy and warm on the finish.

2001 *Estate (tasted in* 2004*):* Brilliant, medium rosy-red; toasted hard spice and vanilla on the nose; sweet, spicy, soft, and rich on the palate; cherry fruit and barrel char; very fine-grained tannin and nicely focused.

DOMAINE CARNEROS
Napa, California

    $ $

Domaine Carneros occupies a 138-acre ranch at the corner of Duhig Road and the Carneros Highway. First planted to vines in 1982 by the Allen family of Sequoia Grove Vineyards, with advice from Tony Soter, the property was purchased in 1986 by a joint venture dedicated to Champagne-method sparkling wine, involving Champagne Taittinger and its American importer, Kobrand Corporation. The joint venture adopted the Domaine Carneros name; built an eye-catching if incongruous winery and visitors' center modeled on the Château de la Marquetterie near Epernay, owned by the Taittinger family; and engaged Eileen Crane, a veteran of Domaine Chandon and GLORIA FERRER, as its winemaker and managing director.

Crane has an unusual background: she taught nutrition and received a diploma from the Culinary Institute of America before she turned to viticulture and enology. In 1986, during her term as president of the Carneros wineries and growers trade group (Carneros Quality Alliance), Crane developed an interest in still pinot noir. Six years later, she and assistant winemaker Dan Karlsen, who had spent several years making pinot (among other things) at DEHLINGER

WINERY, made a few barrels of still pinot experimentally. When Claude Taittinger made his annual visit to Carneros immediately after harvest in 1992, he tasted the experiment and "loved it." Some of the wine was sent to Reims for his personal use and for professional entertaining. When he presented it to fellow members of the board of Relais & Châteaux, a hotel and restaurant group, one of the *convives* impertinently inquired "whether fruit extract had been added to the wine." Nevertheless, Kobrand approved the project after the 1993 vintage had also been made and tasted, and Domaine Carneros became the first of the major sparkling wine houses to make a serious commitment to still pinot.

About half of the 60 acres of pinot noir planted on the Duhig Road site are now used for still wine, as is about 30 percent of the 56-acre Pompadour Vineyard on Napa Road. A third vineyard, called La Rocaille—on the southern side of the Carneros Highway between Cuttings Wharf Road and Stanly Road—was purchased in 1994 specifically for still pinot. The Duhig Road site is a roughly triangular parcel bounded by Highway 121, Duhig Road, and Huichica Creek. Pinot is planted there on the steep north- and west-facing slopes, in thin Diablo clay-loam, at elevations between 100 and 150 feet. The original vines were field selections from Carneros Creek, Newlan (just north of Napa on Highway 29), and Smith-Madrone (on Spring Mountain). Some Swan selection was added in 1991, and Dijon clones have been planted more recently. Although some fruit was sold to Etude and other makers before 1992, Domaine Chandon has used all of its estate grown pinot ever since.

Pompadour, Domaine Carneros's second vineyard, is a flat, rectangular, 70-acre parcel, of which 56 acres are planted, which is used primarily for sparkling wine. The block of Pompadour used for still wine is primarily Swan selection. It is at the vineyard's northern end, where the soils are relatively light and loamy. La Rocaille, the third site, was entirely replanted in 1995 and 1996, aside from a small block of old merlot. This gentle, east-facing slope, with the lightest, loamiest soils of the three, was planted with budwood taken from the Swan, Smith-Madrone, and Madonna blocks in the original estate vineyard. Domaine Carneros's heavy reliance on field-selected heritage "clones" is unusual in Los Carneros.

Vineyards are managed organically, and are expected to be certified in 2008. Still pinot was important enough to Domaine Carneros by 2003 that a dedicated pinot-only production facility was built immediately behind the *château*, featuring temperature and humidity-controlled barrel rooms, mechanically-assisted punchdown devices, and a large solar collection system.

WINES AND WINEMAKING NOTES
Every year since 1993, Domaine Carneros has made two still pinots: a regular bottling called Estate and about 1,000 cases of a limited release called The Famous Gate, which is available only at the winery. (In 1992, The Famous Gate was the *only* release.) A third wine, called Avant Garde, made from the fruit of younger vines, was added to the lineup in 1998.

Winemaking generally follows the consensus protocol, although tanks are plunged more often here than elsewhere for relatively "saturated colors and rich flavors." Barrels are about 40 percent new and are a mix of François Frères, Cadus, Billon, Remond, Saury, and Sirugue. The wine spends about eleven months in barrel and is racked once before bottling. Crane sometimes fines for tannin management

and filters routinely. Domaine Carneros pinots are usually cherry centered, barrel marked, and of medium weight.

TASTING NOTES
2005 *Carneros (tasted in 2007):*
Transparent, medium ruby; slightly funky, slightly meaty nose, with some resin and conifer; raspberry and cherry on the palate; slightly fruit-sweet; texture of polished cotton on the mid-palate with a bit of grip on the finish; of medium weight and length.
2004 *The Famous Gate (tasted in 2007):*
Transparent, medium-dark black-red; herbal, savory, and softly fruity nose; rich and spicy on the palate, with black cherry, *charcuterie*, and raw meat; very barrel marked.

DOMAINE DROUHIN OREGON
Dundee, Oregon

Burgundy *négociant* Robert Drouhin has been involved with Oregon pinot noir almost from the outset—albeit unintentionally. Several Drouhin wines were among the pinots bested by THE EYRIE VINEYARDS'S 1975 South Block Reserve when the latter was entered in a Paris tasting organized by *GaultMillau* magazine in 1979. When Drouhin orchestrated a rematch the following year, presumably hoping to redeem the tarnished reputation of fine Burgundies, the Eyrie wine placed second in an all-Drouhin field. Five years later, Drouhin decided that Oregon might be just the place for his daughter, the first member of her family to be university trained in enology, to do an internship.

Various Oregonian friendships ensued. Véronique Drouhin worked the summer and harvest of 1986 at ADELSHEIM, Eyrie, and BETHEL HEIGHTS. David Adelsheim then told Robert Drouhin that some "interesting" property had come on the market just a stone's throw from Eyrie. And so, in 1987, Maison Joseph Drouhin (MJD)—one of Burgundy's most respected houses and proprietor of almost priceless vineyards in Musigny, Clos de Bèze, and Griotte-Chambertin—established Domaine Drouhin Oregon on a south-facing slope in the Dundee Hills. Additional land was purchased in the 1990s, bringing the estate to a total of 225 acres, of which 98 are planted. A state-of-the-art gravity-flow winery, dug partially into the hillside, was constructed in 1989. Apart from Boisset's subsequent purchase of DE LOACH VINEYARDS in the Russian River Valley, Domaine Drouhin Oregon (DDO) remains the only significant Burgundian investment in North American pinot noir.

Although Robert Drouhin visited Oregon as early as 1961 and says he was struck even then by the climatic and geographic similarities to the Côte d'Or, his mature interest in Oregon was, he asserts, "fundamentally intellectual." An Oregon project forced him to rethink his Burgundian orientations. Why, he says he asked himself, do Burgundians plant at high density? Why do they fertilize their vineyards? Why, in this century, do they trellis their vines? And then, if the *vigneron* were unfettered by Burgundy's "history, regulations, and *mentalité*," how should these practices be adapted for Oregon?

As the Oregon vineyard was planned, Robert placed Véronique (now Véronique Drouhin-Boss) in charge. Decisions were made to plant both sparsely (although what here is called sparse is actually 1 meter by 1.8 meters) and densely (at 1 meter by 1.3 meters), to provide a basis for comparison, and to plant some vines on their own roots, in the Oregon style of the day, and others on resistant rootstock—again for comparison. Drouhin imported cellar equipment from Burgundy, along with Oregon's first row-straddling *enjambeur* tractor. Various Oregon pioneer winemakers were already experimenting simultaneously with rootstocks, planting densities, and cellar techniques, so it is not quite accurate to say, as some have reported, that DDO revolutionized either Oregon's viticulture or its winemaking. Nevertheless, the simple fact that Drouhin had chosen to invest in Oregon gave other vintners confidence in the future and attracted many new players to the field.

Although the earliest plantings at DDO were own-rooted UCD 2A and 5, sourced from nurseries, DDO soon developed its own mother block for rootstocks, and converted to using Dijon clones as scion material in 1990. Dijon 115 and 777 account for the majority of the post-1990 plantings.

WINES AND WINEMAKING NOTES
The 1988 and 1989 vintages of DDO were made entirely from purchased fruit, sourced from eight Willamette Valley vineyards, and were exceptionally well received by the wine press. As the estate fruit began to come online in 1990, most of these sources were progressively abandoned. DDO wines have relied largely on estate grapes for most of the last thirteen vintages, although a small amount of fruit purchased from two neighbors, STOLLER and Durant, is still used to supplement estate fruit in the Willamette Valley cuvée.

A reserve wine, called Cuvée Laurène in honor of Drouhin-Boss's first daughter and made each year since 1992, is produced entirely from estate fruit; it is a barrel selection of lots exhibiting particular depth and complexity. In 1999 a third pinot was added to the DDO portfolio: called Cuvée Louise Drouhin to celebrate Drouhin-Boss's youngest daughter, this wine's production is limited to eight barrels and is selected to privilege elegance and silken texture.

ROBERT DROUHIN'S MATURE INTEREST IN OREGON WAS "FUNDAMENTALLY INTELLECTUAL"

The DDO pinots are invariably elegant, medium-weight wines anchored with aromas of red and black berries when they are young. Cuvée Laurène generally shows more structure than the Oregon cuvée. Although Laurène is built with ageworthiness in mind, both wines appear to age handsomely for at least a decade. My most rewarding personal experiences with these wines have been associated with wines eight or more years old.

At DDO the default protocol is to destem the fruit completely, but small percentages of whole-cluster fruit are sometimes used. Equipped with fermentors of various sizes, the winery is designed to accommodate lots ranging from as little as 500 gallons to as much as 3,500 gallons. The smaller fermentors are jacketed stainless steel open-tops; the largest are custom-designed, horizontal tanks equipped with rotary blades. Apart from a few experimental lots, fermentations rely on resident yeast and are not preceded by a cold soak unless the grapes have arrived warm at the winery. Total vatting time ranges from twelve to twenty-one days, of which the alcoholic fermentation takes from four to ten, with temperatures peaking just over 90°F. In this protocol, postfermentation macerations can last as long as ten days, depending on the vintage. About 90 percent of barrels come from the in-house stocks of MJD in Beaune, which are bought as unmilled wood and are custom coopered for Drouhin by François Frères. Ten percent come from other sources, including, at the moment, a few Hungarian oak barrels for experimental purposes. In the late 1980s Drouhin-Boss used up to 40 percent new wood, but she has now backed off to about 18 percent.

Pinots spend eleven to twelve months in barrel, during which time they are racked once, and then once more to tank before bottling. In some vintages as many as half of the lots may be fined; in other vintages fining is avoided altogether. A light filtration with diatomaceous earth precedes bottling. The Oregon cuvée (see below) is held nine months before release; Cuvée Laurène gets a hefty twenty-one months of bottle aging. Although Drouhin-Boss lives in Beaune and has now assumed "corporate style and memory" responsibilities for MJD, she spends significant time in Oregon, and controls all major decisions involving the DDO wines. Véronique Drouhin-Boss is also the main architect of a related wine called Cloudline. This is a separate brand owned by Dreyfus, Ashby, and Company, which is controlled by Maison Joseph Drouhin. A small amount of DDO fruit is used in Cloudline, but the wine is not made at DDO.

TASTING NOTES

2005 *Willamette Valley (tasted in 2007):* Medium garnet; earth, black raspberry, and some smoke on the nose; pretty and slightly sweet on the palate; turns from fruit to mild, brewed tea with a hint of orange peel after mid-palate; bright, vibrant, high-toned, elegant, and attractive.

2004 *Willamette Valley (tasted in 2007):* Bright, medium garnet; slightly herbal nose; exotic boysenberry with very savory highlights; then, mineral on the mid-palate; almost silky, chamois-like, and lingering; a bit of grip at the end; quite unlike the 2005, but distinctive.

2004 *Cuvée Laurène (tasted in 2007):* Transparent, medium black-red; cherry, sandalwood, and some wet earth on the nose; explosion of intense red fruit on the palate, plus some spice and minerality; nice balance of elegance and concentration; long.

2004 *Cuvée Louise Drouhin (tasted in 2007):* Very transparent, light-to-medium garnet; lovely, expressive nose featuring soft spices and potpourri; extremely elegant and almost gossamer on the palate, with a silky texture and slight barrel-derived smokiness; almost evokes village-quality wines from Chambolle; of medium length and very pretty.

2003 *Cuvée Laurène (tasted in 2007):* Barely transparent, medium-dark black-red with violet highlights; smoky, ripe, dark fruit aromas; ripe black cherry and boysenberry on the palate; slightly sweet, peppery, and smoky; denser and grippier than most editions of Laurène, with properties of strong black tea and a tight finish.

2002 *Cuvée Laurène (tasted in 2007):* Medium-deep garnet; juniper berry, pepper, mocha, and cigar box aromas; very complex overlays of fading fruit with nutmeg, dried tangerine peel, and thyme; some of the remaining fruit has high-toned properties suggestive of persimmon or cranberry; almost creamy on the mid-palate; intense, long, mouth coating, and fine.

DOMAINE SERENE
Dayton, Oregon

In the survey of restaurants, retailers, and reviewers used to select producers for coverage in these pages, Domaine Serene was the most visible American pinot brand of all. It was more visible than quite a few small-production icons and was present on a few more lists than even its most-visible competitors—neighboring DOMAINE DROUHIN OREGON, and TALLEY VINEYARDS and AU BON CLIMAT in California—all three of which have longer histories. This will not surprise consumers who saw the full-page, full-color advertising in which Domaine Serene recently invested, but the advertising followed the visibility, not vice versa.

This enormously successful brand debuted in 1990 when the wines were made by Ken Wright on the premises of Wright's other brand, PANTHER CREEK CELLARS. Few producers have transitioned more elegantly, however, from obscure boutique to hilltop benchmark, and from a program based entirely on purchased fruit to one based almost entirely on estate production, with astonishing vintage-to-vintage consistency, in just a decade and a half. Some of the credit surely belongs to Wright, whose fruit sourcing and winemaking established the brand's initial and fine reputation; but Tony Rynders, the University of California Davis graduate with prior experience at Mirassou, ARGYLE WINERY, and Washington's Hogue Cellars, who has been the winemaker since 1998, has been key. In addition, Domaine Serene's founders' dedication to excellence, and their determination to invest both generously and sensibly in pursuit thereof, has been critical. Ken and Grace Evenstad are a Minnesota couple who had the good fortune to bring pharmaceutical wealth to their passion for Burgundian grape varieties. Grapes for the early vintages of Domaine Serene came, inter alia, from the Carter, Canary Hill, and Freedom Hill vineyards, along with Beaux Frères, Knudsen, and Kircher. This last vineyard was eventually purchased by the Evenstads, and became part of the brand's transition to reliance on estate grown fruit (see below).

In 1990 the Evenstads made their first of several purchases of Dundee Hills property: a 42-acre west-facing parcel on the southernmost of the three Dundee hills. The first estate vineyard, called Mark Bradford, was planted there in 1993, with just over 11 acres of UCD 4 and 2A, spaced 8 feet by 4 feet, high on the slope, between 640 and 760 feet. Nine acres of nearby east-facing slope, named in honor of Grace Evenstad and a tad lower than Mark Bradford, were planted to Dijon 667 and 777 in 1994; these were followed by six acres of Dijon 667 and 777, as well as UCD 4, called Gold Eagle, in 1997, and 4.4 acres of Dijon 667 and 777, called Fleur de Lis, in 1998. Meanwhile, a third land acquisition, in 1997, brought the former Kircher vineyard, upslope from the service road that leads to the aforementioned plantings, into the estate. This parcel—some 13 acres of own-rooted UCD 2A and 4, renamed Côte Sud to describe its orientation—was the site for additional planting from 1999 through 2001 (again Dijon 667 and UCD 4). Spacing throughout has respected the 8-foot by 4-foot beginnings, for which the target yield is 2 tons per acre; but the average as of this writing is just 1.68. Soils throughout are Jory series: weathered, crumbly, reddish basalt. Collectively, these parcels are known as Evenstad Estate. One mile north, on a sister slope, 20 additional acres facing south and west have been planted to Dijon clones. This parcel, called Winery Hill, is also the site for Domaine Serene's new five-level, gravity-flow winery, which was completed in time for the 2001 harvest. The Evenstads also purchased 90 acres on Jerusalem Hill, on the east side of the Eola Hills, of which 55 acres have been planted to pinot noir. Together, the three sites bring Domaine Serene's holdings of planted pinot to an impressive 100-plus acres. All the estate vineyards are dry farmed.

WINES AND WINEMAKING NOTES
Domaine Serene's flagship wine is the Evenstad Reserve. This cuvée is blended first, from the first choice among all available lots, selecting for size, concentration, complexity, and finesse. Generally, these lots tend to have been raised in new barrels, so the overall percentage of new wood in the Evenstad Reserve hovers around 90 percent, and the wine is always bottled with slightly more than twelve months of barrel contact, after the following harvest. From the outset, a second wine has been built from most of the lots not selected for Evenstad Reserve. Until 1998, this second wine was (rather confusingly) also called Reserve, without a modifier, but since 1999, it has been more helpfully known as Yamhill Cuvée. Rynders has created a sharp stylistic distinction between the two wines, bottling the second wine earlier and featuring lots with forward-fruit character. Along with these two blends, there is a "super-high-end" estate cuvée called Monogram, made since 2002, and a variable assortment of single-vineyard wines. A partial list of these includes vineyard-designated wines from the Mark Bradford Vineyard in 1996, 1998, 1999, 2003, and 2004; from Grace Vineyard in 1998, 1999,

2003, and 2004; from Jerusalem Hill in 2002, 2003, and 2004; and from Winery Hill in 2003. Fleur de Lis, Cote Sud, and Gold Eagle have also been made as single-vineyard wines in occasional vintages. The policy is to make vineyard-designates only in very small quantities, only in superior vintages, and only when lots can be spared from the Evenstad Reserve cuvée without any adverse impact on its quality. In 2004, a tiny quantity of white pinot noir, called

---

VERY POLISHED, FINELY STRUCTURED, HANDSOME WINES WITH AN EXCELLENT REPUTATION

Coeur Blanc, was also made by whole-cluster pressing a bit of estate fruit, and then barrel raising it for fourteen months.

Rynders is a believer in rigorous fruit thinning during the growing season. Domaine Serene practices two or three thinnings during the season—one early pass in July to reduce the crop in the heaviest vineyards, and one or two green thinnings before veraison. Rigorous sorting is also done on the crushpad. There, Rynders removes any leaves and second-crop clusters that have been picked with the fruit, as well as clusters that have been affected by rot. He likes a large percentage of whole berries "to moderate tannins," but uses very few whole clusters. His fermentors are 1.25-ton stainless steel open-tops. Following a long cold soak, the tanks are warmed to between 65 and 70°F and inoculated, although some lots are fermented with resident yeast. A custom-built pneumatic device facilitates twice-daily punchdowns. With fermentation temperatures generally peaking in the high 80s or low 90s, the must is usually

dry six to twelve days after the cold soak began. If Rynders detects rough tannins in any lot, he will press before the must is completely dry and allow the fermentation to finish in wood. The free-run and light-press juices are kept separate, but some of the press fraction is used in the Yamhill Cuvée.

In the interest of complexity, barrels from about a dozen coopers are used. Although Rynders employs 75 percent new barrels each year, he does not like oaky flavors, eschews heavy toast and toasted heads, and prewashes new barrels with hot water. Once the wine is in barrel, Rynders finds that a "very antioxidative environment," with little or no racking and with sulfur dioxide as needed, results in better wood integration. Domaine Serene wines are neither fined nor filtered. Barrel time ranges from about eleven to sixteen months, depending on vintage and wine type. Rynders insists that there is "no recipe," and that "the wines let us know when they are ready." Domaine Serene pinots are very polished, finely structured, handsome wines. Relatively long barrel times (except for in the case of the Yamhill Cuvée) and long bottle aging before release reinforce an impression of refinement; they also ensure that these wines are very barrel marked.

TASTING NOTES

2004 *Yamhill Cuvée (tasted in* 2007*):* Transparent, medium garnet; vanilla, smoke, and red fruit on the nose; on the palate, bright, flower-infused red and black fruit in a spicy-peppery wrapper; hints of orange peel, clove, and black raspberry; smooth attack and some grip; peppery flavors dominate the finish.

2004 *Winery Hill Vineyard (tasted in* 2007*):* Deep, black-red; aromas of potpourri and smoke; intense on the palate with tangerine, camphorwood, and tobacco; mouth coating at mid-palate and slightly grippy from mid-palate to finish; almost chewy and briary.

2004 *Evenstad Reserve (tasted in* 2007*):* Deep black-red; gum camphor, sandalwood, and ripe cherry on the nose; cherry liqueur, orange flower water, and smoky chocolate on the palate; very mouth coating and seamless; grippy from mid-palate to finish; substantial and impressive.

2004 *Mark Bradford Vineyard (tasted in* 2007*):* Dark black-red, saturated to the rim; intense, almost explosive barrel-marked aromatics including cedar, cigar box, and allspice; cherry, cola, mocha, and vanilla on the palate; expressive and impressive.

2002 *Evenstad Reserve (tasted in* 2006*):* Transparent, medium rosy-garnet; black cherry and flowers with notes of moss and earth on the nose; a slightly sweet, cherry- and raspberry-centered wine with forward flavors, barrel char, and resin; some grip, heat, and black pepper; serious, nicely structured, medium-long, and still young at age 4.

2000 *Evenstad Reserve (tasted in* 2007*):* Transparent, medium ruby; complex nose of vanilla, barrel char, nutmeg, wintergreen, and menthol; blueberry, blackberry, black licorice, pepper, and coffee on the palate; rich and almost creamy attack; then *eau-de-vie* intense; powerful and elegant in a heavy-velvet sort of way; a tour de force.

DUMOL WINE COMPANY

Orinda, California

P-O

🍷 🍶 ◆ $$$

DuMol began modestly in 1996 when Max Gasiewicz, a Davis-trained winemaker who worked in the 1980s

with Tonnellerie Radoux and in the 1990s for DE LOACH VINEYARDS, negotiated 5 tons of grapes from Warren Dutton's Widdoes and Jewell vineyards for a personal wine project named for his children, Duncan and Molly. The passive investors in this venture were an East Bay businessman, Kerry Murphy, who had "retired" after selling "several companies," and a Walnut Creek restaurateur, Michael Verlander. When Gasiewicz passed away unexpectedly after making just two vintages of DuMol—six barrels each of pinot noir and chardonnay in 1996 and fourteen barrels of pinot only in 1997—Murphy and Verlander reinvented themselves as managing partners. Merry Edwards pitched in on short notice to make the 1998 vintage; Paul Hobbs then signed on as DuMol's primary consultant. Murphy and Verlander, with Hobbs's advice, began to secure and expand the brand's vineyard sources. Andy Smith, a Scot who had once worked in an Edinburgh wine shop and had subsequently studied enology at Lincoln University in New Zealand, made the 1999 vintage under Hobbs's direction, but then joined DuMol full time in 2000 as the brand's main winemaker.

As far as pinot is concerned, since 1998, DuMol's focus has been on Green Valley vineyards and on blended wines, although all of these but one contain fruit from the 14 acres of dry-farmed pinot at Widdoes. Blends are an article of faith with Murphy, who claims that single-vineyard pinots can be "one dimensional" and argues that he wants DuMol focused instead on "repeatable expressions of a wine." Through 2000 the only DuMol pinot was a Russian River Valley blend. In 2001 this cuvée was joined by a second called Finn, which is a blend of Widdoes grapes with fruit from a "mangled clonal trial" on Occidental Road, where Dutton had planted 2 acres to a combination of Swan and Beringer selections, plus budwood from Mondavi's Carneros vineyards, Cambria, and elsewhere. In 2002 it was joined by a third called Ryan, which featured Widdoes fruit combined with UCD 4 clone from Jewell. In 2004, with fruit available from two vineyards on the west side of Green Valley called Wildrose and Sundawg, DuMol inaugurated a fourth blend based on those sources, called Aiden. Meanwhile, a 17-acre estate vineyard was planted in 2004 on three contiguous Occidental Road parcels, using low-vigor rootstocks and tight vine spacing, from which the first fruit was harvested in 2007. The scion material reflects an unusual concentration of old California selections, including Calera and Swan, plus several undocumented imports, and 1 acre said to be CTPS 943. The percentage composition of each pinot varies from vintage to vintage.

WINEMAKING NOTES

Winemaking relies on a bit of whole-cluster fruit and as much whole berry as can be managed—Smith thinks whole-berry fermentations promote "soaring aromatics"—and on a five-to-seven day cold soak, a combination of punchdowns and pumpovers, mostly resident yeast, a few days of postfermentation maceration, and a barrel stock that is composed almost entirely of tight-grained, low-toast offerings from Remond and Ermitage. About 40 percent new barrels are used to raise the Russian River Valley cuvée; at the other end of the spectrum, Finn, the biggest wine, sees 75 percent new wood. The first racking is done, and the blends are made after the wines have been in barrel for nine months; the newly blended wines are then returned to barrel for

another five months, and they are not released until they have accumulated six to twelve months of bottle age. There is no fining or filtration. The wines are simultaneously sweet, solid, and serious, with plush, finely crafted textures that have made them favorites of consumers, critics, and sommeliers.

TASTING NOTES

2002 *Ryan (tasted in* 2005*):* Transparent, rosy-magenta; sweet red fruit and potpourri aromatics; sweet also on the palate, with cherry, raspberry, and a hint of mocha; finishes soft and medium-long with the texture of drape velvet.

2001 *Finn (tasted in* 2005*):* Transparent, medium garnet; tar, black fruit, and ripe figs on the nose; sweet and sober on the palate, with black licorice and Tellicherry pepper; finishes long with just a hint of grip and with considerable slate-y minerality.

DUNAH VINEYARD AND WINERY
Sebastopol, California

After Rick and Diane DuNah sold their electronic components manufacturing company (the main products were backlit liquid crystal displays) in 1992, they purchased 44 acres of apple orchard and horse pasture on a stunning hilltop southwest of Sebastopol. Although still active in the company they had sold, they contemplated retirement. With advice from Ted Lemon (see LITTORAI WINES) and John Ferrington (whose family had sold grapes from a respected Anderson Valley vineyard to WILLIAMS SELYEM for many years), they considered growing grapes, even though they had had no previous experience.

In 1996 both DuNahs enrolled in viticulture classes at Santa Rosa Junior College, and "made friends." They made the right friends, as it turned out. In 1998 the DuNahs planted 7 acres of the orchard and pasture to pinot noir, and 1 acre to chardonnay. The slopes, which wrap around the knoll facing west, south, and east, are steep. The scion material for the pinot is a combination of UCD 4, Dijon 115, and Dijon 667 on 101-14, 110R and (mostly) 5C rootstock, laid out in 8-foot rows with 4 feet between vines, field grafted and cane pruned. Pinot yields vary between 2.5 and 3.0 tons per acre. Until 2003 the fruit was sold entirely to FLOWERS VINEYARDS AND WINERY, where it was used in Flowers's Sonoma Coast cuvée. In 2003 the DuNahs kept half the crop for their own wine (see below); in 2004 Flowers bowed out, and the unretained half of the crop was sold in equal shares to David Vergari (Vergari Wines) and to Peters Family Wines. The DuNahs' winemaker from the outset has been Greg La Follette (see TANDEM WINERY).

When it was first planted, the DuNahs vineyard was entitled only to the Sonoma Coast appellation, but changes to the southern boundary of the Russian River Valley AVA in 2005 gave DuNah the right to either appellation. The DuNahs personally manage both the vineyard and the brand.

WINES AND WINEMAKING NOTES
The inaugural vintage for DuNah wines was 2001: a vineyard-designated wine from the Sangiacomo family's Roberts Road Vineyard on the west side of Sonoma Mountain in the Sonoma

Coast appellation. In 2002 there were two DuNah pinots: a second vintage of Sangiacomo, and a unique vintage of Keefer Ranch. 2003 saw the first release of DuNah's estate pinot, and a continuation of the Sangiacomo, both of which have been made in each vintage since. In 2005 the DuNahs reclaimed all of their estate pinot for their own label, doubling production to about 550 cases.

VISUALLY ATTRACTIVE, INTENSELY AROMATIC, ELEGANT WINES WITH SPICY-PEPPERY HIGHLIGHTS

The winemaking for DuNah pinots follows the La Follette protocol in general terms— basket pressing, resident yeasts for both primary and secondary fermentations, and bottling without fining or filtration— but La Follette explains that the DuNah style was developed to accentuate fruit while de-emphasizing the wild and feral qualities that are often showcased in Tandem wines. The DuNah estate pinot is picked with a much lower sugar accumulation than most Russian River or Sonoma Coast wines—typically between 22 and 24 Brix—creating an exceptionally bright product, while Sangiacomo fruit destined for the DuNah bottling is picked riper than the same fruit for Tandem to create a fleshier, more layered texture and to minimize "wild" aromas.

Cooperage used for DuNah pinots is predominantly Remond, which typically highlights refinement and elegance, of which 40 percent is new for the estate wine, and 20 to 25 percent is new for the Sangiacomo. The estate wine spends two to four months longer in barrel than the Sangiacomo. DuNah pinots are not racked before blending, unless racking is needed to correct a barrel-specific problem. The result is very attractive, intensely aromatic, medium-weight wines.

TASTING NOTES

2005 *Sonoma Coast Estate (tasted in* 2007*):* Brilliant, deep magenta; black licorice and plummy fruit, with floral highlights and a hint of cardamom; simultaneously bright and rich on the palate, with spicy-peppery notes and furniture polish; elegant, intense, long, and slightly warm; fine.

2002 *Keefer Ranch (tasted in* 2005*):* Medium, rosy-garnet, and not entirely limpid; aromas of potpourri, red fruits, and peppery spice; raspberry-strawberry flavors with some wet earth; good structure, and hints of orange peel and minerality on the finish; nice grip behind a generally silky texture.

DUSKY GOOSE
Dundee, Oregon

In 1974 John Bauer began planting vineyard on a perfectly-sited, south-facing slope in the Dundee Hills, straddling the 500-foot contour, on the south side of Worden Hill Road. In the fashion of the day, he set out a bit of cabernet sauvignon, riesling, gamay, and chardonnay, and a bit more pinot noir than anything else. He named the vineyard for the Dundee Hills and sold grapes to an illustrious list of local producers, including ADELSHEIM VINEYARD and REX HILL WINERY. Twenty-eight years after the

first vines were set out, Bauer sold the 17-acre parcel to Neil Goldschmidt, the former mayor of Portland, governor of Oregon, and secretary of commerce in the Carter administration. Goldschmidt engaged David Adelsheim to provide redevelopment advice. The underperforming varieties were replaced between 1999 and 2001, resulting in an all-pinot vineyard about evenly divided between heritage selections (UCD 2A and 5, and Coury) and Dijon clones (mostly 115, plus some 667 and 777.) Unusually, three of fifteen blocks were dedicated to Coury.

In 2002 Goldschmidt launched a partnership with his friend John Carter (a third-generation Oregonian, lawyer, consultant, and executive with Bechtel Corporation), dubbed Dusky Goose, to produce and market estate wines from the Dundee Hills Vineyard—which he had renamed eponymously in 1998. Lynn Penner-Ash (see PENNER-ASH WINES) was selected as the winemaker, owing largely to her experience with the vineyard during her years at Rex Hill, and the first vintage was made in 2003. This was barely in bottle, however, before Goldschmidt sold his interest in the partnership to Carter, making Carter and his wife, Linda Levy Carter, sole owners of the new brand. At about the same time, the Carters bought a second vineyard about half a mile southeast of Goldschmidt's, which they renamed Rambouillet. Rambouillet consists of almost 4 acres of UCD 5 in two blocks, 1.6 acres of an undocumented upright selection, and almost 2 acres of Dijon 777, which was planted after the purchase. Goldschmidt, meanwhile, continued his exodus from the Oregon wine business, selling his vineyard to Bostonians and ex-Fidelity Investments advisers Donna Morris and Bill Sweat in 2006. Morris and Sweat had created Winderlea Wine Company the year before, as a point of entry into the Oregon pinot business. When they acquired the Goldschmidt Vineyard, they also gave it the Winderlea name.

WINES AND WINEMAKING NOTES

The first vintages of Dusky Goose, made in 2003 and 2004, were based entirely on Goldschmidt Vineyard fruit. The 2005 was a blend of lots from Goldschmidt and Rambouillet. In 2006 there were two Dusky Goose pinots: about 200 cases of a vineyard-designated wine from Rambouillet and 1,100 cases of a Dundee Hills wine sourced from both Rambouillet and Goldschmidt. Beginning in 2007, the Dundee Hills wine was even more widely sourced. Because both Goldschmidt and Rambouillet are very early ripening sites, and the first pinot in the cellar at Penner-Ash, where the wines are made, the Dusky Goose fermentations tend to rely on inocula rather than on resident yeast. Lynn Penner-Ash also cold-soaks the fruit for Dusky Goose wines for less time than she gives to most lots of her own label; uses a higher percentage of new oak during élevage, to compensate for very ripe fruit that gives up color and flavor easily; and tends to make wine with a very bold, fruit-driven profile.

TASTING NOTE

2005 *Dundee Hills (tasted in 2007):* Transparent, medium-deep rosy-magenta; interesting nose of nutshells, spring flowers, and hard spice; intense, ripe cherry-raspberry in the mouth suggestive of cherry liqueur, plus infused flowers and a hint of pepper; very clean and fruit driven with the texture of polished cotton; considerable length and a slightly warm finish.

DUTTON-GOLDFIELD WINES

 Graton, California

Dutton-Goldfield is a fortuitous partnership between veteran winemaker Dan Goldfield and Steve Dutton, whose much-respected family owns and farms more than five dozen of the best vineyard parcels in western Sonoma County. Goldfield is a Philadelphian originally; his brother is said to have introduced him to pinot noir through a tasting of 1969 Burgundies. Trained first at Brandeis in chemistry and philosophy, and then at the University of California Davis, in enology, Goldfield worked at ROBERT MONDAVI, Schramsberg, and LA CREMA, then a small Petaluma-based chardonnay and pinot house. When La Crema was acquired by Kendall-Jackson in 1994, Goldfield went with the deal—"the toy in the crackerjack box," he says—and subsequently became the founding winemaker for the Jackson family's nearby Hartford Court venture.

Dutton-Goldfield debuted with the 1998 vintage—300 cases each of pinot and chardonnay. The pinot, labeled as Dutton Ranch–Russian River Valley was based on fruit from two Dutton vineyards: Widdoes Ranch on Sullivan Road and the Jewel Ranch north of Graton, and has varied in composition since that time. In recent vintages, its anchor has been the Maurice Galante Vineyard, a mid-1990s planting of Dijon clones and UCD 4 on Cherry Ridge Road in Green Valley, which has sometimes also been made as a vineyard-designate. Dutton-Goldfield's first vineyard-designated pinot joined the portfolio in 1999, made from the Freestone Hill Vineyard, an extremely cool site that the Duttons farm for Jack Cleary, overlooking the hamlet of Freestone. Freestone Hill is an 8-acre, south-facing slope, planted 8 feet by 5 feet in north–south rows to UCD 2A and Dijon clones 114, 115, 667, and 777.

Vineyard-designated Galante entered the lineup in 2000, along with a single-vineyard wine from Devil's Gulch Vineyard near Nicasio in Marin County. The latter is not a Dutton vineyard, but Goldfield had experience with its fruit during his days at La Crema and Hartford Court. Owned and farmed by Mark Pasternak, Devil's Gulch pinot had been used in some years for champagne-method sparkling wines made by Schramsberg and for still pinots made by Kalin Cellars. Dutton-Goldfield receives fruit only from a new block, planted in 1998 on a very steep, terraced hillside, with 5 feet between vines and two rows on each terrace. The block is 11 acres, planted entirely to Dijon 114, 115, 667, and 777, and its yield is small to derisory. A fourth vineyard-designated wine debuted in 2001, from the McDougall Vineyard in a remote corner of the Sonoma Coast appellation, where Seaview and Tin Barn Roads intersect, north of David Hirsch's vineyard and just inland from Camp Meeting Ridge. McDougall consists of two blocks of vines on a south-facing ridge that Warren Dutton planted in 1998 to Dijon 114 and 115. A fifth, and so far latest, vineyard-designated pinot comes from the Sanchietti Vineyard, a Dutton-farmed, 6-acre site west-northwest of Sebastopol that is also sourced by HARTFORD FAMILY WINES. This debuted in 2002.

The 1998 vintage was made at Windsor Oaks while Goldfield was still finishing his obligations at La Crema and Hartford Court. In 1999 the partners leased space sufficient for 10,000 cases at Martini & Prati, but moved to Balletto Winery after Martini & Prati was sold. Goldfield spends most of his time now on Dutton-Goldfield wines, but is also the winemaker for OROGENY.

A FORTUITOUS PARTNERSHIP OF WESTERN SONOMA'S PREMIER WINEGROWER AND ONE OF CALIFORNIA PINOT'S BEST VETERAN MAKERS

WINEMAKING NOTES

Goldfield picks pinot when the skins taste "soft rather than bitter," which can be anywhere between 23 and 25 Brix. He has experimented with enzymes, but has found that, in general, they increase the "harshness" of cool-climate pinot. He uses whole berries but no stems, enforces a prefermentation cold soak for five to six days with dry ice "to get skin extract without the bitterness that comes from the seed tannins," punches down during both cold soak and alcoholic fermentation, and seeks to achieve peak fermentation temperatures of between 85 and 90°F. Some fermentors are inoculated with an assortment of cultured yeasts, including a syrah yeast that Goldfield likes; others are left to bubble on their own. The 1998 vintage was made in fruit bins; beginning in 1999, the bins were replaced with temperature-controlled, 5-ton stainless steel fermentors. Unlike many makers, Goldfield holds the completely fermented must for four to seven days of postfermentation maceration, arguing that this step creates "more delicacy and spiciness." Inoculation to kick-start the malolactic fermentation is sometimes done, but this is normally not necessary. About one third of the press juice is sold off; the balance is blended with the free-run juice.

About 40 percent of the barrel stock is new each year, with Seguin Moreau, François Frères, Taransaud, and Remond now the favored coopers. Goldfield says he chooses barrels for "nuttiness and spice" rather than for "smokiness or meatiness," and is especially partial to new barrels that have been used just briefly for a chardonnay fermentation before being rededicated, in the same vintage, to pinot noir. This trick is possible only in a very cold mesoclimate; otherwise, pinot ripens before chardonnay. From this point, the wine is little disturbed until bottling, which occurs before the following harvest in the case of the Dutton Ranch cuvée, and in the second spring after the vintage for the single vineyard wines. Deselected lots are culled. There is generally no fining or filtration. The Dutton Ranch cuvée is crafted to emphasize red fruit flavors and to be drinkable at release. The vineyard-designates tend to be denser wines, but Devils Gulch is unfailingly elegant, and the McDougall Vineyard wine as fine as anything from the True Sonoma Coast.

TASTING NOTES

2005 *McDougall Vineyard (tasted in 2007):* Transparent, medium black-red; nutty nose with abundant, ripe red berry fruits; with a mineral-marked mid-palate that is round and silky overall; chalky tannins, however; black pepper; a serious, structured wine that lingers on the finish; attractive.

2005 *Freestone Hill Vineyard (tasted in 2007):* Very transparent, medium-dark garnet; vanilla, cranberry, and violets on the nose; ripe red cherry; black pepper and savory properties suggestive of bay laurel on the palate; bright and linear; finishes long with a hint of grip and warmth; attractive.

2005 *Dutton Ranch (tasted in 2007):* Transparent, medium ruby; strawberry and cherry, with hints of black pepper and orange peel on the nose; dry and structured on the palate; dusty fruit with substantial barrel char and minerality; some grip and grit, but round enough to give the impression of silk; nicely made, high toned, and medium-long.

2004 *Marin County Devil's Gulch Vineyard (tasted in 2007):* Rich, medium-dark blackish red; evergreen and spicy berries on the nose; elegant and firm on the palate with rich flavors of plum, spice, and mocha; layered spice and fruit; simultaneously bright, lively, and exotic; very rewarding.

2004 *McDougall Vineyard (tasted in 2007):* Transparent, rosy-crimson; aromas of earth, wet clay, dark fruit, and mocha; full-bodied and almost creamy; black cherry, graphite, and caramel; serious, long, and fine.

EDNA VALLEY VINEYARD
San Luis Obispo, California

In 1979, a marriage of convenience between Jack Niven (see BAILEYANA WINES) and Philip Woodward (see CHALONE VINEYARD) created a partnership called Edna Valley Vineyard. It happened as follows. In 1972 and 1973, Niven had planted Edna Valley's first large commercial vineyard, called Paragon. In 1973 and 1974, Woodward had built a new, larger "modern" winery at Chalone to replace the repurposed chicken coop that had served there since 1965. In 1976 and 1977, just as cash was needed to pay for the new winery at Chalone, Mother Nature inflicted a monster drought on the Central Coast, which reduced Chalone's crop to a bare trickle of wine. Woodward and his partners reacted by searching for grapes that could be vinified at Chalone but made into wines sold under private labels. The best known of these deals was a batch of 1977 chardonnay made from grapes grown at Paragon that was private-labeled for Mike Grgich at Napa Valley's Chateau Montelena. Less visible, according to Niven's grandson, was a "trial lot" of pinot noir from the same vintage, also made with grapes from Paragon, that became the prototype for Edna Valley Vineyard. In 1979 Chalone Vineyard and Paragon Vineyard established the Edna Valley Vineyard partnership based on the trial lot's success, designed to produce a significant volume of "lower-priced wine [made] in the same style as Chalone" in a facility built on the Paragon site. The win-win, according to the partners, was a wine in the Chalone style from an appellation—albeit not yet officially sanctioned—that "had an identity of its own." While the facility at Paragon was still under construction, inaugural vintages were made at Corbett Canyon in 1979 and 1980. By the early 1980s, however, the new label was well launched, making about 25,000 cases of chardonnay and a dribble of pinot noir, all from Paragon grapes.

Over the next quarter century, Edna Valley Vineyard grew to an annual production of more than 80,000 cases; established an enviable reputation for good chardonnay; became a "center of learning" about winemaking on the Central Coast; and attracted a string of very talented winemakers, including Stephen Dooley (see STEPHEN ROSS WINES) and Eric Laumann, now at the Monterey Wine Company. Laumann's successor and Edna Valley's current winemaker is Harry Hansen, who trained at the University of California Davis, and who previously served as associate winemaker at GLORIA FERRER CHAMPAGNE CAVES.

The Edna Valley Vineyard program consumes about two thirds of the Paragon Vineyard's total production, and of Paragon's 1,225 acres, some of which was planted in 2007 and is not yet bearing. About 225 acres are devoted to pinot noir. The balance of the Paragon crop is sold to other makers. Before the Nivens' Firepeak Vineyard, located a few miles away, came into full production, Paragon Vineyard pinot noir was used in the family's Baileyana brand. In 2005, when the Chalone Wine Group was sold to Diageo Chateau & Estate Wines, Edna Valley Vineyard became a partnership between Diageo and the Paragon Vineyard Company, still owned by the Niven family.

WINES AND WINEMAKING NOTES

A single bottling of pinot noir under the Edna Valley Vineyard label, and designated as Paragon Vineyard wine, has been made in every vintage since 1980. There was also a reserve bottling in some vintages during the 1980s, and the reserve program has been revived since 2005.

Completely destemmed fruit is first cold soaked for two days and then inoculated in large-format, open-top fermentors, where the cap is irrigated with pumpovers and a once-daily rack-and-return. Malolactic starter is introduced after the new wine is barreled. When the malolactic fermentation is complete, the wine is racked barrel-to-barrel to remove heavy lees; it is then filtered and bottled after nine months in 10 percent new oak. Most of the barrel stock is from French forests, but a small percentage of Hungarian cooperage is also used. This results in attractive, medium-weight wines, offered at exceedingly reasonable prices.

2006 Paragon (tasted in 2007): Light-to-medium ruby; very open, floral, red berry nose; bright, peppery, red-fruit dominated palate; primarily cherry and Santa Rosa plum; lightly tart and chewy at mid-palate; plum skin; a very nicely made, medium length, attractive pinot noir.

EL MOLINO WINERY
St. Helena, California

Reginald Oliver's childhood scoutmaster was George Cooper, a NASA test pilot who eventually founded Cooper-Garrod Estate vineyards near Saratoga, California. Under Cooper's influence, Oliver purchased a wine press while he was still a teenager.

Twenty-six years later, following a Wall Street career that gave him "time to think and read about wine, and the financial resources to afford La Tâche and other Burgundies," he restored a tiny, nineteenth-century house and winery that had belonged to his aunt, 3 miles north of St. Helena. The venerable El Molino Winery was then repurposed to accomplish what nearly everyone else in mid- and upper-valley Napa had forsaken a decade earlier: making good pinot noir. Good chardonnay, to be fair, was also pursued— a variety which is a bit less "counter-culture" around St. Helena than pinot, but which is still far from mainstream in a valley where cabernet is king. For two decades, the pinots have been absolutely good enough to have made Oliver's point: sites warmer than the coast and the coastal valleys work fine for pinot as long as the nights stay cool. "The only reason pinot noir has disappeared from mid-valley Napa," Oliver told me in 2001, "is economics. You cannot use expensive land

---

EL MOLINO: A VERTICAL TASTING

2004 (tasted in 2007): Transparent, medium black-red; slightly earthy; slightly savory nose with licorice and citrus peel; pretty, flower-infused attack with lots of bright, serious fruit, pepper, toasty brown spice, and resin; satiny at mid-palate and grippy at the end; long, elegant, and fine.

2003 (tasted in 2007): Medium-dark black-red; earth and dark licorice aromas, but a bit shy; rich, round, and ripe on the palate, with hints of lavender and blackberry; sturdily structured, warm, and grippy, but still elegant, long, and attractive.

2002 (tasted in 2007): Medium-dark black-red; aromas of earth and mushroom; dark fruits and cabinet shop; very concentrated pure cherry flavors on the palate; sweet and rich with hints of mocha, cola, and toasted cinnamon; uncommonly rich for El Molino.

2001 (tasted in 2007): Similar in color; intense and barrel-driven aromas with coal tar and dark fruit; ripe, sweet fruit on the palate, with black licorice and orange peel; mouth coating with noticeable grip; finishes long and warm.

2000 (tasted in 2007): Mahogany with a pinkish rim; expressive of potpourri and leather; a bright wine with citrus and flower infusions; clove-y spice with a hint of tar; then rich with mocha tones at mid-palate; satiny at the end with a bit of grip; long and fine.

1999 (tasted in 2007): Medium garnet core, but slightly pinkish and tiling at the rim; smoky nose with some dense, dark fruit and just a hint of rose petal; rich and flower-infused with some bitter chocolate on the palate; satiny on the mid-palate and slightly grippy at the end.

for a variety that yields only 3 tons per acre." Sadly, Oliver died at his home in St. Helena on June 24, 2005, at the age of sixty-six, but El Molino continues in the hands of his daughter, Lily, and son-in-law, Jon Berlin.

Lily Oliver is no stranger to wine, having traveled the main wine-producing regions of the Southern Hemisphere and worked at New York City's much-respected Sherry-Lehmann Wines and Spirits after college. Berlin holds a postgraduate degree in viticulture and enology from New Zealand's premier wine school (Lincoln University in Christchurch), and has worked harvests and made wine in both hemispheres. In terms of pinot, Berlin has relevant experience at FLOWERS VINEYARD AND WINERY on the Sonoma Coast and at Hamilton-Russell Winery, a pinot and chardonnay specialist in Walker Bay, South Africa.

El Molino's pinot vineyards are a 1-acre "test" site co-located with the winery, and 4 acres carved from a cabernet vineyard on the eastern side of Highway 29, south of Rutherford Cross Road, where Oliver planted pinot between 1991 and 1999. The scion material is a combination of UCD 5 selected from Bouchaine and Saintsbury; Dijon 113, 115, and 777; a field selection "from Abbott Williams in Carneros" that Oliver has dubbed the "El Molino selection"; and cuttings from Larry Hyde's Los Carneros vineyard, credibly said to have come from Bouzeron, near Chagny, just beyond the southern end of the Côte d'Or. These 4 acres are set out in east–west rows, with spacing that ranges from 3 feet between vines in 6-foot rows to 6 feet between vines in 8-foot rows. In 2006 2 adjacent acres of chardonnay were pulled out to make room for additional pinot noir, in north–south rows this time, and all 6 feet by 3 feet. Budwood was field grafted to rootstock here in the spring of 2008. The scion material is Dijon 667, the aforementioned El Molino selection, and a field blend of cuttings taken from existing vines, irrespective of clonal identity, that exhibit the smallest berry size and tightest cluster architecture in the vineyard.

Of the lot, the El Molino selection is the last to ripen each year. Fruit from the Rutherford vineyard made about 80 percent of the El Molino blend until 2000; since then, it has accounted for 90 percent. Most of the purchased fruit has come from Carneros, especially from Larry Hyde's vineyard and CVI (CVI acquired part of the old Stanly ranch circa 1982 and expanded the vineyard surface), but both Lily Oliver and Jon Berlin say that, despite being "committed" to the Rutherford site, they "like the freedom" to add whatever they feel "may improve the cuvée," and find it "fun to buy a little here and there, especially with all the outstanding pinot now available."

WINES AND WINEMAKING NOTES
El Molino makes just a single bottling of pinot in each vintage. The harvest is made in successive *tris;* about three quarters of the fruit is retained and fermented as whole clusters; and the fermentation relies entirely on resident yeast. The Rutherford vineyard is typically picked between 24 Brix and 26 Brix. Fermentors are 1.5-ton, cube-shaped, unjacketed stainless steel open-tops that were custom built. The must is never bled, and there is no use of enzymes; acid is occasionally added to be sure the finished pH stays below 3.65. Free-run juice goes directly to barrel when the must is dry; solids are pressed in a basket press; and the press juice is also used in the cuvée. Barrels are all made with three-year air-dried wood from the Tronçais and other Allier forests coopered by François Frères. Approximately 75 percent new wood is used annually; the rest of the barrels are one year old. The pinot spends a long eighteen months in barrel, is racked once after malolactic fermentation

has completed, and then is egg-white fined (with fresh eggs from the family's flock of sixty-five heirloom hens) and lightly pad filtered before bottling. After bottling, El Molino pinot is held another sixteen months in bottle before release, which occurs almost three years after the vintage.

El Molino pinots are medium-weight, elegant wines with considerable aromatic complexity and a generally silky texture. Aromatic properties vary considerably from year to year, reflecting vintage variation and the evolution of El Molino's fruit sources. My favorites in the tasting below were the 2004 and the 2000, largely because they seemed to speak with significant finished acidity.

ELK COVE VINEYARDS
Gaston, Oregon

In 1974, when Joe and Pat Campbell bought the first piece of the property in the coastal foothills southwest of Gaston that is now home to Elk Cove Vineyards, they had agrarian pursuits in sight, but not necessarily wine. The property had originally been prune orchard and was then planted primarily to cherries. While there were no vineyards in the immediate area, a buzz about wine grapes emanated from the nearby Dundee Hills and from neighboring precincts in the Chehalem Mountains. And so, the Campbells planted grapes and began to make wine as soon as the vines began to bear in 1977. Thirty years later, their toehold had expanded to more than 60 bearing vineyard acres on the original property and adjacent parcels, 50 bearing acres in another vineyard about 5 miles south,

30 acres in the Chehalem Mountains area, and 22 more acres about 20 miles north—and the brand produces 35,000 cases annually. Joe and Pat have retired, and their son Adam is now both winemaker and general manager.

THE WILLAMETTE VALLEY BOTTLING IS A STANDOUT FOR BRIGHTNESS, ELEGANCE, AND COMPLEXITY

Elk Cove is absolutely centered in what is now the Yamhill Carlton AVA, and virtually all its fruit comes from that appellation's characteristically sedimentary soils. The original estate vineyard is still in production and consists entirely of UCD 4 on its own roots. Budwood from this planting, grown into rooted vines in the Campbells' own nursery, was used ten years later to plant the La Bohème Vineyard next door, and the process was repeated in 1993 to plant Roosevelt Vineyard on 3 acres of steep, south-facing slope west of the original estate. In 1996 the Campbells purchased a 22-acre noncontiguous vineyard called Windhill, whose prior owners they had first met when both couples were planting simultaneously in 1975 and from whom they had purchased fruit since 1979. Here, the Campbells grafted several acres of chardonnay to pinot noir, and planted 10 additional acres to pinot, using own-rooted vines propagated from (what else?) the Roosevelt site. Mount Richmond, a 100-acre southeast-facing site near Yamhill, substantially lower in elevation than the other estate parcels, was purchased in 1995 and planted, mostly 1 meter by 2 meters, beginning in 1997. Here, the plant material was a combination of own-rooted plants from Roosevelt and nursery-sourced Dijon 115 and 777 on rootstock. A fifth parcel, called Five Mountain, was purchased in 2005. Five Mountain is 30 acres of own-rooted UCD 4 and Dijon clones planted in 1993 next to Ponzi's Abetina Vineyard on the east side of the Chehalem Mountains.

Although most of Elk Cove's pinot program is based on fruit from these estate vineyards, they buy another 150 acres of fruit from twenty-odd growers, mostly in the Yamhill Carlton appellation, although a few sources are located in the Eola and Dundee Hills AVAs. After growing up on the estate and graduating from Lewis and Clark College in Portland, Oregon, Adam Campbell spent four years managing Elk Cove's vineyards before making wines with his father in 1997 and 1998, and then formally moving into the estate's winemaker job in 1999.

WINES AND WINEMAKING NOTES

Elk Cove has made an estate grown pinot since 1977. In 1979, after the Campbells began purchasing grapes to complement what they could grow themselves, the pinot program morphed from one into two wines: an estate wine, sometimes called an Estate Reserve, and a Willamette Valley cuvée, wherein estate and non-estate fruit were blended. At the same time, Elk Cove began to make vineyard-designated pinots from non-estate sources, including the aforementioned Windhill, and from Dundee Hills (see DUSKY GOOSE) on the south side of Worden Hill Road. In 1989 La Bohème debuted as a separate, vineyard-designated estate wine. In 1993 Elk Cove switched gears, reserving vineyard-designation for estate wines. The Dundee Hills and Windhill bottlings were consequently discontinued, and the "plain" Estate Reserve was not made from 1996 to 1998. At this point Windhill, now an estate vineyard, reappeared as a vineyard-designated wine, along with Roosevelt. Vineyard-designated Mount

Richmond followed in 2000, and Five Mountain debuted in 2005. Estate Reserve, now a blend of Campbell's four favorite barrels from La Bohème and Roosevelt, reappeared in 1999.

Adam Campbell says he tries, now, to pick "beautiful ripe fruit," and he is willing to wait out "rain events" to assure such ripeness. In the winery, winemaking generally follows the consensus protocol for pinot noir. The new wines are pressed off when the must is dry, and are then settled for twenty-four hours before going into barrels. Finding year-on-year qualitative inconsistency in supplies from almost all coopers, Elk Cove spreads the risk by acquiring barrels from at least ten *tonnelleries*. Thirty percent of the barrel stock is new each year, and the wines spend ten months in wood before being blended and bottled. Among the area's blends, Elk Cove's Willamette Valley bottling is a standout for complexity in a bright, elegant package; each of the vineyard-designated wines has a distinct personality, with more weight than the Willamette Valley bottling, and each makes a serious impression.

TASTING NOTES

2005 *Willamette Valley (tasted in 2007):* Bright pinkish-ruby; floral and berry fruit aromas; pleasantly fruity attack; then sober and well behaved on the mid-palate; some savory notes and bright, overall, with just a hint of grip; attractive and nicely made.

2005 *Mount Richmond (tasted in 2007):* Deep, lustrous magenta; earthy, herbal, black fruit nose; very slightly sweet on the palate, with flavors of licorice and black tea; significant grip from mid-palate through the finish; some chalky minerality; long, serious, and quite attractive.

2005 *Roosevelt (tasted in 2007):* Brilliant medium-dark black-red; dark cherry with hints of mint, black pepper, licorice, and earth; earth, cherry, boysenberry, and brewed black tea on the palate; intense, very dark cherry flavors; serious pinot with substantial mid-palate weight, good structure, and length.

EMERITUS VINEYARDS
 Sebastopol, California

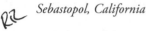

In the early 1990s, Sonoma-Cutrer Vineyards, a hugely successful Sonoma-based, chardonnay-oriented producer, began to feel itself surrounded by pinot noir. Quietly, vineyard manager Kirk Lokka and winemaker Terry Adams planted 2 acres of pinot in a remote corner of the Cutrer Vineyard. A few years later, Brice Jones and the other principals approved a "stealth" project to vinify some of the pinot in-house, experimentally, in a converted shed about a mile from the chardonnay winery. Although no pinot was released under the Sonoma-Cutrer label until 2002, pinot noir was by then grown in all five of Sonoma-Cutrer's vineyards. What was not vinified in-house was sold to other makers, including SCHERRER WINES, which made very nice wines from it.

Even after Jones and other principals sold Sonoma-Cutrer to the Brown Forman Company in 1999, their interest in pinot continued. Two new vineyards, both dedicated entirely to pinot noir, were developed as the basis of what was first called goldridgepinot (yes, written as one word and lower cased) before the project's name was changed to Emeritus Vineyards in 2006. The first vineyard was planted on Don and Marcia

Hallberg's 115-acre apple farm, astride the Gravenstein Highway 2 miles north of Sebastopol, between 1999 and 2003. The other was developed on a 65-acre parcel of steep, rolling hills near Annapolis, in the True Sonoma Coast, and was christened William Wesley Vineyard, using Jones's father's first and middle names.

Hallberg was planted to UCD 4, 5, and 37; five Dijon clones; and two undocumented selections from Burgundy, for which the in-house names are Elite and Cruz. William Wesley is now 35 acres of UCD 23, four Dijon clones, and Elite. The winemaker is Don Blackburn, who originally trained in Burgundy and who is an alumnus of Bernardus Winery in Carmel Valley and Byington Vineyards in the Santa Cruz Mountains. Jones met Blackburn at the famous Focus on Chardonnay conferences he organized through the years with various winemaking luminaries, including Robert Haas, the founder of Vineyard Brands. Blackburn is a gregarious individual with a seemingly insatiable appetite for conversation about the interrelationships between wine, music, and even couture; he also speaks essentially perfect French.

WINES AND WINEMAKING NOTES
Although experimental wines were made as early as 2002, 2004 was the first real vintage, and it was entirely lost in the fire that famously consumed a Vallejo, California, warehouse used by dozens of California producers. In 2005, the first vintage that survived to market, Emeritus made one wine each from its two vineyards: a Russian River Valley cuvée from the Hallberg Vineyard, and a vineyard-designated wine from the William Wesley Vineyard. Blackburn says the former is designed to be fruit-forward and voluptuous, and representative of

the Russian River Valley, for which it is designated, while the Wesley bottling is intentionally leaner and mineral driven.

Picking for both wines starts as low as 23.5 Brix but does not conclude until sugar levels are much higher; as a result, both wines are partially de-alcoholized before the final blends are made. Fermentors are a combination of 5.5-ton stainless steel open-tops and 4-ton wooden vessels in the shape of topless cones. Both allow Blackburn, who is fanatical about certain details, to foot-tread each cuve personally, believing that foot-trodden pinot is always superior texturally to anything that is mechanically plunged. The new wines are generally pressed when the must has gone dry although Blackburn finds that some assertive clones (he calls these "yang" clones) may need to be pressed before dryness. (Conversely, some "yin" clones may benefit from *saignée* to concentrate their flavors.) The wines spend eleven months in barrel, of which about 30 percent are new in each vintage. The coopers of choice are Remond, Rousseau, and Dargaud & Jaeglé.

Blending each wine is a mood-sensitive, artistic exercise for Blackburn, who often defines the profile of the wine he is seeking as a vinous analogy to a particular musical composition, generally selected from classical repertory, and he may play recordings of that piece while the wine is being blended. Considerable amounts of wine are also sold in bulk so that he can optimize the Russian River Valley blend to meet his target profile. With only one vintage available to judge, the shape of Emeritus pinots is not yet clear. The Russian River seems as advertised: flavorful and lush. The William Wesley is, to my palate, a considerably more interesting wine, with more brilliance and more cleanly delineated flavors.

TASTING NOTES

2005 *Russian River Valley (tasted in 2007):* Dark, purplish black-red, almost opaque; briary, mesquite-tinged nose, with understated fruit and some black pepper; broad mid-palate, with raspberry and cherry flavors; slightly sweet and medium weight; some very fine-grained tannin.

2005 *William Wesley Vineyard (tasted in 2007):* Brilliant, very clean, medium-dark black-red; clean licorice on the nose; blacker flavors than the Russian River cuvée; peppery spice, bay laurel, and pomegranate seed; long finish.

ERATH VINEYARDS WINERY
Dundee, Oregon

As Leon Adams (*The Wines of America*, 1978) tells the story, Dick Erath, then a California-based electronics engineer and home winemaker, purchased grapes from Richard Sommer's vineyard near Roseburg during an Oregon vacation in 1967 and "took them home and made them into wine." Within two years, Erath had taken winemaking classes at the University of California Davis, moved to Oregon (but settled farther north than Sommer, in search of cooler weather), purchased the site for his first vineyard on Chehalem Mountain, and planted no less than twenty-three varieties on 4 acres. Three years later, Erath made his first commercial wines, including a pinot noir and a riesling that won gold medals from the Seattle Enological Society.

According to Adams again, Seattle-based lumber magnate Cal Knudsen "stopped by" Erath's place in 1973, tasted the first vintage, and straightaway commissioned Erath to plant a vineyard for him, which was done the following year. The partnership that ensued eventually extended to at least 86 acres of vineyard and contracts to purchase from many others; included a 40,000-gallon winery in the Dundee Hills; and resulted in scores of wines, which bore Erath's name, or Knudsen's, or both. By the middle of the

---

RESPECTED, ATTRACTIVE EXAMPLES OF "CLASSIC" WILLAMETTE VALLEY PINOT NOIR

1980s, the partners had produced several award-winning pinots and had driven production to 35,000 cases of still and sparkling wine combined.

In 1988 Erath bought out Knudsen; in 1994 he hired Rob Stuart, a onetime biochemistry major at Rensselaer Polytechnic Institute, with a passion for pinot and winemaking experience in three states, as co-winemaker. In 2002 Gary Horner, a clinical pharmacist turned winemaker, with experience at BETHEL HEIGHTS, Witness Tree, Washington Hills, and BENTON-LANE, took the winemaking reins entirely. In 2006 Erath sold the Erath Winery and brand to Ste. Michelle Wine Estates, the ninth-largest producer of premium wines in North America, but retained ownership of the Prince Hill Vineyard. Fruit from Prince Hill and various Dundee Hills vineyards that Erath leased remain contracted to the Erath Winery, contributing importantly to a Dundee Hills appellation wine called Estate Selection, and to several made as free-standing vineyard-designated wines.

WINES AND WINEMAKING NOTES
For some years, the core of Erath's pinot program has been an Oregon bottling anchored overwhelmingly with purchased Willamette Valley fruit, but about 10 percent of it is sourced from the Umpqua and Rogue Valleys. An impressive 83,000 cases are made annually. The Oregon wine is built from vineyard selections that privilege fresh fruit, soft tannins, and balanced acidity. The above-mentioned Dundee Hills appellation wine is the property's other blended pinot.

In addition to the blends, Erath also makes several vineyard-designated wines from among its six Dundee Hills sources and from other vineyards in the northern Willamette Valley. In 2005 these were Prince Hill—first planted in 1983 and the site of Erath's personal residence—a vineyard which now consists of mature UCD 4 and younger Dijon clone plantings; Niederberger, a 16-acre hillside 1 mile south of Dundee, planted primarily to UCD 4 and Dijon 777; Juliard, a 10-acre, south-facing hillside on Worden Hill Road planted to UCD 4 in 1986, with Dijon 114 and 115 added ten years later; and Fuqua, a 7-acre, south-by-southwest facing hillside north of Prince Hill planted to UCD 4 in 1984, with Dijon 115 added in 1997. From outside the Dundee Hills, there is one more vineyard-designated wine, from Leland, a 1982 planting of UCD 4 and 2A near Oregon City, which has been an Erath *monopole* since 1987.

Between 2003 and 2005, the following wines, in addition to the Oregon Cuvée, were made in all three vintages: Estate Selection, Prince Hill Vineyard, Leland Vineyard, and La Nuit Magique. In addition, a vineyard-designated wine from Juliard was made in 2003 and 2005 but not in 2004, Fuqua was made as a single-vineyard wine in 2004 and 2005, and a vineyard-designated Niederberger wine was made in 2005 only. The Oregon, Estate Selection and the Prince Hill will certainly also be made in 2006; decisions had not been made at time of this writing about the other single-vineyard wines.

Erath pinots are much respected and attractive examples of "classic" Willamette Valley pinot noir. The Oregon bottling represents excellent value and a bright, low-tannin style. Each of the vineyard-designated wines is distinctive and features modest alcohol. Prince Hill is the most elegant of the lineup, Juliard the spiciest, and Fuqua the warmest and most powerful.

TASTING NOTES

2005 *Oregon (tasted in* 2007*):* Transparent, medium garnet; red fruits on the nose with hints of menthol, cedar, and flowers; cherry, raspberry, and pepper on the palate, and a hint of cocoa at the end; bright, attractive, and sleek, with just a hint of grip.

2005 *Prince Hill (tasted in* 2007*):* Transparent, medium-dark garnet; red fruit aromas with slightly herbal notes; very dark fruit flavors in the mouth, plus licorice and a hint of earth; fruit-sweet but nicely built; elegant, long, rich, and rewarding.

2005 *Niederberger (tasted in* 2007*):* Medium color; barrel-influenced nose with notes of menthol and gum camphor; earthy, chocolaty, and chewy on the palate, with considerable tannic grip from mid-palate to finish; serious but needs more bottle time.

2005 *Juliard (tasted in* 2007*):* Medium garnet; aromas of dried herbs, hard spice, and pinecone; very spicy in the mouth, with cinnamon, allspice, infused bay laurel, and roasted coffee beans; tarry and slate-y notes, too; a considerable load of very fine-grained tannins, and beyond mid-palate; long, structured, and very attractive.

2005 *Fuqua (tasted in* 2007*):* Transparent, very deep garnet; wet clay and citrus peel aromas; slightly fruit-sweet with very dark, ferrous flavors on the palate; some espresso and mocha; enough grip to seem almost gritty; powerful and intense, dense, tightly knit, and long.

2004 *Leland (tasted in* 2007*):* Medium rosy-garnet; earth and tobacco on the nose; sweet on the palate with intense licorice, some pepper, and Kahlua; slightly exotic; silky and mouth coating to mid-palate, then grippy; quite rich and long overall.

1985 *Knudsen-Erath Vintage Select (tasted in* 2007*):* Dark terra cotta with a deep red core; aromas of raspberry, mushrooms, and leather; spicy raspberry on the palate with a hint of citrus peel; silky overall and long, but slightly dry at the end.

ESTERLINA VINEYARDS
Healdsburg, California

Murio and Doris Sterling's four sons, an exceptionally talented cohort with an impressive collection of college and advanced degrees, are all active players in Esterlina Vineyards, the family's youngest business, which was founded in 2000. The family has roots in the Dominican Republic and has wide experience in farming and ranching in several venues—everything from row crops to cattle. In the 1990s, Murio and son Eric, a trauma physician in Santa Rosa, California, who had been increasingly drawn to the wine business that surrounded them, purchased a 30-acre cabernet vineyard in the Alexander Valley. Most of the grapes were sold to area vintners, but father and son also began making small lots of wine for themselves and their friends. As events turned out, this first foray into wine was the thin edge of a wedge: less than a decade later, the family had come to farm four vineyards in two counties and to own two wine brands.

Following the Alexander Valley vineyard, the next step, in 1998, was the acquisition of a 24-acre vineyard on Eastside Road in Russian River Valley that had been planted entirely to the UCD 4 and to Dijon 115 and 667 clones of pinot noir. (The Sterlings replaced some of the UCD 4 with Dijon 828.) Then, in 1999, the family bought the 253-acre Cole Ranch, an exceptional, hard-to-farm, relatively high-altitude site located in a fold of the coastal hills between Boonville and Ukiah, in Mendocino County. Cole enjoys the distinction of containing the country's smallest American Viticultural Area, the Cole Ranch AVA, and the only one owned in its entirety by one proprietor. Since John Cole's first harvest in 1975, its vines have been a favored source of fruit for numerous vintners, including Fetzer Vineyards's Paul Dolan, CHATEAU ST. JEAN'S Dick Arrowood, and NALLE WINERY'S Doug Nalle. Cole Ranch gave the Sterlings some utterly atypical cabernet sauvignon, some much sought-after riesling, and another 10 acres of pinot noir.

The Sterlings' fourth vineyard—the property previously known as Pepperwood Springs, on Holmes Ranch Road overlooking the deep end of the Anderson Valley—was purchased in 2000. Here were yet another 10 acres of pinot, albeit an undocumented selection, plus a bit of chardonnay, planted in 1976 on a stunning, southwest-facing hillside. Pepperwood Springs had two prior owners: Larry and Nicki Parsons set out the vines and established a tiny bonded winery in the basement of their home, and Phyllis Kaliher, a San Franciscan who reinvented herself as a hands-on winemaker, took over after the Parsons' death in 1986. The Pepperwood Springs name, by then contested on the grounds of its infringement on the intellectual property of Don Sebastiani and Sons' Pepperwood Grove brand, was abandoned when the Sterlings bought the property. To replace it, and to cover all wines the family would make from its four vineyards, the Sterlings coined Esterlina, the Spanish adjective for the sterling grade of silver.

Initial vintages of Esterlina were made in the tiny cellar Parsons and Kaliher had used; production was transferred to Everett Ridge Winery in Dry Creek Valley after the Sterlings added Everett Ridge to their list of wine properties in 2006. Eric Sterling, relying on his undergraduate training in microbiology and his home winemaking experience in the mid-1990s, was Esterlina's winemaker until 2006, with assistance from his brother Chris; now the wines are made by Everett Ridge winemaker Dick Schultz, under the Sterlings' overall direction. Schultz knows the North Coast, and pinot noir, extremely well. His wine career began as a laboratory technician for NAVARRO VINEYARDS; subsequently, he worked, inter alia, for Scharffenberger Cellars, for GARY FARRELL WINES, and for MERRY EDWARDS WINES. Chris Sterling, meanwhile, manages all four vineyards; Stephen Sterling handles sales and marketing; and Craig Sterling functions as the brand's general manager and general counsel. Esterlina is *almost* "all in the family."

WINES AND WINEMAKING NOTES
Esterlina's first pinot noir debuted in 2000; this wine, labeled Anderson Valley Estate, is a vineyard-designated wine from the former Pepperwood Springs property. A Russian River Valley pinot, made entirely from the family's Eastside Road vineyard, joined the portfolio in 2002. The first vintage of Esterlina pinot from Cole Ranch fruit was made in 2004. The Esterlina program absorbs all the pinot produced on Anderson Valley property and most of the harvest at Cole Ranch (but Cole Ranch fruit was sold to Vision Cellars in 2004); some of the crop from the Russian River Valley vineyard is sold to other makers.

For each of the three wines, the grapes are entirely destemmed and fermented in 2,200-gallon stainless steel open-tops. A five-day cold soak is followed by about eight days of primary fermentation, during which time the cap is managed with a pneumatic punchdown device. The new wine is pressed off when the must is dry and is barreled on its gross lees. The barrel stock is purchased entirely from François Frères and Remond, and (since 2006) about half the barrels are new in each vintage. The Russian River Valley wine spends at least fourteen months in wood; the Anderson Valley wine up to eighteen months; and the Cole Ranch wine as much as two years.

My experience with Esterlina pinots is limited to the Anderson Valley Estate wine, which is a worthy successor to Kaliher's Pepperwood Springs bottlings: simultaneously earthy, bright, and serious, with considerable aromatic complexity.

TASTING NOTE

2005 *Esterlina Estate Vineyard (tasted in 2007):* Pretty, medium garnet; smoky; earthy and slightly tarry on the nose; bright cranberry-cherry fruit on the palate, with a savory, herb-infused character, hints of pepper and orange peel, and a suggestion of exotic spice; of medium length and very attractive.

ETUDE WINES
Napa, California

Etude was Tony Soter's first personal wine project, launched in 1982. An alumnus of Stag's Leap, Spring Mountain, and Chappelet, and with a formidable reputation as a consulting winemaker for some of Napa's most exalted brands, Soter had become fascinated with pinot noir. He found it a "quixotic and unforgiving grape" that made wines with "transparency." He sometimes characterized it as the "yin" to cabernet's "yang." And this made it, he argued, "the best vehicle for learning about *all* red wine." Very deliberately and reflectively, he decided to call his project Etude, the French noun for a study, a case study, a course of study, or an investigation. Among musicians, the word is also used to denote a genre of musical practice composition that is designed to challenge both composer and performer. All these contexts and connotations seem apt.

Etude was operated as nearly a one-man show from 1982 until 1994, during which time the payroll never exceeded three people, and Soter handled almost everything from grower relations and fermentations to bank loans. In 1995 he handed over the hands-on winemaking to Eric Hamacher for one vintage; Scott Rich (see TALISMAN WINES) succeeded Hamacher from 1996 through 2000. This set the stage for a more substantial change in 2001, when Soter sold Etude to Beringer Blass Wine Estates (which became Foster's Wine Estates Americas in 2005) to make time for a new family and for an Oregon wine project begun as a sidebar, "preretirement" venture in 1997. At this point, the hands-on winemaking duties at Etude shifted again, first to Brian Mox from 2001 to 2004, and then to Jon Priest, a veteran of several Central Coast wine projects that had also been acquired by Foster's, in the spring of 2005. With a corporate structure in place, Soter also stepped away from most of Etude's business decisions, although he accepted a five-year obligation to "run" Etude, and he retained ultimate control over marketing and sales. (Since 2007 Soter's role at Etude has been purely consultative, and he has moved his primary residence to Oregon [see SOTER VINEYARDS]. He still visits Etude monthly, however.)

With the sale, resources became available to move Etude from its motley facilities on Big Ranch Road north of Napa (an eye-jarring, teal-colored structure known in-house as the "*faux château*") to a state-of-the-art production facility on Cuttings Wharf Road in Carneros that had previously been the premises of the RMS Distillery. Most importantly, Etude acquired an enormous estate vineyard: the former Grace Benoist Ranch in the foothills at the south end of Sonoma Mountain. Soter describes the ranch as one of the attractions of the deal with Foster's. It was property he had first seen in 1996 and imagined planting to vineyard; Beringer had since acquired and planted it. By the terms of the sale, Etude was given first choice of its fruit as it came into production in 2002 and 2003.

The first vintages of Etude pinot were made from grapes grown in mid-valley Napa or on Mount Veeder. The first 500 cases, produced in 1982, were sourced from Bruce Newlan's vineyard on Darms Lane, south of Yountville. Despite the growing emphasis, even then, on cool sites for good pinot, Soter found that the fruit then available from Carneros was "not convincingly superior" to mid-valley grapes, having been farmed, in general, to produce a neutral base for sparkling wine. "There was so much lacking in most pinot efforts anywhere in California," he says now, "that a focus on *place* at the expense of technique did not seem the best way to address its shortcomings."

By 1986, Soter began to find more and better resources in Carneros, and gradually came to rely entirely on Carneros for pinot noir. His sources were some of Carneros's best-known independent growers, including Larry Hyde and Lee Hudson, and producers such as DOMAINE CARNEROS (some of whose vineyards were planted in accordance with Soter's suggestions), Domaine Chandon, Artesa, Adastra, CUVAISON, and CASA CARNEROS. In this period, the keystone wine was a blended Carneros cuvée. To maximize its quality, Soter aggressively declassified lots that, once made, did not measure up. Beginning in the late 1990s, along with the Carneros cuvée, Etude made several editions of a cuvée called Heirloom, showcasing selections that did not meet what Soter called "the standard criteria for pinot noir." These were primarily Swan, Calera, and Chalone selections, and a few undocumented imports from Burgundy. Their common characteristic, according to Soter, was small, irregularly shaped clusters and very small berries.

In 2004 the Carneros cuvée was replaced with an estate wine built entirely from Benoist grapes, although the Heirloom program continues to rely primarily (at least for now) on purchased grapes from sites Soter and Rich identified late in the 1990s. Benoist is a 1,250-acre ranch on the western edge of the Carneros appellation, whose topsoils are mostly cobbly loams of volcanic origin atop very old bedrock. Approximately 580 acres have been planted, of which about half are pinot noir. Two thirds of the pinot is claimed by Etude; the balance goes to Beringer and to Chateau St. Jean. The pinot is in fifteen irregularly shaped "vineyards within a vineyard" that follow the hectic contours of the land, with a variety of aspects and exposures, mostly in 7-foot rows with 5 feet between vines. Two blocks have been reserved for Etude's heirloom selections and have been planted with budwood taken from the Carneros vineyards on which the Heirloom program was built; the rest have been planted to UCD 4 and 13, and to most of the currently available Dijon clones.

Priest reports that most parameters of Soter's winemaking continue under the new regime, adjusted for the fact that Priest (and viticulturist Franci Ashton) control winegrowing in the estate vineyard in ways Soter never could in his contracted sites. Picking decisions still hinge primarily on the condition of the vine and on Soter's general rule that, as long as the condition of the vine is not declining, the fruit is probably getting better. In the 1990s this translated into a fairly wide numbers window: sugars as low as 23 Brix or as high as 25.9, and pH values anywhere between 3.3 and 3.6. At Benoist, pH values are typically closer to the low end of this range. The use of whole clusters varies, but hovers between 20 and 30 percent depending on seed and stem maturity. Soter and Priest agree that that stems from vineyards that have experienced, in any given vintage, a curtailed vegetative cycle generally cannot be used because such stems do not lignify.

The assortment of fruit bins and repurposed dairy tanks used as fermentation vessels in the Big Ranch Road facility have been entirely replaced with new 5- and 7-ton jacketed stainless open-tops. Wider than they are tall, these tanks have a naturally high ratio of cap-to-juice contact, which helps with what Soter has always called "the challenge of differential extraction." "You want to get color and fruit and some tannin," he explains, "but there are phenolics you do *not* want, and you want minimal seed tannins." Soter developed, and Priest respects, a yeast-addition technique aimed at encouraging rather than replacing the resident yeast. Sulfur dioxide and chilling are both avoided, but inoculations use only one quarter of the manufacturer's recommended amount of laboratory yeast to induce a slow fermentation that approximates the natural course of native yeast. The result is a natural prefermentation soak lasting three to four days, a primary fermentation lasting another four to five days, during which time temperatures climb into the 90°F range, and one to two weeks of postfermentation maceration—for a total *cuvaison* lasting up to thirty days. The must is both punched down and pumped over. After pressing, the wine is settled for three to five days. Some blending occurs at this time, and some dubious lots are culled.

The unusual barrel regime relies entirely on thin-stave, Bordelais *barriques* from Tonnellerie Nadalie, of which 60 percent are new each year. These are an artifact from Soter's cabernet days, but the thin staves seem to improve concentration, and Etude likes their distinctive fingerprint on pinot. The last vintages made on Big Ranch Road were typically bottled before the following harvest for housekeeping reasons; in the new facility, all the pinots are kept in barrel for twelve to fourteen months. In addition to the estate wine and the Heirloom cuvée, a wine called Deer Camp, made entirely from Vineyard D at Benoist, debuted in 2004. Deer Camp showcases the density and sappy boysenberry flavors of UCD 13 grown in this *terroir*. With the 2005 vintage, Etude introduced a second wine from an individual vineyard/block. Called Temblor, it comes from an alluvial, fog-shrouded parcel that is designated Vineyard 5 at Benoist. The new estate wines seem to have more floral intensity and substantially richer phenolic structure than the old Carneros cuvée. Heirloom remains, as it has been since the outset, an exceptional pinot by any standard.

TASTING NOTES

2005 *Temblor (tasted in 2007):* Medium dark, purplish-ruby; exotic nose of nuts, mace, and barrel char; rich, chewy attack that is also slightly sweet; some mocha and

Mexican chocolate at mid-palate; with an emery texture, and dry after mid-palate; like Deer Camp, it needs time in bottle to soften.

2004 *Deer Camp (tasted in 2006)*: Deep, almost opaque, rusty red; aromas of dark, plummy fruit and barrel char; rich, full, and mouth coating on the palate, with very considerable tannins polished into submission; pervasively black, with notes of mocha and Carborundum; weighty, long, and seemingly monumental, but demanding fortitude to be appreciated now.

EVESHAM WOOD WINERY
Salem, Oregon

Russ Raney was in Germany on a collegiate study abroad program when he discovered wine. He subsequently apprenticed at Weingut Erbhof Tesch in Langenlonsheim, in the Nahe valley, just upstream from its confluence with the Rhine, and earned a degree in viticulture and enology from the state technical school of the Rhine Palatinate (Rheinpfalz), in Bad Kreuznach. After five years selling wines in St. Louis, Missouri, Raney and his wife moved to Portland and searched the Willamette Valley for sites well suited to the Burgundian and Alsatian varieties they preferred. In 1986 the Raneys launched Evesham Wood Winery, named for the Vale of Evesham in the English Cotswolds, which the Willamette Valley landscape recalled for them. Their first release was a 1986 pinot noir made from purchased fruit. They planted 8 acres of vineyard northwest of Salem, in an area known locally as Spring Valley; at the same time, they built a vaguely Tudor-style house overlooking the vineyard and the river beyond. In 1991

a small, full-function winery was built under the house, and Evesham Wood's production was transferred to the estate.

The estate vineyard, called Le Puits Sec, is a gentle, east-facing slope on the Willamette River side of the Eola Hills, between the 300-foot and 420-foot contours. The shallow, rocky soils are iron rich and red tinted and are of volcanic origin. The 1986 planting, which included 3 acres of pinot noir, was laid out in 7-foot, east–west rows, with 4 feet between vines; in a subsequent planting, the intervine spacing was tightened to 3 feet. In 1999 2 acres of 1986 chardonnay were grafted to pinot, bringing the total pinot acreage to 7. Of this, about 4.5 acres are own-rooted UCD 4 or 5 sourced from the Adams vineyard; the balance is mostly Dijon 113 and 115, with very small amounts of 114 and 777. In 2001 an additional acre of

---

RELATIVELY EARLY-PICKED, ELEGANTLY BUILT WINES WITH FINE, SOMETIMES GOSSAMER STRUCTURES AND AROMATIC COMPLEXITY

Dijon 777 was added to the estate, and in 2004 another acre of 4-year-old pinot gris was grafted to Dijon 777.

Le Puits Sec is dry farmed, is certified organic, and normally yields about 2.25 tons per acre. Evesham Wood also purchases pinot noir from other Willamette Valley vineyards, mostly in the Eola Hills as well as in the Coast Range immediately west of these hills, and privileges vineyards that are dry farmed like Le Puits Sec.

WINES AND WINEMAKING NOTES
Evesham Wood's main release of pinot noir is a Willamette Valley bottling, whose fruit

sources have changed over time. The 1986 bottling was made from Seven Springs and Freedom Hill fruit; the 1987, 1988, and 1989 editions relied on Seven Springs and Temperance Hill fruit. From 1990 to 1996, O'Connor Vineyard fruit joined the blend; estate fruit has been used intermittently since 1995. The 1997 Willamette Valley was made from Seven Springs, Temperance Hill, and estate fruits; the 1998 contained some Shea Vineyard fruit, but no estate fruit.

The Collada vineyard was the anchor for the Willamette Valley bottling from 1999 until 2005, when it was replaced by the Ford Vineyard in the foothills of the Coast Range. Meanwhile, as early as 1987, single-vineyard wines began to appear in the Evesham Wood portfolio. Some Seven Springs wine was made as a de facto vineyard-designate—labeled Eola Hills—in 1987; formally vineyard-designated Seven Springs bottlings were made in 1989, 1992, 1994, 1996, 1998, and 1999. Single-vineyard bottlings of Temperance Hill were issued in 1994 and 1998; of Mahonia in 1995 and each year thereafter; and of Shea in 1998 and 1999. Cuvée J (named in honor of Henri Jayer) debuted in 1989. J is Raney's selection of his best barrels, whether from a single vineyard or a blend of several, and has been made in every vintage since it debuted. A 100 percent estate pinot noir, released in 1990, 1992, 1994, 1997, 1998, and 1999 and designated Le Puits Sec after 1997, completes the list.

Barrels destined for the Willamette Valley bottling are identified at the time of the first racking and are bottled early (see above); single-vineyard wines account for most of the remainder, except that Cuvée J barrels are selected out at the very end, just before the second round of bottling. Raney ferments primarily in double-height fruit bins, but also uses one 1,100-gallon open-top stainless steel fermentor. The fruit is entirely destemmed, and the rollers

are set to retain approximately 25 percent whole berries. A prefermentation cold soak lasts three to five days, and it is sometimes enforced with blocks of dry ice to maintain a must temperature of about 50°F. The primary fermentation is started with an inoculation of proprietary yeast on the fifth or sixth day of the vatting.

Raney sometimes adds acid and sometimes chaptalizes, depending on the vineyard source of the fruit. The estate pinot never requires added sugar, according to Raney, whereas the Temperance Hill fruit often does. He chaptalizes only when Brix at harvest is below 22.5. Pumpovers are done twice daily until the cap is firm; thereafter, punchdowns occur once or twice each day, and fermentation temperatures peak at 93 to 95°F. Malolactic fermentation is induced about halfway through the primary fermentation. A single daily punchdown continues through four to five days of postfermentation maceration. The must is pressed at the end of eighteen to twenty-one days' vatting and is settled in tank for twenty-four to forty-eight hours. The press fraction is blended back "for structure."

Use of new wood varies by cuvée. The Willamette Valley blend gets less than 10 percent new oak; most others see 60 to 65 percent in "typical" vintages. In recent years, Evesham Wood has sourced barrels exclusively from François Frères—Raney says he "considers other factors to be more important than barrel variety in achieving complexity in pinot noir." The wines are racked once in May or June after the vintage, and once again at bottling. The Willamette Valley cuvée (see below) is bottled after about ten months in barrel; other cuvées remain in wood until early spring, two years after the vintage. There is no use of concentrators or enzymes, and no filtration, but wines are occasionally egg-white fined for tannin management.

The Willamette Valley bottling is released in February; other bottlings are held until the second autumn after the vintage. Evesham Wood pinots are relatively early-picked, elegantly-built wines with fine, sometimes gossamer structures, aromatic complexity, and personality. Raney's preference for dry-farmed fruit and his light-handed approach in the cellar contribute to exceptionally flattering site expression. In good vintages, Evesham Wood makes some of the finest examples of pinot noir in the state. I have special affection for Le Puits Sec, which is often slightly more nuanced and "exploration worthy" than either Cuvée J or Seven Springs.

TASTING NOTES

2005 *Willamette Valley (tasted from half bottle in* 2007*):* Deep purplish-ruby; pepper, plum, and cherry on the nose; soft and relatively fruit-forward on the palate; red berry fruit and overall spiciness; soft, well-behaved tannins dry out nicely on the finish; light-to-medium weight and medium-long. Exceptional value.

2005 *Le Puits Sec (tasted prerelease from half bottle in* 2007*):* Transparent, medium black-red; orange blossom and other floral aromas; sophisticated, dry, and elegant on the palate with red fruit, black tea, and minerality; very long and mouth coating. Fine.

2005 *Cuvée J (tasted prerelease from half bottle in* 2007*):* Much like Le Puits Sec in color; tar and vanilla on the nose; sleek and silky on the palate with attractive, oak-kissed blackberry; more immediately impressive than Le Puits Sec but not necessarily more satisfying; extremely attractive and fine.

2004 *Seven Springs Vineyard En Dessous (tasted in* 2007*):* Medium black-red; soft spice aromas with hints of cedar and black raspberry; black raspberry tea on the palate; sober, slate-y, and minerally, with a hint of wild, briary underbrush; relatively soft for this vineyard; of medium weight and length; attractive.

2004 *Le Puits Sec (tasted from half-bottle in* 2007*):* Pretty, medium garnet; floral again, like the 2005, but also with notes of evergreen and berry fruit; very slightly sweet attack, then a distinctive mid-palate with roasted nuts and a hint of savory grassiness; round, soft mouth-feel but persistently elegant; the fruit peeks in and out around savory properties and minerality; quite captivating, long, and fine. A personal favorite.

2004 *Cuvée J (tasted from half bottle in* 2007*):* Medium black-red with a pinkish rim; ripe black fruit on the nose with hints of fermented tea leaves, wet stones, and wood smoke; intense and persistent attack with a nice balance of tannin, fruit, and pepper-clove spices; bright with acid; lively, and serious; slightly dry on the finish; likely to impress even more with additional bottle age.

2002 *Le Puits Sec (tasted in* 2006*):* Brilliant, medium ruby; bramble, lacquer, underbrush, and exotic spice aromas; some dark fruit and black pepper on the palate, but predominantly mineral; exhibits a wiry build and is intensely expressive; tannins are fine grained and not gritty.

2002 *Cuvée J (tasted in* 2006*):* Brilliant, medium ruby; wild berries, bergamot, and woodsy-ness on the nose; cherry and minerals dominate the palate; elegant and intense, with considerable grip and fine emery texture; very attractive.

2001 *Cuvée J (tasted in* 2004*):* Brilliant, medium garnet with bluish highlights; aromas of potpourri, dried leaves, and fresh strawberries; intense strawberry-raspberry fruit on the palate, with white pepper, thyme, and bay laurel; taut and structured; elegant with fine-grained tannins; medium weight.

2001 *Le Puits Sec (tasted in* 2004*):* Pretty, transparent, light-to-medium garnet;

slightly exotic flower-and-sandalwood nose with a hint of hard spice; high toned and bright aromatically, but also rich underneath; more black fruit than red in this vintage; minerally like wet slate; long and elegant. Fine.

THE EYRIE VINEYARDS
McMinnville, Oregon

In 1965, armed with a degree from the University of California Davis, some observational experience in Burgundy, and convictions born of examining climates similar to Burgundy's in the New World, David Lett—known to various people in the wine trade as "Papa Pinot"—planted the first few acres of pinot noir in Oregon's Dundee Hills. In 1970 he made 115 cases of wine from his young vines, but the wine was so thin and pale that he called it Spring Wine rather than pinot, and sold it—with difficulty—for $2.65 a bottle. But just half a decade later, Lett succeeded so well with pinot noir that his 1975 South Block Reserve earned very high scores in two blind tastings in France and established the potential of Oregon pinot beyond a reasonable doubt. Lett's choices—south-facing hillside sites, a mix of UCD 2A and 5 clones, and quasi-organic farming—established the model for the first generation of Oregon pinot noir cultivation and attracted a small but steady trickle of co-conspirators to the Willamette Valley. Gradually, Lett and his cohorts, working with secondhand equipment and improvisations worthy of Rube Goldberg, established a pinot-oriented wine industry where walnuts, prunes, and cherries had previously flourished.

Lett's original vineyard, which gave its name to the business, is 20 acres of south-facing slope (of which 6.5 are pinot) between Dundee and Lafayette, in what is now the Dundee Hills AVA. The soil is iron-rich Jory, which often looks red to the eye, and browner Woodburn series clay-loam. The vineyard is planted in a combination of east–west and north–south rows, between about 220 feet and 400 feet above sea level. The vines are loosely spaced 6 feet by 10 feet and are farmed without herbicides, pesticides, or systemic fungicides. The plant material at Eyrie is a combination of 70 percent own-rooted UCD 1A (no longer available; this came from the same mother vines as UCD 2A) and 5, purchased from California increase blocks, and 30 percent own-rooted UCD 18. The first 4 acres were planted incrementally in 1966, 1967, and 1968; an additional 2.5 acres went into the ground in 1970. The so-called South Block, from which some of Eyrie's best pinots have been made, is nine tenths of an acre of this vineyard, which also happens to be entirely UCD 1A. (Lett is a great fan of 1A/2A, which has subsequently fallen out of favor with many American winemakers.)

I NEVER FAIL TO MARVEL AT THE COUNTERCULTURE EXCELLENCE OF THESE EXCEPTIONAL WINES

The second of Lett's vineyards is Stonehedge, planted in 1979 and 1980, uphill from the first. It has 2 acres of pinot noir in a total planting of 15 acres, again a mix of UCD 1A/2A and 5, and again in a checkerboard of row orientations. Stonehedge is very rocky Jory soil and is above 720 feet. Lett varied

the vine spacing here: part of the pinot is
very tightly spaced at 1 meter by 1.5 meters;
the balance is 6 feet by 10 feet.

During the late 1980s, Lett acquired
and planted two additional vineyards
nearby. Rolling Green Farm is 4.9 acres
of pinot noir (plus an acre of pinot gris),
planted 10 feet by 4 feet in north–south
rows, at an elevation of about 600 feet.
The scion material is half UCD 2A and
half UCD 5. Three Sisters, lower in
elevation and thus earlier to ripen, has
4.2 acres of pinot noir in a total planting
of 16 acres. Three Sisters's vine spacing
is 10 feet by 4 feet; the scion material
once again is UCD 2A and 5. In a good
year, yields on all four vineyards amount
to just over 2 tons per acre. Until the
two youngest of the four Eyrie vineyards
came online in 1991, Lett also purchased
pinot noir fruit from Abbey Ridge (see
CAMERON WINERY).

Eyrie's production facility is a
windowless, converted turkey processing
plant in what is now McMinnville's Pinot
Quarter, and Lett has been here since
1970. In 1969 he had commissioned plans
for a modern winery to be built on the
site of his estate vineyard. The architect's
renderings for this unbuilt project still
hang on his office wall. They testify to the
unwillingness of Oregon's banks, at the
end of the 1960s, to invest in the state's
fledgling wine business.

WINES AND WINEMAKING NOTES

From the very first vintage in 1970 until the present, all Eyrie pinots have been made exclusively from estate grown fruit, except in 1982 through 1984, when small amounts were purchased from nearby Abbey Ridge Vineyard. The original Eyrie Vineyard plantings were enlarged with additional plantings at Stonehedge in 1979 and 1980, and at Three Sisters and Rolling Green in 1987 and 1988, thereby completing the current estate. The so-called estate bottling has been made since 1979 from the three younger estate parcels, whereas the reserve wines (including the famous South Block Reserve) come exclusively from the original 1965 planting. A Willamette Valley bottling was made from 1970 to 1990. The secret of pinot says Lett *père*, "is to get pinot noir off the vine at *the* moment of ripeness." His definition of "ripe" would be shared by few makers today, but the house style is firm, dedicated to brilliant, aromatic, and varietally distinctive wines that make it impossible to refute his point.

Fermentations occur in 4- by 4- by 2-foot plastic bins, using no stems but mostly whole berries. Lett believes it is "ill-advised to load pinot noir with a bunch of tannins." Although there has been some experimentation with different yeasts, Eyrie pinots are usually made with neutral champagne yeast. Lett has never added acid, but he chaptalized in 1984 and "here and there" since. Lett would rather pick a bit earlier and chaptalize, he explains, than risk a substantial uptick in pH and a "loss of varietal character" with a later pick. The must is pressed at dryness using a Wilmes press; the clones and vineyards are segregated, but the press fraction of each lot is reintegrated with free-run juice from the same lot.

The unconventional barrel regime uses almost entirely *neutral* oak. Some of Lett's barrels, purchased in 1970, are still in use; an occasional new barrel is purchased from Tonnellerie de Bourgogne. Lett maintains that "the idea of flavoring wine with oak is ridiculous," and that "cutting down an old tree to make three barrels to use for three years is not ecologically correct." Malolactic fermentation occurs spontaneously in barrel, where the estate wine (see below) spends twelve months. The reserve wines spend eighteen to twenty-four months in wood. Racking is minimal; the wines are not fined, and only a few lots are filtered.

Lett's son Jason grew up around the winery, worked at Maison Joseph Drouhin and with Becky Wasserman in Burgundy at the end of the 1980s, earned a degree in plant ecology at the University of New Mexico, and then practiced briefly as a cabinetmaker before succeeding his father at Eyrie in 2005. Although he makes a somewhat gutsier pinot under his own Black Cap label, Jason Lett respects Eyrie's well-established house style. In 2007, as this text is written, Eyrie defines the outer margin of early-picked, aromatically driven, brilliant wines that seem made in Henri Jayer's image of classic, yesteryear red Burgundies. Given the excesses of the other margin, where the wines are huge, jammy, and food hostile, I am personally grateful for Eyrie's example, and I almost never fail to marvel at the counterculture excellence of these exceptional wines.

TASTING NOTES

2004 *Estate (tasted in* 2007*):* Luminous, light-to-medium garnet; lovely nose of dried flowers, white pepper, and exotic woods; bright raspberry attack; then, spicy, elegant, and silky at mid-palate and beyond, with just a hint of grip at the end; lingering and fine.

2002 *Reserve (tasted in* 2007*):* Brilliant, shimmering, and utterly transparent light-to-medium garnet; expressive, refined nose of clove, sandalwood, and potpourri, with a whiff of lemon peel; elegant and silky on the palate with a bit more weight than the 2004 Estate; a quite intense and lingering spiciness and almost a hint of mocha, plus red berries with just a touch of fruit sweetness; dry at the end with a nice balance of acid and grip; very fine.

FAILLA WINES
St. Helena, California

Ehren Jordan discovered wine while working as a part-time stock boy for a Washington, D.C., liquor store, while he pursued a bachelor's degree in art history at George Washington University. Following the wine business to California via ski trails in Colorado, Jordan took a job in the tasting room at Joseph Phelps Winery in 1990. There, he found himself decreasingly interested in the business side of wine but increasingly fascinated with its production. In 1991 he tried his hand making wine, crushing a tiny lot of pinot noir given to him gratis by Angelo Sangiacomo. After this modest beginning, Jordan headed for France, determined to learn winemaking the way most Europeans learn it: on the job. He ended up in Cornas, working for super-*négociant* Jean-Luc Colombo, and he accompanied Colombo on his consulting rounds to other Rhône Valley winemakers. Jordan was lured back to California by Bruce Neyers, whom he had known at Joseph Phelps, and one thing led to another. He became Neyers's partner and the winemaker for Neyers Vineyards; "hung out" with John Wetlaufer, who was then running a retail wine shop in

Calistoga; met Helen Turley and Helen's brother, Larry, through Wetlaufer; and eventually succeeded Helen as the winemaker for Turley Wine Cellars.

Despite this astral success, by 1998 Jordan had decided that he wanted to make wines of his own. With his wife, Anne-Marie Failla, he launched Failla-Jordan Wines (subsequently rechristened Failla Wines, pursuant to an intellectual property settlement with Jordan Vineyards and Winery) with small amounts of syrah and viognier. The following year, Failla produced its first pinot noir: two barrels of vineyard-designated wine from Scott Zeller's exceptional Summa Vineyard, on the spine of the hills between Bodega Bay and Occidental. Pleased with this debut but unable to source grapes from Summa on a continuing basis, Failla and Jordan began a search for western Sonoma vineyards with established reputations for pinot. In 2000 they were able to purchase fruit from Marcy Keefer's much-respected ranch in Green Valley, and in 2001 the source list was expanded to include David Hirsch's almost legendary vineyard on Bohan-Dillon Road west of Cazadero (see HIRSCH VINEYARDS). In 2005 a third Sonoma vineyard (a 1998 planting east of Occidental called Occidental Ridge) was added to Failla's pinot portfolio; at the same time, the couple's sights expanded to the southern Central Coast, where they began working with FOLEY ESTATES'S Rancho Santa Rosa vineyard. The year 2006 saw the first vintage of Failla wine from a fourth Sonoma coast site, PEAY VINEYARDS near Annapolis.

Meanwhile, in 2001, Failla and Jordan had begun planting pinot noir in their own Sonoma coast vineyard about 4 miles from Hirsch and next door to Donnie and Linden Schatzberg's Precious Mountain Vineyard on Creighton Ridge. This vineyard is actually two adjoining parcels, the first of which had been developed between 1998 and 2001 for chardonnay and syrah; both parcels display a wide range of soils, from sand-laced clay to rock with little soil at all. The second parcel, which, like the first, is off the power grid, depends on solar energy to move minuscule quantities of water uphill from natural springs, and which boasts barely 5 plantable acres in a total surface of 40, is dedicated entirely to pinot noir, spaced 6 feet by 3 feet, vertically trellised, cane pruned, and organically farmed. The scion material consisted of two Swan selections (one from Summa and one from a nursery), two Calera selections (one of which came from FLOWERS), and one block of Dijon 777. Because the True Sonoma Coast is anything but an easy place to establish vines, the first harvest from Failla's estate pinot vineyard did not occur until 2006.

Failla's wine production was initially co-located with Turley Wine Cellars in the Napa Valley, but moved in 2007 to dedicated space in a repurposed farmhouse, a re-commissioned old stone winery, and a newly excavated cave on Napa's Silverado Trail. Despite Rhône-oriented beginnings, pinot now represents more than 60 percent of Failla's production.

WINEMAKING NOTES
Failla's pinot-making generally follows the consensus protocol, except that both primary and malolactic fermentations rely entirely on resident yeasts, and there is no filtration. The barrel stock is primarily François Frères, Remond, and Latour, and about 30 percent of barrels are new in each vintage.

TASTING NOTES
2005 *Hirsch Vineyard (tasted in 2007):* Almost saturated, medium-dark black-red; explosive nose of black cherry and blackberries, and strongly floral; lifted, citrus-tinged red berry fruit on the palate, and considerable slate-y minerality; elegant and almost weightless despite the intensity of aromas and flavors, with just a hint of grip on the finish. Very attractive.

2005 *Keefer Ranch (tasted in 2007):* Medium, rosy-black-red; exuberant spice, orange peel, and black tea; intensely fruity and very slightly sweet, with infused flowers, cranberry, and a hint of white pepper; sober, mineral-driven finish. The nose and attack are classic Keefer; the finish is distinctive.

2005 *Occidental Ridge (tasted in 2007):* Opaque, dark black-red; rich, complex impression on the nose with floral, chocolate, and cherry pie components; very sweet on the palate, with inky and almost gritty elements; fine-grained tannins, however, and attractive overall; intense and long.

2000 *Keefer Ranch (tasted in 2003):* Saturated, deep black-red; very ripe fruit aromas with some bramble and beet; sweet on the palate, with plum flavors and roasted root vegetables; emery texture verging on crushed velvet; very long.

FESS PARKER WINERY AND VINEYARDS
Los Olivos, California

Nearly everyone who watched American television in the 1950s and 1960s was exposed to Fess Parker's classic portrayals of the hero-frontiersmen Davy Crockett and Daniel Boone. Far fewer know that the actor had a hugely successful second career in California real estate development, including a major resort and hotel complex on the Santa Barbara waterfront and a 700-acre ranch in Foxen Canyon, where (among other things) he planted a small vineyard in 1989. Rather quickly, the small vineyard grew into a much larger enterprise involving purchased as well as estate grown fruit, a capacious production facility, and one of Santa Barbara County's most photogenic tasting rooms. It absorbed the energies of Parker's son, Eli (who became the winemaker), and his daughter Ashley and Ashley's husband, Tim Snider, both of whom assumed management roles.

Fess Parker Winery and Vineyards was never a pinot-centric enterprise: chardonnay was always the anchor of its portfolio, and Rhône varieties have now become its major preoccupation, but it took pinot noir seriously from time to time, especially when the 212-acre vineyard named for the aforementioned Ashley was planted in 1997 and 1998. Ashley's was a huge project: more than 200 planted acres on a ranch of more than 600 acres. It was also a commitment to pinot noir and a bet on the future of the cool western end of the Santa Ynez Valley, for which the Sta. Rita Hills designation was later approved. Before the investment at Ashley's, the Fess Parker pinot program had relied primarily on purchased fruit from the Santa Maria Valley and from Los Alamos, including blocks G and H at Bien Nacido. In 1995 Fess Parker also purchased 80 acres of the venerable Sierra Madre Vineyard on the Santa Maria Mesa; although some of the acreage had been planted to pinot noir in the 1970s, Sierra Madre's main appeal for Eli Parker was its chardonnay.

Beginning in 1997, Ashley's was planted with great care to UCD 4 and several Dijon clones, and farmed to very low yields, attracting the attention of boutique winemakers searching for superior grapes from the Sta. Rita Hills AVA. Producers such as BREWER-CLIFTON, WILD HORSE, Brophy-Clark, Drew Family, and TANTARA made vineyard-designated wines from Ashley's Vineyard pinots beginning around 2000; the vineyard also came to anchor a new, small-lot pinot program under the Fess Parker label, which was dedicated to a combination of vineyard-designated and clone-specific wines. But by 2006, nine years after the purchase, Ashley's had begun to tie up more capital and human resources than the family wished to invest in cool-climate varieties, and it was sold, subject to a leaseback of 75 acres. This adjustment meant curtailment of the vineyard-designated small-lot program, which was anchored at Ashley's, and the launch (beginning with the 2007 vintage) of a Sta. Rita Hills appellation pinot blended from the contracted acreage at Ashley's (renamed Gaia under new ownership); blocks at Rio Vista (at the extreme east end of the appellation); and Hayes Ranch, which is located almost due south of Ashley's, across Santa Rosa Road from Sanford's La Rinconada property.

WINES AND WINEMAKING NOTES
The first Fess Parker pinot, made from Bien Nacido fruit but not vineyard-designated, was made in 1989. The second, beginning in 1993 after a three-year hiatus, was a county-designated wine made from several Santa Maria Valley sources. The pinot is entirely destemmed; cold-soaked for approximately three days; fermented in vessels ranging from 1.5-ton fruit bins to large, closed-top tanks; started with inoculated yeast; and pressed at dryness. The program relies primarily on François Frères barrels and on varying percentages of new wood, and the vineyard-designated wines spend sixteen months in barrel. Egg-white fining is done as necessary to "polish rough edges," and cross-flow filtration has been standard since 2005.

Eli Parker was the hands-on chief winemaker until 2005. He was succeeded in 2006 (after a short interregnum) by Blair Fox, a "natural" winemaker, who is said to have experimented with grape fermentation as part of high school chemistry. Fox worked at neighboring Sunstone Winery after graduating from the University of California Davis, and briefly in Australia, before joining the cellar team at Fess Parker in 2002.

TASTING NOTES

2005 *Ashley's Vineyard (tasted in 2007):* Medium black-red; open, expressive nose of cherry, toast, and soft spice; soft and slightly fruit-sweet on the palate, with black pepper, barrel marking, and good structure.

2005 *Clone 115 (tasted in 2007):* Distinctive nose of raspberry with a floral, cosmetic-case overlay; very intense in the mouth, with sweet, red-toned fruit; finishes with barrel char and noticeable grip. All the fruit from this bottling came from Ashley's Vineyard.

2005 *Pommard Clone (tasted in 2007):* Brilliant, medium-dark garnet; toasty, soft spice aromas; very silky and intense in the mouth, combining red and black fruit flavors with a bit of roasted red pepper; finished with some grip. This bottling is a combination of fruit from Ashley's and Bien Nacido.

FIDDLEHEAD CELLARS
Lompoc, California

Enology, for Kathy Joseph, was "an escape" from medical school. Headed toward medicine, she had a solid undergraduate background in microbiology and biochemistry. After she worked a summer in Simi Winery's tasting room and learned tasting from the much-respected Zelma Long, her undergraduate work was repurposed as the foundation for a graduate degree in viticulture and enology. Following some early work experience at Long Vineyards and at Joseph Phelps Vineyards, as well as five vintages at the Robert Pecota Winery, Joseph created the Fiddlehead brand in 1989, dedicated to pinot noir and sauvignon blanc. Her business model was a 3,000- to 6,000-case winery with access to fruit from regions that had been "proven by pioneers" but retained "significant growth potential"; long-term contracts with growers; and production at wineries that would agree to custom crush for her. For pinot noir, this framework led her not to "crowded areas" such as Los Carneros or Russian River, but to Oregon's Willamette Valley and Santa Barbara County. Fiddlehead's first release was 100 cases of 1989 pinot from the venerable Sierra Madre Vineyard southeast of Santa Maria. The first Willamette Valley wine was made in 1991.

In 1996, in a departure from the original purchased-fruit and custom-crush model, Joseph purchased 133 acres of field-crop and hillside land between Santa Rosa Road and the Santa Ynez River, across the road from the historic Sanford & Benedict vineyard. To develop this large parcel (100 of the 133 acres have now been planted), Joseph created a separate vineyard company owned equally with Foster's Wine Estates; hired Coastal Vineyard Care as onsite managers; and reached an agreement to split the fruit from each parcel equally with Foster's and to share fruit from Fiddlehead's half with a handful of small pinot-centric wineries, including ARCADIAN WINES, ANCIEN WINES, HITCHING POST WINES, and the Bonaccorsi Wine Company. The

FIDDLEHEAD CELLARS: A VERTICAL TASTING OF THE OREGON WINES

The following tasting of Fiddlehead's Oregon pinots took place in January of 2007. A single wine was chosen to represent each vintage if Fiddlehead had made more than one Oregon cuvée in that year.

2004 *Elton Vineyard:* Brilliant, light-to-medium rosy-garnet; aromas of rose petal, iris, and wild strawberry; more strawberry on the palate in a lovely, silky, elegant package; very fine on the mid-palate; bright with just a hint of grip.

2003 *Oldsville Reserve:* Medium-dark, purplish color; hard spice, sage, and cabinet-shop aromas; then rich, round, ripe, and tannic on the palate; dark and mouth filling, with considerable and atypical mid-palate weight attributable to the exceptionally hot vintage.

2002 *Elton Vineyard:* Medium-dark, pink-rimmed magenta; floral nose again, like the 2004, but also earthy with high notes of peppermint; Italian plum in the mouth; slightly sweet, almost chewy, persistent, and tightly knit.

2001 *Seven Springs Vineyard:* Brilliant, medium black-red; exotic, racy nose of Indonesian spice, tobacco, and *salumi*; sweet, plum-raspberry flavors on the palate with infused violets and dusty tannins; texture of rough silk.

2000 *Elton Vineyard:* Brilliant, medium-dark, blackish-red color; bay leaf, sandalwood, gum camphor, sawdust, crayon, and black fruit aromas; ripe red cherry in the mouth; intense, juicy, bright, and mouth coating, with a powerfully elegant structure and a bit of gentle grip. Fine.

1999 *Oldsville Reserve:* Deep, medium-dark ruby tinged with brick; an earthy, dark edition of the Seven Springs Vineyard's exotic spice; sweet and minerally on the palate, with dark fruit, *charcuterie,* and nice weight.

1998 *Willamette Valley:* Brilliant, medium-dark brick red; earthy and camphory nose; medium-rich and round on the palate, but drying on the finish. Sound but not stellar.

1997 *Willamette Valley:* Medium brick-red with a rosy rim; expansive nose of raspberry, pepper, clove, and nutmeg; black raspberry in the mouth, with chalky tannins that felt alternately silky and grippy; very slightly austere but also very rewarding; an example of lovely maturation from an underappreciated vintage. Fine.

1996 *Willamette Valley:* Brilliant terra cotta; bright nose of potpourri and spring flowers; spicy, racy, and very slightly sweet on the palate, with some hints of orange peel and with a soft, round structure.

1995 *Willamette Valley:* Brilliant terra cotta again; exotic aromas of spice, sawdust, and pumpkin pie; marzipan and cocoa in the mouth; rich, very slightly grippy, and mouth coating; gives an overall impression of subtlety.

1994 *Willamette Valley:* Transparent, dark black-red; aromas of blueberry and cranberry with some mace and intense, camellia-like flowers; black licorice, plum, blackberry, and coffee in the mouth; round, soft, rich, and long; surprisingly youthful and very fine.

1993 *Willamette Valley:* Medium-dark brick-red color; camphor, mushroom, and earthy aromas with ripe Bing cherry underneath; rich and round on the palate, with notes of cocoa, espresso, and Mirabelle *eau-de-vie*; excellent acidity and huge length. Very fine.

1992 *Willamette Valley:* Almost opaque, dark brick-red color; some orange peel on the nose; sweet and rich in the mouth with cocoa, espresso, black cherry, and mint; a big, dark wine with considerable grip and glycerin; nicely structured, nonetheless.

soils in this vineyard, which is now called Fiddlestix, are mainly Botella and Gazos series clay-loams developed from sandstone and shale-derived alluvia. Of the two, the Gazos soils are shallower and are underlain with bedrock shale. The planting, which was carried out over a four-year period from 1998 to 2001, is mostly north–south oriented 7-foot rows with 4 feet between vines (except when an off-angle orientation or slightly different spacing was deemed to better respect soil types). Most of Fiddlestix is very gently sloping benchland, but the eastern end of the vineyard is an impressive, steep-sided knoll. The scion material is roughly one third UCD 4 and 5, one third Dijon 113 and 115, and one third Dijon 667 and 777; the 2001 plantings consist mostly of the trademarked ENTAV versions of 115 and 777. Fiddlestix produced enough fruit to make 300 cases of wine in 2000 and 1,500 cases in 2001. When the vineyard is in full production, Fiddlehead may choose to retain enough Fiddlestix fruit for as many as 3,000 cases.

Throughout the 1990s, Fiddlehead's Willamette Valley wine was a blend that relied on fruit from the Elton and Seven Springs vineyards in the Eola Hills, and from YAMHILL VALLEY VINEYARDS outside McMinnville, where the wine was made through 2002. (The 1991 relied entirely on Yamhill Valley Vineyards grapes.) The Seven Springs fruit has always come from a designated 4-acre block. At Elton (which was once part of Seven Springs), Fiddlehead shares the oldest block, planted in 1983, with KEN WRIGHT CELLARS. At the same time that production of the Oregon wine was shifted from Yamhill Valley Vineyards to dedicated space in Lompoc's wine ghetto, dubbed Fiddle Headquarters, the Yamhill Valley Vineyards fruit was relinquished and replaced with grapes purchased from the Alloro Vineyard in the Chehalem Mountains AVA.

WINES AND WINEMAKING NOTES

A Santa Maria Valley wine was made from 1989 to 1993, exclusively from Sierra Madre fruit, but it was labeled as a vineyard-designate only in 1989. A second Santa Maria Valley wine was made from Santa Maria Hills fruit in 1997 only. The Willamette Valley bottling, made each year since 1991, was joined by an Elton vineyard-designate in 2000 and 2002, a Seven Springs vineyard-designate in 2001, and a vineyard-specific bottling from Alloro in 2005. (The Willamette Valley wine was called Oldsville Reserve in 1999 and 2000.) The first wine from Fiddlestix debuted in 2000, replacing the Santa Maria Valley wine. In 2001 Joseph crafted two pinots from Fiddlestix, a mainstream offering called Seven Twenty Eight (for the 7.28 mile marker on Santa Rosa Road that landmarks her driveway) and a selection of the fattest barrels, called Lollapalooza. A special bottling named for Joseph's husband, Tom Doyle, was made in 2002.

Joseph picks fruit "strictly based on taste," looking for the shift from "simple fruit flavors to complexity," and is sensitive to the uptick in pH that occurs (more or less) when the juice becomes more viscous. Typically, these indicators translate to sugar levels between 23 and 25 Brix. Fermentors are double-height fruit bins. Joseph used about 25 percent whole clusters in early vintages, but she now destems completely. Cold-soaking is lot specific. All lots are inoculated, using a variety of yeast strains, to start the alcoholic fermentation. Punchdowns are done two or three times daily at the outset, and Joseph likes fermentation juice temperatures to peak in the high 80s or low 90s. Pressing is generally done when the must is dry. A light press fraction is reintegrated.

Each year, between 35 and 45 percent new barrels are used. Although a variety of coopers are involved, Seguin Moreau and

Cadus are favorites for their contribution to the wines' aromas and textures. Malolactic fermentations are induced with a second inoculation, after which the wines spend twelve to fifteen months in wood, are sometimes racked after the malo is complete but sometimes not until bottling, and are generally bottled without fining or filtration. Another year of bottle aging precedes release. Joseph says she "cares most about texture" and likes "mid-palate weight and a long finish." Without exception, the Fiddlehead pinots I have tasted when the wines were young display exceptional length and textures reminiscent of upholstery silk or velvet. They are never heavy, although sometimes quite darkly colored, and they age rewardingly.

TASTING NOTES

2005 *Seven Twenty-Eight (tasted in 2008):* Transparent, rosy black-red; slightly fruity, slightly savory nose; very intense and nicely acidic on the palate with strong, spicy fruit flavors that straddle the cusp between black fruit and red; almost creamy at mid-palate; nicely structured and long.

2004 *Seven Twenty-Eight (tasted in 2008):* Transparent, medium rosy magenta; smoke, earth, and spice on the nose; intense, persistent earthy fruit on the palate with notes of gum camphor; exceptionally long finish.

FLOWERS VINEYARD AND WINERY
Cazadero, California

Walt and Joan Flowers were veterans of the wholesale nursery business in Pennsylvania when they found themselves increasingly fascinated by wine. In the 1980s, when they traveled regularly from Pennsylvania to Oregon to inspect or purchase stock for their nursery, they began making side trips to Napa and Sonoma. They were enamored of red Burgundy and impressed by Jensen and Selleck pinots from Calera. When they finally decided they wanted to buy a vineyard, the love of pinot drew them west from Napa and Healdsburg to cool, pinot-friendly sites near the coast. In 1989 an advertisement in *Wine Spectator* for "321 acres with vineyard potential" attracted them to Camp Meeting Ridge, a sometime summer retreat site for various religious groups atop the first ridge inland from the ocean, between Jenner and Fort Ross. This was the proverbial warm site in a cool climate that seemed made to order for pinot noir: full sun pretty much all day; moderate daytime high temperatures and cool nights; and, from a nursery operator's point of view, "lousy" soils. So in 1991, after extensive investigations and with advice from Andy Bledsoe, the then viticulturist for ROBERT MONDAVI WINERY, the Flowerses began planting the first of 35 acres of their spectacular site to vineyard, 1,200 to 1,400 feet above sea level, in Franciscan clay-loam soils irrigated with water from the south fork of the Gualala River.

Vineyard blocks are laid out on the ridgetop itself, on a gentle northwest-facing slope below, and on steeper slopes facing south and southeast. The original rows were oriented east–west; newer plantings are set out in north–south rows, to capture about 60 percent of the morning sunlight and to warm up the soil, while minimizing direct exposure to hot afternoon sun. Clones were selected for rot resistance and open-cluster morphology: two Swan selections, one from Dehlinger, and one from Carneros; three Calera selections, all from the Hyde vineyard in Los Carneros; nursery-sourced UCD 1A, 2A, and 4, as well as some UCD 23; and Dijon 113 and 115. Three spacings were used, all relatively tight: meter-by-meter, 4-foot intervals in 7-foot rows, and 5-foot intervals in 8-foot rows. The meter-by-meter blocks, unsurprisingly, produce a slightly higher yield per acre than those more sparsely planted. Total yield has fluctuated wildly from year to year, from as little as 0.71 tons per acre to as much as 2.67 tons, creating various business headaches for the brand (see below). In 1997 a modern winery was

---

IMPRESSIVE CLARITY AND ELEGANTLY DEFINED FLAVORS PRESENTED WITH A SEDUCTIVE COMBINATION OF DELICACY AND STRENGTH

---

tucked discreetly behind a centenary oak tree on the Camp Meeting Ridge site; ten years later, it remains the only major modern winemaking facility in the True Sonoma Coast.

The 1994, 1995, and 1996 vintages were made by Steve Kistler at his winery in the Russian River Valley; subsequent vintages were made in the Flowers facility. The 1997 through 1999 vintages were made by Greg La Follette (see TANDEM), and the first three in the new millennium by Hugh Chappelle. Ross Cobb (see COBB WINES) took the reins in 2004 after several years' experience as Chappelle's assistant. Since 2005, Tom Hinde, formerly the general manager at HARTFORD FAMILY WINES and LA CREMA, has been Flowers's president.

Four miles south of Camp Meeting Ridge as the crow flies, Flowers acquired a second vineyard site in 1997, which was planted between 1998 and 2001. This site, which is known in its totality as the Flowers Ranch, comprises two separately named vineyards: Sea View Ridge consists of fifteen blocks (about 22 acres) above

the 1,600-foot contour, where the soils are relatively loamy; Frances Thompson includes the twenty blocks (another 22 acres) situated between 1,400 and 1,600 feet, where the soils are primarily weathered red sandstone. As at Camp Meeting Ridge, the clonal assortment is large—Dijon 115, Calera, and UCD 23 budwood from Camp Meeting Ridge; Swan selection from Carneros Creek and Dehlinger; plus nursery-sourced Dijon 667, 777, and 828—on three rootstocks (101-14, 3309, and 420A). No meter-by-meter plantings were attempted at this site, considering the lower-vigor soils; 4-foot intervals in 7-foot rows were used instead. Besides these estate vineyards directly owned by Flowers, two other vineyards are controlled under long-term leases and farmed by Flowers's viticultural team: the DZ Vineyard and Petersen Ranch.

WINES AND WINEMAKING NOTES
All true coastal vineyards require meticulous farming to ensure healthy fruit and full ripeness in what amount to marginal growing conditions. Cobb reports that he spends "enormous time" in the Flowers vineyards, overseeing pruning, shoot positioning, green harvesting, and canopy management. Pinot is picked between 22 and 25 Brix "with attention to seed and skin maturity" and rigorously sorted several times. Most fruit is destemmed, but as much as 30 percent may be retained as whole clusters if a combination of older vines and soil fertility produced ripe, lignified stems. After a four- to ten-day cold soak, primary fermentations are made to rely on resident yeasts. When the musts go dry, the free-run juice is drained directly to barrels, and the remaining skins are pressed in a small basket press. The new wines spend fourteen to sixteen months in barrel (François Frères and Remond

account for a majority of the barrel stock) and are bottled without fining or filtration "when possible."

The Flowers pinot portfolio has evolved considerably since the first vintage was made in 1994. There are now two estate wines from the Camp Meeting Ridge (CMR) Vineyard; two (Sonoma Coast) appellation-driven wines, one of which is known by a proprietary name; a mostly non-estate bottling known by another proprietary name; and a variable number of vineyard-designated wines from Flowers Ranch and estate vineyards controlled under long-term leases. The CMR wines are the flagship Camp Meeting Ridge bottling, made every year since 1994, and a "reserve" bottling, made only in selected vintages, called Moon Select. One of the appellation-driven wines is a Sonoma Coast bottling, blended from a combination of estate and non-estate fruit all sourced on the True Sonoma Coast. The second is the Andreen-Gale cuvée (a fusion of the maiden names of Walt and Joan Flowers's mothers), launched in 2001 as a *second* blend of estate and non-estate fruit, which has gradually evolved into an all-estate wine as the Flowers Ranch vines have matured. The non-estate wine with a proprietary name is called Grand Bouquet and was launched in 2004. The 2005 edition of Grand Bouquet was made entirely from Kanzler Vineyard grapes.

The non-CMR vineyard-designated wine program was begun in 1997 with a bottling from the neighboring HIRSCH VINEYARDS, but vineyard-designated wines from non-estate fruit were abandoned in 2000, except for a Keefer Ranch wine that was made from 2000 through 2003. Since then, this program has featured only estate vineyards, beginning with a wine from the Frances Thompson portion of the Flowers Ranch in 2003, another from the Sea View

Ridge portion of the Ranch in 2004, and a DZ Vineyard wine (DZ is a contracted estate vineyard; see above) in 2005.

Much of this complexity stems from the discovery, soon after the CMR Vineyard began to yield, that true coastal vineyards are notoriously erratic producers, owing primarily to the vagaries of coastal weather during the vines' flowering. Flowers countered this reality by planting a second major estate vineyard and by managing others on long term contracts, making them also into "estate" sources; by supplementing estate fruit with purchased fruit from various sources; and by creating vineyard-designated wines that are increasingly estate-based but have ranged far afield over time. The 2004 vintage may be the best yet at Flowers. The wines have impressive clarity and purity, elegantly defined flavors, and a seductive combination of delicacy and strength. I understand the enthusiasm that many reviewers have expressed for the flagship Camp Meeting Ridge bottling, but this vintage, for me, confirms the suspicion I developed when I first saw the Flowers Ranch site in 2001. This "second" vineyard, with its altitude, steep aspect, and rocky topsoil, may be even better wine terrain than Camp Meeting Ridge. The Sea View Ridge bottling is especially striking and very minerally; Frances Thompson, off the same vineyard, is its fruitier twin.

TASTING NOTES

2004 *Sonoma Coast (tasted in 2007)*: Pretty medium garnet; smoke-, nut- and briar-tinged red fruit aromas; tar, cherry, and raspberry on the palate with a hint of citrus; very clean and elegant, and almost featherweight; well made, long, and attractive.

2004 *Andreen-Gale Cuvée (tasted in 2007)*: A touch blacker in color than the Sonoma Coast bottling and slightly earthier on the nose; more structure than the Sonoma Coast wine, with soft spiciness and a hint of mocha; smooth, almost gripless finish; polished, long, and elegant.

2004 *Sea View Ridge (tasted in* 2007*):* Transparent, deep black-red; very complex nose of rose petals, wet slate, cranberries, and tide pools; black cherry-berry fruit on the palate with ferrous notes; a mouth-coating wine with polish, rounded corners, elegance, and minerality; stunning purity; very fine.

2004 *Frances Thompson Vineyard (tasted in* 2007*):* Transparent, deep brick-red color; fruit-driven nose featuring primarily wild blackberries; clean, intense, and subtle on the palate with tar, mesquite, and a persistent hint of fruit-sweetness; the texture just hints at velvet; long and fine.

2004 *Camp Meeting Ridge (tasted in* 2007*):* Brilliant, medium garnet; expressively aromatic with spring flowers, lavender, and salt marsh smells; rich and ripe on the palate, with notes of boysenberry, coffee, mesquite, and tar; long and lovely, almost creamy, with some minerality.

2004 *Moon Select (tasted in* 2007*):* Transparent, dark brick-red color; red and black fruit aromas with a bit of tobacco and exotic spice; lavender-infused, black and marionberry fruit on the palate with a hint of brightening citrus; some berries-and-cream character; coffee-tobacco throughout; grippy at the end; fine, but very barrel marked.

2002 *Andreen-Gale Cuvée (tasted twice in* 2005*):* Transparent, medium black-red; honeysuckle, wild herbs, mint, fir balsam, cardamom, and rose petal aromas; a sweet core of cherry, black fruit, milk chocolate, and black pepper; considerable barrel marking and some tannin on the finish, but silky, mouth coating, seamless, and long, overall.

FLYING GOAT CELLARS
Santa Ynez, California

Flying Goat Cellars is the personal pinot project of Norman Yost, a University of California Davis graduate in environmental science, who has made wine, or has helped to make wine, for a long list of vintners in the Dry Creek, Napa, Russian River, Willamette, and Santa Ynez valleys since 1981. Influenced by a former college roommate who majored in fermentation science, Yost's wine career was launched with harvest work at E. & J. Gallo's Frei Brothers Winery just months after graduation. Nine months later, he was the assistant winemaker at Napa's Monticello Cellars, taking extension courses in viticulture and enology on the side. Stints as the winemaker for Mark West Vineyards and for the then-new Amberley Estates Winery in Australia's Margaret River region followed, before Yost headed for Oregon to concentrate on pinot noir. From 1991 to 1996, he was the winemaker for Arterberry Winery (sold to Duck Pond Cellars in 1993), and for Flynn Vineyards, a large custom-crush facility, from 1996 to 1998. At this point, entirely by chance, Yost reconnected with Alan Phillips, for whom he had worked at Monticello Cellars sixteen years before. Phillips offered Yost a position at FOLEY ESTATES in Santa Barbara County. Two years later, it was time, at last, for a wine of his own. With enough fruit from the venerable Santa Maria Hills Vineyard to make ten barrels of pinot noir, Yost launched Flying Goat Cellars, named for two pet pygmy goats originally acquired in Oregon to scrub up wild blackberries and other "weeds." By 2004, with production at Flying Goat having grown to 750 cases a year, Yost left Foley Estates to concentrate on a combination of Flying Goat and consulting assignments.

His wine program is based entirely on purchased grapes from carefully selected sources in the Santa Maria Valley, the Santa Rita Hills, and San Luis Obispo County. In 2001 his fruit came from Blocks 3A and 3I (Dijon 115 and UCD 13, respectively) of the 1997 and 1998 plantings at DIERBERG VINEYARD on the Santa Maria Mesa; in 2002 he added Dijon 667 from Block 16 of Foley's Rancho Santa Rosa Vineyard in the Sta. Rita Hills. In 2003 the new sources were Rio Vista, a 1999 planting at the slightly warmer eastern end of the Sta. Rita Hills appellation, and Solomon Hills, the Miller family's late 1990s development on the Santa Maria Mesa. In 2005 the Dierberg fruit was relinquished and a sparkling wine was made from the Solomon Hills fruit. Yost also "diversified," sourcing fruit from the Salisbury Vineyard just off Highway 101 near Avila Beach, a protected microclimate on the coast side of the hills that separate Edna Valley from the ocean. In each vintage, the fruit from each vineyard source is vineyard-designated. This means multiple bottlings each year since 2002: Dierberg and Rancho Santa Rosa in that year; those plus Rio Vista and Solomon Hills in 2003; Rancho Santa Rosa and Dierberg in 2004, plus a clone-specific (UCD 2A) bottling from Rio Vista; and Rancho Santa Rosa and Salisbury in 2005.

WINEMAKING NOTES

Like many makers, Yost says his "first" criterion for deciding when to harvest is "how the fruit tastes," but he admits to checking as well for brown seeds and lignified stems, and to "looking" at Brix and pH. Most fruit is destemmed into fruit bins and layered with dry ice, or put into 3.5-ton, open-top fermentors, which are cooled with jackets;

no sulfur dioxide is added as long as the fruit is in good condition. After two to four days of cold soak and the addition of acid if the must shows a pH higher than 3.7, primary fermentations are started with RC212 or with Assmannshausen isolates. After seven to ten days of action, Yost allows one to three days of postfermentation maceration and presses when all the sugar has been converted. Fermentation temperatures do not exceed 85°F. Water additions "have been employed in the past" when Yost was faced with "excessively high Brix."

After settling for one or two days, the new wines are inoculated with malolactic starter and barreled in a stock that is light on new wood and uses some pieces for as long as five years. The main coopers are François Frères, Rousseau, and Saury; the wood profile is a combination of the Tronçais and Chatillon forests, and a regional wood blend that Rousseau calls MFE, featuring stave wood from forests in the east of France. *Élevage* lasts for twelve to sixteen months, and the wines are held for six to nine months before bottling before they are released. The wines are never fined but are filtered through "old T-shirts" for clarity.

Flying Goat pinots are moderately colored, aromatically expressive, and generally elegant wines that showcase the singularities of the different sites with which Yost works. The Salisbury bottling, new in 2005, seems especially interesting and worth following in future vintages. Overall, these wines are nicely crafted southern Central Coast pinot noir, with considerable finesse.

TASTING NOTES

2005 *Salisbury Vineyards (tasted in 2007)*: Brilliant, pale-ruby; a bit of red fruit and an overall dusty character on the nose; strawberry-raspberry, black pepper, and some barrel char on the front palate;

fruit-peel and fruit-flavored tea at mid-palate; initially fruit-sweet, then dry, quite sober, and minerally; silky, distinctive, and quite attractive overall.

2005 *Solomon Hills Vineyard (tasted in* 2007*):* Transparent, medium ruby; a bit of earth and forest floor on the nose; intense cherry-raspberry on the palate; soft and round texturally with some grip from mid-palate to finish; a bit shy at the moment, but attractive.

2005 *Dierberg Vineyard (tasted in* 2007*):* Luminous rosy-red; forest floor aromas on the nose; intense and resinous on the palate with hard spice; sensation of fruit-and-flower-infused Darjeeling tea; texture of polished cotton at first, then grippy after mid-palate; long.

2005 *Rio Vista Vineyard (tasted in* 2007*):* Medium ruby; potpourri, nutshells, and herbs on the nose, with a bit of ripe fruit; rich, red-fruited, flower-infused, and mocha-tinged tastes on the palate; considerable load of very fine-grained tannins; long and serious.

2000 *Santa Maria Hills Vineyard (tasted in* 2007*):* Brilliant, light-to-medium garnet; dusty floral nose; intense, exotic, and nutty flavors, and a whiff of freshly-ground white pepper against a backdrop of wild raspberry; graceful, elegant, and long; maturing nicely.

FOLEY ESTATES VINEYARD AND WINERY AND LINCOURT VINEYARDS
Solvang, California

Foley Estates Vineyard and Winery is one of two closely connected wineries created by William Foley II, the founder

and chief executive officer of Fidelity National Financial Corporation, in 1996. The other is Lincourt Vineyards. Until 2003 both enterprises cohabited in a repurposed dairy farm on Alamo Pintado Road, near the hamlet of Ballard, that housed J. Carey Cellars from 1973 until the late 1980s. (Several years after the Firestone family purchased J. Carey, and then changed its name to Curtis Winery, the family sold the former Carey premises to Foley in 1995 and relocated Curtis to a new site in Foxen Canyon.) Since 1998 Foley Estates and Lincourt have also shared a single winemaker and general manager, Alan Phillips. Phillips, a graduate of the University of California Davis, previously worked as a consultant at Monticello Cellars in the Napa Valley, and at Byington Winery in the Santa Cruz Mountains. Both Foley Estates and Lincourt produced pinot noir from overlapping vineyard sources beginning in 1996. Lincourt's main offering was a Santa Barbara County blend in most vintages, but small quantities of a Sta. Rita Hills appellation wine from young vines and a Rancho Santa Rosa (see below) were also made after 2002. Until 2001 the Foley Estates pinot program was based entirely on fruit from a portion of the Santa Maria Hills Vineyard that Foley farmed.

Meanwhile, beginning in 1998, Foley planted the first of 240 acres of chardonnay, syrah, and pinot noir on a former thoroughbred horse ranch called Rancho Santa Rosa, which is now home to a new winery and centerpiece for the brand. Rancho Santa Rosa is a beautiful, rolling, 460-acre parcel with elevations reaching almost 1,000 feet on the south face of the Purisima Hills (and the north side of Highway 246), about four miles west of Buellton. Almost exactly half of the planted surface at Rancho Santa Rosa is dedicated to pinot noir, set out in 31 discrete "microblocks" ranging from less than an acre to about 6 acres, mostly at the ranch's higher elevations. As this vineyard began to bear in 2001, Foley's lease arrangements at Santa Maria Hills were terminated, and since 2002 the Foley Estates pinot program has depended entirely on grapes from Rancho Santa Rosa. Fruit from this vineyard has also been sold to other makers, among whom it is much prized, and many Rancho Santa Rosa wines have been vineyard-designated by FLYING GOAT CELLARS, RUSACK VINEYARDS, BREWER-CLIFTON, RICHARD LONGORIA WINES, and Firestone.

In 2007 the former Ashley's Vineyard, farther west on Highway 246, developed by and for the FESS PARKER WINERY in the late 1990s, was acquired for the Lincourt brand, and renamed Lindsay's Vineyard. (Briefly, after Ashley's was sold by Fess Parker and before it was acquired by Lincourt, it was owned by Demetria Vineyards and called Gaia's.) This acquisition may transform Lincourt, as far as pinot noir is concerned, into an entirely estate program based on grapes grown at Lindsay's, but plans were not firm at the time of this writing.

Alan Phillips reports that the Foley Estates and Lincourt wines are made almost identically, following the consensus protocol. Both barrel regimes are based on a variety of coopers and use about one third new barrels in each vintage, except that clone-specific bottlings of Foley Estates (Pommard, UCD 2A, Dijon 115, and Dijon 777) may use up to 50 percent new wood. The important distinction, according to Phillips, is not between Foley Estates and Lincourt but between the pre-2002 period, when both labels were sourced primarily from the Santa Maria Valley, and the post-2002 period, when both became largely Sta. Rita Hills–based. My experience tasting the nationally distributed wines from the 2005 vintage suggests quite different wines (see below).

TASTING NOTES

2005 *Lincourt Sta. Rita Hills (tasted in 2007):* Transparent, medium black-red; aromas of ripe fruit, forest floor, and compost; very sweet, cherry-plum fruit and black pepper on the palate; almost creamy at mid-palate; then considerable grip with a slightly chalky finish.

2005 *Foley Estates Rancho Santa Rosa (tasted in 2007):* Transparent medium-dark ruby; slightly floral but mostly berry fruit–driven nose; sweet, rich cherry and boysenberry in the mouth; big overall, with considerable ripe fruit, alcohol, and very present, ripe tannins; finishes long.

FORT ROSS VINEYARD
San Francisco, California

As vineyards have shifted westward, from the inland coastal valleys and the lee side of the Coast Range to the true coastal valleys and the coast itself, the annals of California winegrowing have been littered with stories of would-be vintners advised not to plant because the site would be too cold or too remote, or because the whole project was just too crazy. It was no different when Lester and Linda Schwartz, both South Africans originally and San Franciscans by adoption, bought 969 precipitous acres south of Fort Ross, overlooking the Pacific, in 1988. As an undergraduate, he was trained in geology, before making a career in law; she was a musician turned arts administrator. Even in South Africa, they had strong orientations to food and wine, and considered planting grapes on their coastal California property as soon as they bought it. Linda took classes in viticulture and enology at Santa Rosa Junior College and at the University of California Davis. The geologist in Lester pondered the site—especially how it disposed of sometimes antediluvian rains.

RIPE BUT NICELY BALANCED WINES THAT SHOW THE MINERALITY TYPICAL OF HIGHER ELEVATIONS IN THE COASTAL HILLS

Between 1994 and 1998, very slowly and without any help from the "consultants or vineyard developers" who advised them solemnly that their project was "not feasible," the Schwartzes (working with their own hands and a small crew) prepared the first seven of twenty-eight small vineyard blocks, installed 7 miles of 6-foot deer fence, and eventually set out vines. The rootstock took two years instead of one to establish, and the field grafting took three years to complete. Like neighboring coastal vineyards, Fort Ross enjoys bright sunshine during the day during most of the growing season, and cold nights, which help to preserve acidity. It is at a higher elevation than most of its neighbors except Flowers Ranch, however, with vines between 1,200 and 1,700 feet.

By 2002 the Schwartzes had 34 acres of pinot noir, 8 acres of chardonnay, and 2 acres of pinotage (these people are from South Africa, after all!) in the ground. The scion material for the pinot is mostly Calera selection, plus Swan selection, a field selection from MARIMAR TORRES ESTATE that was UCD 4 or 13 upstream,

and Dijon clones 115 and 777. The first small crop was picked in 2000; the first commercial vintage came in 2001. The 2000, 2001, and 2002 vintages were vinified by Fred Scherrer (see SCHERRER WINES). All of the small crop in 2000 was made under Scherrer's label; the 2001 and 2002 harvests were divided, more or less evenly, between Scherrer Winery and the Schwartzes' new Fort Ross Vineyard label. In 2003, with 70 tons of fruit harvested, 10 tons went to Scherrer for his own label, 10 to Sherrer for a wine made under the Fort Ross Vineyard label, and 50 to Ed Kurtzman (see AUGUST WEST WINES) for a Fort Ross Vineyard label wine he would make at the Laird Family Winery in Napa. Kurtzman then made all the Fort Ross Vineyard wines from 2004 through 2006; in 2007 the Fort Ross Vineyard torch passed to Helen Kiplinger, formerly the assistant winemaker at FIDDLEHEAD CELLARS.

WINES AND WINEMAKING NOTES
When Scherrer was making the wines in 2001 and 2002, the Fort Ross fruit was made into five wines: "plain" and reserve wines under the Fort Ross Vineyard label; the same under the Scherrer label; and a Fort Ross Vineyard cuvée called Coastal Ridges, crafted to be lighter and more delicate than the other wines. In 2002 Scherrer also blended a bit of Fort Ross fruit with fruit from nearby HIRSCH for a Scherrer Winery blend he called Sonoma Coast, but this wine had no analog under the Fort Ross Vineyard label. In 2003 an intervariety blend called Symposium debuted: a "proprietary" *assemblage* of estate pinot noir with about 4 percent pinotage. Scherrer called the last of the Fort Ross wines made for his label High Slopes. For balance, he made a tiny, special lot for the Fort Ross Vineyard label called Sea Slopes in 2004. With Kurtzman

as the only winemaker in 2003, there was only one cuvée, but the protocol of an estate bottling (for convenience, this is known internally as the FRV cuvée) and a Reserve, plus Symposium, was resumed in 2004. Coastal Ridges was not made in 2003, 2004, or 2005, but was resumed in 2006 as Sea Slopes—using the name Sherrer had coined for his aforementioned last wine under the Fort Ross Vineyard label.

Presently, the final blends are created in the following order: The most intense barrels, destined for the Reserve, are identified first. The balance is then assessed to determine which barrels can be used harmoniously to make the estate wine. Symposium and Sea Slopes are made from the rest. Winemaking generally follows the consensus protocol; new wine is drained and pressed off the must at or just after dryness. The main coopers are François Frères, Cadus, Rousseau, Seguin Moreau, and (for the first time in 2007) Tonnellerie Treuil, a Brive (Corrèze)–based cooper that is part of the François Frères group. Linda Schwartz remarks, as many importers who work with Burgundies have before, that every barrel constitutes an individual lot with its own character and personality. Part of the blending exercise, she observes, is identifying "barrels that get along with each other," making the "ultimate barrel mix both democratic and sociological." About 40 percent of the barrel stock is new in each vintage; the balance has been used previously to raise one, two, or three wines. The wines are made in a ripe but nicely balanced style, and they show the minerality typical of higher elevations in the coastal hills.

TASTING NOTES

2004 *Fort Ross Vineyard (tasted in 2007)*. Transparent medium garnet; bright floral and red fruit aromas followed by attractive cherry-raspberry flavors on the palate; nicely built and quite elegant; almost silky with just a hint of grip; graphite and minerality from mid-palate to finish.

2004 *Reserve (tasted in 2007):* Just slightly darker than the FRV; a spicy, slightly exotic and barrel-marked nose, with hints of pepper and nutmeg; rich, round mouth-feel and slightly sweet; dominance of black fruit, graphite, and minerality; soft grip from mid-palate to finish.

FOXEN VINEYARD AND WINERY
Santa Maria, California

Foxen Vineyard and Winery was established in 1987 by Dick Doré and Bill Wathen on a corner of the horse and cattle ranch midway between Santa Maria and Los Olivos where Doré was raised. Doré, whose first career was in banking, had become enamored of wine when he and his family lived for eighteen months in Europe during the mid 1970s. Wathen, another native of the southern Central Coast, found his way to wine through a degree in fruit science from California State Polytechnic University at San Luis Obispo, worked for Santa Barbara viticultural pioneers Louis Lucas and Dale Hampton, and spent four years as the vineyard manager for CHALONE VINEYARD. The winery is named for Doré's great-great-grandfather Benjamin Foxen, an English sea captain who purchased Rancho Tinaquaic from the government of Mexico in 1837. The logo, a slightly asymmetrical anchor, was the cattle brand for Foxen's ranch. The winery buildings, on the northern side of Foxen Canyon Road, are century-old, repurposed ranch structures (the tasting room is the former black smithy) that give new meaning to the word "rustic." Ground for a new winery was broken early in 2008, and the new facility will be commissioned late in 2008 or early in 2009.

Although Doré and Wathen made a dribble of home wine in 1985 and 1986, the first commercial release came in 1987 and was made entirely from purchased fruit. From 1987 until 1990, only one pinot noir was made, labeled Santa Maria Valley, using grapes from two vineyards on the Santa Maria Mesa. The 1987 and 1989 editions were based entirely on Sierra Madre grapes; the 1988 vintage came entirely from the Santa Maria Hills. In 1990, Bien Nacido fruit entered the Santa Maria Valley blend, and anchored it after 1991. The 1992 through 1995 editions were blends of Bien Nacido, Sierra Madre, and Gold Coast; beginning in 1996, fruit was also obtained from Julia's at CAMBRIA. A vineyard-designate program was launched alongside the Santa Maria Valley wine in 1991, using grapes from the Sanford & Benedict vineyard. A vineyard-designated wine from the Bien Nacido Vineyard then debuted in 1994, using fruit from Block Q. In 1997 Foxen entered into a custom-planting agreement at Bien Nacido for Block 8, a south-facing slope laid out in 8-foot rows with 3.5 feet between vines, using a combination of Dijon 113 and 115, UCD 2A and 4, and Mount Eden selection sourced from Sanford & Benedict. Block 8 produced its first crop in 1999 and completely replaced Block Q in Foxen's Bien Nacido program in 2001. In 2006 three additional acres were planted in Block 8, primarily to Dijon 667 and 777.

The 1999 vintage of Sanford & Benedict was Foxen's last until 2006. Owing to the key role Wathen had played in locating the site and designing the vineyard for Bob David's SEA SMOKE CELLARS property, 6 percent of that vineyard's production has been sold to Foxen since 2002, which has made a vineyard-designated Sea Smoke wine in every vintage.

WINEMAKING NOTES

Wathen says his winemaking has changed substantially since the first vintages in the late 1980s. He now picks riper, cold-soaks, and eschews stems. For a time, he also added enzymes for color extraction and wine clarity, but this is now the exception, not the rule. Brix at harvest is said to be between 24.5 and 25, but with finished alcohols often at or above 15 percent, it is possible that the harvest numbers are higher than 25. The fermentors are 2- and 4-ton stainless steel open-tops. Cold soak lasts from three to five days, at which point each fermentor is inoculated. Pumpovers are practiced as the fermentation starts and continue until Wathen "begins to see seeds;" punchdowns follow until the musts go nearly dry. Wathen adds malolactic starter in the fermentors and presses before the must goes dry. Free-run juice goes directly to barrel; press juice is used only in the Santa Maria Valley wine, and only after settling in tank.

Foxen uses only François Frères barrels. The Santa Maria Valley wine sees about 10 percent new wood and is bottled at the end of ten months; vineyard-designates are raised in 50 to 75 percent new barrels for sixteen months. Lots that will be used for the vineyard-designates are identified in the spring after each vintage, when a single racking is done; the Santa Maria Valley blend is made from deselected barrels. Wines are not usually fined, and filtration is done only "when it is necessary for stability." Recent editions of Foxen pinots, which are popular and sell out quickly once they are released, are very bold, ripe, and fruit-driven wines.

TASTING NOTES

2005 *Block 8—Bien Nacido Vineyard (tasted in 2007)*: Medium-dark, almost purplish-ruby; ripe, slightly tarry nose;

very sweet on the palate, like cherry candy, with undertones of smoke, barrel-derived vanilla, and the black pepper that is often typical of Bien Nacido; big, bold, and warm; impressive and enjoyable in its genre.

2005 *Julia's Vineyard (tasted in 2007):* Medium, luminous garnet; root beer and very strong cinnamon on the nose; dark cherry and black pepper on the palate; almost creamy; big and quite alcoholic, and therefore a trifle hot but not heavy; the most attractive of the Julia's made since 2002.

2003 *Sea Smoke Vineyard (tasted in 2007):* Barely transparent, deep black-red; earthy, slightly ferrous nose; very ripe, rich blackberry and huckleberry fruit with undertones of dark chocolate and brewed coffee; mouth coating and borderline creamy to mid-palate, then grippy from mid-palate to finish; soft, velvety, long, lush, and distinctive.

2002 *Julia's Vineyard (tasted in 2007):* Medium-dark brick-red color; tarry and bramble-y on the nose; sweet, rich, plummy fruit on the palate; substantial chocolate and mocha; a bit of grip and warmth at the end.

2001 *Julia's Vineyard (tasted in 2001):* Medium mahogany; aromas of hazelnut and fading fruit; tar, black licorice, and vanilla flavors, and a bit of remaining cherry; satiny, round, long, and fine.

FRANCIS TANNAHILL
Dundee, Oregon

Francis Tannahill is the Lilliputian, highly personal, countertrend wine project (initially featuring the unlikely combination of *vin-de-paille*–method gewürztraminer and syrah sourced from the extreme north and south ends of Oregon) started in 2001 by Cheryl Francis and Sam Tannahill. Francis was then the co-winemaker at CHEHALEM, and Tannahill handled winemaking for ARCHERY SUMMIT ESTATE. A year later, and having since become a married couple, Francis and Tannahill added pinot noir to their portfolio, while simultaneously forming a partnership with Bill and Debra Hatcher called A TO Z WINEWORKS. (In effect, A to Z, which is a much larger operation, generates the income that makes both Francis Tannahill and WILLIAM HATCHER WINES possible.)

In the 2002 vintage, Francis Tannahill made 250 cases of pinot from a combination of Shea Vineyard (Tannahill also served as the winemaker for SHEA WINE CELLARS in 2002 and 2003) and Momtazi Vineyard fruit. Beginning in 2004, grapes were also sourced from Maresh in the Dundee Hills, and from Poco, a high-altitude planting of Dijon 777 in the Eola Hills. A wider palette was used in 2005, including the CARABELLA VINEYARD on Ladd Hill; the Rainbow Ridge Vineyard northwest of McMinnville; and Pearl, which is Tannahill and Francis's biodynamically farmed estate vineyard in the Dundee Hills. Perhaps appropriately for a biodynamic vineyard, Pearl is named for their resident cow.

Tannahill describes himself and Francis as "relatively late pickers," who look for ripe stems and skins, but compensate by "extracting less in the cellar." "We are looking for power, not size," he explains. There is substantial use of whole-fruit clusters for "tannin contribution" and for "aromatic complexity." Unusually, all fermentors are wood ("I am done with the homogenized flavors that come from stainless steel,"

Tannahill explains), and nothing except sulfur dioxide—no sugar, no acid, no water, and no yeast—is added to the fermenting grapes. After five to ten days of cold soaking and a speedy, fairly hot fermentation, the must is pressed with an old-fashioned basket press when it reaches dryness, and the wine goes straight to barrel "with lots of lees." There is generally no racking until the blends are made, and the wine spends anywhere from ten to eighteen months in barrel. There is no fining or filtration. These are very distinctive and very fine wines with infinitely complicated flavors and aromas.

TASTING NOTE

2004 *The Hermit (tasted in* 2007*):* Medium-dark black-red; stewed rhubarb, spice, and glög aromas; rich, dense, grippy, and simultaneously lively on the palate, with mocha, Darjeeling tea, and orange peel; alongside the richness, there is also elegance, length, and light-to-medium weight. Fine.

FREEMAN VINEYARD AND WINERY

 Sebastopol, California

Ken Freeman's fascination with wine is said to date from supervised childhood visits to Zachys, then morphing from a corner store in Scarsdale, New York, into one of the country's premier wine merchants, and from trips through European wine lands when his parents traveled across the Atlantic. His wife, Akiko, the daughter of a distinguished Japanese academic family in love with wine and food, was exposed to similar infatuations growing up in

Tokyo. After the couple met, married, and moved to San Francisco in 1988, the idea of establishing their own winery gained traction. A decade later, capital generated from the accumulation of stock options in successful entertainment companies, for which Ken Freeman had worked in the interim, provided the necessary financial means. When the former Pomeroy Winery, a tiny, run-down facility on Montgomery Road west of Sebastopol, came on the market in 2001, the Freemans were ready. They bought and remodeled the winery, engaged Ed Kurtzman (who was then preparing to leave TESTAROSSA VINEYARDS after four vintages) as their winemaker, and began working with Kurtzman to source fruit for a pinot noir program based on fine sites in western Sonoma. As proof that the world is, in fact, small, it turned out that Kurtzman had been Ken Freeman's classmate at the University of Massachusetts two decades earlier.

WINES AND WINEMAKING NOTES

The impressive first vintage, in 2002, was made from a single ton of Dijon 115 purchased from the Dutton family's Thomas Road Vineyard, about 3 miles northeast of the Freemans' new winery, and another ton of Dijon 777 and Swan selection from Merry Edwards's 1998 planting, called the Meredith Estate Vineyard, on the south edge of the Sebastopol Hills (see MERRY EDWARDS WINES). This made 350 cases of a Sonoma Coast bottling, and 150 cases of a barrel selection devised personally by Akiko Freeman and appropriately christened Akiko's Cuvée. The same pair of wines was made from the same fruit sources in 2003. The program was expanded in 2004 to include several additional vineyards in the "golden triangle" area in the southwest corner of the Russian River Valley and adjacent parts of the Sonoma Coast AVA, and two additional wines: a Russian River blend, and a vineyard-designated wine from Keefer Ranch, a Green Valley site that has supplied FLOWERS, FAILLA, SIDURI, RED CAR, and TANDEM inter alia. In this scenario, which was repeated in 2005, Freeman's Sonoma Coast wine was anchored with grapes from Thorn Ridge, Ted Klopp's 1998 planting on Thorn Road that was also used by TALISMAN WINES; its Russian River bottling was anchored by a combination of Meredith Estate and Thomas Road Vineyard fruit; and Akiko's Cuvée, which is an exercise in barrel selection each year, was made primarily from Meredith Estate fruit in 2004, while Thorn Ridge was its anchor in 2005.

The winemaking is based on fruit that is 95 percent destemmed, cold-soaked for three to five days, "usually" inoculated but sometimes (Keefer Ranch is a case in point) driven by

---

LUSH, NICELY STRUCTURED WINES SKILLFULLY BLENDED FROM FINE SITES IN GREEN VALLEY AND THE SEBASTOPOL HILLS

---

resident yeasts, and pressed at dryness. The first vintage (in 2002) was held in barrel for fifteen months, but vintages since have been bottled after nine or ten months. The property works with five coopers, primarily Cadus, but also Rousseau, François Frères, Dargaud & Jaeglé, and Remond. There is no fining or filtration. The small winery was usefully and elegantly expanded with a cave bored into the adjacent hillside in 2004, which is now home to barrel cellar space for both Freeman and Kurtzman's other pinot project, AUGUST WEST WINES. In 2007 the Freemans purchased the orchard next door, where they will plant pinot of their

own in 2008, beginning an evolution that will eventually transform Freeman's pinot program into relying primarily on estate grown grapes.

The wine program has already become Akiko Freeman's day job: she is simultaneously Kurtzman's very attentive "winemaker-in-training" and the winery's chief marketer. The wines are attractive exemplars of the modern California style, fully ripe but usually finished to less than 14.5 percent alcohol, lush but nicely structured, with good residual acidity and considerable aromatic interest.

TASTING NOTES

2005 *Keefer Ranch (tasted in 2007):* Brilliant, medium-rosy garnet; strongly floral and exuberantly fruity; red licorice on the palate, with lavender Altoid flavors and citric highlights; intense attack and slightly angular finish, with hints of white pepper and mint.

2005 *Sonoma Coast (tasted in 2007):* Medium-deep black-red with rosy highlights; iodine, lavender, and orange peel aromas; very sweet, cherry-plum fruit in the mouth, with roasted sweet peppers and toasted cumin seed; wild, exotic flavors and some grip; long.

2005 *Russian River Valley (tasted in 2007):* Brilliant, medium ruby; strong floral and red fruit aromas; bright red fruit on the palate, with hints of black pepper and orange peel; silky-to-borderline-creamy mouth-feel; fine-grained tannins and good acidity; finishes long.

2005 *Akiko's Cuvée (tasted in 2007):* Brilliant, medium black-red; mocha, nuts, and dark red fruit on the nose; bright and very fruit driven on the palate, with mint, pepper, spice, and a savory bitterness that is reminiscent of red vermouth; a pretty, round, and complete wine, with persistent intensity and silkiness. Very attractive.

2004 *Keefer Ranch (tasted in* 2007*):*
Light-to-medium garnet; explosive, layered
palate that is fruity on the attack but
then minerally and slightly tannic; lots
of cardamom and clove; nice mid-palate
weight; concentrated and expressive; long
and very attractive.

2004 *Russian River Valley (tasted in*
2006*):* Medium ruby; root beer and spice
cabinet aromas; cherry, raspberry, and cola
on the palate, with black pepper and barrel
char; rich, soft, and elegant.

2003 *Sonoma Coast (tasted in* 2005*):*
Medium-garnet color; aromas of rosehips
with undertones of licorice and smoke;
sweet black cherries combine with mid-
palate hints of cola and cocoa; a riper-than-
usual persona because of late-season heat
and low yields; medium weight.

2003 *Akiko's Cuvée (tasted in* 2005*):*
An expressive nose of incense, tar, and
camphor; black cherries and dark cherry
flavors on the palate; an impressive
combination of softness with structure, and
richness with elegance.

2002 *Akiko's Cuvée (tasted in* 2004*):*
Aromatically impressive with camphor,
sandalwood, and cinnamon; earth, black
fruit, black licorice, and a bit of black
pepper on the palate, with a hint of mocha
at the end; a concentrated and focused
wine that finishes long.

THE GAINEY VINEYARD
Santa Ynez, California

The Gainey family owes its initial wealth
to a successful Minneapolis-based business
that makes and sells the yearbooks, class
rings, and academic regalia with which

schools and colleges celebrate their
annual rites of passage; the family owes
much of its orientation to a passion
for breeding Arabian horses that began
when Daniel C. Gainey (1897–1979) was
given an Arabian pony at a corporate
sales meeting. Both the business and the
passion brought Gainey and his son to
Santa Barbara in the 1950s. In 1962 father
and son purchased an 1,800-acre ranch
at the east end of the Santa Ynez Valley,
where Highway 246 meets Highway
154. The Gaineys gradually replaced
some of the ranch's cattle with a large
number of Arabians, as well as with
alfalfa, wheat, tomatoes, and sugar beets.
After his father's death in 1979, Daniel J.
Gainey's core attention shifted to wine
grapes, although the family maintained
a commitment to diversified farming. At
first he worked with purchased fruit and
hired Rick Longoria as winemaker (see
RICHARD LONGORIA WINES). In 1983
he planted 51 acres of Bordeaux varieties
along the northern boundary of the ranch;
in 1984 he built and opened a large (for
the time and place), Mediterranean-style
winery and tasting room.

In 1996 the Gaineys purchased a second
ranch on Santa Rosa Road in the cool, west
end of the valley, which was dedicated from
the outset to growing Burgundian varieties
and syrah. Initially called the Santa Rosa
Hills Ranch, it was renamed for Daniel C.
Gainey's father, Evan, in 1996. Thirty acres
of chardonnay, pinot noir, and syrah were
planted on Evan's Ranch in 1997, 6 more
acres in 2002, and 6 more in 2005. All the
pinot, which now amounts to 16 acres, is
on north-facing slopes; most blocks are set
out 8 feet by 4 feet, and the scion material
is mostly UCD 4 and Dijon clones. In
2003 the original winery was expanded
to handle 30,000 cases, and updated with
gravity-flow and ambient-temperature-
control capabilities. Meanwhile, Gainey's

pinot program, which had begun with Santa Maria Valley fruit in 1986, began to purchase pinot noir grapes from the Sanford & Benedict Vineyard in 1987. The first estate fruit joined the program in 1999.

Since 1997, the winemaker has been Kirby Anderson, a graduate of the University of California Davis, with prior experience at BUENA VISTA CARNEROS, LA CREMA, and HARTFORD FAMILY WINES in Sonoma, and at Bernardus Winery in Carmel Valley.

WINES AND WINEMAKING NOTES

In 1986 Gainey made just one pinot noir, which was labeled Santa Maria Valley and was sourced from the Sierra Madre, Santa Maria Hills, and Bien Nacido vineyards. From 1987 through 1994, there were two pinots in each vintage, one based on fruit from one or more Santa Maria Valley sources, the other on fruit from Sanford & Benedict. The Sanford & Benedict wine was usually (but not always) sent to market as Limited Selection, sometimes with and sometimes without a vineyard designation. From 1995 to 1998, Gainey's Limited Selection was the only pinot produced, but in this period, the fruit source was Bien Nacido, not Sanford & Benedict. When the first estate pinot became available in 1999, Limited Selection was repurposed, first as a blend of estate fruit with Bien Nacido, and then (from 2001) as a Sta. Rita Hills appellation wine, overwhelmingly anchored with fruit from Evan's Ranch. Small quantities of pinot are purchased from neighboring Sta. Rita Hills vineyards, including Fiddlestix, Huber, and Rancho Santa Rosa. There is still a bit of Bien Nacido in Limited Selection, although not enough to affect the use of the Sta. Rita Hills appellation on its label.

Anderson tries to pick pinot with relatively low pH and high remaining acid. A five- to six-day cold soak precedes

inoculation, and the stainless-steel open-top fermentors are hand plunged two or three times daily. Enzymes are added to the Bien Nacido fruit but not to the Sta. Rita Hills fruit to deepen color. The new wine is pressed before it is completely dry, racked to tank to eliminate the gross lees, and then barreled. Malolactic culture may be added in tank if the primary fermentation has not finished at that point, or in barrel if it has. The barrel stock is mostly from François Frères, with some also from Remond and Sirugue, plus a few "experiments"; about 35 to 40 percent of the stock is new in each vintage. Time in barrel has inched up in recent years, from about ten months to about seventeen. There is no fining or filtration, and the bottled wine is held for six to nine months before release. Since the transition to mostly Sta. Rita Hills fruit, Gainey pinots have gained depth and delineation.

TASTING NOTE

2004 *Limited Selection (tasted in 2007):* Medium dark, almost saturated black-red; incense, dark cherry, some barrel-derived vanilla, and an undertone of earth; then, earthy with sweet, dark fruit on the palate, plus slate-y minerality and some glycerin; good concentration and tame tannins.

GARY FARRELL WINES

 Healdsburg, California

Gary Farrell created his eponymous wine brand in 1982, on a Lilliputian scale, while his full-time job was making wine for DAVIS BYNUM WINES. In fact, Farrell's brand and Joe and Tom Rochioli's brand (see ROCHIOLI VINEYARD AND WINERY) were born simultaneously, from a single transaction, and Farrell was briefly the winemaker for both. Joe Rochioli Jr. had sold his entire crop of pinot noir to Davis Bynum from 1973 through 1981. In 1982, anticipating the construction of a winery on his own property, he asked that part of the crop be vinified under the Rochioli name, on a custom-crush basis, to which Bynum and Farrell agreed. With a separate handshake, but in more or less the same breath, Bynum and Rochioli agreed that

---

WINES WITH GREAT
TRANSPARENCY, SOFT
TANNINS, AND GENUINELY
IMPRESSIVE ELEGANCE

Farrell could also purchase a tiny lot of the same fruit—enough to make two barrels of wine—for a project bearing his own name. And so it happened that 50 cases of 1982 pinot noir from Rochioli's West Block and the North Hill of Allen Ranch launched Gary Farrell Wines.

For many years thereafter, it was, in Farrell's own phrase, "the brand that cash flow built," with the proceeds from the sale of each vintage being used to finance the purchase of grapes and barrels for the next; production inched up until it risked filling every nook and cranny of empty space in the Bynum facility. The wines developed a reputation for excellence that sometimes overshadowed Bynum and which ensured that Farrell was mentioned around the precincts of Russian River in the same breath as Rochioli and WILLIAMS SELYEM.

In 1996 positive cash flow enabled Farrell and his wife to purchase and plant a 25-acre estate vineyard on Starr Ridge, on the eastern side of the Middle Reach, not far from the current western boundary of the Chalk Hill AVA, making the first move toward estate production. All but 4 acres of Starr Ridge were planted to pinot noir, mostly Dijon 115, but also Dijon 114 and 777 as well as UCD 4, planted in 7-foot rows with 4 feet between vines. Four years later, a second estate vineyard was set out between Ross Road and the Gravenstein Highway near IRON HORSE, of which, approximately 12 acres were devoted to Dijon 115 and 777. In 1999, realizing that his brand had outgrown the Bynum facility, Farrell sold a 20 percent interest in the brand to Bill Hambrecht, a veteran player in the ultrapremium segment of the California wine business, in return for help building a dedicated facility on a spectacular hilltop site overlooking the Russian River, 1 mile downstream from Wohler Bridge.

Five years later, the entirety of Gary Farrell Wines (except for the estate vineyards) was sold to Allied Domecq *PLC*, a UK-based wine, spirits, and fast foods conglomerate. When Allied Domecq was sold, in its turn, to France-based Pernod Ricard SA in 2006, some properties, including Gary Farrell, were acquired by the Beam Wine Estates subsidiary of Fortune Brands Inc. Farrell remained as the winemaker for the house that bears his name until just before harvest in 2006, when Susan Reed, who had worked with him since leaving Matanzas Creek in 2003, was named his successor. Early in 2007, Farrell announced plans to team up once again with Hambrecht to establish a new Russian River Valley winery specializing in small-lot pinot noir.

WINES AND WINEMAKING NOTES
Gary Farrell Wines has made a Russian River Valley pinot noir every year

since 1982 and has made small quantities of vineyard-designated pinots every year since 1985—except in 1989, 1993, and 1996, when the only pinot was the Russian River Valley blend. The blend has typically been anchored with fruit from the hillside blocks at Allen Ranch, which are also the source for Williams Selyem's Allen Ranch bottling. Other components of the blend are Rochioli's River Block (see Rochioli Vineyard and Winery and Williams Selyem), OLIVET LANE (see also MERRY EDWARDS WINES and Williams Selyem), the Stiling Vineyard on Vine Hill Road between Kistler and DEHLINGER (where Farrell gets primarily Swan selection planted in the late 1980s), and (since 2000) fruit from Farrell's two estate vineyards. During the 1980s, Allen Ranch was the most frequent vineyard-designated wine, but the fruit for the vineyard-designated lots was typically from Allen's Tri-Corner block, not from the hillside blocks used in the blend. Similarly, when Rochioli wine was made as a vineyard-designate, the lots used were not from the block used in the blend. In more recent years, there were vineyard-designated wines from Stiling in 1997 and 1998, from Starr Ridge since 2000, from Jack Hill Vineyard in 2003, and from the Hallberg Vineyard of EMERITUS in 2005 and 2006.

Farrell's house style has always emphasized elegance, balance, ageworthiness, and structural integrity, and Reed insists that this orientation will continue. To this end, fruit is picked at lower levels of sugar accumulation than other makers pursue—usually less than 24.3 Brix—and vineyards whose grapes show incomplete flavor development at these levels are avoided. Many vineyards are harvested at night or soon after dawn, and there is rigorous sorting to remove leaves, second-crop and underripe berries, as well as the occasional bit of rot. A custom-built,

29-foot-long elevated belt, whose speed is controlled by the sorters and rarely exceeds three bins per hour, is deployed on an exterior but entirely roofed crushpad to expedite the process. Until it reaches the fermentors, fruit is moved entirely by belts to minimize bruising, and is entirely destemmed, but not crushed.

Pinot is fermented in a virtual farm of small, 5-foot-tall by 6.5-foot-in-diameter, jacketed stainless steel open-tops, most of which are filled less than half full. A longish cold soak (up to seven days) is maintained with a combination of the tank jackets and blanketings of dry ice. The fermentors are then heated to 60°F for yeasting with the Assmannshausen isolate, which is said to "enhance color retention and structure, and to contribute notes of spice and fruit flavors" to the finished wines. Plungings occur three times daily, and the must is pressed just before it goes dry. The new wine is then settled in tank, separated from the gross lees, and inoculated for malolactic fermentation before being barreled. New barrels are limited to 40 percent of the stock used for any given wine; the favored coopers are François Frères, Seguin Moreau, and Rousseau. A first racking is done after the malolactic fermentation has finished. The Russian River Valley blend is created just before the next harvest and is bottled immediately. Lots destined for vineyard-designation are held longer in wood.

Farrell was always careful to explain that the Russian River wine was privileged in the course of blending trials and decisions, making the vineyard-designated wines into contingent choices. The latter could be made when lots of extraordinary quality were still available after the blend was built. Reed has embraced this orientation, observing that "it is not unusual for the Russian River Valley selection to be our finest release in any given vintage," and that "though wines designated from a single vineyard may be tremendous wines, they often lack the complexity, interest, and 'completeness' of wines crafted from several vineyards." As a practical matter, however, the twin processes of identifying lots destined for blending and those having obvious vineyard-designation potential proceed in parallel, and some consolidations based on these judgments are made as early as the first racking. There is no enzyme use or fining, but minimal filtration is done when it is "appropriate."

Over the years, Farrell's pinots have enjoyed an enviable reputation among fellow winemakers, wine writers, and consumers. In my experience, they are medium-weight wines with medium to deep black-red color, great transparency, generally soft tannins, and genuinely impressive elegance. There is definition to the flavors, which never seem muddled, and the wines are fruit-sweet without ever being heavy or seeming to have been picked overripe.

TASTING NOTES

2004 *Starr Ridge Vineyard (tasted in 2007)*: Brilliant, medium black-red; very elegant and slightly nutty nose with a dominance of rose petals; rich and intense on the palate, with flavors of freshly brewed Earl Grey tea, lots of infused flowers, and considerable stuffing; long and elegant overall.

2004 *Rochioli Vineyard (tasted in 2007)*: Light-to-medium black-red with pinkish-garnet highlights; nutty and floral like the Starr Ridge wine, but also sweet like cotton candy; rich on the palate, with some mocha, black tea, and *kirschwasser;* well knit and with excellent length, with intense flavors and an elegant architecture. Fine.

2004 *Rochioli-Allen Vineyards (tasted in 2007)*: Transparent, medium rosy-magenta; softly-spiced dark fruit on the nose,

reminiscent of mulled wine, plus violets and tobacco; intense on the palate with grace and complexity; unfolds in layers of allspice, black pepper, and Bing cherry; great concentration on an elegant frame; velvety and long; very fine.

GLORIA FERRER CHAMPAGNE CAVES
Sonoma, California

Gloria Ferrer is the American wine project of Grup Freixenet, the well-regarded Penedès-based *cava* producer whose Carta Nevada and Cordon Negro labels are known around the world. The Carneros project began in 1982, dedicated exclusively to champagne-method sparkling wine, which was made at Piper-Sonoma and at CHATEAU ST. JEAN until 1986. In 1983 and 1986, the Ferrer family bought two adjacent parcels on the western edge of the Carneros appellation and planted 200 acres of chardonnay and pinot noir between 1984 and 1989. Called the Home Ranch, the vineyards occupy mostly flat, clay-loam soils, irregularly laced with gravel and loamier, lower-vigor soils, at the toe of the rolling, east-facing hills. The pinot went into Block D, which borders the Carneros Highway and has now been rechristened Aurora Break; Block B, now called Wind Gap; and, more recently, Blocks E, F, and G, immediately around the winery buildings and above them on the hillside. Row orientation was northeast–southwest, following the natural slope of the land, and vine spacings were originally 10 feet by 5 feet. Various pieces of E, F, and G now carry the names Wingo Vista, Pedragal, Dolores, Carmen

Pilar, and Eagles Fledge. These parcels are known collectively as Gravel Knob and were the source of a block-designated pinot in 2000. The large, Spanish-style winery was built in 1986.

Responding in part to a softening demand for sparkling wine at the end of the 1980s and in part to his conviction that some of the estate fruit had the guts to make good still wines, winemaker Bob Iantosca began thinking about still pinot noir in 1989 and 1990. Uncertain if it would work, he devised a business plan with a quick exit strategy: the pinot could be sold off in bulk without any financial loss if, once made, he and the Ferrers decided it really wasn't good enough to release. A few thousand cases of still pinot, made from the relatively mature vines in Block B, were produced in 1991, and Gloria Ferrer has made still pinot ever since, increasing its production to 10,000 cases in 2000.

Meanwhile, owing to the choice of non-resistant rootstock for the first Home Ranch plantings, a replanting program has been underway since 1992. In addition, Gloria Ferrer has leased and planted 175 acres of the Circle Bar Ranch, less than a mile to the southwest. Despite its proximity and similar range of elevations, Circle Bar is very different from the Home Ranch, with substantially thinner, lighter, stone- and gravel-strewn soils (primarily Pajaro and Laniger series) in hilly swales and saddles that bode well for still-wine fruit. Ninety acres of pinot noir were planted at Circle Bar in 1997 and 1998, in nineteen very heterogeneously sized and irregularly shaped blocks fitted around the natural contours of the land; row orientations follow, variously, the soils, the prevailing wind, and the topography. In 2000 a block-designated pinot was made from one of these blocks, christened Rust Rock

Terrace, a chunk of volcanic soil planted to UCD 2A, UCD 48, and Dijon 115.

To choose scion wood for replanting and new plantings, Iantosca designed extensive clonal trials and selected clones that performed well, in these sites at least, for both still and sparkling wine. This criterion has led to unusual choices. The largest vine populations are now a field selection from Trefethen, UCD 32 (one of the Roederer clones, from Chouilly in Champagne), and UCD 48. Elsewhere (except at GREENWOOD RIDGE VINEYARDS in Anderson Valley), the Roederer clones have not been favored for still pinot, and the selection now known as UCD 48 has been almost ignored both for still and for sparkling pinot as a result of poor performance when it underwent trials in Oregon during the 1980s. At Gloria Ferrer, however, UCD 32 seems to produce, by itself, a nearly complete wine, with deep color, dark fruit flavors, and aromas of leather, furniture polish, and cherry jam. UCD 48, while less complete, gives distinctive aromas of tea leaves, fruitcake, and gingerbread. Other, more popular clones and selections, including UCD 2A, 4, and 13, and Dijon 115, along with some rarities such as UCD 56 (CTPS 927 via British Columbia and Champagne) and 58 (CTPS 779 via British Columbia and Champagne), are also planted on the two ranches. Atypically, Gloria Ferrer has not planted Dijon 667 or 777, which have emerged as must-haves for most winegrowers in California and Oregon.

WINES AND WINEMAKING NOTES
About four fifths of Gloria Ferrer's pinot production is a blend of lots from the Home and Circle Bar Ranches designated Carneros, which has been made annually since 1991 and is nationally distributed.

(About 6,000 cases of a Sonoma Coast wine called Etesian are also made, but are sold exclusively to chain accounts.) Since its debut in 1998, the flagship wine has been José S. Ferrer Selection, named in honor of Gloria's husband; it is sold to restaurants and mailing-list customers, and at the winery. The José S. Ferrer is a barrel selection from four blocks of the Home Vineyard—planted respectively to Trefethen selection, UCD 13 and 32, and Colmar 538—and two blocks of Circle Bar Ranch, planted to Dijon 115 and UCD 2A.

Gloria Ferrer pinots, up to and including 1997, were relatively lightweight and featured slightly herbal properties; beginning with the 1998 vintage, with newer plantings coming online, the fruit has been sweeter, the hue has deepened, and the wines' palate weight has increased. The José S. Ferrer Selection tends toward spiciness with overtones of smoke and has considerable weight. The two block-designates made in 2000 showed exceptionally well in early tastings, combining elegance and minerality with admirable complexity, and were characterized by less fat than the José S. Ferrer.

Pinot for still wine is picked as much as possible between 23.5 and 24.5 Brix, usually around mid-September. Some second-crop fruit (i.e., fruit passed over when the first pick for sparkling wine was done in August) is also used for still wine. Second-crop fruit tends to show smaller clusters than first-crop, to have a high skin-to-juice ratio, and to be a good blending tool, according to Iantosca, although care must be exercised to ensure that the second-crop berries have not raisined. The fruit is completely destemmed. Tanks and open-top fermentors are used, some of which are equipped with automatic punchdown devices. The typical vatting starts with three days of cold soak and ends with one to three days of postfermentation maceration, although some lots are pressed before they are dry. The alcoholic fermentation is started with several yeasts chosen to minimize color absorption; punchdowns or pumpovers are executed three times each day. After pressing, the wine is settled in tank overnight and then inoculated for malolactic fermentation; it goes to barrel fairly clean. The press fraction is segregated, cleaned up, sometimes racked, and used in the Etesian cuvée.

About one third of the barrels are new each year and are sourced mostly from Damy, Cadus, Billon, and François Frères. Iantosca is also experimenting with a few Hungarian oak barrels. The lots are evaluated in February or March after the vintage to make the main Carneros blend; then Iantosca "has some fun" with what's left, creating blends for the other lots. The wine stays in barrel for nine months without racking, except for special lots, which spend up to fourteen months in wood.

All the Gloria Ferrer pinots are attractive wines with mercifully modest levels of finished alcohol. The two block-designated wines, Rust Rock Terrace and Gravel Knob—perhaps especially Gravel Knob—are very nicely made, brightly finished wines of considerable distinction.

TASTING NOTES

2005 *Carneros (tasted in* 2007*):* Brilliant, medium black-red; sweet black raspberry and cherry fruit, with some peppery spice and barrel char; of medium weight and length, with the texture of polished cotton, and with some warmth on the finish.

2004 *Gravel Knob Vineyard (tasted in* 2007*):* Brilliant, rosy-garnet; overwhelmingly spicy nose, with ginger, plum, and rose petal; bright on the palate, with spicy raspberry cream; serious, silky, very elegant, long, almost sensuous, and very attractive.

2004 *Rust Rock Terrace Vineyard (tasted in 2007):* Transparent, medium garnet; lovely nose of crushed berries, flower petals, and exotic spice; cherry and blackberry fruit on the palate; considerable minerality and a hint of orange peel; fills the mouth with a persistent load of very fine-grained tannin; long and attractive.

2004 *José S. Ferrer Selection (tasted in 2007):* Transparent, medium rosy-ruby with a pink rim; earthy, smoky, and spicy on the nose with some violets; slightly sweet, dark cherry fruit, then intense, inky, and smoky on the mid-palate; long and softly gritty from mid-palate to finish.

GOLDENEYE AND MIGRATION
Philo, California

In the beginning, Dan Duckhorn was the king of merlot. Then, in the late 1980s, he and his wife began to realize they were being increasingly seduced, even at their own table, by the charms of pinot noir. Quietly, Duckhorn purchased small lots of pinot grapes from the Elke vineyards in Anderson Valley, and from Sonoma Mountain, and then made some experimental pinots that were not commercially released. He began to look for cool-climate property in Russian River. But when the Obester property, just southeast of Philo, came on the market in 1996, Duckhorn abandoned his Russian River search and settled on Anderson Valley instead. The Obester property came complete with a winery; a winemaker; the 1996 vintage, which was already in barrel; and two and a half acres of bearing pinot

vines, all UCD 13, planted in 1991. The vintage in barrel was repurposed for barrel trials and then released under Duckhorn's second label, Decoy. In 1997 Duckhorn budded Obester's blocks of gewürztraminer and chardonnay to, respectively, UCD 2A and 4, and planted an additional five acres of Dijon 115. On a roll, he also planted new rootstock on the Obester property (renamed the Confluence Vineyard) destined for Dijon 667, 777, 113, and 115; he also planted an additional 16 vine acres on a parcel adjacent to HANDLEY CELLARS, which he called Abel Vineyard.

Three years later, in March 2000, Duckhorn purchased an additional 50-acre parcel bisected by Gowan Creek (and thus named Gowan Creek Vineyard) about 5 miles downstream from Philo and adjacent to Rich Savoy's vineyard, 34 acres of which were later planted to Dijon 667, 777, and 828; to UCD 13, 2A, and 5; and to nursery-sourced Swan selection. In 2003 Duckhorn also acquired Bill Hambrecht's esteemed Floodgate Vineyard at the "deep" northwest end of the valley, which he renamed The Narrows. The 48 planted acres at Floodgate remain almost entirely intact, except that some gewürztraminer and pinot gris were T-budded to pinot noir. By 2007 Goldeneye had become the single largest proprietor of pinot vineyard in Anderson Valley, farming 150 acres divided among no fewer than eighty-four blocks, with twenty-two selections on fourteen rootstocks.

The operation is now almost "pure" estate: non-estate fruit is rarely purchased, and estate fruit is rarely sold. This has been an impressive evolution for a producer that made barely 400 cases of its first release in 1997. Nothing lasts forever, however. Duckhorn Wine Company was put up for sale at the end of 2006, and was sold to a Menlo Park, California–based private-equity firm in 2007. It is not currently known if all of the Duckhorn properties, including Goldeneye, will be maintained intact.

WINES AND WINEMAKING NOTES
An Anderson Valley cuvée is the brand's main release, and it has been made in every vintage since 1997. Migration, a second label, absorbs lighter lots. Although each of the estate vineyards is deemed to have vineyard-designation potential, only Confluence (in 2004 and 2005), The Narrows (in 2004), and Gowan Creek (in 2005) have so far been bottled as single-vineyard wines. Each vineyard-designate is also a barrel selection from among the available lots. Lots destined for Migration are identified first, in the spring after the vintage, and segregated for early blending and bottling. Decisions about the Anderson Valley blend and the vineyard-designates are made several months later through an extended and iterative process.

Bruce Regalia (who had previously made the wines for Obester) served as the winemaker through the harvest of 2002, at which point he was succeeded by Zachary Rasmuson, formerly the winemaker for neighboring HUSCH VINEYARDS. Rasmuson eschews stems, saying that he rarely sees ripe ones, but ferments about 75 percent whole berries in 3-ton, open-top stainless steel tanks. A natural cold soak lasts about two days before the must is inoculated to start the primary fermentation. Hand punchdowns are done twice daily. Rasmuson likes to see fermentation temperatures rise into the low 90s, but this is not always possible given the relatively small size of the fermentors. The must is pressed just before dryness (the whole berries inevitably retain some unfermented sugar), and the wine is settled briefly in tanks before being barreled. Inoculation to begin the malolactic

fermentation is done in the settling tanks. The press fraction is kept separate, but some is normally blended back.

Duckhorn and Rasmuson attach high importance to barrel protocols as a determinant of style. Although they use a large assortment of coopers, Cadus, Remond, François Frères, Billon, Damy, and Rousseau account for more than 80 percent of the barrel stock. In 2001 Goldeneye embraced a policy of pre-purchasing and storing staves, and then paying for coopering in the year of delivery, to get better control over wood sources. Migration is bottled before the following vintage and is bottle aged for six months before release; the other wines spend fifteen to eighteen months in wood and are bottle aged for twelve months. There is no racking until just before bottling, and the wines are neither fined nor filtered.

I find these to be ripe and full-flavored wines overall. I tend to prefer the Anderson Valley bottling, which seems brighter and more typical of Anderson Valley than the vineyard-designated wines.

TASTING NOTES
2004 *Anderson Valley (tasted in* 2007*):* Pretty, transparent, medium black-red; rose petal and black raspberry aromas, with hints of macadamia and licorice; dark berry fruit on the palate with a strong mineral dimension as well; tightly knit, with very fine-grained tannins and a long finish that is slightly hot.

2004 *Confluence Vineyard (tasted in* 2007*):* Dark and barely transparent; dark black cherry, sweet vanilla, and roasted nuts on the nose; sweet on the palate with licorice and brewed black tea; definitely the dark side of pinot; intense and persistent on the palate; mouth coating and long.

2003 *Anderson Valley (tasted in* 2007*):* Transparent, medium-dark brick-red color; intense, sweet nose featuring vanilla and nut meats; a very dense and tightly-knit wine that is black but not fruit driven; dense, integrated, and serious; a slightly sweet attack resolves to a very dry finish; attractive.

1998 *Anderson Valley (tasted prerelease in 2001):* Lighter-colored than the 1997; nose of strawberry, cherry, and smoke; fruit candy, leather, and tobacco highlighted with licorice; aromatic with cedar rather than sweet with chocolate; rich, long, and silky.

1997 *Anderson Valley, made from a combination of estate and purchased fruit, about 60 percent UCD 13 and 40 percent UCD 4 (tasted in 2001):* Transparent, medium-dark black-red; nose of cherries and violets; black fruits, cola, leather, and tobacco; big, round, and chewy, with considerable chocolate; unresolved tannins; rich, long, and velvety.

GREENWOOD RIDGE VINEYARDS
Philo, California

When he is not involved with wine on his ridgetop ranch near Philo, Allan Green practices graphic design, plays center field on an over-50 baseball team named for the winery, and collects wine cans. That's right, wine *cans*. He is the son of Aaron G. Green, a San Francisco architect once affiliated with Frank Lloyd Wright, who designed the Greens' house, winery, and tasting room; he is also the son of an anesthesiologist mother with an abiding interest in the health benefits of wine. His brother, a filmmaker, was the inadvertent catalyst for the family's wine venture. Seized with enthusiasm for the post-hippie back-to-the-land movement, Frank Green encouraged his family to purchase 275 remote acres of ranchland on Greenwood Road in 1971—for weekend retreats. As a teenager, Allan Green spent enough time on the ranch to play softball with some of Anderson Valley's wine pioneers and to become infected with the idea that grape growing could be, well, cool. When Tony and Gretchen Husch decided to sell the warm-weather vineyard parcel they owned adjacent to the Greens' property, the Greens acquired 3 acres of cabernet and 2.5 acres each of merlot and riesling. Jed Steele, a softball chum, talked Green through his first years as a home winemaker, and Greenwood Ridge was bonded in 1980.

In view of its relatively warm ridgetop location, pinot noir was an unlikely variety for Greenwood Ridge. But when Van Williamson was hired as winemaker in 1989, he "*really* wanted to make some pinot," and Roederer Estate (which had planted a large vineyard but had a narrow pick window for sparkling wine) was happy to sell off a few tons of "late harvest" fruit for still wine. Greenwood Ridge's pinot program, therefore, debuted as a non-estate program, and it continued that way until 1999. The fruit source was consistently UCD 32 from Roederer, eventually augmented with UCD 13 from the Corby Vineyard and with small quantities of fruit from the Weir Vineyard in the Yorkville Highlands AVA, except in the 1990 vintage, when grapes were instead purchased from Christine Woods.

Gradually taken with the variety, Green decided to plant his own pinot noir vineyard in 1996, despite the relative warmth of his site. Four acres were developed southwest of the winery, at an elevation of about 1,400 feet, well above the fog line and commanding a stunning view of nearby ridgetops. The pinot vineyard is planted in east–west-oriented

8-foot rows with 5 feet between vines; the scion material is an unusual half-and-half combination of Dijon 115 and UCD 32, with just a bit of UCD 23 (Mariafeld) "for color and seasoning." In 1999 Green made two pinots: the Anderson Valley

---

VERY DISTINCTIVE,
MEDIUM-WEIGHT WINES
WITH SPICY-HERBAL FLAVORS
AND NOTES OF CONIFER

---

cuvée from purchased fruit and the Estate from the first harvest of his own fruit. In 2000 the Anderson Valley bottling was discontinued. The estate wine carries the Mendocino Ridge appellation and is the only pinot produced in that AVA.

WINEMAKING NOTES

Not wishing to grow his total production beyond about 7,500 cases and being essentially unable to afford a full-time winemaker on that scale, Green resumed winemaking duties himself when Williamson left in 1993. He ferments pinot in horizontal, open-top dairy tanks, first destemming completely and then using a combination of whole and slightly crushed berries. He "likes" a two-day cold soak but cannot chill all his tanks simultaneously, so he sometimes gets less. He then lets the temperature rise naturally and inoculates with laboratory yeast. Greenwood Ridge's fermentations generally last five to six days and include punchdowns three or four times a day. The target is to press into tank when the must reaches about 2 degrees Brix, introducing malolactic bacteria simultaneously so that the beginning of the malolactic fermentation overlaps the end of the alcoholic conversion. The press fraction

is reunified with the free-run juice, and the wine is allowed to settle in tank for as little as four days or as long as three weeks before going to barrel.

Greenwood Ridge is a two-cooper shop: it features barrels from Dargaud & Jaeglé and François Frères. Green likes the "different kind of smokiness" in the Dargaud barrels. In July following the vintage, he racks to tank for blending and bottles at the end of the summer, so the wines see only about eight months of wood. Green rarely fines but uses coarse-pad filters for clarity. Six months' of bottle age precede release.

Greenwood Ridge pinots are quite distinctive, nicely built, medium-weight wines that exhibit spicy-herbal flavors and (usually) notes of cedar or other conifers and fir balsam. They also fall into the (sadly) underpopulated category of completely handmade pinots built from estate grown fruit and sold for about $25 a bottle.

TASTING NOTES

2005 *Estate (tasted in 2007):* Pretty, brilliant, medium garnet; opens with forest floor, underbrush, fallen leaves, and earthiness, then gives way to flowers; sweet, spicy, and piney with a hint of mocha on the palate; exceptionally bright and quite intense, but featherweight; slightly exotic, elegantly built, and distinctive.

2004 *Estate (tasted in 2007):* Transparent, medium garnet; shows pine needles, redwood bark, and underbrush on the nose; a cherry-centered palate with some candied ginger and sandalwood; impressively spicy, silky, elegant, and solidly built; very attractive.

2003 *Estate (tasted in 2007):* Transparent, bright brick-red with a hint of umber; distinctive nose of cedar, incense, and tobacco, with a touch of orange peel; very slightly fruit-sweet on the palate with a little avalanche of allspice, cardamom, and nutmeg flavors in a soft wrapper; some elegance; of medium weight; long.

2002 *Estate (tasted in 2007):* Very transparent medium brick-red; nose displays cigar box and pine needles with some very ripe fruit; almost rich on the palate with ripe, plummy, and almost raisiny fruit; flavors of mocha and chocolate, and a suede-like texture; of medium weight, with a nice combination of elegance, richness, and good length, but shows a warm vintage.

GUNDLACH BUNDSCHU WINERY
Sonoma, California

Shortly after the end of Mexican rule in northern California in 1846, quite a few would-be vintners planted vineyards, and some also established wineries in and around Sonoma, the northernmost of the Franciscan missions. Some of the names are familiar, such as Mariano Guadalupe Vallejo, who founded the town of Sonoma around the mission in 1834, and Agoston Haraszthy, the Hungarian nobleman who created BUENA VISTA. But the standout for persistence and durability among these pioneers was Jacob Gundlach, a Bavarian immigrant who had built a successful brewery in San Francisco at the beginning of the 1850s. In partnership with another German immigrant, the architect Emil Dresel, Gundlach purchased 400 acres in the foothills on the east edge of Sonoma in 1857 and planted vineyards (which the partners called Rhine Farm) in 1858. In 1868, Charles Bundschu, a university

graduate from Mannheim, married into the Gundlach family; the following year Emil Dresel died, and his brother Julius came from Germany to take charge of his family's winemaking interests. Six years later, perhaps as a consequence of these events, the Dresels' and Gundlachs' partnership ended, but not before the parties had made enormous investments in the acquisition of fine plant material (Emil Dresel seems to have imported riesling and traminer from his family seat at Geisenheim in the Rheingau as early as 1859) and had developed a reputation for resisting phylloxera by grafting vinifera cuttings onto phylloxera-resistant American rootstock. Almost alone among the American wine ventures begun in the nineteenth century, and against enormous odds, Gundlach Bundschu, originally founded as J. Gundlach & Company in 1858 and reorganized as Vineburg Wine Company from 1933 to 1973, has survived essentially intact and always under family ownership and hands-on direction, for a century and a half. As this book goes to press, the Rhine Farm (now spelled Rhinefarm) Vineyard has been harvested for 148 consecutive years. It produced some of America's finest wines in the last quarter of the nineteenth century, survived phylloxera, won international awards for varietal wines when these were the exception rather than the rule, transferred winemaking to Sonoma after the 1906 earthquake had destroyed its large premises in San Francisco, and maintained the vineyard (although part of it was rededicated to orchard) through Prohibition.

Pinot noir has never been Gundlach Bundschu's preoccupation, but it has likely always been a part of its operations. A map of the vineyard drawn in 1893 shows blocks of pinot noir planted at least that early, a proposition consistent with the appearance, that same year, of a Chambertin vinted by J. Gundlach among California wines shown at the Columbian Exposition in Chicago. Rhinefarm was substantially replanted between 1969 and 1973, and was expanded by acquisition of adjacent land in 1970 and 1997. Pinot noir is now planted in ten blocks, in mostly low-lying, clay-loam soils laced with gravel, underlain with the same hard clay pan that typifies most soils in neighboring Carneros. There are 14 acres of UCD 13, Hanzell selection, and a selection known internally as Hacienda, all dating from the 1970s; there are also 33 acres of UCD 5 and Dijon 115, 667, and 777 planted in 1999 and 2003.

Since 2000 Gundlach Bundschu's chief executive has been Jeff Bundschu, the great-great-grandson of Charles. Jeff is a graduate of the University of Southern California in international relations. One of his signal contributions to the family enterprise has been to appeal to the legendary Zelma Long and her husband Philip Freese for consultation and advice on winemaking and winegrowing matters, an action which led to introduction of a precision farming plan for the family's vineyards. The winemaker, since 1990, has been Linda Trotta, a Southern Californian, who grew up helping her Italian-American grandfather and great-grandfather make wine at home, and who subsequently earned a bachelor's degree in fermentation science at the University of California Davis—with a year spent abroad at the University of Padova in Italy and a harvest's work at Santa Margherita in the Veneto.

WINES AND WINEMAKING NOTES

A single bottling of estate grown pinot noir has been produced at Gundlach Bundschu since 1976. The program was expanded in 2005 to feature very small quantities of clone-based wines. A so-called Pommard and Dijon Clones bottling debuted in 2005, built from selected lots of UCD 5 and the above-mentioned Dijon clones. A Heritage Clones bottling, built from the selections originally planted about 1970, followed in 2007. Winemaking generally follows the consensus protocol. Fermentors vary in size, but none is larger than 9 tons; the cap is managed through "gentle" pumpovers, rather than through punchdowns. Trotta prefers relatively cool fermentation temperatures (between 80 and 85°F), presses the must before it is completely dry, and barrels the new wine immediately so that the primary fermentation finishes in wood. The barrel stock is primarily from Remond, and about 45 percent of the barrels are new in each vintage. Wines are bottled before the following harvest.

Gundlach Bundschu pinots are attractive, medium-weight wines, with a cherry-dominated fruit profile when the wines are young, a classic structure, and some barrel marking.

TASTING NOTES

2005 *Rhinefarm Vineyard (tasted in 2007):* Pretty, medium garnet; slightly smoky, cherry-raspberry flavors; quite intense and very spicy on the palate, with bright red cherry and black pepper; fairly long and structured, with noticeable grip and some heat on the finish.

2005 *Pommard and Dijon Clones (tasted prerelease in 2007):* Transparent, medium-dark magenta; clean, red-black fruit on the nose with a whiff of flowers; sweet, inky, and moderately intense on the palate; cherry and damson plum preserves; the forward fruit turns to grip at mid-palate, and the wine finishes warm and dry.

1999 *Rhinefarm Vineyard (tasted in 2007):* Medium brick-red with a terra cotta edge; very evolved on the nose, with tar and ripe fruit that has turned to *confiture;* elegant on the palate with slightly tarry flavors, slightly organic, and slightly sweet notes, plus "sap and solvent" flavors and a hint of orange peel; velvety, mouth coating, long, and attractive.

GYPSY DANCER ESTATES
Cornelius, Oregon

Gypsy Dancer is Gary Andrus's second Oregon-based pinot noir project, created when he purchased the former Lion Valley Vineyards, in the Tualatin Valley southwest of Portland, in 2002. He had been absent from Oregon briefly in 2001 after the sale of ARCHERY SUMMIT, his first Oregon project, to Leucadia National, a New York investment house. Lion Valley's vineyard was 12 acres planted in 1995, meter-by-meter, on south- and southeast facing slopes, in Laurelwood soils, to Dijon 114 and 115. Gypsy Dancer reports that some of the Lion Valley vines were subsequently grafted to Dijon 667 and 777, and to budwood from the same suitcase clones Andrus first imported to plant the Renegade Ridge Vineyard at Archery Summit, which were subsequently propagated by Argyle. This information does not seem reliable, however. Argyle says it sold Andrus Family Investments–grafted grapevines only, not budwood for field grafting, and only UCD 4 plus Dijon 114 and 777, because the field selections they obtained earlier from Archery Summit were found to be virused and were destroyed. Whatever the real facts about plant material and grafting, Gypsy Dancer has made an estate wine from this site, called Gary and Christine's Vineyard, since 2002,

and a "special" cuvée called Romy, named for Andrus's youngest daughter, Romanée Christine, since 2005.

The winery says Romy is "blended from the same clones and in the same proportion as La Tâche," although it is difficult to imagine how one could measure, much less replicate, the incidence of individual clones in a vineyard that has always been planted and replanted by *sélection massale.* A second estate vineyard is co-owned by Andrus and by Pat Dukes of Dukes Family Vineyards, for which Andrus is also the winemaker. This vineyard, called A&G Estate, is located on Keyes Lane off Red Hills Road in the Dundee Hills, and consists of 4.5 acres of pinot spaced 3 feet apart in 5-foot rows on a southeast-facing slope. It was planted to three Dijon clones plus UCD 4 in 1998 and has been used to make a vineyard-designated wine since 2002. Gypsy Dancer also sources pinot from Bayliss Family Vineyards on Savannah Ridge outside Carlton, which is used mostly for blending, but a small amount was vineyard-designated in 2007. A vineyard-designated wine was also made from BROADLEY VINEYARDS fruit in 2004 and 2005. A blend called Emily's Reserve has been made in all vintages since 2002, absorbing lots not used to make the vineyard-designated wines.

Gypsy Dancer picks fruit ripe, around 25 Brix, and ferments a substantial proportion (40 to 85 percent) as whole clusters. The fermentors are stainless-steel open-tops and large, cone-section oak tanks; fermentations rely on combinations of resident yeast and inocula. Extended macerations typically continue for five days after the must is dry. Wines are raised in a large percentage of new barrels, and some are raised entirely in new wood. My experience is with the 2005 vintage only, where each wine shows the hallmarks of whole-cluster fermentation, very ripe picking, and generous oak treatment. These are definitely serious pinots, grown and crafted with the image of *grand cru* Burgundy from ripe vintages in mind, but they are bold to the point of overstatement.

TASTING NOTES

2005 *A&G Estate Vineyard (tasted in 2007):* Medium, deep ruby; smoky, rich, ripe black fruit aromas with the juniper-berry signature of whole-cluster fermentation; ultrasilky attack that gives way to mid-palate grip; has the character of strong brewed tea; resinated cherry and slate-y minerality; long.

2005 *Gary and Christine's Vineyard (tasted in 2007):* Medium-dark black-red; mesquite and juniper berry on the nose; very tannic front to back, and tightly knit with just hints of fruit and peppery spice; superconcentrated with a dominance of grip.

2005 *Cuvée Romy (tasted in 2007):* Dark black-red; smoky, whole-cluster-dominated nose; almost overpoweringly serious, with extremely dense fruit and huge grip; may become more approachable with more time in bottle.

HALLECK VINEYARD
Sebastopol, California

Ross Halleck, the founder of one of Silicon Valley's premier marketing services agencies in the 1980s, expanded his business late in the decade to help wine producers enhance their brand identities. In addition to household-name technology giants such as Hewlett-Packard, 3Com, and Sun Microsystems, his client list grew to include the likes of IRON HORSE, Beaulieu,

St. Supery, and Kendall-Jackson. Bitten by the proverbial wine bug, Halleck and his wife, Jennifer, then planted a 1-acre pinot vineyard (Dijon 115, 667, and 777) on a steep slope behind their home west of Sebastopol in 1992 and 1993, to "serve as a college fund" for their prospective children. They harvested their first grapes in 1999 and sold fruit the 2000 and 2001 vintages to TANDEM WINERY, which produced exceptional vineyard-designated Halleck pinots that attracted considerable attention.

The first wine made under the Hallecks' own label came in 2002, when Tandem and Halleck shared the tiny harvest. In 2003 a non-estate wine called Three Sons was added to the Halleck portfolio, based on fruit from The Farm and Hallberg vineyards, both located on the Gravenstein Highway near Occidental Road; small amounts of The Farm and Hallberg fruits were also made as vineyard-designated wines beginning in 2005. (Halleck also makes a bit of sauvignon blanc and dry gewürztraminer from other purchased fruit.) Tandem's Greg La Follette was the winemaker until 2004, when the reins were passed to La Follette's colleague Rick Davis. Beginning in 2007, Jennifer Halleck, a committed and serious student of vineyard practices, winemaking, distribution, and retailing almost from the outset, began assisting Davis with parts of the hands-on winemaking. From the beginning, the estate vineyard produced stunning wines, displaying explosive but very fine intensity, as well as the firm acidity that typifies Sebastopol Hills pinots generally.

WINEMAKING NOTES

Fruit is harvested when the berries taste ripe, generally between 24.5 and 25.5 Brix. Clusters with lignified stems are used whole; the rest of the fruit is destemmed after sorting. Fermentations rely on resident yeast, so the fruit soaks cold for three or four days, during which time acid levels are adjusted, if necessary, "for flavor." Fermentation temperatures are normally capped at 85°F, and nutrients are added only if this is deemed necessary to maintain a healthy population of yeasts.

EXCEPTIONAL WINES WITH GREAT PURITY OF FLAVOR AND INTENSE, ELEGANT STRUCTURES

The free-run and light-press fractions are combined and settled briefly before barreling, but the hard-press fraction is evaluated before blending.

Barrels are primarily from Remond and Cadus, with smaller percentages from the Spanish cooper Toneleria Magrenan, and from François Frères, Louis Latour, Damy, and Billon. Wood sources, "when given a choice," are the Tronçais and other Allier forests. About 30 percent of barrels are new in each vintage, and another 30 percent have been used for one previous wine; the rest are older than one year. After the cuvées are made, the barrel stock is rotated to reflect how the wines have reacted, to that point, to the barrels in which they have been raised. There is no use of enzymes, usually no fining, and just minimal filtration for stability.

These are exceptional wines, with great purity of flavor and with intense, elegant structures. In 2005 the Hallberg bottling was especially impressive.

TASTING NOTES

2005 The Farm Vineyard (tasted in 2007): Bright, medium garnet; aromas of ripe cherry, soft spice, and incense; intense

and forward red fruit and spicy flavors on the palate, plus lively notes of sage and bay laurel; nicely built and balanced; long and attractive.

2005 Hallberg Vineyard (tasted in 2007): Brilliant, pretty, light-to-medium garnet; aromas of herbs, sassafras, and wood smoke with background red fruit; bright, high-toned strawberry and raspberry on the palate, with peppery herb notes and a hint of citrus peel; very slightly sweet on the mid-palate with brewed tea toward the finish; extremely attractive and fine.

2004 Estate (tasted in 2007): Transparent, medium-dark black-red; earth and ripe blackberry on the nose; fruit-sweet, sturdy, and tightly knit on the palate, with concentrated blackberry, soft spice, and a hint of espresso; very intense black-fruited pinot with serious structure; long and fine.

HAMACHER WINES
Carlton, Oregon

Eric Hamacher is a 1960s child who discovered wine while his contemporaries were consuming six-packs of standard American beer. Raised on California's Monterey Peninsula, he studied viticulture and enology at the University of California Davis in the 1980s. Because his roommate was an Oregonian, a few bottles of Oregon pinot noir infiltrated their regular weekly tastings of French Burgundies. In 1987 he worked the crush at REX HILL VINEYARDS and fell decisively in love with Oregon. "I saw," he recalls, "Oregon's incredible potential for pinot noir." What was missing, he thought, was "consistency." He liked what he calls

Oregon's "Wild West" culture: a second generation of *arrivistes* who "looked at the Ponzis and at Dick Erath and said, 'Wow, me too.'"

After the 1987 harvest, Hamacher returned to California to "make some money." He worked briefly as a research enologist for ROBERT MONDAVI, studying the effects of sunlight on various chemicals, and put in four years at CHALONE VINEYARD and a year working for Tony Soter at ETUDE WINES. He remembers the year at Etude as an incredible learning experience: such a "cocktail" of projects, consultants, and winemakers that every day was "like being in school."

Hamacher returned to Oregon in 1995 to launch his own brand and to marry Luisa Ponzi, whom he had met at the Steamboat pinot noir conference in 1993. From the outset, by necessity, he was involved with various winery facilities projects and with campaigns to modify Oregon law so that multiple wineries could share a single physical facility. This involvement culminated in the creation of the Carlton Winemakers Studio, a built-from-scratch, 15,000-square-foot facility designed to accommodate multiple independent boutique-scale winemakers, which opened on the eve of harvest in 2002. The studio has deservedly attracted huge attention. The project has been explicitly green from the outset, incorporating passive solar technology; high-efficiency windows; captured rainwater from roof runoff, using efficient, gravity-based production capabilities; and top-of-the-line equipment. It is dedicated to being the sort of environment in which small makers can craft wines of the highest quality, simultaneously and side by side.

The Hamacher label was launched in 1995 and was dedicated exclusively to chardonnay and pinot noir. The 1995, 1996, and 1997 vintages were made at the Medici Winery in Newberg; 1998, 1999, and 2000 at LEMELSON VINEYARDS outside Carlton; and 2001 at ADELSHEIM. Hamacher moved to the Carlton Winemakers Studio in 2002.

WINES AND WINEMAKING NOTES
Hamacher's main pinot noir is a blend built from a handful of Willamette Valley vineyards, most of them within the confines of Yamhill County. The consistent sources are the Durant Vineyard, a 1973 planting of own-rooted UCD 4 in the Dundee Hills, and Manuela, a 15-year-old vineyard uphill from Abetina (see PONZI VINEYARDS) near the top of Chehalem Mountain. Over the years, he has also used fruit from ELK COVE'S Windhill Vineyard; the Wahle family's Holmes Hill Vineyard in the Eola Hills; and (very recently) LAZY RIVER VINEYARD in the Yamhill Carlton AVA.

Although he has been a strong advocate for blending over vineyard-designation, arguing that most Oregon vineyards are too young to display consistent *terroir* and that most winemakers have too little experience with individual sites to showcase site specificity appropriately, Hamacher moved to small bottlings of vineyard-designated wines in 2006, using vineyards more than 25 years old. Hamacher is guided by two main stylistic parameters. First, he seeks what he calls "complete, elegant, and supple" wines. He believes that texture is paramount with pinot, and he aims for what he calls "liquid silk." Second, he insists on "embracing the vintage," by which he means that style is subordinated to vintage variations. The 1995 and 1997 wines, therefore, are quite different from the 1998s and 1999s.

Because of Oregon's marginal climate, Hamacher believes in a "super" sorting table designed to feed the destemmer as evenly as possible. He destems almost completely and prefers medium-size, 4-ton fermentors with excellent heating and chilling capabilities. Most winemakers, Hamacher asserts, "follow the temperature curve Mother Nature provides." Hamacher's fermentors give him the opportunity to achieve higher fermentation temperatures faster, but then to cool the must for a longer and more extended finish. This schema translates to a five-to-seven day cold soak while the resident yeasts "get going," and to least five days of postfermentation maceration. To avoid what Hamacher calls "forward, fruit-sweet character," the wine is not pressed or barreled until the must is fully dry.

Cooperage is mixed but primarily of Sirugue barrels—Hamacher likes Sirugue's "clove-cinnamon spiciness"—whose staves have been air dried for three years; about 35 percent are new each year. The pinots spend eighteen to twenty months in barrel; they are racked once barrel-to-barrel using compressed air after malolactic fermentation has completed, and once more when the blends are made prior to bottling. Blending is an elaborate process: Hamacher tries out as many as three dozen possible blends before narrowing the field, and he often ends up declassifying many lots. Declassified lots are finished and bottled, but sold under private labels or as "H," which is Hamacher's own second label. (In 1995 and 1997, Hamacher declassified half of his lots, finding that these vintages had been too weak to tolerate the percentage of new wood he had used; in 2003, which was pathologically hot on Oregon 70 percent of lots were declassified. The remaining 2003 wine, however,

received the highest score *Wine Spectator* has ever awarded to an Oregon pinot.) Hamacher fines or filters, or both, if necessary, although he prefers to avoid both processes. Each of the four vintages I have tasted has been impressive for its integration, balance, and elegance.

TASTING NOTE

2002 *Oregon (tasted in 2005):* Brilliant, light-to-medium garnet with pinkish highlights; engaging and slightly exotic nose of dried leaves and potpourri, with wild berries and a whiff of citrus peel; spicy, briary, and very elegant on the palate, with just a hint of fruit-sweetness; of medium weight and very long. Fine.

HAMEL WINES
Healdsburg, California

Kevin Hamel earned a bachelor's degree in fermentation science from the University of California Davis in 1978. Unconventionally, he began his career at Cockburn's, in Portugal. From Cockburn's he moved into wine retailing, managing the wine department of Corti Brothers Market in Sacramento for the legendary Daryl Corti; thence to wholesale wines sales; and finally to wine production, first at Santino Winery in the Sierra Foothills, and then at Preston Vineyards in Dry Creek Valley. At Preston he established an enviable reputation for nicely-crafted wines made from Rhône Valley grape varieties, which became his specialty. In 1994, while still at Preston, he launched his own label, initially dedicated to cool-climate editions of syrah. While sourcing syrah from vineyards on the True Sonoma Coast, however, proverbial word-of-mouth led him to the Campbell Ranch near Annapolis, on the third ridge inland from the ocean, where the owners had begun planting pinot noir in 2000—after their erstwhile business milling lumber had collapsed with the rest of the area's forest products activity.

In 2002 Campbell custom planted a small parcel for Hamel, using entirely Dijon 667 and 777, and Hamel added a Campbell Ranch pinot to the Hamel Wines portfolio in 2003. In 2005 Hamel's day job shifted from Preston to the Pellegrini Family Winery (see OLIVET LANE VINEYARD), and he brought Hamel Wines with him. He assumed responsibility for making Pellegrini's Olivet Lane pinot, as well as handling oversight duties for Pellegrini's custom-crush clients. The Hamel pinot is made, according to Hamel, following more-or-less the same protocol used for the Olivet Lane wine, with a bit less new wood during *élevage*. The wine is a substantial but is still a bright and elegant edition of pinot noir, signed with the wild aromatics of the True Sonoma Coast.

TASTING NOTES

2005 *Campbell Ranch (tasted prerelease in 2007):* Slightly peppery nose, with aromas of earth and underbrush over ripe plum; rich, intense, and bright on the palate, with some wild mint and plenty of peppery spice; a very pretty, medium-length wine.

2004 *Campbell Ranch (tasted in 2007):* A shade darker than the 2005; peppery-spice aromas again; intensely spicy flavors with briar, mesquite, and hints of tar; more mouth-weight, body, and slightly more power than the 2005; satiny finish. Impressive.

HANDLEY CELLARS
Philo, California

Milla Handley entered the University of California Davis intending to study art. Six years later, she graduated with a degree in fermentation science, one of the first such degrees awarded to a woman. After three years with the legendary Dick Arrowood at CHATEAU ST. JEAN, she moved to Anderson Valley in 1978, working first at Edmeades for Jed Steele. In 1982 she obtained a bond for the converted cellar in her house, northwest of Philo (now the premises for Claudia Springs Winery), and made 250 cases of Handley North Coast chardonnay from a combination of Mendocino and Dry Creek Valley fruit. The wine won awards, and Handley Cellars was launched.

Pinot noir came rather later, after sparkling wine and several vintages of sauvignon blanc. In 1983 Handley went to Burgundy and found (apparently to her surprise) that she "really liked the wine." In 1986 she planted 4 acres of pinot on the former Holmes Ranch, a long stone's throw from the house *cum* winery. In 1989 the second crop from this vineyard, which had previously been picked for sparkling wine, was used to make an experimental batch of still pinot. The exercise was repeated in 1990. In 1991 the first "real" Handley pinot noir was made. Then the 4 acres of estate pinot noir grew to 12. The original parcel of estate pinot, southeast of the winery building on a mostly south-facing slope, is UCD 13 on a vertical trellis, planted in north–south-oriented 10-foot rows with 6 feet between vines. A second block, planted in 1990, is lyre-trellised

UCD 2A in northeast–southwest rows. In the newest plantings, Handley is working with Dijon clones. In 1999 planting began at a hillside site above the winery to the east, at the 900-foot contour that was later dubbed RSM (for Rex Scott McClellan, Handley's husband).

The Handley program also relies on grapes purchased from numerous Anderson Valley vineyards, including Ferrington (see WILLIAMS SELYEM), Corby (located where Greenwood Road meets Route 128), Klindt (the site of Handley's original house *cum* winery), Carol Pratt's little vineyard above Philo, Romani (at the foot of Holmes Ranch Road), Day Ranch, the Iron Oak Vineyard in Potter Valley, and Oppenlander Vineyard in Comptche's Surprise Valley. Handley's co-winemaker since 2004 is Kristen Barnhisel, the daughter of a home-winemaker father and microbiologist mother, who majored in biology and Italian literature as an undergraduate before earning an MS in viticulture and enology at the University of California Davis.

WINES AND WINEMAKING NOTES
Until 2004, estate fruit was divided between an Estate Reserve bottling (made in 1992, 1993, 1995, 1996, 1998, 2001, and 2004) and an Anderson Valley cuvée. The Anderson Valley wine is Handley's "main" release of pinot noir. In some vintages during the 1990s, there was also a blend of pinot noir and pinot meunier called Cuvée Primo, but this entry-level wine was replaced in 2001 with a Mendocino County bottling of 100 percent pinot, sourced from a combination of Potter Valley, Comptche, and Anderson Valley vineyards. In 2005 a second "reserve" wine was added to the portfolio: a special bottling of lots from the RSM hillside vineyard. In 2000 Handley also purchased pinot from River Road

Vineyard in the Santa Lucia Highlands, which was vinified separately.

At Handley, fruit is generally picked between 23.5 and 24.5 Brix, depending on taste. The grapes ferment in cylindrical, stainless steel open-tops and in converted horizontal dairy tanks that hold from 1.5 to 7 tons each. The winery has largely abandoned whole clusters, and now uses no stems unless they are "very ripe." A cold prefermentation maceration lasts one or two days, enzymes are sometimes added to stabilize color and to improve settling after the new wines are pressed, and the must derived from the estate UCD 2A is often bled to help "concentrate flavors." Punchdowns are done two or three times a day, and pumpovers sometimes once, during a plus-or-minus twelve-day fermentation, with peak temperatures of about 90°F. The must is pressed at dryness, and settled for three or four days to avoid racking later. Malolactic bacteria are normally introduced in tank during settling.

Barrels are mostly Latour, Cadus, François Frères, Rousseau, Remond, Dargaud & Jaeglé, and Seguin Moreau; between 25 percent and 30 percent are new in each vintage. Each barrel is stirred until the malolactic fermentation has finished in midwinter. The wines are then allowed to settle, and the blends are made, at which point the new blends are racked into tanks. The Mendocino and Anderson Valley wines are usually bottled directly from tank. Reserve lots may be bottled without filtration "if they are visually clear and microbially stable." The Anderson Valley cuvée is bottle aged for twelve months before release; the Reserve gets eighteen months.

The reputation of Handley pinots grew steadily in the second half of the 1990s, buttressed by favorable reviews and competition medals. The Mendocino cuvée is a fruit-forward, soft-tannin wine of exceptionally good value. The Anderson Valley wine is layered and complex, but nicely sized and built. Overall, the wines are bright, fruit-driven, complex, and moderately long.

TASTING NOTES

2005 *Mendocino County (tasted in 2007)*: Brilliant, light-to-medium garnet; softly nutty and spicy on the nose, with dark red fruit; sweet on the palate, with cherry fruit and mild black tea; attractive and easy drinking.

2005 *Anderson Valley (tasted in 2007)*: Medium, rosy-ruby color; slightly earthy nose, with crushed berry fruit and a hint of balsamic condiment; sweet and fairly rich, with deep cherry flavor, a hint of mocha, and some pepper; very fine-grained tannins make it almost satiny on the mid-palate.

2005 *RSM (tasted in 2007)*: Deep ruby; cranberry and blueberry on the nose; sweet, ripe-fruit-driven wine, but also grippy and minerally, with attractive structure; notes of strongly brewed black tea; almost silky at mid-palate despite the grip.

2004 *Estate Reserve (tasted in 2007)*: Transparent, medium-dark black-red; slightly peppery and slightly floral red-fruit nose; sharply spicy and peppery on the front palate; barrel marked and smoky at mid-palate; then, warm and very slightly grippy.

HANZELL VINEYARDS
Sonoma, California

Hanzell occupies 200 acres in the foothills of the Mayacamas Range above Boyes Hot Springs to the west and Sonoma to the south. Often described as a "jewel"

or "millionaire's plaything," Hanzell gives the impression of a well-manicured estate dedicated to gracious living, where the owners just happened to plant a few acres of vines. The original winery building was explicitly modeled on a courtyard façade in Burgundy's Clos de Vougeot. Without this referent, it resembles an elegant, small barn, its entrances turned discreetly away from the "farm" and residence. James D. Zellerbach, a San Francisco forest products magnate, acquired this property in 1948, preceding his appointment as United States ambassador to Italy, to serve both as a country home and as a venue for his aspirations to produce in California chardonnay and pinot noir as good as Burgundy's. Zellerbach's original pinot vineyard sits on a saddle of land downhill from the winery.

There were originally two blocks of pinot noir here, planted in 1953 and 1957, both using 6-foot intervals in arc-shaped, 10-foot rows on a well-drained, mostly south-facing, clay-loam slope that looks more fertile than it is in fact. The provenance of Hanzell's scion material is not entirely clear. In the most likely scenario, it is Mount Eden selection via the Stelling vineyard in Napa. In another version of the story, however, the budwood Hanzell took from Stelling may have come from the old Inglenook planting in St. Helena via the university's experimental vineyard at Oakville.

The vineyard was completely dry farmed until the mid 1970s, when drought conditions led to the installation of drip irrigation, but the drip system is not often used, so quasi-dry farming has prevailed over the life of the vineyards. The 1957 block was replanted to chardonnay in 1998, but the 1953 block is still in production for pinot. (This 4.04-acre block is now, as far as I know, the oldest pinot vineyard in North America still in production.) In 1976 a second pinot vineyard—named de Brye in honor of Hanzell's new owners post-1975—was planted on another south-facing slope east of the original blocks. Budwood was taken from the 1953 and 1957 blocks to plant de Brye. Most recently, a third planting of pinot, called Sessions Vineyard, has been developed near the property's eastern edge, on an east-facing slope overlooking Norrbom Road. There, the vine spacing has been tightened to

---

DEEPLY-COLORED, VERY
AGEWORTHY WINES IN
WHICH EARTHY AND MINERAL
FLAVORS ARE MORE
DOMINANT THAN FRUIT

3.25-foot intervals in 8-foot rows, and only part of the budwood was taken from the older blocks. The rest of this vineyard is dedicated to "experiments" with a variety of California field selections, Davis clones, and Dijon clones. Sessions fruit is now said to contribute "structure" to the Hanzell blend. Yield from the mature blocks ranges from barely 1 (for the 1953 block) to 2 tons per acre.

On the whole, Sonoma Valley is better known for cabernet and zinfandel than for pinot noir, and much of the valley is believed to be too warm for pinot. But Hanzell, close to the valley's southern end and ventilated with marine air derived from San Pablo Bay and the Petaluma Gap, is not typical of Sonoma Valley. Overnight lows during the summer average in the low 50s, and the morning fog that often blankets the valley floor occasionally rises to Hanzell's elevation. No one knows now whether mesoclimatic considerations were an important criterion in Zellerbach's choice of site, but harvest dates at Hanzell are not much earlier than for most of

Carneros, and the fruit attains good physiological ripeness at approximately 25 degrees Brix. Sessions thinks the site may have been cooler fifty years ago than it is now—he remembers two substantial snows in the 1970s but only the lightest dusting in the 1990s.

Hanzell's handsome wood-and-stone winery, designed with the assistance of his first winemaker, former E. & J. Gallo Winery researcher Brad Webb and built in 1956, was used to make every vintage through 2004. A half century later, it is hard not to be amazed by Zellerbach's and Webb's radical departures from the prevailing principles of winemaking and winery design, and by their clairvoyance. Save for an initial uphill pump from the crushpad to the fermentors, the winery is entirely gravity flow. A row of small, shallow, rectangular, temperature-controlled stainless steel fermentors (custom made for Zellerbach by a foundry in Fresno) meets virtually all the requirements of today's exacting maker of small-lot pinot. The space reserved for a "cellar" of French oak barrels on the ground floor followed Burgundian practice and the example of Martin Ray, but antedated nearly everyone else in California wine by at least a decade. The 1956 facility, unused since 2005, is now something of a museum, fermentations having been moved to a new, roofed, open-air facility about 50 feet away, and *élevage* to a new barrel cave dug into the hillside behind the winery between 2002 and 2004. It is often assumed that these moves were in response to the discovery, when the 1999 vintage was released in 2002, that the original winery had been infected with TCA, the chemical that causes so-called cork taint in wine. In fact, however, the new facility was conceived earlier, largely to relieve congestion associated with surge space built in the 1970s, and to make way for a modest increase in production when the Sessions and (later) the Ramos Vineyards (the latter being devoted entirely to chardonnay) began to bear in and after 2002.

If the Hanzell story is remarkable in part for Zellerbach's and Webb's prescience and for Zellerbach's willingness to invest in expensive solutions at a time when there was little money in the California wine business, it is remarkable also for its historical continuities. In sixty years, the property has known only three owners, and neither its objectives nor its scale has significantly changed. The so-called Hanzell style has also been remarkably consistent. On the winemaking side, Webb's association with Hanzell lasted almost twenty years. Kim Giles (who went on to the winemaking job at Mount Veeder Winery) and Tom Dehlinger represent a brief interregnum from 1967 through 1972, but then Bob Sessions, who had been the winemaker at Mayacamas Vineyards, signed on in 1973. In a consulting capacity, Webb overlapped with Sessions, transmitting methodological and stylistic parameters. Daniel Docher—a native of Clermont-Ferrand and a 1986 graduate of the École nationale d'ingénieurs des travaux agricoles de Bordeaux—worked with Sessions for eight harvests before taking the winemaking reins for two years from 2003 to 2005. In January 2005, Docher was succeeded by a close neighbor—Michael Terrien—who had been at ACACIA WINERY in Carneros since 1996. Sessions, meanwhile, assumed the mantle of "winemaker emeritus."

WINES AND WINEMAKING NOTES
Tank records, painstakingly maintained by hand in notebooks, exist for every vintage from the beginning. One interesting fact that emerges from examining these records is that Hanzell has picked its grapes, at least for pinot noir, at about the same level of ripeness for a half century. Brix at harvest has varied from year to year, but the trend line has moved barely 1 degree, from 24 to 25 Brix, and even this change has occurred only in tiny increments. Experiments notwithstanding, fermentations and *élevage* have not changed much either, save for a move to include 15 to 20 percent of whole clusters, which were avoided entirely at the outset but have been *de rigueur* since the late 1980s.

Apart from the whole-cluster lots, pinot noir has been crushed and pumped into the small fermentors, inoculated right away, and sometimes acidulated. The must has been punched down by hand and fermented for seven to ten days at very cool temperatures—generally under 80°F. The must has sometimes been bled to increase concentration. Arguing that "the worst time to press is around dryness," Sessions usually pressed with a bit of remaining sugar but sometimes permitted a postfermentation maceration instead, if he discerned any lack of "the right flavors." Unlike anyplace else I know, new wines have not been merely settled in tank but have been left there for at least the duration of the malolactic fermentation, sometimes for as little as six weeks and sometimes for as long as six months, meaning that the wines rarely have any contact with oak until the spring, the summer, or even the autumn after the vintage.

The barrel regime has been unusual, too. The sole cooper has been Sirugue, only 25 to 30 percent of the stock has been bought new in each vintage, and all barrels have been used until they were three-plus years old. The pinot has then spent a full two years in barrel, has rarely been racked except at bottling, has sometimes been fined "to take the edge off," and has usually been put through a coarse-pad filter. Another twelve months of bottle aging has preceded release, which has occurred about three and a half years after the vintage.

With some mixed feelings and great respect for the house style, Terrien has modified the Zellerbach-Webb-Sessions protocol in some significant, if not earthshaking, ways. Effective as of the 2005 vintage, a one-week cold soak has been implemented before primary fermentations begin, fermentation temperatures have been about 8 degrees warmer, and the warmer temperature has then been maintained through a two-week extended maceration. Malolactic fermentations still occur in tank, but the new wines are now in barrel by December. The percentage of new wood has been increased slightly, and time in barrel has been shortened from twenty-four months to eighteen—still reasonably long by pinot noir standards. Fining and filtration were abandoned in 2003. The point, Terrien explains, is to maintain the traditional ageworthiness of Hanzell's pinot noir balance between wines that "taste good" soon after release but remain reliably ageworthy, while adapting winemaking protocols to evolutions in viticulture and to new winemaking equipment. Terrier argues that the comparative "gentleness" of the modern equipment installed in 2004 "needed to be considered in the winemaking decisions in order to protect the historic ageability of the wines."

As it has from the beginning, Hanzell still makes a single pinot in each vintage, always the product of barrel selection with deselected lots sold off. The sole exceptions are the 1963 and 1964 vintages, which (following Zellerbach's death in 1963) were sold, via an intermediary, to Joe Heitz, who bottled them as Heitz Cellars Pinot Noir, and 2003, when a small amount of wine from the 1953 block was bottled separately as the Ambassador's Anniversary Cuvée.

Over the decades, Hanzell pinots have been curiously controversial. In the 1960s and 1970s, the wines enjoyed considerable acclaim and sold out quickly to waiting connoisseurs, but the Vintners Club tasting notes from the period 1973 to 1987 are by no means universally complimentary. Some observers say the wines declined in the 1980s; others argue that they were simply eclipsed by the emergence of newer cult wines. Occasionally, they are described as "portlike," a comparison that may contain an element of truth—if the reference is to the aromatic properties of very fine, 20-year-old tawny. The Hanzell pinots I have tasted, including a substantial selection of older vintages, have been consistently rewarding. They display medium to deep color, and complex flavors and aromas, and they age very slowly. Mineral flavors are often more dominant than fruit, although some tasters believe that the wines of the 1990s have been more fruit driven than those of earlier vintages. The 1965 and 1966 vintages, tasted in 2002, testify eloquently to the structure and ageworthiness of these exceptional wines.

TASTING NOTES

2005 *Estate (tasted prerelease in 2007):* Medium, rosy-crimson; decidedly earthy nose with some dark cherry fruit; brewed black tea, with infused blackberry and flowers, and with some hard spice on the palate; texture of rough silk; long.

2004 *Estate (tasted in 2007):* Rosy-crimson again; dusty, minerally nose with some raspberry, but a trifle closed at the moment, even double decanted; blackberry tea again; elegant with some grip and considerable mid-palate flesh; dries quickly on the finish, at least for now.

2003 *Estate (tasted in 2007):* A bit darker than the preceding wines; nut shells and nut meats (peppered cashews?) on the nose, with some black raspberry; atypically fruity mid-palate with some properties of creamed black tea; suave and attractive; significant grip on the finish.

2002 *Estate (tasted in 2007):* Light-to-medium rosy-crimson; extremely complex nose of fruit, flowers, cumin, and caraway seed, plus some intense gum camphor; bright, lightweight, and very dry on the mid-palate; ultra-elegant but simultaneously a little hollow; finishes dry and dusty. Owing to housekeeping exigencies, this wine was held in tank for eighteen months before being bottled.

2001 *Estate (tasted in 2007):* Brilliant, light-to-medium garnet with a rosy edge; slightly nutty, hickory-shells nose with a hint of caraway; attractively fruity attack, then rosewater and savory notes on the mid-palate and finish; some grip; very attractive.

2000 *Estate (tasted in 2007):* Color quite similar to the 2001; an elegant, floral nose with some soft spice and a hint of orange peel; very bright and elegant in the mouth; hints of resin and pepper; some grip and a long, dry finish. Fine.

HARTFORD FAMILY WINERY
Forestville, California

Hartford Family Winery (which did business as Hartford Court until 1999 and still uses the Hartford Court name on some bottlings) was created in 1994 by Don Hartford. Hartford, a son of strawberry farmers in western Massachusetts, once taught English as a second language in Spain, and then practiced law in San Jose, San Francisco, and Tokyo. He came to wine through the law and by marriage: his wife, Jennifer, is Jess Jackson's daughter. Don, Jennifer, and Jennifer's sister, Laura Jackson-Giron, own Hartford Family Winery, which is supported by Jackson Family Farms, an independent marketing, public relations, and vineyard management company established in 2000 by Jackson *père.* Jackson Family Farms also provides management support to CAMBRIA WINERY in Santa Maria and to Edmeades in Anderson Valley, and is run separately from Kendall-Jackson Wine Estates Ltd., Jess Jackson's large, international, multilabel, multitier business widely known as K-J.

The first winemaker at Hartford was Dan Goldfield (see DUTTON-GOLDFIELD WINES), who had entered the Jackson wine universe when Kendall-Jackson acquired the undercapitalized, Burgundy-oriented LA CREMA WINERY in 1993. When Goldfield left to create his own label in 1997, he was succeeded briefly by Bob Cabral, who moved on to WILLIAMS SELYEM after a short tenure; then by Mike Sullivan, a Fresno-trained winemaker with experience at DE LOACH, Chappellet, Landmark, and La Crema; and then in 2005 by Jeff Mangahas, a Dutton-Goldfield (full circle!) alumnus with an unusual background in cell biology and cancer research.

Hartford Family Winery, from the outset, was oriented to tiny lots of very high-end, single-vineyard pinots and chardonnays, made under the Hartford Court label. The main estate vineyards for pinot are Arrendell Vineyard on Atascadero Creek northwest of Sebastopol, once contracted to La Crema, but later purchased outright by and for Hartford; a Carneros vineyard called Sevens Bench, a high-density planting of Dijon clones 667 and 777 on the east side of Duhig Road opposite Robert Mondavi's Carneros holdings; the Seascape Vineyard, on a ridge-top west of Occidental next to Coastlands; and a vineyard planted in 1999 about two miles south of Annapolis. Fruit is also purchased from other vineyards in the Sonoma Coast AVA, and until 2005 it was purchased from Rich Savoy's vineyard in Anderson Valley, northwest of Philo, as well.

WINES AND WINEMAKING NOTES

Hartford Family Winery asserts that it emphasizes low yields and "*terroirs* that are distinctive expressions of site." Fruit is hand sorted both in the vineyard and at the winery to remove botrytis and sunburn when either occurs, as well as to remove stem fragments; the fruit is completely destemmed. Fermentors sized 4 and 6 tons are used. A long, five-to-seven-day, 50°F cold soak is practiced, with a combination of cooling jackets and dry ice used to ensure that a completely anaerobic environment is maintained in the tank's headspace. Alcoholic fermentations are allowed to begin with resident yeast. Some cuvées, such as Sevens Bench, escape without any inoculation; others are inoculated in the interest of obtaining "higher-toned fruit." Fermentation temperatures are capped at 85°F "to avoid volatilizing too many esters." Punchdowns are the main means of managing the cap and of mixing cap and juice, but pumpovers and rack-and-return are practiced "on a case-by-case basis." The must is pressed at dryness, using a Marzola basket press, is settled overnight, and is racked to barrels.

Depending on vintage, between 35 and 75 percent new barrels are used, sourced primarily from François Frères, Seguin Moreau, Cadus, Rousseau, and Remond. Blends are made in the spring following the vintage, and the Land's Edge and Fog Dance wines (see below) are bottled before the following vintage, but the vineyard-designates are held in barrel for fourteen to sixteen months. Very small lots are racked just once before bottling; larger lots are racked twice. The wines are neither fined nor filtered.

Vineyard-designated wines have been made in most vintages from the Arrendell, Sevens Bench, and Savoy Vineyards (Hartford called its Savoy bottling Velvet Sisters, but the final vintage, made in 2005, was a blend of Savoy fruit with unidentified "estate" parcels), and a block-designate has been made since 2004 from a parcel within the Arrendell Vineyard named for Don Hartford's daughter Hailey. (Hailey's is labeled as a Green Valley wine, whereas Arrendell carries the Russian River Valley designation; the vineyard is entitled to both appellations.) A wine called Jennifer's, named in honor of Hartford's wife, was made in 1998, 1999, and 2005 from purchased fruit grown in a single, unnamed vineyard at the south end of Sebastopol off Bloomfield Road, in a cool and windy site planted primarily to UCD 23. A Marin wine, an undesignated single-vineyard bottling from Mark Pasternak's Devil's Gulch Vineyard (see Dutton-Goldfield Wines) was made until 2001.

In addition, two blends debuted in 2005, made in slightly larger quantities than the single-vineyard wines. These are the Land's Edge Vineyards bottling, created from grapes grown in the estate vineyards at Occidental and Annapolis, and from fruit purchased from growers in the True Sonoma Coast; and the Fog Dance Vineyards bottling, anchored with fruit from the estate vineyard on Ross Road, plus a few lots from Arrendell. The Fog Dance bottling carries the Green Valley appellation.

Hartford pinots are always polished, professionally crafted wines with considerable barrel marking that fall into the mainstream of ripe-picked, warm-finished, high-end California pinot noir.

2005 *Fog Dance Vineyards (tasted in 2007):* Transparent, medium black-red; nutty nose with some cardamom and mace; bright red berry fruit with hints of citrus on the palate, plus some hints of white fruits such as apple and pear; very high toned with notes of white pepper; clean, intense, light-to-medium weight, and very slightly hot; of medium length; attractive.

2005 *Land's Edge Vineyards (tasted in 2007):* Dark black-red; dark fruit and toasty notes on the nose; very ripe on the palate; simultaneously silky, dense, and mouth coating; rich to the edge of heaviness, slightly spirity; challenging at this point; may resolve attractively with additional time in bottle.

2005 *Velvet Sisters (tasted in 2007):* Transparent, rosy-ruby color; intense aromas of red berries, pine tar, and tobacco; slightly sweet on the palate; cherry, pepper, graphite, and barrel char; soft, almost creamy, and of medium weight; finishes quite warm.

2005 *Far Coast Vineyard (tasted in 2007):* Medium-dark rosy black-red; very forward nose of pine needles, forest floor, wet moss, and rose petals; exuberant palate exhibiting abundant cherry fruit, barrel char, and vanilla, plus hints of blueberry and pepper; a wild, organic character overall; soft grip from mind-palate to finish; warm and medium long.

2005 *Arrendell Vineyard (tasted in 2007):* Transparent, dark ruby; slightly smoky nose; bright, primary fruit flavors on the palate, especially raspberry, red cherry, and griotte; overlay of cinnamon and nutmeg; rich on the back palate, with a bit of lavender and tobacco; peppery-alcoholic bite at the end.

2005 *Hailey's Block (tasted in 2007):* Transparent, light-to-medium rosy-garnet color; aromas of nut shells and potpourri; slightly sweet, delicate red berry flavors with mace, other spices, and orange flower water; elegant impression overall; long and very attractive.

WILLIAM HATCHER WINES
Dundee, Oregon

This microboutique brand was created in 2001 when Bill Hatcher, a midwesterner and one-time director of strategic planning for May Department Stores, left DOMAINE DROUHIN OREGON, where he had spent fourteen years as the project's chief architect and general manager, to begin a small business with his wife, Debra. William Hatcher Wines, known as Hatcher Wineworks until 2006, works with just a few dozen barrels of wine, many of which are eventually redirected into the A TO Z brand the Hatchers co-own with Cheryl Francis and Sam Tannahill. Each year, about sixteen barrels enter the Hatchers' own program, where they are crafted into a single blended edition of pinot noir, and (since 2004) also into a minuscule release of chardonnay.

As a passionate believer in "the virtues of blending" for pinot noir, Hatcher says he "cannot ever foresee" making his pinot as a single-vineyard wine. The idea, he explains, is not to "cull" lesser barrels, but rather to "find the most harmonious blend." In fact, to ensure a "big palette" of blending options, Hatcher deliberately sources pinot from widely scattered vineyards. In 2002 these included Goldschmidt (see DUSKY GOOSE) and two Ponzi-owned vineyards on the on the north slope of the Chehalem Mountains; in 2003 and 2004, they included the Chehalem Mountain Vineyard, Momtazi in the Coast Range west of McMinnville, and Bella Vida, adjacent to Maresh in the Dundee Hills. Stoller, at the base of the Dundee Hills near Lafayette, was used in every vintage through 2005. The 2006 cuvée is now a combination of Amity Hills Vineyard, Momtazi, Rainbow Ridge (a late 1990s planting of Dijon 115 and 777 near Momtazi), and CARABELLA VINEYARD (a 1996 planting on Parrett Mountain.) Carabella, according to Hatcher, provides the "forward prettiness" he had been seeking from Stoller and Bella Vida. My experience is limited to the 2005 vintage, which is aromatically complex and very nicely made.

TASTING NOTE

2005 *Willamette Valley (tasted in 2007):* Transparent, medium-dark garnet; evergreen and cigar box aromas, with dried pecan shells and some ripe berries; cherry-like and very slightly sweet on the palate; tightly knit and nicely balanced; long, borderline chewy, and slightly barrel marked; long.

HIRSCH VINEYARDS
Cazadero, California

In 1980 David Hirsch, a veteran of the clothing business with no background in wine, purchased 800 acres of remote, rugged, disused sheep ranch at the end of a dirt-track *cum* road, which was off the power grid, 8 miles north of the Russian River and about 3 miles as the crow flies from the Pacific Coast. The site met his criteria for the antithesis of civilization, but given that coyotes had finished off the sheep, and that loggers had cut all

the trees suitable for lumber, it was not clear what, if anything, could be done with the all-but-abandoned land.

THE FIRST VINEYARD ON THE TRUE SONOMA COAST TO SET OFF GRAND CRU MURMURINGS AMONG PINOTPHILES

Hirsch commissioned a study of potential uses, which examined possibilities such as mushroom farming. In the end, it was Jim Beauregard, a friend and grape grower from Hirsch's previous life in Santa Cruz, who suggested he plant pinot noir. Other ranchers in the area had already planted small vineyards, but Hirsch's planting was the first to attract serious attention and set off "*grand cru*" murmurings among pinotphiles. In numerous, discontinuous blocks so different one from another that they could pass under objective criteria as entirely separate vineyards, 3 acres were planted in 1980, followed by 43 acres between 1990 and 1996, and 26 acres in 2002 to 2003. All but 4 acres of the 72-acre total are pinot noir. The grapes were sold, over the years, to an extraordinary list of luminary pinot makers, including WILLIAMS SELYEM, LITTORAI WINES, and SIDURI, who simultaneously established the reputation of Hirsch Vineyards and the promise of the True Sonoma Coast.

Vineyard-designated wines from Hirsch are found on nearly every list of the best American pinots, and the vineyard sports the same cachet as Sanford & Benedict in the Santa Rita Hills or PISONI in the Santa Lucia Highlands. In 2002 Hirsch took the next logical step: he created his own brand and began to make his own wine—in a small facility built onsite, at the end of the aforementioned dirt-track *cum* road. The winemaker for the first two vintages was Vanessa Wong (see PEAY VINEYARDS); the torch then passed to Mark Doherty, who was previously the winemaker at DAVIS BYNUM, in 2004.

WINES AND WINEMAKING NOTES

In each vintage through 2005, Hirsch made an estate wine, bottled simply as Hirsch Vineyards, and a second wine called The Bohan Dillon (this is the proper name for Hirsch's dirt road), crafted from declassified barrels of estate wine, press wine, and (sometimes) fruit purchased from Hirsch's immediate neighbors. In 2006 a second estate wine will be made, called M. In addition, a "reserve-quality" barrel selection may be culled and released separately if and when "a few barrels exhibit exceptional quality in a given vintage." This reserve wine has been named The Rauschen Reserve, for a noted painter who lived on the ranch in the nineteenth century, but it has not yet been made. All of the new blocks planted in 2002 and 2003 have been reserved for use in the above wines and constitute about two thirds of them, but Hirsch also holds twenty-five of the forty-five older blocks, three of which were replanted in 2007, for "house" use.

Hirsch explains the large palette is useful since the cuvées that express the site best, in any given vintage, are those made from "compatible" barrels drawn "from all the blocks and fermentation lots." The main estate wine privileges structure, as it is made to be cellared, while M relies on a preponderance of "friendlier" lots. Hirsch describes The Bohan Dillon as a "new-world bistro wine," but at $30 a bottle, it seems to redefine that category a bit grandly.

Most vintages are picked exceptionally early by prevailing California standards—at less than 24 Brix. The fruit is entirely destemmed, fermentations rely exclusively on resident yeast, there are no additions of enzymes or acid, and there is no extended maceration. Wines are raised in mostly François Frères and Remond barrels, with some Cadus and Marsannay thrown in; about 40 percent of the barrels are new, and the wine stays in them for up to eighteen months. Wines are neither fined nor filtered. Each vintage of the estate wine has been different—no surprise, given how radically growing seasons vary in true coastal vineyards—but all have genuine elegance and transparency, and display bright, high-toned aromatics.

TASTING NOTES

2005 *Hirsch Vineyards (tasted in 2007):* Rosy, transparent, medium black-red; intense nose of cherry pie; rich and mouth coating, with bright acidity and a fair load of very fine-grained tannin that makes for a dry finish; raspberry, tree bark, and barrel char play subordinate roles; elegant.

2004 *Hirsch Vineyards (tasted in 2007):* Very transparent rosy-red; aromas of rosewater and orange peel; raspberry with citrus notes on the palate; bright, dry, and elegant; of light-to-medium weight, and very long.

2003 *The Bohan Dillon (tasted prerelease in 2005):* Medium ruby with a rosy rim; aromas of ripe black cherry and barrel char, with some pecan shells; rich, chocolaty, and intense on the palate, with medium weight and good length.

2002 *Hirsch Vineyards (tasted in 2005):* Dense, opaque brick-red color; high-toned cedar and subtle, nutmeg-like aromatics; coffee and ripe cherry-plum fruit flavors; tight, dense, and smooth, with considerable end-of-palate grip; impressive.

HITCHING POST WINES
Santa Maria, California

In the 1970s, when Frank Ostini Jr. returned from college (he had studied environmental planning at the University of California Davis) to his family's restaurant business in Casmalia, near Lompoc, he tended the restaurant's bar. Having been around wine in college, conscious that northern Santa Barbara County was spawning vineyards and wineries with increasing speed, and looking for a creative way to have some fun, Ostini got the idea to improve the restaurant's unimpressive list of basic Paul Masson varietals with good value, local wine that—in an unusual twist on the "house brand" story—he would make himself. In 1981, having been offered 3 tons of merlot grapes that nearby Firestone Vineyards had decided not to pick, Ostini recruited a friend—who was also a neighbor, a carpenter, a commercial salmon fisherman, and a sometime customer of the family's restaurant—and reinvented himself as a part-time home winemaker. Two years later, Hitching Post Wines became a bonded, commercial proposition. From 1984 to 1989, Ostini's then partner, in life and in wine, was Lane Tanner, who founded her own label (see **LANE TANNER WINES**) after the couple separated. In 1991 Ostini appealed once again to the friend who had helped with his home-winemaking project initially. Gray Hartley became Ostini's business and hands-on work partner in a second incarnation of the Hitching Post brand, which is made by Hartley Ostini LLC.

With Hartley as the de facto cellarmaster and Ostini handling fruit sourcing and "executive" winemaking, Hitching Post

wines became much more than the family restaurants' (a second Hitching Post had been opened in Buellton in 1986) house brand: the wines developed a national market and reputation. From 2003 to 2005, production more than tripled, benefiting in part from the restaurants' role in the movie *Sideways*. Virginia Madsen's character in the movie was a waitress at Hitching Post II, in Buellton, and Hartley made cameo appearances in several scenes. Despite his substantial role in Hitching Post Wines, Ostini self-identifies as a chef, and is often seen deftly tending a mobile grill at high-profile wine events. Interviewed together, Ostini and Hartley exude how-did-we-get-so-lucky enthusiasm for their common enterprise, which ranks high on nearly everyone's list of American pinot success stories.

DARK EDITIONS OF PINOT WITH RICH FLAVORS AND NICELY CRAFTED TEXTURES MADE FROM THE BEST VINEYARDS

WINES AND WINEMAKING NOTES
Hitching Post's are among the many pinots once made using a percentage of whole clusters that now depend (since 1994) entirely on destemmed fruit. Cap manipulation relies on pumpovers during the period of cold soak, followed by punchdowns thereafter, except for the Santa Barbara cuvée (see below), which is made entirely in 20-ton, stainless steel tanks and is pumped over from start to finish. The wines are pressed at dryness and go to barrel on their gross lees without significant settling. The press fraction is reintegrated with the free-run juice. Although the Santa Barbara cuvée is bottled after only eleven to twelve months in barrel, the other pinots

spend a comparatively long sixteen to eighteen months in wood.

The cooperage is almost entirely François Frères, with the largest percentage of new oak going into the Highliner cuvée. Malolactic fermentations are left to happen spontaneously, and these generally run late into the spring after the vintage. Most Hitching Post pinots are egg-white fined, and the Santa Barbara cuvée, given its shorter barrel time, is sometimes also filtered for clarity.

Overall, the brand is focused on blends, which account for about 70 percent of total volume; Ostini observes that, as a chef, he "likes putting things together." A Santa Maria Valley wine debuted in 1991, initially anchored with fruit from the historic Sierra Madre vineyard. In 1991 the Sierra Madre fruit was blended with fruit from the Bien Nacido Vineyard; in later vintages fruit from the Riverbench and Gold Coast vineyards entered the blend. In 1998, Sierre Madre fruit disappeared from the Hitching Post palette entirely and was replaced by fruit from the Santa Maria Hills Vineyard. Fruit from Julia's Vineyard has also been used in this wine since 1996. A Santa Barbara County wine, born in 2000 and christened Cork Dancer since 2004, was first assembled from Gold Coast and Santa Maria Hills grapes, to which sources Rio Vista, Bien Nacido, Riverbench, and Kickon (in Los Alamos) have been added progressively since 2003. Hitching Post's highest-priced wine, a blend of "the best barrels from our best vineyards" called Highliner, specifically designed as a marriage of the Santa Maria Valley's elegance with Sta. Rita Hills' raciness, debuted in 1996. An all-Santa-Rita-Hills blend dubbed Saint Rita's Earth debuted in 2001. This wine began as a bit of all the Sta. Rita Hills' vineyards to which Hitching Post had access (Fiddlestix, Sanford & Benedict, Cargasacchi, and Clos Pepe in 2001), but was a subset of the whole by 2005, when it claimed fruit only from Rio Vista, Fiddlestix, and Richard Sanford's newest vineyard, called La Encantada (see ALMA ROSA WINERY AND VINEYARDS).

In addition to the blends, the partners make no less than six (as of 2005) vineyard-designated wines: Bien Nacido (UCD 13 from N Block and UCD 4 from Q Block), made since 1992; Julia's, made since 1996; Sanford & Benedict, made since 1985, except in 1986 and 1990; Fiddlestix, made since 2001; Cargasacchi, made since 2002; and Rio Vista, made since 2003. Vineyard-designated wines were also made from Sierra Madre from 1984 through 1990, and from Clos Pepe in 2001 and 2002. All told, there has been a marked south- and westward shift in the focus of Hitching Post's vineyard attentions in the two decades since the brand was launched, and virtually all of the new volume since 2003 has come from vineyards in Los Alamos and in the Santa Rita Hills. The wines are (generally) dark editions of pinot noir, with rich flavors and nicely crafted textures made from the best vineyards available. They are poster children for the top quintile of mainstream-styled pinots from the southern Central Coast.

TASTING NOTES

2006 *Cargasacchi Vineyard (tasted in 2008):* Brilliant light-to-medium magenta; nutmeg, rose petal, and smoke on the nose; round and intense on the palate with some minerality; very persistent and attractive; finishes long and warm.

2005 *Cork Dancer (tasted in 2006):* Dark black-red; very floral nose; cassis with strong mint, some black pepper and some tar in the mouth; very full bodied with medium weight and length.

2005 *Saint Rita's Earth (tasted in 2006):* Transparent, dark black-red; ink, cherry cola, mint, resin, sweet fruit, and anise, with some hard spice; smoky and briary impression overall, with a long finish and noticeable grip.

2005 *Cargasacchi Vineyard (tasted in 2006):* Light-to-medium black-red; sandalwood and Indonesian spices on the nose; bright, cedary red fruit on the palate; a high-acid, high-tanning profile typical of Sta. Rita Hills wine; considerable structure in an elegant wrapper; bright, long, and intense; very attractive.

2005 *Bien Nacido Vineyard (tasted in 2006):* Dark, barely transparent black-red; violets and black pepper on the nose; sweet black raspberry on the palate; elegant, refined, and long, with a suede-like texture.

2004 *Highliner (tasted in 2007):* Transparent, medium-dark black-red; aromas reminiscent of glög; very fruit-sweet, featuring black cherry; soft and round, with some grip from mid-palate to finish; serious, but also accessible and attractive; medium in length.

2004 *Sanford & Benedict Vineyard (tasted in 2006):* Opaque, dark black-red; sweet, dark, and brooding; inky and intense, with flavors of tar and boysenberry; satiny and long; young at this tasting, but very a impressive wine from very old vines.

2003 *Highliner (tasted in 2005):* Deep rosy-red; leathery licorice and dusty, slightly raisined fruit; intense, sweet fruit on the palate, with cloves and noticeable tannin; medium in length, with some glycerin; very slightly hot on the finish.

HUSCH VINEYARDS
Philo, California

When Tony Husch, a Harvard-educated urban planner, bought a 60-acre ranch in Anderson Valley in 1968, he retreated symbolically from the city to the land. When he then planted 22 of the 60 acres to gewürztraminer, chardonnay, and pinot noir, he unleashed a slow but remarkably durable revolution. Except for Donald Edmeades's earlier block of gewürztraminer, these were the first plantings of the grape varieties destined to make the reputation of Anderson Valley. Three years later, having decided to make wine from his own grapes, he established Anderson Valley's first bonded winery and made its first estate-bottled wine.

Across thirty vintages, most of Husch's 1971 block of pinot has remained in production, used exclusively for varietally designated, estate-bottled pinot noir. Since Husch sold the business in 1979, much of the credit for this remarkable consistency goes to Hugo Oswald Jr., a Williams College graduate, who married into a pear-farming business in California's Santa Clara Valley in the 1950s; he subsequently relocated to Ukiah when the area around Santa Clara became nearly completely paved with housing tracts and silicon. Oswald purchased Husch, consolidated its operations with his La Ribera Ranch in Talmage, and then invested repeatedly in facilities and additional land. Almost as durable a figure as Oswald is Al White, who worked with Tony Husch on some of the initial plantings, served quietly as interim winemaker at the end of the 1970s, and piloted the interplanting and vineyard modernization efforts of the last decade.

Husch was his own winemaker at the outset; Hugo Oswald's son H. A. Oswald III was responsible for the vintages 1980 through 1983; Mark Thies served as winemaker from 1984 through 1994. Fritz Meier, with the unusual (for an American) background of Geisenheim training in enology, joined Thies as assistant winemaker in 1987 and was named winemaker in 1994. Meier was succeeded, in July 2001, by

Zachary Rasmuson, a graduate of St. John's University in Maryland and a veteran of Stag's Leap Wine Cellars and ROBERT SINSKEY VINEYARDS. Jeff Brinkman, an alumnus of Atlas Peak, held the reins for the 2003 and 2004 harvests, before Brad Holstine, Hugo Oswald Jr.'s grandson-in-law and Amanda Robinson Holstine's husband, was named winemaker in 2005.

Although pinot noir accounts for only about 15 percent of Husch's total production, it is the main product made in the Anderson Valley facility. Husch's sauvignon blanc and chardonnay are made at La Ribera. The original estate vineyard on the Nunn Ranch, halfway between Philo and Navarro, was planted on a modest south-facing slope, rising up from the northeastern bank of the Navarro River. Known in-house as The Knoll, this site was planted with scion material from Wente's Arroyo Seco vineyard. The thin, well-drained soils at this location are perched atop a shale outcropping. Interplanting with Dijon 667 began in 2001. A second block, unimaginatively called Middle, occupies a steeper portion of the site. A third block, called Meadow, has been withdrawn from the pinot program and replanted to chardonnay. From 1988 through the mid 1990s, 22 additional acres of pinot were planted on the nearby Day Ranch after this property was acquired by Hugo's son Ken Oswald. Here, the Apple Hill (1.6 ac) and East (2.8 ac) blocks were planted to UCD 15; Highway block (4 ac) to UCD 16; Main Block (10.1 ac) to a combination of UCD 13 and 15; and Tony's Block to UCD 32. (Tony's bears no relation to Tony Husch; it takes its name from Tony Sanchez, the Day Ranch foreman.) The average yield on these blocks is about 5 tons per acre, which is high for Anderson Valley.

When Hugo Oswald Jr. and his wife died, ownership in the winery was spread among various members of the next two family generations. In 2003 the grandchildren, Zac Robinson and Amanda Holstine, found financing to buy out shareholders who wished to exit the business, and assumed control of the winery, although members of the second generation retained ownership of the Day Ranch. At the same time, recognizing that some blocks at Day Ranch were threatened by phylloxera, then winemaker Zach Rasmuson recommended that the family diversity its fruit sources for pinot noir. The upshot was three long-term leases for pinot from new sources, including Ferrington Vineyard, long used by WILLIAMS SELYEM; Corby; Valley Foothills; Henneberg (on Guntley Road near HANDLEY CELLARS); and Nash Mill, a new planting in the hills behind Roederer Estate. Now that three fields at Day Ranch have lost their battle with phylloxera but have not been replanted, Husch's pinot programs depends less on Day and more on the newly contracted sources; nevertheless, its single largest source remains, as always, the estate vineyard itself. From 2003 the Anderson Valley cuvée has been built from this wider array of sources.

WINES AND WINEMAKING NOTES

Husch's main release is the aforementioned Anderson Valley cuvée, of which about 6,000 cases are made in a typical vintage. In addition, much smaller quantities of The Knoll were made in 1999, 2004, and 2005, and a reserve blend was made in 2001 and 2005. The Knoll is the only vineyard-designated wine. The reserve is a genuine barrel selection, and the selected lots have involved estate and non-estate fruit since 2003.

Holstine continues the house tradition of relatively early picking—between 23 and 24.5 Brix. Fruit is largely destemmed, but the destemmer-crusher rollers are set apart to maximize whole berries, and "a fraction" of the grapes are fermented as whole clusters, following an initial cold soak. Fermentors are all small, three-quarter-ton bins; fermentations rely on inocula, and plunging is done by hand. Holstine describes his winemaking, overall, as "gentle" and "reductive" to help keep "the essence that is pinot noir alive and kicking." The barrel program is restrained—the Anderson Valley cuvée sees only about 24 percent new wood—so that "the fruit, subtle nuances, and textural magic take center stage." Preferred coopers include François Frères, Rousseau, Remond, Mercurey, and Sirugue.

Husch pinots are generally understated, medium-weight, elegant wines that do not always show well in their youth, but which age faithfully and gracefully. In general, their texture is more silky than plush. The Reserve (and now the vineyard-designates) is distinguished from the Anderson Valley bottling by somewhat greater weight and softer mouth-feel, along with a core of sweeter fruit. All Husch pinots exhibit great complexity, which increases with a few years of bottle aging. Library wines from the 1979 through 1998 vintages, tasted in 2001, were showing wonderfully with only one exception.

TASTING NOTES

2005 *Anderson Valley (tasted in 2007):* Intense ruby red; smoky, black cherry nose; bright, almost tart, cherry-raspberry-pomegranate fruit on the palate, with mint, menthol, and black pepper; smooth, almost silky, and long.

2005 *Reserve (tasted in 2007):* Barely transparent, dark black-red; red fruit and pine pitch on the nose; very intense black cherry and some rosewater in a smooth, round package; slightly sweeter and weightier than the appellation wine; soft grip at the end.

2004 *Knoll (tasted in 2007):* Transparent, medium garnet; exotic sandalwood, gum camphor, tar, and tobacco aromas; cherries and mesquite on the palate, plus a herbal-savory note with some tangerine peel; silky but substantial; nicely and elegantly built; very fine.

2003 *Anderson Valley (tasted in 2007):* Almost opaque, dark, rosy black-red; some earth and wet clay on the nose, with a hint of nuts, but slightly closed at this tasting; intense and slightly sweet on the palate, with briary, peppery cherry, and a slight hint of tobacco; grippy after mid-palate and medium long; nicely built overall.

INMAN FAMILY WINES
Santa Rosa, California

Simon and Kathleen Inman's story reads like a fairy tale. The couple met when he (an Englishman on vacation) visited the Napa Creek Winery's tasting room where she (an art history major at the University of California Santa Barbara) had a summer job. A transatlantic courtship led to marriage, followed by fifteen years of living in Yorkshire and working in London, where she was a finance executive and he was a lawyer. Both were serious wine drinkers, however, and both developed a preference for pinot noir above all other wines. In 1998, with some self-confessed mixed emotions, they pulled up their English roots, moved to California, and began searching for vineyard land that would be suitable for pinot noir and pinot gris. In 1999 they found 10 acres of sandy loam and gravel on Olivet Road not far from DE LOACH VINEYARDS—which they christened Olivet Grange Vineyard, to memorialize their erstwhile English residence near Elvington in Yorkshire, known locally as The Grange.

In the summer of 2000, the Inmans planted 7 acres of their new parcel to four Dijon clones of pinot (114, 115, 667, and 777) and less than an acre to pinot gris, which they laid out in 6-foot rows with 4 feet between vines. Kathleen Inman reinvented herself as a grape grower and winemaker, with help from courses at the University of California Davis. In 2006 an additional half-acre was planted to Dijon 828, sourced via Jim Platt's Cornerstone Vineyard near Sebastopol. Although Inman

---

ELEGANT, EARLY-PICKED
WINES WITH FLORAL
AROMAS AND RED FRUIT
FLAVORS

Family Wines uses the vast majority of its estate fruit, small quantities of pinot noir are sold to Pali Wine Company, where Brian Loring is the winemaker, and to Atalanta Wines, a brand created by Angie Riff, formerly the assistant to Helen Turley. These fruit clients refer to the Inman's vineyard as the Inman Olivet Vineyard, but the Inmans have removed references to Olivet Grange Vineyard from their front labels, replacing those words with OGV as part of an intellectual property settlement with Southcorp Wines of Australia, which had sought to protect its interests in the Penfolds Grange name.

WINES AND WINEMAKING NOTES
From 2003 to 2005, Inman Family Wines produced a single pinot noir in each vintage, made entirely from Olivet Grange fruit. In 2006 the program was expanded to include purchased fruit (initially from

Ted Klopp's Thorn Ridge Vineyard, which is also used by FREEMAN VINEYARDS AND WINERY and by TALISMAN WINES, among others) a part of a plan to develop a portfolio of up to three vineyard-designated wines and a Russian River blend. The Inmans "like low alcohol" and pick early, but at picking, as they say, the seeds are already "more than 80 percent brown," the stems show "some browning," and skin pigments "stain our fingers when the berries are crushed." (In 2005 the average Brix at picking was 22.6, and the finished alcohol was 13.2°! The fruit is entirely destemmed, cold soaked for three days with help from cooling jackets and some dry ice, inoculated with RC 212 yeast, and fermented (for seven to ten days) before being pressed in a Diemme bladder press. In the first vintage, the Inmans had only two fermentors, and therefore co-fermented the 114 and the 777, and the 115 and the 667. By 2004 there was enough fruit to justify four fermentors, allowing them to ferment each clone separately.

Cooperage comes from Sirugue, Billon, François Frères, and Remond, and about 30 percent of barrels are new in each vintage. Kathleen Inman has developed a preference for barrels coopered from trees grown in Vosges Mountains forests, so these make up a growing percentage of the cellar stock. New barrels are inoculated to start the malolactic fermentation; older barrels start spontaneously. The wine is bottled before the following vintage. Since 2004 the pinot has been cross-flow filtered. The inaugural vintage in 2003 produced a beautiful wine with red fruit flavors, soft tannins, gentle notes of spice and herbs, and admirable elegance.

TASTING NOTES
2005 OGV (tasted in 2007): Luminous, very transparent, light garnet; nose bespeaks

orange peel; on the palate, Indonesian spices in the garam masala family and some wet earth; a touch rounder, earthier, less fruity, and less floral than earlier vintages; hints of resin and tar; satiny, with medium weight; elegant and long.

2004 *Olivet Grange Vineyard (tasted in 2007):* Luminous, light-to-medium garnet; soft spice and red fruit on the nose; lovely, intense, medium-bright cherry-raspberry fruit, white pepper, infused flowers, and toasted hard spice; silky, elegant, and long.

2003 *Olivet Grange Vineyard (tasted in 2005):* Medium rosy-ruby color; cinnamon and rose petal on the nose; then, cranberry, cherry, and raspberry fruit, with hints of herbs and forest floor; light-to-medium in weight, and silky.

IRON HORSE VINEYARDS
Sebastopol, California

Iron Horse sits astride Green Valley Creek about 8 miles north of Sebastopol, far removed from most other stirrings in the Russian River valley until the 1990s, but now almost the epicenter of the pinot centric interest in Green Valley. The ranch was "discovered" in 1971 by Rodney Strong, whose Windsor Vineyards brand secured an option to buy it. Strong tapped Forrest Tancer, a Berkeley graduate who had grown up on a farm and vineyard in the Alexander Valley and had learned winemaking on the job at Windsor Vineyards, to redevelop the ranch as vineyard. When Windsor Vineyards was caught in the general recession and wine bust of the mid-1970s and was unable to exercise its option, Iron Horse was put up for sale. Barry Sterling, an attorney with an international practice

in Los Angeles and Paris, and his wife, Audrey, who had previously considered purchasing a *château* in the Haut-Médoc, heard about the offering at a dinner party in San Francisco. Despite a driving winter rainstorm, their first visit to Iron Horse, it is said, resulted in love at first sight.

The Sterlings bought the ranch and hired Tancer, who became their vineyardist, winemaker, and eventually partner, until his retirement in 2006. The original vineyard, planted between 1971 and 1973, covered about 110 acres, evenly divided between chardonnay and pinot noir. After the Sterlings' purchase, in February 1976, it was systematically rehabilitated with new trellising, drip irrigation, and some replanting, and was then dedicated primarily to sparking wine, on which the reputation of the Iron Horse brand was built in the 1980s. Even before the first grapes were crushed for sparkling wine, however, Iron Horse made a still edition of pinot noir in 1979, and Tancer experimented with small lots of still pinot noir throughout the 1980s. The 1980 pinot has a legendary reputation in the family, and those made in 1985, 1986, 1987, and 1988 from a rocky, low-yielding knoll near the winery building called Block G are said to have been especially good.

In 1985 hopes for a new generation of still pinot were pinned on the south-facing slope of a butte about a quarter mile northeast of the winery called Block Q—which from the winery looks like the back of an armadillo—and on Block N, also known as the Corral Block, on an adjacent ranch the Sterlings acquired in 1984. Q is a magnificent, 3.5-acre site overlooking Green Valley Creek, where the Sterlings' son, Laurence, had once imagined building a house; it was planted in 1985, first in 10-foot rows with 8 feet between vines to UCD 5 from ADELSHEIM VINEYARD in Oregon, and then interplanted with UCD 4, so that the spacing was effectively tightened to 10 feet by 4 feet. Unlike the rest of the Iron Horse vineyard, which is on very friable Goldridge soils, Block Q is Josephine soil, weathered from a geologically older material, once uplifted from seabed, which is richer both in iron and in clay.

From the outset, Block Q demanded patience: the vines were slow to become established there, and it has often displayed a propensity to give angular, high-tannin wines. At the end of the 1980s, as part of a short-lived joint venture with the French champagne firm of Laurent Perrier, pinot was also planted in a declining apple orchard along Thomas Road, on the high western side of the ranch. These plantings of UCD 13, known around Iron Horse as the P2–P9 blocks, were originally intended for the production of sparkling wine, but the westernmost half of P6, which is more benchland than slope, and all of P7, have turned out to produce excellent fruit for still red wine.

At the end of the 1990s and in the beginning of the new millennium, Iron Horse began a Herculean project to redevelop all its remaining original plantings. Five acres of chardonnay in E Block came first in 1997, rededicated to Dijon 113 in 12-foot rows with 5 feet between vines; then Block I, 7 acres of existing pinot noir, was replanted to Dijon 115 in 2000; 13 acres of chardonnay in the B North and B South blocks followed in 2001, dedicated to Dijon 777 and 667 set out 9 feet by 5 feet and 8 feet by five feet, respectively. Eleven acres in Block G were replanted to Dijon 115 and 667 in 2002, followed by 7 acres in Block K in 2003. Two final pieces of redevelopment were underway at the time of this writing: Block H, where 22 acres of original pinot was in the process of being converted to about 15 acres of as yet unselected clones of pinot, and two of chardonnay; and Block J, destined to see a combination of Dijon 667 and 777.

This transformation has been guided by Daniel Roberts, the former director of winegrowing and research for Jackson Family Farms, who has established an impressive reputation for pinot-centric viticultural consulting in western Sonoma; it has been effectively advanced by the emergence of Laurence Sterling, who was trained as a lawyer, as the estate's hands-on vineyard manager.

Viticultural practices have changed along with the replanting. Sterling and David Munksgard, an alumnus of CHATEAU ST. JEAN who succeeded Tancer as winemaker in 2005, now strive for uniform ripening through vine training and pruning protocols (rather than relying on green harvesting of clusters at veraison), and tailor viticultural practices to the circumstances of each individual vine. Sterling is said to be inseparable from a small utility vehicle acquired in 2002 that fits neatly between the narrowest of the property's vineyard rows.

WINES AND WINEMAKING NOTES

Since early in the new millennium, just over 10 acres of Iron Horse vineyard have been reliably dedicated to the production of still pinot: half of Block P6, all of P7, and all of Q; other blocks of pinot shift between the still and sparkling programs vintage by vintage. Since 1996 an estate bottling and a Thomas Road bottling (a barrel selection from the P6 and P7 blocks on Thomas Road) have been made each year, except that there was no Thomas Road in 1999. A Corral Vineyard wine was made once only, in 2000. A new block-designate wine debuted in 2005 from Block Q.

Deliberately experimenting to get better fruit expression, and to obtain soft tannins even in warm years when sugars spike up before the grapes are physiologically mature, Munksgard adopted a new, untraditional, and decidedly interventionist protocol soon after he arrived at Iron Hose in 1996. Enough of "letting the wine make itself"—a proposition of which Munksgard disapproves. Cold-water jacketing and layers of dry-ice pellets are used to make sure the destemmed but uncrushed grapes macerate for seven full days before the yeasts wake up, so that the extractive properties of water and acid, not alcohol, work first. On the seventh day, the must is heated and inoculated with a Brunello strain of laboratory yeast, which produces more "forest floor" flavors than most Burgundian isolates, according to Munksgard, and then fermented for about five days in closed tanks, mostly at about 75°F, although "a few hours" at 85°F are permitted once during this period. In lieu of punchdowns, a rack-and-return system is used to keep the must in contact with the skins, while Munksgard evaluates aromas and flavors. When the fermentation is between 60 and 80 percent complete— and juice Brix somewhere between 10 and 2—the juice is drawn off the skins and transferred to barrel, where the fermentation finishes in contact with wood. Further intervention comes in the form of lees stirring and racking. The wines then spend upward of ten months in mostly new, medium-toast barrels from the Rousseau cooperage. They are not fined and are only coarsely bug filtered before bottling.

I have no experience with Iron Horse pinots before 1996. The 1996 debut vintage of the Thomas Road cuvée—an elegant, medium-weight wine that (in pinot-typical Jekyll and Hyde fashion) actually *gained* both weight and complexity four years after the vintage—was consistently a personal favorite, through multiple tastings between 1997 and 2001. The 2005 wines described below are a new generation at Iron Horse. Medium dark in color, they are rich in aromatic interest and distinctive in flavor.

After tasting barrel samples for a decade, I have always been impressed by Block Q, which has now been block-designated.

TASTING NOTES

2005 *Estate (tasted in* 2007*):* Transparent, medium ruby; tarry and savory aromas with hints of bayberry; slightly sweet on the palate, with cherry and briary wild fruit; peppery like arugula and slightly bitter like dandelion green on the palate, but still persistently fruity to the end; medium in weight and length.

2005 *Thomas Road (tasted in* 2007*):* Medium garnet; nutty, softly spicy, and slightly exotic on the nose; sweet with blackberries, walnuts, and cashews on the palate; briefly velvety and almost plush; then like strong tea and dry on the finish. This is the most immediately appealing of the Iron Horse pinots, but very ripe fruit interferes with its expression of *terroir,* and it is warmer on the finish that earlier editions of this wine.

2005 *Q (tasted in* 2007*):* Transparent, medium-dark black-red; clove, bubblegum, volatile aromatics, and flowers on the nose; a huge, broad satiny palate seems to surmount a big, bold structure; muscular acidity and very fine-grained tannins; very distinctive, intense, and lingering.

J. K. CARRIÈRE
Newburg, Oregon

Nearly everything about Jim Prosser, the thoughtful and well-spoken principal behind J. K. Carrière pinots, seems simultaneously deliberate, admirable, and unlikely. In the middle of the 1990s, he put his first career in real estate finance, along with its monetary perks and "designer Italian suits," firmly behind him. Figuratively, he returned to his childhood roots in Bend, Oregon, where the family's hardware business inspired him to reconsider vocations where one works with one's "head and hands." He explored professional cooking and winemaking.

Once focused on wine, Prosser pursued it with systematic dedication, arranging internships with Oregon's best producers, followed by time in New Zealand and Australia. Then he worked for no less than Christophe Roumier, in Chambolle-Musigny, for most of 1998. It was Roumier,

---

IMPRESSIVE, RIPE AND
HIGH-ACID WINES WITH
SMOOTH TANNINS THAT
ARE MADE TO AGE WELL

---

according to Prosser, who finally sealed his commitment to wine, telling him to "go make your own." Prosser admits to enthusiasms, above all, for skiing and fly-fishing; makes his wine in a rented centenarian barn outside Newberg where the restroom is in an adjacent building; and sounds unambiguously happy that, albeit on a tiny scale, his business is "profitable" and that he has "no debt." His logo is adorned with the image of a wasp, reminding Prosser that he is allergic to this constant concomitant of winemaking. Fittingly, perhaps, his wines are countercultural, too: his pinots are high-acid, smooth-tannin editions made to age.

WINES AND WINEMAKING NOTES
The first vintage of J. K. Carrière was made in 1999: 500 cases of a Willamette Valley wine made with grapes from Chehalem's

Corral Creek Vineyard, Knight's Gambit Vineyard in the Dundee Hills, and Stony Mountain Vineyard in the Coast Range. In addition to the Willamette Valley wine, Prosser made fifty cases of a cuvée called Isabella in 2000, exclusively from Stony Mountain. Isabella was named for Prosser's very young niece, and was crafted to be drunk on her twenty-first birthday. Glass, a white pinot made like no other rosé in the world—whole cluster pressed and fermented bone dry in neutral barrels, its color stripped out by adding lees left over from fermentations of chardonnay—debuted in 2001, along with Antoinette, a wine not unlike Isabella, selected from individual barrels of uncommon elegance. In 2002 J. K. Carrière launched Provacateur to showcase the barrels with which Prosser was "least thrilled." In 2004 the first vineyard-designated pinots debuted, from the Shea and Anderson Family vineyards. Along the way, the fruit of other vineyards was added to the Willamette Valley blend, notably Gemini and Momtazi in the McMinnville foothills.

The winemaking relies on some use of whole clusters, indigenous yeasts, very hot fermentations in 3-ton, stainless steel open-tops, and short postfermentation macerations. Barrels are primarily from Remond, Rousseau, Sirugue, and François Frères with a preference for wood from the Bertranges forest; new wood is limited to between 18 and 20 percent. Wines are racked entirely to neutral barrels after malolactic fermentation has finished and are not bottled until nineteen months after the vintage. Prosser avoids both fining and filtration. J. K. Carrière pinots are always ripe but never overblown, and fruit shares the organoleptic space with herbs, pepper, and resin, giving the wines a savory aspect. Cellaring is rewarded, and most J. K. Carrière pinots should be decanted if they must be drunk young.

TASTING NOTES

2004 *Willamette Valley (tasted in 2006):*
Transparent, medium black-red; aromas of
potpourri, cassis, and blackberry; earth and
bay laurel on the palate, with the intensity
of jam against a stone-dry ground; slightly
creamy, concentrated, and long.

2002 *Willamette Valley (tasted in 2004):*
Transparent, deep black-red; clean, frank
nose of black cherry, raspberry, and toast,
with a whiff of orange peel; slightly sweet
attack, but then very structured mid-palate
with a rush of very fine-grained tannin;
nice acidity, and very black flavors of ink
and pencil lead; long and youthful.

1999 *Willamette Valley (tasted in 2006):*
Transparent, medium-dark garnet; earthy
nose, with hints of iodine and tar; bright,
elevated cassis and blackberry flavors that
give way to orange peel on the finish; full
bodied and mouth coating; satin textured
but reinforced with a bit of grip. Fine.

J VINEYARDS AND WINERY
Healdsburg, California

Judy Jordan's father—an oil entrepreneur
from Colorado—established Jordan
Vineyards and Winery, dedicated to Sonoma
cabernet and chardonnay, on the south side
of the Alexander Valley in the 1970s. In
1986, two years after Judy Jordan graduated
from Stanford with a degree in applied earth
science, father and daughter entered into a
separate partnership to make sparkling wine.
At the outset, the new company, called J
for Judy, used space in the Jordan facility,
but Jordan *père* then gave his daughter two
vineyards and a vintage prune-processing
plant on Eastside Road, establishing J's
separate identity and premises.

In 1996 J acquired the former Piper-
Sonoma facility along with Piper-Sonoma's
110 acres of Russian River Valley vineyards.
Having made two barrels of still pinot
in 1994 and liked them, and with a large
palette of vineyard sources now at hand,
J made pinot its second raison d'être, and
expanded production dramatically. By
2006 the fruit for its pinot program came
from five noncontiguous estate sites and
was also purchased from five non-estate
vineyards.

Nicole's Vineyard, a 42-acre hillside
site on the east side of the Middle Reach,
about 150 feet above the valley floor where
striations of gravel seem to engender vine
stress and intense flavors, is planted mostly
to UCD 2A and to Dijon 113 and 115. This
is J's self-professed crown jewel, and the
source of a single-vineyard bottling, as
well as fruit for the Russian River Valley
blend. Typically, the single-vineyard
Nicole's comes from Block 4—UCD 2A
from Domaine Chandon's nursery in Los
Carneros—where the surface soil is visibly
red Goldridge series, similar to soils in the
Laguna Ridge area of the Russian River
Valley, but unusual on the eastern side of
the Middle Reach.

Robert Thomas Vineyard, an exceptionally
cool site about 1 mile south of Wohler
Bridge on Westside Road, between the road
and the river, is a 23-acre planting of Dijon
113 and 115, UCD 32, and UCD 4 taken
from Rochioli's nearby vineyards, in silty,
clay-loam soil densely strewn with gravel. A
vineyard-designated wine is also made from
Robert Thomas, privileging the vineyard's
upslope side, while grapes from the vineyard's
bottom half are used in the Russian River
blend and in the sparkling wine program.
Robert Thomas ripens almost three weeks
later than vineyards in the heart of the
Middle Reach. The combination of longer
hang time, yields capped at about 4 tons per
acre, and Rochioli budwood appears to create

wines of considerable concentration, spiciness characteristic of the Middle Reach's west side, and velvety softness. Only about 12 percent of the Robert Thomas fruit goes into the vineyard-designated wine.

The balance of J's pinot comes from 32 acres, planted to seven clones, in the Eastside Ranch Vineyard, where alluvial soil is deposited over a bed of gravel by the river's seasonal flooding; Teardrop Vineyard, a half-acre demonstration vineyard adjacent to the winery; and Nonny's Vineyard, another east-side, valley-floor site where 73 acres of Dijon 115, 667, 777, and 828, along with Calera selection, were planted in 2000. Additional non-estate sources are also used.

J has had only two winemakers since its inception. Oded Shakked, raised in Israel and bitten by the wine bug while surfing of the coast of Bordeaux, then Davis-trained, made every vintage through 2005. George Bursick, a 21-year veteran of Ferrari-Carano, whose 2002 Fume Blanc was "biographied" in Mike Weiss's 2005 book *A Very Good Year,* succeeded Shakked in 2006.

WINES AND WINEMAKING NOTES

Nicole's Vineyard was J's first pinot noir, and the only pinot made in the 1994 and 1995 vintages. The Russian River blend debuted in 1996 and has been made each year since, as has Nicole's. The Robert Thomas bottling was introduced in 1997.

Throughout Shakked's tenure, J's house style was based on relatively early picking, careful sorting, complete destemming (except for part of Nicole's Vineyard, which was sometimes fermented as whole clusters), and no addition of enzymes. Fermentations were preceded by several days of cold-soaking and were jump-started with a combination of Williams Selyem and Assmannshausen yeasts. After pressing,

which occurred at dryness, a combination of free-run and light-press juice went into 30 to 35 percent new medium-plus-toast barrels with toasted heads from Seguin Moreau, Mercurey, and François Frères. Shakked tried not to filter, but sometimes felt forced to; there was no fining except in 1995, when Shakked mistakenly fermented too high a percentage of whole clusters, generating too much tannin—a situation which demanded remediation.

There was no finished wine from the Bursick regime at the time of this writing, but changes can be anticipated, given aspirations toward a "new" style, "darker black fruit with really concentrated flavors," and "powerful" although "not aggressive" wines. Already, Bursick has embraced longer and cooler fermentations based on especially slow-acting yeasts, some postfermentation maceration, and increased use of new wood. The percentage of new barrels has already doubled to between 60 and 70 percent of the stock in use.

Until the regime change, J's were elegant, quintessential pinots that displayed great finesse and cascading layers of flavor, in a light- to medium-weight frame. The wines were also transparent, brilliant, and unsaturated. The Russian River bottling typically showcased high-toned fruit and floral notes, Nicole's had a tendency to feature *charcuterie,* and Robert Thomas was distinctively though elegantly spicy. The wines tended to divide reviewers; some found them "dead ringers for Burgundy," whereas others were critical of their feminine structure and unsaturated robe. The new regime wines may be different— time will tell.

TASTING NOTES

2005 *Russian River Valley (tasted in 2007):* Transparent, light garnet; aromas of sweet berry fruit and vanilla, with tarragon highlights; pretty cherry-raspberry flavors in the mouth, with some white pepper, red licorice, and resin; briary and peppery on the finish; elegant, lean, moderately intense, and very attractive.

2001 *Russian River Valley (tasted in 2004):* Brilliant, light-to-medium garnet, rosy at the rim; dried leaves and spicy berries on the nose; soft on the palate; cherry, raspberry, clove, black pepper, and black tea, and hints of turmeric, cumin, and coriander seed; long elegant, and complex. Fine.

1997 *Robert Thomas Vineyard (tasted in 2004):* Brilliant, light-to-medium garnet with rosy highlights; spice potpourri on the nose; rich, refined, and intense on the palate with flavors of clove, pepper, cinnamon, and cured meat; silky at mid-palate, then grippy toward the end; medium-long and impressive.

JOSEPH SWAN VINEYARDS

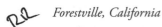 *Forestville, California*

Joseph Swan (1922–1989) was a commercial pilot, amateur artist, avid reader, and the first boutique producer of estate-grown pinot noir in the Russian River valley. The son of teetotaler parents in North Dakota, he read about wine as a child and became fascinated. Swan's first "wine" was reportedly made from rhubarb crushed in the wringer of his mother's washing machine, fermented in the barn, and then secreted in the family's attic. Rather later, he is supposed to have made zinfandel in Utah and to have planted a vineyard in the foothills of the Sierra Nevada. In 1967, at the age of 45, he bought a farm on Laguna Road in the Russian River valley: it contained 13 acres of old zinfandel;

some fruit trees and pasture; a barn; and a centenary house that had once housed the post office, telephone exchange, and general store for the now-extinct hamlet called Trenton. The property looked good to Swan. It looked as if it ought to be good for vineyard. It wasn't flat. And the soil was poor: 1 to 3 feet of decomposed sandstone surmounting bedrock.

Swan made wine from the existing zinfandel vines in 1968. In 1969, cognizant of the pioneer plantings at Bacigalupi and Rochioli and encouraged by his friend and mentor, André Tchelistcheff, he began replanting the dying zinfandel vineyard to pinot noir, chardonnay, and a bit of cabernet sauvignon. The budwood Swan used for pinot has been a matter of some dispute, since Swan is quoted variously by other growers who later obtained their cuttings from him; in fact, the wood almost certainly came from Mount Eden via the University of California Experiment Station in Oakville. Swan briefly parked the first generation grafts on property he owned in the Sierras until he was ready to commence planting at Trenton.

Swan's first block of pinot, planted in 1969, was done in the fashion of the day: 12-foot rows with 6-foot intervine spacing, on a south-facing slope. A second block, south of the first but facing north, was planted in 1974 with slightly tighter 6-foot by 10-foot spacing. The very shallow topsoil is the same Goldridge series that prevails across a large portion of Laguna Ridge, but here, near the northern edge of the formation, it forms an especially thin layer. In 1973, from the 1969 planting, Swan produced a pinot of legendary beauty. Those who had the chance to taste it in its prime say it had balance, elegance, and "Burgundian complexity." Along with the wine DAVIS BYNUM WINES made the same year from Joe Rochioli's fruit, it was a benchmark in the evolution of Russian River pinot noir.

Swan's models for Russian River pinot were always French. He traveled often to France and interviewed Burgundian *vignerons* exhaustively. He seems to have believed that "if it was French, it had to be good." Swan is said to have walked his vineyard whenever he received visitors from Burgundy; if a knowledgeable visitor raised critical questions about the appearance of a particular vine, Swan immediately marked it for removal after harvest. Bits of additional planting were done this way over the years, including a few vines of Dijon clones, the scion material for which was given to Swan by a helpful Burgundian vintner, who spared Swan the need to wait until the plant material officially imported via Oregon State was released in California.

BERGLUND CAN COAX WINES OF HONESTY, PURITY, ELEGANCE, AND SOUL FROM HIS RAW MATERIAL

Happily, Swan seems to have learned a number of good lessons from his French travels and visitors: a vineyard should be small enough that a single person can tend it; the winery should be small enough that one winemaker can maintain complete control; and low-production vines planted in low-vigor soil should be pruned and thinned rigorously.

Swan's first vintages were made in the cellar of the old farmhouse, then in the adjacent barn. In 1974 Swan built the present winery building, which has come to be called "the tin shed." With only a few amenities added over time—wider doors, a lab, a bathroom, and a concrete crushpad in back—the tin shed is still in use.

Since Swan's death in 1989, winemaking has been in the hands of his son-in-law, Rod Berglund. Berglund, whom Swan introduced to winemaking after Berglund discovered wine during his service in the United States Navy, was later the founding winemaker at La Crema Viñera (see LA CREMA). Berglund has kept faith with the founder on all basic matters: boutique size, consummate attention to the vineyard, and ceaseless experimentation. Swan, Berglund remembers, was "always thinking, always evolving." He has also expanded Swan's practice of purchasing fruit to make non-estate wines, including several non-estate pinots, and has begun the process of replanting the estate vineyard. In 1996 an especially stressed 3.5-acre block of this vineyard, consisting of cabernets, chardonnay, and some pinot noir was replanted entirely to pinot noir, primarily using the estate's own budwood, plus Dijon 113, 114, 115, 667, and 777. Vine spacing was dramatically tightened to 3 feet by 6 feet. This drove this block's notoriously parsimonious yield from about 1.6 tons per acre to a whopping 2.5.

Apart from the estate vineyard (now called the Trenton Estate Vineyard), the main sources for vineyard-designated pinots in the 1990s were Saralee Kunde's eponymous vineyard near the Sonoma County Airport, Lone Redwood Ranch, and the Steiner and Wolfspierre vineyards on Sonoma Mountain. At Saralee's, the Swan program was originally anchored with a single row of Dijon clone vines originally planted in 1991 as pinot meunier and subsequently grafted to pinot noir. (A sign now designates this as "Rod's Row.") Since the beginning of the new millennium, a larger selection of fruit has been taken from Saralee's, including some UCD 4, 29, and 37. A property almost adjacent to the estate vineyard called Trenton View was partially vineyard-designated in

2004; Great Oak, a spectacular site on the lower slopes of Black Mountain, west of the Middle Reach, which Berglund helped develop, made a vineyard-designated wine in 2004 and 2005. Great Oak is between 7 and 8 acres of pinot scattered in six non-contiguous blocks, planted entirely to Dijon clones and budwood from Trenton Estate.

In the 1990s Berglund also began making blended pinots. In 1994 there was a Sonoma Mountain pinot made from a combination of fruit from Steiner and neighboring Wolfspierre, just across Sonoma Mountain Road. In 1996 Lone Redwood Ranch and Hopkins River Ranch (on Eastside Road in Middle Reach) fruit was blended to create a Russian River valley cuvée. Cuvée de Trois debuted in 1999, using Saralee's and Lone Redwood fruit, plus the first crop from the young 1996 vines on the Trenton Estate Vineyard. Over time, the Cuvée de Trois has evolved into Swan's principal blend. Its composition varies year to year as Berglund evaluates the available components, and assesses which lots can stand alone as vineyard-designated wines.

WINES AND WINEMAKING NOTES

Winemaking at Joseph Swan is fairly traditional and does not change radically from year to year. The prefermentation maceration lasts two to three days, and the entire vatting continues for three to three and a half weeks. The estate pinot almost always relies on resident yeast; other pinots may be inoculated, depending on the vintage and the condition of the fruit. The use of whole clusters rose to 100 percent in the late 1980s but has since dropped back to between 15 and 20 percent; berries in the destemmed fruit are kept whole as far as possible. Berglund punches down in open-top fermentors during the primary fermentation, which usually tops out at

90 to 93°F. Toward the end of the vatting, when most of the action is postfermentation maceration, the cap is manipulated just enough to keep it wet and to keep the wine safe. The use of some whole clusters means that some residual fermentation continues until the wine is barreled.

Pinots spend nine to fifteen months in various combinations of new barrels with one-, two-, and three-year-old ones. The estate pinot gets half to two thirds new oak, depending on the vintage; other pinots take about 30 percent new wood. The wines are racked once before bottling, are rarely fined, and are never filtered. The barrels are now mostly Remond, representing a variety of French regions and forests. Berglund says he is more inclined to "push the envelope" with the estate wine than he is with pinots made from purchased fruit, partially because he knows better how to read the vineyard, and partially because he is reconciled to this wine taking longer to come together. Pushing the envelope means more new barrels, more whole clusters in warm years, and longer fermentations.

Swan pinots are often made in lots so tiny that they give a new dimension to the term *boutique*. A single barrel, or two, may be all that's made. With its small size and parsimonious yield, the estate vineyard has never made more than a few hundred cases. The wines are the antithesis of house style: each vineyard and each vintage is allowed self-expression—which is an article of faith for Berglund, who insists that "at all cost, winemaking must not obscure the vineyard." In general, however, Swan pinots show more minerality and nuance than bold fruit, and they are never heavily extracted.

The flagship wine is the Trenton Estate Vineyard, made entirely from the original 1969 and 1974 plantings until 2002, when a small amount of young-vines fruit from the 1996 replanting also began to be used.

In most years, the estate wines are angular, tannic, and a touch backward in their youth, but they open up and soften two to four years after the vintage, displaying an avalanche of fruit, earth flavors, and pepper. Ten years of positive evolution before the wine peaks is not unusual, and several vintages from the 1970s are still in good condition. A recent tasting of Swan pinots from the 2004 and 2005 vintages was hugely impressive.

The Cuvée de Trois represents extraordinary value. The Great Oak vineyard-designate, especially in 2004, is one of the finest California pinots I have ever tasted. The 2004 estate reminds us that, whether by genius or by dumb luck, Swan seems to have stumbled on one of the grandest spots for pinot in California. Overall, the ensemble is evidence that Berglund can coax wines of honesty, purity, elegance, and soul from his raw material.

TASTING NOTES

2005 *Cuvée de Trois (tasted in 2007):* Luminous, medium ruby; floral and red berry aromas with a hint of spice; slightly sweet, cherry-cranberry fruit, with a layer of mild but spicy cherry-cola flavors underneath; a serious wine with admirable structure, just a hint of grip, and more complexity than anything else in this price range. Bravo.

2005 *Great Oak Vineyard (tasted in 2007):* Brilliant, medium black-red; huge nose of Assam tea with floral, spice, and tobacco highlights; rich and very elegant on the palate, with spice and cherry; tightly knit, velvety, and well integrated; complex and rewarding; very fine.

2004 *Great Oak Vineyard (tasted in 2007):* Brilliant, almost scarlet wine; engaging aromatics with notes of camphorwood and toasted cumin; a palate-filling, tightly knit wine with a Vosne-like richness; tar and blackberry; persistently bright and very elegantly built, with very understated alcohol; stupendous.

2004 *Trenton Estate Vineyard (tasted in 2007):* Transparent, medium black-red; ripe aromatics with hints of spicy molasses and cola; lovely and creamy on the palate; dense with dark cherry; almost tarry at times; grippy on the mid-palate and finish; statuesque and elegant, very serious; borderline great.

KAZMER & BLAISE
Oakland, California

Kazmer & Blaise, the middle names of Peter Molnar and Michael Terrien, was launched in 1998 to make one wine only, a pinot noir, from one block of a single vineyard. The wine was made from 1998 through 2002, and again after 2005; the interruption was caused by phylloxera-forced replanting. The Molnar family, which fled Hungary after the aborted revolution in 1956, joined forces with financial partners to purchase Los Carneros pasture land in the 1960s, developed an 83-acre vineyard in 1973, planted it to UCD 13, and sold the fruit to Napa and Sonoma wineries.

Peter Molnar and Michael Terrien, introduced by a common friend, began the Kazmer & Blaise partnership when Terrien enrolled in the enology program at the University of California Davis, and Peter assumed responsibility for the Carneros vineyard from his father. Terrien joined ACACIA WINERY, a couple miles to the west, after getting his degree, but he continued to make the Kazmer & Blaise wines, as he did following his move from Acacia to HANZELL VINEYARDS in 2005.

The Molnars' vineyard is adjacent to the Carneros Marina and is bound on the west by the Carneros Creek. Its maritime climate is determined by its proximity to the river, the marsh, and San Pablo Bay. The soils, typical of Carneros, are composed of clay throughout most of the acreage, but it is from a particular slope referred to as Primo's Hill that the Kazmer & Blaise pinot grapes are harvested. The slope measures less than 100 feet from bottom to top, but the soil is lighter in color and pebblier than the surrounding terrain. Terrien says the vines respond to these better-drained soils with diminished vigor and a naturally restricted fruit-set. Working "sympathetically" with the "tannin-rich" grapes, Terrien fashions a distinct pinot that is very stylish and perhaps not typical of the region's expression of pinot noir.

WINEMAKING NOTES

To achieve his unique results, Terrien ferments destemmed and crushed grapes at relatively warm temperatures, but presses while the must is 1 to 3 Brix and immediately barrels the wine without settling. The barrels are kept warm during the first several weeks of *élevage* to encourage the fermentation to finish completely; to this practice Terrien attributes the strong aromas of peat smoke and meatiness (dry-cured sausage) that are the hallmarks of Kazmer & Blaise wines. One racking to separate the wine from its heavy lees (containing plenty of grape solids in addition to expired yeast, according to Terrien) is performed after fermentation is complete, and then the wine is allowed to age undisturbed in all-new oak barrels from the Tokaj region of Hungary. (The Molnar family owns the Hungarian cooperage Budapesti Kadar Kft.) Bottling occurs after roughly eighteen months of barrel aging, and the wines are released six months after bottling.

Production is small, with just over 200 cases being made in a given vintage. However, grapes from the land around Primo's Hill are vinified and bottled under the Molnar Family label, another venture of the Tricycle Wine Company, which owns the Kazmer & Blaise label. The Molnar Family label is a sturdy, dense pinot, quite marked by the Hungarian barrels in which it is raised. It is utterly unlike the wines Terrien makes at Hanzell, but it is nicely made.

TASTING NOTE

2005 *Primo's Hill (tasted in 2007):* Deep, barely transparent brick-red with scarlet highlights; aromas of smoke, peat moss, and evergreen; ripe, rich, extracted, and mouth coating, with a huge load of very fine-grained tannin, like strong, long-brewed tea; sturdy, but not sappy or sweet.

KELLER ESTATE WINERY
Petaluma, California

Trained as an engineer, successful in the business of manufacturing automobile interiors and upholstery, and always enamored of good wine, Arturo Keller, a third-generation Mexican of Swiss-German descent, purchased several hundred acres of pasture on the east side of the Petaluma River plain in 1983. Not quite twenty-five years later, 89 acres have been redeveloped as vineyard; an elegant winery (designed by award-winning architect

Ricardo Legorreta, famous inter alia for the Solana complex in Solana, Texas) has been created in a draw between grass-covered hills; and a gleaming, impeccably-restored 1956 Mercedes SL convertible has been added as the centerpiece of the winery's handsome tasting room. Keller's granddaughter, a Stanford University graduate who now handles media relations for the winery, explains—leaving only a few lacunae—that Keller *grandpère* had always been passionate about vintage cars, thought the ranch was large enough to serve as an off-road course, and liked good wine.

Thirteen acres of chardonnay were planted first, in 1989. It ripened so well and tasted so good that the family added 3 acres of pinot noir in 1994 and 1995. The first vintages were vinted by Greg Graham at Rombauer Vineyards in St. Helena, which also purchased Keller Estate grapes for other projects. More pinot was planted in 1998, 1999, and 2000 (as was more chardonnay). Arturo's daughter Ana became the general manager of a commercial wine estate; the family engaged Ted Lemon (see LITTORAI WINES) as its winemaker; and the first Keller Estate wines were made in 2000, using an outdoor crushpad and a cave for barrel storage. The vineyard, which is called La Cruz for the large wooden cross erected on one of its hillocks, consists of 68 mostly southwest-facing acres on the lower hills of the ranch, of which 26 are pinot noir. The soils are the same Diablo and Haire clay-loams that are found throughout Carneros, whose southwestern corner is only 5 miles away as the crow flies, at the southernmost end of Sonoma Mountain.

The oldest pinot blocks here were planted to UCD 4; later plantings relied primarily on Dijon 115, 667, and 777. In 2000 the family began to develop the ranch's high east side as well, planting an additional 20 acres of pinot noir in lighter, loamier soil around the 425-foot contour, facing mostly northeast. Here, the assortment of scion material is broader. In addition to the selections used in blocks 1–9, as the lower blocks are known internally, the higher-elevation Block 10 includes some acreage devoted to Dijon 114 and 828; to Swan selection from Camp Meeting Ridge Vineyard (see FLOWERS VINEYARD AND WINERY); and to an incompletely documented selection (indirectly from PISONI in the Santa Lucia Highlands), here called LT. The hilltop vineyard is considered part of La Cruz, but is known in-house as El Coro, for the grouping of sandstone church-choir figurines set out next to a grove of olive trees. As El Coro has come into full production, it has come to constitute a majority of the fruit used for the estate pinot. An increasing proportion of fruit from the older blocks is sold to an illustrious list of fruit clients, including Flowers, Landmark, TESTAROSSA (which makes a vineyard-designated La Cruz Vineyard wine from Block 4), Mayo Family Winery, Adrian Fog, and Zepaltas Wines (the sidebar project of Ryan Zepaltas, the cellarmaster at SIDURI WINES).

WINES AND WINEMAKING NOTES
Since 2000 Keller Estate has made a single blend of pinot noir in each vintage, although a single, "best" barrel has been reserved since 2003 for a special, magnums-only reserve bottling called Precioso. More than half the fruit used for the 2004 and 2005 editions of the blend came from the El Coro blocks.

Winemaking begins with a five-to-seven day cold soak in 3-, 4- and 6-ton, stainless steel open-top fermentors, and relies mostly on resident yeasts. Punchdowns are done three times daily until the juice measures about 10 Brix, at which point their frequency is reduced. The new wine is drained and pressed with some residual sugar, although experiments have also been done with extended macerations. The blend is raised in barrel for ten to eleven months. The barrel stock is mostly from Cadus, Remond, and Dargaud & Jaeglé, with an emphasis on stave wood from Allier forests.

Ted Lemon was the winemaker for the first three vintages. Michael McNeill, a veteran of R. H. Phillips, CHALONE VINEYARD, SAVANNAH-CHANELLE, and SILVAN RIDGE in Oregon, has been the winemaker since December 2002. The wines are exceptionally handsome editions of pinot that display brilliant, deep colors, deep earth and cherry flavors, and an elegant silky or chamois-like mouth-feel.

TASTING NOTES

2005 *La Cruz Vineyard (tasted prerelease in 2007):* Brilliant, medium-deep black-red; fruit aromas wrapped in forest floor and wet earth; brighter fruit than the wine that follows; red-toned fruit with red licorice, and a hint of strawberry with bay leaf; chamois-textured, long, and elegant.

2004 *La Cruz Vineyard (tasted in 2007):* Brilliant, medium crimson; earth, forest floor, and tobacco aromas; rich, deep cherry on the palate, with some tar and anise but no substantial sweetness; finely etched, minerally and silky; very attractive.

2003 *La Cruz Vineyard (tasted in 2007):* Transparent, medium black-red; earth, forest floor, and pine needles on the nose; scents of conifer and animal fur mingle; rich and intense on the palate, with deep cherry flavors and dark minerality; silky texture; a hint of mocha on the finish.

KEN BROWN WINES
Lompoc, California

Ken Brown spent his first years after college selling computers and real estate, reading wine books, and making wine at home. In 1974 he went back to school (at California State University Fresno) to study viticulture and enology, and directed the research program for the school's vineyard and winery. In 1977 he became the founding winemaker at Santa Barbara County's seminal winery Zaca Mesa, and then a founding partner and winemaker at BYRON VINEYARD AND WINERY after 1984. When the ROBERT MONDAVI WINERY, which had purchased a controlling interest in Byron in 1990, prepared to sell it in 2003, Brown set out on his own once again, establishing a much smaller, eponymous wine project in a Lompoc warehouse. Here, Brown makes some syrah and chardonnay, but the core of his production is pinot noir from respected vineyards in the Sta. Rita Hills.

The focus on the Sta. Rita Hills fruit is deliberate and fundamental: Brown remembers that his original epiphany with respect to pinot and the southern Central Coast, in 1976, was the inaugural vintage made by Richard Sanford and Michael Benedict at Sanford & Benedict. He also limits total production to about 2,500 cases so that he can make and market the wines by himself.

WINES AND WINEMAKING NOTES

Brown makes ripe, 14-to-15-percent–alcohol pinots from grapes picked around 25.5 Brix and handled to "avoid seed tannin extraction." The fruit is completely destemmed, cold-soaked with dry ice, and inoculated and fermented in fruit bins (Brown thought the best pinot at Byron came from the smallest fermentors). The cap is managed by plunging, and the maximum fermentation temperature is kept around 86°F to "maintain pinot's perfume." If the berries are largish, or if the fruit has come from very young vines, Brown bleeds the must slightly to increase concentration and to generate a small volume of (rather tasty!) *vin gris.* Acid additions are avoided—Brown says he has "always regretted acidification." The must is pressed at dryness, and malolactic bacteria are introduced in barrel. The main coopers are Boutes and Remond, 33 to 40 percent of barrels are new, and most wines stay in barrel for about fifteen months. (If a wine based on Santa Maria Valley fruit is made, it is bottled before the following harvest; see below.) The wines are not usually filtered, and are fined only if the tannins "need polishing."

The core fruit sources are long-term contracts with Clos Pepe, where Brown gets a 3-acre block of UCD 4 near the top of the estate's landmark hill; Peter Cargasacchi's vineyard in Sweeney Canyon below Fe Ciega; the Rio Vista Vineyard at the appellation's east end; and the T-6 block at Sanford & Benedict, where an old planting of own-rooted riesling was replaced, in 1999, with Dijon 667 in north-south-oriented rows. Based on this quartet of sources, vineyard-designated wines have been made from Clos Pepe in every vintage since 2003, from Cargasacchi since 2004, and from Sanford & Benedict since 2005.

An appellation blend has also been made in every vintage since 2003, anchored with Rio Vista fruit and seasoned with deselected barrels of Clos Pepe and Cargasacchi, plus some fruit from Fiddlestix in 2003 and 2004, and from young vines in José Bear's La Viña Vineyard above La Encantada (see ALMA ROSA WINERY) beginning in 2007. In addition, in 2003 only, there was a vineyard-designated wine from Block F at Bien Nacido. A Santa Barbara County wine was also made in 2004 and 2005. (In 2004 the county bottling was a blend of Bien Nacido with deselected barrels of Sta. Rita Hills wines; in 2005 it was made from lighter lots of wines that would otherwise have been used for the Sta. Rita Hills blend, sacrificed to create a wine suitable for shorter *élevage* and early release.) In my experience to date, Ken Brown pinots have been deeply colored wines with lifted aromatics, polished tannins, plush textures, and some barrel marking.

TASTING NOTES

2005 *Cargasacchi Vineyard (tasted in 2007):* Pretty and luminous ruby; lifted nose of floral esters, tea, and bright fruit; intense and very slightly sweet on the palate, with cherry, raspberry, fruit-infused tea, and vanilla; silky with a suggestion of mild chocolate; attractive and long.

2005 *Sta. Rita Hills (tasted in 2007):* Light-to-medium rosy-garnet; earth, flowers, and spice on the nose; intense, spirity, and fruit-sweet attack, like cherry *eau-de-vie*; a fleeting impression of cream approaching mid-palate; then warm from mid-palate to the end; dark, wild berry flavors with some clove-y spice; nicely made and very typical of the Sta. Rita Hills appellation.

2004 *Santa Barbara County (tasted in 2005).* Nearly opaque, medium-dark garnet; black fruit and evergreen aromas; more black fruit, soft spice, and vanilla on the palate; slightly sweet, full, and concentrated, with velvety tannins.

KEN WRIGHT CELLARS
Carlton, Oregon

Ken Wright is engaging and passionate about pinot noir and an indefatigable champion of its Oregonian editions. He is also almost an icon among pinot noir's many producers, having created, from scratch, no less than three brands of persistently high reputation: PANTHER CREEK CELLARS, DOMAINE SERENE, and Ken Wright Cellars. At one point when Wright was the winemaker for both Domaine Serene and Ken Wright Cellars, those houses (which then cohabited) were simultaneously Robert M. Parker Jr.'s choices for Oregon's two "outstanding" producers of pinot noir.

Wright's road to wine is no less likely than a score of others. He says he was "hooked" on pinot while waiting tables in Lexington, Kentucky, working his way through college. The restaurant's owner was determined to educate his serving staff about wine and repeatedly broke out a few of his best bottles for systematic tastings. Struck with the discovery that Domaine de la Romanée-Conti was "infinitely more interesting than Lancer's," Wright transferred from the University of Kentucky to the viticulture program at the University of California Davis and embarked—albeit with no financial assets—on a career in wine. After eight years making, in his phrase, "very average" pinot noir for wineries in California's Central Coast, he moved to Oregon, waited tables again to make ends meet, and launched Panther Creek in 1986—with just ten barrels of wine.

Within a few years, Wright was transformed from a skillful blender into a champion of vineyard-designation. By the time he founded Ken Wright Cellars in 1994, vineyard-designation had become the core of his program: in some vintages, as many as twelve individually designated pinots were made. As of 2007, the list stands at ten: three estate sites, one vineyard leased for fifteen years, and six acreage contracts for non-estate fruit. The three estate vineyards are Abbott Claim, on an east–west-oriented ridge east of Carlton, in sedimentary soils of remarkably consistent depth, which Wright shares with Soter Wines, where 15.5 acres of UCD 4, as well as Dijon 115 and Dijon 777, were planted in 2000 and 2001; Canary Hill, about ten miles west of Salem in the Eola Hills, planted in 1983 and acquired by Wright in 2006, which consists of 20 acres of UCD 4, and Dijon 114 and 777; and Savoya, 17.5 acres of UCD 2A and 4, and Dijon 115, 667, and 777, plus a bit of chardonnay, planted in 1999 on a 40-acre parcel on Blackburn Road east of Yamhill. The long-term lease is 7.5 acres of McCrone Vineyard, another

STRUCTURED, HEFTY WINES THAT ARE ALSO SERIOUS, SENSUOUS, AND TRANSPARENT TO TERROIR

Blackburn Road site, planted in 1991, 3 feet by 6 feet, to Dijon 115, 667, and 777, which typically display dense, black fruit flavors and considerable power. McCrone is owned by an American couple who also own a vineyard in Martinborough, New Zealand, from which Ata Rangi makes a vineyard-designated wine.

Wright has worked with some of the acreage-contract sites for many years.

Nysa is a dense planting of UCD 2A and 5 between Domaine Drouhin and Archery Summit, in the Dundee Hills, set out in 1990. In the Eola Hills, he gets fruit from Carter Vineyard, where his parcel is a combination of UCD 2A and 4, planted in 1983, and Dijon 667 and 777, planted in 2001, and from Freedom Hill, where he gets 4 acres of UCD 2A and Dijon 777. Near the winery in Carlton, the persistent sources are Guadalupe, a 1989 planting of UCD 5 spaced 7 feet by 5 feet in exceptionally well-drained shallow dirt where volcanic soils transition to sedimentary material, and SHEA, the iconic vineyard on the east side of the new Yamhill-Carlton appellation, first planted in 1989 and substantially replanted since. In the McMinnville foothills area, Wright uses fruit from four designated acres of the Meredith Mitchell Vineyard, a widely spaced 1988 planting of UCD 5 in especially shallow sedimentary soils surmounting basaltic mother rock.

The vineyards that Wright's crews farm meet or exceed organic standards, and no herbicides or pesticides of any kind are employed. Vines at the end of rows, which are typically more vigorous and later to ripen than mid-row vines, are harvested separately to ensure that all the vineyard's fruit reaches the same level of maturity. Many winegrowers reduce the vines' crop load at veraison, but Wright has found that concentration is improved when this is accomplished earlier in the season, so some fruit is dropped soon after set whenever the set is average or above. The target is 1.5 to 2.25 tons per acre.

WINES AND WINEMAKING NOTES
Wright's large portfolio of vineyard-designated wines unfolds as follows. In 1994 he made pinots from Freedom Hill Vineyard, Abbey Heights Vineyard (which was renamed Guadalupe the following year), Canary Hill Vineyard, Carter Vineyard, and Shea Vineyard. In 1995 he added Kircher, which was then purchased by Domaine Serene. The 1996 vintage saw the debut of his Abbey Ridge, Whistling Ridge, and McCrone bottlings. Elton Vineyard joined the lineup in 1997. In 1998 Wright began a four-year run with Archery Summit's Arcus Vineyard and also began acquiring fruit from the Nysa and Wahle vineyards. The Meredith Mitchell Vineyard in the McMinnville foothills debuted in 2001. With the exceptions of Kircher, which was made for one year only, in 1995; Abbey Ridge, which was not made in 1997 and was relinquished in 1999; Whistling Ridge, which was relinquished after the 2000 harvest; Elton, which was relinquished in 2006; and Arcus, which was no longer available after 2001, Wright has stuck with every vineyard he has tried, and each new vineyard has been an addition to his lineup.

In 2005, probably on a one-time-only basis, Wright also made a wine called Angela's from a combination of fruit from the Abbott Claim and Savoya vineyards. This was intended to be the inaugural release of a new brand called Angela's, owned by Wright's friend Antony Beck (a South African with a degree from the University of London) and a partner. In due season, Angela's is to be based on a vineyard adjacent to Abbott Claim that Wright developed and farms for Beck and his partner. A second vintage of the Abbott Claim and Savoya blend was made in 2006 and will "probably" be bottled under the Angela's brand.

Asserting that "there is no human way to sort fruit in the vineyard," Wright insists on a meticulous sorting regimen in which eight to ten people are deployed around a shaker table. The objective is to eliminate "every leaf, whether brown or green; every bit of mold; and all second-crop berries." The sorted fruit is then destemmed—apart from about 20 percent whole clusters, which are layered on the bottom of each fermentor—but not crushed. All fermentors are 1.25-ton, food-grade fruit bins. Since 1994, he has practiced a five-day cold soak, enforced with a single application of dry ice. After the ice has evaporated, he uses an inserted flag (a flat, rectangular panel laced with tubes that is used to warm or chill the must by circulating hot or cold water through the tubes) to warm the must to about 60°F, at which point 80 percent of the lots are left to ferment with resident yeasts. Two vineyards, at this writing, have not yet proved that their yeasts were reliable; fruit from those lots is inoculated. During the cold soak, the must is left pretty much alone. One or two punchdowns a day are done once fermentation starts, and the fermentation temperature peaks in the high 80s. Wright does not bleed the must—he compares this procedure to doing surgery with a hacksaw and says it can make the wines tannic. He has abandoned postfermentation maceration, having found that it often produced bitterness. The must is pressed when dry, and the press fraction is reintegrated unless the pH is high, in which case it may be kept separate.

Barrels are between 65 percent and 70 percent new; the balance is one year old. Wright likes Vosges wood for the "sweetness" it imparts to the wine; he uses mostly house-toast barrels from Cadus and Sirugue, in roughly equal percentages. Malolactic fermentation is started by inoculation with Hansen freeze-dried bacteria, although this practice may change once a resident yeast population has become established in the new facility, completed in 1998. The wine is racked once at bottling, is neither fined nor filtered, and is bottled before the next year's vintage. Release occurs at the annual Thanksgiving open house. Any lots that fail to meet the winery's standards for vineyard-designated wine are sold to the bulk market. Wright says he has "no intention of bottling a blended pinot noir" of any kind.

Ken Wright Wines have developed a reputation for dark colors, plush textures, and substantial tannins. Some fellow vintners say Wright is the "author" of the low-yield, ripe-picked style of Oregon pinot, which now represents a substantial fraction of the market. There is no question that his wines have a hefty, serious profile. But they are not gravely tannic, like many wines from BRICK HOUSE and WILLAKENZIE ESTATE. They are sensuous instead, are often finished well under 14 percent alcohol, and are transparent to *terroir*.

TASTING NOTES

2005 *Nysa Vineyard (tasted in 2007)*: Medium deep, translucent but not transparent black-red; intense earthy nose of wet clay and rich red fruit; a bright mineral-and-fruit–driven wine, with Queen Anne cherry and savory notes; mouth coating but not heavy; bright but also serious; persistent fruit; long and very attractive.

2005 *Canary Hill Vineyard (tasted in 2007)*: Medium-deep magenta; explosive nose of fresh flowers and funky earth, with aromas of Tootsie Roll and tar; slightly more angular than the Nysa cuvée; sweet on the attack and at mid-palate; then serious, dry, and intense; more tar and cherry after mid-palate, plus Indonesian spice and cardamom; a lively and elegant impression overall, with medium weight and length.

2005 *Abbott Claim Vineyard (tasted in 2007)*: Dense, barely transparent dark brick-red; a spice and cherry-driven nose; sweet, tightly knit, and mouth coating on the palate, with infused violets and dark red fruit; a bit of chalk after mid-palate; rich and velvety at the end; needs time.

2005 *Savoya Vineyard (tasted in* 2007*):* Translucent, deep black-red; slightly funky, slightly peppery, and predominantly earthy on the nose; bright cranberry and dark cherry fruit on the palate, with notes of tarragon and mint; bright and serious throughout; considerable grip after mid-palate; intense, medium in weight, and medium in length; a hint of dissolved carbon dioxide.

2005 *McCrone Vineyard (tasted in* 2007*):* Opaque black-red; herbs and conifer foliage on the nose; rich, slightly sweet boysenberry-marionberry flavors on the palate; tightly knit, intense, and long, with good acidity and grip at the end. Given its structure, the wine seems likely to mellow with time.

2005 *Carter Vineyard (tasted in* 2007*):* Opaque, purplish black-red; a shy, brooding nose suggestive of wet earth, ripe fruit, and forest floor aromas; sweet and rich on the palate, with clean flavors of espresso and mocha; the fruit-sweetness persists to the finish; there is strong grip at the end. Like the McCrone bottling, this wine seems likely to soften with additional bottle age.

KOSTA BROWNE
Sebastopol, California

Kosta Browne is cut from the same cloth as SIDURI and TESTAROSSA, among others: boutique size, non-estate production; wines made and marketed hands-on by passionate food-and wine people with little previous experience in winemaking, and

wild success almost overnight characterize this producer. But there the sameness ends: Kosta Browne's meteoric rise dwarfs even the impressive record of those most like it. Four years after its first vintage of pinot noir, one of its blended wines took the number seven spot in *Wine Spectator*'s Annual Roundup of the Year's Most Exciting Wines for 2006 with 96 points, and five of the nine top spots on the *Spectator*'s list of California's thirty best pinots, published in the December 15, 2006, issue. *Wine Spectator*'s Jim Laube, reviewing the 2005 vintage in 2007, scored all of Kosta Browne's ten pinots 91 or higher, with the top two wines pegged at 97 points. The magnitude of this success allowed Kosta Browne's initial mailing-list customers to arbitrage their allocations for as much as ten or eleven times the price of purchase, and unleashed a confetti of want-to-buy-at-almost-any-price advertisements on the web for *any* bottle of the brand's pinot with which its first owner was willing to part.

The eponymous principals of Kosta Browne are alumni of Sonoma County's benchmark restaurant, John Ash & Company, located just north of Santa Rosa on the site of the Vintners Inn, in partnership with Chris Costello, a 1997 graduate of UCLA with a degree in economics, whose family members have been active players in San Francisco Bay Area real estate development for a generation. Michael Browne is the winemaker. He is a native of Washington State who worked variously as a cook, barman, and sommelier at John Ash, before becoming a winemaker in 1996. Dan Kosta, born and raised in Santa Rosa, was also a sommelier at John Ash; he is the brand's effective and genial chief marketer.

The first vintage, all sauvignon blanc, was made in 1999; the first pinot noir, from the Cohn Vineyard, a 1975 planting on Westside Road, debuted in 2000. Through 2006, the pinot program focused almost exclusively on vineyards in the Russian River Valley and Sonoma Coast appellations. In addition to the vineyard-designated Cohn bottling, Sonoma Coast and Russian River appellation wines were added to the lineup in 2001. A second single-vineyard wine, from the Kanzler Vineyard on Watertrough Road west of Sebastopol, in the Petaluma Gap, debuted in 2002. (Kanzler pinot is also sourced by Landmark Vineyards, by RHYS VINEYARDS for its Alesia label, and by ROESSLER. Landmark's assistant winemaker, Greg Stach, makes a small amount for Kanzler's owners under a Kanzler Vineyard label.) A third vineyard-designated wine, from the Koplen Vineyard—a young (2000), 5-acre, family-owned planting of Dijon 667 off Olivet Road near the geographic center of the Russian River Valley appellation—followed in 2003, along with an appellation wine from the Santa Lucia Highlands in Monterey County, and a "best barrels" blend called 4 Barrel.

Amber Ridge, a planting of Dijon 115, 667, and 777 on the east side of the Middle Reach, northwest of the Sonoma County Airport, debuted as a single-vineyard wine in 2004. In addition, 2005 saw the debut of two vineyard-designated wines from the well-known Garys' and Rosella's (see ROAR WINES) vineyards in the Santa Lucia Highlands, and a Green Valley site called Miron. The year 2004 was the last vintage in which Kosta Browne received fruit from the Cohn Vineyard, where its program had begun five years earlier.

WINEMAKING NOTES

Winemaking generally follows the consensus protocol. To compensate for very ripe picking, the musts are generally adjusted with added acid. The barrel regime involves sixteen months in about 40 percent new barrels, most of which are acquired from Remond. Although Kosta says he "grew up on Burgundy," Kosta Browne pinots are quintessentially and unapologetically New World editions of the variety. They are bold, ripe-picked, and substantially extracted, with a signature of intense and sweet fruit, full body, plush texture, and considerable concentration. The aromatic properties of the wines are typically intense and fruit dominated, but floral, herbal, and earthy veins are also common. Kosta explains that the partners strive to get "as much out of pinot as possible, while maintaining elegance." Whether elegance is always successfully maintained rests in the palate of the beholder, but the appeal of these wines to critics and to many consumers is beyond question. The wines seem to me to be structurally reminiscent of DUMOL, although they are even lusher and richer, with some inspiration from Siduri and Testarossa.

TASTING NOTES

2004 *Amber Ridge Vineyard (tasted in 2006)*: Medium, rosy black-red color; huge nose of rose petal and raspberry; raspberry and cherry candy on the palate, with briary and peppery hints toward the end; full-bodied, concentrated, and satiny.

2004 *Koplen Vineyard (tasted in 2006)*: Transparent, dark garnet; vibrant fruit-forward impression emphasizing red and black berries; some tar, merbromin, and smoke; sweet, concentrated, and of medium length.

2004 *Cohn Vineyard (tasted in 2006)*: Dark but still transparent rosy-magenta; violets, cassis, and blackberry on the palate, plus a hint of chocolate; intensely silky texture but also weighty; full bodied and slightly grippy, with not quite resolved tannin.

2004 *Kanzler Vineyard (tasted in* 2006*):* Flowers and beetroot on the nose; rich, sweet, and earthy in the mouth with a spicy bite; black fruit cola, resin clove, and black pepper; medium- to heavy-weight, texture of upholstery silk, and some grip; long.

2004 *Russian River Valley (tasted in* 2006*):* A blend from all three of Kosta Browne's Russian River vineyard sources plus fruit from the Bly Vineyard; a rich, round, spicy cocktail of cherry fruit and cloves; red-fruit dominated, but brighter and more lifted than the single-vineyard wines; borderline tarry at mid-palate with a hint of orange peel, licorice, and Indonesian spice.

2004 *Sonoma Coast (tasted in* 2006*):* Transparent, medium-deep, rosy black-red; root vegetables, intense fruit, and slate-y minerality, with infused violets, cherry, raspberry, and black fruit; briary notes plus a hint of mint; satiny finish.

LA CREMA WINERY
Windsor, California

In the dark ages of American pinot noir, back in 1979, when only lunatic-fringe winemakers pursued this variety, no fewer than three producers devoted to the duo of pinot and chardonnay came onstream in a single year. Two of these, ACACIA and Kistler, have survived more or less intact ever since, although Acacia has changed ownership twice. The third, La Crema Viñera, for which Rod Berglund (see JOSEPH SWAN VINEYARDS) was the founding winemaker, was reorganized in 1991 as La Crema Winery, and was moved from its initial base in Petaluma

to Sebastopol. Two years later, the brand was acquired by the Jess Jackson family, and production was moved to Laughlin Road near Windsor. Early vintages of the former La Crema Viñera's vineyard-designated pinots came from Winery Lake in Carneros; Ventana Vineyard in Monterey; and three vineyards in the Russian River Valley—Roberts Vineyard on Willowside Road, Arendell (now owned by HARTFORD FAMILY WINES), and PORTER CREEK.

In its current incarnation, owned by Jennifer Jackson, Jess Jackson's daughter and her sister Laura Jackson-Giron, La Crema still specializes in Burgundy's two main varieties and still sources grapes from coastal Northern California (but not from Monterey). La Crema has given up vineyard-designated wines, and has also moved past a stage in which it made widely-sourced California blends, in favor of making appellation wines from Anderson Valley, Sonoma Coast, Russian River Valley, and Los Carneros. A number of talented winemakers have passed through La Crema since it was acquired by the Jackson family, including Dan Goldfield (see DUTTON-GOLDFIELD WINES), who held the reins until 1996, and Jeff Stewart, who moved on to BUENA VISTA CARNEROS in 2003. Since January 2004, Melissa Stackhouse, a Michigan native trained at the University of California Davis, with subsequent experience at Peter Michael Winery, at Hardy's Tintara Winery in McLaren Vale (South Australia), and at Joseph Phelps Winery, has been in charge.

WINES AND WINEMAKING NOTES
The backbone of La Crema's pinot portfolio since 1999 has been the appellation wines mentioned above. The Anderson Valley wine is anchored with fruit from the Jackson-owned Falk

Vineyard northwest of Philo, a 58-acre hillside site planted to UCD 2A and 4 and to Dijon 115, 667, and 777. The Russian River sources are the Laughlin and Piner vineyards on the Santa Rosa Plain near the winery, and the Ross Vineyard in Green Valley. The Carneros wine relies mainly on grapes (UCD 2A and 4, and Dijon 115, 667, 777, and 828) from the Ahmann Ranch on the Napa side of the AVA, just south of the Carneros Highway. In addition to its appellation wines, La Crema also produces small quantities of a barrel selection designed to showcase each *vintage*, typically built from the brand's Russian River Valley vineyards.

La Crema is remarkable for using small-winery protocols for relatively large-volume wines—between 2,500 and 6,000 cases of each appellation wine are made in most vintages—including careful hand-sorting on the crushpad; completely destemmed fruit; fermentations in small, open-top tanks that are plunged manually; several days of postfermentation maceration; and nine months' *élevage* in all-French barrels, of which one third are new in each vintage. The wines are ripe, fruit-sweet, and sometimes a little warm on the finish, but they represent varietally correct, appellation-typical, mainstream editions of pinot noir, offered to the market at fair price points.

TASTING NOTES

2005 *Los Carneros (tasted in 2007):* Medium-deep black-red; floral-berry nose; mostly red and black cherry in the foreground, with smoke and earth behind; a broad-shouldered wine with a noticeable load of very fine-grained tannin from mid-palate to finish.

2005 *Russian River Valley (tasted in 2007):* Dark black-red; sweet fruit, substantial spice, and a hint of coffee on the nose; predominantly Bing cherry and Italian plum on the palate; creamy with overtones of alcoholic warmth; mouth coating and medium long; noticeable grip from mid-palate to finish.

2005 *Anderson Valley (tasted in 2007):* Medium, rosy black-red; nose marked with volatile aromas of mint and conifer; very sweet, almost unctuous on the palate; intense, cherry-plum flavors plus infused violets; evokes cherry liqueur; round, fleshy, and warm at the end.

2000 *Sonoma Coast (tasted in 2003):* Transparent medium ruby; dusty nose with some geranium, cherry, and raspberry; sweet on the palate, with dark cherry, black pepper, and wet slate; angular, medium in weight, and medium long.

LA ROCHELLE WINERY
Livermore, California

The Mirassou family has been involved with California wine since Pierre Mirassou (1856–1889) married Henriette Pellier, Pierre Pellier's daughter. From her father, Henriette had inherited one of the Santa Clara Valley's first important wine estates, as well as the legacy of a hugely significant nursery business that imported grape vine cuttings, among other things. The estate, near Mount Hamilton, became the foundation for a Mirassou wine business than has continued, more or less unbroken, across six generations.

In 2003, when controlling members of the family's fifth generation sold the Mirassou name and inventory to the E. & J. Gallo Winery, and then had difficulty imagining what they might do outside the world of wine, they created a new brand, vaguely focused on Monterey County grapes. They called the new brand La Rochelle, for the French port from which their family (and the Pelliers) had embarked for California 150 years earlier. Almost immediately, in 2004, Steven Mirassou, a member of the family's sixth generation who had gone to college on the East Coast and majored in English literature but had worked in the family winery as a kid, and Tom Stutz,

---

A SINGLE-VINEYARD PROGRAM BUILT ON VINEYARDS BEYOND THE EDGE OF THE USUAL LIMELIGHT

---

who was the winemaker for the Mirassou brand before it was sold, "reformulated" La Rochelle as a house dedicated to small lots of mostly vineyard-designated pinot noir, sourced from up and down the state as well as from Oregon.

The La Rochelle's business plan is unconventional but is reminiscent of WILLIAMS SELYEM's: nothing is produced in large volume, only a few wines are destined for distribution of any sort, and most sales are to individuals who join a "club" and buy direct. Stutz, who makes the wines at Wente's small-lot, custom-crush facility in Livermore, has a long history with California pinot that began at HANZELL VINEYARDS in 1978.

WINES AND WINEMAKING NOTES
La Rochelle's inaugural releases were a 2004 pinot noir from Garys' Vineyard in the Santa Lucia Highlands, a Monterey appellation pinot, and some Monterey chardonnay. In 2005 the small-lot pinot-only program was firmly launched with

six vineyard-designated pinots plus appellation pinots from the Santa Lucia Highlands and Arroyo Seco. Three of the vineyard-designated wines are from the Santa Lucia Highlands: Sarmento Vineyard (see CAMPION WINES); Paraiso Vineyards, a 1973 planting of UCD 13 near the appellation's south end; and Sleepy Hollow Vineyard, another old planting of UCD 13 near the appellation's colder, north end. There is also a blend from the San Vicente Vineyard on the east side of Highway 101 near Soledad, Deer Park in the Pleasant Valley district of the Santa Cruz Mountains, and the Anindor Vineyard in Oregon's Umpqua Valley.

Winemaking follows the consensus protocol, except that the fermentors are 4-foot plastic-lined wooden cubes, of the kind typically used for olives in the Central Valley; there are extended postfermentation macerations; and some wines are held in barrel for up to eighteen months. Barrel regimes rely on different coopers for different wines and often involve shifting the wine from one barrel set to another, and sometimes from one cooper to another, after the first racking. Although the wines are quite different one from another (that is the point, after all, of a program built on multiple vineyard-designated wines), most are bright and precisely built with good transparency, elegant structure, and aromatic interest. It is especially useful to have a single-vineyard program built not on the usual suspects, but on extremely interesting and well-farmed vineyards a bit beyond the edge of the usual limelight.

TASTING NOTES
2005 *Sarmento Vineyard (tasted in 2007)*: Light-to-medium rosy-ruby; cinnamon, aromatic wood, and roasted fennel aromas;

intense and slightly angular on the palate; silky and almost creamy at midpoint; some raspberry, but increasingly granitic toward the finish, with a dry character and moderate grip. Attractive.

2005 *Paraiso Vineyard (tasted prerelease in 2007):* Very transparent light ruby; vaguely custardy nose with herbal notes; elegant and silky mid-palate with dominant cherry-raspberry fruit; finishes slate-y and granitic.

2005 *Deer Park Vineyard (tasted in 2007):* Pretty, medium-dark rosy-ruby; intensely floral and herbal with a combo of cosmetic-case and eucalyptus aromas; spicy cherry in the mouth, with allspice and juniper berry; vibrant, mid-palate fruit plus freshly brewed tea; very slightly sweet; extremely attractive. My favorite among these wines.

2005 *Sleepy Hollow Vineyard (tasted prerelease in 2007):* Brilliant, medium rosy-ruby; herbal-mineral nose; sweet, intense peppery cherry in the mouth; mostly savory toward the finish; some minerality and very slightly warm; nicely made.

2004 *Garys' Vineyard (tasted in 2007):* Transparent, rosy-ruby color; rose petals and white pepper; moderately rich on the palate with a hint of caramel cream; very peppery, long, and serious, with wet slate at the end; elegant.

LACHINI VINEYARDS
Newburg, Oregon

Ron and Marianne Lachini say they drafted the initial business plan for their pinot venture in 1994, when they were living in the San Francisco Bay area, and he was working in the pharmaceutical industry.

Although they first explored pinot-friendly sites in California, Oregon pinots appealed to them more, so they relocated northward at the end of the 1990s. In February 1998, they purchased a 45-acre parcel on Calkins Lane northwest of Newburg, on the south face of the Chehalem Mountains, where they planted 27 acres of pinot noir beginning in 1999, in gently sloping sedimentary soils with little capacity to hold water, mostly in 6-foot rows with 4 feet between vines. The easternmost of three blocks was planted first, entirely to UCD 4; the "middle" blocks are dedicated to Dijon 113, 114, 115, 667, and 777; the westernmost block is a combination of UCD 2A and 4, and Dijon 115, 777, and 828. The vines are sustainably farmed with growing use of organic and biodynamic protocols, and yields are limited to 2 tons per acre. The first vintage—just 150 cases—was made in 2001, and production has grown significantly as the progressive plantings have come online.

Since 2004, Lachini has also purchased pinot grapes from the Ana Vineyard in the Dundee Hills, from which a vineyard-designated wine has been made, plus a bit of other varieties. The winemaker for the first three vintages was Isabelle Dutartre, an enologist who worked at Maison Joseph Drouhin in Beaune and at DOMAINE DROUHIN OREGON, and now assists with several Oregon labels. Dutartre was succeeded by Laurent Montalieu, formerly the winemaker for WILLAKENZIE ESTATE, and the wines are now made at Montalieu's custom-crush facility in McMinnville. Estate fruit is sold occasionally in very small quantities; SINEANN has made a vineyard-designated Lachini Vineyards wine consistently since 2002, however.

WINES AND WINEMAKING NOTES
In most vintages, three pinots are made from the estate vineyard. The Lachini

Family Estate and a sister wine called "S" are blends made from the three estate blocks and their clonal components. The Estate is distinguished for having been picked relatively early and for being made with enough acid to age; "S" is an experiment, using the youngest blocks, to determine if "different viticultural practices" and "longer hang times" are beneficial with certain clones or blocks. "S" is picked ten to fourteen days later than the Estate and exhibits a significantly riper style, but Lachini explains that he is seeking *terroir* expression and will therefore pick at modest Brix unless the seeds are "not ripe" or the tannins are "astringent." In 2004 a third pinot was added to the portfolio. Cuvée Giselle is a selection of the eight "best barrels" in the cellar and is generally built from the Dijon-clone blocks. In addition to these estate wines, the Ana vineyard-designate has been made since 2004.

Fermentations are done with small amounts of whole-cluster fruit and rely on resident yeasts. Relatively cool temperatures are preferred, the musts are sometimes bled for concentration, enzymes are usually added for color extraction, and maceration extends for several days beyond dryness. "S" is also acidified. The barrel stock is mostly Mercurey, Sirugue, and François Frères, plus a few others, and the wines are bottled before the following vintage. Except for "S," these are big, dense, extracted wines, dark in color, and with a very significant tannic load.

TASTING NOTES

2006 *"S" (tasted in 2007):* Transparent, light-to-medium ruby; juicy, bright, raspberry aromas; very bright and fresh on the palate; fruit-driven first, then serious

from mid-palate to finish, with some pepper, grip, and graphite; light weight and easy drinking.

2005 *Lachini Family Estate (tasted in 2007):* Transparent, dark black-red; resin, cherry, earth, and underbrush aromas; dark, brooding ripe fruit on the palate, and very slightly fruit-sweet with a cherry-cocoa character; strong minerality dominates at and beyond mid-palate; texture of polished cotton; long.

2005 *Cuvée Giselle (tasted in 2007):* Very dark and nearly opaque; dominantly black fruited on the nose and palate; intense, very tightly knit, big, serious, and long to finish; considerable load of fine-grained tannin overpowers fruit from mid-palate to finish.

2004 *Lachini Family Estate (tasted in 2007):* Barely transparent; dark cherry, merbromin, boot polish, and cinnamony-spice aromas; slightly sweet but seriously structured, with a hint of peppery spice and juniper berry at mid-palate; mouth coating but dry on the finish; nicely balanced overall, but challenging.

2003 *Lachini Family Estate (tasted in 2007):* Dark black-red; aromas of gum camphor, mint, and very ripe fruit; tarry on the palate, with some raspberry and cherry fruit; creamy at mid-palate but quite tannic thereafter; long.

LAETITIA VINEYARD AND WINERY
Arroyo Grande, California

Laetitia Vineyard and Winery occupies an enormous, 1,900-acre site astride Highway 101 at the mouth of the Arroyo Grande Valley that was first developed early in the

1980s as Maison Deutz, a joint venture of Wine World Estates, then the parent of Beringer, Château Souverain, and several other American brands, and Champagne Deutz, a then family-owned producer based in Ay. Maison Deutz, dedicated almost exclusively to Champagne-method sparkling wines, faltered when the American market for these wines failed to keep pace with rapid increases in production.

In 1987 the vineyard was sold to one of its original investors, Jean-Claude Tardivat, who renamed it for his daughter Laetitia and began its reorientation toward still wines. The following year the property was sold again, this time to a partnership involving Nebil Zarif—born in Turkey, educated at Oxford, and a Francophile with a master's degree in energy management—and Selim Zilkha, an Iraq-born investor in the banking, petroleum, and recorded music businesses. Zarif sold his share in Laetitia in 2001, leaving the Zilkha family as its sole proprietors.

The estate vineyard now consists of about 623 planted acres of which two thirds are pinot noir. The vineyard is situated on several rolling hills, encompassing a variety of shale-y, silty, and sandy clay-loam soils, between 3 and 5 miles from the Pacific Ocean, where marine fog dominates the morning weather during most of the growing season. Selections include UCD 2A and 13, Dijon 115 and 667, and (unusually) CTPS 459 from the Jura. Some estate fruit is sold to other winemakers and labels, including AU BON CLIMAT and TANTARA WINERY.

The property has had several winemakers over time, and sometimes two at the same time when responsibility for the still- and sparkling-wine programs has been kept separate, but those with the longest and most significant tenure are Christian Roguenant (see BAILEYANA WINERY), who was largely responsible for establishing the fine reputation of Maison Deutz's sparkling wines between 1986 and 1999, and Eric Hickey, who trained on-the-job at Laetitia from the age of sixteen. Hickey first worked as a cellar rat, apprenticed widely, was named winemaker in 2000, and became general manager in 2003.

WINES AND WINEMAKING NOTES

The still pinot program, always based entirely on estate grown fruit, began in 1995 under Roguenant's direction and the Maison Deutz label. An estate wine and a reserve wine have been made in every vintage since. The latter has always been a barrel selection; from 1995 through 1999, the selection was made entirely from new and well-toasted François Frères barrels. The first of Laetitia's block-designated pinots, called La Colline, was made entirely from the UCD 13 vines in Block J, just southeast and downslope of the winery building; it also debuted in 1995, but it was not made in 1997 or 1998. A second block-designated wine debuted in 1999: Les Galets is built from the UCD 2A and Dijon 115 in Block V on the east side of the vineyard. A third block-designate was added to the portfolio in 2006. It is called La Coupelle and is made from the CTPS 459 in Block X, northeast of Block V.

Winemaking generally follows the consensus protocol, but Hickey tends to pick a trifle later than most, preferring to see sugar accumulations over 25 Brix; adds enzymes for color extraction and tannins for color stability; and filters "everything" with isinglass before bottling. Atypically, Laetitia's fermentors are stainless cylinders, 7 feet high by 7 feet in diameter, with only 3-foot top openings; as a result, cap management relies primarily on pumpovers rather than punchdowns. Until 1998 the pinots were bottled after ten months in barrel; since 1998, *élevage* has been extended to fourteen months. Although almost all grapes are destemmed before fermentation, Hickey has experimented with whole-cluster fermentation for the Les Galets wine.

Overall, Laetitia pinots are darkly colored, fruit-forward, barrel-marked wines that tend to show well in comparative tastings. The first vintage of La Coupelle seems especially mineral driven and may show over time as the most distinctive wine in the portfolio.

TASTING NOTES

2006 *Estate (tasted in 2007):* Barely transparent, medium-dark purplish-garnet; conifer, red fruit, and gum camphor on the nose; fruit-forward minty and cherry flavors, with some black pepper and a bit of bite at the end; medium length with just a hint of grip.

2006 *Reserve (tasted in 2007):* A shade darker and blacker than the Estate; rose petals and plums dominate the nose; sweet, cherry-plum flavors on the palate, with considerable smoke and vanilla from *élevage;* slightly inky; round, ample, mouth coating and medium long.

2006 *Les Galets (tasted in 2007):* Almost opaque, deep black-red; smoke and vanilla on the nose; sweet, creamy cherry *clafouti* on the palate; considerable barrel char and some grip from mid-palate to finish; some minerality; warm overall.

2006 *La Coupelle (tasted in 2007):* Very rosy, medium-dark ruby; violets, smoke, and plummy red fruit on the nose; pleasant palate; more mineraly and less sweet than Les Galets; properties of wet slate and Carborundum; substantial load of very fine-grained tannins from mid-palate to finish; long.

LANE TANNER WINES
Santa Maria, California

In 1980 André Tchelistcheff inadvertently recruited Lane Tanner into the wine business. A chemist whose first career was focused on air pollution control, Tanner was temping in Konocti Winery's laboratory in her hometown of Kelseyville, California—and considering alternative careers—when Tchelistcheff arrived on a consulting visit. As Tanner tells the story, her temporary employers, presumably reluctant to tell their illustrious consultant that, in fact, they employed no dedicated lab staff, introduced her to Tchelistcheff as "the new enologist."

A year later, on Tchelistcheff's recommendation, Tanner became an enologist for real at the Firestone Winery in Santa Barbara, and in 1984 she began making wines for HITCHING POST WINES, then the private label of a steakhouse in Casmalia, near Vandenberg

---

RESEMBLES WHAT PATRICE RION CALLS BURGUNDY'S "TRADITIONAL WINES OF LACE AND POLISH"

Air Force Base. In 1989 she launched her own wine project, which was dedicated entirely to pinot noir until 1996, when she reluctantly diversified into syrah. Over the years, Tanner has sourced pinot from most of Santa Barbara County's best pinot vineyards, including Sierra Madre, Bien Nacido, Julia's, and Sanford & Benedict, using long-term contracts wherever possible to guarantee consistent access to specific rows of fruit. The wines are made at the Central Coast Wine Services facility in Santa Maria.

WINES AND WINEMAKING NOTES

In 1989 Lane Tanner made two pinots: a Santa Barbara County cuvée made entirely from Sierra Madre fruit, and a Benedict vineyard-designate from Sanford & Benedict fruit. In 1990 there was only one wine, from Sierra Madre. In 1991 and 1992, the Santa Barbara County bottling was made mainly from Sierra Madre fruit, but with a touch of Bien Nacido added "for color"; from 1993 through 1996, this bottling was replaced by a Sierra Madre Plateau wine that used fruit from the Gold Coast Vineyard as well as from Sierra Madre. Simultaneously, from 1991 through 1994, a Sanford & Benedict vineyard-designate was made. The 1993 vintage saw the debut of a vineyard-designated Bien Nacido cuvée, which has been made annually ever since, from UCD 13 fruit in Bien Nacido's Block N. The first vintage of a Julia's Vineyard wine was 1996; this wine also continues.

Tanner's Santa Maria Valley cuvée, made from Bien Nacido blocks X, Y, and Z, plus the aforementioned 5 percent syrah, debuted in 1997, was made for four vintages, disappeared in 2001, and was revived in 2005. From 2000 through 2003, Tanner made a vineyard-designated wine from the Melville Vineyard on Highway 246, built from a block custom planted, as she specified, to an unusual combination of UCD 2A, 9, and 16. The Santa Maria Valley wine is now Tanner's main release, with single-vineyard Julia's and Bien Nacido wines reliably present in each vintage.

Tanner is an early picker of pinot noir, sometimes taking fruit off the vine as low as 21.5 Brix, and generating wines with relatively low pH and high total acidity, at which levels the aromas are, she believes, "more exciting." (That said, she picked later in 2000 and 2001, although still earlier than almost everyone else.) She ferments barely crushed but completely destemmed berries in double-height, plastic-lined, plywood fruit bins, using a bit of dry ice and argon but no sulfur to ensure one or two days of prefermentation cold soak. The alcoholic fermentation is kicked off with an inoculation of Assmannshausen yeast, which Tanner describes as "a slow grower" that "never sticks" and "does not infringe on the flavor of the fruit." Punchdowns are done three or four times daily at the beginning of the fermentation, but the frequency decreases as the fermentation slows down. Tanner inoculates for malolactic fermentation and presses very gently just before the cap sinks, always leaving a bit of juice for some other (and less fussy) winemaker.

Barrels are two-year-air-dried, medium-toast *pièces* from François Frères, of which 20 to 35 percent are new each year. The wines are racked once in February after the vintage, barrel to tank and tank back to barrel for uniformity, and once again before bottling, which occurs in August after the vintage. The wines are not fined, but are coarse-pad filtered for visual clarity. The Santa Maria Valley cuvée (see below) is released in October; other wines are held until January of the second year after the vintage. The Santa Maria Valley cuvée is blended with 5 percent syrah "just to make it different"; the others are 100 percent pinot noir. No enzymes are used.

With only a few pathological exceptions such as the 2005 Julia's, Lane Tanner pinots are light- to medium-weight wines with strong aromatic profiles, suave textures, and considerable length. Tanner sometimes describes her pinots as "chick wines," to differentiate them (quite properly) from some blockbuster exemplars of the pinot genre. Actually, they are closer to what

Patrice Rion (Domaine Daniel Rion in Prémeaux-Prissey) calls "traditional wines of lace and polish." Tanner's wines should remind us that, overwhelmingly, style is a choice, not a necessity imposed by the fruit. These understated wines also age beautifully, and many early vintages of Lane Tanner pinot are now in their prime.

TASTING NOTES

2005 *Santa Barbara County (tasted in 2007):* Transparent, light ruby; red berry and herb aromas; moderately intense, bright, strawberry-cranberry fruit with a hint of white pepper; light-to-medium weight and pretty; the finish betrays the bit of syrah added to the blend.

2005 *Bien Nacido Vineyard (tasted in 2007):* Medium ruby; deep briary cherry-raspberry fruit aromas with licorice; savory fruit and rosewater on the palate, with hints of fruit-sweetness, clove-y spice and tangerine peel; of medium length, and attractive.

2005 *Julia's Vineyard (tasted in 2007):* Medium ruby; earthy and slightly smoky red fruit on the nose; initially sweet, but then sober and serious on the mid-palate; floral-infused red fruit character; almost minerally; definitely warmer and slightly weightier than is usual for Lane Tanner pinots, but still nicely built, with medium length and a hint of grip.

LANGE ESTATE WINERY
Dundee, Oregon

Don Lange has successfully co-managed two careers for most of his adult life. In his first persona, he is a poet, songwriter, guitarist, and recording artist. In the second, he is a winegrower, dedicated especially to pinot noir. While playing clubs in Santa Barbara in the late 1970s, Lange met his wife, Wendy, a singer who was also working Santa Barbara clubs. The couple took day jobs in local wineries to supplement the income derived from music gigs. In 1980 Don worked his first crush—at the tiny winery Richard Sanford and Michael Benedict had rigged in their vineyard on Santa Rosa Road—graduated to assistant winemaker jobs at Ballard Canyon Winery and Santa Barbara Winery, and made wine at home. When the home winemaking got "out of hand," the Langes resolved to "go pro." Fixated on pinot, they moved from California to Oregon in 1987, made their first commercial wine from purchased fruit, and planted a vineyard in the northeast corner of the Dundee Hills. This first estate vineyard, next door to the Fuqua Vineyard on Buena Vista Drive, now consists of 40 dry-farmed acres, of which 36 are pinot noir, on a southeast-facing slope between the 775- and 625-foot contours, planted 8 feet by 5 feet.

The Langes feel strongly that dry farming makes a considerable contribution to *terroir* expression once the vines have reached their fourth leaf. The first plant material was UCD 2A field-selected from Fuqua (which is supposed, in its turn, to have come from David Lett's original planting in 1965), UCD 4, and cuttings from the Bien Nacido Vineyard in the Santa Maria Valley, supplemented later with additional 2A and four Dijon clones.

A second estate vineyard on Red Hills Road was acquired in 2006—already planted but not yet bearing—and another 12 acres will be added to the main estate vineyard in 2008 and 2009. Fruit for Lange's pinot program, which debuted in 1987, is also sourced from the Durant Vineyards (adjacent to Sokol Blosser), YAMHILL VALLEY VINEYARDS, and the Temperance Hill and Freedom Hill vineyards in the Eola Hills.

The Langes' son Jessie, whose introduction to pinot noir is said to have occurred at age six when he drank new wine from the spout of the Santa Barbara home winemaking project's basket press—and liked it—now shares the commercial winemaking duties with his father and functions as the estate's general manager and vineyard manager. He prepped for these roles with a degree in agriculture

STRONG MINERALITY, BRIGHT REFRESHING STRUCTURE, AND GREAT AROMATIC INTEREST

from Oregon State University, including a half-year's exchange in viticulture and enology at New Zealand's Lincoln University, where he "solidified his interest in making wine into [a] full-fledged career," fly-fished for "giant trout," and "made friends for life." Meanwhile, Don Lange's work as a recording artist continues in a basement studio in the couple's home, and a new CD, *A Change in the Air*, was released by Poppycock Records in 2006.

WINES AND WINEMAKING NOTES
Before the estate vineyard began to bear in 1992, Lange's pinots relied on purchased fruit, and especially on the esteemed Freedom Hill Vineyard, which anchored their wines in the first vintages. A Willamette Valley blend, which still depends primarily on purchased grapes, is the property's largest-volume pinot, and purchased grapes have also played an anchor role in the Reserve bottling from its debut in 1991. The first vineyard-designated pinot, from the family's estate vineyard,

was added to the portfolio in 1993, and has been made in every vintage since. The second vineyard-designated wine was made from Yamhill Vineyards fruit in 1994, and again after 1996. As a single-vineyard wine, Freedom Hill debuted in 1996, and has been made annually since, but some of Lange's Freedom Hill fruit is used in the Reserve cuvée. In 1997 the family was unable to resist a temptation to blend a bit of Freedom Hill wine for structure, estate wine for minerality and acidity, and Yamhill wine for softness and savory properties, and voilà—Three Hills Cuvée was created and has been made in every vintage since.

Winemaking generally follows the consensus protocol. There is no extended cold-soaking or extended postfermentation maceration; fermentors are almost entirely 1.5-ton open-tops, and free-run juice is bucketed into the press at the end of the primary fermentation to avoid pressing any bitter seeds. The Willamette Valley and reserve wines are raised almost entirely in one-year-old and older barrels and are bottled before the following vintage; the single-vineyard and Three Hills wines, held in wood for thirteen months, see about 40 percent new wood. Based on experience in prior vintages, barrels are chosen specifically to complement the flavor and structural properties of individual wines.

Overall, Lange pinots display great aromatic interest, strong minerality, and bright, refreshing structure. The Three Hills Cuvée is quite approachable early on, whereas the Dundee Hills Estate wine and, especially, the Freedom Hill Vineyard bottlings benefit from additional bottle age.

TASTING NOTES
2006 Three Hills Cuvée (tasted in 2007): Luminous medium garnet; fragrant, flowers-and-red-fruit nose; intense, slightly peppery, and edgy attack; red fruit

and spice on the mid-palate; bright and attractive overall, with a hint of citrus and the texture of polished cotton.

2005 *Dundee Hills Estate (tasted twice in* 2007*):* Luminous, medium ruby color; earthy minerality and crushed flower petals with a whiff of tangerine peel on the nose; black and red fruit with sage-like notes, some allspice, and a citric accent on the palate; slightly sweet but dominantly mineral; soft, rich, round, and mouth coating; nicely built, with good acidity and grip.

2005 *Freedom Hill Vineyard (tasted in* 2007*):* Almost opaque, medium-dark black-red; aromas of conifer foliage, incense, and mentholated fruit; camphor, black pepper, and wet-slate minerality on the palate; considerable grip and intensity from attack through finish; a serious wine that has been built to age.

LAZY RIVER VINEYARD
Carlton, Oregon

Ned Lumpkin, a Seattle-based general building contractor who discovered wine during his military service in Germany at the beginning of the 1960s, recalls that he and his wife, Kirsten, first considered planting a vineyard, in Washington's Walla Walla Valley, more than thirty years ago. Instead, in 1999, the couple acquired 146 very pretty acres northeast of Yamhill, Oregon, where they fell in love with views of the Coast Range, along with a stand of white oaks; a barn; a granary; a stream; some cow pasture; and quite a few acres covered with Scotch broom, thorny Himalayan blackberries, and feral cherry trees. Steven Price, a horticulturist and longtime key figure in Oregon

viticulture, and Andy Gallagher, a soils engineer, helped evaluate the site's vineyard potential. Locals said it was exceptionally cool—cool enough that spring freezes could be problematic—and backhoe pits revealed a preponderance of the same red, volcanic soil series that had made the initial reputation of Oregon pinot noir fifteen miles away in the Dundee Hills.

So, in the spring and fall of 2000 and the spring of 2001, the Lumpkins planted 28 acres of pinot noir and 1.3 of pinot gris across the site's sunniest, south-facing slope, between the 250- and 425-foot contours. For scion material, they chose mostly Dijon clones with some of the Oregon workhorse selections, UCD 2A and 5. (In 2007 they also deployed two giant wind machines after two years of cold spring weather froze the vines' first buds.) They also remodeled the granary to serve as their second home for six months out of every twelve.

As the vines began to bear in 2002, the news was better than they had had any right to expect: the exceptionally low-vigor soils delivered vines requiring little canopy management or crop thinning, and their fruit consisted of compact clusters and very small berries. Some of Oregon best labels— SOTER VINEYARDS, ANDREW RICH WINES, PANTHER CREEK CELLARS, and PONZI VINEYARDS —developed an interest in the Lumpkins' grapes. Meanwhile, with vines in the ground and the aspiration to make wines, not just to grow grapes, the Lumpkins searched for a winemaker. A Seattle distributor suggested they speak with Eric Hamacher (see HAMACHER WINES). As it happened, Hamacher, who had successfully lobbied the Oregon legislature in the 1990s to permit winemaking facilities that housed multiple wineries, was also looking for the wherewithal to build the first example of the shared facility that had newly been permitted by law. The synergy was clear to both parties. The Lumpkins joined forces with Hamacher and his wife, Luisa Ponzi, to design and build the Carlton Winemakers Studio.

Lumpkin's Seattle-based construction firm became the project's general contractor, and Hamacher signed on as winemaker for the Lumpkins' new Lazy River brand. Within a few years, the Lumpkins' son Jeff had left his job in business development at Microsoft to take over management of the Studio, while Jeff's wife, Ruoh-Shin, a Singaporean, who, like Jeff, had an MBA, set about studying for the diploma granted by the International Sommelier Guild, on her way toward the marketing and brand development responsibilities for Lazy River's wines.

WINES AND WINEMAKING NOTES

A Lazy River estate pinot has been made in every vintage since 2002. In 2003 there was also a reserve bottling called Famille Neuville, in honor of French friends who are also investors in Lazy River. There have been no significant departures from the consensus protocol for making pinot, except that the 2002 and 2003 reserve wines were made and raised with no new wood at all, and more recent vintages with very little. These wines are exceptionally elegant editions of pinot noir with smooth, satiny textures, attractive overlays of red berry fruit, floral aromas and peppery spice, and intensity without weight.

TASTING NOTES

2005 *Estate (tasted in 2007):* Transparent, medium ruby; aromas of raspberry, strawberry, flowers, and white pepper; bright, soft, red berry fruit on the palate; good acidity, considerable elegance, and admirable length.

2004 *Estate (tasted in 2007):* Brilliant, light-to-medium garnet; raspberry, soft spice, cherry-pie fruit, and peppery licorice aromas; a sturdier and slightly bigger wine than the 2005 with some black licorice; satiny and elegant, with just a hint of grip on the finish.

2003 *Estate (tasted in 2007):* Medium ruby color; bright and citrus marked on the nose, against a backdrop of cherry-cranberry fruit and a hint of earth; suave and almost rich textured, but still creamy on the palate; no hint of the hot weather that made this vintage aberrant in most of Oregon.

2003 *Famille Neuville Reserve (tasted in 2007):* Rosy-ruby tint and just slightly darker than the regular estate bottling; nose of wet earth and slate-y minerality; light weight but intense on the palate; very well built, with good acid and good grip; still very young.

2002 *Estate (tasted in 2007):* Medium ruby; potpourri and black raspberry aromas, plus elements of fresh wildflowers and sage; creamy, elegant, and fruit-driven mid-palate, buttressed with minerality; considerable grip but very dusty, fine-grained tannins on the finish; astonishing quality from third-leaf vines; fine.

LEMELSON VINEYARDS
Carlton, Oregon

Eric Lemelson's grandfather was a New Jersey physician. His father (1923–1997), a prolific inventor, is said to have held more United States patents than anyone since Thomas Edison. Lemelson was the first of his family to move west, initially for an undergraduate education at Reed College. In and after college, and eventually in law school as well, he turned to overlapping and successive careers and avocations in rock music, political activism, legislative analysis, and environmental law. In 1990 he moved from Portland to a farm on Parrett Mountain, the southernmost peak in the Chehalem Mountains, not far from newly planted vineyards. Inevitably, perhaps, he was approached by local vintners, who offered to buy grapes if he, too, would plant vines on his farm's most suitable slope. Lemelson was not a wine person at this point, nor was there any history of wine connoisseurship in his family. But he remembers tasting a then-recent vintage of BEAUX FRÈRES pinot noir in 1994 that he describes, now, as a "head-turner." Thereafter, matters progressed quickly.

In 1995 he planted 1.5 acres each of pinot noir and pinot gris on the Parrett Mountain site he calls Chestnut Hill. Seven years later, he had come to own or farm 120 acres of sustainably managed, mostly pinot noir, grapes, certified organic in 2004, on six sites in the Yamhill-Carlton, Chehalem Mountains, and Dundee Hills AVAs. In that same time period, he built a state-of-the-art, 10,000-case winery northeast of Carlton, designed with the assistance of Eric Hamacher (see HAMACHER WINES), and became sole proprietor of the thirtieth-largest wine brand in Oregon.

The original Chestnut Hill site grew to 15 acres, including five clones of pinot noir on three rootstocks planted between 1995 and 2007. The Stermer Vineyard, where the winery is located, consists of 31 planted acres of pinot noir (six clones on three rootstocks planted in 1997 and 1998) in sedimentary, Willakenzie-series soil where the Stermer family grew plums and wheat in the 1940s and raised cattle in the 1950s. Two other vineyards, Johnson and Briscoe, are within 2 miles of the winery and share similar soils. Johnson is a south-facing slope, sited

between 250 and 450 feet, planted to 24 acres of pinot noir and 3 acres of chardonnay; Briscoe is a near-plateau at an elevation of about 500 feet, with a slight south-to-southwest slope where Lemelson set out 19 acres of pinot in 2001 and 2002. A fifth pinot vineyard is located on the Meyer farm in the Dundee Hills. This 70-acre site boasts 26 acres of pinot in Jory and Nekia-series soils planted between 2000 and 2007 on steep, south-facing slopes, between the 560- and 780-foot contours. All of Lemelson's estate vineyards consist entirely of vines planted since 1995; Lemelson accurately describes his enterprise as a "young-vines winery"— mostly because mature sites were not on the market in the late 1990s.

WINES AND WINEMAKING NOTES
Although Lemelson is a strong proponent of *terroir,* and the brand specializes in single-vineyard wines, two blends have been made in each vintage since the launch in 1999. Thea's Selection, named for his mother, features the most precocious and most highly perfumed barrels in the cellar. Jerome Reserve, named for his father, is its mirror opposite: a home for the deepest, most complex, and most concentrated lots.

The first of many vineyard-designated wines, a bottling from the "home" vineyard's Wädenswil vines, debuted the same year. A second vineyard-designate, added to the portfolio in 2000, and an exception to Lemelson's twin orientations toward estate grown wines and young vines, was a Reed & Reynolds Vineyard bottling based on fruit sourced from a twenty-year-old vineyard 4 miles west of Carlton, planted entirely to own-rooted UCD 2A and 5. In 2002 a bottling from Lemelson's 1995 planting on Parrett Mountain (Chestnut Hill Vineyard) debuted, and the name of the Reed & Reynolds wine was changed to Resonance, following the vineyard's sale to Kevin Chambers. (CALERA WINE COMPANY objected to the Reed & Reynolds name because of its similarity to the name of Calera's Reed Vineyard.) A vineyard-designated wine from the Meyer Vineyard was added in 2003, as was a non-estate wine called Anderson from a vineyard next door to Meyer in 2005; at that time, the Reed & Reynolds/Resonance bottling was discontinued. Over time, Thea's Selection became Lemelson's largest bottling, accounting for nearly half the label's total volume, and it made use of fruit from nearly all its vineyard sources; the Jerome Reserve came to rely increasingly on fruit from Lemelson's volcanic soils sites.

Winemaking involves rigorous sorting to privilege the ripest clusters, entirely destemmed fruit (except in the case of the Dundee Hills wines), small- and medium-size fermentors, five to seven days' cold soak, resident yeasts, 90°F fermentations, and a fourteen-month *élevage* in barrel stocks that range from about 50 percent new oak for Thea's Selection to 100 percent new oak for the Jerome Reserve and for several of the single-vineyard wines. The favored coopers are Sirugue, Remond, and François Frères. New wines are neither fined nor filtered.

Thomas Bachelder, a Quebec native with experience in Burgundy, was Lemelson's winemaker from 1999 through 2002, when he left to take the reins at Le Clos Jordanne in Ontario, Canada. Bachelder was succeeded in 2003 and 2004 by Paul Pujo, a young New Zealander who had worked several vintages for Kuentz-Bas in Alsace, and in 2005 Eric Lemelson made the vintage himself. Anthony King, formerly the winemaker at ACACIA WINERY in Carneros, came on board in 2006. The wines—even Thea's, which is supposed to privilege precocious lots—are deeply-colored, concentrated, long-to-finish, and often grippy editions of pinot noir that require time to show their best.

2005 *Thea's Selection (tasted in 2007):* Medium-deep black-red; dusty, macerated berries on the nose; rich and round on the palate, with intense red fruit, peppery spice, and some mocha; grippy at the end.

2005 *Stermer Vineyard (tasted in 2007):* Aromas of fennel fronds, earth, and floral elements; bright acid and red fruit on the mid-palate; silky at first, then quickly grippy, with a long, dry finish.

2005 *Meyer Vineyard (tasted in 2007):* Camphor and citrus-peel aromas, with the juniper-berry signature of whole-cluster fermentation; bright, intense, citrus-infused, cranberry-plum fruit in the mouth, with hints of clove, cinnamon, and creaminess; long.

2002 *Thea's Selection (tasted in 2007):* Brilliant ruby-red; slightly herbal nose; soft, intense cherry-raspberry fruit on the palate with peppery highlights; fine.

2002 *Stermer Vineyard (tasted in 2007):* Brilliant, medium rosy-garnet; a lifted nose featuring both herbs and flowers; bright raspberry and licorice on the palate, with hints of nutmeg, mace, and allspice; fine.

2000 *Jerome Reserve (tasted in 2007):* Transparent medium ruby with a rosy rim; leather, camphor, and sandalwood on the nose; tobacco, raspberry, boot polish, spicy plum, and black pepper on the palate; deep, intense, and very pretty.

LITTORAI WINES

Sebastopol, California

The path from suburban Westchester County in New York, where he grew up, to winemaking in western Sonoma County took Ted Lemon through an undergraduate major in French literature at Brown University, a junior year abroad in France, a postgraduate fellowship to study enology at the Université de Bourgogne, and apprenticeships at Domaine Dujac, Domaine Roumier, and Domaine Bruno Clair. In 1982 Lemon was hired to make wine for the house of Guy Roulot in Meursault—as far as

---

ELEGANT, DEEPLY FLAVORED, NUANCED, AND COMPLEX; BENCHMARKS FOR NORTH AMERICAN PINOT NOIR

---

anyone knows, the first and only time an American has been employed, not as a consultant or harvest worker, but as the winemaker and vineyard manager by a highly regarded Burgundy estate. Back from France in 1984, Lemon became the founding winemaker for Napa-based Chateau Woltner.

In 1991 and 1992, he traveled up and down the Pacific Coast, from Oregon to Santa Barbara, examining vineyards and tasting extensively, searching for fruit on which to base a label of his own. He found himself drawn to what he calls the "true" North Coast, located within a few miles of the ocean north and south of the Russian River and in Anderson Valley. The quality of the fruit from these sites impressed him, he recalls, "even when the wines were not especially well made." In 1992 Lemon left Chateau Woltner to begin a consulting career, working inter alia with several wineries, including Franciscan Estates's Estancia operation and Oregon's ARCHERY SUMMIT, which aspired to make top-quality pinot noir. In 1993 Lemon and his wife, Heidi, founded Littorai—a plural derivative of the Latin

littor, meaning "coasts"—a boutique-sized project dedicated to coastal pinot noir and chardonnay.

Littorai's first pinot noir was the 1993 One Acre, Lemon's designation for a piece of Rich Savoy's Deer Meadow Ranch, at 1,600 feet on the crest of a northwest-facing ridge on the northeastern side of the Anderson Valley, above Boonville. This vineyard was planted in 1986 in 9-foot rows with 3 feet between vines, in shallow, loamy soil overlaying uplifted marine sandstone. The scion material is UCD 13 and 2A clones, along with Mount Eden selection, and the yield ranges from 2 to 3.5 tons per acre. In 1995 Littorai added a second Anderson Valley vineyard to its pinot portfolio: Savoy's main ranch, on the northern side of Highway 128, west of Philo. There, Littorai gets fruit from blocks planted in 1991, 1992, and 1993 at the toe of the hill, in Boont and Pinole loam soil overlaying Franciscan shale. The plant material is a mix of Dijon 114 and 115, and UCD 4, plus Swan selection. Also in 1995, Littorai began sourcing pinot noir from David Hirsch's well-known vineyard northeast of Jenner, in the Sonoma Coast AVA. (See below for more about the block-specific sources of Littorai's fruit from HIRSCH.)

In 1997 Littorai began sourcing pinot from the Thieriot Vineyard, a 2-acre parcel at 1,200 feet between the Fay and Tannery Creek drainages, overlooking the town of Bodega Bay, five miles from the ocean. There, in a thin layer of Goldridge sandy loam surmounting fractured sandstone, Cameron Thieriot planted Swan selection in 1991 and Dijon 114, 777, and 667, along with UCD 4, in 1994. Littorai now has a 25-year lease on this site. A custom-planted block in the Cerise Vineyard, not far from Deer Meadow Ranch in Anderson Valley, was added to the portfolio in 2001; other additions were the much-respected Summa Vineyard on the ridge between Occidental and Bodega Bay, and Roman Vineyard, a 2-acre site custom planted for Littorai in 1999, high on Holmes Ranch Road northwest of Philo, both in 2002. In 2006 Lemon received his first fruit from the Platt Vineyard in the Petaluma Gap.

The new millennium also saw the beginning of estate winegrowing at Littorai. The first estate vineyard was planted in 2001, on Willow Creek Road west of Occidental, to 4 acres of pinot noir, a half acre of chardonnay, and a half acre of "mixed whites." Littorai calls this site "The Haven Vineyard," and its first pinot noir was made in 2004. A second estate vineyard is located off Goldridge Road between Sebastopol and Freestone. Three acres of pinot have been planted there, but the vines are not yet bearing, and the site has not yet been named. The estate sites are farmed biodynamically.

In addition to the vineyard-designated wines, which are the core of Littorai's program, Lemon began making a Sonoma Coast appellation wine in 2002, using lots of Hirsch and Theriot declassified from the single-vineyard program, and drifted into a similar arrangement for Anderson Valley beginning in 2003. Anticipating that 2003 would be the last vintage made from One Acre before phylloxera forced replanting there, and finding the wine lesser in quality that its vineyard-designated predecessors, Lemon called it, rather soulfully, Les Larmes and billed it as the last wine from One Acre until after the site was replanted. But the vineyard had a mind of its own, producing one more vintage of indisputably single-vineyard quality in 2004, so One Acre was revived for that year. Having established the precedent of a bottling called Les Larmes for less than single-vineyard quality from Anderson Valley, Lemon rebirthed Les Larmes in 2005 as a home for declassified

barrels of Savoy, Roman, and Cerise, and as the presumptive vehicle for handling the first young-vines fruit from One Acre after replanting.

As of 2007, Littorai's production facility is the Black-Sears Winery on Howell Mountain, where space is shared with Black-Sears and the Howell Mountain Winery. The as-yet-unnamed estate vineyard on Goldridge Road is the site for a new winery to be built in time to receive the 2008 harvest.

WINES AND WINEMAKING NOTES
The fruit sources for Littorai's four vineyard-designated pinots have been consistent, except that Block 6 was added to Blocks 5, 7, and 9 at Hirsch beginning in 1996; a block of Dijon 115 was exchanged for a block of UCD 13 at Savoy beginning in 1996; and the UCD 4 block was added to the Swan block at Thieriot in 1998. In 1997 tiny quantities of Hirsch Blocks 5, 7, and 9 were bottled separately. These wines have been misunderstood in some circles as super-vineyard-designates; in fact, the block-designates were kept separate for analytic purposes only.

Lemon tailors winemaking to the vineyard and the vintage, paying particular attention to tannin management. Fruit is sorted repeatedly: in the vineyard before harvest, at the destemmer, and again between the destemmer and the fermentor. Whole-cluster percentage varies from wine to wine and year to year, and is taste-based, but is always lower in cool years. The fermentors are all jacketed stainless steel, and most are open-tops, ranging in size from 400 to 1,200 gallons. Nevertheless, Lemon argues that closed-top tanks can be an advantage in the case of very small volumes, because they help both to sustain temperature and to maintain an anaerobic environment, so he purchased a few in 1999.

Because Littorai's vineyards are some distance from the winery, the fruit is picked into refrigerated trucks, where it is chilled to 45°F. On the crushpad, the fruit typically gains about 5 degrees, going into the fermentors at about 50°F. Lemon then seeks to maintain the 50° temperature during a three- to ten-day cold soak, and thereafter begins to warm the fermentors. The resident yeasts on which Littorai relies tend to start slowly and spike late—a fermentation curve that Lemon finds conducive to good palate length. Hand punchdowns are *de rigueur*, but Lemon may taper off their frequency, convert to pumpovers, or desist altogether when he is confronted with tannic lots. At one extreme, he may press before the must is dry and go directly to barrel without settling the juice; at the other extreme, he may permit as much as seven to ten days of postfermentation maceration before pressing. In early editions of Littorai, the press juice was reassembled; now, press wines are generally excluded and bulked out. Malolactic fermentations rely on resident bacteria.

On average, about 50 percent of barrels are new, but the mix varies considerably from wine to wine. Most of the cooperage comes from François Frères, Remond, Damy, and Rousseau; medium to medium-plus toast is favored, and there is a preference for a mix of barrels that have been air-aged for two years rather than three. Littorai pinots have not been fined since 1997, and the 1993 One Acre was the only wine ever filtered. Wines spend eleven to fifteen months in barrel as necessary to polymerize the tannins. The release date is two years after the vintage.

Overall, Littorai's editions are benchmarks for North American pinot: invariably elegant, medium-weight, deeply flavored wines, each of which showcases its respective *terroir*. Aromas and flavors are always nuanced, layered, and complex, and there is always much more at work than fruit. Lemon has chosen sites where optimal flavor development occurs at very reasonable levels of sugar accumulation, so only a few of the finished wines exceed 14 percent alcohol. Savoy has a tendency to brilliant cherry fruit and chewiness, Thieriot to spiciness, and One Acre to dried flowers and exotic berries. Hirsch is the most tannic, the wildest, and the smokiest of the lot, and it is generally the last to soften. The wines are standards for fine North American pinot noir, expressing organoleptic complexity and purity of fruit with just enough flesh and ripeness to make them elegant and lovely.

TASTING NOTES

2005 *Sonoma Coast (tasted in 2007)*: Transparent, light rosy-garnet; citrus, potpourri, and raspberry aromas; cherry and some earth, but bright overall on the palate; intense peppery spice and a hint of nuttiness; substantial but bantam weight; long and very attractive.

2005 *Roman Vineyard (tasted in 2007)*: Brilliant, deeply tinted, scarlet-brick color; elegant, engaging nose of spicy cherry with notes of citrus peel; toasted South Asian spices with a hint of tobacco; exceptional palate of clean, persistent, cherry-based fruit; very nice grip with hints of mocha, tar, and merbromin; persistently bright, long, intense, and very fine.

2004 *The Haven Vineyard (tasted in 2007)*: Stunning rosy-scarlet; explosive and complex nose of resin, morello cherry, tar, and nut shells; intensely fruity on the front palate, with pure, cherry *eau-de-vie* flavors, some earth, and brewed black tea; beautifully built, elegant, impressive, and distinctive.

2003 *Les Larmes (tasted in 2006)*: Exotic Indonesian spice on the nose, plus mushroom and moss; bright and high toned on the palate with a sweet-tart character; round and elegant at mid-palate, with hints of orange flower water and thyme; long and distinctive.

2000 *One Acre (tasted in* 2007*):* Transparent, deep black-red; characteristically exotic nose again, this time redolent of cinnamon, sandalwood, and cashews; an exceptionally deep, earthy, and brooding edition of One Acre; flavors of orange peel and Darjeeling tea; soft, elegant, and long, and truly the last wine from this site before replanting.

2000 *Hirsch Vineyard (tasted in* 2005*):* Limpid, dark black-red; very strong perfume with a marked note of citrus peel; very structured with dark chocolate and mocha; velvety now, but also tightly woven, rich, mouth coating, and long.

1999 *One Acre (tasted in* 2007*):* Dense mahogany color; spice, earth, and tobacco aromas; deep spicy cherry on the palate; fruit so pure it resembles *kirschwasser;* dark, Vosne-like earth marked by wet clay and Tootsie Roll; considerable mid-palate weight; good grip, but now beginning to soften; very distinctive, elegant, long, and fine.

LONDER VINEYARDS
Philo, California

Larry Londer's near-lifelong fascination with wine began in medical school, when he worked in a small liquor store stocking shelves and running deliveries. Later, as an ophthalmologist in Albuquerque, New Mexico, Londer and his wife, Shirlee, began to collect good Bordeaux and California cabernets, and eventually red Burgundies, and he took extension courses at the University of California Davis to learn more. In the 1990s, when his wife served as general chairman of the New Mexico Symphony's wine auction and he chaired its wine committee, the Londers made numerous trips to California "to beg and plead for donations" and to look for retirement property where they could plant a vineyard of their own in due season. Their sights landed eventually on the Anderson Valley, which was "ideal" for pinot and gewürztraminer, the two varieties they aspired to grow, and affordable. The pieces came together in May 2000, when the Londers moved to Anderson Valley, purchased a 55-acre parcel that had been developed a few years before as an organic vegetable, stone fruit, and berry farm, and began planning a 15-acre pinot vineyard. Economics pushed them beyond grape growing right from the outset, however. Having met Greg La Follette (see TANDEM WINERY) in 2000, and finding themselves confronted with an opportunity to be among La Follette's first custom-crush clients at the new Tandem facility, the Londers used purchased fruit to create their own wine brand in 2001—the same year their first pinot vines went into the ground. La Follette was their principal winemaker for the first three vintages; in 2004 he was succeeded by Rick Davis, one of La Follette's associates. The estate vineyard, which is located about 4 miles northwest of Philo, between the old Edmeades property and Husch, was planted to UCD 2A and 4, Dijon 115 and 777, and Swan selection; it produced its first significant crop in 2004.

WINES AND WINEMAKING NOTES
Although most of Londer's pinot program is based on Anderson Valley fruit, a small amount of vineyard-designated Van der

Kamp was made in 2001 (owing to La Follette's contacts with Martin Van der Kamp), and a vineyard-designated Keefer Ranch was made in 2003 and 2004. A blended Anderson Valley wine has been made from the outset, sourced from the Ferrington (see WILLIAMS SELYEM), Donnelly Creek, and Valley Foothills vineyards; a barrel selection from Ferrington and Valley Foothills only, called Paraboll, debuted in 2002. Since it began to bear in 2004, the estate vineyard has been used primarily to make an estate grown wine, although some of it winds up in the Anderson Valley blend. Londer admits to picking relatively late, while he waits for "brown seeds, fragile skin, and flavors." Some fruit is fermented as whole clusters "if the stems are lignified and brown." Acid is added "if necessary," and fermentations normally rely on resident yeast, following three to five days of cold-soaking. The barrel regime consists primarily of Cadus, François Frères, Remond, and Latour barrels, most coopered from wood grown in Allier forests, of which one third are new in each vintage. The wines are not usually fined or filtered.

Londer pinots are made in a ripe-picked, fruit-forward, dark-flavored style and display very polished tannins and soft impressions. Paraboll shows these parameters almost to a fault, while the estate grown cuvée is, to my palate, the most interesting of the Londer wines.

TASTING NOTES

2005 *Anderson Valley (tasted in 2007):* Medium-dark black-red; earth, cherry, and gum camphor on the nose; spicy, slightly peppery, black-toned fruit with fine-grained tannins; nicely knit, suede-like texture; long and attractive.

2005 *Londer Estate (tasted in 2007):* Transparent, medium-deep black-red; very ripe black cherry and cassis on the nose, plus a bit of smoke; sweet, slightly resinated black fruit on the palate; brewed black tea properties with slight hints of spice; very silky, soft, and long.

2005 *Paraboll (tasted in 2007):* Medium black-red again; reticent aromatically, with just hints of boot polish and dark fruit; very rich and sweet on the palate, but big loads of mocha and espresso; smooth and almost creamy on the mid-palate and finish; soft and warm.

2004 *Anderson Valley (tasted in 2007):* Barely transparent, medium-dark black-red; dark, slightly earthy, and slightly smoky nose featuring ripe black fruit; intense and very black on the palate, with a slightly fruit-sweetened graphite, mineral, and tannin core; dries quickly on the finish.

2004 *Londer Estate (tasted in 2007):* Purplish, medium black-red; aromatically tight, with hints of cherry, camphor, and black licorice; very ripe cherry on the palate, with resin and clove-cinnamon spice; grip at mid-palate and beyond; promising.

2004 *Paraboll (tasted in 2007):* Medium dark, black-red; ultraripe, plummy-cherry nose; soft, smooth, sweet, and almost creamy on the palate, with notes of pomegranate, pencil lead, and wet slate; finishes warm, long, and astringent.

RICHARD LONGORIA WINES
Los Olivos, California

Richard Longoria's wine credentials go back to 1974, when he worked at the historic BUENA VISTA winery in Sonoma. Two years later, he became cellar foreman for the Firestone Vineyard near Los Olivos. Experience at Chappellet in Napa, J. Carey, and THE GAINEY VINEYARD (the last as its founding winemaker) followed. Meanwhile, he and his wife established Richard Longoria Wines in 1982, producing just 500 cases of pinot noir and chardonnay. The family business

---

ELEGANT, PRECISION-CRAFTED, AND VISUALLY STRIKING PINOTS FROM THE SOUTHERN CENTRAL COAST

---

finally grew into a full-time project at the end of the 1990s, simultaneously inhabiting an unglamorous production facility in Lompoc and a quaint tasting room on the main street of Los Olivos.

Richard Longoria Wines has produced pinot noir in every vintage since 1982, except for 1990 and 1992, but the ebb and flow of fruit sources illustrate the vicissitudes that were visited upon small, landless, Santa Barbara–based producers until very recently. The legendary Sierra Madre Vineyard southeast of Santa Maria was the anchor for the earliest vintages, from 1982 through 1986. Longoria's 1982, 1983, and 1984 Santa Maria Valley bottlings were 100 percent Sierra Madre fruit; a Santa Maria Hills vineyard-designated wine was also made in 1983.

Reflecting Longoria's demanding new assignment as winemaker for The Gainey Vineyard beginning in February 1985, as well as some avowed frustration with fruit sources, his release letter for the Longoria 1984 vintage announced that it would be his last effort under that label; however, the retreat was short lived. Longoria pinot noir was made in 1985 after all. In that vintage and the next, however, the pinot carried a Santa Barbara County designation on the

label, confirming that the fruit was sourced from both the Santa Maria and the Santa Ynez valleys (the 1985 was a combination of Sierra Madre and Sanford & Benedict Vineyard; the 1986 was widely sourced). In 1987 Longoria made two pinots, a Santa Maria Valley wine once again sourced entirely from Sierra Madre, and a Santa Ynez Valley–Benedict Vineyard wine. In 1988 and 1989, the only pinot was a Santa Ynez Valley wine sourced from Sanford & Benedict. In 1991 the Santa Maria Valley rubric returned, made from a combination of Sierra Madre and (for the first time since 1986) Bien Nacido fruit. The year 1993 marked the beginning of vineyard-designated wines from Bien Nacido Blocks G and N, and these have been made in every vintage since, except that in 1997 the fruit from Block G was kept separate and bottled as a block-designated, lighter-weight wine.

At the end of the millennium, much of Longoria's attention turned to the newly approved Sta. Rita Hills AVA, close to his production facility in Lompoc. He was the architect of a 1998 project to plant a new vineyard called Fe Ciega, at around the 400-foot contour on the northern bank of the Santa Ynez River. This 7.75-acre parcel consists of two blocks, one laid out in east–west rows to accommodate topography; in the other, the rows run north–south. Vines are spaced 4 feet apart in 8-foot rows, and the scion material is evenly divided among UCD 5, Dijon 115, and Dijon 667. An additional acre will be planted at Fe Ciega in 2008 with budwood taken from some of the original vines at Mount Eden.

From 2001 to 2004, Longoria also sourced pinot from the Mount Carmel Vineyard, but Mount Carmel entered into an exclusive agreement with BREWER-CLIFTON in 2005, ending fruit supplies to other producers. Sanford & Benedict also returned to the list of sources for Longoria pinot from 2002 to 2006. These sources enabled Longoria to reduce his commitment at Bien Nacido, where his rows of Block G were released after the 2000 harvest, but he returned to Bien Nacido (Block N this time) in 2005. Also in 2005, Longoria began to source pinot from Foley's Rancho Santa Rosa Vineyard, using blocks planted to UCD 4 and Dijon 667. The emphasis is now firmly on vineyard-designated wines, but Longoria will make a blended Sta. Rita Hills wine in most vintages as a home for declassified lots of Fe Ciega, Rancho Santa Rosa, and (through 2006) Sanford & Benedict.

WINES AND WINEMAKING NOTES

Longoria is one of the many winemakers who say they pick by flavor, but he admits that until the mid 1990s, he tried to pick at sugar levels lower than 24 Brix. This choice put him, he recalls, "in the middle position" for picking at Sierra Madre and Bien Nacido—later than early birds such as LANE TANNER, but earlier than many very-ripe-fruit makers. Since the mid 1990s, he has been more tolerant of higher sugars. He fermented entirely in fruit bins through 2001, but added one small, 2-ton, stainless steel tank to his cellar in 2002. He destems completely, allows about two days of cellar-temperature cool soak, and inoculates almost all fermentations. Fermentation temperatures usually peak in the high 80°F. Longoria admits that a few degrees warmer might be better, but a fruit bin is not large enough to build juice temperatures much higher than 90°F. He normally delays pressing until about five days after the primary fermentation has completed, reunifies the free-run and press fractions, and settles briefly in tank.

A mix of medium-toast barrels is used, mostly from François Frères, Remond,

and Billon. About one third of the barrels are new each year, although the Sta. Rita Hills wines are raised in a higher percentage of new wood than is the Bien Nacido. A few barrels are inoculated to kick off the malolactic fermentation; this is usually sufficient to start the rest. The pinots spend eleven or twelve months in barrel, and are not racked until time for bottling, just before the next harvest. Egg-white fining and 1-micron pad filtration are standard.

Longoria reports that 2005 will be the largest-volume vintage for the foreseeable future as he readjusts vineyard sources to optimize for quality. His elegant, precision-crafted, and visually striking wines are fine examples of pinot from the southern Central Coast, and Fe Ciega seems an exceptional site for complex wines with great depth of flavor.

TASTING NOTES

2005 *Rancho Santa Rosa Vineyard (tasted in 2007):* Brilliant, medium ruby; dusty, floral nose; raspberry and cherry on the palate, with toast and minerality; nicely structured, serious, and very slightly sweet, with good acid and end-of-palate grip.

2005 *Sanford & Benedict Vineyard (tasted in 2007):* Stunning, bright, rosy-garnet; slightly shy but very precisely etched aromas of black raspberry and rose petal; unfolds slowly on the palate through cinnamony spice, licorice, and infused savory herbs; barely perceptible sweetness, understated elegance, and rewarding length; silky and lovely throughout; very fine. A personal favorite.

2005 *Bien Nacido Vineyard (tasted in 2007):* Brilliant, medium-dark magenta; aromas of unroasted nuts, earth, thyme, and mace; quite sweet (almost honeyed) red berry fruit flavors on the palate, with characteristic Bien Nacido black pepper, hints of blood orange, and ground hard spice; long and round, featherweight velvet wrapper; nicely structured. Fine.

2001 *Mount Carmel Vineyard (tasted in 2004)*: Dark, saturated, purplish-red; aromas of morello cherry, sarsaparilla, and herbs; sweet cherry-blackberry fruit on the palate, with wet slate and pepper; structured, medium in weight, and full bodied, with the texture of crushed velvet.

LORING WINE COMPANY
Lompoc, California

Brian Loring, a software engineer who specialized in military applications, confesses that he has been a "wine geek" since he was eighteen years old. In 1997 and 1998, he cut a deal with the proprietor of Santa Barbara's Cottonwood Canyon Winery to "hang out" during crush, where he could absorb hands-on experience. In 1999 Cottonwood Canyon sold him 3 tons of pinot noir for a personal start-up project. The wine Loring made from these grapes was enthusiastically reviewed by the usual suspects, making these editions of American pinot into an almost instant cult. Loring, modestly, credits his overnight success to "amazing fruit" from his vineyard sources and to "blind luck" in connecting, at the very launch of his brand, with a platinum list of growers, including both of Monterey's famous Garys (Pisoni and Franscioni), Sta. Rita Hills growers Wes Hagen (Clos Pepe Vineyard) and Peter Cargasacchi, and Green Valley's Marcy Keefer—just for starters. By 2004 his renown was sufficient that both he and his wife could forsake day jobs in greater Los Angeles, move to the Santa Barbara wine country's new central core in Lompoc, and concentrate on wine full time.

In both word and deed, Loring plainly does not pursue Burgundian parameters for pinot. On the contrary, he picks very ripe, tells mailing-list customers that his wines "are built to drink right away," argues that high alcohol is a perfectly acceptable counterpoint to "big fruit," writes admiringly of "soft tannins" and "tasty fruit," and punctuates his remaining advice to consumers with smiley-face icons. Critics have responded in kind, extolling "deep purple colors," "deep aromas," and "amazing depth." Asked if pinot is as difficult to make as is generally reputed, Loring replies that the maker's job is easier than the grower's, in part because grapes picked "riper" are "less fragile in the winery." (Quite a few vintners would argue that point.)

In the winery, Loring generally follows the consensus protocol, completely destemming all berries, fermenting in double-height fruit bins with inocula, and bucketing the new wine into a basket press when the must is dry. The barrel regime is roughly half new barrels and half once used barrels, and the main coopers are Sirugue and François Frères. Loring uses the caves at Cottonwood Canyon for *élevage*.

Many Loring pinots I have tasted from the 2002, 2003, and 2004 vintages have displayed overtly pruney aromas from super-ripe picking, enough fruit-sweetness to masquerade as late harvest, and almost enough alcohol to qualify as port. The 2005s, however, are atypical but delicious. Loring denies any "stylistic" change, claiming vintage variation instead. These wines may not be "elegant," he asserts, but no one will "mistake them for syrah." True enough. Most of these wines display alcohol levels under 13 percent and acid levels that are very attractive; they are completely free of raisiny flavors. At this point in the life of the brand, in addition to the vineyards mentioned above, Loring sources pinot from Rancho Ontiveros in the Santa Maria Valley, from Brosseau Vineyard and Naylor's Dry Hole Vineyard in the Chalone AVA, and from the renowned Durrell Vineyard on the Sonoma Valley flank of Sonoma Mountain.

TASTING NOTES

2005 *Clos Pepe Vineyard (tasted in 2007):* Transparent, dark black-red; ripe, blackberry-boysenberry fruit on the nose, with notes of mint and pepper; fruit *confit* on the palate, with fig and Italian plum preserves; creamy texture, and rich, velvety, dense, and long; mouth coating but still nicely structured.

2005 *Brosseau Vineyard (tasted in 2007):* Transparent, dark black-red; dark black fruit, underbrush, and tree bark on the nose; slightly sweet attack, with some plum skins and black tea; then grippy with substantial tannin that persists and dominates the brooding fruit; needs time (Loring says it does not, but it does!) to soften.

2005 *Cargasacchi Vineyard (tasted in 2007):* Transparent, medium rosy-ruby; assertive nose of gum camphor and conifer leaves; sweet on the palate, with black earth and black cherry flavors; medium in length, and with the texture of polished cotton.

2005 *Garys' Vineyard (tasted in 2007):* Very transparent light-to-medium black-red; spicy raspberry and incense on the nose; slate-y, with hints of orange peel and Assam tea on the palate; sober and serious texture; lifted, bright flavors; reminiscent of mineraly and masculine wines from Gevrey; very attractive and long.

2005 *Rosella's Vineyard (tasted in 2007):* Brilliant medium magenta; explosive, cascading nose of potpourri, cherry-raspberry, vanilla, and cigar tobacco; intensely fruity on the palate, with strong minerality and cherries; bright and serious; lively throughout; linen textured with just a hint of grip; medium long and quite impressive.

2005 *Keefer Ranch (tasted in 2007):* Brilliant magenta; incense, fir balsam, and the exuberant fruit for which Keefer is known; vanilla and red fruit on the palate; bright, moderately intense, and long; almost spirity, with some sweet cherry pie flavors and some excellent acidity that lengthens the finish.

2002 *Rancho Ontiveros (tasted from a half bottle in 2004):* Deep black-red; aromas of ripe fruit, spicy *charcuterie*, and orange peel; very sweet blackberry and plum flavors with barrel char and black pepper accents; mouthfilling, round, and tannic; long, warm finish.

LYNMAR WINERY
Sebastopol, California

In 1980 Lynn Fritz purchased Quail Hill, a 42-acre vineyard, on the ridge that separates the Gravenstein Highway from the Laguna de Santa Rosa. Quail Hill was first planted in 1971 with scion material from Joseph Swan's Trenton Estate Vineyard—and with considerable help from Swan himself. A San Francisco native and Georgetown University graduate, Fritz was in the process, in the 1980s, of transforming a small, family-owned, San Francisco company that specialized in shipping documentation and customs clearance for Chinatown merchants into a Fortune 1000 enterprise handling transportation, warehousing, and transaction processing for national accounts like Boeing, Sears, and Microsoft, whose businesses depended heavily on import-export transactions. Along the way, he and his then wife, Mara, are said to have become enamored of red and white Burgundies, but they were mainly interested in Quail Hill as a retreat from urban life.

Throughout the 1980s, the Fritzes continued the practice of Quail Hill's previous owners, selling grapes to a stable of luminary producers, including Merry Edwards (see MERRY EDWARDS WINES) when she made wines for Matanzas Creek, and Tony Soter, who founded ETUDE WINES in 1982. But in 1990 Fritz took the next logical step: he created Lynmar Winery (eliding and contracting he and his wife's given names) to produce estate wines from Quail Hill.

Noncommercial vintages were made at Lynmar from 1990 to 1993. The first commercial wines were made in 1994 and released in 1996. In 2002, following the sale of his (now) global logistics business to United Parcel Service, Fritz began to invest heavily in Quail Hill with the intention of transforming his small, estate-driven brand into a 20,000-case winery in the same class as neighbors such as ROCHIOLI VINEYARDS and WILLIAMS SELYEM. An impressive building program produced a new fermentation building downhill from the original winery, a seven-bore cave for barrel storage, and a stunning board-and-batten tasting room *cum* visitors' center that also accommodates seminars associated with Fritz's "other" retirement project: a not-for-profit organization dedicated to improving the efficiency of worldwide disaster relief.

Paul Hobbs (see PAUL HOBBS WINES) signed on as consulting winemaker in 2003, and Hugh Chappelle (who succeeded Greg La Follette at FLOWERS VINEYARD AND WINERY) took over the day-to-day winegrowing and winemaking reins in 2004. Detecting some "weakness" in the vineyard, the new team designed an aggressive replanting and redevelopment program; acquired land for a second estate vineyard on the west side of the Gravenstein Highway; and made contracts with several Russian River and Sonoma Coast vineyards to purchase premium pinot and chardonnay fruit, both for the long term, and to compensate for estate production temporarily lost because of replanting.

As of 2007, the Quail Hill site was home to 23 acres of pinot noir in eight blocks, including 2 acres of Swan selection on St. George rootstock planted in 1974, 1.8 acres of Swan planted in 1997 with budwood taken from the 1974 block, and about 4 acres of Dijon clones and UCD 4 set out in 1996. The balance is a variety of clones and selections planted in 2000 and 2004. Except for a single, low-lying block at the edge of the Laguna, the soils are universally Sebastopol sandy loam, a close cousin of Goldridge sandy loam. Three of the eight blocks, including the block that contains the old Swan vines and the 1.8 acres of UCD 37, are used primarily to make Lynmar's estate pinot, which has been called Quail Cuvée since 2001.

WINES AND WINEMAKING NOTES

All Lynmar pinots from 1994 through 2002 were made entirely from Quail Hill fruit. In 1995 there was only a single cuvée, called Quail Hill; in all other years, at least two wines were made, of which one was "reserve quality." In addition, a cuvée called Five Sisters, named for Fritz's daughters, was made in 1997 and 1999, and an all-estate appellation (Russian River Valley) wine was bottled separately in each vintage from 1997 through 2002.

In 2003 the first fruit from contracted, non-estate sources entered Lynmar's pinot program. Most of these grapes feed the Russian River Valley bottling, which morphed immediately into a predominantly non-estate blend. Some purchased fruit also goes into the Five Sisters wine, which was rebirthed in 2004 as a "reserve-quality" appellation wine. The 2004 Five Sisters was anchored with fruit from the Jenkins Vineyard on Pleasant Hill Road just west of Sebastopol, but from 2005 it relied on a kaleidoscope of western Sonoma sources. In 2005 Lynmar also began a series of vineyard-designated wines from non-estate fruit, debuting this program with a small Jenkins Vineyard bottling, followed in 2006 with a second edition of Jenkins and a first edition of Hawk Hill Vineyard, a windy, late-ripening site near Freestone planted to Dijon 115 and UCD 4.

Since his arrival in 2004, Chappelle has embraced a "feminine and delicate" style for Lynmar estate pinots, believing that the site is not destined to make "muscular" wines. He picks when the skin tannins "are no longer chalky" and the pulp "has flavor," which usually means Brix levels between 23 and a bit over 25. He is content to have some lots riper than others, so that lots of lower-alcohol wines can be back-blended with higher-alcohol lots later.

As much as 30 percent of the harvested fruit is retained in the form of whole clusters because stems can "moderate extraction and generate aromatics." A half gram of acid per liter is sometimes added to the must, but enzyme additions are very rare. A three- to ten-day cold soak is standard and is enforced with dry ice. The fermentors are jacketed, stainless steel open-tops, and fermentations rely mostly on resident yeasts. The dry ice can return toward the end of the primary fermentation, in bags deposited on top of the cap, as a way to keep the cap fresh, to maintain an anaerobic environment, and to preserve "delicate fruit and floral aromas" when fermentations extend beyond about fifteen days. If any water has been added to compensate for Brix levels over 25, Chappelle compensates in turn for these by bleeding the must. The new wines are pressed off using a basket press, settled for twenty-four to seventy-two hours to eliminate "gross sludge," and barreled.

Two thirds of the barrel stock is either Remond or François Frères and relies mostly on wood from the Tronçais forest, never toasted more than medium, and never augmented with toasted heads. Between 40 and 45 percent of the estate wine and non-estate vineyard-designates are raised in new wood for sixteen to eighteen months. The appellation wine spends a few months less in barrel and sees a lower percentage of new wood. Generally, Lynmar pinots are neither fined nor filtered, but turbidity is measured with a nephalometer before bottling, and Chappelle strives to ensure that it stays under 20 NTUs. Overall, Chappelle explains that he is trying to "capture the purity of pinot noir" and to work "naturally but with sensitivity to the biochemistry of the wine."

Chappelle is making some extremely pretty pinots, and the brand's expansion to include vineyard-designated wines from sites other than Quail Hill helps to showcase his talent. Tasted in their youth, the estate wines from Quail Hill sometimes seem to lack the clarity of expression that one expects from Laguna Ridge. A recent tasting of library wines was reassuring, however: a few years of bottle age help enormously (see below).

TASTING NOTES
2005 *Quail Hill Vineyard (tasted twice in 2007):* Transparent, medium

garnet; slightly exotic nose that displays mixed red fruit laced with hints of nuts and violets; opens with brewed black tea infused with bits of dried fruit and flowers; turns creamy, peppery, and slightly warm at mid-palate; warmth persists to the finish; medium in length.

2005 *Jenkins Vineyard (tasted in 2007):* Transparent, medium-dark purplish-ruby; fruit-driven nose of blueberry, cranberry, Italian plum, violets, and herbs; intense and nicely delineated on the palate, with the tar and fruit-essence profile that often typifies the Sebastopol Hills; nicely structured mid-palate; long and attractive.

2005 *Five Sisters (tasted in 2007):* Luminous, medium-deep magenta; allspice, tar, and licorice on the nose; rich, round, and elegant on the palate; slightly fruit-sweet with dark cherry on the mid-palate; wet slate and quite black at the end; substantial but still elegant, with grip.

2005 *Russian River Valley (tasted in 2007):* Transparent, medium black-red; aromas of hard spice and dried ancho chili; dark cherry, black pepper, and black licorice on the palate; slightly sweet, soft, silky, and round, with barely a suggestion of fine-grained tannin at the end.

2002 *Quail Cuvée (tasted in 2008):* Very transparent, medium black-red verging toward mahogany; aromas of fading raspberry, wood smoke, gum camphor, and creosote; bright raspberry on the palate with good length and medium weight; fine.

1994 *Quail Hill Cuvée (tasted from magnum in 2008):* Well-developed mahogany color, orange at the rim; leather and boot polish on the nose; intense on the palate with some faded fruit, cocoa, and milk chocolate; soft, rich, ripe, and fully mature with a satiny texture; fine.

MAHONEY VINEYARDS AND FLEUR DE CALIFORNIA
Napa, California

Francis Mahoney, a native San Franciscan drawn to the wine trade by postcollegiate travels in Europe and seasoned with experience importing European wines and managing vineyards for Mayacamas Winery, purchased a ravine in the ranchland of Los Carneros in 1972. The hilly terrain and rocky subsoils reminded him of Burgundy; the morning fog and cool days seemed to assure a long growing season. Construction of a winery building began in 1973. Although Louis Martini had preceded him in Carneros and André Tchelistcheff had encouraged him, Mahoney's venture, in which he was joined by his wife Kathleen and partner Balfour Gibson, was still a pioneering effort, waged against the consensus of specialist opinion, and its heart and raison d'être was pinot noir.

Unique among the pinot pioneers of the 1970s, Mahoney suspected that, after soil and climate, clones might be the third most important factor in making great pinot. Simultaneously, he planted about 7 acres to best-bet clones selected for their performance in other vineyards, and a 1.5-acre plot dedicated to tiny, experimental replicates of 20 clones and field selections. This second plot, known variously as the Clonal Selection Plot and the Carneros Creek Clonal Trial, was a seminal event in the evolution of North American pinot noir, even though it was ultimately overtaken by interest in the clones that became available from France in the 1990s. It provided systematic comparative data on clonal performance, a planting guide for further vineyard development at Carneros Creek, budwood for dozens of other vineyards throughout California, and eventually the plant material for further trials and subsequent dissemination via Foundation Plant Services at the University of California Davis. Its third phase is actually still under way.

In the 1980s and 1990s, Mahoney planted vineyards around his residence on Dealy Lane, east of the winery; on a 37-acre site on the upslope side of Dealy Lane, known sometimes as Las Lomas and sometimes as the Mahoney Ranch; and finally at Las Brisas, a 95-acre site consisting of gently sloping sand and gravel, on Ramel Road. Because Las Lomas is a warmish site for Carneros, Mahoney eventually planted a bit of syrah in its warmest northwestern corner. Las Brisas, first planted entirely to various selections of pinot noir, chosen primarily on the strength of their performance in the trial, eventually also became home, after a visit with his wife's Italian family in 2000, to small plantings of vermentino, montepulciano, and tempranillo. Both estate vineyards are distinguished by a preponderance of Swan selection, UCD 107, and something called Carneros Creek selection, all of which have a tendency to ripen unevenly. These selections seem to favor red fruit characteristics even when they are picked at relatively high Brix levels.

Alongside the vineyards, Mahoney's pinot program also expanded to include two initiatives designed to produce substantial volumes of entry-level wines, called Côte de Carneros and Fleur de Carneros, made primarily from purchased fruit. Côte de Carneros was abandoned in 2000; Fleur, established in 1987, is still alive and well. It is a smaller program than it was in the 1990s, however, and has been renamed Fleur de California.

In 1998, to finance further expansion, Mahoney sold a majority share in Carneros Creek to Bill Hambrecht, a San Francisco–based investment banker with several decades of close involvement with California wine. This infusion of funds was followed, rather rapidly, by a whirlwind of changes. Melissa Moravec, who had managed Mahoney's clonal trials in the 1980s and served as winemaker since 1989, departed. Mahoney retired from all activity save farming. Hambrecht acquired most (though not all) of Mahoney's remaining interest in the winery, whereas Mahoney retained ownership of all the vineyards, except the original 10-acre parcel immediately adjacent to the winery building on the downslope side of Dealy Lane. Scott Rich, who had been the day-to-day winemaker at ETUDE, took over Carneros Creek's winemaking duties in 2001, with a mandate to reverse the 1998 expansion and reposition the brand. Barely a year after his appointment, Rich was succeeded by Ken Foster, longtime winemaker at DAVID BRUCE. Hambrecht, whose Hambrecht Vineyards and Wineries (HVW) enterprise was forced to sell key assets in the economic downturn that followed 9/11, reduced his majority share in Carneros Creek at the beginning of 2003, at which point Mahoney resumed control. In 2004, Mahoney sold the Carneros Creek brand to the newly formed Briarcliff Wine Group, LLC; two years later the winery itself was sold to Folio Fine Wine Partners, which uses it as a production facility for their I'M, Oberon, and Hangtime brands. For the 2006 vintage, Carneros Creek, now owned by Briarcliff, and Mahoney Vineyards, still owned by Francis and Kathleen Mahoney, were tenants in the winery they previously owned; as of 2007 they are producing the wines in a new Carneros facility, although the aforementioned Ken Foster is still the winemaker for both. In 2007, Mahoney Vineyards owned 162 planted acres in Carneros, of which 149 were dedicated to pinot noir. In addition to supplying the Carneros Creek and Mahoney Vineyards brands, Mahoney Vineyards also sells fruit to a variety of smaller producers, many of whom make vineyard-designated wines from the Las Brisas Vineyard.

WINES AND WINEMAKING NOTES
The first vintage under the Mahoney Vineyards brand was vinted in 2004, although Carneros Creek made a Mahoney Estate wine beginning in 1991, sold primarily in the Carneros Creek tasting room and to the Ireland market. Initially there were three pinots made from estate-grown fruit. The two flagship wines are vineyard-designated cuvées from the Mahoney Ranch and Las Brisas vineyards, respectively, and a Carneros bottling blended from the two sites. From 2002 to 2004 there was also a Haire Vineyard bottling, from Jim Haire's nearby ranch.

The Mahoney Vineyard wines are essentially a barrel selection from among the 25 to 30 lots made from the estate vineyards. Typically these are fermented in lots of 8 to 14 tons, in a mix of open-top, auto-punch, and closed-top tanks. All fruit is destemmed. Assmannshausen, RC212, and BRL97 yeasts are used, and vattings average twelve days. Only free-run juice is used in the Mahoney Vineyards wines. New oak is on the decline, now between 10 and 30 percent, and the barrel regime is moving toward greater reliance on lighter levels of toast that "respect fruit character." The wines are not racked until blending, just before the following vintage, at which point lots destined for the two vineyard-designated bottlings are returned to barrel for an additional four or five months in wood. The wines are not fined, but cross-flow filtration is practiced before bottling. Existence of the Fleur and Carneros Creek brands (even though the latter is not owned by Mahoney Vineyards) means that only about 20 percent of total production goes to Mahoney Vineyards wine. They are elegant and attractive pinots, nicely built and typical of Carneros.

TASTING NOTES
2004 *Las Brisas Vineyard (tasted in 2007):* Pretty, brilliant light-to-medium garnet; earthy-floral nose with a hint of soft spice; soft and silky on the palate with some earthy depth and intensity; background of raspberry; light-to-medium weight and medium length; elegant and attractive.

2004 *Mahoney Ranch (tasted in 2007):* Transparent, medium garnet; aromas of cherry, raspberry, and barrel char; slightly sweet and fruit-forward impression with considerable clove and cinnamon spice, and a hint of orange peel; medium-weight, soft, and lightly mouth-coating with good length and a peppery bite at the end.

MARIMAR ESTATE
Sebastopol, California

Marimar Torres is the youngest child and only daughter of Miguel Torres Carbó (1909–1991), the distinguished winemaker and entrepreneur who built Bodegas Torres—a Catalan firm anchored in the Penedes—into the largest family-owned wine business in Spain. Known internationally for proprietary blends like Viña Sol, Sangre de Toro, and Gran Coronas, Bodegas Torres was founded in the middle of the nineteenth century, when Miguel's great-great-uncle worked his way to the Americas as a cabin boy, and then parlayed a fortuitous investment in Cuban oil into the beginnings of a wine empire.

Marimar joined the family firm in 1967, armed with a degree in business and economics from the Universitat de Barcelona and fluency in six languages. Although she worked initially as export

---

A PANOPLY OF FLAVORS AND AROMATIC INTEREST IN AN ELEGANT, NICELY BALANCED PACKAGE

---

director, and then as Torres's resident representative in North America, she followed the American wine scene with enough attention that, early in the 1980s, the family firm was persuaded to expand its business beyond Spain and Chile to include grape growing and winemaking in California.

At this point Marimar was not especially passionate about pinot noir, and the family's experience elsewhere was concentrated in warm-climate varieties, but the purchase in 1983 of a 56-acre parcel west of Graton, just 10 miles as the crow flies from the Pacific Coast, argued for a wine program focused on pinot and chardonnay. This so-called Don Miguel vineyard, named in honor of Marimar's father, is a narrow, northeast–southwest-oriented parcel fronting on Graton Road about halfway between Graton and Occidental. The upslope, which faces mostly eastward, is fairly steep, gaining about 400 feet from roadside to hilltop. The soils are almost entirely Goldridge loam, reddish in some spots, yellowish in others.

The first 14 acres of pinot noir were planted in 1988 and 1989; 2.5 acres were added between 1992 and 1994. Ten additional acres of pinot were added in 1995, 1996, and 1997, at which time 4 acres of chardonnay were also grafted to pinot. A small (0.9-acre) block, planted 3 feet by 3 feet, was set out in 2000.

The 1980s plantings were made with field-selected budwood from various North Coast sources. For the 6 acres planted in 1988, Torres used wood from the Eliot Vineyard on Big Ranch Road in Napa that was first dubbed Beringer Selection for its presumed upstream source. Now called Cristina 88, it is probably none other than one of the Martini clones distributed by FPMS in the 1960s. The balance of the 1980s plantings were Swan selection from DEHLINGER WINERY, Lee selection from IRON HORSE VINEYARDS, and UCD 4 from ADELSHEIM VINEYARD in Oregon via SAINTSBURY. Dijon 115, 667, and 777 were added in the 1990s, along with more Swan and UCD 4 propagated from the 1980s plantings. Typical spacing is 2,000 vines per acre, though several blocks are set out 3 feet by 3 feet, and about 3 tons are harvested per acre, or 3 pounds of fruit per vine.

An entirely separate second vineyard, located in rugged terrain near Freestone and named Doña Margarita in honor of Marimar's mother, was planted to 10 acres of pinot in 2002. Since 2003 both vineyards have been farmed organically and have been certified organic since 2006.

WINES AND WINEMAKING NOTES
Apart from a special bottling of so-called Vineyard Selection made once in 1992, only one pinot was made at Marimar Estate until 2002. The winemaking team, which consists of Torres, technical director Bill Dyer, and cellarmaster Tony

Britton, is said to have felt that the best wine from the Don Miguel vineyard was, consistently, a blend made from all the producing blocks, without special selection or deselection.

Beginning in 2002, however, and perhaps stemming from the beginnings of the property's transition to organic farming, one block of the aforementioned Cristina selection seemed to stand out for separate attention and has been made on its own in every vintage since. Torres observes that the vineyard has been healthier, and the vines in better balance, since organic protocols were adopted, making for more even ripening and slightly fleshier wines that, in her words, have "more personality."

Additional block-designated wines, called Earthquake (for the visible fault line that bisects the block) and Stony Block, debuted in 2003, and a wine from the Doña Margarita Vineyard made its first appearance in 2004. Although the block-designates tend to be a bit blacker, bigger, and weightier than the main estate bottling, and Doña Margarita displays the wilder properties often associated with the True Sonoma Coast, the Marimar pinots are elegant, medium-weight wines overall, with long finishes and great organoleptic complexity. They also age very rewardingly; see the note on the 1996 wine below, tasted in 2007.

The fruit is normally destemmed and slightly crushed, although the Lee selection grapes, which are usually the last to be picked, sometimes display stems ripe enough to be retained as whole clusters. A three-day cold soak precedes inoculation, and primary fermentation temperatures peak between 85 and 90°F. The must is pressed at dryness, and the press fraction is recombined with the free-run juice. The barrel regime involves about 33 percent new oak for the estate wines, 50 percent for the Earthquake Block, and up to 80 percent for the Cristina.

Since 1998 the main sources of cooperage have been Rousseau, Radoux, and Seguin Moreau. All lots are inoculated to initiate the malolactic fermentation, and the wine spends between twelve and fourteen months in wood. A first racking is done as soon as the malolactic fermentation is over "so that the wine will not need to be filtered," and the blends are established. A second racking is done prior to bottling. The 1997 vintage was fined with egg whites both for clarity and for tannin management, but there has been no filtration since 1996. The wine is held in bottle for twelve months before release.

The estate blend from the Don Miguel Vineyard remains my favorite of the Marimar Estate pinots, despite the recent appearance of block designates, and the first vintages from the newer Doña Margarita Vineyard. The estate blend can be shy in its youth, but it tends to blossom quite beautifully after four or five years in the bottle, displaying a panoply of flavors and aromatic interest in a nicely balanced, very food-friendly package.

TASTING NOTES

2004 *Earthquake Block (tasted in 2007):* Very deep, barely transparent black red; sage and bay laurel on the nose; slightly sweet, dark fruited attack; then smoky, mouth coating and noticeably grippy; impressive, almost daunting structure; probably a *vin de garde*.

2004 *Stony Block (tasted in 2007):* Transparent, medium magenta; preponderantly earthy and minerally aromas with highlights of red fruit; intensely fruity attack featuring very pure essence of fruit like *eau-de-vie*; noticeable fine-grained tannins; a mineral-driven wine on the mid-palate and finish; leaves a serious, almost austere, impression; finishes long.

2004 *Cristina (tasted in 2007):*
Transparent, medium-deep garnet; cherry-plum aromas with hints of herb and citrus; sweet attack followed by intense minerality; cherry-plum flavors persist; mouth coating with a solid load of very fine grained tannins; long and nicely structured; overall impression of crushed velvet.

2004 *Doña Margarita Vineyard (tasted in 2007):* Deep, barely transparent blood red; underbrush, black fruit, plum skin, and mesquite on the nose; rich dark fruit with tar and earthy properties and black cherry; silky mid-palate gives way to a slightly gritty finish with considerable fine-grained tannin; serious, dense and weightier than the Don Miguel wines.

2002 *Cristina (tasted in 2006 and 2007):* Deep crimson just barely turning toward mahogany; dark fruit aromas with black pepper and resin; on the palate, camphor, mint, and pepper wrapped around dried cherry and plum flavors; lots of wet slate and related minerality; dense and velvety.

1996 *Don Miguel Vineyard (tasted twice, in 2007 and 2008):* Deep, brilliant crimson; engaging nose of pepper and spice with floral highlights; an intense and very precisely built wine with attractive structure, bright cherry flavors, and minerality, plus a hint of roasted red pepper; almost velvety at mid-palate, then a bit of grip from mid-palate to finish; very fine and possibly nearing the apogee of its evolution.

MAYSARA WINERY
McMinnville, Oregon

Moe Momtazi is an Iranian-American engineer trained at the University of Texas Austin, who has made his life in the United States since the fall of the Iranian monarchy in 1979. The family's Tecna Industries, Inc., which manufactures trusses for residential construction, has thrived in McMinnville, Oregon since 1995.

In 1997 Momtazi and his wife Flora purchased 500 acres southwest of McMinnville, in the foothills of the Coast Range, consisting partially of forest and partially of abandoned wheat farm, where they set about developing a vineyard the following year. The property covers a large range of elevation, from about 250 feet to about 860 feet, and includes multiple soil types, including the volcanic Nekia and Jory series, and the sedimentary Peavine and Yamhill series.

Thirteen acres of own-rooted UCD 4 were planted first on easy-to-cultivate lowland; more vineyard was then planted in the abandoned wheat fields at the property's high end; the forested, hillside sectors in between have been tackled bit by bit along the way. Some new blocks have been planted each year since 1999, with grafted vines. The grafted vines were bench grafts created in Momtazi's onsite nursery operation. The first of these involved purchased rootstock and Dijon clones; a second phase used budwood taken from the original UCD 4 vines.

Farming has been resolutely sustainable; the vineyard has renounced pesticides and herbicides from the outset, grown a variety of plants and herbs for compost teas, maintained multiple compost piles, and largely followed biodynamic protocols. In 2007 the vineyard consisted of more than 200 planted acres, planted in 7-foot rows with 5 feet between vines, of which about three quarters are dedicated to the UCD 4 and Dijon clones of pinot noir. About 60 percent of the vineyard's fruit is sold to other makers, among whom it has established an enviable reputation for meticulous farming and for the highest possible quality. SCOTT PAUL WINES, BELLE VALLÉE CELLARS, FRANCIS TANNAHILL, and other makers use Momtazi fruit.

Maysara Winery was founded in 2000, when the vineyard was beginning to bear, and its first vintage was 2001. Like the nursery, the production facility is located onsite. The late Jimi Brooks was the founding winemaker, and also the manager of the Momtazi Vineyard. Brooks made the 2001, 2002, and 2003 vintages; his assistant

---

A SUCCESSFUL COMBINATION OF MODEST ALCOHOLS, BRIGHT FLAVORS, AND A FRUIT-DRIVEN PROFILE

Chris Williams finished the 2003s and made the 2004s; Todd Hamina, who was previously at PATTON VALLEY VINEYARDS, finished the 2004s and made the two subsequent vintages. In 2007 the reins passed to Tamina Momtazi, Moe Momtazi's daughter, who had been the assistant winemaker for several years. She was trained in fermentation science at Oregon State University, and she apprenticed with several Willamette Valley producers.

WINES AND WINEMAKING NOTES
Although Maysara purchases some fruit for its pinot gris and rosé programs, the pinot noir program has been based entirely on estate grown grapes from the beginning. From 2001 through 2003 there were three pinots: an estate cuvée and a barrel selection called Delara, both made from the 1998 planting of own-rooted UCD 4, and a Willamette Valley Reserve,

drawn from all bearing blocks. In 2004 the name of the Williamette Valley cuvée was changed to Jamsheed. In 2005 a fourth wine debuted, called Mitra. This is a barrel selection from among the lots otherwise destined for Delara: just four barrels of Mitra were made in 2005, and six in 2006.

Many, but not all, of the pinots are fermented with some whole clusters intact, and the tank caps are managed with the same Pulse-Air system used at BENTON-LANE WINERY. Peak fermentation temperatures range between 88 and 92°F, and extended macerations are typical; the new wines are barreled without settling, are kept in wood for less than twelve months, and are racked just once before bottling. Use of new barrels is conservative, ranging from less than 10 percent for Jamsheed to a maximum of about 45 percent for the estate cuvée.

The wines are an interesting and successful combination of modest alcohols, bright flavors and a fruit-driven profile that makes them appealing, approachable, and quite food-friendly.

TASTING NOTES
2005 *Jamsheed (tasted in 2007):* Transparent, intense, medium-deep ruby; expressive nose of dusty fruit and soft spice with a hint of roasted nuts; intense on the palate, with bright cherry-cranberry fruit, a hint of plum, and some ink; a few notes of hard spice and juniper berry; nicely built with attractive grip and acidity. Very good value.
2005 *Delara (tasted in 2007):* Transparent, medium-deep blackish ruby; lovely nose of fresh flowers, citrus peel, and berry fruit; intense and bright on the palate; a substantial load of very fine-grained tannins; almost velvety impression at mid-palate; bright acidity and a slightly chalky finish; very attractive.

2005 *Mitra (tasted in 2007):* Almost opaque ruby-aubergine color with rosy highlights; elegant nose redolent of slightly dusty red and black fruit with vanilla; lavish, almost exuberant attack; then serious and well structured at mid-palate; a bit of pencil lead and peppery spice; long and extremely attractive.

MELVILLE VINEYARD AND WINERY

Lompoc, California

Ron Melville remembers discovering wine, as a counterpoint to his contemporaries' enthusiasm for beer, when he was enrolled at Pasadena City College in 1959. Then, over a four-decade career as a floor specialist for the Pacific Stock Exchange, he developed a substantial passion for California cabernets. After the stock market's meltdown in 1987, he acquired a vineyard in Knight's Valley to "diversify" his assets. The site, which was too cool for the grape varieties to which it had been planted, was a better learning experience than investment.

In 1992 Melville found himself dining in an Aspen, Colorado, restaurant that had decided to feature Santa Barbara County pinots for a month-long promotion. With no cabernet in sight, he chose an early vintage of AU BON CLIMAT pinot noir, and "flipped out." Within a year, he was looking for a place to grow pinot of his own. In 1996 he moved (from Laguna Beach) to Santa Barbara. Then, in rapid-fire succession, Melville bought two parcels "of sandy, depleted soil" just west and east of BABCOCK WINERY AND VINEYARDS, planted pinot, chardonnay, syrah, and viognier; was joined in the new business

by his sons Chad and Brent; decided not just to grow grapes but also to make wine; hired Greg Brewer, then at Santa Barbara Winery, as winemaker-to-be; and exchanged the Knight's Valley vineyard for a parcel in Cat Canyon where he planted 53 additional acres.

By 2005 Melville Vineyards was farming 135 acres of vines in a combination of the Sta. Rita Hills and the Los Alamos Valley, and using 95 percent of its total crop for an estate wine program under the Melville label. Although several blocks on the Sta. Rita Hills site were originally custom planted for other winemakers, by 2005 the only fruit clients for Melville's pinot were Bonaccorsi Wine Company, BREWER-CLIFTON, WHITCRAFT WINES, and Samsara. Samsara is the personal project of Chad Melville and his wife Mary, devoted to syrah and (since 2005) to pinot noir.

The Sta. Rita Hills vineyard adjacent to Babcock consists of about 63 acres of pinot in eighteen small blocks. Fourteen selections—possibly the largest palette in any single California vineyard—are planted in mostly deep but well-drained, gritty, alluvial soils, although a few hilltop blocks display shallow clay-loam over a hard pan. Vine spacings are mostly tight: either 4- or 8-foot rows with 3-foot intervine spacing. Despite the large repertory of selections, the majority tenant is Dijon 115, which anchors the Melville pinot program. The first fruit from the Los Alamos vineyard, named for Ron Melville's mother Verna, appeared in 2001.

WINES AND WINEMAKING NOTES
Melville has made an estate pinot since 1999, and this bottling has carried the new Sta. Rita Hills appellation since 2000. In addition, since 2000, Melville has set aside a few barrels of pinot for what it calls the "Small Lot Collection." From one to four

barrels produced from the highest density plantings have been released as Estate Pinot Noir—High Density. A single fermentor has also been held aside for an indigenous yeast fermentation, and the four-barrel product from this fermentor has been released as Estate Pinot Noir—Clone 115 Indigène. A block-designated pinot named Carrie's, made from one of the estate's veins of clay-loam soil planted entirely to Dijon 114 and 115, debuted in 2001. Terraces, another block-designated release from a steep portion of the vineyard farmed in narrow belts that follow the contour of the slope with (consequently) almost every imaginable row orientation, and combines two California heritage selections of pinot (Swan and Mount Eden) with three Dijon clones, was first made separately in 2002. Beginning in 2004, Melville has also made microscopic quantities of single-clone pinots, drawing on the vineyard's unusually large repertory. One barrel each of Clone 5, Clone 667, and Clone 113 was bottled separately in 2004; two barrels each of Clones 9, 777, and 828 followed in 2005.

The small lot program is possible only because all fermentations at Melville are done in small, 1.5-ton, double-height fruit bins, each of which is pressed separately to four barrels of which only one is new, and because each lot of four barrels is kept separate—until the final choices have been made for both the small lot program and the estate blend—after the first racking in the spring following the vintage. Other peculiarities of viticulture and winemaking at Melville are a substantial reliance on whole clusters (the estate wine tallies to between 25 and 50 percent whole clusters depending on the vintage); aggressive leaf-pulling both to maximize phenological development and to encourage stem lignification; no sprayed sulfur in the vineyard after fruit set; no use of sulfur dioxide in the wines until after the first

racking; a long vatting consisting of a week's cold soak, two weeks' fermentation, and a week of extended maceration; process additions limited to yeast and yeast nutrients only; a barrel regime that relies on just three coopers: Sirugue, Rousseau, and Mercurey; and bottling that is done by gravity.

Melville pinots almost always clock in above 15 percent alcohol, but are attractively balanced otherwise, thanks to the good acid retention that typifies Sta. Rita Hills wines overall, with silky, long-chain tannins apparently encouraged by the extended maceration. The mark of whole cluster fermentations is clear, but the effect is salubrious, giving wines that are aromatically complex and often marked by notes of orange/spice tea.

TASTING NOTES

2005 *Verna's (tasted in* 2006*):* Brilliant light-to-medium rosy-magenta; perfumed with potpourri, rose petals, and red berries; more strawberry and raspberry on the palate with licorice and white pepper; light-to-medium in weight, and very slightly grippy; medium length.

2005 *Estate (tasted in* 2006*):* Medium black-red; potpourri and dried leaves on the nose; cherry, resin, and tar on the palate with hints of tree bark, clove, and licorice; concentrated, medium-long, and suede-textured.

2004 *Terraces (tasted in* 2006*):* Transparent, medium-dark garnet; rose petal and earth aromas; cassis and blackberry fruit dominate the palate; some licorice, black pepper, resin, and even fruit jam, with notes of mocha; sweet, grippy, and warm on the finish; satiny in texture.

2004 *Carrie's (tasted in* 2006*):* Transparent, medium-dark black-red; some floral notes and some resin; very sweet on the palate, with black cherry, cassis, blackberry, and cola, plus a tar-y note; smooth, almost creamy texture; long and warm.

MERRY EDWARDS WINES
Windsor, California

Merry Edwards is something of a legend in the California wine business, a trail blazer for many women who have become winemakers since, and a near-pioneer in its pursuit of fine pinot noir. An avid cook and food scientist whose fascination with yeast led her from bread to beer and then to wine, she was an amateur winemaker even before she graduated from the University of California Berkeley with a degree in physiology. Fascinated to discover, soon thereafter, that formal coursework and "real" academic degrees were offered in her avocation, she enrolled in the then-obscure program at the University of California Davis, where she earned a master's degree in food science with an emphasis in enology in 1973. Her class was the first to graduate women, and Edwards was the only one of her female classmates to pursue winemaking as a career. As a winemaker, she is credited with the development of two well-respected California brands: MOUNT EDEN VINEYARDS in the Santa Cruz Mountains and Matanzas Creek Winery in Sonoma's Bennett Valley. Subsequent ventures in the mid and late 1980s—a family enterprise called The Merry Vintners, and Domaine Laurier, the child of an ill-fated investment company that built the winery now used by HARTFORD FAMILY WINERY—both succumbed to economic recession, but Edwards worked successfully throughout

the 1990s as a consultant to various California wineries, including Liparita, Nelson Estate, Lambert Bridge, B. R. Cohn, and Pellegrini Family.

Edwards made legendary pinot noir at Mount Eden. The 1974, 1975, and 1976 vintages of this wine, along with the 1973 made by Dick Graff, were turnaround benchmarks as pinot noir clawed its way back from the qualitative nadir of the late 1960s and early 1970s. She also made pinot for three of the seven years she worked at Matanzas Creek, using fruit from the Quail Hill Vineyard (see LYNMAR WINERY) in the Russian River Valley. In 1997 Edwards launched a new all-pinot venture called Meredith Vineyard Estate, a privately held corporation created to underwrite the planting of her Meredith Estate vineyard and the production of Merry Edwards Wines. In that year, she purchased fruit from several mature vineyards around Russian River and planted a 24-acre parcel just outside the then-existing southern periphery of the appellation, on Burnside Road, southwest of Sebastopol.

The mature sources were the Klopp Ranch on Laguna Road, a 1989 planting of Swan selection and UCD 4 in the Laguna Ridge section of Russian River, and Robert Pellegrini's OLIVET LANE VINEYARD. Windsor Gardens, a stand of 33-year-old UCD 13 leased by Lee Martinelli, was added in 1999. Edwards has continued to source pinot from Olivet Lane and Klopp Ranch and has added two other non-estate sites to her list: Tobias Glen, a cool, southeast-facing 6-acre vineyard near Forestville, and Flax, which is adjacent to Allen Ranch on Westside Road.

Meredith Estate, the first of Edwards's estate vineyards, is a cool, south-facing slope heavily influenced by marine air sucked in from the ocean through the Petaluma Gap. The scion material here is Dijon 115, 667, and 777, plus Swan and

UCD 37, a certified clone propagated from budwood Edwards personally selected at Mount Eden. Meredith Estate produced its first significant crop in 2000.

In 2001, having finally downsized her consulting business, Edwards planted a second estate vineyard bearing her husband's name. This Coopersmith Vineyard is 9.5 acres of south- and southeast-facing hillside where the Gravenstein Highway intersects Graton Road. Coopersmith is planted to a combination of UCD 37 and *soi-disant* Dijon 828 sourced from Archery Summit in Oregon, and the vineyard is configured in 8-foot rows with 5-foot spacing between vines. Its first small crop was harvested in 2003.

A third estate vineyard, called Georganne, planted entirely to UCD 37 on 7 acres of leased land on Westside Road, will begin bearing in 2008; a fourth, called Cresta d'Oro, is 8 acres immediately adjacent to Meredith Estate planted in 2005 to UCD 37 and Dijon 667, plus a bit of sauvignon blanc to feed the white wine program Edwards launched in 2001.

Winemaking was itinerant from 1997 through 2006. The first vintages were made at Lambert Bridge and Michel Schlumberger in Dry Creek Valley, the 2003 and 2004 at Taft Street Winery in Sebastopol, and the 2005 and 2006 at Moshin Winery. The Pellegrini facility on Olivet Lane was used to make all Edwards's wines in 2001 and 2002, and the Olivet Lane wine through 2006. A custom-built facility co-located with the Coopersmith Vineyard was finished in time to receive the 2007 harvest.

WINES AND WINEMAKING NOTES
The pinot program is based on a combination of blended and vineyard-designated wines. A vineyard-designated wine from the Olivet Lane Vineyard, and a

Russian River Valley cuvée, blended from three to seven sources that have varied from year to year, have each been made in every vintage since the brand debuted in 1997. Klopp Ranch and Windsor Gardens joined the list of vineyard-designated wines in 1999. Windsor Gardens was produced until the vineyard fell victim to a developer's bulldozers in 2003; Klopp was vineyard-designated in 1999, 2000, and 2003, but has played an important role in the Russian River blend throughout. In 2000 ten barrels of the first harvest from the Meredith Estate vineyard were made as a vineyard-designated wine, and a Meredith Estate wine has been made in each vintage since. (Until 2005 the Meredith Estate site was inside the boundary of the Sonoma Coast appellation, but outside the boundary of the Russian River Valley AVA; since 2005 it has carried the Russian River Valley designation.) Meanwhile, a Sonoma Coast appellation wine was launched in 2001, built from lighter lots of Meredith Estate fruit and from purchased fruit in the Sebastopol Hills area. Vineyard-designated wines from Tobias Glen and Flax debuted in 2006.

Edwards picks by taste and says she finds that Russian River pinot generally tastes ripe somewhere between 24 and 25.5 Brix. Rows destined for vineyard-designation, identified before harvest, are segregated, fermented in 4.5- and 5-ton stainless steel open-tops, and punched down manually or with the aid of pneumatic *piges*. The rest of the fruit, which is used in the Russian River or Sonoma Coast blends, is fermented in conventional 10-ton tanks, in which juice from the bottom of the tank is pumped over the cap. Interestingly, this difference in technique, often described as fundamental, seems to have only a modest impact on the style of the resulting wines.

Edwards reports that, in recent vintages, she has reduced the proportion of fruit she ferments as whole clusters and reduced the length and intensity of her cold soaks. She still prefers relatively warm fermentations with cultured yeasts because she "likes to be in control." Edwards argues that "if you get grapes really ripe, you must add acid," and she does. Asked about persistent reports that she de-alcoholizes some lots before making her final blends, Edwards replied that "some of my winemaking techniques are proprietary and not up for discussion."

The must is generally pressed at dryness, although some lots have seen extended macerations since 2001. Barrel regimes are tailored to each cuvée—"with time," Edwards explains, "it becomes clear that certain barrels work better for certain wines." Across the board, she uses only new and one-year-old barrels from six cooperages—François Frères, Dargaud & Jaeglé, Mercurey, Tonnellerie Doreau (a Cognac-based cooper), Cadus, and Remond. The barrels are ordered in several different toastings. The Russian River Valley cuvée sees about 60 percent new oak from a mix of the aforementioned coopers; about the same percentage is used for the estate wine, but in this case, most of the barrels are Mercurey. Olivet Lane sees about 85 percent new wood, also from the mix of coopers, but Dargaud & Jaeglé barrels were preferred for the Windsor Gardens bottling when it was made.

Lees are sometimes stirred in barrel, and all wines are racked and blended in the spring after the vintage, and then returned to barrel until bottling, which takes place just before the following vintage. Wines are rarely fined—Edwards "abhors" the technique, believing it invariably results in a loss of aroma—but all wines are filtered (generally with diatomaceous earth) on the theory that such treatment "improves the brightness of the wine's aromas." Edwards describes her ideal pinot noir with words like *luscious, opulent,* and *concentrated.*

Her emphasis on "perfectly ripe fruit" and a high percentage of new oak yields big wines, and some vintages of some wines have been heftily tannic in their youth. Although she was not around to taste them, Edwards says she has "a mental image" of what old Burgundies were like, and that these old Burgundies serve her as a model. From the very first vintage, Edwards's wines have received high praise from the wine press and from fellow winemakers, one of whom described her 1997 Russian River Valley cuvée as his image of the "perfect" California pinot noir. I was personally fond of the Windsor Gardens wine while it was made and have especially liked several vintages of the wines anchored with Meredith Estate fruit.

TASTING NOTES

2004 *Russian River Valley (tasted in 2007):* Transparent, medium ruby; roasted dark fruit and toasted nuts; peppery, slightly sweet, and slightly creamy, but an overall impression of omnipresent, fine-grained tannin; finishes warm.

2001 *Olivet Lane (tasted in 2004):* Transparent, medium garnet; explosive nose of pine sap, gum camphor, and cinnamon over very ripe fruit; viscous, mouth coating, and rich on the palate, flavors of pepper, hard spice, and dark cherry but not predominantly fruity; hints of orange peel, chocolate, and underbrush; long, full bodied, and almost velvety.

2001 *Klopp Ranch (tasted in 2004):* Medium-dark purplish-red; aromas of cinnamon, tobacco, and orange peel; black cherry, ripe plum, black pepper, and Carborundum in a rich, plush, and slightly chewy package; very full bodied, long, and warm.

MINER FAMILY VINEYARDS
Oakville, California

Miner Family Vineyards has its origins in the Oakville Ranch Vineyard, on the east side of Napa Valley's Oakville appellation, which Dave Miner's aunt and uncle acquired and planted in the 1980s; in the software industry, where both segments of the family accumulated financial resources; and in Miner's passionate interest in wines as various as sangiovese from Mendocino, viognier from the Central Valley, and pinot noir from the Santa Lucia Highlands. Although the core of the portfolio consists of cabernet- and merlot-based wines from Napa, it was an unusual edition of chardonnay fermented with resident yeasts, first made in the 1997 vintage, that established the brand's reputation.

The winemaker, from the outset in 1996, has been Gary Brookman, a southern Californian with prior experience at Joseph Phelps Winery and at Franciscan Estates. It was Brookman's time at Franciscan, where he crafted (among other things) the Monterey-based wines sold under the Estancia label, that defined Miner's path of entry to pinot noir. Brookman had purchased pinot noir from Gary Pisoni (see PISONI VINEYARD AND WINERY) for Estancia; in 1997 he returned to Pisoni for a few tons of fruit to launch Miner's pinot program. Almost immediately, Pisoni's explosive popularity among cult makers of California pinot limited the quantity of Pisoni fruit Miner could expect to receive. Pisoni's joint venture with friend and neighbor Gary Franscioni, called Garys' Vineyard (see ROAR WINES), generated an alternative.

Miner made vineyard-designated pinots from the Pisoni Vineyard in 1997 and 1998, and a blended pinot from a combination of Pisoni and Garys' fruit in 1999; thereafter, Garys' anchored the program, joined by a second vineyard-designate, from Franscioni's Rosella's Vineyard, in 2002. A special bottling of wine, made from the Dijon 777 planting at Rosella's, was made beginning in 2003.

Brookman's characterization of the three wines is apt: Garys' makes the "older brother" wine, Rosella's resembles the feminine sibling, and the clone-specific bottling of Dijon 777 seems like Rosella's eligible but still unmarried younger sister. All three wines display consummate respect for pinot's distinctive varietal character. They are lovely, restrained, elegant editions of California pinot made for people who don't want to wonder if their glass has been filled with syrah-in-disguise.

All Miner pinots have been resident-yeast fermented since 2005—Rosella's was made this way from the beginning—and all fermentations take place in tiny, half-ton fruit bins. After four to five days of cold-soaking, the must is gently warmed to unleash the fermentation, and exceptionally gentle *pigeage* is done by humans with elbow-length gloves. Yeast nutrient is added to "give the wild yeasts an advantage over bacteria." Seven to ten days of extended maceration (after the must measures dry) precedes pressing, and the new wine goes to barrel quickly and dirty. The barrel regime lasts for fourteen to fifteen months, in 65 to 70 percent new oak that was primarily coopered by François Frères, with minority components from Latour and Sirugue.

TASTING NOTES

2005 *Garys' Vineyard (tasted in 2007):* Transparent, deep black-red; aromas driven by fruit and phenols; rich and almost creamy on the palate, with a strong impression of ripe cherries, sweet strawberries, and vanilla custard with some mocha; soft tannins with a bit of grip on the finish; lingering.

2005 *Rosella's Vineyard (tasted in 2007)*: Medium garnet; aromas of fading flowers and rosewater; mostly black raspberry on the palate, with fruit-sweetness, silky texture, and attractive length. An elegant but substantial wine.

2005 *Rosella's Vineyard 777 (tasted in 2007)*: Pretty, transparent, medium garnet; nutmeg and exotic spice, plus orange peel and rosewater on the nose; light-to-medium weight, and a chamois-like texture in the mouth; flavors of raspberry and orange flower water; intense and very appealing.

MIURA VINEYARDS
Santa Rosa, California

Emmanuel Kemiji is a Master Sommelier with impressive experience in hospitality management and retail wine sales. Like his high school friend and college roommate Byron Kosuge (who went on to a career in winemaking [see B. KOSUGE WINES]) Kemiji discovered wine in college, but in his case, outside the classroom. In fact Kemiji and Kosuge seem to have shared an autodidactic wine education during their time at Davis. Kosuge reports that the pair ate Top Ramen so that they could afford to drink bottles of very good wine, which they found, often unintentionally aged and gathering dust, on the so-called "Reserve Shelves" at Ernie's—a chain of large wine and spirits stores spread across northern California in the late 1970s.

Some years later, building on the contacts and expertise that people in the on-premise wine business forge with producers, Kemiji was tempted to try winemaking on his own, using a ton of pinot noir grapes from Roederer Estate

---

IMPRESSIVE WINES THAT DISPLAY AN ATTRACTIVE COUNTERPOINT OF SWEETNESS AND GRIP, FRUIT AND HERBS, BODY AND ELEGANCE

---

in Anderson Valley. This noncommercial debut, which was largely given away to Kemiji's friends in the wine and hospitality trades, was followed by a commercial release of chardonnay, made at TALLEY VINEYARDS from Talley grapes, in 1997.

By 1999 Kemiji had launched a successful wine label—Miura. (The name honors one of Spain's best-known breeders of fighting bulls.) The new label made small lots of quite a few wines, but its pinot program debuted with a vineyard-designated bottling from the well-known Pisoni Vineyard in the Santa Lucia Highlands. Miura's Pisoni comes from three separate blocks: Old Block, Hermanos Block, and Camper Block.

A pinot from Garys' Vineyard was added to the Miura portfolio in 2000; vineyard-designated pinots from Lee Hudson's Carneros vineyard and from David Hirsch's Sonoma Coast vineyard followed in 2002. In 2003 Kemiji added a Talley Vineyard pinot, using a seven-year-old block of Dijon 115 and 777 from the Rincon Vineyard's west hill, and a vineyard-designated wine from Robert Silacci's vineyard near Chualar in Monterey County, a cool and late-ripening site that had been planted with budwood from the Pisoni Vineyard in 1999. (The Hudson and Hirsch wines were discontinued after the 2003 harvest, leaving the brand focused pinot-wise on wines from the Central and Southern Central Coast.)

In 2001, when Kemiji's old friend Kosuge left SAINTSBURY, where he had been the winemaker since 1996, Kosuge became the hands-on winemaker for Miura. Kosuge describes the winemaking as "typical small-lot California protocol," except that he often ferments a significant portion of the grapes as whole clusters and relies entirely on resident yeasts. The balance of winemaking is "as non-interventionist as the vintage will allow." Overall, the wines are impressive and nicely focused. Many show a counterpoint of tension between sweetness and grip, fruit and herbs, body and elegance.

TASTING NOTES

2005 *Garys' Vineyard (tasted prerelease in 2007)*: Brilliant, light-to-medium ruby; explosive nose of bay laurel and cardamom; intense fruit-sweetness on the attack, almost suggestive of white- and yellow-fleshed stone fruits, with just a hint of bitterness at the end; very pretty with a long finish.

2005 *Pisoni Vineyard (tasted prerelease in 2007)*: Brilliant, rosy-ruby color; talc-like potpourri aromas with a hint of earthy underbrush; rich and mouth filling on the palate, with flavors of cherry and raspberry; almost lean, however, especially for this site; impressive elegance.

2004 *Silacci Vineyard (tasted in 2007)*: Transparent, but not quite limpid, medium rosy black-red; explosive rosy-floral nose with wild raspberry and a hint of herbs; sweet on the palate, with more infused herbs, dark red fruit, minerality, some grip, and a long finish.

2004 *Talley Vineyard (tasted in 2007)*: Brilliant, rosy-ruby color; red-fruit nose with a citrusy highlight; elegant, silky, and slight sweet attack, with a note of molasses, but dry on the finish; very fine. A personal favorite.

2003 *Garys' Vineyard (tasted in 2005)*: Dense, medium-dark, slightly purplish garnet; explosive nose of potpourri and black raspberry with hints of tangerine peel and black pepper; slightly sweet on the front and mid-palate, then grippy toward the end; black fruit, black pepper, and a hint of toffee.

MORGAN WINERY
Salinas, California

Daniel Morgan Lee's roots are at Turlock, in California's central valley, and he began college, at the University of California Davis, intending to study veterinary medicine. Before he graduated, however, he had discovered enology. After earning a master's degree in viticulture and enology, he went to work for Jekel Vineyards, a near-pioneer producer in Monterey County, and later for Durney Vineyards in Carmel Valley.

In 1982 Lee and his wife, Donna (a southern Californian banker, some of whose business involved financing wineries and vineyards), created Morgan Winery, which was initially focused on chardonnay. Lee's first pinot noir, a 50–50 blend of fruit from CVI in Carneros and from Rich Smith's Paraiso Springs Vineyard at the south end of the Santa Lucia Highlands appellation, was made in 1986, and the pinot program relied on both Carneros and Monterey fruit (vinified separately) until 1999.

The turning point for Morgan, however, was the purchase of a 65-acre parcel at the cool, north end of the Santa Lucia Highlands appellation in 1996, which Lee began planting the following year to chardonnay and pinot noir. The site, which the Lees named Double L, short for Double Luck (for their identical twin daughters, then five years old), consists of a lower field that begins on the property's River Road boundary and features sandy-loam soil, and an upper field based on more clay and less sand. The parcel was planted in 6-foot rows with 5 feet between vines and farmed organically from the outset. Most of the pinot (15 acres) was planted straightaway in 1997, but 4.5 acres followed in 1998, 4 more in 2001, and (most recently) 2.5 acres in 2003. The scion material for the pinot noir is five Dijon clones plus UCD 2A, 4, 5, 12, and 23, along with some of the suitcase selection said to have been imported by Gary Pisoni.

In 2000 Morgan translated the emergence of the estate vineyard and contracts to purchase fruit from very close neighbors into a single vineyard program, featuring vineyard-designated wines from Double L, Gary Franscioni's Rosella's Vineyard (see ROAR WINES), and the Franscioni-Pisoni joint venture called Garys' (see PISONI VINEYARDS AND WINERY). A single vineyard wine from the Pisoni estate vineyard had been made in 1998 and 1999. A fifth vineyard-designated wine, sourced from the Tondre Vineyard (see CAMPION WINES for additional information) debuted in 2005.

Lee functioned as his own winemaker from 1982 through 1986, at which time the reins were passed to Joe Davis (see ARCADIAN WINERY). In 1995 Dean de Korth replaced Davis, and in 2002 David Coventry replaced de Korth. In 2005 Gianni Abate, who shares Central Valley roots and Davis training with Lee, and who amassed winemaking experience in the ROBERT MONDAVI'S Woodbridge and Central Coast programs, became Morgan's winemaker.

WINES AND WINEMAKING NOTES
In addition to the single-vineyard wines, Morgan has made a blended Santa Lucia Highlands wine called "Twelve Clones" since 2003. Slightly more than half of this blend originates from the Double L Vineyard; the balance comes from Garys', from Rosella's, and (since 2005) from Tondre.

Winemaking at Morgan follows the consensus protocol except that only about half of each vintage is cold-soaked due to space constraints, and resident and laboratory yeasts are used in combination. Most of the barrel stock comes from François Frères, Cadus, and Meyrieux, and the ratio of new wood to once- and twice-used varies from about one third to one half. Wines are bottled before the following harvest. Always fruit-forward, varietally correct, sweet, and appealing, Morgan pinots are a good mainstream expression of the Santa Lucia Highlands appellation.

TASTING NOTES
2004 *Rosella's (tasted in 2007):* Brilliant, light-to-medium orangey-scarlet; nutshells and flowers on the nose give a slightly exotic impression; sweet, bright, and fruit-driven on the palate with some black pepper and infused rose petal; some glycerin; persistent white pepper on the finish; slightly warm; attractive.

2004 *Double L Vineyard (tasted in 2006):* Transparent, deep black-red; very barrel-marked and slightly reduced nose of cola and beetroot; rich, sweet, and very ripe on the palate; notes of pepper, and Tootsie Roll; long and almost chewy.

2001 *Rosella's Vineyard (tasted in 2005):*
Transparent, rosy black-red; licorice,
smoke, and black pepper on the nose;
dusty and slightly minty black fruit on
the palate; very slightly sweet; medium in
weight, with some grip; a bit hot and very
long. Rather atypical of Rosella's, which
usually shows a more feminine personality.

2001 *Garys' Vineyard (tasted in 2005):*
Transparent, medium-dark black-red;
aromas of very ripe fruit and wet earth with
hints of fir balsam and orange peel; sweet,
dark cherry with spicy herbal notes; brewed
black tea at mid-palate and beyond; soft,
almost unctuous, like heavy upholstery
silk; warm on the finish and long.

2001 *Double L Vineyard (tasted in 2005):*
Transparent light-to-medium ruby; quite
expressively floral on the nose with notes of
mint and sarsaparilla; very forward red fruit
in the mouth, noticeable barrel char; warm
at the end.

MOUNT EDEN VINEYARDS
Saratoga, California

About 2 air miles south of the Stevens Creek
Reservoir, at the very edge of Silicon Valley's
suburban sprawl, Table Mountain rises 2,000
feet above the town of Saratoga, in the shape
of a U, open to the east. La Cresta, Paul
Masson's mountain winery—now empty of
wine but a favorite site for executive events,
weddings, and summer concerts—is on the
southern side of the U. A narrow, vertiginous
dirt road snakes up the northern (and
much higher) side of the mountain, where,
beginning in 1943, Masson's protégé Martin
Ray cleared enough chaparral and poison
oak to make room for five small vineyards
of cabernet sauvignon, chardonnay, and

pinot noir; two houses; and a winery. The
houses were the venue for Ray's interminable
and infamous bacchanalian fests, attended
variously by academics from the University
of California Davis, screen stars from
Hollywood, aspiring winemakers, and others

ELEGANT, MEDIUM-BODIED
WINES THAT COMBINE JAMMY
BERRY FLAVORS WITH AN
AVALANCHE OF EARTHY,
MEATY NOTES

willing to endure Ray's filibusters about all
and sundry, but most especially, we are told,
about the pitiful state of American wine, his
own excepted.

Ray's years on Table Mountain,
chronicled in 1993 by his widow, Eleanor,
in *Vineyards in the Sky* (Heritage West
Books, 1993), were apparently a more
or less constant struggle against the
elements, destructive fires, insufficient
insurance, inadequate financial resources,
and personal enemies. In the 1960s Ray
conceived the idea of simultaneously
financing new vineyard development
and surrounding himself with a "club
of compatible people" by selling shares
in an enterprise he called Mount Eden
Vineyards. Almost from the outset,
however, Ray quarreled with his
investors, eventually setting off waves and
counterwaves of litigation.

When the legal dust settled in 1971, the
original hilltop vineyard Ray had planted
in 1943 and the hilltop ranch house, with
its wide verandahs overlooking Santa
Clara Valley, plus considerable acreage
lower on the mountain, had all passed to
a subset of the investors, while Ray and
his family retained a second house on the
midslope between the two, along with a

small vineyard downslope from the house. This small vineyard now belongs to Ray's stepson, Peter Martin Ray.

From these tumultuous beginnings, Mount Eden Vineyards, first a partnership, then a corporation, produced its first vintage of pinot noir in 1972, using fruit from Martin Ray's 29-year-old vines. CHALONE VINEYARD founder Dick Graff was the winemaker for a single vintage; he was followed by his brother, Peter Graff. The baton then passed to Merry Edwards, who established the brand's reputation for voluptuous, mineral-laced chardonnay, and later to Bill Anderson and Fred Peterson.

For the past twenty-seven vintages, Jeffrey Patterson has made the wines. An autodidact in wine matters who took some courses at the University of California Davis in 1979–1980 and supported his postcollegiate self-study of fine wine with odd jobs painting houses and repairing cars, Patterson has brought a steady hand, a huge passion, and a site-specific dedication to Mount Eden's wines. He and his family live in the hilltop house.

There are now seven pinot vineyards at Mount Eden, counting the one that is actually owned by Peter Martin Ray. Of the original 7 acres of hilltop vineyard, 5 have been replanted to pinot noir: 1 acre to cuttings taken from the original planting, in 1996; 1 acre each to Dijon 115, 667, and 777, planted in 1998; and another acre of the Old Mount Chardonnay Vineyard to Dijon 115, planted in 1999. In other words, most of Ray's original hilltop pinot, which had been sourced from La Cresta and grafted to rootstock by a local nursery, was kept in production until 1997, and the acre replanted in 1996 will preserve the original Paul Masson pedigree indefinitely.

The hilltop vineyards share a moderate, east-facing slope of friable, well-drained Franciscan shale. (Martin Ray likened the shale to "fine Parmesan cheese" for its granularity and tendency to fracture simultaneously in orthogonal directions.) Yield was down to a measly quarter-ton per acre on the hilltop before the old vines were removed; the target for the replanted blocks is 2 tons per acre.

The other two vineyards are 400 feet downslope, on the northern side of the access road. One is the 1.5-acre Peter Martin Ray vineyard already discussed. It is a sparsely planted parcel—10-foot rows with 10 feet between vines, untrellised— and the budwood was a field selection from Winery Lake Vineyard in Los Carneros, but it has not been used in the Mount Eden wines since 2000. The other vineyard is a 1-acre parcel set in 10-foot rows with 6-foot intervine spacing, whose scion material was taken from the hilltop site. The soils in these lower vineyards contain a bit more clay, so the yield is slightly higher, ranging from 1 to 3 tons per acre.

Together, the seven vineyards produce only enough fruit for about 400 to 600 cases of wine, which makes pinot noir less than 4 percent of Mount Eden's total production. (The rest of Mount Eden's program is chardonnay and cabernet sauvignon.) A single bottling of pinot has been made each year since 1972, except for 1992, when no pinot was released, and 1997, when 200 cases of a wonderful Cuvée des Vieilles Vignes were separately bottled, to honor the last vintage from Ray's original planting. Fruit from the replanted hilltop vineyards rejoined the pinot program in 2000.

Mount Eden has been a favored source when pinot growers elsewhere in California have field-selected budwood. It has been known variously as the Paul Masson selection, the Martin Ray selection, and the Mount Eden selection; additionally, budwood taken from Mount Eden by Merry Edwards has been released by FPS as UCD 37. In these pages, as in *North American Pinot Noir*, I have standardized the nomenclature for the field selections as Mount Eden, but UCD 37 is still UCD 37.

WINES AND WINEMAKING NOTES

Pinot is usually picked at Mount Eden during the first half of September at Brix levels ranging from 23 to 25. Patterson ferments in 120-gallon bins and 1,000-gallon stainless steel open-tops. The 1995 and 1998 vintages were made in tank, the 1996 and 1997 in bins. Since 1998 fermentors have been matched opportunistically with lot sizes. Use of stems has changed over the last decade. Patterson's predecessors followed a 100-percent whole-cluster protocol. In 1983 Patterson eliminated stems entirely. Early in the new millennium, he crushed most of his fruit, but used between 5 percent and 10 percent whole berries, "some of which have stems"—so the must is getting a light seasoning of stems. Now he destems but does not crush, except that he retains 20 to 30 percent of fruit as whole clusters. "It's a moving target," he asserts. He is also experimenting with cold soaks, which run for as few as two days to as many as seven.

Fermentation is jump-started with Assmannshausen and Burgundian yeasts, and acid is added to the must about two years out of three, to compensate for high levels of juice potassium. The must is punched down four times daily, and the primary fermentation normally takes about seven days. Patterson favors a fairly hot alcoholic fermentation (between 85 and 90°F) to gain "earth, mushroom, and cheese flavors, and some sexiness," but he argues that fermentation temperature is a stylistic rather than a qualitative parameter with pinot. Two to five days of postfermentation maceration are permitted before the must is pressed and sent to barrel, where the malolactic fermentation is allowed to begin naturally. The press fraction is settled in tanks before being reintegrated with the barreled wine. Patterson uses 50 percent new barrels, mostly medium-plus-toast François Frères. Barrel time is a fairly long eighteen to twenty months. One racking is performed after malolactic fermentation has ended; a second is done at bottling. There has been no fining since 1984, but Patterson sometimes filters to control brettanomyces.

In the 1990s, Mount Eden pinots were complex, elegant, medium-bodied wines with jammy berry flavors upfront and an avalanche of minty, earthy, and meaty notes on the mid-palate and finish. A few tastings of older vintages suggest that the wines usually age very well, peaking ten to fifteen years after the vintage. Vintages from early in the new millennium are impressive for their seamless intensity, and they remain bright and nicely structured.

TASTING NOTES

2004 *Estate (tasted in 2007):* Transparent medium ruby color; dark red fruit on the nose; some sweet, cherry-plum fruit with brown spice and tea on the palate; rich and bright with the tiniest hint of espresso and tar; mouth coating, serious, and tightly-knit; long, rewarding, and fine.

2003 *Estate (tasted in 2007):* Transparent medium ruby color; soft spice and earth aromas; sweet but very serious on the palate with dark cherry, Italian plum, and hints of orange peel and clove; almost creamy but still bright on the mid-palate with some minerality; tightly-knit with very fine-grained tannins; some overall smokiness; a long and richly elegant finish. Fine.

2000 *Estate (tasted in 2006):* Transparent, brick-red color; spicy, cigar-box nose; hints of fallen leaves and marinated cherries; very structured, silky, elegant, and very fine. A transitional vintage at Mount Eden, made partially from the hilltop block replanted in 1996 and 1998, and partially from the lower vineyard.

NALLE WINERY
Healdsburg, California

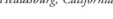

Doug Nalle, a Southern Californian with an undergraduate degree in history from the University of Redlands, and his wife, Lee, a University of California Berkeley– and University of California San Francisco–educated nurse practitioner and daughter of Dry Creek Valley ranchers, created Nalle Winery in 1984. By this time Nalle had amassed over a decade of hands-on experience on the production side of the wine business, including five years of service as the co-winemaker at Balverne Vineyards and Winery and a four- year stint at Quivira Winery, plus a formal education in wine science that featured such luminary instructors as Dick Arrowood, and a master's degree from the University of California Davis.

The brand focused, unsurprisingly, on Dry Creek Valley zinfandel, some of which was grown on land Lee's family owned, but Nalle dabbled in small quantities of other varieties as early as 1987. (The first of Nalle's non-zinfandels was a Bradford Mountain cabernet sauvignon.) Nalle says that long ruminations with his friend, Mike Hin, a soulmate who published important research on pinot noir during the 1970s, sparked his interest in pinot, which was then buttressed when another

friend, Steve Edgar, trekked from Arizona to California every year to help with the harvest, dividing his time between Nalle and WILLIAMS SELYEM. Edgar shared Burt Williams's pinots with Nalle, evening after evening and harvest after harvest. When Bob Hopkins, yet another longtime friend, who had grown up with Lee, planted a bit of pinot noir on his Russian River Valley ranch to fill out a vineyard block initially designated for pinot meunier, Nalle cut a handshake deal for a ton of grapes. The first successful vintage, in what is now an unbroken string of ten, was made in 1998. In 2002, the Nalles' son Andrew entered the family business and is now its winemaker; Andrew confesses to a special affection for pinot despite the brand's historic and very successful focus on elegant editions of zinfandel.

WINES AND WINEMAKING NOTES
Nalle's one and only pinot noir is a single vineyard wine from the aforementioned Hopkins Ranch, where six parcels, totaling 14 acres, are dedicated to pinot, in soils classified as Yolo loam. The vineyard is not certified organic, but organic protocols are respected. Of the six parcels, Nalle uses fruit from three;

AGEWORTHY, FOOD FRIENDLY, AND VERY REWARDING PINOTS, MADE WITH ADMIRABLE RESTRAINT

---

the balance is sold to other producers, including MERRY EDWARDS WINES and Kendall Jackson.

The first two vintages were made entirely from the rows planted in 1989 to budwood taken from Joe Swan's nearby estate vineyard. As blocks planted to Dijon 115 and 667 in 2000 came into production, Nalle experimented with those in varying percentages, but has now decided that the original Swan selection gives the best results of all, displaying a "gamey, rhubarb" quality that father and son both like. Since 2003, the Nalle wine has relied mostly on Swan, with a minority share of Dijon 667, "for deeper fruit."

The grapes are typically picked at about 24.5 Brix and are sorted on the crush pad to eliminate clusters that fall outside a narrow bandwidth of "just properly ripe." (The same discipline is applied to Nalle zinfandel, which substantially explains its elegant profile.) Cold soaks last from two to five days in small open-top fermentors; Assmannshausen yeast is used to start the primary fermentation; the cap is hand plunged; and fermentation temperatures generally push but do not exceed 90°F. Great care is taken at pressing, first to exclude any "heavy lees paste" entirely and then to cease pressing immediately at the first sign that seed tannin has found its way into the new wine. The wine is raised in François Frères and Alain Fouquet barrels for approximately eleven months.

Following a first racking in the spring following the vintage, some barrels first used for chardonnay are repurposed for pinot noir, so that the percentage of "new" barrels used to raise the pinot is almost impossible to calculate precisely. There is no use of enzymes or fining. Filtration, if any, is minimal.

This regime yields wines of great visual clarity, pale garnet color, and finished alcohol levels between 13.4 and 13.9 percent. The restraint used in the winemaking, plus rational farming in the vineyard, makes the wines transparent to a panoply of aromas and flavors. The wines are demonstrably ageworthy, food friendly, and very rewarding.

TASTING NOTE

2003 *Hopkins Ranch (tasted twice, in 2005 and 2007):* Completely transparent, light rosy garnet; explosive nose that combines fresh flowers, potpourri, Indonesian spice, and hints of pepper and raspberry; cherry and raspberry with notes of smoke, tea, rosewater, and macerated orange peel on the palate; featherweight and silky, but intensely flavored; very elegant and fine.

NAVARRO VINEYARDS
Philo, California

Ted Bennett and Deborah Cahn, husband and wife, moved to Anderson Valley in 1974. They had sold a successful retail business in the Bay Area, and they shared strong counterculture values. In Anderson Valley they raised sheep and even paid the obstetrician who delivered their first child with lambs. They also planted grapes: gewürztraminer and pinot noir. Bennett loved gewürztraminer. As for the pinot, well, he remembers needing a red grape that could ripen in a cool mesoclimate. A quarter-century later, having outlasted Anderson Valley's other wine pioneers, Bennett and Cahn are still planting grapes, raising animals, and selling most of their wine from the tasting room they built on Highway 128.

Their son, Aaron, and daughter, Sarah, became co-owners of the estate in 2007, and both have assumed active roles in the winery's business. Sarah, who is now Navarro's enologist, holds a master's degree in viticulture and enology from the University of California Davis. She did her dissertation work on the phenolic structure of Anderson Valley pinots, uncovering an exceptionally wide band of variation within the appellation and even among blocks in the same vineyard. One of Sarah's former classmates and a specialist on rootstocks, Jeff Wheeler, joined Navarro in 2006 as viticulturist. The familial character of Navarro seems secure for at least one more generation.

Bennett made his first pinots under the Edmeades label—he was an early investor in Edmeades—in 1975 and 1976. The grapes for these wines were sourced from the Redwood Valley, northeast of Ukiah. In 1977 fruit from the same source was used to make Navarro Mendocino Pinot Noir, which was the first pinot to carry the Navarro name. Meanwhile, the 4 acres of pinot Bennett had planted on the Navarro Ranch in 1975—the block is now called South Hill—began to bear, and an estate pinot debuted in 1978. The 1980s concentration was on white wines, however, and Navarro did not increase its stake in pinot until 1990. At that point, Bennett planted a new block called Hammer-Olsen, which consisted of 3.5 acres of UCD 13 and 3 acres of a field selection from Chalone, plus 1.5 additional acres of the same UCD 4 that had been planted on South Hill. In 1992 the Hammer-Olsen planting was expanded to include an acre of Dijon 115.

By 1995, when it was obvious that pinot noir was now *very* marketable, Navarro began an ambitious planting program, crawling gradually up the hillside that marks the northeastern boundary of the Anderson Valley appellation. Upper Garden Spot was planted in 1995: a 3.9-acre block devoted primarily to Dijon 115, with some 113 and 114. At the same time, the 1.3-acre Lower Garden Spot was planted to UCD 4. In 1996, the Omega vineyard, 1.8 acres between the 400- and 600-foot elevation contours, were planted to Dijon 667 on 3309 rootstock. Another 1.3 acres of Dijon

667 were planted on a site called Fox Point at the 1,000-foot elevation; and 2.2 acres, called Middle Ridge, ranging from 1,000 to 1,300 feet, were planted to Dijon 114 and 777. The following year the so-called Upper Marking Corral (remember that this property was originally a sheep ranch), at 1,500 feet on mostly rocky, thin soil, was planted to 5.5 acres of Dijon 113, 114, and 115, along with a bit of UCD 4.

The 1998 project was the Lower Marking Corral: 2.3 acres of Dijon 115 and 667 on 101-14 rootstock, Dijon 777 on 3309, and Clone 459 on St. George. The 459 was replaced in 2001 with Clone 238. The top of South Hill was replaced in 2002, owing to phylloxera, and its upper rows, once devoted to a test planting of muscat and a trellis trial for gewürztraminer, were converted to Dijon 777 on 101-14, planted 3 feet by 3 feet and trellised in a double-T to better protect the fruit from direct sunlight and heat.

Never indifferent to their environment (this is antidevelopment Anderson Valley, after all!), the family replaced mechanical farming with animal activity in 2007. A leased flock of babydoll sheep, used to mow the weeds and sucker the vine trunks, has now been replaced with a permanent, resident flock, and a mobile hen house dubbed "Chickenmobile 1" introduces chickens to each vineyard block after the sheep have been moved on to the next, to scratch the ground, bury the sheep dung, and control weeds.

Off the estate, Navarro also became a buyer of Anderson Valley pinot noir in the 1990s, acquiring fruit from its nextdoor neighbor on Highway 128, Valley Foothills Vineyards, and from Bemposto and Corby, across from Navarro on the southwest side of Highway 128, creating an aggregate of about 30 acres of estate grown pinot noir and contracts for about 15 more, which are used as a palette for blending—Navarro's approach to pinot noir.

Although Bennett maintains that it took ten years' experience before Navarro was able to make a pinot that "really excited us," the original South Hill planting still provides the anchor for the property's reserve wine, called Deep End Blend. Arguing that "*terroir* is a winemaking tool, not an end in itself," Navarro winemaker Jim Klein explains that the allocation of lots among Navarro's three pinot releases changes from year to year, and that wind and temperature may favor first one site, then another. Klein—a Southern Californian and onetime certified public accountant who did coursework at the University of California Davis and made wine in both Santa Barbara and Israel—has been at Navarro since 1992.

WINES AND WINEMAKING NOTES
Navarro makes three pinots: about 1,200 cases of a reserve wine called Deep End Blend, about 6,000 cases of an Anderson Valley bottling called Méthode à l'Ancienne, and a variable quantity of Pinot Mendocino. Increasingly, the Deep End Blend privileges fruit from the highest elevation vineyard blocks. Estate and purchased fruit are used in the Anderson Valley wine. Despite its name, Pinot Mendocino is no longer built substantially from inland (Potter and Redwood Valleys) fruit, but mostly from grapes grown at the Boonville end of Anderson Valley, and from Comptche, about 20 miles due north of Navarro.

Klein says that a "smorgasbord" of factors shapes Navarro's decisions about picking: the numbers, of course; how the fruit tastes; whether the seeds have lignified; and always, whether there is rain in the forecast. He is a strong believer that grapes should be sorted in the field, and that it is far better to invest in multiple pickings than to invest in sorting tables at the winery.

Navarro used to ferment with about 15 percent whole clusters; now the grapes are completely destemmed. The must is cold-soaked in fruit bins and small stainless steel open-tops for three to five days. Fermentation usually starts spontaneously, but Klein inoculates all lots anyway, using a red grape yeast isolated in Bordeaux. To minimize bitterness from seed tannins, he likes to press well before the must is dry and then move the wine to tank. If it is clean, he will transfer it from tank to barrel when sugar is still about 1 or 2 degrees Brix; or he will let the fermentation finish completely in tank and do one clean racking before barreling the wine. Either way, the wine is still turgid and a little foamy when it gets to barrel.

Klein gets 95 percent of the winery's barrel stock for pinot from Remond, coopered from forests in the Allier. For the Deep End Blend and Anderson Valley wines, one third of the barrels are new each year. Malolactic fermentation is started by inoculation, in barrel. Some barrels finish secondary fermentation as early as November; others subside for the winter and finish in the spring. Klein likes to keep the wine on its lees until spring anyway. A single racking, to tank, is then done just before bottling.

Klein always fines with egg whites, both for clarity and for tannin management (he calls this step "polishing" and says it gives the wine "a touch of sheen"). In most vintages, some of the Anderson Valley blend is bottled unfiltered (and is so labeled), but Klein and Bennett are not great fans of brettanomyces, so they will filter with pads or cartridges if they detect signs of it.

The two high-end wines are classic Anderson Valley pinots, dominated by bright cherry flavors, and quite elegantly built. Alcohols are moderate, so the wines are food friendly. The Deep End Blend is the more immediately appealing of the two, but the Anderson Valley cuvée is very nicely built and ages exceptionally well. The Mendocino bottling should not be neglected, however. Sold for a very modest price, it varies by vintage but is frequently a delicious, light-to-medium weight pinot noir, perfect for warm weather and salmon.

TASTING NOTES

2005 *Mendocino* (tasted twice in 2007): Brilliant, medium ruby; explosive nose of flowers, red fruit, licorice, and orange peel; bright and fruit-driven on the front palate with hints of tree sap and resin; then, sober and dry on the finish; silky and attractive.

2005 Anderson Valley (tasted in 2007): Bright, medium ruby; slightly exotic nose showing notes of mesquite and tar; rich cherry-cocktail flavors on the palate with a bit of earthiness and a slightly ferrous quality; substantially minerally; dry from mid-palate to finish; tasty, attractive, and nicely built.

2005 *Deep End Blend (tasted in 2007):* Luminous, medium garnet; riper nose than the Anderson Valley bottling; elegant, slightly creamy, rich, and tightly-knit on the palate; again, bright cherry dominates; there is some fruit-sweetness and a hint of mocha on the back palate; appealing, well behaved, and medium in length, with a bit of grip from very fine-grained tannins.

THE OJAI VINEYARD
Oak View, California

The Ojai Vineyard, founded in 1983, is Adam and Helen Tolmach's small, family-owned wine project in the hilly canyon that ascends from the Pacific coast at

Ventura to the pretty resort town of Ojai. The Tolmachs planted a syrah vineyard there in 1981, but it succumbed to Pierce's disease in 1995 and has not been replanted, so the brand has since lived entirely on purchased fruit. The inaugural vintage was made at AU BON CLIMAT in Los Olivos, where Adam Tolmach and Jim Clendenen were partners, but a winery was built and bonded on the Oak View site in 1984, and it has been the venue for winemaking ever since. After the Au Bon Climat partnership was dissolved in 1991, Tolmach added pinot noir to the Ojai Vineyard portfolio, sourcing fruit from the Bien Nacido Vineyard. Tolmach was trained in fermentation science at the University of California Davis and was the enologist at Zaca Mesa Winery before he and Clendenen founded Au Bon Climat in 1982.

WINES AND WINEMAKING NOTES

All Ojai pinots are vineyard-designated wines. The Bien Nacido bottling, made from grapes grown at the east end of Block Q, a widely-spaced planting of UCD 13 converted to a vertical trellis system in 1993, debuted in 1991. A PISONI VINEYARD wine was added in 1996 and was made until 2001. Two neighboring vineyards in what is now the Sta. Rita Hills appellation—Clos Pepe and MELVILLE— were added in 2000 and 2001, respectively, but the Melville wine was discontinued after 2002. A third Sta. Rita Hills site, Rick Longoria's Fe Ciega Vineyard (see RICHARD LONGORIA WINES), debuted in 2003, as did Solomon Hills, a Santa Maria Mesa site close to Sierra Madre, farmed by the Miller family of Bien Nacido fame and used by numerous Santa Barbara producers, in 2004. In 2007 the Presidio Vineyard was added to the lineup. Presidio, tightly spaced, low trellised, and biodynamically farmed, is located on Purisima Road near Lompoc, just beyond the west edge of the Sta. Rita Hills "AVA.

In most of the vineyards he works with, Tolmach finds that he is now among the earliest winemakers to pick, though he was among the latest twenty years ago. The difference, he explains, is not the chemistry of the grapes at harvest,

---

THE SWEET SPOT FOR PINOT COMES WHEN NATURAL ACIDITY IS SUFFICIENT TO KEEP THE FLAVORS FROM SEEMING DULL
—*Adam Tolmach*

---

which has changed little, but "the times." Tolmach thinks the sweet spot for pinot comes around 24 Brix, when the skins have not begun to shrivel, and when natural acidity is sufficient to keep the flavors from seeming "dull."

His fermentors are unjacketed 3.5-ton stainless steel open-tops. He now destems completely, having discovered that stems tended to drive up the must's pH, forcing him to acidify, and that the added acid then caused "bad tastes." A cool room facilitates a four- to six-day cold soak before the alcoholic fermentation begins with resident yeast. Fermentation temperatures peak between 90 and 95°F, and the must goes dry within six to ten days. After twenty-four hours in tank to settle the grossest lees, the wine goes to barrel fairly dirty. The barrels are mostly François Frères, though some Sirugue barrels are also used, and about 33 to 40 percent of the total stock is new.

New barrels are steamed briefly before they are filled "to minimize wood flavors." The cellar is kept quite cool, so malolactic fermentation is usually slow to start and long to finish. Tolmach says he likes a wine's flavors better if it is held in barrel until after the next harvest, so the usual regime is about 15 months. Ideally, he says, he never racks, and generally avoids both fining and filtration. He has also learned to minimize the use of sulfur throughout the winemaking process. Not only does sulfur, in his experience, affect pinot noir's flavors more than it affects other varieties, but it also tends to interfere with oxygen absorption by the wine's tannins, which can make the wines taste harder.

Although Tolmach describes the 2005 vintage as "something of a new direction with pinot," with a bit less brawn than earlier vintages, Ojai's pinots remain, comparatively speaking, large-framed, darkly colored wines that display considerable tannin when they are young. Unusually, however, Ojai pinots' size relies more on structure than on ripeness, positioning them to benefit from bottle age.

TASTING NOTES

2005 *Solomon Hills Vineyard (tasted in 2007):* Almost opaque, deep, blackish ruby; peppermint, black pepper, ripe plum, and lavender on the nose; rich, intense, blueberry, boysenberry, and black licorice on the palate; round at mid-palate; dry and a little grippy from mid-palate to finish; long.

2005 *Bien Nacido Vineyard (tasted in 2007):* Dark purplish-red; slightly herbal, savory aromas of fennel and roasted beets; intense, sleek, and peppery attack; berries on the mid-palate; a soft, slightly sweet core; warm and grippy toward the end; needs time.

2005 *Fe Ciega Vineyard (tasted in 2007):* Barely transparent dark ruby; aromas of peppery *charcuterie*, merbromin, and ripe fruit; very sweet, deep, dark, and serious on the palate with considerable earthiness and minerality; rich overall, and considerably extracted, but retains some fruit-sweetness to the end.

2005 *Clos Pepe Vineyard (tasted in 2007)*: Medium-dark color; clove, pepper, allspice, and juniper berry on the nose; simultaneously bright, intense, brooding, and fruit-sweet on the palate; mostly cherry and Santa Rosa plum; mouth coating and tightly knit; very fine-grained tannins; a peppery-alcoholic bite at the end; a massive wine.

OLIVET LANE VINEYARD AND PELLEGRINI FAMILY VINEYARDS
Santa Rosa, California

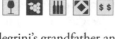

Robert Pellegrini's grandfather and great uncle entered the California wine business around 1925, when that business consisted of shipping grapes to home winemakers, many of them Italian immigrants, around the country. After Repeal, in 1933, the family acquired the Buchignani Winery in Dry Creek Valley, established the Pellegrini Wine Company in San Francisco, and set about making private label wines for various San Francisco restaurants and shops.

Forty years later, Pellegrini's parents purchased 70 acres of apple orchard on West Olivet Lane, west of Santa Rosa, accessed via an allée framed with olive trees. In 1975 they replanted 65 of these 70 acres to two thirds chardonnay and one third pinot noir—the only red variety anyone would advise them to attempt. The scion material was UCD 13, grafted to the nonresistant rootstock of the day, widely spaced and allowed to flop from above two horizontal wires, in the trellising configuration later known informally as California sprawl.

Alas, the Pellegrinis found few takers for their pinot. Some was vinted by Pellegrini Wine Company as "Vintage Red"; the rest was sold to Geyser Peak Winery, then recently acquired by the Schlitz Brewing Company and making an estimated 1 million cases annually, and to Sebastiani Vineyards, another expanding wine enterprise owned and operated by immigrants from Tuscany, which turned out about a half-million cases during the 1970s wine boom. At both destinations, the Olivet Lane grapes disappeared anonymously into blends.

Robert Pellegrini suggested to his father that they graft the pinot to chardonnay, but his father patiently demurred. "Thank God," says Robert now. In 1987, the same year that judges for the California State Fair named WILLIAMS SELYEM, then operating from a garage, as the state's Winery of the Year, Burt Williams agreed to buy 15 tons of pinot from Olivet Lane and to vineyard-designate the resulting wine. This wine won many awards and clinched the reputation of the vineyard.

The arrangement with Williams Selyem lasted for ten years, until the latter was sold in 1997, at which point the same 15 tons of pinot were sold to Merry Edwards, who had launched MERRY EDWARDS WINES the same year. Edwards had already become the Pellegrini's in-house winemaker, had helped the family to design a new winery on the Olivet Lane site, and had built a sturdy reputation for Olivet Lane as one of pinot's most successful value brands. As in-house winemaker, Edwards was succeeded by Scott Covington, an alumnus of Sonoma-Cutrer and MARIMAR ESTATE, and then by Kevin Hamel (see HAMEL WINES) in 2005. During this period, the new winery became host to a half-dozen small custom-crush clients.

Olivet Lane pinot, most of which is sold to restaurants, is made from mostly destemmed fruit with 15 to 20 percent whole clusters. It is pressed about two days after the must goes dry, barreled for ten months, and raised in about 33 percent new oak.

TASTING NOTES

2005 *Olivet Lane (tasted in* 2007): Pretty, bright, pinkish cherry-red; flowers, raspberry, and strawberry on the nose; very bright, red-berry oriented palate with irresistible charm; excellent acidity with no manipulation whatsoever; excellent value.

1998 *Olivet Lane (tasted in* 2001): Pretty, transparent, medium black-red; red and black cherries on both nose and palate; sweet fruit core with a bit more black fruit than red; notes of black pepper, cinnamon, and tree bark; linen-like texture; medium-long.

OROGENY VINEYARDS
Napa, California

In 2002, Tom Selfridge, then president of the Chalone Wine Group, decided that a Russian River Valley pinot noir would complement the Salinas Valley, Edna Valley, and Carneros programs already represented in Chalone's portfolio. A partnership was established with the Dutton family to source grapes from Dutton-owned or Dutton-managed vineyards in Green Valley, which is the Russian River Valley's coolest corner, and Dan Goldfield, already partnered with the Duttons in DUTTON-GOLDFIELD WINES, was engaged as the new brand's winemaker.

A single Green Valley pinot blended from four vineyards (Dutton's Barron Vineyard, on Green Valley Road about a half-mile northwest of Keefer Ranch; Marty Gregori Vineyard on Thomas Road just north of Barron; Lorenzo Vineyard on the Gravenstein Highway at the corner of Ross Station Road; and the Fox Den Vineyard in the hills northeast of Occidental) was made in 2002, 2003, and 2004. In 2004, alongside the blend, the project was expanded to include a vineyard-designated wine from the aforementioned Fox Den Vineyard and another vineyard-designated wine from outside Green Valley. The latter was the Redding Ranch, a 2001 planting of four Dijon clones on 23 hillside acres near Nicasio in Marin County. The Redding Ranch wine was not made in 2005 but was resumed in 2006.

Although it was designed as a pinot-only project, Orogeny embraced chardonnay from 2005 and now makes more chardonnay than pinot. In 2005 the brand was part of the sale of the Chalone Wine Group to Diageo Chateau and Estates Wines.

WINES AND WINEMAKING NOTES

Winemaking follows the consensus protocol in most respects, although Goldfield will sometimes let fermentations start (and sometimes even finish) with resident yeasts. Limited experience suggests that Orogeny pinots will usually display the richly extracted and texturally generous style that has come to characterize pinots from much of western Sonoma excluding the true Sonoma Coast.

TASTING NOTES

2005 *Sonoma County Green Valley (tasted in* 2007): Medium ruby; very ripe fruit and potpourri; sweet, ripe, plummy cherry fruit with bright citrus and cranberry highlights and noticeable brown spice on the palate; round, soft, and long.

2002 *Sonoma County Green Valley (tasted in* 2004*):* Transparent, dark ruby; underbrush, nutmeg, and candle wax on the nose; intense and slightly sweet on the palate; cherries and red licorice with briary undertones; round at mid-palate; tannin and barrel char on the finish.

ORTMAN FAMILY VINEYARDS
Pismo Beach, California

In 1968, while Chuck Ortman was studying graphic design at Oakland's California College of Arts and Crafts, he chanced to taste a friend's homemade wine and was instantly fascinated. He moved his young family to the Napa Valley, took a cellar-rat job with the legendary Joe Heitz, and learned winemaking from the bottom up. Within a few years, he had moved from Heitz Cellars to Spring Mountain Winery, and then into wine consulting, working with luminary brands like Cain Cellars, Far Niente, and Fisher Vineyards in the formative years of each and establishing a reputation for wizardry and innovative techniques with chardonnay.

In 1979 Ortman launched an eponymous label, Charles Ortman Wines, that was renamed Meridian in 1984, acquired by Wine World Estates (later Beringer Blass Wine Estates, and Foster's Wine Estates after 2005), and evolved into a successful producer of moderately priced chardonnay, pinot noir, syrah, and cabernet sauvignon based on Central Coast grapes. In 2001, Ortman and his son Matt, who had dabbled briefly in beer before focusing on

wine, founded Ortman Family Vineyards, dedicated to small batches of (mostly) chardonnay and pinot noir sourced from vineyards in the southern Central Coast. The first vintages of Ortman Family pinot, in 2001 and 2002, were Santa Barbara County bottlings anchored with fruit from White Hills Vineyard.

In 2003 the pinot program evolved toward three wines in each vintage: a vineyard-designate from Fiddlestix Vineyard (see FIDDLEHEAD CELLARS) grapes, a Sta. Rita Hills wine anchored with Fiddlestix fruit, and a Willamette Valley wine anchored with fruit from the renowned Temperance Hill Vineyard in the Eola Hills—a mid-1980s planting, organically farmed, that is used by many of Oregon's top producers.

The Sta. Rita Hills fruit is harvested very ripe "for enhanced concentration and color;" fermentations are preceded by a three- to four-day cold soak; fermentors are 1.5-ton fruit bins; fermentations are hand-plunged; a small percentage of the Willamette Valley grapes are fermented as whole clusters; and the juice temperatures of one lot in five is allowed to rise as high as 95°F. The result is very attractive wines, overall, sourced from fine sites, and thoughtfully vinified with skill and restraint.

TASTING NOTES

2005 *Sta. Rita Hills (tasted in* 2007*):* Pretty, light-to-medium ruby; spicy and slightly smoky nose; bold, violet-infused black fruit on the palate, lifted with notes of resin and citrus; satiny through mid-palate, then structured and slightly grippy. A classic Sta. Rita Hills pinot, but quite well-behaved.

2005 *Fiddlestix Vineyard (tasted in* 2007*):* Deep, transparent garnet; slightly exotic nose of camphorwood, hard spice, licorice, and violets; intense, mostly black fruit on the palate, slightly sweet attack; round and almost unctuous at mid-palate; then, a considerable load of very fine-grained, sweet tannins persists to the end. A very pretty wine from a young, expressive vineyard.

2004 *Willamette Valley (tasted in* 2007*):* Medium garnet; chalky, slightly floral nose; a nicely built and mineral-dominated wine that also displays cherry-raspberry-pomegranate fruit and a hint of citrus; lightweight, but anchored with good grip from mid-palate to finish. Attractive.

PANTHER CREEK CELLARS
McMinnville, Oregon

In the more than two decades since it was founded by Ken Wright in 1986, Panther Creek Cellars has changed hands twice. In 1994, after Wright's original partnership dissolved in an acrimonious dispute, the business was acquired by a couple from Des Moines, Iowa, with a taste for red Burgundies and French cuisine. Ron Kaplan was a successful construction lawyer; his wife Linda was a writer and reporter. The story of their stewardship of Panther Creek is engagingly told in Linda Kaplan's memoir, *My First Crush* (The Lyons Press, 2005). Although the couple remains actively involved with the winery's operation thirteen years later, all of its assets, save the underlying real estate, were sold to Chambers McMinnville LLC in 2005. Chambers McMinnville is the same entity that owns SILVAN RIDGE WINERY near Eugene.

At the beginning of the 1990s, Panther Creek's wine program also shifted gears quite visibly, as Wright moved from a concentration on blended wines to a preoccupation with vineyard-designates. Since 1994, however, there has been more continuity than change at Panther Creek, and the brand seems increasingly comfortable in a wine program that is now concentrated almost entirely on pinot noir, and whose portfolio consists of a single Willamette Valley blend plus a quite stable array of vineyard-designated wines that depend (mostly) on long-term contracts for specific rows and blocks.

Michael Stevenson, who has been the brand's full-time winemaker since 1999, has been in the cellar since the Kaplan's purchase in 1994; from 1994 to 1999, Stevenson worked as the cellarmaster while Mark Vlossak (see ST. INNOCENT WINERY) held the overall winemaking reins. Stevenson, who came to Oregon from North Carolina because it was the "American mecca for microbrewing," transitioned from brewing to winemaking at St. Innocent before making the move to Panther Creek. The

---

SINCE 2000, ELEGANT AND FINELY CRAFTED WINES WITH MODERATE LEVELS OF FINISHED ALCOHOL

Panther Creek premises are where they have been since 1990, in a repurposed power station in uptown McMinnville that looks surprisingly like a bank.

WINES AND WINEMAKING NOTES
Since 1994 vineyard-designated wines have been made in every vintage from the Freedom Hill Vineyard in the Eola Hills; the Shea Vineyard on the east edge of the Yamhill-Carlton AVA (see SHEA WINE

CELLARS); and the Bednarik Vineyard, a tiny planting on the north side of Patton Valley west of Gaston. There is also a long-term lease for fruit from Temperance Hill, just north of Bethel Heights. Occasional vintages of vineyard-designated wines were also made during the late 1990s and early 2000s from the Nysa Vineyard in the Dundee Hills and from the Youngberg Hills Vineyard southwest of McMinnville. LAZY RIVER VINEYARD northwest of Yamhill, and Vista Hills, a new planting at the very summit of the Dundee Hills, between Domaine Serene and Domaine Drouhin, joined the lineup in 2006.

Meanwhile, the blend side of the portfolio has consisted of a single assemblage called Winemaker's Cuvée since 2000. From 2000 through 2005, this carried an Oregon designation because it was anchored with fruit from the Melrose Vineyard northwest of Roseburg in the Umpqua Valley; but Melrose was replaced by the aforementioned Lazy Creek Vineyard in 2006, pulling the entire Panther Creek portfolio within the confines of the Willamette Valley appellation. Picking decisions are made based "on flavor," and the harvested fruit is completely hand-sorted on the crushpad to eliminate leaves, second-crop fruit, and botrytis.

Until 1999 the sorted fruit was completely crushed and pumped into fermentors; now, gentle and partial crushing leaves between 30 percent and 40 percent of the berries uncrushed, and as much as 17 percent in whole clusters. Fermentors are a mix of 6-ton and 9-ton stainless steel open-tops, and double-height fruit bins. After a one- to three-day cold soak, fermentations are started with multiple strains of laboratory yeast, all of which are chosen for their slow action. Until 2001 the must was left alone during the cold

soak; now, punchdowns are started during this phase. There have been no extended macerations since 2002. The winery employs a membrane press and settles the wine in tank before racking it to barrel. Although barrels from Seguin Moreau and Cadus predominate, Panther Creek relies on a large mix of coopers and prefers three-year-air-dried wood that is toasted medium-plus or heavy. New barrels constitute between 30 and 35 percent of the stock in each vintage. Malolactic fermentations are left to start and finish naturally, and the wines are racked after the secondary fermentation has finished. Pinots spend ten to sixteen months in wood before bottling. There is generally no fining, but wines may be coarse-pad filtered "as necessary."

Among the vineyard-designates, Freedom Hill is almost always the densest and darkest wine, demanding the most time before it softens, whereas Bednarik exhibits the most persistently exotic flavor profile. In my experience, vintages up to and including 1999 were very considerably extracted, large-framed wines that were often tough in their youth; now the winery seems to be making polar opposite wines: elegant, finely crafted, and moderate in alcohol. The 2003 and 2004 editions of Freedom Hill, for example, though they are scarcely timid wines and are still the densest bottlings in the Panther Creek portfolio, are both approachably structured, while the 2004 Temperance Hill Vineyard is truly elegant and quite beautiful. It is also instructive to compare the Freedom Hill wines with the wines Michael Stevenson makes under his own label (see STEVENSON-BARRIE).

TASTING NOTES

2006 *Winemaker's Cuvée (tasted in 2007)*: Deeply tinted purplish ruby; intense and very ripe cherry and berry fruit aromas, plus violets; sweet, rich fruit is overcome by an avalanche of very fine-grained tannins at mid-palate; classy, showy, and young, and quite unlike the single-vineyard wines from 2003 and 2004 described below.

2004 *Temperance Hill Vineyard (tasted in 2007):* Brilliant light-to-medium garnet; cosmetics-case nose; intense, resinous red and black fruit on the palate; notes of mesquite; silky at mid-palate, then some grip from mid-palate to finish; insistent minerality; long and attractive.

2004 *Shea Vineyard (tasted in 2007):* Medium rosy-garnet with a shy nose; rich, almost creamy attack with notes of cherry and blackberry pie; infused orange peel and rose petals; considerable attractive grip from mid-palate through the finish; elegant, long, and fine.

2004 *Freedom Hill Vineyard (tasted in 2007):* Brilliant, medium-deep garnet, turning toward mahogany; aromas of ripe fruit, spice, and nutshells; creamy, rich, ripe black fruit on the palate; soft, with some mocha; fine-grained tannin, too; long and very attractive.

2003 *Freedom Hill Vineyard (tasted in 2007):* Transparent, medium black-red; an earthy nose with toasty campfire notes; intense, rich, and chewy on the palate; tannin intensive, but with enough creaminess to cover it; chalky minerality and considerable length; a very good effort in a hot and difficult vintage.

PAPAPIETRO PERRY WINERY

Healdsburg, California

Like Burt Williams, who founded WILLIAMS SELYEM in 1980, Ben Papapietro spent most of his career with the San Francisco Newspaper Agency. In fact, Williams and Papapietro were friends, and Williams offered advice when Papapietro, who had grown up drinking his Italian grandfather's homemade wine with meals, decided to make some wine of his own in his San Francisco garage. Williams was not involved, however, when Papapietro and Bruce Perry, another friend from the paper, and Perry's wife, Renae, turned their joint, twelve-year-old home winemaking venture into a commercial project, with seventy-five cases of pinot noir produced in a custom crush facility near Windsor. Both Papapietro and Perry are also passionate cooks who say they cannot imagine wine without food.

By 2004 the Papapietro Perry brand's production had grown to about 5,000 cases of pinot noir and zinfandel sourced from vineyards in western Sonoma and Anderson Valley. The core sources for pinot are Randy Peters's fog-laced, 25-acre ranch in the Sonoma Coast appellation west of Sebastopol, where 20-plus acres of UCD 4, Dijon 115, and Dijon 777 were planted (along with a bit of chardonnay) in 1989, and the Leras Family Vineyard off Woolsey Road in the Laguna Ridge section of the Russian River Valley, planted to a combination of UCD 4 and three Dijon clones. Papapietro Perry also sources pinot from the Elsbree Vineyard on a steep knoll east of Windsor, where a dozen clones of pinot are farmed, and (beginning in 2006) from the Charles Ranch northwest of Boonville in the Anderson Valley.

WINES AND WINEMAKING NOTES
Ben Papapietro is the hands-on winemaker. In 2004 the brand made vineyard-designated wines from the Peters, Elsbree, and Leras Family vineyards; a barrel selection from the Peters Vineyard named

for Randy Peters's father-in-law Tom Mukaida, who actually owns and farms the ranch; a Russian River appellation wine blended from Leras Family, Elsbree, and a single block of Dijon 115 grown in the Windsor Oaks Vineyard near Elsbree; and a clone-specific wine called Pommard Clones. This last was blended from a combination of Leras Family and Peters lots. The Anderson Valley wine debuted in 2006.

Fruit is normally harvested between 24 and 26 Brix, and each clone and vineyard is handled as a separate fermentation lot. After two or three days of cold soak, most lots are inoculated. The frequency of hand-plunging is adjusted as a function of must temperature: warmer musts are plunged more frequently than cooler musts. Acid is added in warmer vintages. Like Williams Selyem, AU BON CLIMAT, and a few others, Papapietro Perry relies entirely on François Frères barrels, and new wines stay in wood for ten to twelve months.

The wines are pretty, ripe, fruit-forward, spice-flavored, and barrel-marked, and they have a tendency to finish warm with noticeable grip.

TASTING NOTES
2004 *Elsbree Vineyard (tasted in 2007):* Brick-red color; slate-y, earthy, and briary aromas; rich and smoky with a hint of stick cinnamon on the palate; overall impression of extraction and heat; considerable grip; long.

2004 *Peters Vineyard (tasted in 2007):* Transparent, pretty, medium garnet; cherry pie nose; sweet, fruit-driven attack; rich and very slightly creamy mid-palate; impression of tannin and alcohol-derived warmth on the finish.

2004 *Sonoma Coast "Pommard Clones" (tasted in 2007):* Transparent, medium-dark black-red; sweet blueberry and black cherry nose with floral and herbal highlights; nicely balanced combination of sweet fruit and enlivening acidity; rich, elegant, plummy, and spicy with a hint of mocha; almost luscious at the end.

2004 *Russian River Valley (tasted in 2007):* Light-to-medium rosy-magenta; aromas of bay laurel, resin, and dark fruit; hard spice and coffee flavors overlay slightly sweet black fruit in the mouth; warm, long, and grippy at the end.

PATRICIA GREEN CELLARS
Newburg, Oregon

Patricia Green Cellars was created in 2000 when Patty Green and her business partner Jim Anderson bought the former Autumn Wind property, which sits adjacent to Beaux Frères on the west flank of Ribbon Ridge. Green had begun transitioning into winemaking fifteen years earlier from a prior career in forest management and reforestation, working first for several wineries in southern Oregon, and then (from 1993 to 2000) as the winemaker and "sole employee" of TORII MOR WINERY in McMinnville. Anderson, a Maine native with a background in finance and accounting, had the experience of only a single harvest (1994) worked at AMITY VINEYARDS when Green hired him as Torii Mor's "second employee."

Now their estate vineyard consists of 26 planted acres (of which the oldest blocks date to 1983) on a 52-acre parcel, but Green and Anderson also source fruit from vineyards throughout Oregon for an extensive portfolio of vineyard- and block-designated wines and for two or three blends, one of which is a selection of the cellar's "best barrels." The partners farm or control the farming for most of the non-estate vineyards they use and have worked with some of them since their days at Torii Mor. An interesting common denominator is that all the vineyards (or at least the selected blocks) from which Green and

GREEN'S RICH, RIPE, STRUCTURED STYLE BENEFITS ENORMOUSLY FROM SEVERAL YEARS OF BOTTLE AGE

Anderson source fruit are predominantly planted to UCD 4 and 5. Although these selections were anchors for most of Oregon's first-generation pinot vineyards, they have lost ground to Dijon clones in the last decade.

Green's wines have an enviable reputation for deep color and a full spectrum of organic flavors with an emphasis on red fruits, earthy minerality, and good acidity. Green is also not shy about tannins, which are substantially present even in Patricia Green wines from volcanic soil sites; she and Anderson even strive to create some tannin-based structure in their earliest-drinking wine (see below).

WINES AND WINEMAKING NOTES
In every vintage since 2001, Green has made an Oregon blend, a "best of the new barrel(s)" selection called Notorious, one or more estate wines, two *monopole* bottlings from the Balcombe Vineyard and one from the Eason Vineyard, and one or several vineyard-designated wines from Shea Vineyard. The Oregon wine has been consistently anchored with fruit from the Bradley Vineyard (near Elkton, a

small town on the Umpqua River 30 miles from the Pacific) and is raised entirely in one- or two-year-old barrels. The Balcombe Vineyard and Eason Vineyard are both sited on Breyman Orchard Road in the Dundee Hills, and were planted in the 1990s to UCD 4. Except in 2004, a vineyard-designated pinot was also made from the Four Winds Vineyard in the Coast Range west of McMinnville. (Four Winds is also Green's sole source of fruit for a small, tasty, and vaguely Chablisian chardonnay program.)

Beginning in 2002, Green also made tiny quantities of vineyard-designated wine from blocks of the Goldschmidt Vineyard (see the DUSKY GOOSE profile for details); from Quail Hill, a twelve-acre vineyard in Laurelwood-series soil near Rex Hill; and from Anden, the name since 2001 for a vineyard that was formerly part of Seven Springs: a steep, southeast facing slope in the Eola Hills. The 2003 vintage saw the debut of a wine made from Green's upslope neighbor in Ribbon Ridge, Dick and Patricia Alvord's Whistling Ridge Vineyard. Croft Vineyard, another Eola Hills site used by many serious producers, was added to the portfolio in 2004. Ana, a 1976 Dundee Hills planting adjacent to Goldschmidt and Arcus, debuted in 2005. A Reserve blend was made in 2002, 2004, and 2005, when Green and Anderson were able to identify barrels that showed "more oomph" than they customarily seek in the Oregon blend, but less "nuance" than they associate with the vineyard-designates.

Estate fruit has been increasingly segregated into cuvées with differing block origins, as Green and Anderson have worked to rectify poor farming and to achieve the site's full potential. By 2005 the "plain" estate wine came to feature primarily fruit from vines less than fifteen years old. Alongside this "plain" estate wine, Green and Anderson fashioned three additional estate bottlings. The first was an estate "Old Vine" cuvée, based on three blocks that were nineteen, twenty, and twenty-two years old, respectively, to which they added gross less in barrel in an unusual protocol aimed at increasing softness and richness. There were also two block designates: Bonshaw Block, from the warmest and steepest corner of the vineyard, and Etzel Block, from the block closest to the property line with Beaux Frères. Exceptionally, Green also made a non-Oregon pinot in 2002, from the HIRSCH VINEYARDS near Cazadero on the Sonoma Coast.

Green makes decisions about whole-cluster retention based on the vineyard and the vintage, but often opts for a substantial percentage of whole clusters "to accentuate aromatics and make the tannins finer." Acid additions are common, to "keep the fruit bright" and to compensate for high sugar levels at picking. Fruit bins are used for all fermentations. Prefermentation maceration can last for as little as forty-eight hours or as much as eight days, and the must is pressed when a bit of sugar remains. After two or three days' settling, alcoholic fermentations are allowed to finish in barrel "to develop aromatics." Since 2002, the barrels have all been sourced from Cadus, and across the cellar, one third to one half of the barrels are new each year. The wines are not racked until the barrels are sorted between vineyard-designation and blends, and all cuvées are bottled before the following vintage. Nothing is fined, but some lots may be filtered for clarity.

Of the non-estate vineyards, Ana gives perhaps the most elegant and feminine wine, whereas Eason comes closest to the classic, silky red fruit profile of the Dundee Hills. Four Winds is Green's most exotic wine, combining dark berry fruit with brambles and barnyard. Green's rich, ripe style benefits enormously from several years of bottle age, especially considering its short barrel time and early release schedule.

2005 *Ana Vineyard (tasted in 2006):* Dark black-red with rosy highlights; floral and black tea aromas; strawberries and earth on the palate; a medium-bodied wine with intense chalky tannins.

2005 *Eason Vineyard (tasted in 2006):* Brilliant deep black-red; aromas of violets and red cherry; then, cherry, cassis, cola, clay, and earth in the mouth; concentrated and medium in weight with fine-grained tannins.

2002 *Oregon (tasted in 2006):* Brilliant, medium garnet; rose petals and dried leaves on the nose; then, earthy in the mouth with intense flavors of cherry and cassis and hints of licorice and game; light-to-medium in weight and softly tannic with good length.

2000 *Estate (tasted in 2006):* Pretty, rosy-garnet color; aromas of flowers, dried leaves, and gum camphor; then, raspberries in a silky wrapper with only a hint of grip.

PATTON VALLEY VINEYARD
Gaston, Oregon

Patton Valley is a wedge-shaped, east–west oriented valley whose mouth is found just north of the town of Gaston in a major branch of Tualatin River drainage, and whose thin end stretches into the lee side of Oregon's Coast Range. The valley's south side is included within the perimeter of the Yamhill-Carlton AVA, but there were few vineyards on the north side until quite recently.

In 1995 two friends from their student days at Northwestern University's Kellogg School of Management (who cruised Chicago's better wine shops in pursuit of a vinous education alongside their conventional studies in business administration) bought 72 acres here, and began planting vines two years later. Prune and cherry orchard were replaced with two 5-acre blocks of pinot noir. Additional acreage was dedicated to vines each year from 1998 through 2003, until 24 acres had been planted. Most of the plant material is Dijon clones, but there are also some of the Oregon workhorse selections, UCD 2A and 4—with the UCD 4 consistently delivering some of the property's finest results. The soils are Laurelwood series—wind-blown sedimentary material that is widely distributed on the inland face of the nearby Chehalem Mountains—which can also be found on the inland faces of other outcroppings in the immediate environs.

Monte Pitt, the founding duo's more active partner, had done undergraduate work in aerobic fermentation prior to graduate studies in business administration and a career in biotech analysis, and had invested three "slave years" with Michael Etzel at BEAUX FRÈRES, which provided him with sufficient background to be able to make Patton Valley's first vintages hands-on, in 1999 and 2000. Pitt was succeeded as winemaker by Todd Hamina, who left for MAYSARA, southwest of McMinnville, in 2004; Hamina was followed by Jerry Murray, a man with "culinary experience" who grew up around agriculture and taught physiology in Ohio before learning winemaking at ERATH VINEYARDS AND WINERY, PANTHER CREEK CELLARS, and J. K. CARRIÈRE. For good measure, he also worked at Highfield Estates in

New Zealand and at the well-known house of Selbach-Oster at Zeltingen, in the Mosel Valley. Patton Valley's other partner is David Chen, whose career involves management consulting and venture capital, but whose business-related move to Portland in the early 1990s focused the partnership decisively on Oregon sites suitable for pinot noir.

Farming has been organic *almost* from the outset. Limited drip irrigation, installed when the first vines were laid out in 1997, has been abandoned in favor of complete dry farming since 2000. The vines, which have been planted in 6-foot rows with 5 feet between vines on each of the east-, south- and southwest-facing slopes, are remarkably self-regulating despite relatively deep topsoil, so that canopy management and green harvesting are both minimal.

WINES AND WINEMAKING NOTES
Grapes are generally picked between 24 and 25 Brix. The fermentations rely on resident yeasts, which seem to leave a signature of exotic Asian spice in the wines. Once pressed, the wines go to barrel without settling, on their gross lees, and are racked only if necessary. They spend eleven months in wood, primarily Cadus, Damy, and François Frères, of which a decreasing percentage is new in each vintage. (The first vintages of Patton Valley were made using up to 80 percent new oak; this percentage has now dropped to between 45 and 50 percent.)

The property makes two wines, both entirely from estate fruit. The main release is a Willamette Valley cuvée, but three or four barrels in each vintage are set aside for a reserve wine called Lorna Marie. Typically, Lorna Marie is disproportionately reliant on UCD 4, while the Willamette Valley cuvée is anchored with Dijon clones. In the early years, estate fruit was also sold to Beaux Frères (which used it in the Belles Soeurs blend) and to Elk Cove, but such sales had all but ceased by 2006. The wines are very impressive, with reliably good acidity, bright flavors, an intense display of exotic spice, and considerable elegance.

TASTING NOTES

2005 *Willamette Valley (tasted in 2007):* Medium ruby-garnet color that is red to the rim; a fruit-driven nose of black cherry with Asian spice; on the palate, it is fruit forward with a slightly grippy edge; nice acid, dusty tannins, and impressive length.

2004 *Willamette Valley (tasted in 2007):* Very light, brilliant garnet; aromatic evolution already with notes of mushroom; bright red cherry with some raspberry and thyme on the palate; nice length and very attractive; fine.

2004 *Lorna Marie (tasted in 2007):* Color much like the Willamette Valley cuvée; strong aromas of Asian spice and camphorwood; slightly fruit-sweeter than the Willamette Valley, with strong notes of rose flower water; very pretty, elegant wine. Fine.

2002 *Willamette Valley (tasted in 2007):* Light-to-medium garnet that is red to the edge; intensely earthy and strongly spicy nose redolent of camphorwood and cedar; enormously deep flavors of spice and cherry; now losing the baby fat of a relatively warm vintage; elegant.

2001 *Willamette Valley (tasted in 2007):* Light-to-medium terra cotta; intense, clean scents of gum camphor, Asian spice, vanilla, and assorted cosmetics; solid but softening tannins on the palate with good structure and notes of orange peel. Fine.

2000 *Willamette Valley (tasted in 2007):* Light-to-medium terra cotta; evolved aromatically with earth, forest floor, peat, vermiculite, and sphagnum moss; still some bright berry fruit on the palate, with orange peel; bright with attractive grip.

PATZ & HALL WINE COMPANY
Napa, California

Donald and Heather Patz, James Hall, and Anne Moses created the Patz & Hall Wine Company in 1988, which was focused initially on chardonnay made from purchased fruit, and which operated on about the same scale as a medium-sized *propriétaire-récoltant* in the Côte d'Or. Hall and Moses are the winemaking side of the venture, with experience (between them) at Flora Springs, Honig, Far Niente, Spring Mountain, and MARIMAR ESTATE; the two Patzes contribute hands-on expertise in sales and marketing. Donald Patz and James Hall met when they both worked at Flora Springs, as national sales manager and assistant winemaker, respectively, in the mid 1980s. A 1985 Flora Springs experiment called Leaping Lizards, involving the musqué clone of chardonnay finished with full malolactic fermentation but not filtered, was part of the inspiration for the partners' new venture.

In the tradition of this experiment, Patz & Hall focused from the outset on the importance of clones and selections, of gentle handling as a determinant of aging potential, and of the circumstances in which wines can be safely bottled without filtration. From the first release in 1988, the brand made only chardonnay until 1995, when the first pinot noir was added to its offerings. Patz explains that they considered other red varieties initially, but "were very interested in how [pinot noir] was improving all over the cooler areas of California."

Pinot fruit was purchased from the Aquarius Ranch, a 1992 planting on the downslope side of Westside Road near Porter Creek, in the Russian River valley, in 1995, and was made and bottled as Russian River Valley pinot noir. A Russian River Valley bottling was then made in each subsequent vintage except in 1999 (see below), but the fruit sources have evolved considerably. In 1996 and 1997, the wine was a blend of lots from Aquarius Ranch and Saralee's Richard's Grove vineyard. In 1998 Saralee's Richard's Grove was the sole source. The 1999 edition, though anchored with Russian River valley fruit, contained enough wine from Patz & Hall's Mount Veeder source that it was bottled as a Sonoma County wine. The Russian River sources in 1999 were Saralee's Buggy Patch parcel, planted to a mix of UCD 2A and UCD 23; Catie's Corner vineyard near Windsor; and Keefer Ranch, a Green Valley site planted entirely to Dijon clones that is also used by FLOWERS VINEYARD and TANDEM WINES. The 2000 Russian River was once

CAREFULLY CRAFTED, DEEPLY COLORED, MEDIUM WEIGHT WINES WITH RIPE FRUIT AND WELL-BEHAVED TANNINS

again anchored with the Buggy Patch parcel of Saralee's Vineyard, plus Catie's Corner, Keefer Ranch, and a block called Pie Shaped Piece farmed by Lee Martinelli. With the 2001 vintage, fruit from Dutton's Thomas Road Vineyard was added to the mix of Saralee's, Catie's Corner, and Pie

Shaped Piece. In 2002 the blended wine was rechristened Sonoma Coast, reflecting the use of a substantial quantity of fruit from PEAY VINEYARDS near Annapolis and from the McDougal Vineyard north of Flowers, complementing the Russian River and Green Valley sources that anchored the 2001 blend. Fruit sources for the Sonoma Coast blend have continued to evolve. Peay, McDougal, and Keefer are no longer used.

Meanwhile, in 1996, the partners began purchasing fruit from Larry Hyde's Los Carneros vineyard, which emerged as Patz & Hall's first vineyard-designated pinot. In 1997 vineyard-designated wines from the PISONI VINEYARD in the Santa Lucia Highlands and from the Alder Springs Vineyard, a 2,100-foot site near the hamlet of Laytonville in Mendocino County, about 7 miles from the Pacific Coast, were also introduced. A wine from Lee Martinelli's Burnside Road Vineyard, and east-facing parcel in the Sebastopol Hills planted to Dijon 115, has been vineyard-designated since 2002. Another vineyard-designated wine from Charlie Chenoweth's vineyard, which is seven acres of Dijon clones in Green Valley, in Goldridge series soils, debuted in 2004. Fruit from the Jenkins Vineyard, which Patz & Hall call the Jenkins Ranch Vineyard, planted to Dijon 115 and 777 and located on a ridge overlooking Sebastopol (a site also used by LYNMAR WINERY for vineyard-designated wine), joined the lineup in 2005. With the exceptions of Hyde and Pisoni, the common characteristic of Patz & Hall's fruit sources for pinot is relatively young plantings of Dijon clones.

The wines were made in rented space at Honig Cellars in Rutherford through 2006. A purpose-built winery and elegant tasting "salon" in Sonoma were ready in time for the 2007 harvest.

WINEMAKING NOTES

Hall explains that "no single factor" governs the picking decision, but he defines *mature grapes* in terms of "mature tannins," "ripe seeds," and good acidity. His subsequent decisions about length of fermentation, punchdowns, and fermentation temperature all revolve, he says, around the type, quantity, and maturity of tannins in the fruit. That said, Hall finds that he usually ends up picking pinot between 24 and 25 Brix.

Somewhere between 5 percent and 25 percent whole clusters are then layered on the bottom of each fermentor, with the exact percentage dependent on acid levels, stem maturity, how much red fruit aroma is typical of the vineyard, and how much tannin can be tolerated in the specific vintage. Destemmed grapes, poured directly from macro-bins, are then layered on top of the whole clusters. The combination of whole clusters and whole berries promotes slower fermentations at higher temperatures, which Hall finds conducive to "better tannin extraction" with "softer and more complex tannin polymers." The fermentors are very wide open-tops that handle 4 to 6 tons each.

There is only the briefest of cold soaks, since primary fermentations usually start within two days. Inoculation with RC 212 yeast is typical. Hall adds acid if the finished wine will have a pH value higher than 3.7, and "often" also adds a color-extraction enzyme. The must is pumped over on the first day of primary fermentation and then punched down three to five times daily, but sometimes a mix of punchdowns and pumpovers is practiced, depending on the condition of the berries and how the tannins are being extracted. Peak juice temperatures during fermentation range between 80 and 84°F, and Hall uses heaters to maintain this temperature even toward the end of the fermentation, which lasts seven to twelve days. The must is usually pressed at about zero Brix, goes into barrel with all its lees the day after pressing, and finishes its primary fermentation in wood. Malolactic starter is added in barrel six to eight weeks later. Various unspecified strategies are used to compensate for what Hall admits are "high Brix levels."

Preferred coopers are François Frères, Seguin Moreau, and Meyrieux, but small numbers of other barrels are also used. From François Frères, Patz & Hall purchases stave wood in advance, which is air-dried for three years before being coopered, making for "more sweet spice" and "less drying oak tannins." Between 55 and 80 percent new wood is used, depending on the weight of each wine. Barrels are considered new if they are either entirely new or have previously been used only for chardonnay.

The wines are left on their lees until one month before bottling, with weekly stirrings before and during the malolactic fermentation. At this point the wines are racked off their lees and are immediately returned to barrel for a final month in clean wood. Total barrel time is ten to eleven months. The wines are rarely fined and, so far, never filtered.

Patz & Hall pinots are medium-weight, rich, and impressive, with uncharacteristically strong minerality. They are carefully crafted, deeply-colored, medium-weight wines that generally display ripe-picked fruit and well-behaved tannins. The high percentage of new barrels used for *élevage* is generally reflected in very noticeable barrel-derived aromatics. Although each bottling is distinctive, there is considerable stylistic consistency across the portfolio.

2005 *Alder Springs Vineyard (tasted in 2007)*: Luminous, but deeply-tinted, black-red; an exotic nose of cumin, mace, and coriander, plus dark cherry and black licorice; sweet, clean, and intense attack; blackberry and hard spice at mid-palate; grippy at the end; warm, full bodied, and mouth coating.

2005 *Sonoma Coast (tasted in 2007)*: Medium black-red; briar, hard spice, and shy fruit on the nose; bright, red berry flavors on the palate with some pomegranate and infused lavender, plus a hint of black pepper; satiny in texture, and especially food friendly.

2005 *Chenowith Ranch (tasted in 2007)*: Medium-dark black-red; mostly rose petal and violets on the nose; bold, menthol- and briar-tinged dark red fruit and fruit-seasoned tea on the palate; a bit of minty spice as well; bright overall with a bit of bite at the end.

2005 *Jenkins Ranch (tasted in 2007)*: Transparent dark black-garnet; dusty berry aromas and some floral notes in a generally shy nose; blackberries and cream on the palate with red fruit, mesquite, and pepper in the background; sturdy, serious pinot with some grip at the end.

2005 *Pisoni Vineyard (tasted in 2007)*: Luminous medium-dark garnet; sweet, ripe nose with a whiff of dried currants; very sweet, raisiny flavors on the palate; some mocha and chocolate; rich, briary, and long; good with cheese, perhaps, but too sweet and alcoholic to be generally food friendly.

2003 *Hyde Vineyard (tasted in 2006)*: Dark garnet; expressive nose of flowers, cherry, raspberry, and citrus peel; racy and fruity on the palate with peppery notes, a clove-y finish, and considerable barrel-marking; nicely built and long overall, with attractively lingering flavors.

PAUL HOBBS WINES
Sebastopol, California

Paul Hobbs was raised on an upstate New York farm where his family replaced part of an apple orchard with a vineyard in 1969. In college, at the University of Notre Dame, he took botany (and wine tasting) from a Christian Brother who had worked previously as a winemaker in California; after college, he earned a master's degree in food science (with an emphasis on enology) at the University of California Davis. His thesis on the chemistry of wine maturation in oak barrels attracted attention from California vintners, whose use of new barrels for *élevage* was then exploding.

His career was then almost meteoric, beginning with a rapid succession of increasingly responsible positions at ROBERT MONDAVI WINERY; through two jobs at Simi Winery, of which the second was vice president and winemaker; to responsibility for a highly visible project to make world-class chardonnay for Nicolas Catena in Argentina's Mendoza Province, and consulting for some of California's best-known wine labels; and finally to a winery and label of his own, created in 1991. Although Hobbs's own cabernets, merlots, chardonnays, syrahs, and pinot noirs attract a good deal of very positive attention, his partnership with Luis Barraud and Andrea Marchiori in the Mendoza, his import company, and a continuing string of consultancies on three continents are arguably more visible, creating the impression of a man in almost perpetual motion, in quite exalted circles.

After several years of itinerant existence in leased and shared spaces, Paul Hobbs

Wines settled into dedicated facilities on the Gravenstein Highway, north of Sebastopol, in 2002. The winery was constructed on the site of Hobbs's estate vineyard on Laguna Ridge, where 14 acres of pinot noir were planted in 1998. The site, called Lindsay Vineyard, is a gently rolling hillside facing mostly south and southwest, in Goldridge series soils, and the scion material is a combination of UCD 10, Dijon 115 and 777, and Swan and Calera selections, on three rootstocks. The first crop was harvested in 2002.

WINES AND WINEMAKING NOTES

The cornerstone of the pinot program is a vineyard-designated wine from the Hyde Vineyard in Carneros, made in every vintage since 1991. In exceptional years like 1999, 2000, 2001, and 2002, a reserve quality wine was also made from Hyde fruit. This cuvee, called Agustina, is first a vine-by-vine and cluster-by-cluster selection from among Hyde's Calera vines, which Hobbs likes especially for their naturally low pH even in warm vintages, and then also a barrel selection in the cellar to privilege barrels with special concentration. When the estate vineyard began to bear in 2002, a Russian River Valley appellation wine was added to the Hobbs portfolio, crafted from a combination of the first estate fruit and grapes purchased from a few neighboring sites. Frank Darien's Amber Ridge Vineyard near Windsor (which has also been sourced by KOSTA BROWNE, SIDURI WINES, and SONNET WINES) was used from 2002 through 2005; Anderson-Ross was used in 2002 only; Terry Gibson's vineyard on Ross Road in Green Valley has been used since 2003. A second Russian River Valley appellation wine called CrossBarn is crafted from declassified barrels. Two Russian River

Valley vineyard-designated wines debuted in 2005 and have been made in every vintage since. One of these is Hobbs's own Lindsay Estate Vineyard; the other is a Ulises Valdez Vineyard wine. Valdez, which is located about 2 miles north of Lindsay on Laguna Ridge is planted mostly to Calera selection. It is also used by Mark Aubert for a single vineyard bottling called UV.

Hobbs has a reputation for very ripe picking. He explains that he looks for "full enological ripeness" and ripe tannins, and therefore postpones picking until he sees lignified stems and seeds, and "senescence of canopy." In cool years such as 2005 and 2006, he says he can pick "around 25 Brix," but admits that sugars have sometimes risen much higher. When this happens, water may be added to some musts to ensure that fermentations can finish dry and reduce the alcoholic content of the finished wine. Reverse osmosis was used "once" to reduce alcohol, but Hobbs says he dislikes this process. Although he destemmed all fruit until recently, he reports "going back to some whole cluster" in recent years, looking for "more than fruit" in the finished wines. No enzymes are added. Acid is added "only in very hot years." A three to four day cold soak is followed by primary fermentations that rely on resident yeasts. The new wines are pressed off when they are dry and barreled for between eleven and sixteen months. Wines are left on their gross less for seven to eight months without any stirring, and are then racked to clean barrels. Remond and François Frerés account for a majority of the cooperage, but barrels from Cadus and Damy are also used. There is no fining or filtration. The wines described below are rich, extracted, very mouth filling, and quintessentially New World editions of pinot noir.

TASTING NOTES

2005 *Hyde Vineyard (tasted in 2007):* Medium-dark, black-red color; aromas of violets, citrus peel, barrel char, and vanilla; sweet black fruit on the palate that ranges from dark cherry through marionberry to huckleberry; utterly mouth filling, as if the wine were determined to fill every crevice; a substantial load of very fine-grained tannin creates a chalky feeling overall; warm, rich, and intentionally impressive.

2005 *Lindsay Estate Vineyard (tasted in 2007):* Opaque, very dark purplish black; a dark, brooding nose of wet earth, violets, and lacquer; very sweet attack with an avalanche of ripe red and black fruit; very large-framed and richly textured; some flavors of chocolate and berry pie; massive.

2005 *Russian River Valley (tasted in 2007):* Opaque, dark black-red; roasted root vegetables, ripe dark fruit, smoke, and wet clay on the nose; rich chocolate-mocha flavors and some graphite in the mouth; utterly mouth filling again; the fruit gives way to a large load of tannin from mid-palate to finish; warm.

PAUL LATO WINES
Santa Maria, California

Paul Lato is a Polish expatriate who left Poland in its last two years under Communist rule, and went first to Sweden, then to Spain, and finally to Canada, where he studied hospitality management and became a successful sommelier. In 1996, determined to make wine of his own, he assembled very modest savings and moved from Toronto to California's southern Central Coast. Now he works miscellaneous jobs around wine (including the tasting room at TALLEY VINEYARDS) to support himself in an exceedingly modest style, sublets space for his barrels and equipment from other winemakers at Central Coast Wine Services in Santa Maria, cooks occasionally and generously for friends, and devotes all the time he can to making infinitesimal quantities of superb syrah and pinot noir.

The first pinots were based on fruit from Gary Burk's Gold Coast Vineyard (see COSTA DE ORO) on Santa Maria Mesa, beginning in 2002. He calls this wine *duende,* a Spanish word that commonly translates as ghost, goblin, or genie, but which denotes charisma by figurative extension, and signifies what Lato calls "the demon that possesses you." And Lato does seem possessed, albeit calmly and quietly, with the ineluctable genius of wine and with a passion to make it very well indeed. A second pinot, from the Miller family's new millennium planting at Solomon Hills, debuted in 2005. In 2006 Fiddlestix Vineyard (see FIDDLEHEAD WINES) became Lato's third source for pinot. Each of these is made as a vineyard-designated wine.

Lato says he thinks long and hard about ripeness and picking, and looks for a "sweet spot" that will produce finished wines between 14 and 14.7 percent alcohol. In the cellar, Lato favors complete destemming, a long cold soak of up to seven days, a hot fermentation, and some postfermentation maceration. He has experimented with resident yeasts and likes the results, but typically inoculates with RC 212. The new wines are kept on their gross lees, without racking, until August following the vintage, at which point the wines are returned to barrel for another two to seven months. New barrels account for half to three quarters of the cellar's stock.

The final blends are made just before bottling, and even with the tiny quantities that characterize his operations to date, entire barrels are declassified if they are "just good" and not "exceptional." The first editions of Duende are substantial, but also elegant, seamless, and impressive.

TASTING NOTES

2005 *Gold Coast Vineyard Duende (tasted in 2007):* Medium garnet; intense nose of ink and caramel over black raspberry; then, silky, rich, elegant, and long, with notes of mocha and tangerine peel.

2003 *Gold Coast Vineyard Duende (tasted in 2006):* Medium garnet with pink-orange highlights; aromas of rose petals and aromatic herbs; sweet, black raspberries on a ground of wet earth and bay laurel; very intense, clean, and elegant with precisely defined flavors and a long, silky finish. Very fine. A personal favorite.

2002 *Gold Coast Vineyard Duende (tasted twice, in 2005 and 2006):* Very slightly hazy medium garnet; nutty and softly spicy in 2005, but brilliantly aromatic with gum camphor, white pepper, and dried, savory herbs in 2006; bright, intense black raspberry, pepper, and spice on the mid-palate, plus flavors of toasty wood and infused flowers; medium in weight, beautifully structured, concentrated, and long. Fine.

PEAY VINEYARDS
Cloverdale, California

In 1997 and 1998, Nick and Andy Peay planted the first modern vineyard overlooking the Wheatfield Fork of the Gualala River, near the hamlet of Annapolis, 4 miles from the Pacific, in the extreme northwest corner of the Sonoma Coast appellation. The brothers were raised in Cleveland, in a wine-drinking family, and their mother was a serious cook. Nick is a Bowdoin College graduate in Far Eastern History, with a college-classmate connection to Hugh Davies, the son of

WINES WITH CONSIDERABLE AROMATIC COMPLEXITY AND AN ADMIRABLE JUXTAPOSITION OF INTENSITY AND ELEGANCE

Jack and Jamie Davies, who had founded Schramsberg Vineyards in the 1960s. After college a harvest's work at Schramsberg, on-the-job training with Bill Smith at La Jota Vineyard Company, and viticulture classes at Santa Rosa Junior College led to degree work in enology at the University of California Davis, and then to a position as assistant winemaker for Storrs Winery in the Santa Cruz Mountains.

By 1994 Nick and Andy (a onetime banker with an MBA from the University of California Berkeley) began searching the California coast for sites that seemed well suited to their emerging passion, which was pinot noir. The Annapolis ranch, which consisted of about 80 acres of one-time timber farm redeveloped as apple orchard and sheep pasture early in the twentieth century, appealed because of its cool, fog-influenced mesoclimate, moderately steep slopes, well-drained and low-vigor sandy loam soil with a mildly calcareous underlay of uplifted seabed, and west and southwest orientation. These properties seemed to meet the Peay's desiderata better than sites near the Petaluma Gap or in the southern Central Coast; Nick thought the true coastal site promised (inter alia) good physiological ripeness without excessive sugar, and good acid retention.

The first 30 acres were planted in 1998; 18 more followed in 2001 and 2002. Of these 48, 33 were committed to nine selections of pinot noir on six rootstocks. In 2008 the numbers increased to 35 acres of pinot in a total planted surface of 50 acres.

Meanwhile, as Andy assumed duties focused on marketing a new brand, Nick married Vanessa Wong, another Davis-trained winemaker, with European experience at Domaine Jean Gros in Vosne-Romanée, who had established an enviable reputation for distinguished editions of several varieties at the venerated Peter Michael Winery. In 2001 Wong left Peter Michael to make the inaugural vintage at Peay: small quantities of marsanne, roussanne, chardonnay, and syrah.

The Peays' 2001 pinot crop was sold to FLOWERS VINEYARDS AND WINERY, PATZ & HALL, and WILLIAMS SELYEM, and limited pinot fruit sales continued to assortments of those and other producers (including ROESSLER CELLARS, Ryan Cellars, and FAILLA WINES) in succeeding vintages, even as Peay built its own pinot program from 2002. By 2006 Peay's only remaining fruit clients for pinot noir were Williams Selyem, which took blocks of Dijon 777, UCD 4, and Calera selection, and Failla, which received a small amount of Dijon 115. Simultaneously, Peay's own production reached 2,000 cases of pinot.

WINES AND WINEMAKING NOTES
From 2002 to 2004, Peay made a single pinot, simply called Estate. In 2005, with viable fruit from the 2001 and 2002 plantings joining fruit from the 1998 blocks, Wong saw an opportunity to craft two quite different estate blends. The first

of these, called Pomarium, is based on a preponderance of Dijon clones 667 and 777. The second, dubbed Scallop Shelf, is anchored with a near-majority of UCD 4 selection. In principle, Pomarium is a brighter wine intended to emphasize red fruit over black, while Scallop Shelf is deeper flavored, fuller bodied, and built to last. My own tasting experience differs slightly, however (see below).

Thus far in the pinot program, Wong has destemmed almost all Peay pinot, except that she experimented with 10 to 30 percent of whole clusters on five lots in 2006. She cold-soaks the fruit as whole berries for four to six days in (mostly) 1- and 3-ton stainless steel open-tops; presses when the must tests dry, or even twenty-four to forty-eight hours thereafter; uses about 40 percent new oak in a ten-month barrel program that features an assortment of coopers; and bottles without fining or filtration. (Wong says she "remains open" to a longer barrel regime as the vines mature and has sized the new winery—in Cloverdale—such that 50 percent of the pinot can be held in barrel until after the succeeding vintage if necessary, but she finds that fruit from young vines can develop cherry-cola flavors if such wine stays too long in barrel.)

In all vintages to date, Peay has declassified barrels deemed unsuitable for the estate blends. These are used for a second label offered entirely to restaurants for use in by-the-glass wine programs. Overall, Peay pinots are nicely structured wines with more texture than fruit-sweetness, considerable aromatic complexity, and an admirable juxtaposition of intensity and elegance.

TASTING NOTES
2005 *Scallop Shelf (tasted in 2007):* Transparent, medium magenta; nose dominated by exotic spice and

sandalwood; slightly sweet (compared with the Pomarium cuvée) on the palate; substantial, grippy, and mouth coating, with flavors of dried cherries and conifer foliage. Hefty but balanced.

2005 *Pomarium (tasted in* 2007): Slow to open but eventually gives up some red fruit aromas and jasmine tea; dark fruit with some glycerin in the mouth; very mouth coating, broad shouldered, and velvety to grippy at the end, intense and long.

2004 *Estate (tasted in* 2007): Transparent, medium black-red; slightly reticent nose; intense, bright, dark cherry fruit, with overtones of cranberry on the palate; notes of French-roast coffee and mocha, light tannins; fine length and elegance. A warm growing season seems to have given an especially fine wine here, which is a personal favorite.

PENNER-ASH WINE CELLARS
Newburg, Oregon

Lynn Penner-Ash's first undergraduate major, at the University of California Davis, was botany. Before she graduated, it had changed twice: first to viticulture, and then to fermentation science with an emphasis on enology. After graduation, she worked first at Stag's Leap Wine Cellars in the Napa Valley, and then at Oregon's REX HILL VINEYARD. Hired initially as Rex Hill's winemaker, she became its president and chief operating officer in 1993.

In 1998, still at Rex Hill, she and her husband Ron, a career teacher in public schools and self-styled passionate cellar rat, created their own wine brand,

dedicated to small amounts of hand crafted syrah and pinot noir. The brand relied on purchased fruit, and on space at Rex Hill, until 2002, when the Penner-Ash's joined forces with Chris Dussin and his wife Tyanne. The Dussins were anchored in the Oregon restaurant business (Portland's famous Old Spaghetti Factory restaurant) and were interested in developing a vineyard.

Together, the couples found a suitable site on the east edge of the Yamhill-Carlton AVA and a stone's throw from Dick Shea's eponymous vineyard, but looking mostly east and southeast over the Chehalem Valley. In the course of a five-year partnership, the two couples designed and built a stunning winery and tasting room on this site, established access from Ribbon Ridge Road, and developed 15 acres of vineyard around the winery, facing primarily southeast, in a propitious combination of volcanic and sedimentary soils. The scion material was UCD 4, UCD 5, and Dijon 114, 115, 667, and 777. The 2002, 2003, and 2004 vintages of Penner-Ash were made at the Carlton Winemakers Studio while the new winery was in design and under construction; the new vineyard produced its first crop in 2005. In 2007 the Penner-Ash's bought the Dussin's interest in the Penner-Ash brand and the winery.

WINES AND WINEMAKING NOTES
From 1998 to 2001, Penner-Ash made only one pinot, a Willamette Valley blend anchored with fruit from the Seven Springs Vineyard in the Eola Hills. Lynn Penner-Ash describes this wine as the brand's "flagship," blended before any lots are earmarked for single-vineyard treatment. Beginning in 2002, however, four vineyard-designated wines were made alongside the Willamette Valley cuvée: Seven Springs, Goldschmidt,

Bethel Heights, and Shea. To this portfolio, a Dussin Vineyard wine from the aforementioned estate planting was added in 2005, as were wines from the CARABELLA VINEYARD (a Parrett Mountain site) and from Palmer Creek (on the west flank of the Eola Hills) in 2006.

The house style is focused on "upfront elegance," and "monstrosities" are eschewed, but grapes are typically picked quite ripe. Most fruit is destemmed, but 10 to 20 percent of the Seven Springs grapes are sometimes retained as whole clusters. Long cold soaks are enforced with dry ice, and Lynn Penner-Ash will add acid if necessary, but never enzymes, to the must. Primary fermentations rely on resident yeasts, but Penner-Ash believes that long, slow malolactic fermentations contribute to the upfront elegance she seeks in pinot noir so the barrel cellar is kept cool through the winter after the vintage. The new wines stay in barrel for nine or ten months, and the barrel stock consists of approximately 35 percent new oak. The wines are typically riper, more concentrated, and more intensely flavored than the pinots Penner-Ash made at Rex Hill, and they have been very well received by critics.

TASTING NOTES

2005 *Willamette Valley (tasted in 2007):* Brilliant medium garnet, aromas of lavender and violets; intense, sappy cherry-plum flavors in the mouth with a strong impression of black tea; very bright with good acidity, some grip, and medium in length.

2005 *Dussin Vineyard (tasted in 2007):* Brilliant, medium rosy-garnet with an almost orange rim; freshly-turned spring soil and dusty minerality on the nose; chewy, sappy, rich, cherry pie flavors on the palate with plenty of grip; needs time to soften.

2005 *Shea Vineyard (tasted in 2007):* Aromas of flowers, hard spice, and black tea; rich and sweet on the palate, with fruit-coated tannins; a broad-shouldered and mouth-coating wine but not at all a heavyweight; long.

1998 *Willamette Valley (tasted in 2007):* Pretty red-mahogany color; nutshells, mocha, and leather on the nose; camphor, sandalwood, caramelized sugar, and Tootsie Roll flavors on the palate, substantially evolved but still very sound, with significant remaining grip.

PEY-MARIN VINEYARDS
AND
PEY-LUCIA VINEYARDS
San Anselmo, California

Marin County, north of San Francisco, across the Golden Gate Bridge, is better known for picturesque waterfront suburbs than for dairy farms and oyster beds, and then better for the pastures and oysters than for vineyards. The truth is, however, that vineyards have existed in Marin for almost two centuries, and that noteworthy pinots have been made from Marin grapes since the 1980s. Surrounded on three sides by water, and its west side bathed in morning fog for much of the growing season, Marin enjoys warmer winters and cooler summers than all except the true coastal part of neighboring Sonoma, creating the sort of environment that seems propitious for cool-climate grape varieties.

Jonathan and Susan Pey—he an agronomist by training, with vineyard experience in Burgundy, Australia, and California, and she a wine buyer for the respected Il Fornaio restaurant group—grow pinot on an 8-acre site on the county's west side that was developed in 1990, part of which was T-budded to pinot noir in 2004. The couple began producing a small quantity of Marin County pinot noir from two neighboring vineyard blocks in 2002. Estate fruit from their converted 1990 vineyard entered the program in 2005.

The Peys call their Marin pinot "Trois Filles," in honor of their three young daughters. They say it is a blended wine "by design" rather than necessity, since they believe in general that "blending produces superior wine." The 2002 and 2003 editions of "Trois Filles" relied entirely on Dijon clone fruit; the use of fruit from their estate vineyard beginning in 2005 added Swan selection (taken from Carneros Creek) to the palette.

Clusters are entirely destemmed, although 5 percent of whole berries are retained; resident yeasts take fermentations to their mid-point before cultured yeasts are added to finish them; and acid adjustments are "minimal." The new wine is normally pressed before the must goes dry so that fermentations finish in barrel for "creaminess." The barrel regime relies on about 35 percent new oak from Cadus, Remond, and François Frères, and the wines stay in barrel for about twelve months before bottling, depending on the vintage. There is usually no racking, but frequent lees stirring is routine.

A second Pey family pinot program, called Pey-Lucia, is based on Santa Lucia Highlands fruit grown in the Lone Oak Vineyard next to Gary Franscioni's Rosella's Vineyard in the appellation's midpoint; this will be released in 2008. (The Peys also make an impressive, bright, mineral-laden dry riesling from estate fruit, and warmer climate varieties under the Mount Tamalpais Vineyard label.) The pinots to date have been intense, nicely-built, high-toned wines with complex aromatics, modest alcohols, and admirable elegance.

TASTING NOTES

2002 *Trois Filles (tasted in* 2004*):* Brilliant, light-to-medium ruby with a pink rim; engaging nose of cherry, raspberry, and flowers; light-to-medium body and weight, with intense berry flavor and a hint of leather; slightly short finish but very elegant.

2004 *Trois Filles (tasted in* 2006*):* Brilliant rosy-garnet; a concerto of intense red berry, conifer, and smoke on the nose; high-toned cherry-berry fruit, with hints of resin and spice in the mouth; some fruit-sweetness and some grip; enough weight to be serious and enough restraint to be elegant; very attractive and impressive.

PISONI VINEYARDS AND WINERY AND LUCIA
Gonzales, California

Gary Pisoni, a colorful, outspoken, and passionate hedonist once described (by New York City wine merchant Peter Morrell) as "the personification of Bacchus," is a watershed figure in the transformation of the northern Salinas Valley into serious wine country. Far from the first person to plant vineyards on the valley's west side, and not yet a winegrower when the Santa Lucia Highlands AVA was established, Pisoni is significant as the fulcrum on which the area's fortunes were tied to pinot noir and as the magnet that first attracted a phenomenal stream of talented boutique winemakers to Santa Lucia Highlands fruit.

He represents the third generation of a Swiss-Italian family that settled in the dusty hamlet of Gonzales at the end of the nineteenth century, and the son of parents who built a very successful family business on huge fields of lettuce, onions, broccoli, cauliflower, and celery after World War II. In 1979 Pisoni's parents used celery profits to finance the purchase of some pretty oak-studded upland at the south end of the appellation, overlooking the fertile valley,

---

THE MAGNET THAT ATTRACTED A PHENOMENAL STREAM OF TALENTED WINEMAKERS TO THE SANTA LUCIA HIGHLANDS

---

as pasture "for a couple of horses and a few head of cattle." But their son, who had discovered wine in Puerto Rico when his parents took him along on a trip intended to sell potatoes—a fussy sommelier stimulated Pisoni to ascertain whether "the wine thing was real or bunk" (!)—thought the ranch had promise as vineyard.

In 1982 he planted 6 acres of chardonnay, merlot, cabernet franc, own-rooted cabernet sauvignon, and pinot noir, and irrigated the struggling vines with trucked-in water. Simultaneously he began making a bit of wine at home. When a productive well was finally drilled on the property in 1991, Pisoni set about planting additional vineyard, consisting entirely of pinot noir. The 17-acre Tessa Block (also known as Big Block) came first; followed by Hermanos (5 acres), Camper (2.5 acres), and Tina (a 1.2-acre experiment in lyre-trellising) in 1994; Elias Block (4.5 acres) in 1995; and Mommies block (2.5 acres) in 1999. Elevations and orientations vary, and the soils differ from block to block in terms of rockiness, sandiness, and vigor. With each planting, Pisoni experimented methodically with different vine spacings, trellising schemes,

and row orientations, and specifically tested the performance of grafted versus own-rooted vines. He claims the own-rooted vines produce better wine and reserves one of the own-rooted blocks, Elias, for his estate wine (see below).

The scion material used for all the pinot-only plantings was originally reported to be a field selection from La Tâche in Vosne-Romanée, imported personally and illicitly by Pisoni, but Pisoni himself no longer makes this claim, having bowed to pressure from attorneys representing the French Institut national des appelations d'origine contrôlée who charged that, irrespective of the facts, use of the La Tâche name to identify the source of the budwood constituted infringement on the intellectual property right that inheres in French vineyard and appellation names. Other well-informed sources assert that Pisoni's budwood was not a direct import from La Tâche or any other French vineyard; on the contrary, they say, its proximate source was a vineyard in nearby Carmel Valley. The two versions of the story may or may not conflict, but neither can be confirmed.

In 1997 Pisoni's viticultural enterprise expanded beyond his parents' ranch to a second, lower-elevation site about 8 miles away, in the very heart of the Santa Lucia Highlands appellation. Here, Pisoni joined forces with his old friend and schoolmate Gary Franscioni to plant a 50-acre vineyard of which 42 acres are pinot noir, appropriately called Garys', on rocky, sandy-clay benchland formerly used to graze sheep. The same budwood (whatever its true origin) used since 1991 at Pisoni was also used on this site, and the vineyard is farmed with the same attention to detail for which Pisoni had already become legendary. The first crush at Garys' was in 1999.

WINES AND WINEMAKING NOTES

In the wake of the stellar reputation established by Pisoni fruit in the hands of top-tier California pinot-makers including Joe Davis (ARCADIAN WINERY), James Hall (PATZ & HALL WINE COMPANY), and Luc Morlet (Peter Michael Winery), it was probably inevitable that Pisoni would eventually gravitate to a label of his own. So-called "Pisoni-Pisoni," Pisoni vineyard grapes vinified by Pisoni Vineyards and Winery, debuted in 1998.

The first vintages were made at the Peter Michael facility in Calistoga, first by then-winemaker Marc Aubert and thereafter by his successor Vanessa Wong who is now the winemaker for PEAY VINEYARDS, but in 2002 Pisoni's son Jeff, a recent graduate of California State University Fresno in enology, took the winemaking reins and moved production first to the Copain facility in Santa Rosa, then to the Peay Vineyards winery in Cloverdale, and finally to a dedicated facility in 2007.

Picking decisions are based on whether the seeds have turned brown and whether the berries have a "rich, jammy taste." Generally this translates to Brix levels between 25.5 and 26. Fruit is entirely destemmed, cold-soaked for two to three days with a bit of dry ice, and fermented in two- or three-ton stainless-steel open-tops with a combination of resident yeasts and isolates of Assmannshausen and RC 212. The must is pressed after twelve to fourteen days, when it is dry, but the press juice is not used in the finished wine. Between 60 and 70 percent of the barrel stock is new—it relies mostly on the cooperages of François Frères, Latour, and Remond, and on stave wood from Allier forests—and the wines are bottled after about sixteen months in barrel. There is no fining or filtration.

A "sister" label (Lucia) was created in 2000, to cover pinot noir made from blends of Pisoni "estate" fruit with fruit from Garys' Vineyard, a vineyard-designated pinot from Garys' Vineyard, and other varieties. Lucia pinots tend to rely on Remond and Taransaud barrels, to spend less time in barrel than does the estate wine, and to benefit from a small percentage of whole clusters.

TASTING NOTES

2005 *Lucia Garys' Vineyard (tasted in* 2007): Transparent, dark black-red; cherry cola, cedar, and licorice aromas, with nutmeg and floral highlights; intense and phenolic on the palate with an emphasis on high-toned, black, inky fruit, deep flavors, and a long, smooth, silky finish.

2005 *Pisoni Estate (tasted prerelease in* 2007): Dense, inky-rich wine tinged with espresso; hints of cherry *eau-de-vie* on the palate, simultaneously bright, deep, and rich; some grip; long and very masculine. Not for timid palates, but manna for fans of rich and very serious pinots.

2000 *Pisoni Estate (tasted in* 2007): Camphor, tar, and mocha on the nose; then, blackberries and India ink on the palate; intense, long, rich, and barely evolved, but also showing some brawny elegance; grippy at the end. No reason to rush; this wine should age well for at least another decade.

PONZI VINEYARDS
Beaverton, Oregon

When Dick Ponzi left a lucrative career in mechanical and aeronautical engineering—he designed rockets, jet fighters, and rides for California's Disneyland—to grow grapes in Oregon, there were just four wineries in the entire state. "If you had made a business plan," he likes to recall, "you would not have started." In 1969 he and his wife, Nancy, planted their first vines on a 20-acre parcel in the

LUISA PONZI INSISTS THAT
YOUNG PINOT IS ABOUT
"THE COMPONENTS" OF
GREATNESS, MATURE PINOT
ABOUT "INTEGRATION"

Tualatin Valley, just half an hour's drive from downtown Portland. Being close to Portland was an important criterion in their choice of site because they thought Portland would be the winery's main market. The next year they founded Ponzi Vineyards; in 1974 they produced their first four barrels of pinot noir.

Ponzi's Estate vineyard, which includes 2 acres of pinot noir, is close to the meandering Tualatin River, on relatively flat, deep, sandy benchland soils in the Hillsboro loam series. The pinot is own-rooted UCD 4 from Wente's Arroyo Seco increase block, and UCD 18 from another increase block farmed by Mirassou. The original spacing was 7 feet between vines in 9-foot rows, but this density was doubled by interplanting in 1980. The winery, which is just east of the vineyard, is an attractively expanded and remodeled edition of the family's first house in Oregon, built more or less with their own hands.

In 1981 the Ponzis were able to purchase a 20-acre parcel 10 miles west of their estate, at the crest of the Chehalem Mountains, facing southeast and commanding a beautiful view of the Cascade Range. Two acres of this parcel had been planted in 1975 as a joint venture of the state's

fledgling wine industry with Oregon State University, for trials of various clones of pinot noir. This vineyard, named Abetina for its surrounding stand of fir trees, is planted in 8-foot rows with 4 feet between vines, is own-rooted, and is footed in Laurelwood series soil. Madrona, the Ponzis' third vineyard, is 10 acres just downslope from Abetina in identical soil, of which 8 acres were planted in 1985 exclusively to own-rooted UCD 4.

In 1991 a fourth estate vineyard was established on a 65-acre parcel on Highway 219 between Scholls and Newberg, which was christened Aurora for its spectacular views of the dawn. Aurora is another southeast-facing site in Laurelwood soils, on gently rolling hills between the 300- and 600-foot contours. Over the decade between 1991 and 2001, roughly half of Aurora was planted to Dijon clones 113, 114, 115, and 777, as well as to UCD 4, using several spacings, ranging from 4 by 8 feet to 3 feet by 5 feet, and using (on an experimental basis) several rootstocks as well as own-rooted plants. Most recently, a fifth vineyard (as yet unnamed) was established on a 40-acre, northwest-facing slope, about 3 miles southwest of the first estate site, on Highway 219. Of its 40 acres, 20 have been planted, 10 of them to pinot noir. About half of the pinot is a field blend of budwood taken from the old clonal trial block at Abetina; the rest is Dijon 777; both have been grafted to riparia gloire rootstock; the configuration is 6-foot rows with 40 centimeters between vines. Ground was broken here in 2007 for a new winery, long overdue, that should be ready for the 2008 harvest.

Part of Aurora was fitted for drip irrigation in 2000, and the fifth vineyard has been irrigated from the beginning; otherwise the Ponzis' vineyards are dry farmed, and all are Low Impact Viticulture and Enology (LIVE) certified.

In addition to the five estate vineyards, Ponzi purchases fruit from other vineyards for its pinot program. Durant Vineyard, directly below Domaine Drouhin in the Dundee Hills, and Temperance Hill vineyard in the Eola Hills were consistent sources for many years. The main sources now are Gemini Vineyard in the McMinnville AVA; LAZY RIVER VINEYARD near Yamhill; Alloro Vineyards, a southwest-facing site on Laurel Ridge in the Chehalem Mountains, planted in and after 1999 to Dijon clones and UCD 4; and Dion Vineyard, an instance of Laurelwood soils off Highway 219 near Hillsboro that was planted in 1971.

The youngest son of immigrant Italian parents, Ponzi learned the basics of winemaking as a child and functioned as his own winemaker until he passed the reins to his daughter Luisa, following her return from wine-related studies in France in 1993. He also leveraged his professional training as an engineer to design and fabricate the winery's first press, to rebuild its first tractor, and to pioneer—long before they became *de rigueur*—gravity-driven protocols for moving wine.

Luisa not only grew up in and around wine; she was also formally trained. After graduating from Portland State University in 1990 with a degree in biology, she spent a year of specialized study and apprenticeship in Burgundy. At Beaune's Centre de formation professionnelle et de promotion agricole (CFPPA), she earned a *brevet professionelle d'oenologie et viticulture*; her internship was at Domaine Georges Roumier in Chambolle-Musigny.

WINES AND WINEMAKING NOTES
Despite its major investment in vineyards, Ponzi has always been a strongly blend-oriented house. In most vintages before 2001, two pinots were made: a Willamette Valley wine and a reserve. In 2001 the Ponzis introduced a third blend, this time very moderately priced, called Tavola. Although the reserve program is nominally a barrel selection privileging slightly darker, weightier, and more complex lots, the Ponzis' thirty-plus years of experience with many of their fruit sources have led to the reserve wine being regularly anchored, even before individual barrels are evaluated, in the Abetina and Madrona vineyards. The Willamette Valley wine claims most of the remaining estate fruit, as well as a considerable portion of the purchased grapes. Since 1998 a few single vineyard bottlings have been made from time to time, notably from the Abetina Vineyard.

Dick Ponzi recalls trying "every possible combination of winemaking techniques" during his first ten years as a winemaker. The list of tried and discarded manipulations includes the use of a high percentage of whole clusters, destemming and then returning stems to the fermentors, very long macerations, and fermentations at very high temperatures.

Now, with the accumulated experience of two generations at hand, adjustments are made to fit each vineyard and vintage, but the general practice is to destem completely—though a small percentage of whole clusters is used in warm years when the stems are truly ripe—and to cold soak for about seven days without sulfur dioxide. Luisa Ponzi uses both 1.5-ton bins and 3-ton jacketed stainless steel open-tops, but is developing a preference for the latter. Fermentations start naturally with resident yeasts, and the goal is a nice bell-shaped fermentation curve. Lots destined for the Willamette Valley blend are pressed before the must is dry; other lots are allowed some days of extended maceration before pressing. The hard press fraction is kept separate and is excluded from both the Willamette Valley and the reserve programs.

Overall, about 50 percent of barrels are new. Until 2000 Luisa Ponzi used mostly François Frères barrels; beginning with the 2001 vintage, the majority share is an eclectic assortment, but always 100 percent French. The Willamette Valley blend stays in barrel for eleven months, gets just a single racking, and is bottled before the next vintage. Reserve wines are also racked at the eleven-month mark but are returned to barrel for another six-plus months, at which point they are racked again and bottled. Ponzi pinots are not filtered, but some barrels are egg-white fined for clarity. The wines are held six to seven months in bottle before release. Luisa Ponzi's experience in Burgundy is responsible for various winemaking changes after 1993, including the introduction of a sorting table on the crush pad, a shift to resident-yeast fermentation, and racking pushed with plain compressed air rather than inert gas.

All Ponzi pinots I have tasted have been fruit-intensive, mildly spicy, and nicely built. While the close-knit character of Oregon's pioneer winegrowing group in the 1970s and 1980s birthed many mutual influences on style and method, it can be argued that Ponzi, more than any other, is responsible for the combination of generosity and high-toned elegance that typifies the best of mainstream Oregon pinots today. The wines are enjoyable young, but (in most vintages) they also age superbly. This duality has become a Ponzi mantra. Luisa Ponzi, like her father, insists that a good pinot should show "all the components" of great pinot young, and that mature vintages should demonstrate "integration."

TASTING NOTES

2005 *"Tavola" (tasted in 2007):* Light-to-medium ruby; red berry fruit with some vanilla on the nose; strawberry, raspberry, and Queen Anne cherry flavors on the palate; grip, acidity, and earth with a bit of spice; lightweight but complete; comparable structurally and qualitatively to a good village wine from Nuits-Saint-Georges.

2005 *Reserve (tasted in 2007):* Medium black-red; finely perfumed nose with some sandalwood and gum camphor; red cherry fruit and red licorice on the palate; bright, nuanced, and slightly sweet, with a suggestion of vanilla flan; satiny texture to mid-palate, then some grip; very nicely built; fine.

2004 *Reserve (tasted twice, in 2006 and 2007):* Transparent medium ruby; aromas of dusty red berries with notes of flowers, sweet vanilla, and sandalwood; slightly fruit-sweet and very elegant on the palate, with notes of Indonesian spice, black licorice, and vanilla; very silky with a hint of grip; a soft and attractive wine that seems lightly polished; fine.

2004 *Willamette Valley (tasted in 2006):* Pretty, medium garnet; cherry-raspberry fruit aromas with a hint of smoke; bright cherry, black raspberry, and black pepper on the fruit-driven mid-palate; elegant, fairly intense, and nicely structured, with the texture of polished cotton.

2002 *Reserve (tasted in 2007):* Medium brick-red color; café au lait and allspice on the nose; in the mouth, raspberry that is just beginning to fade, plus infused dried flowers and black pepper; slight creaminess on the mid-palate; tannins softening nicely, but still some grip; elegant, very attractive, and fine.

PORTER CREEK VINEYARDS
Healdsburg, California

Porter Creek is a 34-acre ranch on Westside Road, about a half-mile upstream from Wohler Bridge, now almost completely surrounded by E. & J. Gallo's MacMurray Ranch Vineyard. Reached by an unpaved driveway and untouched by wine-biz glitz, it looks and feels like an outpost. Production is tiny. Porter Creek, however, produces some of California's loveliest and most elegant pinots.

George Davis bought Porter Creek in 1979 as a career change. For twenty years he had designed and built sailboats in Berkeley and Maui. His plan, when he moved, was to grow and sell grapes. Two parcels on the Porter Creek property had already been planted to pinot noir, but the variety was not much in demand, so Davis planted a bit of chardonnay to supplement the pinot. The hilly site was a parsimonious producer, however, and even the chardonnay remained persistently unprofitable.

So in 1982, Davis decided to make his own wine, hoping to improve the economics of his career change. Like so many others in Russian River during the early years, he was a self-taught winemaker. He was also self-financed. Porter Creek grew slowly: a barn was converted to a winery; new French oak barrels were purchased one by one; refrigerated storage space was cobbled together from old, freestanding, insulated storage units; and a roof was finally constructed over the crushpad area to minimize the infiltration of leaves and dust into the open-top fermentors. To this day, the winery's tasting facility is a tin-roofed, redwood-beamed farm building alongside a dusty driveway; the only seating space is a bench outside the front door.

Before the 1997 vintage, Davis decided to concentrate his personal energies on the vineyard and passed the winemaking role to his son Alex. The younger Davis grew up surrounded by grapes, wine, and neighboring winemakers, and graduated from the viticulture and enology program at California State University Fresno. He apprenticed at Sonoma-Cutrer, a benchmark producer of chardonnay, which was something of a mecca for visiting European wine folk. Using Sonoma-Cutrer contacts, Alex Davis soon took off for France, bent on experience with handmade, tiny-volume, top-quality wines. He could scarcely have picked a better mentor than Christophe Roumier of Domaine Georges Roumier in Chambolle-Musigny, one of Burgundy's leading young lights and, in his late thirties, just half a generation older than Davis. Davis also repeated the enology curriculum he had already completed in Fresno, this time in French, at the Université de Bourgogne, and spent an additional year working for the Rhône house of Guigal, where he developed a taste for syrah as well.

The French experience made him a devout *terroir*-ist. He argues, quite properly, that *terroir* is not enough explored in the New World. "We don't know," he observes, "which *terroirs* will produce wines that are better young, and which will produce something ageworthy. Even Bonnes-Mares can be very linear in its youth." And demonstrating a plainspoken modesty uncharacteristic of the California wine business, Davis says candidly, "If Porter Creek turns out to be a great site for pinot noir, we will have to admit to dumb luck."

Until 2002 Porter Creek farmed two pinot vineyards, simply and descriptively called Hillside and Creekside. Planted in 1974, Hillside is a moderately steep 3-acre parcel on fine-particle clay soil, between 175 and 200 feet above the valley floor. Yields are declining as time passes, and there is now only enough fruit from Hillside to make about 150 cases of wine. It is no surprise that the vineyard is not profitable, and that Davis wonders if it should not be replanted soon—and perhaps to syrah. For the moment it is UCD 13 on St. George rootstock, planted sparsely in the fashion of its day—about 450 vines to the acre. but gradually coaxed from California sprawl to a semblance of verticality. Because it sits above the fog line, Hillside ripens early.

Creekside, which straddled the creek at the entrance to the property, was traded to Gallo in 2002—not as a fruit source but as the site for a new access from Westside Road into MacMurray Ranch—in exchange for a nice, 7-acre, hillside block of pinot noir that Gallo had planted in 1997. This block of thin rocky soil underlain with fractured shale, rechristened Fiona Hill by the Porters, is planted 8 feet by 5 in rows oriented northeast–southwest to reduce sunburn during the hottest part of the day, and the scion material is entirely UCD 2A. Fiona Hill replaced Creekside in Porter Creek's pinot portfolio in 2002.

Both vineyards are almost completely dry farmed and cover cropped, and have been treated following biodynamic protocols in recent years.

WINES AND WINEMAKING NOTES

Through 2001 Creekside and Hillside were made as two separate, vineyard-designated wines. Since 2002 the program has become a bit more complicated because the Fiona Hill lots have been distributed over as many as three bottlings. The main Fiona Hill wine is a "plain" vineyard-designate, but some lots have been declassified into a "basic" estate bottling, and some have been isolated to make 100 to 200 cases of a "reserve" wine.

Winemaking at Porter Creek is low-tech and straightforward. Grapes are picked when the stems crack audibly when snapped and when they no longer taste bitter when chewed. The Hillside vineyard (see below) is typically picked between 23 and 23.5 Brix; Fiona Hill is picked between 23.5 and 25. The Hillside fruit is usually completely destemmed, but as much as 20 percent of the Fiona Hill fruit is fermented as whole clusters. Fermentors are 6-foot, unjacketed stainless steel open-tops. The fruit comes in cold and usually macerates three to four days before fermentation begins naturally with resident yeasts; there is no addition of enzymes. Davis rarely adds acid, but when exceptionally warm weather drives sugar levels too high, acid goes in before fermentation begins. The vatting now lasts for twelve to twenty days and sometimes includes a period of extended maceration. Cap management involves both punchdowns and pumpovers. Generally about 25 to 35 percent new oak is used—Cadus and Rousseau are the favored coopers—and the wine stays in barrel for about eighteen months. Davis racks the wines once after natural malolactic fermentation has finished, does not filter, and occasionally fines with egg white for suppleness. Davis subscribes to the unconventional idea that pinots made with *some* air contact may display increased resistance to oxidation later in life, making them more ageworthy. This hypothesis reinforces Davis's belief in open-top fermentations and means that he sometimes racks with compressed air rather than inert gas.

My 2007 tasting of Porter Creek pinots, which I have always liked enormously, convinced me that this house is now making, bar none, some of the most stunning pinots in California. The fruit is picked early enough that the wines can develop and display a full array of floral and fruit aromas, beautiful structure, and drop-dead gorgeous elegance. Hillside is an heirloom, to be savored for the vintages it can still produce, and Fiona Hill, in Alex Porter's hands, is truly impressive. Caveat, however: some bottles of older vintages display the musty properties associated with large populations of brettanomyces.

TASTING NOTES

2005 *Russian River Valley (tasted in 2007):* Very transparent, luminous garnet; floral and lightly spicy on the nose; bright, intense red cherry and raspberry flavors; with the clove-y, cinnamony, peppery-spice medley that typifies Westside Road pinots; modest grip and medium length. Entirely from Fiona Hill.

2005 *Russian River Valley Reserve (tasted in 2007):* Brilliant, light garnet; slightly closed, with just hints of dried flower petals, citrus peel, and red raspberry; bright, engaging berry fruit dries to a bit of grip on the mid-palate; large-framed but very restrained and sophisticated; silky, gossamer-like, and engaging; serious underneath; fine. Entirely from Fiona Hill.

2005 *Fiona Hill Vineyard (tasted in 2007):* Brilliant, light-to-medium rosy-ruby; floral again, with hints of orange peel and white pepper underneath; intense and moderately fruit-driven attack; plenty of structure; a silky mid-palate before grip takes over; almost exuberant but also serious, gentle, and sophisticated; very long and very fine.

2005 *Hillside Vineyard—Old Vine (tasted in 2007):* Utterly transparent with a beautiful rosy rim; highly perfumed and mostly floral nose with the tiniest hint of blackberry; barely steeped Assam tea on the palate; very pretty, *griotte*-like red berry fruit; majestically satiny with very gentle but insistent grip; elegant and very, very fine.

2004 *Fiona Hill Vineyard (tasted in 2007):* Brilliant light-to-medium ruby with a touch of terra cotta; aromas have turned from primary to secondary with leather and potpourri; hugely seductive palate; a spicy base, with a floral-leathery-evergreen overlay; substantial grip at mid-palate, and an earthy, wet-clay aftertaste; long and very fine.

1998 *Creekside Vineyard (tasted in 2007):* Light, transparent terra cotta; evolved nose of citrus peel, leather, boot polish, and fading berry fruit; deep, slightly earthy, and almost satiny, with a substantial load of very fine-grained, ripe tannins; large-framed but very elegant; very fine.

R. STUART & CO.
McMinnville, Oregon

Rob Stuart, a Rensselaer Polytechnic Institute graduate in biochemistry with graduate training in fermentation science at the University of California Davis, made wine for at least four wineries in three states—and most recently at ERATH VINEYARDS WINERY in Dundee, Oregon, from 1994 to 2002—before establishing a project on his own. In a repurposed granary in what he and others call (with some justice) the "Pinot Quarter" of McMinnville, R. Stuart & Co. now crafts pinot noir, pinot gris, and sparkling wine from about a dozen vineyards in the northern Willamette Valley, and from the Melrose Vineyard near Roseburg.

The still pinot program consists of two blended wines—Big Fire, which is designed to be bright and fruit forward, and Autograph, a "reserve quality" wine that is a bit more texture driven and exotically aromatic—and a small array of tiny (sometimes no more than two barrels each) single-vineyard bottlings. Fruit sources generally fall into two categories: vineyards chosen specifically for Big Fire, which are typically low-elevation sites just off the valley floor that display "less interesting *terroir*," and "reserve quality" sites located around mid-slope of the Dundee or Eola Hills formations that "can stand on their own" in most vintages. When Autograph has been blended from the latter, but enough remains to do small, vineyard-designated bottlings, those are produced as well. The most common vineyard-designated sources are Temperance Hill just north of BETHEL HEIGHTS Vineyard; Daffodil Hill Vineyard, a relatively warm, southwest-facing site around the 400-foot contour, 3 miles south of Bethel Heights on the west side of the Eola Hills, where Stuart gets about 6 acres of dry farmed Dijon 667 and 114, planted in 2000; Goldschmidt Vineyard (see DUSKY GOOSE); and the Weber Vineyard in the Dundee Hills. The Weber and Ana vineyards are two parts of the same property owned and farmed by Andy Humphrey; Weber is the east-facing slope, and Stuart's block is UCD 4 planted between 1985 and 1987 on its own roots. The first vintage for R. Stuart pinots was made in 2001.

WINEMAKING NOTES
Stuart destems all his fruit but retains as many whole berries as possible, adds a small amount of sulfur dioxide at the destemmer, begins punchdowns immediately, and cool-soaks without dry ice for twenty-four hours. At this point he adds yeast, but his yeast has (quite unusually) been cultured in-house during the weeks preceding harvest. Two weeks before harvest, as Stuart collects field samples for analysis, he presses their juice, adds a bit of sulfur dioxide, and then adds more pressed juice as additional samples are collected, and then more sulfur, in a cumulative process that nets, by harvest time, a starter culture of mixed "native"

yeasts collected from his various source vineyards. This culture is the inoculum for his first musts and the yeast population that subsequently kicks off fermentation in all the lots that follow. RC 212 is added, but only after the mixed native yeast fermentation is well under way, so it functions mostly as an insurance policy should some recalcitrant fermentation be tempted to stick later.

Fermentors are never covered, and high temperatures are encouraged in an effort to evaporate some of the newly generated alcohol and to reduce the alcoholic content of the finished wine. Punchdowns, in the fruit bins used as fermentors, continue until the juice reaches between 5 and 6 Brix, and the seeds begin disengaging from the manipulated berries. At this point, using a gentle peristaltic pump, he moves the juice from each fermentor to another, passing it through a coarse screen to remove seeds. This process is important to Stuart, who wants his pinots (and especially his reserve quality wines) to age well. Stuart thinks that ageworthiness in warm vintages depends primarily on tannin (while acid may be the main guarantor of attractive aging in cooler years), and he wants to be sure that the final tannins in the wine are supple and skin derived, not harsh and seed derived. When vessel-to-vessel racking is complete, and most loose seeds have been removed from the must, the musts are allowed to finish primary fermentation, and are then pressed, settled, and barreled.

Stuart is not a fan of new oak, using only about 1 percent of it annually, and he keeps most barrels in service for five to eight years. He likes Claude Gillet barrels because they have been made with a long, cool toasting, but he is preparing to experiment with some locally coopered François Frères barrels as well, providing these can be made for him with the same long, cool toast practiced by Gillet. All wines are bottled before the following vintage.

Big Fire is a bright, cheery wine that seems reminiscent of Dôle, the once-ubiquitous blend of tank-raised pinot noir and gamay made in Switzerland's Valais; Autograph is quite serious pinot with a resinous signature, nice complexity, and good structure.

TASTING NOTES

2006 *Big Fire (tasted in 2007)*: Transparent, medium ruby; red cherry nose with a hint of citrus peel; cherries and red berries on the palate; fruit forward and easy drinking, with a tiny hint of spice and black pepper, light-to-medium weight, and medium length.

2005 *Autograph (tasted in 2007)*: Brilliant, medium garnet; juniper berry, resin, and tree bark aromas; cherry-cassis fruit on the palate with some sappy, mesquite flavors and a bit of brown spice; nicely structured and bright throughout, with a bit of grip at the end.

RADIO-COTEAU WINE CELLARS

 *Forestville, California*

Eric Sussman, a New Yorker who discovered wine while studying agriculture at Cornell University in the 1980s, created Radio-Coteau in 2002. He learned winemaking on the job, working first in Washington's Yakima Valley, then in 1995 for the various enterprises of Baron Philippe de Rothschild in Bordeaux, and finally in 1996 for *régisseur* Pascal Marchand at the Domaine du

Comte Armand in Pommard. From 1998 to 2002, Sussman was the associate winemaker at DEHLINGER WINERY. Radio-Coteau, which is a partnership with Bill and Joan Smith (see W. H. SMITH WINES), is focused geographically on western Sonoma County, although

DISTINCTIVE PINOTS WITH GREAT TRANSPARENCY AND LAYERS OF SUBTLE AROMATICS

Sussman also sources fruit from Mendocino's Anderson Valley, and varietally on pinot noir, although some syrah, chardonnay, and zinfandel are also made.

Sussman is an eloquent champion of site specificity in winemaking, and he works closely with growers to identify those individual rows that present "the best possible expression" of each vineyard. However, he also makes one blended pinot, called La Neblina, which is typically assembled from a combination of Russian River Valley and True Sonoma Coast fruit. The Radio-Coteau name is a Rhône localism connoting information passed among the growers and winemakers of the Côte Rotie by word of mouth. From their first release, Radio-Coteau's shapely wines have impressed virtually all serious observers of the American pinot scene.

WINES AND WINEMAKING NOTES

Sussman typically picks "for seed and flavor maturity," which he usually finds at a bit over 25 Brix. The fruit is mostly destemmed and enjoys a relatively extended cold maceration. A bit of sulfur dioxide is used to suppress "less desirable yeasts," but the primary and maloloactic fermentations are otherwise indigenous. Thus far, Sussman has avoided both acidification and addition of enzymes, which tend, he believes, to obscure the expression of *terroir*. Sussman uses both bladder and basket presses, and keeps the press fractions separate until they can be assessed. Barrels are about 50 percent new, mostly from Remond, François Frères, and Cadus, and made from staves that have been air dried for three years before being coopered. Pinots usually stay in barrel for about sixteen months, and lees are sometimes stirred while the malolactic fermentation is in progress. Wines may be racked once in the summer after the vintage, or not at all until bottling, and they are never fined or filtered.

In 2002 and 2003, the vineyard-designated wines were from the Marsh and Hellenthal vineyards, respectively south and north of the Russian River in the True Sonoma Coast, and from Rich Savoy's hillside vineyard west of Philo in the Anderson Valley. In 2004 vineyard-designated wines from the Alberigi Vineyard on Vine Hill Road, in the heart of the Russian River AVA (previously used for the La Neblina blend but not vineyard-designated), and from Terra Neuma, a block in Benziger's new, biodynamically farmed De Coelo Vineyard near Bodega, replaced the Marsh and Hellenthal bottlings in the Radio-Coteau portfolio.

In many vintages, the Savoy bottling has been a personal favorite, but the 2005 edition seems much riper, blacker, and sweeter than usual. Radio-Coteau pinots are distinctive across the board, exhibiting vivid colors, great transparency, and layers of subtle aromatics, always wrapped in an elegant, tasteful, understated package. They testify to the uncompromising purity of Sussman's winemaking style.

TASTING NOTES

2005 *La Neblina (tasted in 2007):* Medium black-red; aromas of red berries and fresh flowers; intense, peppery, and spicy attack; almost silky on the mid-palate with some grip at the end; bright overall; a serious, nicely crafted wine.

2005 *Alberigi (tasted in 2007):* Transparent, almost brilliant brick-red; citrus peel, dark cherry, and meadow flowers on the nose; intensely flavorful attack featuring spice and earthy minerality in the foreground, with red fruit in the background; silky and moderately long; attractive.

2005 *Terra Neuma (tasted in 2007):* A transparent but very deeply colored and almost black-centered wine; nose combines resinous herbs with black berry fruit; rich, dark, and feral on the palate; resolutely fruit-sweet through mid-palate; dries to an intense elegance on the finish; strong minerality; texture of heavy upholstery silk; distinctive.

2005 *Savoy (tasted in 2007):* Saturated, nearly opaque black-red; intense, very ripe nose of red and black berries, with notes of gum camphor; very fruit-sweet attack that is overtaken with a strong grip of very fine-grained tannins at mid-palate, plus graphite and earth; muscular and almost massive structurally; very seriously made.

RAPTOR RIDGE WINERY
Carlton, Oregon

Raptor Ridge is the very hands-on, evenings-and-weekends wine project of Scott Shull, a strategic and business planner for Intel Corporation, and his wife, Annie, who also worked for Intel until Raptor Ridge grew large enough to demand full-time attention. Scott Shull was reportedly fascinated, early on, by bees, beer, and anything that could be made to ferment, and was a home winemaker as early as 1989.

Raptor Ridge was founded in 1995 with enough fruit for 500 cases of pinot noir and chardonnay from the Wahle Vineyard in the Yamhill-Carlton AVA, Murto in the Dundee Hills, and the Eola Hills Vineyard. Since then, the list of fruit sources has expanded to nine, including parts of five blocks at Hawks View Vineyard, a Chehalem Ridge site sourced by numerous makers; 3 acres (Block 11) in the Shea Vineyard; 4 acres of UCD 4 at Meredith Mitchell in the McMinnville AVA; 4 acres of UCD 4 at Stony Mountain Vineyard, another McMinnville site; and 10 acres of UCD 2A and Dijon clones at Yamhill Springs Vineyard, tucked into Peavine series soils 10 miles west of Yamhill, in the foothills of the Coast Range. Meanwhile, the Shulls

---

RIPE-PICKED BUT
MODERATELY EXTRACTED
WINES THAT COMBINE
WEIGHT AND ELEGANCE

---

planted another 18 acres, including a small amount of grüner veltliner and pinot gris, on the 27-acre parcel where they live, a mostly forested ridge on the northeast side of the Chehalem Mountains 10 miles north of Newburg. The pinot noir on this site, which the Shulls call Tuscowallame, is in six blocks dedicated to UCD 2A and 4, and Dijon 114, 115, 667, and 777, set out in 8-foot rows with 5 feet between vines, on a mostly north-facing slope, in the loess-based, Laurelwood series

soils that predominate on this side of the Chehalem Mountains. A new, leased production facility serving Raptor Ridge and Carlton Cellars, for which Shull is the consulting winemaker, located in the heart of Carlton, was ready for the 2007 harvest.

WINES AND WINEMAKING NOTES
Raptor Ridge's main blend, made since 1996, was called the Yamhill County Cuvée until 2003, when the inclusion of grapes from Washington County required that it be rechristened as Willamette Valley. This blend aims at bright fruit and relative precociousness, and is priced to succeed in restaurant by-the-glass programs. A vineyard-designated wine from the Shea Vineyard also debuted in 1996, as did a Meredith Mitchell bottling in 2000, a Stony Mountain wine in 2001, and a reserve in 2002. (Compared to the Willamette Valley wine, the Reserve is deeper, richer, more extracted, often more tannic, and intended to support cellaring.) In addition to these "regulars," Yamhill Springs Vineyard was made as a vineyard-designated wine in 2005 and 2006, and Harbinger in 2000, 2003, and 2006. The estate vineyard produced its first crop in 2006, 40 cases of which were bottled as a vineyard-designated wine.

Shull picks relatively ripe, "by taste," with post-facto chemical analysis "to let us know what we got." Most fruit is hand sorted and destemmed; as many berries as possible are kept whole and uncrushed, but some whole clusters may be layered into the fermentors "depending on vineyard and vintage." Following a four- to five-day cold soak, most lots are inoculated, although some may ferment with resident yeasts, but in no case is an entire bottling based on "wild yeast" fermentations. There is no use of enzymes and generally very little acidification. The must is pressed at dryness and barreled in between 25 and 50 percent new oak for ten to eleven months. Most of the cooperage is purchased from Remond, Ermitage, and Marcel Cadet. The final blends are made early, soon after the malolactic fermentation has finished, at which point the wines are returned to barrel. The choices are confirmed toward the end of *élevage,* whereupon the barrels destined for each cuvée are assembled in a blending tank for "a couple of weeks" before bottling. The wines, at least in the 2006 vintage, are a fairly rare combination of quite modest extraction with high alcohol, resulting in medium-weight, almost elegant wines that finish very warm.

TASTING NOTES

2006 *Willamette Valley (tasted in* 2007*):* Light-to-medium, very transparent garnet; dusty cherry-raspberry nose with some floral notes; slightly sweet and slightly resinous on the palate, with peppery red fruit and some cola notes; modestly extracted but warm, with medium weight and length.

2006 *Reserve (tasted in* 2007*):* Transparent, medium ruby; shy nose of nut shells and spice; slightly sweet red and black fruit on the palate, then, inky and intense; peppery and almost bitter when the initial sweetness has dissipated; something of a Manhattan cocktail/sweet vermouth character; long, and medium in weight.

2006 *Shea Vineyard (tasted in* 2007*):* Medium rosy-garnet; dusty, floral nose; rosewater, strawberry, raspberry, and some fruit-infused black tea in the mouth; licorice and pepper; almost satiny; the most elegant of the 2006 bottlings.

2006 *Yamhill Springs Vineyard (tasted in* 2007*):* Medium deep black-red; nose combines spice and earth; very dark, intense, and earthy on the palate; dark

fruit flavors; some mesquite, root beer, and touches of pepper and licorice are almost overwhelmed by strong minerality and a hefty load of very fine-grained tannins; finishes very warm and spirity.

2006 *Meredith Mitchell Vineyard (tasted in* 2007*):* Medium-dark black-red; resinous and savory aromas highlighted with violets and gum camphor; sweet and rich on the palate; evokes chocolates filled with cherry liqueur; long and warm; feels almost like an after-dinner wine.

2006 *Stony Mountain Vineyard (tasted in* 2007*):* Volatile aromatics like pine sap; slightly sweet black berries on the palate; rich and voluptuous; begins suede-like but turns chalky after mid-palate owing to the considerable load of very fine-grained tannins; massive, muscular, and firm.

RED CAR WINE COMPANY
Culver City, California

Red Car is the creation of a former film producer and talent scout, and a former screenwriter (now sadly deceased) that is Hollywood-esque in more ways than the career backgrounds of its founders. The project began in Carroll Kemp's Beverly Hills driveway in 2001, with enough grapes from vineyards in Paso Robles and Santa Maria to make two barrels of syrah. Kemp's winemaking credentials were limited to his volunteer work at Central Coast Wine Services in Santa Maria and a few community college courses, so he relied quite a bit on a "consulting winemaker" named Tim Spear, a University of California Davis–trained enologist with experience at Justin Winery and Tablas Creek in Paso Robles.

When the fifty cases of finished wine were barely available commercially but offered to a mailing list, the wine was discovered by the Martini House restaurant in St. Helena, and by bloggers and mainstream critics, all of whom loved it. More or less overnight, Red Car became the sort of quintessential instant, unlikely, outsider success at which wine business insiders with huge marketing budgets shake their heads. By January 2004, Kemp had moved from movies to wine on a full-time basis, had become a winemaker, and had replaced his consulting winemaker before the 2004 harvest. By the end of 2004, Red Car had made no less than eighteen different wines and was able to source fruit—syrah and pinot noir—from some of the most prestigious vineyards in the state.

It is impossible to deny that Red Car itself is a story, and that stories, as movie people know and Kemp repeats, "are key." Within the brand, each wine is treated as a story, illustrated in promotional materials with artwork designed to evoke the classical era in Hollywood, and each vintage is billed as a chapter in the story. The main release of pinot noir, so far at least, is called Amour Fou, which debuted in 2002, sourced from Green Valley's Keefer Ranch and from the Cloud's Rest Vineyard in the Petaluma Gap. The 2003 "chapter" was a blend of Keefer Ranch with fruit from the Zio Tony Vineyard on Frei Road east of Highway 116, which is farmed by Lee Martinelli. Zio Tony persisted as a component of the 2004 edition of Amour Fou, but fruit sources have evolved and will continue to evolve—at least until the vineyard Kemp acquired on the Sonoma Coast begins to produce "estate" pinot. Meanwhile, a less expensive pinot called Boxcar was added to the portfolio in 2004, and a single-vineyard pinot called The Aphorist, sourced from the Bartolomei Vineyard in Forestville, debuted in 2005.

The wines are made at Central Coast Wine Services in Santa Maria.

Winemaking generally follows the consensus protocol, but the fermentations rely entirely on resident yeast, and the barrel regime is a bit longer than most, at about fourteen months. Kemp says that the first two vintages of pinot were "made like syrah," but that the protocol changed in 2004 to emphasize "nuance" and "complexity." Having tasted only the 2004, I cannot comment on stylistic evolution, but the 2004 remains a very ripe-picked, big, and lushly structured wine.

TASTING NOTE

2004 *Amour Fou (tasted in 2006):* Dark, slightly hazy black-red; spice, cedar, sandalwood, and black fruit on the nose; sweet, rich, and concentrated on the palate, with an emphasis on blackberry and black cherry fruit, plus cinnamon and clove; medium long and suede textured.

REX HILL VINEYARD
Newburg, Oregon

Rex Hill Vineyard was created in 1983 by Paul Hart and Jan Jacobsen. Hart was a local actuarial consultant, and Jacobsen was a high school mathematics teacher before she and Hart married; he "retired" to start Rex Hill, whereas she became a full-time artist. Determined to be personally involved in the area's growing wine business, the couple purchased a disused nut-drying barn north of Newburg, intending to repurpose it as a winery and to surround it with vineyards. But since grapes grown in existing, mature vineyards were going unpicked at the time, the brand was launched instead with purchased fruit from underappreciated sites that are now in high demand, such as the Maresh Vineyard in the Dundee Hills. Estate vineyards, on the original site and nearby on the south face of the Chehalem Mountains, came later.

From 1983 to 1988, Rex Hill's winemaker was David Wirtz. Lynn Penner-Ash (see PENNER-ASH WINES) followed Wirtz. Penner-Ash was succeeded by Aaron Hess, who had also joined Rex Hill in 1998 as its enologist, and Hess was succeeded by Ryan Harms, who began his winemaking career as a Rex Hill intern.

In recent vintages, Rex Hill has produced a large, variable portfolio of pinot noirs, plus a significant quantity of pinot gris and chardonnay. The largest-volume wine is an Oregon cuvée, sourced mostly from Willamette Valley vineyards, plus vineyards in the Umpqua and Rogue valleys. Other wines, made in much smaller quantities, include a vineyard-designated wine from the estate-owned Jacob-Hart Vineyard, located on Hillside Drive about 5 miles west of the winery; vineyard-designated wines from non-estate parcels including Maresh and CARABELLA; and an assortment of blends.

In 2006, when Hart decided he wanted to retire for real, Rex Hill—brand, winery, vineyards, equipment, and inventory—was sold to A TO Z, with whose principals Hart and Jacobsen had been friends since late in the 1980s. A to Z, which had been making some of its wine in the Rex Hill facility for several years and needed additional space to accommodate growing production, says it expects to maintain the Rex Hill brand, which will continue to be made side-by-side with A to Z wines (albeit with separate staff) in the Rex Hill facility, to "return to Rex Hill's original focus on pinot noir" and "hone the number of offerings to a more reasonable number."

With the 2007 vintage, Rex Hill's anchor pinot will be based entirely on Willamette Valley fruit. There will also be a reserve, a

Dundee Hills appellation wine, and several vineyard-designates confined to winery-direct sale. Some fruit is being redirected from the A to Z program to Rex Hill and vice versa. Historically, the house style has cleaved to modestly extracted pinots with soft flavors.

TASTING NOTES

2004 *Reserve (tasted in* 2007*):* Transparent, medium brick; aromas of dusty, red berries; intense, fruit- and mineral-driven attack with a hint of herbs, then a soft mid-palate with some floral elements; cherry flavors; medium in length with a hint of fine-grained grip.

2004 *Maresh Vineyard (tasted in* 2007*):* Very transparent, light-to-medium garnet; earthy, animaly, and feral aromas; sweet, fading berry fruit with minty earthy undertones; rosewater; complex, elegant, and quite serious, with a silky-creamy texture and a lightweight frame; long and attractive.

2004 *Jacob-Hart Vineyard (tasted in* 2007*):* Very transparent, medium rosy-garnet; minty nose; bright, clean, hard spice, and pepper on the palate; slightly sweet with mint and menthol; considerable intensity in a lightweight architecture; just a bit of cocoa and smokiness; medium in length, and attractive.

RHYS VINEYARDS
AND
ALESIA WINES
Woodside, California

Kevin Harvey, a Rice University graduate whose first Silicon Valley company (Approach Software) was sold to Lotus

Development Corporation when he was barely twenty-seven, and whose venture capital enterprise funded such name brands as Priceline.com and WebVan a few years later, is also a self-described "nut" about pinot noir. The 1990 pinots from GARY FARRELL WINES, WILLIAMS SELYEM, and ROCHIOLI VINEYARD AND WINERY were the first wines to capture

---

VERY SERIOUS PINOT
WITH THE INTENSITY THAT
COMES FROM LOW YIELDS
AND TERROIR, NOT
WINEMAKING

---

his attention; after this introduction to the variety, he turned to red Burgundies from the 1991 and 1993 vintages. In 1995 he planted a tiny, quarter-acre pinot vineyard in his Woodside, California, backyard (which he talked his wife into doubling a few years later, so that he could harvest enough grapes to make at least a single full barrel of wine).

By 2001 he had become fascinated with the impact of site on wine and enamored with the rocky soils just uphill from his home in the Santa Cruz Mountains. "Around the world," he observes, "interesting wines are grown on rocks." His tastings of older Santa Cruz Mountains pinots—from the Santa Cruz Mountain Vineyard, MOUNT EDEN VINEYARDS, and DAVID BRUCE— revealed, to his palate, a Gevrey-like earthiness that seemed promising. The Santa Cruz Mountain area, Harvey observes, "was a promised land, and a land that time forgot." Harvey, at least as far as wine is concerned, is a quiet, reflective personality, utterly without bravado, who describes his subsequent

investments in wine as "experiments," marches to an untraditional drummer, and adjusts everything he does, repeatedly, in the light of experience.

In 2001, 2002, and 2003, Harvey planted the first of four vineyards in the Santa Cruz Mountains, in sites explicitly chosen for their different soils, exposures, and microclimates. The first vineyard, called Alpine Road, consists of 1.5 acres of chardonnay and 11.5 acres of sixteen, mostly undocumented selections of pinot (although some of the scion material was Swan, Calera, UCD 4, and Dijon 777). It is a very steep (up to 52 percent), south-facing slope between 1,200 and 1,400 feet, planted in north–south oriented rows. The soils are Purissima series. In 2003 he also planted a 6-acre vineyard called Family Farm.

In 2004 his attentions—always in the service of experiments with multiple and very different *terroirs* very close to each other—shifted to a 17.5-acre site called Horseshoe Ranch Vineyard, which was essentially virgin soil previously used for pasture. Here, he planted 10 acres of vines on an upper, east-facing slope at about 1,600 feet, and 7 acres on a lower slope at about 1,350 feet. A fourth vineyard, and the highest of all at 2,400 feet, is called Skyline. It was also planted in 2004 and features 1.5 acres in an east-facing block, planted 3 feet by 3 feet, plus 1 acre of the tightest pinot planting in the world as far as I know: 3-foot rows with 2 feet between vines. In each of these mostly inhospitable sites, Harvey laid the vineyards out in very small, half-acre blocks, each of which (at a target yield of 2 tons per acre) generates enough fruit to fill *one* of Rhys's 1-ton, jacketed stainless fermentors and make (if kept separate) *one* barrel of wine. All sites are watered minimally and farmed biodynamically. Until 2005 the wines were made in Harvey's garage and raised in a cellar beneath it. Then, after two years' tenancy in a San Carlos industrial park, the brand moved to a completely subterranean facility, located at the Alpine Road Vineyard, in 2008.

Although Harvey was his own winemaker in the early, precommercial years of the Home Vineyard from 1996 to 2003, Jason Jardine, a Davis-trained winemaker who had previously worked at DOMAINE SERENE and at several Rogue Valley (Oregon) wineries, including Eden Vale and Griffin Creek, came on board at the end of 2003. In 2006 the hands-on winemaking mantle shifted again, this time to Jeff Brinkman, previously the winemaker at HUSCH VINEYARDS in Anderson Valley; at that time, Jardine became Rhys's general manager, assuming primary responsibility for the vineyard management and development. Along with the estate wines, all from the Santa Cruz Mountains and San Francisco Bay appellations, made under the Rhys label, Harvey, Jardine, and Brinkman make several pinots (and some syrah) from purchased Sonoma Coast fruit under a second label called Alesia.

WINES AND WINEMAKING NOTES
In 2004, Rhys's first commercial vintage, there was one barrel of wine from the Home Vineyard, one from Alpine Road Vineyard, and four from Family Farm. In 2005, owing to disastrous weather in the Santa Cruz Mountains, no estate wines were made, but vineyard-designated pinots were made from the Sonatera, Chileno Valley, and Kanzler vineyards in the Petaluma Gap, and a blended Sonoma Coast wine was made from all of the foregoing, all under the Alesia label. The year 2006 saw new editions of the same Santa Cruz Mountains wines that were made in 2004, as well as the addition of a Falstaff Road bottling to the portfolio

of Sonoma Coast pinots; in 2007 wine was made, for the first time, from all the estate vineyards.

Winemaking is unconventional by contemporary California standards. Grapes are picked as early as 22.5 Brix; there are no additions of yeast, nutrients, enzymes, or even water except in extraordinary circumstances; between 25 and 100 percent of fruit is retained as whole clusters; all fermentors are foot trodden; and the barrel stock (entirely François Frères since 2007) is custom coopered from staves that have been air dried for four years. Wines stay in barrel for fifteen to eighteen months and are usually bottle aged for another year before release. The result is very serious pinot that runs the gamut of color from gossamer garnet to deep black-red; typically finishes under 14 percent alcohol; is rarely fruit forward; shares organoleptic space with strong minerality, spice, and flowers; and displays the restrained intensity that comes not from winemaking, but from low yields and intrinsically interesting *terroirs*. Although few of these wines had made an appearance in the marketplace as of press time, they are hugely promising. A tasting of 2006 components in barrel early in 2007 was inspirational; two finished wines tasted prerelease in 2008 confirmed first impressions.

TASTING NOTES
2006 *Alesia Falstaff Road Vineyard (tasted prerelease in 2008):* Pretty, rosy-ruby color; dusty, granitic rose-petal aromas; a very intense expression of minerals and red fruit; lightweight and satiny; very attractive.
2006 *Alpine Vineyard (tasted prerelease in 2008):* Medium-dark black-red; noticeable signature of partial whole-cluster fermentation manifested as hints of juniper berry and cinnamon, plus flower petals;

strongly mineral, like cherries on slate; a tiny hint of fruit-sweetness; palate-filling and intense to the end; long, fine, and impressive.

2005 *Alesia Falstaff Road Vineyard (tasted prerelease in* 2007*):* Nearly opaque; spring meadow flowers with hints of gardenia, tarragon, and evergreen; dark cherry, boysenberry, and lingonberry on the palate; rich with a hint of mocha, but beautifully built with a creamy mid-palate and a long, sturdy finish.

2004 *Rhys Home Vineyard (tasted in* 2007*):* Medium-deep black-red; dense, complex nose scented with briar, ferrous earth, and forest floor; rich and very intense on the palate with some dark cherry, mocha, and a hint of grip, but also very bright, elegant, and long. Just 13 percent alcohol. A personal favorite.

RIVERS-MARIE
Calistoga, California

Rivers-Marie is the first of two Sonoma Coast pinot projects undertaken by Thomas Rivers Brown, a South Carolinian educated at the University of Virginia, whose California winemaking career had meteoric beginnings. Having discovered wine (and especially Burgundy) both as a pleasure of the palate and as an object of intellectual interest, Brown moved to Napa on a shoestring in 1996, where he worked briefly for a wine shop in Calistoga. Ehren Jordan (see FAILLA WINES) offered Brown a cellar rat job for the 1997 harvest at Turley Wine Cellars; then, Jordan hired Brown as his assistant. Within three years, and with no formal training in viticulture or enology, Brown inherited some of

Jordan's high-profile, custom-crush projects, including Tra Vigne restaurateur Michael Chiarello's new wine venture, and Schrader Cellars, successor to Colgin-Schrader Cellars, which had produced cult Napa cabernets early in the decade.

But Brown says that he "always knew" he "loved pinot noir." He secured a place on the mailing lists of WILLIAMS SELYEM, ROCHIOLI VINEYARD, and DEHLINGER WINERY. In 2002 he "reconnected" with Scott Zeller, whom he had first met at Turley in 1999. Zeller and his wife, Joan, own the Summa Vineyard, one of the first pinot vineyards planted at the south end of the True Sonoma Coast, west of Occidental, overlooking Bodega Bay, and the fruit source for some of Williams Selyem's best coastal pinots. Zeller told Brown he thought some of the 2002 pinot at Summa might be "available." Unable to resist, Brown and his then girlfriend, now spouse Genevieve Marie Welsh birthed Rivers-Marie. (Brown is also the managing partner in a second Sonoma Coast pinot project called Ridgetop, where Fred Schrader is a second partner. Ridgetop planted a mostly pinot vineyard near Annapolis in 2001.)

WINES AND WINEMAKING NOTES
Rivers-Marie made minuscule quantities of two pinots in 2002 and 2003, both from the Summa Vineyard. The "main" release, called simply Summa Vineyard, came from a block planted in 1999. A Summa Old Vines bottling was made from the original block planted in 1978. In 2004 a third wine, labeled Sonoma Coast, was made from Summa vines planted in 2002 and fruit from a neighboring vineyard called Joya. All of these are uncommonly and impressively bright, high-acid, red fruit–oriented pinots with intense aromatics and silky textures, although the 2004 is a

bit blacker and riper than its predecessors. In each vintage, the Old Vines bottling is an especially intense sibling of the "plain" Summa wine, possessed of genuinely astonishing depth and length.

The wines are made at Nicholson Ranch in Carneros. Brown picks the Summa pinot when the grape flavors are still "fairly shrill." This has always translated to less than 25 Brix, and sometimes *much* less. The 2003 was picked at just 22.2! The fruit is entirely destemmed, but berries are kept largely intact. Tiny lots are fermented in fruit bins; slightly larger lots go into 3-ton, stainless steel open-tops. A cold soak is maintained in an ambient, cool environment until Brown "can smell ethyl acetate," and then the temperature of the must is raised until resident yeasts trigger fermentation. The vattings are hand-plunged, and the *cuvaison* lasts fourteen to twenty-one days. The wine is pressed based on taste and barreled straightaway on its gross lees. Malolactic fermentation relies on indigenous yeasts and finishes in barrel.

Half to two thirds of the barrels used for the Summa bottling are new, as are all of those used for the Old Vines cuvée. The majority cooper is Tonnellerie Remond, but Brown also uses some Cadus and Taransaud barrels. The wines are racked first after the malolactic fermentation is complete, and again after ten months in barrel, when they are bottled. There is no fining or filtration. Another eight months of bottle age precedes release. This regime produces slightly hazy wines with intense aromatics, deserving of serious attention.

TASTING NOTES

2004 *Summa Vineyard (tasted in 2006):* Medium garnet color; floral and gamy on the nose, then strawberries, raspberries, Queen Anne cherries, and rosewater in the mouth, with hints of white pepper,

Indonesian spice, and a hint of tannic grip; slightly riper and blacker than the 2002 and 2003, but still impressively elegant, long, and satiny.

2003 *Summa Old Vines (tasted in 2006):* Very intense aromas of rosewater and dried citrus peel; then, a fusion of wild strawberry, black raspberry, white pepper, briar, and iodine on the palate. Light-to-medium in weight, very modest in alcohol, and with a long, silky finish with just a hint of grip.

2002 *Summa Vineyard (tasted in 2006):* Light-to-medium, hazy rosy-garnet; aromas of rosewater, tangerine peel, and potpourri, with hints of truffle and iodine; bright flavors of wild strawberry and tangerine peel; engaging high-acid, low-pH profile; medium weight; long, silky finish.

ROAR WINES
Soledad, California

Even before Gary Franscioni and Gary Pisoni (see PISONI VINEYARDS AND WINERY) joined forces to develop Garys' Vineyard in 1997, Franscioni had followed his friend's lead, diversifying from the row crops that had made their parents successful, into wine grapes. Franscioni planted his first vineyard, named for his wife, Rosella, and co-located with their residence on River Road, just south of its intersection with Gonzales Bridge Road. Rosella's is 50 acres of southeast-facing benchland, dedicated entirely to pinot noir. Like the Pisoni estate and Garys', it is impeccably farmed, and the fruit is in huge demand from cult winemakers throughout California; unlike Pisoni and Garys', however, it is planted to Dijon 113,

115, 667, and 777, and to UCD 4 on 101–14 rootstock. Beginning in 2001, Franscioni followed his friend's lead once again, committing to make a small quantity of his own wine. His partners in this venture are Adam and Dianna Lee, who are also fruit clients, making critically acclaimed and widely appreciated vineyard-designated pinots under the SIDURI WINES label from both Rosella's and Garys'.

Four Roar pinots are made in each vintage: a Santa Lucia Highlands blend derived from Garys', Rosella's, and the Pisoni estate vineyard, and vineyard-designated wines from each of those three sites. At Garys', the Roar fruit comes from Block 1 at the uphill end of the vineyard; at Rosella's, the Roar wine uses the vineyard's entire planting of Dijon 113 and some of most other planted clones; and at Pisoni, the Roar "block" is a single acre within Tessa's Block, which dates to 1991. The Franscionis control the picking decisions for the Roar wines, as well as the stylistic parameters of winemaking. The Lees make sure that the wines are well raised technically.

Despite their common vineyard origin, once allowance is made for different assortments of clones and blocks, *élevage* in the same cellar, and oversight by the same team, the Roar and Siduri editions of each vineyard-designated wine are quite different. Roar pinots rely almost entirely on destemmed berries and are fermented in a larger proportion of stainless steel tanks; the Siduri wines are made mostly in fruit bins where Lee believes he can manage extraction more easily. Roar's barrel program is confined to cooperage from François Frères and Remond; Siduri uses a much wider assortment, and Lee tailors his choices on a vineyard-by-vineyard basis. The Roar wines usually spend sixteen months in barrel, whereas their Siduri cousins are usually bottled before the following harvest. Most importantly, when the final blends

are made, the Franscionis privilege lots that, in combination, exhibit plush textures and near-term drinking pleasure; the Lees, for Siduri, prefer a bit more structure in the service of ageworthiness. Overall, the Roar pinots are impressive, large-framed, ripe wines with the good breeding that comes from fine sites and with appealing, plush textures that range from creamy to chewy.

TASTING NOTES

2005 *Santa Lucia Highlands (tasted in 2007):* Transparent, deep black-red; nuts, baked fruit, and even roasted root vegetables on the nose; rich, soft, suede-like, and almost chewy on the palate, with notes of mocha and a fruit presence that seems like cherry *eau-de-vie* in a chocolate truffle.

2005 *Rosella's Vineyard (tasted in 2007):* A more feminine wine than the blend, and slightly lighter in color; roasted chestnut aromas; intense and lightly spicy in the mouth, with cherry-raspberry fruit with hints or orange peel and mocha; almost creamy in texture and quite long.

2004 *Garys' Vineyard (tasted in 2007):* Transparent, medium red; a concerto of aromas reminiscent of evening meals in winter: baked fruit, roasted nuts, rendered bacon, mocha, and chocolate; dark cherry, black raspberry, earth, and cured meat on the palate; finishes rich, creamy, and long.

ROBERT MONDAVI WINERY
Napa, California

In the annals of fine California wine, no name is better known than Robert Mondavi. His story has been told and retold, not least in his own autobiography (*Harvests of Joy: How the Good Life Became Great Business* [New York, 1998]), and in Julia Flynn Siler's *The House of Mondavi: The Rise and Fall of an American Wine Dynasty* (New York, 2007).

Mondavi was the son of Italian immigrant parents who grew grapes in California's Central Valley in the first half of the twentieth century. The family relocated from Lodi to the Napa Valley in 1943, when his father purchased the

---

THE SENSITIVITY OF PINOT IMPACTED OUR WORK WITH ALL THE VARIETIES WE TOUCHED
—Tim Mondavi

Charles Krug Winery from its then owner, James Moffitt. Robert quarreled famously with his older (and reputedly quieter) brother, Peter, early in the 1960s, left Krug, and founded Robert Mondavi Winery as an independent enterprise in 1966. From that point on, he was known for a relentless—sometimes egomaniacal—pursuit of parity with the greatest wines in the world, and for partnerships with famous European wine dynasties.

A decision to take the Robert Mondavi Winery public in the 1980s led to his eventual separation, along with his sons, from the business that bears his name and to the sale of that business to drinks giant Constellation Brands in 2004. What is much less appreciated is the substantial investment Robert Mondavi Winery made, almost from the outset, in research and development, in the experimentation that led to widespread use of new oak barrels for *élevage* and to the adoption of computers to manage fermentation temperatures, and

the extraordinary stable of winegrowing talent that was nurtured chez Mondavi over three decades. Dozens of Mondavi alumni moved into leadership positions across the California wine industry and elsewhere. Perhaps the best kept secret of all is how much of the family's and the company's attention was focused on pinot noir—even though benchmark pinot was rarely made under the Robert Mondavi label.

Robert's younger son, Tim, who was the company's director of winegrowing from 1976 to 2003, told me parts of the pinot noir story in 2000. He described a trip to Burgundy in 1973 with his father and brother, when the trio tasted through Côte de Nuits cellars beginning chez Louis Trapet in Gevrey-Chambertin, finding that "each wine we tasted was better than the last." Tim Mondavi said he discovered "the mystique of *terroir*" in Burgundy and came home "bitten by the pinot bug." (Initially, he conceded, he mistook *terroir* for "some kind of terrier.") He explained that the orientation of Napa Valley winemaking, after the Repeal of Prohibition, was "repression of fault technology," including heavy doses of sulfur and cool-temperature fermentations, and that "cabernet was a variety that could get through [such treatments] while pinot could not." In a 2001 interview with *Wines & Vines*, Mondavi said, "For us, pinot noir is the grape that began to help us make a change to a more natural way of looking at wine, and a greater understanding of *terroir*."

In its early years, Mondavi's pinot program was based on fruit from the Stags Leap district; the orientation shifted gradually to Carneros in the 1980s, beginning with the purchase of grapes from the Winery Lake Vineyard. In the cellar, 1974 was the first vintage fermented at a significantly higher temperature than the norm. Mondavi experimented with whole-cluster fermentation and stem retention beginning in 1976 and with some use of new oak for *élevage* in 1978. In Tim Mondavi's memory, the "late 1970s vintages" were "the beginning of recognition that California could produce good pinot noir." "We spent a lot of time on pinot noir," Tim Mondavi explained, because "the sensitivity of pinot demanded close attention. Cabernet did not demand it, but [cabernet and pinot both] loved it. The sensitivity of pinot impacted our work with all the varieties we touched." Those who tasted samples Mondavi winemakers brought from time to time in the 1980s to the annual Steamboat Conference in Oregon, where unfinished and problem wines were group-critiqued behind closed doors, say that nothing was more impressive than the repeated improvements seen in Mondavi wines, year after year.

Late in the 1980s, the company made its first viticultural investment in Carneros, acquiring an estate off Duhig Road, south of the Carneros Highway, close to the line that separates Napa and Sonoma counties. Fifteen acres of pinot were planted there in 1989, 52 in 1990, 56 in 1991, and 21 in 1998. Although no fewer than fifteen selections of pinot were used, emphasis was placed on Swan selection from the Hyde Vineyard, and on Dijon clones 115, 667, and 777.

Late in the 1990s, a cavernous farm structure on the Carneros property was refitted as a pinot-only winery, and Steven Leveque, an associate winemaker at Mondavi since 1992, was dedicated full time to pinot until he left to assume the winemaking duties at Chalk Hill Estate in Sonoma in 2003. The rustic Carneros facility was then abandoned, and production shifted to newly refurbished facilities in Oakville. Gustavo Gonzalez, a member of the winemaking team since 1995, assumed responsibility for pinot noir when Leveque departed; he now handles

pinot, along with all red varieties, under the overall direction of Geneviève Janssens, the company's director of winemaking since 2003. Janssens is a Morocco-born, France-raised, and Bordeaux-educated enologist who first worked at Mondavi from 1978 to 1979 and has been involved continuously since 1989.

The company's other pinot ventures— BYRON VINEYARD AND WINERY in Santa Maria, acquired in 1990, and Robert Mondavi Coastal, a mid-priced brand sourced primarily from Santa Barbara and Monterey counties, were divested, or ceased, after Constellation Brands acquired Mondavi in 2004.

WINES AND WINEMAKING NOTES
During the 1970s and 1980s, the mainstays of Mondavi's pinot program were a Napa Valley bottling and a reserve. A Carneros appellation wine was first made in 1991, and it soon replaced the Napa Valley bottling as the program's anchor. A small-lot program named Huichica Hills for the winery's Carneros property debuted in 1998 but was short lived. A non-estate, vineyard-designated pinot noir was made from the Hyde Vineyard in 2002 and 2003. PNX, another small-lot wine sourced from the Rancho Carneros Vineyard, a thirty-year old planting on resistant rootstock, debuted in 2004. The sum of the Carneros bottling, the Reserve, and PNX is about 22,000 cases annually, which is approximately 5 percent of the brand's total production.

Grapes are typically picked between 25 and 26 Brix, and are fermented in a mix of oak and stainless steel open-tops. Unlike many small-lot operations where clones and vineyard blocks are fermented separately, the practice at Mondavi is to co-ferment clones "for complexity." Some fruit is retained as whole clusters "for spice and depth," and fermentations rely on a combination of resident and inoculated yeasts. Extended macerations are normal. The Carneros wine spends about seven months in barrels, of which just 16 percent are new; the reserve spends nine months in 75 percent new barrels. The wines are not normally filtered, but many lots are fined with egg whites.

The small-lot program undertaken at the end of the 1990s was indicative of Mondavi's seriousness about pinot noir. I have less experience with recent Carneros and reserve bottlings, but the 2005 Carneros is a commendable effort.

TASTING NOTE

2005 *Carneros (tasted in* 2007*):* Medium transparent, rosy-garnet; spicy, slightly exotic nose redolent of red fruit and resin; briar, cherry-cranberry fruit, and conifer foliage on the palate; considerable barrel marking; bright overall with a hint of macerated plum skin at the end; attractive.

ROBERT SINSKEY VINEYARDS
Napa, California

Robert Sinskey, a Los Angeles ophthalmologist, was one of the original investment partners in ACACIA WINERY. After his initial investment when the Acacia partnership was created in 1980, Sinskey also provided capital to finance an intended but stillborn expansion into Bordelais varieties in 1984. In addition to these investments, he purchased land near Acacia's new facility on Las Amigas Road in 1982, where he planted merlot,

chardonnay, and pinot noir the following year, planning to sell grapes to Acacia for its vineyard-designation program. The sales never happened. Acacia sailed into troubled waters at mid-decade and was sold to Chalone Inc. in 1986. At this point, Sinskey's investment in Acacia's forthcoming expansion was "exchanged" for a piece of that expansion—a 5-acre parcel of volcanic shale and rocky clay in Napa's Stags Leap district, where he built a state-of-the-art winery in 1988. This transaction explains how Robert Sinskey, always a Burgundy-focused producer with extensive holdings in Los Carneros, came to be domiciled in the heart of Napa's cab country and to make a benchmark cabernet sauvignon on the side.

When the winery was completed, Sinskey appealed to his son, a New York–trained photographer, to "take a six-month vacation" and "make a business and distribution plan" for Robert Sinskey wines. Rob Sinskey took over management of the winery and, in effect, never looked back. Twenty years later, he is the winery's owner, "daydream believer," and evangelist. In 1997 Sinskey *fils* married Maria Helm, then the executive chef at San Francisco's Plumpjack Café, who became the nexus of a tight alliance between cuisine and Sinskey wines, and eventually the culinary director for the winery.

Sinskey's original plantings of pinot noir—about 15 acres on the southwestern corner of Las Amigas and Milton Roads, and facing the northern side of Las Amigas—are part of what the winery now calls the Three Amigos vineyards. These were in 10-foot rows with 4 feet between vines, in the Haire series, clay-loam soils typical of the area, using scion material from the Iund and St. Clair vineyards. In 1988 Sinskey acquired a second Carneros vineyard, called Vandal, close to the northern edge of the appellation, due west of the city of Napa. Eighteen acres of pinot noir were planted there, using nursery-sourced UCD 4 and St. Clair selection taken from the Three Amigos vineyards. Nine more acres of pinot were planted on a property known as the Capa Vineyard, on Buhman Avenue near Henry Road, in 1993. This west-facing site is the warmest and most precocious of Sinskey's Carneros vineyards. It is laid out in 8-foot rows with 6 feet between vines—except that one block of Dijon 115 was planted 3 feet by 3 feet—to UCD 4 and field selections from Hanzell and Chalone.

Then, in 1996 and 1997, more land was acquired on the eastern side of Old Sonoma Road south of Saintsbury's Brown Ranch, dubbed simply O.S.R. Vineyard, for Old Sonoma Road. Thirteen acres of pinot noir were planted there (alongside a similar quantity of merlot) to Dijon 114 and 115, as well as to UCD 4. At the same time, more land was purchased adjacent to the old plantings on Las Amigas Road, which was now dubbed Three Amigos. Some of this acreage was also planted to pinot noir. Expansion continued as Sinskey planted more pinot (along with pinot blanc, pinot gris, riesling, and gewürztraminer) on the Sonoma side of Los Carneros in 2001 and 2002, in a vineyard on Ramal Road just east of Carneros Creek's Las Brisas vineyard. The winery calls this parcel Scintilla Sonoma.

In 1990, alarmed by the spread of phylloxera in neighboring vineyards and by the dead, wormless look of his own earth, Rob Sinskey began the slow conversion of Sinskey's vineyards from chemical herbicides and nitrogen-based fertilizers to sustainable and organic viticultural practices. This change, according to the principals, has produced more consistent year-by-year yields, longer hang times, healthier late-season development, better-colored grapes,

more intensely flavored wines, and better expression of *terroir*.

Winemaker Jeff Virnig joined the Sinskey team in 1988, initially as assistant to then winemaker Joe Cafaro. A 1984 graduate of California State Polytechnic University at San Luis Obispo with a degree in agricultural business management, Virnig had learned winemaking on the job at Mayacamas and Joseph Phelps. He has been Sinskey's winemaker since 1991.

WINES AND WINEMAKING NOTES
Sinskey has made an estate grown Los Carneros of Napa Valley pinot in every vintage since 1987, except for 1989. (Sinskey's 1986 first release of pinot noir was made from purchased fruit.) Until 1990 the Los Carneros wine was made entirely from Three Amigos fruit. In 1991 Vandal Vineyard fruit entered the blend, as did Capa Vineyard fruit beginning in 1996. Meanwhile, in 1990, for one vintage and again after 1993, Sinskey also began making a reserve bottling in addition to the Los Carneros wine. In 1998 the Reserve was renamed Four Vineyards. Under both names, it has been a barrel selection, anchored with fruit from the Three Amigos vineyards. Beginning with the 2001 vintage, Sinskey launched an array of single-vineyard wines: Three Amigos, Vandal Vineyard, and Capa Ranch. (Three Amigos and Vandal were also made in 2002; Capa was not.) The single-vineyard wines debuted at the expense of the Four Vineyards program, whose volume was substantially reduced after the 2000 vintage. Unfortunately, all of the 2002 and 2003 vintages of Three Amigos, the 2003 single-vineyard wines from Vandal and Capa, and the 2003 Four Vineyards blend were completely destroyed before release in an offsite warehouse fire.

Stylistically, and therefore also in cellar technique, Virnig and Sinskey *fils,* a bit like David Lett in Oregon, take the road less traveled. They are champions of elegance, proponents of wine that combines well with food, and enemies of the competitions that measure wine quality in terms of point scores. It follows that Virnig picks pinot early, typically between 22.5 and 24.5 Brix. Since 1998 the fermentors have been mostly 8.8- and 6.5-ton open-tops, although some lots are fermented in half-ton fruit bins, and a few closed tanks remain. A two- to three-day cool soak not enforced with tank jackets or dry ice typically precedes the onset of fermentation, which may be powered entirely by resident yeasts or buttressed with selected isolates. Because of its early ripening character, the Capa Vineyard fruit sometimes demands acidification, but otherwise, acid additions are avoided, and there is no use of enzymes. Punchdowns are done in all the open-top fermentors (and cap irrigation is practiced in a few closed-top tanks) until sugars reach 1 percent or less, at which point the must is pressed. Depending on the vintage, the press fraction may be fined or not and is then reassembled with the free-run juice.

One-, two-, three-, and four-year-old barrels are used to raise the wine, and between 25 percent and 30 percent of barrels are new each year. François Frères is Sinskey's "base cooperage," but barrels are also purchased from Taransaud and from the boutique operations of Michel Toutant and Claude Gillet. Sinskey and Virnig say the "sweet spot" in their barrel regime is a one-year-old barrel coopered from Bertranges wood by François Frères. Malolactic starter is added when the new wine is barreled, and malolactic fermentations usually finish before Christmas. Racking is done "as needed"—

two or three times. Blends are made in June after the vintage, but the wines usually stay in barrel until January or February of the second year after the vintage. "One or two lots out of ten" are fined with egg whites, and cross-flow filtration has been practiced since 1999. Twelve to twenty-four months of bottle aging precede release, so Sinskey pinots are typically at least one and sometimes two years later to market than the norm.

Sinskey pinots display persistent elegance, satiny texture, and a rich palate of secondary flavors happily unmasked by dominant fruit, heavy extraction, or high alcohol. The Three Amigos bottling was a particular favorite when I tasted through the 2004 wines; the Vandal Vineyard bottling tends to be the darkest and ripest of the pinots, but dark and ripe for Sinskey is still not very dark or very ripe in the greater scheme of things.

TASTING NOTES

2005 *Los Carneros (tasted twice in* 2007*):* Brilliant, light-to-medium garnet with a rosy rim; rose, violet, and hibiscus aromas, with a hint of resin and fresh-sawn tropical wood; raspberry, black licorice, and soft spice in the mouth; light-to-medium weight, satiny, and elegant with a hint of grip at the end. Very attractive.

2004 *Four Vineyards (tasted twice in* 2007*):* Transparent, medium garnet; intense nose marked with vanilla, cabinet-shop aromas, and slightly herbal berry fruit; black cherry, raspberry, pepper, and clove on the palate, with considerable depth, some creaminess, and a hint of peppermint; firm at mid-palate; long and attractive.

2004 *Three Amigos Vineyard (tasted twice in* 2007*):* Transparent, medium ruby; resin, orange peel, moss, fir balsam, and dried flowers on the nose; pretty, red-black fruit with undertones of earth and tar on the palate; gentle grip from mid-palate to finish; very serious, elegant, and long; extremely attractive.

2004 *Vandal Vineyard (tasted in 2007):* Medium garnet; conifer foliage with hints of mint and smoke on the nose; the ripest and blackest of the Sinskey pinots on the palate; a hint of Medjool dates on the attack; very slightly sweet before mid-palate; strong grip and minerality from mid-palate to finish; Gevrey-like and very serious; needs time.

2002 *Four Vineyards (tasted in 2007):* Brilliant brick-red color; earth and cherry on the nose, with a hint of toast; rich and substantial on the palate, with hints of sweet fruit, orange peel, licorice, and soft spice; intense; very pretty finish.

ROCHIOLI VINEYARD AND WINERY

Healdsburg, California

Despite an explosion of activity throughout the appellation since 1990, Joseph Rochioli Jr.'s 160-acre estate on Westside Road, about 7 miles from Healdsburg, remains the incontrovertible nexus of pinot noir in the Russian River Valley. For almost four decades, his vineyards have provided fruit for some of the area's most talented pinot makers, including Davis Bynum, Gary Farrell, Burt Williams, and his own son Tom, whose collective craftsmanship is substantially responsible for the appellation's impressive reputation. Budwood from his so-called West Block has been the basis for important plantings in neighboring vineyards. The adjacent Allen Ranch—which Rochioli also farms, exactly as he farms his own—is WILLIAMS SELYEM'S home turf. And the 8 acres of pinot that Rochioli planted on his own ranch at the end of the 1960s are today, virus and phylloxera notwithstanding, *the* benchmark for the rich, complex pinots grown on the west side of the Middle Reach.

The beginnings were scarcely grand. Joe's father, Joseph Rochioli Sr., had leased the present estate in the 1930s, before he accumulated the resources to purchase it outright. He sold its yield of zinfandel grapes, hops, and hay for cash, and raised nearly everything the family needed to live—fruits, vegetables, pigs, and chickens—plus a few cows and horses in addition to the cash crops. When the hops business deteriorated in the 1950s, he replaced the hops with Blue Lake green beans and then, as the market for wine grapes improved, interplanted the beans with vinifera—mostly colombard and cabernet sauvignon. In 1959 he planted a 10-acre block of sauvignon blanc close to the center of the ranch that is still in production. "The colombard and cabernet were the wrong choices," Joe Jr. told me in 2002. "But in 1960 we didn't even know what region we were in. I had no clue. No one else had a clue, either. I got the University of California farm adviser to put in a weather station in 1962." By the time his father died in 1966, Joe Jr. had learned Russian River's cool-weather truth, so in 1968 he began the process of replacing the colombard and cabernet with pinot noir and chardonnay. When his first crop of pinot was picked in 1971, however, winemakers were hardly standing in line. According to Joe Jr., he was forced to sell that harvest and the next to Martini & Prati, who "sent it on to Gallo," where it seems to have finished ignominiously in Hearty Burgundy.

The picture brightened substantially in 1973. Former San Francisco newspaperman Davis Bynum (see DAVIS BYNUM WINES) purchased a nearby hops kiln, transformed it into a more-or-less modern winery, purchased Rochioli's entire crop of pinot, vinified it as a varietal wine, and put Rochioli's name on the label. Beginning in 1979, some fruit was also sold to Williams Selyem, which made Rochioli's fruit genuinely famous.

In 1976 Joe Jr. briefly tried his own hand at winemaking, working in Davis Bynum's facility, where he made 1,000 cases each of pinot noir and chardonnay under a label called Fenton Acres. Then in 1982, Rochioli agreed to sell a very small quantity of pinot to Gary Farrell, Davis Bynum's winemaker, for a project that would carry Farrell's name (see GARY FARRELL WINES); in return,

---

THE INCONTROVERTIBLE NEXUS OF PINOT NOIR IN THE RUSSIAN RIVER VALLEY

Farrell agreed to make 150 cases of pinot noir on a custom-crush basis to launch the Rochioli brand. Soon thereafter, Joe Jr.'s son Tom returned to the family farm from a short-lived career in banking. He applied his training in business and finance to plans for a new, 10,000-case winery and home for Rochioli wines, which was built on the Rochioli estate in 1985. To his father's surprise, Tom also became a hands-on winemaker, so the custom-crush arrangement with Farrell and Bynum was allowed to expire, making Rochioli both an estate winery and an all-in-the-family enterprise.

The estate vineyard now consists of approximately 128 planted acres, of which

half are pinot noir. The oldest pinot vines are 4 acres in East Block, planted in 1968, and another 4 acres in West Block, set out the following year. The scion material for East Block is said to be a combination of UCD 4 and a field selection taken from a vineyard "south of St. Helena on the east side of Route 29," whose particulars Joe Jr. can no longer recall. The budwood for West Block was acquired from Karl Wente. Joe Jr. thinks he remembers being told that these cuttings came from Wente's estate vineyard in Livermore, and before that directly from France, but Karl's son, Phil, believes this scenario is unlikely. Phil Wente thinks any budwood obtained from Wente at the end of the 1960s would have been taken from the winery's increase block in Arroyo Seco—which was planted entirely to UCD selections. Indeed, several winegrowers familiar with West Block fruit believe it is morphologically consistent with UCD 4; others disagree, leaving the matter of provenance open.

Both East and West Blocks feature east-facing, deep alluvial soil, although West Block is on slightly higher ground and is less vigorous; the vines were planted, in the style of the day, in widely spaced, 14-foot rows with 8 feet between vines. The vines sprawl, and the rootstock is nonresistant AxR1. East Block yields about 4 tons per acre; West Block typically produces less than 3 tons per acre. No more pinot was planted at Rochioli until 1985, when a rise between West Block and Westside Road was planted to cuttings from the West Block vines. These 2.2 acres of rocky soil are called Little Hill. A 3.7-acre block, called Three Corner for its triangular shape, is Rochioli's southernmost vineyard, bordering Little Hill and West Block on their southern edge. This 1974 planting of nursery-sourced UCD 4, planted in 12-foot rows with 8 feet between vines and laid out uncharacteristically in east–west rather than north–south rows, was part of the Allen Ranch until 1999, when Howard Allen deeded it to Rochioli. Joe Jr. says the gift was a thank-you for his two decades of stewardship over Allen's vineyards.

In the mid 1990s, 13 acres between East Block and the river, called River Block, were planted with cuttings taken from West Block, as were 2.8 acres on the uphill side of Westside Road. (This was the first pinot noir planted on the western side of the road, which had hitherto been used only for cabernet, zinfandel, gamay, and chardonnay.) More pinot was added at the end of the 1990s and in 2000, in several blocks on both sides of Westside Road, using (variously) cuttings from West Block, Swan selection, and nursery-sourced Dijon 115 and 777. Collectively, Rochioli calls the blocks on the uphill side of Westside Road the Sweetwater Ranch.

East Block fruit is the basis for the Rochioli pinots made by Bynum called Le Pinot, as well as Rochioli's own East Block vineyard-designate (see below). A mix of East Block, West Block, and Three Corner Vineyard fruit has also been sold to Farrell, who has made the components into single-vineyard wines or blended them to create a Rochioli–Allen Vineyards blend. Some West Block and Three Corner fruit was sold to Williams Selyem until 1997. Williams Selyem used most of the West Block grapes for a vineyard-designated wine called simply Rochioli Vineyard, and bottled most of the Three Corner as Allen Ranch–Tricorner Vineyard. Since 1997, the only Rochioli fruit sold to Williams Selyem has come from the younger River Block planting.

West Block is the most reputed of the Rochioli blocks, which explains its use as a source of budwood for several younger blocks. Some winemakers,

including Farrell, refer to it as Rochioli's "mother block." East Block, however, has a reputation for making the longest lived of the Rochioli wines.

WINES AND WINEMAKING NOTES

An estate pinot noir has been made under the Rochioli label in every vintage since 1982, in quantities ranging from just 150 cases in the first years to about 4,000 cases in the most generous of recent vintages. Until 2002 the estate blend was anchored with fruit from River Block and Little Hill; more recently, the new Sweetwater Vineyard has accounted for 80 percent of it. The reserve wine was made in 1986, 1989, 1990, and 1991 from a selection of West Block lots; something called Special Selection was made just once, in 1988, also from West Block lots. The now-famous block-designates debuted in 1992, effectively replacing the reserve program. A West Block wine and a Three Corner Vineyard wine have been made in every vintage since. A block-designated wine from East Block was made in 1993, 1994, and every year since 1997; a vineyard-designated wine from the Little Hill Vineyard debuted in 1995.

Picking decisions at Rochioli are based on "visual maturity and stats." The fruit is sorted both in the vineyard and on the crushpad. Fermentations are done in 3-ton, open-top tanks. A three-day cold soak precedes inoculation with a combination of Montrachet and RC 212 yeasts. The primary fermentation normally takes eight to ten days at temperatures in the low 80s, during which time the cap is plunged three times daily. Malolactic inoculation is done in the fermentors. Wines are barreled directly from the fermentors without settling, and there is no postfermentation maceration. Barrels are preponderantly medium-plus toast from François Frères, and the percentage of new oak used for each wine varies from 30 percent to 100 percent, with the block-designated wines getting a disproportionate share of the new barrels. All wines spend fifteen months in barrel, are racked once prior to bottling, are never fined, and are rarely filtered. The estate blend is held three months after bottling before release; the single-vineyard wines are held for eight.

By convention, the winery labels the estate blend as "Rochioli" and the single-vineyard wines as "J. Rochioli." The estate wine is beautifully crafted, quintessential Russian River Valley pinot, perhaps with a bit more berry fruit and less stone fruit now that this wine is anchored with grapes from the Sweetwater Ranch side of the estate. The block-designates are an excellent lesson in *terroir* variations across small distances: each is distinctive despite the close proximity of each of the blocks to the others. The wines are ripe picked, intensely flavored, and noticeably barrel marked, but they are still very elegantly made.

TASTING NOTES

2005 *Estate (tasted in* 2007*):* Pretty, transparent, rosy-garnet; aromas of fruit tea, strawberries, and raspberries; rich, sweet, and elegant on the palate; bright and attractively built; finishes with a cascade of very fine-grained tannin; quintessential Russian River Valley pinot; fine.

2005 *Three Corner Vineyard (tasted in* 2007*):* Brilliant medium ruby; walnut, macadamia, and other exotic nut aromas; rich and exotic on the palate, with inky, dark-fruit notes that suggest designer coffees; creamy, soft, and round on the mid-palate; seductive and distinctive.

2005 *Little Hill (tasted in* 2007*):* Brilliant medium ruby; huge nose of smoky fruit and spice; cherry, cinnamon, clove, black pepper, and a hint of juniper berry on the palate; mouth filling, intense, and rewarding.

2005 *West Block (tasted in* 2007*):* Color much as above; briar, cherry, and mocha on the nose; rich, intense, and complex, but more fruit forward than the Little Hill or Three Corner; slightly bigger structurally and more muscular; tightly knit and symphonic, with a bit of tannic grip at the end.

2005 *East Block (tasted in* 2007*):* Darkest of the four block-designated wines; ink, blueberry, and gum camphor on the nose, with a slightly savory note; bright fruit with (nonetheless) very dark flavors; intense white pepper, some mace, nutmeg, and infused violets; mouth coating to the end with just a bit of grip; very long and fine.

RODNEY STRONG VINEYARDS
Healdsburg, California

Rodney Strong (1928–2006) was perhaps the only successful dancer of classical ballet and Broadway theater to have made a second, and mostly successful, career in wine. Born to a winemaking family in the Rheingau, Strong returned to wine when, at the age of thirty-three, he created a storefront firm in Tiburon that specialized in small lots of custom-labeled wines. In 1962, after his retirement from the theater, he purchased a winemaking operation between Windsor and Healdsburg and began to acquire vineyard land throughout Sonoma County.

By the early 1970s, Strong owned no fewer than 6,500 acres and had built one of California's first wine production facilities designed from the ground up for tourism: an avant-garde structure shaped vaguely like an incomplete pyramid, at the corner of Eastside Road and Old Redwood Highway. The wine glut of the mid 1970s nearly ruined Strong's business, however. Although most of his vineyards were sold, and investors assumed a majority interest in the remaining enterprise, there was still room for a joint venture with Piper-Heidsieck in 1980, dedicated to the production of champagne-method sparkling wine. This partnership resulted in the construction of a second winery next door to the pyramid that was subsequently sold to J VINEYARDS AND WINERY. In 1989 Tom Klein—a Stanford MBA with farm roots in the Central Valley near Stockton, who knew Strong from an earlier management consulting assignment— purchased the company from its then owner, Guinness American Inc. Production soared during the 1990s. By 2004 Rodney Strong was the twenty-third largest wine company in America.

Strong planted his first pinot noir about 1967 in what is now called the River East vineyard, on the site of the winery. The plant material was a field selection from Louis Martini's plantings on the Stanly Ranch. The pinot program then began in the 1970s, albeit somewhat erratically, with some fruit from River East and some from the IRON HORSE VINEYARDS near Sebastopol, which Strong then controlled. Strong seems to have believed that any "serious" winery would produce pinot noir perforce, and an additional 80 acres of pinot (mostly Wente selection and Pommard clone) were planted on the western side of the Middle Reach, in a parcel now known simply as River West. This vineyard has since been sold but remains under long-term contract, although no pinot has been sourced there since 1999. Still, pinot noir was a hard sell in the 1970s, and most of Strong's pinot fruit ended

up in a rosé wine, which was sold, it is said, "by the truckload." Fortuitously, Strong's sparkling-wine venture with Piper-Heidsieck had an almost bottomless appetite for pinot fruit, reducing the still pinot program to modest (and therefore salable) dimensions throughout the 1980s and into the early 1990s.

Although the River East vineyard was the sole source of fruit, Rodney Strong pinots were labeled Russian River Valley River East Vineyard; the "River East Vineyard" part of the designation was dropped when the River West plantings came online. With still pinot finally popular and the Piper-Heidsieck venture sold, most of River East (except the legacy Martini block) was replanted, and in 1998, 63 acres of pinot noir were planted in a third vineyard site, called Jane's Vineyard, on Woolsey Road west of Santa Rosa. An additional 33 acres were planted there in 2002, and 11 more in 2006. The scion material in Jane's is UCD 2A, 23, 44, 46, 71, 72, 73, and 91.

Rodney Strong's winemaker since 1979 has been Rick Sayre. In the 1970s, Sayre worked at Simi, where the *éminence grise* was André Tchelistcheff, then recently retired from Beaulieu. Simi struggled to produce good pinots in this period, handicapped by fruit grown in the warm Alexander Valley, but Sayre had the benefit of Tchelistcheff's perspective on pinot noir, and the opportunity to work with a coterie of amazingly talented young winemakers. Sayre's long tenure at Rodney Strong shows: his hand is sure.

WINES AND WINEMAKING NOTES
Two pinots, an estate wine carrying the Russian River Valley appellation and a Reserve, have been made in every vintage since 1997. Initially the Reserve was anchored with fruit from River West. In

2001, when Jane's Vineyard came online, a vineyard-designated wine from Jane's effectively replaced the Reserve. The estate bottling is built from a combination of River East and "declassified" Jane's fruit. Both wines are made in stainless steel tanks that range in capacity from 5 to 28 tons. (The smaller tanks are housed in a new facility called the "Luxury Wine Cellar," a part of the main winemaking facility formerly used for barrel storage that has been repurposed as a "winery within a winery" for smaller lots.) Gary Patzwald, formerly at Matanzas Creek, has overseen winemaking in this facility, under Sayre's direction, since it was carved out and set up separately in 2005.

All tanks, regardless of size, are pumped over, not punched down. Sayre argues the minority view that, in his experience, punchdowns and open-tops do not make better pinot. In a further departure from classical pinot protocol, Sayre adds a small percentage of syrah to the estate pinot, mostly for color, but also in the belief that good syrah "can have the same meaty quality" as good pinot. Sayre lets the crushed fruit cold soak for up to four days, and then inoculates with cultured yeast. Thereafter, fermentation temperature is allowed to rise to about 82°F, and the must is pressed when it is nearly dry. One day to one week is allowed for settling in tank, whereupon the wine is barreled. After a period of using some American oak "for mouth-feel" in the 1990s, Rodney Strong pinots are now raised entirely in French barrels, including François Frères, Charente-based Tonnellerie Marchive, and Dargaud & Jaeglé among others; about 25 percent new oak is used on the estate wine and 50 percent on Jane's. The wines spend seven to thirteen months in barrel, and are fined and filtered "only if necessary." The finished wines are varietally

correct, reliable, and agreeable. They show attractive color, balance, sensible extraction, and medium weight, as well as a pleasant mix of fruit, spice, and flower-related aromatics.

TASTING NOTES

2005 *Estate Vineyards (tasted in 2007):* Brilliant, medium rosy-black-red; vanilla, spice, and red berries on the nose; slightly sweet attack, then with the weight and character of briefly brewed black tea; soft and supple texture, but still a hint of grip; cinnamon and orange peel give a suggestion of mulled wine; attractive and food friendly.

2005 *Jane's Vineyard (tasted in 2007):* Transparent, medium garnet; dusty and predominantly floral nose with some spice and red fruit; bright, forward red fruit on the palate, then with flavors of vanilla and barrel char; soft, medium in weight, and agreeable, with a hint of grip.

ROESSLER CELLARS
Sonoma, California

In 2000 Roger Roessler, a longtime restaurateur with projects spread across the western part of the country, and his brother Richard, an electrical engineer and hobbyist winemaker, created Roessler Cellars, dedicated primarily to the kind of food-friendly pinot noir on which Roger had built wine lists for his restaurants. Roger's restaurant interests included a share in the historic Swiss Hotel on Sonoma's town square, where the Sangiacomo family, Carneros's largest independent grape growers, were regular customers. When it occurred to Roger that he might like to make wine, Angelo Sangiacomo did not hesitate to offer him 4.5 tons of pinot noir.

On the strength of this offer, the Roessler brothers formed a company that they own in equal shares and enlisted Wells Guthrie (see COPAIN WINE CELLARS) as their winemaker (and part owner). They began an explosive expansion that, five years later, encompassed no fewer than twelve vineyard-designated pinots sourced from northern Mendocino County to the Sta. Rita Hills, four appellation pinots with proprietary names, and a dribble of chardonnay. Not content to function entirely as *négociants,* in 2001 the Roesslers also purchased 40 acres near Annapolis, at the north end of the True Sonoma Coast, where they planted 3 acres of pinot noir in 2003. The vineyard, called Ridges, will eventually consist of 13 planted acres on the slopes of three distinct and separate ridgelines. The first 3 acres, on the westernmost of the ridges, facing southwest, are laid out in south-southwest oriented rows 6 feet apart with 4 feet between vines; the scion material is an even mix of Dijon 115 and 828, with slightly lesser amounts of Dijon 777 and

---

AN UNCOMMONLY LARGE PORTFOLIO OF RIPE, RICH, LUSH WINES MADE WITH TALENT AND RESTRAINT

UCD 4. The first harvest from Ridges made one single barrel of wine in 2005. In 2006 Scott Shapley, Guthrie's brother-in-law and the former assistant winemaker at SIDURI WINES, replaced Guthrie as Roessler's hands-on winemaker. Further growth of the brand, primarily with respect to the appellation wines, is anticipated, as

is construction of a dedicated winemaking facility. Unsurprisingly, considerable attention is given to restaurant placements.

WINES AND WINEMAKING NOTES
Within the portfolio of single-vineyard pinots, the Sangiacomo wine was made from 2000 to 2003; a Peay Vineyards (a neighbor to Ridges) wine in 2003 and 2004; a Pisoni Vineyard, wine in 2003 only; and a Kanzler Vineyard (see KOSTA BROWNE WINES) wine in 2004 only. A Russian River Valley wine called Dutton Ranch, from the Duttons' Thomas Road Vineyard, has been made in every vintage since 2001, and an Anderson Valley wine from the Savoy Vineyard (see LITTORAI WINES) since 2000. Vineyard-designated wines from Alder Springs (see PATZ & HALL WINE COMPANY), Griffin's Lair near Lakeville, and Sanford & Benedict debuted in 2004, as did wines from the Widdoes Vineyard in the Russian River Valley AVA, the Brosseau Vineyard in the Chalone AVA, and Hein Family in the Anderson Valley AVA in 2005. Among the appellation wines, a Sonoma County wine called Red Label has been made since 2001, an Anderson Valley blend called Blue Jay since 2002, a Sonoma Coast wine called La Brisa since 2003, and a Sta. Rita Hills wine called Peregrine since 2005.

On the crushpad, almost all of the fruit is destemmed, although some is retained and fermented as whole clusters "depending on the flavor profile of the vineyard and the quality of the stems." Fermentations rely on a deliberate combination of resident and cultured yeasts, and the must is bled if water has been added at the outset to compensate for high sugar levels. The Roesslers find that California-grown pinot, picked ripe enough for their taste, can often end up, after malolactic fermentation, without enough acid to pair well with food, so they add tartaric acid (as well as water) before the alcoholic fermentation begins.

Roessler sources most barrels from François Frères, Remond, and Ermitage, and uses between 30 and 40 percent new wood on each wine. Since the appellation wines and the vineyard-designates are mostly sourced from the same vineyards, decisions are made in the spring after each vintage regarding which lots go into which wines. Once those decisions are made, the final blends are constructed, and the blended wines are returned to barrel. Most wines are bottled unfined and unfiltered before the following vintage, but a few are held up to fifteen months in barrel. Although Roessler pinots are made with enough talent, restraint, and sensitivity that the underlying *terroirs* are expressed, as a group they are ripe, rich, and lush wines, with forward flavors, and finished alcoholic strength between 14 and 14.5 percent.

TASTING NOTES

2005 *Sanford & Benedict Vineyard (tasted in 2007):* Transparent, medium ruby; conifer, exotic, fragrant woods and ripe berry fruit on the nose; fruit and minerality compete for bandwidth on the palate; the fruit ranges over red, blue, and black berries; suede textured and slate-y. A nicely made, refined edition of Sanford & Benedict that is simultaneously sturdy and elegant.

2004 *Savoy Vineyard (tasted in 2007):* Transparent, medium-dark ruby; aromas of tar, lavender, and brambly fruit; bright red fruit and black tea on the palate, with a hint of hard spice. A serious, nicely structured wine with substantial mineral underlay; very attractive, long, and slightly grippy at the end.

2004 *Griffin's Lair (tasted in 2007):* Medium-dark brick-red color; aromas of very dark, black-toned fruit with notes

of underbrush; sweet and intense on the palate; toasty, concentrated, and quite barrel marked; notes of raisined fruit and resin; moderately tannic on the finish; long and warm.

2004 *Red Label (tasted in 2007):* Pretty, medium garnet; nuts and exotic spice on the nose; sweet and fruit forward in the mouth, with cherry, strawberry, pepper, and licorice; silky mid-palate and very slightly grippy at the end.

RR WINERY
Newburg, Oregon

RR, first called Ribbon Ridge Winery but renamed after the Ribbon Ridge AVA was approved, is the personal pinot project of Harry Peterson-Nedry, founder and winemaker at CHEHALEM. It is based entirely on fruit from his Ridgecrest Vineyard and is made in the Chehalem facility. Peterson-Nedry explains that the barrels destined for RR are identified at the same time barrels are chosen for the Chehalem reserve—"at the end of multiple blind tastings over the previous six months." Lots not selected for either the Chehalem reserve program or RR become candidates for Chehalem's Ridgecrest Vineyard bottling or, one step farther along the selection tree, for the Three Vineyards blend.

In the first cut, the best barrels of Ridgecrest are divided: those that display "the more feminine representation of pinot noir" are tagged for the Chehalem reserve; "the more masculine projection becomes RR." At harvest and afterward, Peterson-Nedry says he tries not to tie winemaking choices to the program in which the finished wine will likely star, but experience has shown him that lots fermented with a higher percentage of whole clusters, or treated with "higher extraction regimes," or that are "less elegantly styled" end up being tapped for RR. These lots, and those used to make the Chehalem Reserve, are "inevitably" from Ridgecrest's oldest blocks, which means they feature UCD 2A and 4—the Oregon workhorse clones—and are farmed to 2.5 tons per acre or less. RR wines display black fruit, some tar and petrochemical aromatics, and significant tannins, but the vintages I have tasted have also been uniformly bright and attractively structured. These are true, old-vines pinots from an exceptional site.

TASTING NOTES

2005 *Ridgecrest Vineyards (tasted in 2007):* Transparent, medium garnet; herbal and savory aromas, with some cranberry and some dark berry fruit; slightly sweet on the palate, with an avalanche of marionberry and lingonberry flavors and lavender water; medium in weight but with huge intensity; balanced, bright, long, and fine.

2004 *Ridgecrest Vineyards (tasted in 2007):* Transparent, medium black-red; aromas of blackberry, dried flowers, and creosote; cherry-blackberry fruit on the palate, with significant grip and minerality; bright and nicely structured, if slightly warm and peppery at the end; long.

2002 *Ridgecrest Vineyards (tasted in 2007):* Brilliant, medium-dark, slightly bricky red; herbs, gum camphor, and lavender on the nose; soft attack, then quite intense on the mid-palate, with some black cherry, minerality, and tar; perceptible load of very fine-grained tannins; persistent and long.

RUSACK VINEYARDS
Solvang, California

After high school in California and before matriculating at Maine's Bowdoin College, Geoffrey Rusack drove the delivery truck for a Santa Monica wine shop. A few years later, in law school at Pepperdine University in Los Angeles, he dated the daughter of a pioneering Napa Valley vintner. When he married Alison Wrigley—older sister of the present CEO of Chicago's Wrigley Company—he considered planting a vineyard on the Wrigley family's ranch, which happened to be located on an atoll about twenty miles off the California coast. However unlikely, this last project was finally consummated many years later, abetted by a gaggle of consultants, with a "ceremonial planting" of three vineyard blocks on Santa Catalina Island—some of it pinot noir—from which the first grapes are expected in 2009.

Meanwhile, aboard a flight from Chicago to Los Angeles in 1992, Santa Barbara wine pioneers Brooks and Kate Firestone told Rusack about a defunct winery in Ballard Canyon, but advised him against buying it, because the vineyard consisted of mostly declining blocks of muscat, riesling, and cabernet, and the barn *cum* winery was infested with rodents. The Rusacks bought the Ballard Canyon property anyway, however, created the Rusack brand 1995, and made their first pinot in 1998 "with a lot of advice from Rick Longoria." In 2001, they hired the husband-and-wife team of John and Helen Falcone, both professionally trained winemakers with experience (variously) at Atlas Peak, Chimney Rock, and Artesa, to handle their winemaking. By

2005 Rusack was making about 5,000 cases of wine annually, of which a bit less than half was pinot noir.

Since the Ballard Canyon site is too warm for pinot, Rusack pinot is sourced from the Miller family's Solomon Hills Vineyard on the Santa Maria Mesa, from Fiddlestix (see FIDDLEHEAD CELLARS), from Rancho Santa Rosa (see FOLEY ESTATES VINEYARD), and from Huber Cellars, in the Route 246 corridor of the Sta. Rita Hills appellation, near Babcock Winery.

WINES AND WINEMAKING NOTES
John Falcone says Rusack pinot is picked "in perfect condition" between 24.5 and 25 Brix, completely destemmed (there have been "no ripe stems in California in twenty-nine years," according to Falcone), cold-soaked for forty-eight hours, treated with Colorpro enzymes, and fermented warm (but not hot) for about six days. The wine is barreled before the must is dry "to retain fruit character;" is raised in a combination of Dargaud & Jaeglé, Cadus, François Frères, and Sirugue barrels, of which 30 to 40 percent are new in each vintage; is racked once after the malolactic fermentation is finished; and is bottled after eleven months in barrel. The wines are filtered as necessary "for stability and clarity."

Three wines are made: a Sta. Rita Hills reserve cuvée anchored with Fiddlestix fruit, a Santa Maria Valley wine based 95 percent on Solomon Hills grapes, and a Santa Barbara County wine made from lots not selected for the Sta. Rita Hills or Santa Maria Valley cuvées. My experience with Rusack pinots is limited to the 2003 and 2006 vintages in bottle and to barrel samples of the 2004.

TASTING NOTES
2006 *Santa Maria Valley (tasted in 2008):* Bright ruby color; barrel-marked red fruit nose; attractive, fruit-oriented mid-palate with some elegance and finesse; a bit sweet, soft, and round overall, with a long warm finish.

2006 *Sta. Rita Hills (tasted in 2008):* Very transparent ruby color; structured, earthy, and dense; mostly black-toned fruit on the palate; slightly grippy from mid-palate to the end; intense and warm.

2003 *Santa Maria Valley (tasted in 2005):* Saturated, dark, rosy-magenta color; plum, blackberry, and earth aromas, with hints of cinnamon and clove; cassis and blackberry on the palate, with more wet earth and black pepper; fairly weighty, full bodied and slightly sweet.

2003 *Sta. Rita Hills Reserve (tasted in 2005):* Dark and saturated again, but with a floral nose, with notes of wild strawberry and raspberry; cassis, red fruit, and cola on the palate, with hints of cinnamon and clove, plus smoke and tree bark; long and full bodied, this wine finished slightly warm and grippy.

SAINTSBURY
Napa, California

Saintsbury, named for the English man of letters who wrote *Notes on a Cellar-Book,* was founded in 1981 by David Graves and Dick Ward, two winemakers trained at the University of California Davis, who dedicated themselves explicitly to proving that the contemporaneous critics were wrong—that genuinely good pinot noir really could be made in California. For the first five years, Saintsbury worked entirely with fruit purchased from other growers in Los Carneros, including the Lee Vineyard on Los Carneros Avenue, the Stanly Ranch, and Zach Berkowitz. In 1986 the partners planted their first estate vineyard (12.5 acres) adjacent to the present winery buildings at the corner of Withers Lane and Los Carneros Avenue, which they now call the Saintsbury Home Ranch. Ten acres were added on leased land near the

---

THE FLAGSHIP CARNEROS BOTTLING STRIKES AN ATTRACTIVE BALANCE BETWEEN BRIGHT FRUITINESS AND SOLID STRUCTURE

RMS Brandy Distillery in 1991. In 1992 Saintsbury acquired the 40-acre Brown Ranch on Old Sonoma Road, in the Carneros banana belt, where the soils show both volcanic and sedimentary origins.

The original estate vineyard at the winery is a low-density planting of UCD 5 from Adelsheim in Oregon, with some field selections from the nearby St. Clair and Madonna vineyards. It is reported to be one of the first vertically shoot-positioned vineyards in California and is trellised as an open lyre. In contrast, Brown Ranch is more densely planted, and here the UCD 5 is used in combination with Dijon 115, 667, and 777. The combination of Dijon clones and partially volcanic soils causes Brown Ranch to throw fruit with dark, black flavors, while the original estate fruit tends toward the red flavors of strawberry and cherry.

The year 1995 was a watershed for all Saintsbury pinots. Brown Ranch fruit began to dominate all the wines save the Garnet blend (see below), bringing the stamp of a new *terroir* and a change in clonal composition. About the same time, Saintsbury made fundamental changes to its farming and irrigation programs. Chemical additives were minimized, and

the emphasis shifted toward compost, cover crops, and mulching to maintain the vines' health. Irrigation was rescheduled from the beginning of the growing season to the tail end, changing the flavor curve and making for brighter fruit flavors overall. Since 1995 the vines' water requirements have been precisely monitored. Often, there has been no irrigation until after veraison, and in some years, the vines have not been irrigated at all.

Although the founding partners were their own hands-on winemakers in Saintsbury's early years, a talented succession of individuals has been involved since 1991. Byron Kosuge, a Davis-trained enologist who began college as an English major, held the reins from 1991 to 2000, when he left to handle consulting and the B. KOSUGE brand. Mark West, who joined Saintsbury in 1998 as assistant winemaker, served from 2001 to 2004, when he departed for the Rominger West Winery in Davis. Since 2004 the job has belonged to French-born Jerome Chery, a graduate of the Université de Bourgogne in Dijon, who had previously worked with Ted Lemon at LITTORAI WINES.

WINES AND WINEMAKING NOTES
About 45,000 cases of pinot noir are now produced annually by Saintsbury—up from a mere 2,000 in 1981. Almost 80 percent of this volume is associated with two blends: a Carneros appellation wine and an entry-level, proprietary blend called Garnet. Since 1995, the Carneros wine has been heavily anchored with fruit from Brown Ranch, whereas the Garnet is made mostly from fruit purchased from a dozen independent growers in Carneros, with a small admixture of Monterey County grapes. A reserve bottling debuted in the 1980s; after 1995 this was composed almost entirely of Brown Ranch fruit. In 1996 Saintsbury introduced its first vineyard-designated wine, made

entirely from Brown Ranch grapes. In 2005 the reserve was replaced with a trio of non-estate, vineyard-designated wines from Carneros vineyards—Lee Vineyard, Stanly Ranch, and Toyon Farm—and, in a radical departure from tradition, a single-vineyard wine from the Cerise Vineyard near Philo in Mendocino's Anderson Valley. In 2004 there was also an appellation wine from Anderson Valley.

Saintsbury says that "taste, seed maturity, and the weather forecast" all play a role in its picking decisions. Once picked, the mantra here as elsewhere is to handle the fruit gently. Through the 1997 vintage, fermentations were carried out in closed-top tanks with pumpovers. The first open-top fermentors with punchdown capability were installed in 1998. Varying amounts of whole clusters, up to 100 percent, are used "as a way of increasing complexity." The winery is now working with its third destemmer, which Richard Ward describes as "a step forward from its predecessor and a huge improvement over the first." A prefermentation cold soak lasts between two and three days, but the must is thereafter warmed deliberately to between 65 and 70°F. Chery says that "if you don't warm the must, the fermentation will not get warm enough for optimal extraction of color and tannin." The yeast strategy is described as "pretty catholic:" sometimes native yeasts are allowed to take their course; sometimes isolates are added. According to Graves, this approach yields "an interesting palette of wines for blending." Graves says that Saintsbury is now "much less interested" in adding acid than it was in the past, because the incoming fruit has "generally better chemistry"—owing primarily to the changes in the irrigation calendar and to better soils management. Some lots are bled to increase concentration and to produce the 1,000 or so cases of *vin gris* that the winery now sells as Vincent Van Gris.

Barrels are primarily Nevers and Allier wood coopered by François Frères and Taransaud "because these coopers tend to age their wood longer, and longer-aged wood produces softer and rounder wines." Lots destined for the Garnet blend are raised in about 25 percent new barrels; those headed for the Carneros wine see closer to a one-third share of new barrels. Malolactic fermentations occur in barrel and are generally finished in February. After about five months in barrel, the lots are tasted, and those chosen for the Garnet blend are finished early. Lots destined for the single-vineyard bottlings are raised in about 40 percent new wood for up to fifteen months. Most Saintsbury pinots have been cross-flow filtered since 2005.

The Garnet blend, which has been made since 1983, is many critics' choice for an "entry-level" pinot, expressly crafted to be relatively light in color, with fresh, forward fruit and an open, perfumed nose. The flagship Carneros bottling has grown darker over time, and it now strikes an attractive balance between bright fruitiness and solid structure. The vineyard-designated wines are exceptionally well crafted, with distinctive profiles. Toyon Farm, at least in 2005, is a personal preference, and is interesting to compare with the ANCIEN WINES bottling from the same site.

TASTING NOTES

2005 *Carneros (tasted in* 2008*):* Medium garnet; fresh flowers and red berry fruit aromas; bright, fruit-driven attack with a hint of citrus on top of the red fruit, then dry with a bit of grip on the back palate; light-to-medium in weight, and food friendly; medium in length.

2005 *Cerise Vineyard (tasted in* 2007*):* Brilliant rosy-ruby; intense, bright strawberry-cherry nose, with some notes of tea and briar; a hint of fruit-sweetness on the attack, silky at mid-palate, and slightly chewy from mid-palate to finish; the back palate seems marked with quinine, like Bitter Lemon.

2005 *Toyon Farm (tasted in* 2008*):* Medium garnet; distinctive, slightly smoky, vaguely fruity nose, with notes of nut shells and orange peel; rich, serious, and tightly knit on the palate; minerally with an underlay of dense, black fruit; texture of crushed velvet; medium-long finish.

2005 *Lee Vineyard (tasted in* 2007*):* Brilliant medium magenta; pepper, raspberry, and cotton candy aromas; cherries and red licorice in the mouth; a bit of peppery bite after mid-palate; long, silky, and quite intense overall.

2005 *Brown Ranch (tasted in* 2008*):* Transparent, dark black-red; smoky, peppery, and slightly floral nose with black fruit hiding underneath; cherry liqueur, mocha, and chocolate on the palate; considerable structure creates the impression of a round, full-bodied wine with a texture that straddles velvet and fine emery; long.

2003 *Carneros (tasted in* 2005*):* Transparent medium ruby; resinous wood, beetroot, and cherry aromas; cherry and strawberry in the mouth with Chinese five-spice; a hint of grip and a linen-like texture; nicely balanced; medium in weight and length.

SANFORD WINERY
Lompoc, California

There has been no Sanford at the Sanford Winery since 2005. That year, Richard Sanford, the brand's namesake and founder, and his wife, Thekla, sold their remaining interest in the name and winery to Anthony Terlato, Terlato's sons Bill and John, and the Terlato Wine Group, a family-owned wine production, sales, and marketing corporation based in Chicago, which had assumed an initial ownership interest three years earlier. Since 2006 Sanford's longtime winemaker, Bruno Alfonso, has been gone, too, replaced by Steve Fennell, a University of California Davis-trained winemaker and Santa Barbara native with prior experience at Trefethen Vineyards and Voss Vineyards, working under the direction of Doug Fletcher, the Terlato Wine Group's vice president of winemaking.

The Sanford & Benedict Vineyard, the iconic planting where Richard Sanford, then partnered with Michael Benedict, had established his original beachhead at the west end of the Santa Ynez Valley, in 1971, is a more complicated story. When Sanford and Benedict's partnership was dissolved in 1980, the vineyard remained initially with Benedict but then was sold to London-based industrialist and wine collector Robert Atkin in 1988. Atkin asked Richard Sanford to manage the vineyard, and a significant share of its crop was used to make Sanford wines for more than a decade. In 2007 the Terlato Wine Group purchased the vineyard from Atkin, which restored its connection to the Sanford name and brand.

Sanford Winery, established in 1981, established a reputation for chardonnay, sauvignon blanc, and pinot noir made from purchased fruit, which was vinified at EDNA VALLEY VINEYARD in 1981 and 1982, and in a Buellton warehouse after 1983. In 1983 Sanford and his wife purchased a second ranch, El Jabali, on Santa Rosa Road, 3 miles east of the Sanford & Benedict Vineyard. The Sanfords used El Jabali primarily for entertaining and as a tasting room—which was later featured in the *Sideways* movie—but a small vineyard was also planted, giving Sanford a bit of estate fruit.

The main step toward making Sanford Winery into the estate-based operation Sanford & Benedict had been at the outset came in 1995, when the Sanfords purchased the 485-acre ranch just west of Sanford & Benedict. This southwestern corner section of the original Rancho Santa Rosa land grant, called La Rinconada, consists of about 130 planted acres, set out in 1995 and 1996, of which approximately half are pinot noir. It is a modern planting, in 8-foot north–south rows with 4-foot intervine spacing, vertically trellised. The scion material is mostly Dijon clones, but there is also some UCD 2A and 4, along with some Mount Eden selection from Sanford & Benedict. La Rinconada is also the site of Sanford's spectacular winery, constructed from recycled quarried dolomite, old-growth timber from sawmills in Oregon and Washington, and adobe bricks that were manufactured onsite. An attractive tasting room on this site replaces the rustic facility previously located at El Jabali, which now serves Richard and Thekla Sanford's new brand, ALMA ROSA.

WINES AND WINEMAKING NOTES

A blended Santa Barbara County bottling has been made since 1981. Until 2001 this wine relied mostly on purchased fruit, much of it from Bien Nacido, some (within the legal limit) from Mendocino County, plus a bit from El Jabali; after 2001 enough fruit was available from La Rinconada to support it as a primarily estate grown wine. Sanford & Benedict fruit, purchased after 1990, was mostly used to feed a vineyard-designated bottling, but some was also used in the Santa Barbara County wine. Vineyard-designated La Rinconada debuted in 1999. A Sta. Rita Hills wine, blended from La Rinconada

and Sanford & Benedict fruit, joined the portfolio in 2005. Since 2004, when production moved from Buellton to the new winery at La Rinconada, all Sanford pinots, including the Santa Barbara County cuvée, have been made in relatively large, open-top stainless steel fermentors that can be raised and lowered on hydraulic lifts, creating gravity flow in a primarily one-level winery.

New wines are pressed off at dryness, settled, and barreled in French oak purchased from an assortment of cooperages. The Santa Barbara County wine and the Sta. Rita Hills wine spend from ten to fourteen months in wood, of which 10 to 30 percent is new in each vintage; the La Rinconada and Sanford & Benedict bottlings may spend up to eighteen months in barrel, and the latter is sometimes raised entirely in new wood. The wines are typically not filtered before bottling.

These are somewhat Jekyll and Hyde wines. The Santa Barbara County (now Sta. Rita Hills) wine is bright, red fruited, and floral; the vineyard designates are dark, very ripe, and brooding.

TASTING NOTES

2005 *Sta. Rita Hills (tasted in* 2007*):* Transparent medium garnet; attractive, floral nose, with some red fruit and slightly citrus notes; bright, soft, and slightly peppery red berry fruit on the palate; medium in weight; texture of polished cotton; warm on the finish.

2004 *La Rinconada Vineyard (tasted in* 2007*):* Transparent, very dark black-red; strong aromas of tobacco and camphor that are probably barrel derived; very ripe, plummy, red and black fruit flavors; dark cherry, some cola, and an impressive load of brown spice; tightly knit, rich, and dense; medium long.

2004 *Sanford & Benedict Vineyard (tasted in* 2007*):* Brilliant, medium-dark black-red; sarsaparilla and a hint of citrus on the nose; dark flavors on the palate beginning with mocha and very ripe fruit, then merbromin, smoke, and a hint of orange peel; mouth filling and intense, with considerable grip from mid-palate to finish.

SAVANNAH-CHANELLE VINEYARDS
Saratoga, California

Savannah-Chanelle is the fourth life of property in the hills above Saratoga that was first planted to vines in or about 1892. The original developers were Pierre Pourroy (1866–1960) and his brother Eloi (1868–1957), *émigrés* from Gap, in the French *département* of the Hautes-Alpes. The brothers appear to have cleared several tens of acres and to have planted zinfandel and cabernet franc inter alia, some of which remains and is still producing. The family farmed the vineyard and operated a winery in a concrete "villa" erected on one of the property's lesser hilltops until sometime in the late 1950s.

In 1971, overgrown, neglected, and all but abandoned by the Pourroys, the property was acquired by Victor Erickson, who restored the *faux château*. Five years later, Erickson formed a partnership, called Congress Springs Vineyard, with Daniel Gehrs, a newlywed and aspiring winemaker, who had been working at nearby Paul Masson. Erickson and Gehrs reportedly worked "arm in arm" to restore the vineyards one vine at a time, and to make wines from both estate and purchased grapes, achieving considerable success with several varieties. The partnership was dissolved in 1988,

however, when Erickson bought out Gehrs. Erickson then leased the property to members of the family that had founded the Mariani Packing Company, who made wines there under the Mariani Winery label. But as Erickson grew older—he turned eighty in 1990—the property seemed burdensome, and in 1996 he sold it to Michael Ballard and his wife, Kellie. (Ballard's UUNet Technologies had been sold to MCI Corporation, generating substantial personal capital.)

The Ballards established the fourth incarnation of the Pourroy estate, which they named Savannah-Chanelle for their two young daughters. (In truth, the second daughter's name was Chanel, but the House of Chanel, a French luxury brand, objected on grounds of trademark dilution, so Chanel became Chanelle.) Another round of attention was then lavished on the heritage vineyard, from which zinfandel, cabernet franc, and chardonnay (planted during the Gehrs-Erickson era) were produced, but the Ballards chose to refocus their brand on pinot noir. In 1998 they hired Michael McNeill (see KELLER ESTATE) as winemaker, and McNeill made the first generation of Savannah-Chanelle's pinots, from 1998 through 2002. He was followed by Tony Craig (see SONNET WINE CELLARS), who became the full-time winemaker just prior to the 2003 harvest. In 2001, as part of the pinot focus, the first pinot noir was planted in the estate vineyard, on an especially steep slope, where yields will always be parsimonious. The scion material is all Dijon 667, except that some vines whose grafts failed have been regrafted to Dijon 115.

WINES AND WINEMAKING NOTES
The first Savannah-Chanelle pinots were a Central Coast wine made from 1998

through 2001, initially anchored with fruit from River View in the Salinas Valley, a Garys' Vineyard (see ROAR WINES) bottling that was made through 2002, and a Sleepy Hollow Vineyard wine made in 1998 only. A single-vineyard wine from the Armagh Vineyard in the Chileno Valley between Petaluma and Tomales Bay was added in 1999. An appellation wine from the Santa Lucia Highlands debuted in 2000, a Corda Vineyard wine from Marin County was made for one year in 2001, and a Russian River Valley blend was launched in 2002.

With the transition from McNeill to Craig, the pinot program was substantially reoriented to North Coast fruit, plus the first grapes from the aforementioned 2001 planting on the estate. Only the Armagh wine has been a consistent feature of the portfolio across both winemaking regimes. In 2003 Savannah-Chanelle began working with the Tina Marie Vineyard, a 2000 planting of Dijon clones in Green Valley; Gunsalus, on the south side of Green Valley Creek followed in 2004.

Craig follows essentially the same winemaking regime here that he observes for his own brand, picking by taste, skin maturity, and "cluster tightness." Craig finds that pinot clusters are tight until just before the fruit is ready to pick, but then, without any shrivel of the berry skins, they shrink just enough to create a slight looseness in the total cluster; he argues that this phenomenon tends to coincide with the perfect time to pick.

All fruit is normally destemmed, although some whole clusters are retained from some vineyards in some years, and a hydraulic plunger is used during the cold soak. Once yeast is added, Craig converts to *pneumatage* for cap management during most of the primary fermentation. The new wine is pressed when the wine tannins taste ripe, which is usually when the must

is dry, but sometimes before. The gross lees are settled out after pressing so that Craig can stir the barrels throughout the period of malolactic fermentation. This is important, he believes, to combat pinot noir's tendency to display "a doughnut-shaped structure" and a "short palate," and so that the remaining yeast cells can release glycerols, softening tannins and contributing to "round" and satiny texture. At this point the wines are sulfured, racked, and bottled—after fourteen to seventeen months in barrel—with no fining or filtration. Very unusually, the barrels are mostly Hungarian oak; see the Sonnet Wines profile for details.

Whatever else this regime may induce, each wine is quite distinctive. The common properties seem to be relatively smooth tannins, little barrel marking, and very pretty color. The estate is quite different from the Sonoma County wines: it is darker, chewier, and loaded with more tannin.

TASTING NOTES

2005 *Tina Marie Vineyard (tasted in 2007)*: Brilliant, intense ruby; conifer, vanilla, red berry fruit, and earth on the nose; rich, deep, stunning cherry and black pepper on the palate, with just a hint of chocolate; smoky overtones; satin texture. Very impressive.

2005 *Armagh Vineyard (tasted in 2007)*: Light-to-medium, intense rosy-ruby; bramble-y raspberry aromas with a hint of mint; inky and wild at mid-palate; slightly dry tannins contribute to some grip at the end.

2005 *Gunsalus Vineyard (tasted in 2007)*: Transparent, light-to-medium, scarlet-tinged-garnet; intense nose of conifer, mint, and potpourri; marionberry and blackberry on the palate; slightly grippy and long.

2005 *Estate (tasted in 2007)*: Medium rosy-ruby; strong aromas of violets; rich, mouth filling, and chewy on the palate;

sensation of strong, long-brewed black tea; pinot flavors but almost the structure of syrah; grippy at the end.

SCHERRER WINERY
Sebastopol, California

Fred Scherrer grew up in his father's Alexander Valley vineyard, from which he was permitted to make some wine, at home, in the 1970s. Following proper training in fermentation science at the University of California Davis early in the 1980s, Scherrer worked first at GREENWOOD RIDGE VINEYARDS in Anderson Valley, and then for Tom Dehlinger (see DEHLINGER WINERY) from 1988 to 1998. His own label was launched briefly as a sidebar project during his time at Greenwood Ridge, using zinfandel grapes from his father's vineyard, but was then suspended until 1991, when it began a second phase.

By 1997 Scherrer Winery was ready for dedicated space in a repurposed apple-packing facility north of Sebastopol, and its first pinots were made in 1999: twin cuvées of Russian River Valley wines made from grapes farmed by Sonoma-Cutrer, dubbed Big Brother and Little Sister to evoke their respective weights and stature; a Hirsch Vineyards wine poetically called Diaphanous; and a Sonoma Coast bottling made from a combination of leftovers and the first small crop from HALLECK VINEYARD in the Sebastopol Hills. Big Brother and Little Sister were collapsed into a single Russian River Valley cuvée in 2000; in the same year, a small bottling from Don and Patricia Helfer's 1993 planting on Laguna Ridge was added to the lineup. In 2001 Scherrer

began sourcing pinot from the new FORT ROSS VINEYARD (and also making wine for the owners' own label), making two vineyard-designated cuvées, and adding a barrel of the Fort Ross wine to his Hirsch-dominated Sonoma Coast blend.

In 2003 a modestly-priced Sonoma County bottling joined the portfolio; in 2004 there was also one tiny half barrel from the Hallberg Vineyard on the Gravenstein Highway. By 2005 the Fort Ross fruit was no longer available, but one barrel of pinot was made from Don Bliss's vineyard before Bliss returned to his native Texas and sold the vineyard to LYNMAR WINERY. The year 2006 brought an almost entirely new assortment of fruit sources to the Scherrer portfolio: the first vintage from the vineyard Lewis and Joan Platt had planted in 2003 and 2004 at the mouth of the Petaluma Gap; a small amount of fruit from Keefer Ranch in Green Valley; some Dijon-clone fruit from Keefer's neighbor Gunsalus, a source also used by TALISMAN WINES.

If this picture seems volatile, it is. Scherrer reports that demand for pinot has made it extremely difficult for small producers to secure supplies reliably. Producers such as Scherrer, who believe in *terroir* and build tiny releases of vineyard-designated wines as an article of faith—even in Burgundy it is extremely rare that anyone produces just a half barrel of any single wine—respond by adjusting their program annually, releasing wines once that they know they can never reproduce, creating blends that are never the same from one year to the next, and attempting blends but then abandoning them in favor of yet more tiny bottlings because the components "just didn't work" when they were blended.

Few winemakers read vineyards and their wines as carefully as Scherrer, who tastes reflectively, respects the evolution of every fermentor and every barrel, and "trusts" every wine, in the end, to reflect its origin—and its vintage. In addition to pinot, Scherrer still makes cabernet sauvignon and zinfandel from his parents' vineyard, including a phenomenally elegant zinfandel with pinot-esque character called Shale Terrace; chardonnay from both estate and non-estate sources; and an assortment of rosés from cabernet, zinfandel, and pinot.

SCHERRER "TRUSTS"
EVERY WINE, IN THE END,
TO REFLECT ITS ORIGIN
AND ITS VINTAGE

WINEMAKING NOTES

Scherrer sorts "everything" no matter how clean the fruit appears when it arrives on the crushpad, because "there is always something more to remove." Almost immediately, however, the tempo slows, so that calm, observation, patience, and reflection prevail He describes using a "lazy cool soak," so that the first fruit to arrive does not start fermenting right away. A bit of sulfur dioxide helps delay things, too, giving Scherrer time to decide which native fermentations will be viable on their own, and which will require inoculation to finish. Either way, he likes to have control over the yeast residues, which have important aromatic and textural signatures, and insists that the wine go "bone dry." This means that extended macerations are the usual rule, and he takes time to decide when to press, centrifuging samples and tasting the clean wines from the centrifuge.

Once started, pressing is an all-day process with a bladder press, executed slowly, with zen-like patience and constant tasting. Meanwhile Scherrer contemplates his sixteen possible combinations of coopers (the main suppliers are François Frères,

Seguin Moreau, Dargaud & Jaeglé, and Ermitage) and forests to achieve the most felicitous pairings of new wines and barrels. The barrel regime itself is front-loaded with up to 45 percent new wood—but new barrels may be switched out in favor of older wood after the first racking, which is done just before the following harvest. When the blends have been determined, the wines are returned to barrel for another nine months before going once more to tank, and from tank to bottle. There is no fining or filtration. These are exceptionally pretty wines with impressive aromatic complexity and an elegant mouth-feel. Despite Scherrer's need to pursue unstable fruit sources, these pinots seem to get better, more or less, with each passing year.

TASTING NOTES

2004 *Sonoma County (tasted in* 2007*):* Very transparent, medium blackish-ruby; softly spicy, cherry-plum fruit with savory herbal highlights on the nose; sweet, fruit-intensive attack that turns sober and dry mid-palate; a lithely built, light- to medium-weight wine, with excellent concentration and flavor intensity; an astonishingly good value.

2004 *Russian River Valley (tasted in* 2007*):* Pretty, medium-dark ruby; the signature spicy-cherry nose typical of Russian River Valley pinots; cherry and blackberry fruit on the palate, with spice and black pepper; tightly knit and sleekly textured; finishes soft and elegant, but seriously structured, with attractive grip.

2004 *Hallberg Vineyard (tasted in* 2007*):* Transparent but nearly saturated magenta; aromas of exotic, tropical woods, tobacco, and berry fruit; very intense, almost explosive flavors of gingerbread, pepper, and camphor on the palate; the intensity persists after mid-palate, with slate-y minerality and attractive grip. Fine.

2003 *Russian River Valley (tasted in 2006):* Luminous, medium brick-red color; aromas of mace and orange peel; partially fruity and partially savory on the palate, seeming to combine sweet black cherry and even a hint of blueberry with braised fennel; richly flavored and intensely spicy; slightly smoky also, and peppery at the end; mouth coating; medium in weight, and long.

SCHOOL HOUSE VINEYARD
St. Helena, California

The School House Vineyard is a 160-acre property located at the 1,500-foot contour on Spring Mountain, overlooking the north end of the Napa Valley, personally tended since 1991 by its owners, John Gantner and Nancy Walker. Gantner's father (John O. Gantner Jr., 1909–2002, principal in the family's San Francisco knit goods firm) purchased the property in 1940. In addition to the one-room schoolhouse that gave the ranch its name, the property was also home to a 50-acre vineyard, planted to the usual zinfandel-dominated California field blend. Gantner *père* seems to have been passionate, however, about pinot noir. No later than 1953, he planted pinot at School House, using budwood taken from vines at Inglenook, given to him by Inglenook's owner, John Daniels. Daniels and Gantner *père* had been college friends at Stanford University. An oral history interview conducted in 1984 seems to imply that School House had been acquired for the express purpose of accommodating the pinot, and that both Daniels and the legendary Frank Schoonmaker (1905–1976) had "approved" the ranch for this vocation,

but this testimony may not be reliable. Gantner *fils* says the cuttings were not taken until 1952, were bench-grafted to St. George rootstock "by Emilio's Nursery in Napa," and were planted in 1953. In any case, the budwood source was almost certainly the same vine block from which Louis Martini took cuttings circa 1950, from which the Martini clones were derived. However, although Martini propagated individual clones, Gantner seems to have performed a traditional field selection.

Varietal pinot noir was then made under the School House label beginning in 1957, first by Fred McCrea at nearby Stony Hill Vineyard, and then by a succession of other Napa-based winemakers, including Bo Barrett and Ric Forman. Between 1953 and 1991, the vineyard was allowed to deteriorate, and the original planting was eventually pulled out, in stages. In 1991 about 20 percent of a second planting, said to have been done in 1965 with budwood from the 1953 planting, was salvaged, using a combination of individual vine replacements and tender loving care. This restored vineyard is the source for School House pinots made since 1992, in tiny quantities, by Gantner *fils* and Nancy Walker. Since 1998 the winemaker has been Bob Foley of nearby Pride Mountain Vineyard, where the wines are vinified. These pinots are the product of an eighteen-month *élevage* followed by a year of bottle age before release. They are distinguished by modest levels of alcohol, always under 14 percent, intense flavors, and elegant structures.

TASTING NOTE
2002 *Spring Mountain District Estate Pinot Noir (tasted in 2006):* Brilliant medium garnet; intense floral nose with highlights of *charcuterie;* elegant attack;

flavors of black fruit, tar, tobacco, briar, and black pepper; medium in weight, and concentrated, with a long, silky finish. Fine.

SCHUG CARNEROS ESTATE
Sonoma, California

Walter Schug, raised on the premises of the Staatsweingut Assmannshausen in the German Rheingau, where his father oversaw production, and later trained formally in enology and viticulture at the nearby Forschungsanstalt Geisenheim, is among the least celebrated of pinot's pioneer champions in California, despite an early start and a significant market presence. Schug crossed the Atlantic in 1959, handled grower relations in North Bay counties for the E. & J. Gallo Winery in the 1960s, and became the founding winemaker at Joseph Phelps's new Napa Valley winery in 1973. Although his reputation at Phelps hinges mostly on Insignia, said to have been California's first proprietary Bordeaux blend, and on several distinguished single vineyard cabernets, he also presided over a pinot noir program until Phelps discontinued it in 1980. At this point, Joe Phelps agreed that Schug could continue working with pinot under his own name, and the first three vintages of Schug pinot were made in Phelps's winery. In 1983 Schug left Phelps to work full time on his personal project, whose focus shifted increasingly toward Carneros.

In 1989 Schug bought 50 acres at the base of Sonoma Mountain on the west side of Carneros, about 6 miles southwest of the town of Sonoma, where he eventually planted 42 acres of chardonnay and pinot noir in Haire, clay-loam soils. The

pinot occupies about 23 of the 42 acres and six of eleven vineyard blocks. The main selections of pinot are UCD 5, UCD 13, and Swan, with smaller amounts of UCD 12, and Dijon 115 and 667. Most blocks are set out in 9-foot rows with 6 feet between vines, but a few blocks, some of which were replanted later in the 1990s, benefit from tighter spacing. An onsite winery was completed in 1991; barrel caves were added in 1995. Since 1996, when Schug withdrew to chief executive and "winemaster" roles, the hands-on winemaker has been Michael Cox, an alumnus of UCLA and the University of California Davis, with prior winemaking experience at De Moor Cellars in Napa and Dry Creek Vineyards in Sonoma.

WINES AND WINEMAKING NOTES
Schug's first pinots were sourced from the same fruit used in the Phelps program: the Heinemann Mountain Vineyard on the east side of the Napa Valley. Schug's commitment to Carneros began in 1983, when he started purchasing grapes from Andy Beckstoffer's Las Amigas Vineyard, which had originally been planted by Louis P. Martini. The former made a vineyard-designated Napa Valley bottling from 1980 to 1990, when the Heinemann property was sold and replanted entirely to cabernet; the latter made a vineyard-designated Carneros bottling from 1983 to 1990. A Carneros blend, using a combination of purchased and estate fruit, then debuted in 1991, and has been made in every vintage since. Since 1992 there has also been a Heritage Reserve bottling, which is a barrel selection, from essentially the same sources. The main non-estate sources for the last decade are the aforementioned Beckstoffer parcel, the Iund Vineyard (see ACACIA WINERY), the Brown Vineyard east of downtown Sonoma on the site of the old

Buena Vista estate, and the Sangiacomo family's Tall Grass Vineyard, which is located nextdoor to Schug's estate.

A Sonoma Valley bottling was also made from 1997 to 2001; this was replaced with a Sonoma Coast bottling from 1992. Both are second-quality wines made from deselected lots. Of the estate fruit, blocks 8 and 10, toward the top of the property, often migrate disproportionately into the reserve wine, as do some lots from the Iund Vineyard.

Schug's winemaking departs in several significant respects from the consensus protocol. Cold soaks are normally limited to between twelve and twenty-four hours, and all fermentations are done in closed-top, 8-ton "plunger tanks," designed and manufactured by Rieger Behälterbau GmbH in Beitigheim-Bissingen (near Stuttgart, in Germany). These so-called Volltaucher tanks plunge the cap with an internal device resembling a paddle wheel. Both the duration of each plunging and the interval between plungings can be preset and automatically executed. Schug also practices extended macerations on some lots, adding dry ice and sealing the tanks for as long as thirty days after the primary fermentation has finished.

After the wines are pressed and settled for twenty-four to forty-eight hours, they spend about one month in large, neutral oak casks—a German approach—where the malolactic fermentations take place, before being transferred to barrels, about 20 to 25 percent of which are new in each vintage. When purchasing barrels from coopers not domiciled in Burgundy, Schug asks for barrels coopered from Allier- and Vosges-sourced wood; Burgundy-based coopers are asked for a "Burgundy blend." Favored Burgundy-based coopers are Mercurey and Marsannay. (Some lots destined for the Sonoma Coast bottling

are blended directly from the large-format casks and are never barreled.)

Blends are made in June after the vintage; the Carneros wine is bottled in August, and the Reserve is held in barrel for an additional four to six months. Schug pinots are, by design, slightly leaner and more structured than the California mainstream, with a touch more minerality, but they are also graceful, food friendly and relatively ageworthy. The Sonoma Coast cuvée is especially lightweight, but is still an attractive, every-day pinot. The Heritage Reserve wine, in the vintages I have tasted, is the most barrel marked.

TASTING NOTES

2006 *Sonoma Coast (tasted in* 2007*):* Transparent, light-to-medium garnet; potpourri, red berries, and a hint of citrus peel on the nose; slightly chalky, slightly peppery red berry flavors in the mouth; lightweight and bright, with modest alcohol and a slight bite on the finish.

2006 *Carneros (tasted in* 2007*):* Transparent, but a shade deeper than the Sonoma Coast wine; slightly smoky, slightly resinous red and black fruit aromas with minty, talc-like highlights; nicely built and fairly round at mid-palate; mostly cherry-blackberry flavors with some minerality, good acid, and noticeable grip; attractive overall.

2005 *Heritage Reserve (tasted in* 2007*):* Pretty, deep ruby; barrel-derived vanilla and a bit of tobacco on the nose; dark cherry, cinnamon, and conifer foliage on the palate; smooth and satiny to mid-palate; then grippy, long, and intense, and slightly warm at the end.

1999 *Heritage Reserve (tasted in* 2007*):* Deep mahogany color; tiling at the rim; leather, *charcuterie,* boot polish, and rhubarb aromas; slightly sweet, slightly tarry dark fruit on the palate; some smoke, considerable spice, nut shells, and a hint of tangerine peel; evolving nicely but perhaps nearing its apogee.

SCOTT PAUL WINES
Carlton, Oregon

Scott Paul Wright left a career in media and entertainment marketing to pursue his self-described "passion"—red Burgundies and American pinot noir. In 1999 he teamed with Greg La Follette, then the winemaker at FLOWERS VINEYARD, to make three barrels of pinot noir from the iconic Pisoni Vineyards in the Santa Lucia Highlands. When he moved to Oregon as the general manager for DOMAINE DROUHIN in 2001, his eponymous wine project began a transition from Californian beginnings to a focus on Oregon fruit.

In 2001 and 2002, Wright made both California and Oregon editions of pinot. By 2003 the project was entirely Oregon based. It outgrew the available space at Domaine Drouhin and moved to Eric

---

LOVELY EDITIONS OF AMERICAN PINOT THAT PRIVILEGE PERFUME, FINESSE AND BALANCE

Hamacher's Carlton Winemakers' Studio. In the summer of 2006, it moved again, this time to a handsome brick office, tasting room, and retail sales space adjacent to Carlton's abandoned grain elevator operation, and to a winery space across the street. The tasting room and offices are also home to Scott Paul Selections, a tiny business dedicated entirely to importing infinitesimal quantities of superb red Burgundies. Since 2004 Wright has shared the winemaker title with Kelley Fox, who previously worked with David Lett at THE EYRIE VINEYARDS.

Wright's Oregon pinot program was initially built around fruit from three blocks in the Stoller Vineyards, including some of the original plantings of UCD 4 done between 1995 and 1997; half of Dewey Kelly's 9-acre Ribbon Ridge Vineyard; and two blocks of Shea Vineyard, including Block 21, which is still planted to the own-rooted Pommard that Shea set out in 1989.

Beginning in 2005, in order to increase production from just over 1,000 cases in 2004 to the eventual target of 3,500, Wright began adding new vineyard sources, including 2.5 acres of own-rooted UCD 2A in the Maresh Vineyard on Worden Hill Road in the Dundee Hills, and in 2006, about 5 acres of Dijon clones in the Momtazi Vineyard, and 4 acres of Zena Heights, in the Eola Hills near Bethel Heights.

WINEMAKING NOTES
Fruit is picked slightly early by Oregon standards—sometimes under 23 Brix—to privilege elegance. To the usual assortment of small, stainless steel open-tops and double-height fruit bins, Wright added one 3-ton Taransaud oak fermentor in 2006. Both primary and malolactic fermentations rely entirely on naturally present organisms. To avoid the reductive tendencies frequently associated with wines that are raised in contact with gross lees, Wright sometimes settles wines before barreling. The primary cooper is François Frères, joined with small quantities of Remond and Taransaud, and about 20 percent of barrels are new in each

vintage. There is no fining or filtration, and wines can be completely brilliant or slightly hazy depending on the vintage.

The bulk of Scott Paul production is a cuvée cleverly called La Paulée, playing simultaneously on Wright's middle name and the "*paulée*," or harvest festival, held annually in many Burgundian communes. A barrel selection that Wright describes as a "texture-driven" wine with "Hepburn-esque qualities" is blended and bottled separately as Audrey. In 2004 Audrey was made from Shea, Three Sisters, and Stoller fruit; in 2005 it was all Maresh. The fruit of younger vines, press lots, and lots that turn out (for whatever reasons) to show less complexity go into a cuvée called Martha Pirie. The barrels for Audrey are identified first; La Paulée follows. Wright's pinots are, like most red Burgundies, perfume-driven wines whose structures feature length and elegance in lieu of weight and fleshiness.

TASTING NOTES

2005 *La Paulée (tasted in* 2007): Transparent, medium black-red; nose bespeaks subtle, clean black fruit and minerality; intensely fruity attack, then sober and serious on the mid-palate; tightly knit; light as a feather, but simultaneously substantial, long, and very attractive.

2004 *La Paulée (tasted in* 2006): Transparent, medium, rosy-garnet; dominantly floral aromas with an underlay of black raspberry; fruit-sweet and minerally on the palate, with notes of white pepper, clove, and earth; light to medium in weight, concentrated, and silky.

2004 *Audrey (tasted in* 2006): Brilliant garnet; aromas of rose petal, strawberry, and raspberry with substantial barrel-derived vanilla; resin, tar, licorice, white pepper, and clove in the mouth; medium in weight, and intense. An exceptionally pretty wine.

SEA SMOKE CELLARS
Lompoc, California

In 1998 Bob Davids, a devoted collector of red Burgundies and CEO of a Hong Kong–based company with a dominant share of the market in handheld computer games, acquired 350 acres of horse ranch and bean field on the south face of the Sta. Rita Hills, overlooking the Santa Ynez River, which was part of a land grant known locally as Rancho Chahuchu. He knew want he wanted—shallow, clay-laden hillsides and a south-facing exposure. He had been looking for several years, and had found the site with help and intermediation from Bill Wathen, the winemaker partner at FOXEN VINEYARD AND WINERY. Davids immediately redeveloped 100 of the 350 acres as vineyard: twenty-five blocks of vines roughly laid out in two mid-slope crescents that hug the river's right bank, at elevations between 360 and 650 feet, dedicated almost entirely to pinot noir. The view across the river is spectacular. Kathy Joseph's Fiddlestix Vineyard (see FIDDLEHEAD CELLARS) commands the foreground, while the historic Sanford & Benedict Vineyard and Sanford's newer La Rinconada Vineyard rise up the face of the Santa Rosa Hills on the southern horizon.

Sea Smoke Cellars's vineyard is planted to ten selections of pinot on rootstocks chosen to privilege low yields. forty-one selection-and-block combinations are vinified separately. The ten selections are the usual suspects plus CTPS 459 and soi-disant 828; UCD 2A, 9, and 16; and Mount Eden. Soils are dark-hued clay-loams, mostly in the Botella, Gazos, and Lopez series. The winemaker, until 2007, was is Kris Curran, a graduate of California State Polytechnic University at San Luis Obispo in animal science, who subsequently earned a degree in enology from California State University Fresno. In early 2008, Curran was lured from Sea Smoke to Foley Estates—and to a bit more time for her personal project, called Curran Wines. At Sea Smoke the "deck chairs" were then "rearranged," according to Victor Gallegos, the property's general manager. Gallegos, who is a product of the University of California Davis and partner in an interesting project in Spain's Priorat DOC, became director of winemaking as well as general manager, while Don Schroeder, Curran's former assistant, assumed the "winemaker" mantle.

Of all the American pinot ventures new since about 2000, few have ascended so quickly from debutante to full-blown stardom. The first vintage, made in 2001, sold out almost immediately, and subsequent vintages are all so tightly allocated that, according to Curran, even she must pay for the few bottles set aside for her personal cellar. Six percent of each harvest, however, goes to Foxen, in recognition of Wathen's role in the birth of the estate.

WINES AND WINEMAKING NOTES
Sea Smoke fruit is picked quite ripe, between 24 and 27 Brix, when the seeds are visibly brown and "separate easily from the pulp" and is entirely destemmed (Curran explained that she did not like "edges" and "would do everything possible to avoid green flavors"), and the wine is made according to a clean, modern protocol that minimizes risk. Ozone is used to kill wild yeasts, two to four days of cold soak precedes the start of fermentation, both primary and secondary fermentations are started by inoculation (Curran believed wild malolactic bacteria produced excessive histamines), enzymes are

added to enhance clarity, and every effort is made to ensure that the wine goes into barrel as clean as possible. Vattings are typically ten to fourteen days in length, "except for one lot each of Dijon 115 and 667," which are allowed extended maceration. The wines spend eighteen months in barrel and are never fined or filtered.

Three wines have been made in each vintage since 2002: Botella, intended to be "fruity and quaffable" with soft tannins; Southing, crafted to be darker, more "brooding" and "slower to come around"; and Ten, made from a single "favorite" barrel of each of the ten clonal selections grown on the ranch. Ten carries the highest price tag and is intended for cellaring. (In 2001, the inaugural vintage, only Botella and Southing were made.) The team says Southing is "what we are after," while Botella absorbs lesser lots. Ten, they confess, can seem like "high testosterone." The forty-one fermentor lots are earmarked for one of the finished wine programs on the basis of weight, intensity and mouthfeel, before *élevage* begins. Lots destined for Botella are then raised in barrels of which 40-50 percent are new; lots destined for Ten go into entirely new barrels. The typical percentage of new wood used for lots in the Southing program ranges between 60 and 75 percent. Until 2005, the CTPS 459 lots were mostly excluded from Ten; now more are included, and increasingly esteemed. Comfirming some exogenous experience but contravening received wisdom, the UCD 2A lots also impress the Sea Smoke team, year after year, with their ability to make "a complete end-to-end wine."

The ripe-plus picking protocol translates into wines that emphasize black rather than red fruit. Extractive winemaking ensures full-bodied and concentrated wines with dark, complex structures, and the site seems to mark all Sea Smoke bottlings with earth and smoke, although Southing and Ten can also exhibit strong floral properties. Most tasters find Botella easy to like, and the wine is exceptionally successful on restaurant lists; however, the 2002 Ten is my favorite Sea Smoke to date, owing largely to especially lifted aromatics and brightness of flavor, despite its large and grippy frame.

TASTING NOTES

2006 *Botella (tasted pre-release in 2008):* Transparent, deep brick red; intense nose of spring flowers, incense, cigar box and white pepper; bright cranberry-plum fruit on the front palate, with a hint of sweetness, then black, smoky and barrel-marked at mid-palate, eventually warm, dry, peppery and persistent.

2006 *Southing (tasted pre-release in 2008):* Medium-dark garnet; sarsaparilla, bay laurel, and wood smoke aromas with hints of blackberry and tobacco; bright, herbal, dry and serious on the palate like medium-brewed Darjeeling tea; clean and elegant impression with considerable intensity.

2006 *Ten (tasted twice pre-release in 2008):* Medium ruby; vanilla, cigar box, floral elements and a hint of peppermint on the nose; intense ripe blackberry and infused flower flavors against a background of sweet vanilla; soft and rich at first, then spirity, chalky and long; very barrel-marked and not yet "together," potentially impressive with some time in bottle.

2005 *Botella (tasted in 2008):* Medium-deep black-red; subdued and nuanced aromas with undertones of hard spice, roasted beets minty fruit and barrel-marking; rich, slate-y and intense in the mouth with some lifted flavors at mid-palate; elegant and very fine-grained tannins from mid-palate to finish; very attractive.

2002 *Ten (tasted in 2005):* Dark, brooding aromatics lifted with floral components, barrel marking, India ink, and flower-scented tea; slightly spicy palate

with ripe, dark fruit; an intense, almost dramatic wine, with good acidity and substantial tannins.

2001 *Botella (tasted in 2005):* Brilliant, medium black-red; black cherry, black pepper, and smoky aromas; infused flowers on the palate; medium in weight and length; linen-like in texture, with a good shot of soft tannins on the finish.

2001 *Southing (tasted in 2005):* Almost saturated, medium-dark black-red; smoky, meaty blackberry dominates the nose; black tea, licorice, and some cinnamon on the palate, with some dried blueberries; an intense, full-bodied rendition of pinot, with good length and some grip.

SHEA WINE CELLARS
Portland, Oregon

Dick Shea developed an interest in American wines during his first career as a New York investment banker. With two East Coast partners and advice from Oregon winemakers, he purchased a 200-acre parcel of filbert orchard northwest of Newberg in 1988, and began setting out vines in 1989. Shea credits Mark Benoit, whose father owned Château Benoit (now ANNE AMIE VINEYARDS) with the initial insight that the sedimentary soils in what is now the Yamhill-Carlton District could produce wines as good or better than the red, volcanic soils near Dundee, on which many of Oregon's first-generation pinot pioneers had relied. Eventually, 140 of the 200 acres were planted on two adjacent hillsides separated by a deep ravine, mostly to pinot noir. The grapes attracted attention almost from the outset for a fruit profile that covered the entire spectrum from strawberry to cassis, for their propensity to ripen relatively early, and for subtle tannins. Within a few years, vineyard-designated pinot noir made from SHEA fruit by winemakers such as Ken Wright (see KEN WRIGHT CELLARS) and Mark Vlossak (see ST. INNOCENT WINERY) began to garner

---

A VINEYARD KNOWN
FOR FRUIT THAT COVERS
THE ENTIRE RED
SPECTRUM FROM
STRAWBERRY TO CASSIS

---

impressively high scores from the ratings mavens. In 1995, Shea, who had been the vineyard project's only active partner from the outset while commuting continually between New York and Oregon, bought out his partners.

Emboldened by the combination of independence and critical acclaim, Shea launched his own label, Shea Wine Cellars, the following year, with a single barrel of wine made by Michael Stevenson at PANTHER CREEK CELLARS. Three barrels (again made by Stevenson at Panther Creek) followed in 1997. Production grew to twelve barrels in 1998, some made by Stevenson and some made by Ken Wright. The winemaking baton was then passed several times. Wright made the 1999 and 2000 editions of Shea Wine Cellars pinot at Ken Wright Cellars. Patricia Green (see PATRICIA GREEN CELLARS) handled the 2001 vintage in her new facility on North Valley Road; and Sam Tannahill (until then winemaker at ARCHERY SUMMIT) took over in 2002. In 2004 Tannahill withdrew to consulting status, ceding full responsibility for hands-on winemaking to Chris Mazepink beginning in January 2005.

With the construction of a dedicated winery building on the vineyard's East Hill in 2006, the nomadic production phase of Shea Wine Cellars's history ended. The brand now takes about 75 tons of the vineyard's total crop, which is sufficient for 4,000 cases, of which 95 percent is pinot noir.

WINES AND WINEMAKING NOTES
Mazepink uses 2- and 4-ton stainless steel fermentors and makes decisions about whole-cluster usage on a vintage-by-vintage basis. He reports that, on the Shea site, the Dijon 115 and UCD 2A selections have the greatest propensity to develop lignified stems, and therefore to be used in whole-cluster form, and that "5 to 10 percent of whole clusters in the final blend can enhance our style." The barrel regime is based on 45 to 50 percent new wood overall, with the estate wine hovering around 33 percent new wood, the block-designates between 50 and 60 percent, and the Homer cuvée (see below) between 70 and 80 percent. Wines are racked and blends are made in May following the vintage, and blended wines go back to barrel for one month before bottling in August. Barrels are acquired from seven coopers, of which none is dominant.

Through 2000 only one pinot was made in each vintage, but 2001 saw the debut of a second wine, called Homer. Shea is partial to baseball metaphors, and Homer, short for home run, denotes a selection of the cellar's "best" barrels, chosen to showcase concentration. Compositionally, Homer usually features fruit from the vineyard's oldest vines, enlivened with a small amount of younger Dijon-clone fruit. It has been made in every vintage since 2001. A block-designated wine from Block 23 on the West Hill was also made from 2001 to 2004 and "will return" after replanting, according to Shea; a second block-designate from Block 32 (on the north side of the West Hill) was made from 2001 to 2003. In addition to these block-specific wines, a Pommard clone wine was made in 2002 and 2005, and an East Hill blend, based primarily on Dijon-clone fruit, debuted in 2004. The constant in all this is that, in addition to the Estate wine and the Homer cuvée, there is always at least one wine anchored with UCD 5, and one with UCD 2A. These are attractive, nicely-structured wines that showcase the red fruit and flowers profile of this remarkable site.

TASTING NOTES

2005 *Estate (tasted in* 2008*):* Deep black-red; exotic nose of rose petal, white pepper, and cinnamon; cherry and raspberry on the palate, plus Constant Comment tea; structured, serious, seamless, and mouth coating, but also intense, long, and bright overall, with some grip at the edges; very attractive.

2005 *East Hill (tasted in* 2008*):* Deep ruby; mossy and earthy aromas in the foreground; smoke and floral elements in the background; on the palate, sweeter than the Estate; primarily cherry and plum fruit with a bit of pepper; nicely structured with soft, ripe tannins from mid-palate to finish; attractive and likely to improve with time.

SIDURI WINES
 Santa Rosa, California

Adam and Dianna Lee met at Neiman Marcus in Dallas when he was the store's wine buyer, and she was the food buyer. They married and moved to California in 1993 "to do something in wine." After a year working in tasting rooms, the Lees wrote a 1-acre contract with the Rose Vineyard in Anderson Valley, hauled the grapes to rented space at Lambert Bridge in Dry Creek, and made the first 4.5 barrels of Siduri pinot noir. Their formal training in winemaking was limited to Dianna's single course in viticulture at Sonoma State and to a weekend course

OREGON GRAPES TEACH YOU TO "WORRY LESS ABOUT SUGAR," SAYS ADAM LEE

at the University of California Davis, but they liked their first pinot.

In 1995, when they heard that Robert M. Parker Jr. was a guest at the Meadowood Resort in nearby Napa, they decided to leave a sample bottle with the concierge. Parker loved the wine. In 1995 the Lees added to their portfolio fruit from the Muirfield Vineyard in Oregon and from David Hirsch's much-admired vineyard in the True Sonoma Coast, beginning their evolution toward the longest and most geographically extensive list of single-vineyard pinots made by any winery in North America. By 2006 their fruit sources ranged across five vineyards in the Chehalem Mountains of Oregon, ten in western Sonoma County (including Sonoma Mountain), three in the Santa Lucia Highlands, and two in the Sta. Rita Hills. In principle, all vineyards are sourced with a view to vineyard designation, but not all lots make the grade. Deselected barrels are made into no fewer than seven appellation wines.

To accommodate this formidable array of wines and Novy Wines, a separate label dedicated to syrah and other varieties, and to give themselves time to raise a family, the Lees expanded their staff early in the new millennium to include an assistant winemaker (Ryan Zepaltas, an alumnus of LA CREMA WINERY and New Zealand's Villa Maria), a cellarmaster, a general manager, and a growing complement of harvest interns. This leaves the principals time to concentrate on their vineyards and to perform barrel-by-barrel evaluation in the cellar. The production facility is a converted, unglamorous warehouse on the north edge of Santa Rosa.

WINES AND WINEMAKING NOTES

Siduri's portfolio is too large and too volatile to be cataloged here, vineyard by vineyard and vintage by vintage. In Oregon, the anchor tenant from the beginning has been the Muirfield Vineyard, now described as a block of the Hawks View Vineyard, with Laurelwood soils on the north face of the Chehalem Mountains. (This is in fact a *monopole*, since Siduri is the only fruit client for Muirfield pinot.) In the Russian River Valley, Marcy Keefer's Green Valley vineyard has been made by Siduri since 2002. The Van der Kamp Vineyard on Sonoma Mountain and David Hirsch's remarkable estate west of Cazadero have also been persistent sources, as have the well-known and well-respected Garys' and Pisoni vineyards in the Santa Lucia Highlands.

In 2006 Siduri also made vineyard-designated pinots from the Arbre Vert, Beran, Hawk's View, and Shaw Mountain vineyards, all (like Muirfield) in the Laurelwood soils that prevail on the Tualatin Valley side of the Chehalem Mountains; from the Sapphire Hill, Lewis, and Amber Ridge vineyards in the Russian River Valley's "Middle Reach"; from the Ewald Vineyard on Laguna Ridge; and from the Parsons Vineyard on the Santa Rosa Plain. There are also two Petaluma Gap sources, Terra de Promissio and Sonatera (the latter is also used by RHYS VINEYARDS for its Alesia label),

as well as two in the Sta. Rita Hills: Peter Cargasacchi's planting overlooking the Santa Ynez River and Clos Pepe in the Highway 246 corridor. The regional blends are a Chehalem Ridge bottling of barrels from Beran, Muirfield, and Arbre Vert, and a Willamette Valley cuvée that absorbs whatever remains; a Russian River Valley cuvée that is composed of deselected barrels from Keefer, Parsons, and Ewald; a Sonoma Coast wine made from deselected barrels of all three sources in that appellation; a Sonoma County wine containing a bit of almost all the contracted vineyards in Sonoma; and cuvées to absorb deselected barrels from the Sta. Rita Hills and Santa Lucia Highlands, respectively.

Adam Lee explains that the two-tier approach to the appellation wines has given him latitude to deselect very rigorously when he, Dianna Lee, and assistant winemaker Ryan Zepaltas assemble the vineyard-designated wines. This means that some of these wines use only a small percentage of the lots available, and that the single-vineyard wines sometimes see disproportionately new or older wood. It is worth noting that the so-called broader appellation wines—the Willamette Valley and Sonoma County bottlings—are offered to the market at exceedingly reasonable prices and represent exceptional value.

With few exceptions, all of Siduri's contracts are per acre rather than per ton, so the Lees have control over matters such as leaf pulling, crop thinning, and picking date. In each vineyard, one of them is always present the day before picking begins to supervise the discarding of any clusters they want to exclude from the crush. The fruit is sorted manually when it arrives in Santa Rosa, mostly to remove leaves from the California fruit and stem rot from Oregon grapes. Adam Lee says that making pinot from Oregon fruit has helped teach him that ripeness must be flavor based, not sugar based. "You learn," he explains, "to worry less about sugar." With the Central Coast fruit, in which sugars rise very early, Lee has learned to wait for flavor in the fruit and to exercise a bit of legerdemain in the cellar to compensate for the high alcohol that results.

Fermentations are done in open-top tanks and in plastic fruit bins. Lee reports that he is increasingly picky about the use of whole clusters and makes many wines from entirely destemmed fruit; however, he will still use up to 50 percent whole clusters if the stems are sufficiently lignified. After a three- to five-day cold soak, one third of the fermentors are made to rely on resident yeast, but a large assortment of isolates are used to inoculate the rest. Acid is added, if necessary, to the California wines; conversely, the Oregon wines are sometimes chaptalized. The must may be pressed and barreled dry, or with a bit of residual sugar, and some lots have been subjected to extended maceration in some years.

Siduri's barrel stock is about 60 percent new in each vintage, of which most is from François Frères and Remond. Ermitage, Billon, Gamba, and Sirugue account for a large percentage of the rest. Malolactic fermentation is allowed to begin naturally "unless there is a problem." Depending on vineyard and vintage, Siduri wines spend ten to seventeen months in barrel. They are racked only if necessary to clarify the wine, and are not fined or filtered. Commercial success allows the Lees the luxury of bottle aging before release, so the wines are typically released the spring or fall of the second year after the vintage.

On reflection, Siduri pinots seem to me to be the original poster children for a category of hedonistic, expressive, fruit-sweet, nicely textured, appealing American pinots that would be populated later by producers such as DUMOL and TESTAROSSA. Meanwhile, Siduri itself seems to have evolved toward slightly soberer, more elegant wines that are more expressive of their individual *terroirs*.

TASTING NOTES

2005 *Sapphire Hill Vineyard (tasted in* 2007): Transparent, medium garnet; very aromatic, with highlights of nuts and bay laurel; slightly sweet on the palate, silky, and medium in length, with good acidity.

2005 *Muirfield Vineyard (tasted in* 2007): Medium garnet; aromas of forest floor and conifer needles, with hints of citrus peel and caramel; very tasty; simultaneously savory and bright; roasted meat, considerable hard spice, and black pepper; silky, long, layered, and distinctive.

2005 *Van der Kamp Vineyard (tasted in* 2007): Saturated medium-deep ruby; feral nose that features *charcuterie* and potpourri; very intense and distinctive on the palate, with strong earthiness, black fruit, and mineral-driven flavors; rich, impressive, and very serious in a very slightly sweet envelope; long finish.

2005 *Rosella's Vineyard (tasted in* 2007): Medium rosy-garnet color; earth and moss on the nose; sweet, richly textured, almost creamy, and mouth coating on the palate; considerable ripe berry fruit, and some cherry on the attack and at mid-palate; some gentle grip toward the end; very likeable and appealing.

2005 *Keefer Ranch Vineyard (tasted in* 2007): Brilliant light-to-medium garnet; nose displays some reduction, flowers, and citrus peel; rich, spicy cherry-raspberry on the palate; intense, seamless, and slightly fruit-sweet; some fine-grained grip on the back palate; spice, pepper, and some sensation of heat at the end.

SILVAN RIDGE WINERY
Eugene, Oregon

The Silvan Ridge brand was created in 1992 when Carolyn Chambers and her family purchased Hinman Vineyards (established in 1979) from its founder, Doyle Hinman. Chambers, a Eugene businesswoman involved with several family projects, was the president of Chambers Communication Corporation, which owned, among other things, a multimedia production house, three television stations, and an Internet service provider. In 2005 the family extended its wine base to include PANTHER CREEK CELLARS in McMinnville, a distinguished brand originally founded by Ken Wright, but Panther Creek is operated separately, aside from an occasional joint promotional event.

Silvan Ridge makes about 25,000 cases of wine annually, including the white varieties and pinot noir that are grown in the Willamette and Umpqua valleys, plus cabernet, merlot, and syrah sourced from southern Oregon, all from purchased fruit. In most years, there are two pinot noirs: an Oregon blend and a Reserve. The blend is sourced from Craemer Farms and Whispering Heights on the east side of the Willamette Valley (the former near Woodburn, the latter farther north and high in the foothills of the Cascade Range), from Mark Cleaver's vineyard in the Coast Range near the town of Cheshire, from Elton Vineyard (see WILLAMETTE VALLEY VINEYARDS), from Doerner Vineyards in the Umpqua Valley, and from Bradshaw Vineyard southwest of Monroe. The Reserve is a barrel selection from any or all of the above. In 2002 and 2005, Silvan

Ridge also made a vineyard-designated pinot from the Bradshaw Vineyard.

From 1991 to 1995, the winemaker was Joe Dobbes, who went on to Willamette Valley Vineyards and then to create his own label. Bryan Wilson succeeded Dobbes, but since 2004, Jonathan Oberlander, a San Diego State University graduate who worked in sales for Youngs Market Company and then learned winemaking at Bernardus Vineyards in Carmel Valley, has held the reins.

WINEMAKING NOTES
Winemaking involves 5 to 10 percent use of whole clusters, two to three days of cold-soaking, cool fermentations to avoid excessive extraction of tannins, *saignée* "when necessary" to improve concentration, and addition of enzymes to help break down the skins and deepen color. Small fermentors are hand-plunged; cap management in larger tanks relies on rack-and-return and on bubbled oxygen. Barrel times vary between eight and fourteen months. The Oregon cuvée sees only a small percentage of new wood; the reserve and vineyard-designated wines may be raised in as much as 40 or 50 percent new barrels. My experience with Silvan Ridge is limited to the two wines described below, which are varietally correct and soundly made.

TASTING NOTES
2006 *Willamette Valley (tasted in 2007):* Transparent ruby; spring bulb flowers and peppery berries on the nose; bright, strawberry-cherry fruit with a savory note at mid-palate; almost satiny at first, then lightly grippy from mid-palate to finish; straightforward, with medium weight and length.
2005 *Reserve (tasted in 2007):* Transparent, medium ruby; a bit spicier and less floral than the 2006 Willamette Valley; soft fruit and dusty spice on the palate; black raspberry and barrel-derived

vanilla; bright overall and nicely balanced; almost creamy at mid-palate.

SINEANN
Newburg, Oregon

During the second half of Peter Rosback's twenty-one-year career as a mechanical engineer, he was also a committed home winemaker. He took a few classes in enology "here and there," worked harvests at ELK COVE VINEYARDS, peppered winemakers with questions, and figured out what he calls "the grape thing"—the persistent truth that really good wine comes only from really good grapes. In 1994 a harvest-season conversation with David O'Reilly (who then had marketing responsibilities at Elk Cove and subsequently founded the much-respected Owen Roe label)—and a tasting of Rosback's homemade zinfandel—persuaded Rosback that he should try making wine commercially.

Zinfandel came first. Four years later, in 1998, Rosback produced the inaugural vintage of Sineann pinot noir, a vineyard-designated wine from the Resonance vineyard—then known as Reed and Reynolds—planted in 1981 in an uncommonly warm, weather-protected site on the western edge of what is now the Yamhill-Carlton District, owned and biodynamically farmed by Kevin Chambers. From this quantitatively modest but qualitatively uncompromising debut, the Sineann pinot program expanded to no fewer than twelve separate bottlings by 2005, including a special cuvée made for Napa Valley's globally respected French Laundry restaurant.

All but two of Sineann's pinots are vineyard-designated wines. Covey Ridge and Phelps Creek bottlings were added to the portfolio in 2000; Whistling Ridge in 2001; Wyeast, Lachini, and Schwab in 2002; Able and Schindler in 2004; and Maresh in 2005. Of these, Phelps Creek, Wyeast, and Able are sites in the Hood River Valley—the Hood empties into the Columbia about 35 miles upstream from Portland—where higher altitude offsets what would otherwise be a substantially warmer climate. Rosback champions the Hood River Valley for pinot, and the Sineann editions suggest that his confidence may be justified. O'Reilly, Rosback's inspiration back in 1994, has been a partner in Sineann from the outset. The partners, who share an Irish heritage, have embraced nomenclature that showcases their roots: Sineann is Gaelic for the River Shannon, which empties into the Atlantic on Ireland's west coast.

WINES AND WINEMAKING NOTES
Rosback explains his overall orientation as "Old World with respect to *terroir* and New World for ripeness." He argues that low crop loads tend to showcase *terroir,* and he insists that vines be pruned to one cluster per shoot. He is also an unapologetic ripe picker, explaining that he "will take high alcohol to get ripe flavors." Stylistically, Rosback privileges texture, saying that he "wants to feel the wine" and is "very sensitive to astringency on the back palate."

All Sineann pinots are made from completely destemmed fruit. Some native yeast actions start during a five-day cold soak, at which point Rosback inoculates the fermentors with yeasts chosen to maximize color extraction, aromatics, and strength (and thus to avoid fermentations that stick in the high alcohol environment that his ripe fruit produces). Pressing is timed to ensure that the tail end of the primary fermentation finishes in barrel. Anchor coopers are Taransaud, Rousseau, and Damy—and Radoux for its "best barrels." Only new and 1-year-old barrels are used, in ratios that vary between 10 and 100 percent, depending on the vineyard and vintage. The barrel cellar is kept relatively warm at first, so that both primary and malolactic fermentations finish promptly.

At this point, which is sometimes as early as January following the vintage, Rosback adds sulfur dioxide and racks barrel-to-barrel once. Rosback "may filter to moderate tannins" but never fines. The blends (except for the Oregon cuvée, which relies on sites purchased specifically for blending), which are derived by culling vineyard-specific barrels that do not quite measure up, are made in June; the wines are bottled in August and released in September. On release, which occurs barely eleven months after the vintage, Sineann pinots emerge as very dark, ripe, extracted, and assertive wines with great concentration, density, and sometimes off-putting backbone; within a year or two of bottle age, however, the wines acquire significant finesse. Across the large portfolio of vineyard-designates, the wines display more consistency of style than *terroir*-based variation, however. Minerality shares organoleptic space at least equally with fruit, and the wines are not heavy.

TASTING NOTES

2005 *Schindler Vineyard (tasted in 2007):* Transparent, very dark purplish-red; ripe and plummy fruit on the nose; blackberry and Italian plum on the palate with some tart, citrusy highlights; attractive minerality and acidity; relatively lightweight in the mouth; noticeable grip on the finish.

2005 *Able Vineyard (tasted in 2006):* Especially approachable Sineann pinot; transparent, medium black-red color; sweet mid-palate, with black fruit and cola; moderately concentrated; a huge load of fine-grained tannins and considerable extraction; almost velvety, but also grippy.

2005 *Oregon (tasted in 2006):* Exotic sandalwood nose, with sweet blackberry and dusty cherry flavors in the mouth; concentrated and grippy, but approachable.

2005 *Resonance Vineyard (tasted in 2007):* Nearly opaque black-red; intense nose of black cherry, tar, and infused flowers; a mineral and fruit-driven wine overall; nicely structured and serious; mouth coating without heaviness; medium in length.

2005 *Maresh Vineyard (tasted in 2007):* Dark black-red; resinated black fruit on the nose; berry fruit predominates on the palate; very slightly fruit-sweet, with infused flowers and nice acidity; graceful, attractive, and serious; perhaps my favorite among the Sineann offerings.

2004 *Schindler Vineyard (tasted in 2007):* Medium-dark brick-red with rosy highlights; aromas of smoke, earth, and exotic spice; very ripe on the palate, with cocoa and cinnamon, like Ibarra chocolate; medium in weight and length.

2004 *Wyeast Vineyard (tasted in 2007):* Transparent, medium-dark brick-red; floral on the nose with a dominance of spring meadow flowers; intense, bright red fruit on the palate, including clove-spiced cranberries; black pepper, too; nicely structured; almost silky; grip only on the finish; attractive.

2004 *Whistling Ridge Vineyard (tasted in 2007):* Transparent, medium garnet; white pepper, raspberries, flowers, and citrus on the nose; rich, ripe, caramel-, mocha- and spice-tinged cherry and plum fruit flavors; a hint of black licorice; soft, fine-grained tannins on the mid-palate; elegantly built; finishes warm.

SKEWIS WINES
Healdsburg, California

Hank Skewis, a Colgate University graduate and onetime VISTA volunteer, turned his attention toward the wine business by happenstance. A friend offered him a job looking after a Sonoma vineyard. Skewis then worked part time in a winery tasting room, took viticulture classes at Santa Rosa Junior College, landed a job as assistant winemaker for Lambert Bridge Winery in Dry Creek Valley, and (getting really serious) worked the 1993 harvest for Dominique Lafon in Meursault. At this point, Skewis was hooked, on wine in general and on pinot noir in particular. In 1994 he signed on as winemaker for Mill Creek Vineyards in the Russian River Valley and simultaneously launched an eponymous label—using three barrels of pinot sourced from the Floodgate Vineyard in Anderson Valley.

Today, Hank and Maggie Skewis make barely 1,000 cases of elegant, understated, and hugely rewarding pinot noir in a tiny, repurposed mushroom farm facility in the Alexander Valley. Fruit is sourced from a handful of Anderson Valley and Russian River vineyards where Skewis is intimately involved with all aspects of farming. This is as hands-on, honest, and purpose driven as American winemaking gets.

WINES AND WINEMAKING NOTES
Skewis likes to pick pinot by a combination of flavor and chemical markers, slightly early by mainstream California standards, when sugars have reached between 24 and 25 Brix, and acids are still fairly high. For the Russian River vineyards, this means

pH values of 3.4 to 3.5; for Anderson Valley fruit, the typical pH is closer to 3.6. Yields are kept quite low, and the grapes are picked by hand into half-ton bins. In Skewis's Lilliputian facility, there is one 4-ton stainless steel fermentation tank, which Skewis says he rarely uses; the rest of the fermentations take place in fruit bins. Grapes are destemmed (stems add "more bad than good," according to Skewis), soaked cool for two days, and inoculated with Assmannshausen yeast. Acid is often added in the fermentors before inoculation, especially for Anderson Valley lots. Fermentations run eight to ten days; juice temperatures top out at about 90°F; and the new wine is pressed directly into barrels to create a "better marriage with new oak."

Beginning in 2005, most tanks have been bled to produce a rosé, which has the effect of concentrating the remaining red wine. Skewis uses barrels from Seguin Moreau made with staves air-dried for two years, and from Cadus made with staves dried for three years, 33 to 40 percent of which are new. Malolactic bacteria are introduced in barrel; the wines are racked barrel-to-barrel once or twice, and are racked again to tank before bottling.

AS HANDS-ON, HONEST, AND PURPOSE DRIVEN AS AMERICAN WINEMAKING GETS

With a long *élevage*—sixteen to nineteen months—Skewis pinots settle very clear without fining or filtration.

All Skewis wines are vineyard-designated. The Floodgate bottling, from a well-known vineyard in the cool, "deep" end of Anderson Valley, has been made in every vintage since 1994. It was rechristened Anderson Valley Reserve in 2004 after Bill Hambrecht, an investment banker with long involvement in the California wine scene, sold the vineyard to the Duckhorn Wine Company for the latter's Anderson Valley pinot project (see GOLDENEYE). A Russian River Valley wine, from the tiny (just two thirds of an acre) Montgomery Vineyard on Olivet Lane opposite DE LOACH, was added in 1996. (Montgomery was planted ca. 1986 with "undocumented" plant material.) Two other Russian River vineyards—Salzgeber (Salzgeber-Chan beginning in 2004), a 1996 planting of Dijon 115 on the uphill side of Westside Road, and Bush, a low-yielding benchland site on the south side of River Road near Fulton—joined the portfolio in 1999 and 2001, respectively. In 2000 Skewis began sourcing grapes from Chris Demuth's 1990 planting at the 1,600-foot contour on Deer Meadow Road above Boonville, and in 2005 he added Mark Lingenfelder's planting of UCD 13, located not far from Bush on the Santa Rosa Plain.

Although Skewis would prefer that all his pinots display alcohols under 14 percent, and the entire portfolio is indeed modest by California standards, recent vintages of many wines clock in over 14. The wines show rewarding elegance, nice structure, and avalanches of subtle flavors and aromatics.

TASTING NOTES

2004 *Anderson Valley Reserve (tasted in 2007):* Transparent, medium magenta; exotic aromas of nut meats, beeswax, and red fruit; sweet, cherry-pie flavors in the mouth, with hints of hard spice, apple cider, boot polish, black licorice, and mulled wine (!); slightly heavier than most Skewis pinots and perhaps best kept for a few years; long and very good.

2004 *Demuth Vineyard (tasted in 2007):* Light-to-medium rosy-garnet; aromatic avalanche of herbs, citrus, cherry *eau-de-vie*, and rose petal; soft, round, and almost creamy on the palate, but also persistently bright and well structured; slightly resinous with a hint of bitterness on the finish; a very pretty wine.

2004 *Bush Vineyard (tasted in 2007):* Very transparent, light-to-medium black-red; intense nose of fresh flowers, gum camphor, incense, and earth; beautiful and slightly sweet on the palate with tarry, licorice-infused, and tobacco-tinged notes; mouth coating but not mouth filling; finishes bright and clean; very attractive.

2004 *Montgomery Vineyard (tasted in 2007):* Brilliant medium magenta; aromas of flowers, wood resin, orange peel, and Brazil nuts; elegant and very slightly sweet on the palate, with paprika (!) and hints of espresso. Nicely built; great clarity of flavors; a personal favorite.

2003 *Bush Vineyard (tasted in 2007):* Brilliant scarlet; cherry, cranberry, and a cascade of soft, Indonesian spice on the nose; dominant spice on the palate; elegant and velvety, with just a hint of grip on the finish. Fine.

2002 *Floodgate Vineyard (tasted from a half bottle in 2005):* Brilliant monochrome garnet; bright rosehips and cherry aromas; intense, mineral rich, essence-of-fruit on the palate, with strong pepper and hard spice flavors, some grip and the stamp of sweet oak.

2002 *Salzgeber Vineyard (tasted in 2007):* Transparent, medium mahogany with rosy-crimson highlights; beginning to mature; sweet, exotic Indonesian spice aromas, with suggestions of furniture polish and pine needles; elegant, spicy, and peppery on the palate; undertones of wet earth, mushroom, and some orange peel; complete, fine, and enjoyable, with some high-toned acid to maintain its brightness.

2002 *Montgomery Vineyard (tasted in 2007):* Brilliant, light-to-medium rosy-magenta; explosive nose of exotic spice and cardamom; silky, raspberry flavor with some black pepper; finishes stylish and dry; intense rather than weighty.

2001 *Bush Vineyard (tasted in* 2005*):* Brilliant, medium black-red; funky, forest-floor aromas with some minty conifer; then, cherry and ginger in the mouth; intense smoky fruit; rewarding length and persistence; texture of rough silk.

2001 *Montgomery Vineyard (tasted in* 2005*):* Brilliant pretty garnet with a rosy-orange rim; nose of tar and Indonesian spice; a background of black fruit on the palate, but a dominance of slate-y minerality and black tea, with substantial grip at the end.

2000 *Montgomery Vineyard (tasted in* 2005*):* Transparent, medium garnet; aromas of vanilla, mesquite, and thyme; strawberry and red cherry flavors, with a hint of fruit-sweetness over strong minerality; some grip but still silky; very fine. A personal favorite.

SOKOL BLOSSER WINERY
Dayton, Oregon

According to Susan Sokol Blosser, the vineyard she and Bill Blosser planted in 1972 was born of Bill's brainstorm, in the unlikely context of a flea market near Lancaster, Pennsylvania, as the couple drove a Volkswagen van from North Carolina to Oregon. Its surprising resonance seems to have traded on their mutual interest in wine, which had been Susan's father's hobby, on Bill's college year abroad in France (where wine was always close at hand), and on the 1960s notion that socially conscious people might do good in the world by living close to the land. Within

five months, as Bill took up a career teaching urban planning at Portland State University, the Blossers applied themselves to meeting the handful of pioneers who had already committed to grow grapes in Oregon's Willamette Valley, to the acquisition of an abandoned orchard in the Dundee Hills, and to weekend, do-it-yourself farming with secondhand equipment.

With hands-on help from family members in the spring of 1972, the Blossers set out an acre each of riesling, Muller-Thurgau, and chardonnay, and two acres of pinot noir. They produced the first Sokol Blosser wines in 1977, with California microbiologist Bob McRitchie as winemaker, and opened Oregon's first tasting room in 1978. Additional land was acquired and planted in 1975, 1976, and 1977, and again in 1989, 1998, 2000, and 2001. The winemaker since 1998 has been Russ Rosner, a ten-year veteran of ROBERT MONDAVI WINERY in Napa, who made extensive changes in the vineyard and cellar after his arrival, including the termination of filtration and fining regimes, and the installation of a new, gentler destemmer and a new sorting table. The whole story is charmingly told in Susan Sokol Blosser's memoir, *At Home in the Vineyard* (University of California Press, 2006).

WINES AND WINEMAKING NOTES
From 1977 to 1997, Sokol Blosser's pinot program consisted of a Yamhill County bottling and a reserve wine called Redland—plus substantial amounts of a very tasty, dry rosé. In 1998 and 1999, the Yamhill County wine was joined by small quantities of three block-designated wines featuring some of the estate's oldest vines: Watershed (planted in 1976 to 1977), Old Vineyard Block (planted in 1972), and Twelve Row Block (planted in 1975.) The

block-designates were not made in 2000, but they were resumed in 2001, when the estate cuvée, made from a 65 to 35 percent blend of old-to-young-vines fruit, also debuted. Watershed, Old Vineyard Block, and Estate Cuvée were made in 2002, while the Willamette Valley wine was renamed Dundee Hills. Watershed was not made in 2003, but Twelve Row returned to the lineup. In 2004 a new block-designate called Goosepen, based on nursery-sourced Pommard clone planted in 1998 not far from the original 1972 planting, replaced Twelve Row Block.

Rosner prefers short cold soaks and very extended macerations. After the primary fermentation has been completed, the fermentors are topped with carbon dioxide, sealed, and tasted daily until they show signs of a "changed tannin structure"; at that point, they are pressed. A long barrel regime follows, during which just the lees and very small doses of sulfur dioxide protect the wine; there is no racking until the blends are made just before bottling, which occurs in March two years after the vintage. The Dundee Hills wine sees about 40 percent new wood; the other bottlings average about 60 percent.

Whether by virtue of the very extended macerations or for other reasons, Sokol Blosser pinots always seem understated to me, and perhaps shyer that this extraordinary site should give. They are elegant, however, and since Rosner's arrival, extremely well made. Many pre-Rosner vintages have seemed to age prematurely; vintages made since the full repertory of his changes have been implemented may do much better.

TASTING NOTES

2004 *Watershed Block (tasted in 2006):* Transparent, medium garnet; slightly reticent nose of chamomile flowers; resin, tar, tobacco, licorice, and *lapsang souchong* tea on the palate; strong mineral core; light-to-medium weight; suede-textured and long.

2004 *Goosepen Block (tasted in 2006):* Transparent, medium rosy magenta; slightly closed aromatically; mint, resin, tar, white pepper, and a hint of clove on the palate; full bodied and slightly creamy; texture of rough silk.

2004 *Old Vineyard Block (tasted in 2006):* Transparent, medium black-red; hints of wild strawberry and raspberry on the nose; more berry fruit in the mouth with notes of mint, resin, earth, and pepper; concentrated, smoky, and round with a satiny finish.

2004 *Dundee Hills (tasted in 2007):* Brilliant, medium garnet; fir balsam, tangerine peel, and hard spice aromas; more herbal than fruit driven on the palate, with bite that is reminiscent of dried green peppercorns; good weight and structure; quite dry from mid-palate to finish.

2003 *Dundee Hills (tasted in 2007):* Light-to-medium rosy-garnet; dried flowers and wet chalk on the nose; very ripe, sweet fruit and quite grippy tannins at mid-palate; dry from mid-palate to finish.

2002 *Dundee Hills (tasted in 2007):* Light-to-medium rosy-garnet; hickory shell, cranberry, and raspberry aromas; bright, understated berry fruit and citrus peel on the mid-palate, with black pepper on the finish; engaging and lingering; attractive.

SONNET WINE CELLARS
Los Gatos, California

In the 1980s Anthony Craig was an aspiring actor, studying drama at the College of Arts and Technology in Newcastle-upon-Tyne, and working part-time in the city's

Theatre Royal. There, he was discovered by a director of the Royal Shakespeare Company on tour and encouraged to further his studies in London. In London he met and married a young, would-be actress, who also happened to be an American from Los Gatos. Tired of English weather, the couple decided to pursue their careers in California. When they eventually divorced, Craig thought a career change would be well advised; he searched the classified ads in the Los Gatos *Weekly Times* for opportunities and was promptly hired as a cellar rat in the DAVID BRUCE WINERY on Bear Creek Road. In a meteoric rise, he became Bruce's cellarmaster just fourteen months later and then its enologist; in 1995 he became the co-winemaker, in which capacity he was the principal architect of the brand's small-lot, vineyard-designation program.

In 2001, still on the job at David Bruce but now independently passionate about pinot noir, Craig founded his own boutique brand, which he called Sonnet in honor of his Shakespearian beginnings. The first vintage, in 2001, was 95 cases of vineyard-designated wine from the River View Vineyard on Metz Road east of Soledad. Since 2002 the stable source has been Tondre's Grapefield in the Santa Lucia Highlands (see CAMPION WINES for more detail on Tondre). In 2002, 2003, and 2005, however, Craig also sourced fruit from the Amber Ridge Vineyard, a young planting of Dijon clones on the east side of the Russian River's "Middle Reach" that is also used by KOSTA BROWNE and SIDURI WINES, and in 2004 and 2005 from the Kruse Vineyard (belonging to Jack Creek Cellars) in the York Mountain AVA, located in the Templeton Gap west of Paso Robles. In 2005 Sonnet's first Santa Cruz Mountains pinot debuted, sourced from Ed Muns's very high-altitude, 13-acre vineyard on Loma Prieta Mountain planted almost entirely to Dijon clones. Since Craig left David Bruce in 2004, the Sonnet wines have been made at Silver Mountain Winery, for which Craig consults, and for which Craig makes a second edition of Muns Vineyard pinot, with a rather different *élevage*.

WINEMAKING NOTES

Craig departs in some interesting and significant ways from the consensus protocol. During fermentation, in lieu of either pumpovers or punchdowns, Craig uses *pneumatage* (see BENTON-LANE for additional information), which he finds gentler than conventional methods. The barrel regime relies on a large percentage of Hungarian oak because Craig finds its grain to be tighter than the wood available to the American market from most French forests. Given that Craig also keeps his pinots in wood for fourteen to seventeen months (until the thirteenth month, pinots have "a tendency to taste like gamay," according to Craig), tight grain is an important defense against excessive barrel marking. There is no racking or blending until just before bottling, and all Sonnet pinots are bottled without fining or filtration.

Sonnet's wines are mostly dark, serious pinots, some of which take ripeness to the edge of raisiny flavor. The wines are extremely well made, however, and have serious fruit- and mineral-rich structures.

TASTING NOTES

2005 *Muns Vineyard (tasted twice in 2007):* Transparent, deep garnet; very ripe nose, with a whiff of raisins, plus conifer foliage and rose petals; floral-fruit character on the front palate; intense and tightly knit; grippy on the back palate and dry at the end; some bright hints of citrus; attractive overall; medium in length.

2005 *Amber Ridge Vineyard (tasted in 2008):* Luminous medium garnet; aromas of flowers, cranberry, and pine tar; very bright and high-toned on the palate, with notes of Queen Anne cherry and citrus oil, plus a hint of white pepper; elegant, silky attack, then dry after mid-palate; long and attractive.

2005 *Kruse Vineyard (tasted in 2008):* Transparent, dark black-red; coal tar and black cherry on the nose; very slightly sweet, tightly knit, and intensely flavored on the palate; hint of creaminess on the attack; then supple, mouth coating, and velvety from mid-palate to finish; long; testifies to an exceptionally interesting site.

SOTER VINEYARDS
Carlton, Oregon

Soter Vineyards, the second major pinot noir–based wine project of Tony Soter's distinguished career, is headquartered in a repurposed 1940s barn on a ranch devoted partially to vineyards, but primarily to wheat fields and pasture, about 3 miles due east of Carlton, Oregon. The contrast with the discordant, teal-colored *faux château* on the north edge of Napa, California's urban sprawl that was home for more than a decade to Soter's first pinot project, is both stark and significant. That project, ETUDE WINES,

---

SOTER VINEYARDS: A VERTICAL TASTING OF FIVE VINTAGES FROM BEACON HILL

This vertical tasting of wines made from the Beacon Hill site was based on samples furnished by Soter Vineyards in the spring of 2007.

2003: Transparent, medium-deep black-red with rosy highlights; dominant, ripe-fruit nose, with rose, lilac, and lavender; then intense, rich, and mouth coating with both red and black fruit; the fruit gives way to grip and minerality; tannins are ripe but substantial—inevitable, perhaps, given the vintage; the wine finishes warm.

2002: Medium-dark black-red; predominantly floral aromas are wrapped in red berry fruit and soft Indonesian spice; pretty, bright, and seductive on the palate; abundance of cherry-berry fruit with orange flower water; very slightly fruit-sweet; silky at first, then grippy on the finish.

2000: Medium garnet evolving toward brick-red; floral and carpenter-shop aromas, with a hint of caramel; lovely in the mouth with a combination of opulence and brilliance; perfect juxtaposition of ripeness and acid-lifted aromatics; cherry-cranberry fruit with some citrus; silky and long, with just a hint of grip at the end; very fine.

1999: Dark brick-red; intense nose of ripe blackberry and marionberry, with briar and creosote; sweet, extracted, and rich, but also tannic and dry even on the mid-palate; little sign thus far of softening; may need more time.

1998: Very dark brick-red; this vineyard's signature nose of flowers, minerals, and mocha plus a bit of toasted cumin; rich, sweet, dark, and grippy in the mouth, with black licorice and black tea; more resolved than the 1999.

was founded in 1982 and sold to Beringer Blass (now Foster's Wine Estates) in 2001.

Several years before the sale of Etude Wines, however, Soter began to lay groundwork for his Oregon venture, which he conceived initially as a "homestead" and retirement project "with "entertainment value," close to his childhood roots in

---

SOTER SAYS THE
OREGON ENVIRONMENT
BRINGS "GREATER
INHERENT STRUCTURE"
TO PINOT NOIR

Portland. The first step was a 6-acre pinot and chardonnay vineyard, in the valley carved by the north fork of the Chehalem River east of Yamhill, which Soter and his wife, Michelle, had purchased in 1997 and augmented with new plantings in 1998 and 1999. They called this site Beacon Hill, for a wood-shingle structure on its hilltop that seemed suggestive of a lighthouse. The second step was taken when proceeds from the sale of Etude became available in 2001. These effectively transformed the erstwhile retirement project into something substantially more ambitious.

As the new and larger focus for their renewed energies, the Soters chose a 245-acre ranch known locally as Mineral Springs, on a rise overlooking the Yamhill River valley east of Carlton, where the trappings of a wine culture are gradually replacing abandoned grain elevators. Soter believes that about 50 acres of Mineral Springs can eventually be planted to pinot noir. He has already planted 32 acres and dug two cement-lined caves for barrel storage. The site is an east–west-oriented ridgeback with commanding views, mature trees, established agriculture, and perhaps

most significant, substantially sandier soil than Beacon Hill. The new vineyard covers the ridgeback in rows oriented about twenty degrees off due north–south; plant material consists of the UCD 2A and 4 selections that anchor most Oregon pinot vineyards, plus the "heirloom" selections on which Soter came to rely for his best Etude wines: Swan, Mount Eden, and Calera.

Soter is plainly positive about Mineral Springs as a venue for sustainable farming in a biodiverse environment, but he saves special enthusiasm for the uncommonly well-drained, sand-and-siltstone soils that seem (thus far at least) to produce silkier and more elegant wines than most of the sedimentary terrain north and west of the Dundee Hills. In 2005 the Soters made their first vineyard-designated wine from Mineral Springs and sold the Beacon Hill property, subject to a leaseback agreement that secured its fruit for Soter Vineyards through 2006.

WINES AND WINEMAKING NOTES
The first Soter Vineyards wines, made in 1998, were a vineyard-designated pinot and a sparkling rosé (made from a combination of pinot noir and chardonnay grapes) from Beacon Hill. The still Beacon Hill pinot remained in the portfolio until 2006, except for the 2001 and 2004 vintages, when the wine from this site was declassified. A second still pinot noir bottling, called North Valley, was inaugurated in 2003. North Valley is anchored with purchased grapes but also is used as a vehicle for handling young-vines fruit from estate vineyards as well as declassified lots. The vineyard-designated wine from Mineral Springs debuted in 2005.

Soter is a thoughtful winemaker, formed by two decades of Californian experience with pinot noir; he is adjusting to the "greater inherent structure" the Oregon environment brings to pinot, and to the happy truth that "Oregon-grown grapes seem to taste better at lesser sugar levels than grapes grown in California." Most wines are made with "some measure of whole clusters," although this varies "by vintage and vineyard." Indigenous yeasts are "encouraged" but augmented with small inoculations of cultured yeasts, as they were at Etude. Soter (and his associate winemaker James Cahill) practice extended macerations when they believe the wine has a potential for long life, but otherwise press at dryness. Time in barrel ranges from ten to eleven months for the North Valley wine to as much as fourteen to sixteen months for the estate wines; the percentage of new oak fluctuates between 30 and 70 percent, with the North Valley cuvée at the low end of the range. Soter describes a gradual "evolution away from new oak." Filtration is "avoided." All the Beacon Hill pinots are serious, structured wines in some vintages; the first vintage from Mineral Springs is handsome and impressive.

TASTING NOTE

2005 *Mineral Springs (tasted in* 2008*).* Luminous ruby color; intense, savory, herbal nose; explosive on the palate with strong earthy-cherry flavors and notes suggestive of infused rose petals; silky to mid-palate, then some gentle grip; minerally, elegant overall, long and fine.

ST. INNOCENT WINERY
Salem, Oregon

Mark Vlossak says he had his first sip of wine at the age of seven, and drank or tasted wine pretty continuously thereafter until he left home for college. His father imported wine, so most of the product served at home was good, better, or best, and his mother fell into serious cooking, creating a near-epicurean environment. But Vlossak had other preoccupations in college

---

THE ST. INNOCENT EDITIONS ARE OFTEN THE MOST VIVIDLY SITE EXPRESSIVE OF ALL THE WINES MADE FROM ANY GIVEN VINEYARD

---

and immediately afterward, shifting from an early concentration in chemistry to a major in theater arts. After college, when he was working for the Opera Company of Boston, he discovered a pioneering, Colorado-based program that trained physician assistants to practice in pediatrics, and he decided to make a wholesale career change. During his internship, he traveled to Oregon and determined that it was a place "he would never leave." While working in Salem, he rediscovered his fascination with wine and decided to try his hand at making it. As an amateur, he made three vintages of sparkling wine at home. To gain professional experience, he then apprenticed for two years at the Arterberry Winery (later purchased by Duck Pond.) A proper formation in enology came from time at Napa Valley's Wine Lab and extension courses at the University of California Davis.

In 1988 Vlossak founded St. Innocent Winery, named for his father, who had been born on All Innocents Day. The first vintage involved crushing 10 tons of grapes for about 550 cases of wine: pinot noir, chardonnay, and sparkling. From 1994 to 1999, Vlossak was also the winemaker for PANTHER CREEK CELLARS, reinforcing its reputation for fine pinot noir. His career in pediatrics continued until 1998, when he felt able to focus entirely on St. Innocent. The winery now makes almost 7,000 cases, including chardonnay, pinot gris, and pinot blanc, but its stellar reputation comes mostly from an impressive portfolio of single-vineyard pinots made from purchased fruit. In 2002 three of these pinots earned 94-point scores from *The Wine Advocate,* catapulting Vlossak and St. Innocent into the wine public's eye.

Meanwhile, a fortuitous chain of events began in 2003 when Tim Ramey, a Wall Street investor and loyal St. Innocent customer, purchased the former O'Connor Vineyard on the north side of Zena Road in the Eola Hills, from which Vlossak had sourced pinot between 1989 and 1998. This began a chain of events that transformed St. Innocent into a partially estate-based producer. In 2006 St. Innocent purchased a 25 percent interest in Ramey's vineyard, the vineyard's name was changed to Zenith, and fruit from 20 acres of new planting was dedicated to St. Innocent under long-term contract. Vlossak also agreed to make wine for Zenith Vineyards, Ramey's new label, and construction began on a 10,000-case winery, on the site of the vineyard, to be the shared premise of the Zenith and St. Innocent brands.

WINES AND WINEMAKING NOTES
The first St. Innocent pinot noir, in 1998, was a Willamette Valley blend anchored with fruit from the Seven Springs Vineyard. In 1989 the first vineyard-designated wine, from the aforementioned O'Connor Vineyard, debuted, joining the Willamette Valley cuvée. Vineyard-designates from Seven Springs were added in 1990, from the Freedom Hill and Temperance Hill Vineyards in 1994, from BRICK HOUSE WINE COMPANY in 1995, and from the Shea Vineyard in 1998, which was also the

last year for O'Connor. In 2001, when Seven Springs was divided between two owners and the lower part of the vineyard rechristened Anden, Vlossak added an Anden Vineyard wine to the St. Innocent list, plus a single-vineyard wine from the WHITE ROSE VINEYARD, his first foray into the Dundee Hills. The year 2001 was the last vintage for Brick House, 2004 the last for the original planting at Freedom Hill (which succumbed to phylloxera and went out of production until 2008), and 2005 the last for Shea; however, Justice Vineyard, the tightly spaced 1999 to 2001 planting of Dijon 777 owned by the principals in Bethel Heights Vineyard, was added in 2004.

The year 2002 marked the debut of St. Innocent's Villages Cuvée, built on fruit from the Vitae Springs Vineyard in the Salem Hills and on young-vines fruit from vineyards otherwise used to make single-vineyard wines. Villages effectively replaced St. Innocent's earlier Willamette Valley bottling. A vineyard-designated pinot from the Maresh Vineyard was made for one year only in 2005; Momtazi, in the McMinnville foothills, was added to the portfolio in 2006, along with the first edition of vineyard-designated wine from Zenith. Because the owners of Seven Springs Vineyard wrote a new contract in 2007 that obligates virtually all the crop to a restaurant group, neither St. Innocent nor very many of the vineyard's other small-winery fruit clients will have access to its grapes after 2006.

Vlossak chooses to work with growers who share his goals and values. These growers agree to work with Vlossak to customize viticultural practices: to hedge the vines as late as possible in the season, to pull leaves conservatively, and to drop fruit based on estimates of yield that Vlossak makes himself, inter alia. Most of the growers farm sustainably, organically, or biodynamically. Picking decisions are based on Vlossak's "taste memory"—actually, meticulous notes on his experience tasting grapes in the weeks before each year's harvest at each site, which are consulted as maturity approaches in each new year to pinpoint the perfect time to pick.

At the winery, fruit is completely destemmed (Vlossak respects and enjoys some Oregon pinots from other makers who rely heavily on whole-cluster fermentation, but he does not like stems in his own wine) and fermented without any addition of sulfur dioxide unless the skins have been compromised by rot. Without sulfur, the quarter-dose of Epernay II, a white wine yeast that he customarily adds to each cuve after a short, cold maceration, leaves most resident yeasts alive and well, while the inoculum helps to ensure a "stable, slow and calm fermentation that consistently goes completely dry." (Dry wine is the best defense against brettanomyces, according to Vlossak.) To avoid racking later, which disrupts the anaerobic environment that seems to correlate with a wine's capacity to evolve— in the bottle and in the glass after the bottle is uncorked—the new wines are settled after pressing and sent "clean" to barrel.

The wood program is tailored, as far as possible, to the properties of each vineyard and each vintage, but all the vineyard-designated wines spend two winters in wood and are not bottled until sixteen to twenty months after the vintage. Only the Villages Cuvée is permitted a shorter *élevage*. Wines are rarely racked, fined, or filtered.

The overall orientation, Vlossak explains, is "to use winemaking techniques to achieve specific results based on the needs of specific vineyards in specific years, but not to drive a particular style of wine." He is clear about what he wants, however: complex wines that show their *terroir* (he observes that *grand cru* wines are distinguished from lesser cousins by their ability to "reveal the details of *terroir* more intimately than other wines") and that can evolve (see above). He is uncommonly successful at both. St. Innocent editions are often the most vividly site-expressive of all the wines made from any given vineyard in a given year, exhibiting perfect balance, great finesse, and finely chiseled structures.

TASTING NOTES

2005 *Justice Vineyard (tasted in* 2007*):* Transparent, medium blackish-ruby; earth, graphite, and wet slate on the nose; blackberry, cinnamon, clove, and slate on the palate; very slightly creamy at mid-palate; finishes with very fine-grained tannins.

2005 *Shea Vineyard (tasted in* 2007*):* Brilliant deep garnet; intensely floral nose encompassing roses, violets, and lavender; red fruit on the palate; an elegant, long, mineral-driven wine with impressive finesse; sadly, St. Innocent's last vintage from a substantially old-vines block at Shea.

2005 *White Rose Vineyard (tasted in* 2007*):* Brilliant medium black-red; a startling nose of white wildflowers, smoked meat, and incense; slightly sweet, briary fruit in the mouth, already dominated by secondary flavors; mouth coating but still elegant, intense, finely chiseled, and long; fine.

2005 *Seven Springs Vineyard (tasted in* 2007*):* Deep, transparent crimson; aromas of exotic spice and minerality; on the palate, a layer of blackberries and cream on an underlay of wet slate; very young, expresses unresolved tannin; needs time.

2001 *White Rose Vineyard (tasted in* 2005*):* Pretty, medium rosy-crimson; bright floral aromas wrapped in earth, softly exotic spice, and a bit of barrel char; intense, brightly etched flavors of infused flowers, sweet oak, and black cherry; satin mid-palate; dominant minerality and some grip on the finish; beautifully built and very elegant; very fine.

STEPHEN ROSS WINE CELLARS

San Luis Obispo, California

Stephen Ross Dooley, a Minnesotan and Davis-trained winemaker, did his formative wine work at Napa's Louis M. Martini Winery before moving to the EDNA VALLEY VINEYARD as winemaker and president in 1987. In 1994 he created the Stephen Ross brand. His pinot program began with an Edna Valley blend anchored with fruit from the Edna Ranch Vineyard, to which a Bien Nacido bottling (using grapes from interplanted vines in Blocks G and N) was added in 1995. Early in the new millennium, the Edna Ranch sources were replaced with fruit from other Edna Valley vineyards, notably Jean-Pierre Wolff's 1998 planting on the former Andy McGregor site, and 9 acres, leased for a twenty-five-year period, in the Stone Corral property on Edna Valley's southwest edge, developed, owned, and sustainably farmed under contract to the lessees by TALLEY VINEYARDS. The vines here are a combination of Dijon clones and UCD 2A propagated from Talley's Arroyo Grande plantings; the property is divided among Talley, Stephen Ross, and Kynsi Winery such that each party gets fruit from part of each distinctive vineyard block.

Since 2004 Dooley also has made vineyard-designated wines from Stone Corral and a true coastal vineyard south of Arroyo Grande called Aubaine. This steep, south-southwest facing site overlooking the town of Nipomo consists of about 13 acres of Dijon 667 and 777 planted in 2000. Declassified barrels from Stone Corral, Wolff, Bien Nacido, and Aubaine—primarily the press fractions of each—augmented with wines purchased on the bulk market, are used for a Central Coast blend, bringing the total number of Stephen Ross pinots, in each vintage since 2004, to five.

Each of the wines has a distinctive personality. The vineyard-designate from Stone Corral displays power and concentration, while the Bien Nacido wine, true to that site's *terroir,* shows a soft, approachable persona with a bit of black pepper at the edges. The Aubaine is typically a very dark wine with a low pH and very smooth tannins. Overall, the wines are ripe and deeply colored. Except for the Bien Nacido cuvée, they seem serious, even powerful, and can be challenging when they are young.

WINEMAKING NOTES

Dooley argues that it is possible to pick pinot from the sites he uses at or below 24.5 Brix "if you farm well." He tries to avoid acidification, but his hand is sometimes forced at Stone Corral. Processing begins with a seven-day cold soak that ends with inoculation, followed by a coolish fermentation (approximately 82°F) in a combination of 5-ton and 2.5-ton jacketed stainless steel open tops. Since 2005 the fermentors have been drained directly into a newly purchased basket press, from which the new wine is transferred to barrel after settling overnight.

The stock of cooperage relies primarily on François Frères with some Sirugue, and averages up to 25 percent new barrels across the cellar. The blends are made in April following the vintage. The Bien Nacido and Central Coast wines are then bottled after eleven months in barrel, while other wines are held for as long as sixteen.

There is no fining or filtration. Stephen Ross pinots have a considerable following among pinot noir cognoscenti, and Dooley ranks high among southern Central Coast producers.

2005 *Edna Valley (tasted in 2007):* Aromas of black cherry and high-toned, spicy fruit; spirity; intense, chewy, and highly extracted on the palate; finishes with the texture of polished cotton.

2005 *Stone Corral Vineyard (tasted in 2007):* Deep, almost opaque black-red; superripe cherry and plum aromas; dark, saturated, and slate-y on the palate; mineral driven, overall, and grippy at the end.

2005 *Aubaine Vineyards (tasted in 2007):* Nearly opaque, dark black-red; nose marked with anise and black earth; sweet, black licorice in the mouth with some grill-charred red peppers; minerally black fruit gives an inky and tarry impression; dense and tight; a very distinctive, one-of-a-kind pinot.

2003 *Stone Corral Vineyard (tasted in 2005):* Nearly opaque; violets, rose petal, and India ink on the nose, with hints of blackberry and wet stone; black fruit on the palate; extracted and tannic, with huge grip.

STEVENSON-BARRIE
McMinnville, Oregon

Stevenson-Barrie is the personal pinot project of Michael Stevenson, the winemaker at **PANTHER CREEK CELLARS**, and his business partner Scott Barrie, who is a legislative lobbyist for the Oregon Home Builders Association.

The label was created in 1995, just after Stevenson arrived at Panther Creek, and has been made in the Panther Creek facility ever since. From 1995 through 1997, there was one wine only, made from the Glasgow Vineyard outside the town of Cheshire, northwest of Eugene.

VERY SUCCESSFUL AND ELEGANT WINES FROM SOME OF OREGON'S MOST RESPECTED SITES

In 1998 Dick Shea's vineyard (see **SHEA WINE CELLARS**) replaced the Glasgow Vineyard as the brand's fruit source. In 2003 a second vineyard-designated wine (from the Freedom Hill Vineyard) was added to the portfolio. A third wine, from Temperance Hill, was added in 2004; and a fourth, from Momtazi Vineyard (see **MAYSARA WINERY**) in 2007. This makes the Stevenson-Barrie portfolio remarkably similar to Panther Creek's—and enables interesting comparisons.

Stevenson says he manages the crop load on vines destined for the Stevenson Barrie program to a higher tonnage per acre than his target for vines destined for Panther Creek wines. A slightly larger crop tends to slow ripening and reduce intensity, making the Stevenson-Barrie wines a bit more elegant and a bit lower in finished alcohol. Fermentations are done entirely in 1-ton fruit bins and "tend to be on the cool side." There is also zero use of new wood for *élevage*. Overall, Stevenson says he is striving for "pretty, balanced wines" that are "an homage to the Eyrie-Erath style that founded the Oregon industry." Recent vintages suggest he has accomplished his objectives perfectly. The wines can be recommended as very successful and elegant editions from some of the most respected sites in Oregon, offered at extremely attractive price points.

TASTING NOTES

2006 *Shea Vineyard (tasted prerelease in* 2007*):* Pretty, transparent, medium rosy-ruby; intense, predominantly floral nose; lovely red berry and cherry palate, with notes of moss, earth, and a hint of gum camphor; unfolds gradually from mid-palate to finish; elegantly built, light to medium in weight, and slightly peppery at the end; genuinely beautiful and a fine example of Shea.

2006 *Freedom Hill Vineyard (tasted prerelease in* 2007*):* Brilliant, medium garnet; savory, aromatic nose featuring rose petals and a briary, garrigue-like character; wet earth and intense dark fruit on the palate; silky, clean, and almost creamy at mid-palate; serious and elegant, with some grip and considerable length.

2005 *Temperance Hill Vineyard (tasted in* 2007*):* Brilliant, light-to-medium rosy-garnet; exotic nose of nut shells, garam masala, clove, and dried flowers; bright, serious, and spicy on the palate, showing raspberry and white pepper; very elegant and satiny, intense with very little weight; medium in length, and very attractive.

STOLLER VINEYARDS
Dayton, Oregon

Bill Stoller grew up on and around what is now Stoller Vineyards, a 373-acre parcel on the southwest flank of the Dundee Hills, near the town of Lafayette. From the 1940s until 1993, the land was operated as a turkey farm, and Stoller's father and uncle at one point operated the largest turkey farm in Oregon. In the 1980s, Stoller and his wife, Cathy, who was successful in an international personnel services business, signed up for a wine-tasting class taught by Judy Peterson-Nedry, a founder of *Northwest Palate* magazine. This contact led the Stollers first to partner with Judy's husband, Harry Peterson-Nedry, in the creation of CHEHALEM, then to invest in the Corral Creek Vineyard and former Veritas Winery when Chehalem acquired these assets in 1995, and finally to purchase the family's newly defunct turkey farm for a vineyard of their own.

The vineyard, which consists almost entirely of high-density (5-foot spacings in 7-foot rows, and 3-foot spacings in 5-foot rows) plantings of pinot noir, chardonnay, pinot blanc, and riesling, functions as a third estate vineyard for Chehalem (which takes half of each harvest, and all of the pinot blanc and riesling). It is also an important source of pinot noir and chardonnay for numerous other producers, including DOMAINE DROUHIN, ARGYLE WINERY, BROADLEY VINEYARDS, SCOTT PAUL WINES, and A TO Z. The pinot consists primarily of Dijon clones on 101-14 and 3309 rootstocks, but there are also 18 acres of UCD 5 and 4 acres UCD 2A.

In 2001 the Stollers launched their own wine brand, which they describe as a "sister" to Chehalem, and moved winemaking operations to an onsite facility in 2005. The 2001 and 2002 editions of Stoller Vineyards pinot and chardonnay were made at Chehalem by Peterson-Nedry and Cheryl Francis; the 2003 and 2004 wines were also made at Chehalem but by Melissa Burr, formerly of COOPER MOUNTAIN WINERY, whom the Stollers engaged as their dedicated winemaker in the summer of 2003. In 2006 the Stoller brand was consuming 20 percent of the vineyard's total output.

WINES AND WINEMAKING NOTES

Stoller made small quantities of a single pinot from 2001 to 2003, relying primarily on fruit from some of the vineyard's oldest (1995 and 1997) plantings. In 2004, in addition to the Estate wine, Burr made a second cuvée, called JV (for *jeunes vignes*) to showcase the fruit of younger vines, and a block-designate called Cathy's Cuvée that uses grapes from a mid-slope, medium-density block of UCD 2A planted in 1997.

Winemaking involves a relatively long (seven- to-ten-day) cold soak, a short alcoholic fermentation, and an occasional postfermentation maceration. Burr adds both acid and enzymes during fermentation, the latter to increase extraction. Barrels are sourced from Rousseau, François Frères, Bouchard, Damy, and Sirugue, and Burr tends to match cooperage styles with individual clones. The UCD 2A, for example, seems to demand a "gentle" barrel such as Sirugue, whereas the UCD 5 benefits from something "more muscular" such as François Frères. Burr says she aims for wines that display a balance of earthy aromas and "ripe, red, juicy fruit." In my experience, the wines to date display a dominance of smoky, briary, wet-earth-and-stone aromas, as much black fruit as red, creamy textures, and silky tannins.

TASTING NOTES

2004 *Estate (tasted in 2006):* Transparent, medium garnet; aromas of rose petal and dried leaves; slightly sweet, dark red fruits on the palate, with overtones of wet slate and briar; nice, silky texture but rich, and noticeably grippy at the end.

2002 *Estate (tasted in 2006):* Medium-dark black-red; sweet, wet earth and dark fruit aromas; black pepper and black fruits in the mouth, plus a bit of citrus peel, cocoa, and caramelized sugar; rich (even slightly fat); long and satiny apart from a bit of grip and bitterness at the end.

T. R ELLIOTT
Sebastopol, California

Ted Elliott, a San Francisco–based management consultant in the 1970s, was one of several investors in a cabernet-based project at the end of Moon Mountain Road in the Mayacamas Range between Sonoma and Napa, first called Glen Ellen Vineyard, later renamed Carmenet. (Carmenet was acquired by Gavilan Vineyards Inc., then the parent company of CHALONE VINEYARD and EDNA VALLEY VINEYARD, eventually Chalone Wine Group, in 1981.) Almost immediately thereafter, Elliott joined forces with Brice Cutrer Jones, who was in the process of transforming his Sonoma-Cutrer Vineyards from a vineyard-only enterprise to estate-based, state-of-the-art wine production specializing in chardonnay. After Sonoma-Cutrer was sold to Kentucky-based Brown-Forman Corporation in 1999, Jones and Elliott became co-investors a second time—this time in a new vineyard dedicated entirely to pinot noir and a pinot-based wine project targeted at 25,000 cases within ten years. The project released its first vintage in 2006 (see EMERITUS VINEYARDS).

Meanwhile, in 2002, Elliott created an eponymous brand of pinot based on grapes from Sonoma-Cutrer's Vine Hill Vineyard, where pinot had been quietly planted in 1994, and on fruit from the Hallberg Vineyard, which is home to Emeritus. UCD 5 and Dijon 115 come from the C Block at Vine Hill and the C Block at Hallberg, which is Elliott's favorite. (In 2005, owing to a poor set, Elliott's Hallberg came from the nearby M Block.) From these, Elliott currently fashions two wines with proprietary names: Queste and Three Plumes. Neither is a vineyard-designate, but Queste is anchored overwhelmingly with Hallberg fruit, while Three Plumes comes predominantly from Vine Hill. (In 2002 and 2003, only a single wine was released; the two proprietary names debuted in 2004.)

T. R Elliott wines are made at the Pellegrini Family Winery, pursuant to a custom-crush arrangement. Winemaking follows the consensus protocol for pinot overall, although there is some use of whole clusters, and only free-run juice is used in the final blends. The two Elliott pinots are quite different, but both are made in a similar, modestly extracted, medium-weight, elegant style.

TASTING NOTES

2005 *Queste (tasted in 2007):* Bright rosy-ruby; white pepper, brown spice, and blackberry on the nose; elegantly wrapped boysenberry and blackberry on the palate, with some herbs and a hint of almond; structurally fairly dense, but nonetheless a very pretty wine.

2005 *Three Plumes (tasted prerelease in 2007):* Again, bright rosy-ruby; floral nose with some high notes of citrus peel; bright, strawberry-cranberry fruit on the palate with hints of tarragon; silky texture and medium-long finish; attractive.

TALISMAN WINES
Sonoma, California

Scott Rich's first career, in the 1980s, was in landscape architecture and environmental planning. In 1989, however—disenamored with work for land developers and the deadlines associated with regulatory approvals—Rich reexamined his interests and priorities, thought seriously about the red Burgundies he had tasted from his father's cellar, and returned to his alma mater, the University of California Davis. This time his field was food science, with an emphasis on enology. Following stints as a research enologist for Robert Mondavi's Woodbridge facility and subsequently for R. H. Phillips, Rich was named winemaker for Mont St. John Cellars in 1992. In 1993 Mont St. John agreed that 3 tons of fruit from its much-respected Madonna Vineyard in Los Carneros could be part of Rich's compensation as winemaker. This was the debut of Rich's own, Carneros-centered pinot noir project called Talisman Wines.

In 1993 and 1994, Talisman's total production was eight barrels of Madonna Vineyard pinot. In 1995, following his move from Mont St. John to ETUDE WINES, Rich began sourcing fruit for the Talisman project from the Truchard Vineyard, not far from Mont St. John. His fruit sources expanded beyond Los Carneros to the Russian River Valley AVA in 1999, and to the Sonoma Coast in 2000. Meanwhile, Rich's day job changed, too. He left Etude to assume the winemaking mantle at Carneros Creek Winery in 2001, and then moved on to focus on Talisman and Moraga Vineyards— an unusual vineyard project in Los Angeles' elegant Bel Air neighborhood dedicated to Bordeaux varieties—beginning in 2002.

WINES AND WINEMAKING NOTES

In 1993 and 1994, the only Talisman wine was a Carneros bottling, made entirely from Madonna Vineyard fruit. Thereafter, the Carneros fruit source(s) shifted. Truchard's old block of Swan selection was used exclusively in 1995, while the 1996 was a blend of that block with an old UCD 4 block at Domaine Chandon. In 1997 Sasaki's old Pommard block (on the Sonoma side of Carneros) replaced the Domaine Chandon block, blended again with Truchard's Swan. In 1998 and 1999, the Carneros wine was made entirely from Truchard fruit (as it had been in 1995), but in 1998, some UCD 4 was added to the Swan; from 1999 through 2002, fruit from a new, mixed-clone block was also used. In 2003 Talisman shifted its Carneros focus to Steve MacRostie's Wildcat Mountain Vineyard, a new planting of Dijon clones and Swan selection in pebbly, clay-loam soils overlaying decomposed volcanic material at the south end of Sonoma Mountain above Gloria Ferrer, from which a vineyard designated wine was made in 2003, 2004, 2006, and 2007. Adastra Vineyard, a 1994 planting on Las Amigas Road that was previously used by Etude, was added to the portfolio from 2005. Meanwhile, a Russian River Valley bottling debuted in 1999, based entirely on fruit from Ted Klopp's Ranch on Laguna Road, and this wine was labeled as Ted's Vineyard from 2002 to 2004.

Beginning in 2005, the Hawk Hill Vineyard west of Sebastopol replaced Ted's. Another Klopp property, the Thorn Ridge Vineyard southwest of Sebastopol in the Sonoma Coast AVA, debuted in 2001, and was made in every vintage through 2006. Thorn Ridge is an exceptional site northeast of English Hill, planted in 1995 to a mix of Swan selection, UCD 4, and Dijon 115, in 9-foot rows with 6 feet between vines. It is cold and windblown, virtually dry farmed, and always yields parsimoniously, but the fruit displays astonishing intensity. A Sonoma Mountain wine, from a 10-acre planting of UCD 4 as well as Dijon 115 and 777, called Red Dog, located 2,000 feet above Bennett Valley on a north-facing slope, was added in 2004. (Rich shares Red

---

BRILLIANT, FULL-FLAVORED, ELEGANT, TERROIR-DRIVEN WINES THAT AGE VERY REWARDINGLY

Dog with Ken Bernards; see ANCIEN WINES.) Two more Russian River Valley vineyards—Mil Vistas, 2.2 acres near the intersection of Coffee Lane and Occidental Road near Graton, planted in 1996 to UCD 4, Dijon 115, and an undocumented selection; and Gunsalus, a Green Valley site off Graton Road that was planted in 2001 to Dijon 115, 667, and 777—were added in 2007, along with a second Sonoma Coast wine from the Clary Ranch on Middle Rock Road in the Petaluma Gap that is often bathed in fog.

An average of 25 percent whole clusters is used, and the fermentors are 5-, 7.5-, and 8-foot in diameter, 3-and 5-ton jacketed stainless open-tops and some 1-ton fruit bins. Two to three days of 58 to 60°F "lukewarm" soaks with just a bit of sulfur dioxide precede inoculation with a quarter-strength dose of laboratory yeast. Using 25 percent of the recommended inoculum ensures that the commercial yeast population lags behind the resident yeasts until late in the fermentation, but that the fermentation still finishes. As soon as the fermentation has begun, the temperature in each fermentor is increased to between 93 and 95°F and then slowly decreased. The must is punched down quite vigorously at the beginning of the alcoholic fermentation, when the majority of extraction is aqueous rather than alcoholic; Rich then reduces the frequency of punchdowns as the fermentation continues and its temperature falls. A long postfermentation maceration follows, so that the total time from pick to press is twenty-eight to thirty-five days. Rich no longer separates the press fraction from the free-run juice except in very tannic years, having found that the press fraction's high pH made it difficult to manage independently, and because it makes "an important contribution in terms of aroma and texture."

After settling briefly in tank, the wine is barreled, using between 60 and 100 percent new wood. Dargaud & Jaeglé (and its special selection of three-year air-dried stave wood called Marcel Cadet) is Rich's favorite cooper, but he also uses some from Cadus, François Frères, and Remond. Malolactic starter from Matanzas Creek is added to each barrel. Barrel times range from fourteen to eighteen months. The wines are sometimes fined in naturally high-tannin years, or if clarity is a problem, but Rich does not filter if he can "sleep comfortably" with the wine unfiltered.

Talisman pinots are visually transparent, full-flavored, elegant, *terroir*-driven wines that typically finish around 14 percent alcohol. Each wine from each site is unique, and most age rewardingly.

TASTING NOTES

2004 *Thorn Ridge Vineyard (tasted in 2007):* Medium black-red; on the nose, a mini-concerto of spring flowers, nutty spice, and just-ripe berries; impressively fruity on the palate with some hard spice, merbromin, and barrel char; long and elegant, but also intense and sturdy, with the texture of heavy silk. Fine.

2004 *Ted's Vineyard (tasted in 2007):* Transparent, pretty, medium black-red; floral aromas overlay red berry fruit; clove and allspice on the palate; slightly sweet with intense, clean, finely focused flavors; some minerality on the finish; lingers pleasantly; very attractive.

2004 *Red Dog Vineyard (tasted in 2007):* Barely transparent, deep black-red; blackberry jam and Carborundum on the nose, with some high notes of citrus peel; sweet and earthy on the palate, with black licorice, huge minerality, and considerable grip. Not for the faint of heart, but serious, intense, and broad shouldered.

2004 *Wildcat Mountain Vineyard (tasted in 2007):* Evergreen and vanilla over black-red fruit; slightly sweet, with allspice and juniper berries; long with considerable grip, but an underlying texture of polished cotton.

2003 *Ted's Vineyard (tasted in 2007):* Light, rosy-mahogany; huge nose of nut shells, flower petals, and berry fruit; orange peel, leather, and some hints of evolution on the palate; intense flavors, but featherweight and satiny; beautiful, very elegant, and very fine. A personal favorite.

2001 *Thorn Ridge Vineyard (tasted several times in 2005, 2006, and 2007):* Brilliant, luminous magenta; once decanted; an explosive nose of red and black fruit, with hints of roasted cashews and hazelnuts; bright and rich on the mid-palate, with black tea and exotic Indonesian spice flavors; some peppery cherry from mid-palate to finish; most recently, also notes of furniture polish and sandalwood; velvety, elegant, and long; very fine. A personal favorite.

TALLEY VINEYARDS
Arroyo Grande, California

Oliver Talley began farming vegetables in the Arroyo Grande Valley soon after World War II. Three decades later, aware that vineyards had been developed in the nearby Edna and Santa Maria valleys, Oliver's son Don began to explore whether the hillsides above the family's vegetable fields could be successfully planted to wine grapes. In 1981 five quarter-acre test plots were set out with cabernet sauvignon, riesling, chardonnay, pinot noir, and sauvignon blanc. A quarter century later, although Talley Farms remains an important player in the field of specialty produce, and is especially known for the quality of its bell peppers, the vineyards are Don Talley's most impressive legacy (he passed away in 2006 at the age of 66) and his son Brian's major preoccupation.

Talley's estate grown chardonnays and pinot noirs command attention in all markets. The great majority of fruit is used in the estate wine program, but small amounts are sold to AU BON CLIMAT and Sinor-LaVallee. Talley's pinot noir plantings are divided now among three vineyards: Rincon, the site of Don Talley's original test plots; Rosemary's, about 1 mile west of Rincon, overlooking Talley Farms vegetable coolers; and Stone Corral, a 2001 planting in nearby Edna Valley.

Rincon has grown to 86 acres, of which 37 are pinot noir. The oldest pinot is 3.6 acres of vines on Rincon's West Hillside—a steep, south-facing slope planted 6 feet by 12 feet in east–west rows, originally planted as own-rooted sauvignon blanc in 1983 but grafted to UCD 2A in 1992. Just over 5 acres of pinot noir were planted on Rincon's East

Hillside between 1984 and 1986, similarly spaced but in north–south rows; again, the scion material was UCD 2A, and again the vines were mostly own-rooted. The Rincon vineyard is about 8 miles from the Pacific Coast and is routinely fog shrouded until midday; both hillsides consist of shallow, rocky, clay-loam soils. The West Hillside contains some subsurface limestone; the East Hill is underlain with fragmented sandstone. These two plantings at Rincon were the basis for Talley's first pinots, beginning in 1986. Planting resumed on the East Hillside of Rincon in 1999, 2000, and 2001, using a combination of UCD 2A selected from Rosemary's vineyard (see below) and Dijon clones 115, 667, and 777, this time on predominantly 101-14 rootstock.

Rosemary's is a slightly cooler site. The soil here is also underlain with fragmented sandstone, and the surface layer is mostly a rocky loam, weathered in place from the sandstone. Planting at Rosemary's began in 1987 on a northwest-facing slope and continued throughout the 1990s, wrapping around the hillside to southwest- and south-facing exposures. The first Rosemary's plantings were, like early Rincon, set out 6 feet by 12 feet, on a combination of their own roots and AxR1, but vine spacing was tightened to 8 feet by 4 feet in the 1990s. In 2000 there were about 17 acres of pinot noir at Rosemary's. As at Rincon, the 1990s plantings have been split between field-selected UCD 2A and Dijon clones.

Stone Corral is now home to 28 acres of Dijon 115, 667, and 777, plus scion material from Rosemary's, on three rootstocks. The vineyard is divided among five blocks, and each block is split evenly into thirds, with one of the thirds reserved for Talley Vineyards. (Talley custom-farms the other two thirds for STEPHEN ROSS WINE CELLARS and Kynsi Winery, respectively.)

Appropriately for an enterprise founded on farming, the rule at Talley is sustainable

Every year since 1993, Talley has made a vineyard-designated wine from one or more blocks of Rosemary's, the cooler of its two estate sites in the Arroyo Grande Valley. In most vintages, the vineyard-designated wine has been anchored with fruit from Blocks 5 and 6, which were the first blocks planted on this site in 1987 and 1988. (See below for the exceptions, which are 1999 and vintages after 2004.) The scion material was entirely UCD 2A, taken from Talley's earlier plantings around the Rincon Adobe. This vertical tasting was done before Talley's regular Thursday staff lunch, on an impeccably stunning December morning in 2006.

2004: Medium-deep, rosy-magenta color; slow to open; then notes of nut meats, nut shells, barrel char, and vanilla; rich, ripe, and creamy on the palate; intense and inky; some grip throughout; discernibly impacted by exceptionally hot late-season weather.

2003: Deep, rosy, black-red color; predominantly smoky and earthy nose, with floral highlights and hints of caramel; tremendous underlying black raspberry fruit; intense wine but less graceful than some earlier vintages.

2002: A darker and blacker aspect that the preceding vintages; intensely earthy nose, with menthol and conifer underbrush; brettanomyces at work but quite attractively; soft, rich, and earthy on the palate, with an unmistakable note of really good espresso. Uncharacteristic but impressive.

2001: Huge, explosive nose with a hint of reduction; rose petals, earth, and black raspberry; considerable licorice with some tar and boot polish in the mouth; elegant, racy, long, intense, and quite fine. Another personal favorite.

2000: Medium, very transparent black-red with ruby highlights; rose-petal, black raspberry, and smoky overtones; then sweet, rich, and soft on the palate; a crowd-pleasing pinot with consistent and persistent soft tannins throughout the mid-palate; just a bit of bite from a combination of tannin and alcohol at the end.

1999: Extremely low yields tempted Talley and Rasmussen to invert the usual ratio of vineyard-designated wine to estate wine, and to include not only Rosemary's blocks 5 and 6, but also fruit from blocks planted in 1995 and 1996. Deep, saturated ruby color; nose of cola, sarsaparilla, and earth; intense, dark berry fruit with hints of mocha on the palate; agreeable acidity gives the wine a lively mouth-feel; lean structure and a long finish.

1998: Medium-dark brick-red; very fragrant nose filled with rose petals, spring bulbs, and black raspberry, slightly evolved now with hints of truffle; extremely bright fruit, almost evoking cranberries; intense, persistent, and clean, with just a hint of something savory like ripe olives; long to finish and utterly enjoyable; a personal favorite.

viticulture that uses onsite compost and cover crops and that minimizes the use of pesticides. The vineyards are tended by a full-time, year-round labor force that is devoted entirely to grapes. Yields in both vineyards are managed to between 2 and 2.5 tons per acre.

WINES AND WINEMAKING NOTES
Until 1989, Talley made just one pinot noir in each vintage: an estate bottling derived entirely from Rincon Vineyard fruit. In 1990 Rosemary's fruit entered the estate wine. In 1993 Talley added vineyard-designated Rincon and Rosemary's wines

to the portfolio. These wines have gradually evolved into quasi–block selections: Rosemary's is made primarily from 2.6 acres of the oldest, northwest-facing rows on that site, whereas Rincon is anchored with fruit from the grafted, own-rooted sauvignon blanc vines on West Hillside. The first two vintages of Stone Corral fruit were used to make an Edna Valley wine, but a vineyard-designated wine from Stone Corral was added to the portfolio in 2004.

The pinots are mostly fermented in 1-ton, plastic-lined plywood bins, but the winery sometimes also uses a 6-ton or a 9-ton stainless steel open-top. Until 1995, 25 percent whole clusters was the rule; the approach in subsequent vintages has been less rigid, with whole clusters being used only for vineyard blocks where good stem lignification is observed. A four- to five-day cold soak precedes five days of alcoholic fermentation at 85 to 92°F, relying entirely on resident yeast. Punchdowns are done by hand twice daily. The must is pressed when it is dry or just before, and the juice is settled overnight before being barreled. Malolactic fermentation takes place in barrel without inoculation. The entire barrel room is cold stabilized for one month each winter. Pinots spend fifteen to eighteen months in barrel, and are racked once during the spring or summer after the vintage. Barrels were all François Frères until 1999, mostly medium- or heavy-toast staves from the Allier and Vosges forests, but Talley has now begun to source some barrels from other coopers on an experimental basis, and he uses just 35 to 40 percent new oak.

For the first twenty years, Talley's winemaker was Steve Rasmussen. Rasmussen was succeeded in January 2007 by Leslie Mead, a University of Michigan graduate in aquatic resources who worked at Bonny Doon before joining Talley as enologist and assistant winemaker.

Talley pinots are ripe, deeply colored, intensely flavored, and richly textured wines, emphasizing black rather than red fruit characteristics that belie the vineyards' reliance on UCD 2A. In my experience, the wines age well, with the 1991s showing especially well ca. 2002.

TASTING NOTES

2005 *Arroyo Grande Valley Estate (tasted in 2007):* Brilliant medium ruby color; expressive nose of red fruit, rose petals, and smoke; peppery fruit cocktail on the palate with some orange peel; satiny attack and some grip on the back palate; noticeable barrel marking; bright overall.

2005 *Rincon Vineyard (tasted in 2007):* Deep, rich black-red; aromas of black fruit, mesquite, and tar; blueberry-blackberry on the palate; intense and slightly fruit-sweet, with dusty tannins; soft, warm, and peppery at the end.

2005 *Stone Corral Vineyard (tasted in 2007):* Very dark, purplish black-red; dark fruit and wet-slate aromas with some barrel-derived vanilla; rich, mouth coating, and slightly sweet on the palate; smooth at mid-palate but not silky; dense, arguably monochromatic, and quite grippy at the end. Much of this profile is site-driven; many of the same properties are also displayed in the Stephen Ross wines from this vineyard.

TANDEM WINERY
Sebastopol, California

Two Gregs, La Follette and Bjornstad, with intersecting careers and continuous association beginning when they worked

together at FLOWERS VINEYARD AND
WINERY from 1997 to 1999, founded
Tandem Winery in a repurposed fruit-
processing plant on the Gravenstein
Highway north of Sebastopol just
before the harvest in 2000. La Follette
is a Davis-trained winemaker with
a background in biochemistry, who
built a stellar reputation with pinot
at (sequentially) LA CREMA WINERY,
HARTFORD FAMILY WINES (where,
along with Dan Goldfield and Susan
Doyle, he was a founding winemaker),
and Flowers. Bjornstad is a viticulturist
and winemaker initially trained at
Colorado State University in agronomy,
with subsequent experience at Newton
Vineyard and Joseph Phelps Winery
in Napa. In addition to Tandem, to
make the small business viable, the two
Gregs also operated Greg & Greg Inc.,
a custom-crush operation that made
the first vintages for many labels that

have since established independent track
records, including HALLECK VINEYARD,
SCOTT PAUL WINES, DUNAH,
MACPHAIL, and LONDER. La Follette
calls this Tandem's "catch-and-release"
program. (Greg & Greg was sold to John
Tracy, a laser engineer with two wine
brands of his own, in 2004.)

The first Tandem pinot, in 2000,
was made using grapes from the highly
regarded PISONI VINEYARD in the Santa
Lucia Highlands and was vinted at Laird
Estate in the Napa Valley. Pinots from
the Van der Kamp Vineyard on Sonoma
Mountain, Keefer Ranch in Green Valley,
Ross and Jennifer Halleck's one-acre
vineyard in the Sebastopol Hills, and
the Sangiacomo family's 1998 planting
on Roberts Road in the Sonoma Coast
AVA, all followed in 2001. The Van der
Kamp and Sangiacomo bottlings have
been made in every vintage since, but
the Pisoni was discontinued after 2001,

the Halleck after 2002, and the Keefer after 2004.

To replace these sources, a Silver Pines Vineyard wine was produced in 2004 and 2005; a Hellenthal (see W. H. SMITH WINES) Vineyard bottling on a one-time basis in 2004; and a Chris Lee Vineyard wine, sourced from a vineyard near Van der Kamp on the north slope of Sonoma Mountain, on a one-time basis in 2005. A special cuvée called Auction Block (a blend of the best barrels in the Tandem cellar), destined primarily for donation to various charity auctions, was also made in tiny quantities from 2002 to 2004, and in slightly larger volume in 2005. Fruit from EMERITUS Vineyards' Hallberg site anchored the Auction Block wine for its first two years; thereafter, it tended to rely more on the Sangiacomo parcel, Silver Pines, and Van der Kamp, with "bits" of other wines added in.

Bjornstad exited the management of Tandem in 2005 to start his own label, Bjornstad Cellars, focused in pinot and chardonnay, using some of the same fruit sources the Gregs used at Tandem. He remains a partner in Tandem.

WINEMAKING NOTES AND WINES

La Follette is an eloquent and passionate champion of California pinot, whose discourse combines wine chemistry and poetry. He explains picking decisions as a "dialogue with the vines" that requires "learning to see flavors." Visual measures of the fruit's ripeness include how much of the berry flesh sticks to the stem when the latter is pulled away, how firm and crunchy the seeds seem when crunched in the mouth, whether the shoot tips are becoming "crispy," and whether the skins have begun to yield color easily. But La Follette also admits to shifting, as he "gets older," to slightly earlier and

less-ripe picking protocols. Interestingly, however, when Tandem pinot numbers (including Brix at picking) are compared across all vintages from 2000 through 2005 and across all vineyards, the wines are astonishingly consistent. Of the twenty-six

---

LA FOLLETTE EXPLAINS PICKING DECISIONS AS A "DIALOGUE" WITH THE VINES AND "LEARNING TO SEE FLAVORS"

Tandem wines made in this period, only four were picked at or above 25 Brix, while nine wines were picked below 24 Brix, and 13 were in the middle. Final wine chemistries also varied in a very narrow range, with total acidities generally between 6.4 and 7.3 grams per liter, virtually undetectable residual sugar, and finished alcohol levels between 14 and 14.5 percent.

Essentially all fermentations are executed with resident yeasts, in jacketed stainless steel open-tops, following long cold soaks lasting up to ten days, and using dry ice to maintain anerobic conditions. La Follette believes that a wine's aromatic signature depends in large measure on compounds created by yeasts that are about to die. Since resident yeast populations always consist of multiple organisms, it follows that resident yeast fermentations generally produce more complex and distinctive aromas than yeast inoculations that depend on a single strain of sacchromyces. Tandem musts are always hand plunged, fermented relatively warm, basket pressed before dryness, and sent to barrel without settling. The new wines are raised on the gross lees for at least nine to ten months before bottling, and some vintages of some wines are kept in wood for as long as sixteen months, but in this case they are racked off their gross lees before the following harvest. With the exception of the two Halleck wines and the 2001 edition of Pisoni, new wood has been a minority player in Tandem's cellar, with most wines raised in 25 to 33 percent new oak, drawn from many cooperages. (The Van der Kamp has usually relied primarily on François Frères barrels, however.) Most Tandem wines are neither fined nor filtered.

Although Tandem typically makes only about 1,300 cases of pinot, it also turns out twice that amount of an unusual and quite delicious pinot-based blend called Peloton that generally includes (in addition to the pinot) some sangiovese, chardonnay, and sometimes even a whiff of gewürztraminer! These are very serious, *terroir*-driven wines, but they are also ripe and large-framed.

TASTING NOTES

2005 *Sangiacomo Vineyard (tasted in 2007)*: Brilliant black-red; strongly floral nose; then, meaty, rich, and soft on the palate, with a long, elegant, and rewarding finish.

2005 *Silver Pines Vineyard (tasted in 2007)*: Transparent, medium black-red; aromas of orange peel and boot polish; infused flowers, subordinated fruit, and a substantial load of very fine-grained tannins.

TANTARA WINERY
Santa Maria, California

The story of William Cates and Jeffrey Fink is another instance of unlikely individuals eventually being attracted into the orbit of fine wine. Cates's roots were in cameras, free-lance photography, political activism, and the professional theater. In the 1970s, he "dropped out" and became a grower of American hybrid grapes near Roanoke, Virginia. Fink, initially a musician who later became an architect, met Cates around 1980 when he dated Cates's daughter. Both remember late-evening conversations about great red Burgundies, although Fink's first wine "epiphany" was Robert Mondavi's 1974 cabernet sauvignon; he also remembers having become excited about 1970s pinots from MOUNT EDEN VINEYARDS and CHALONE VINEYARD before he had tasted Burgundies.

After Fink moved to California in 1984, he hung around the edges of wine, frequenting the annual Masters of Food and Wine in Carmel. He befriended pinot makers. In 1992, as a home winemaker, he made a vintage of Russian River Valley pinot from grapes sourced via Burt Williams. In 1994 he "hooked up with" Bryan Babcock and became linked to grapes grown at LAETITIA VINEYARD and at Bien Nacido on the Tepusquet Bench. Jeff Wilkes, then Bien Nacido's director of grape sales, showed Fink a crumbling shed on the ranch. "You are an architect," he said, "maybe you could do something with this building." So with 4 tons of pinot and 2 of chardonnay, fifteen barrels, a handful of essential equipment, and borrowed space at Laetitia while the shed at Bien Nacido was being rebuilt, Cates's and Fink's partnership to make "the very finest" Central Coast pinot and chardonnay they could manage began.

The project was named Tantara, for a filly Cates had owned in Virginia that had lived to an unexpectedly ripe old age. The partners made 250 cases of pinot from Bien Nacido's N Block in 1997 and somewhat larger quantities (from Block G) in each of the years that followed. By 2002 the wines had infiltrated award-winning restaurants' lists in New York, Boston, Atlanta, San Francisco, and Los Angeles. By 2005 Tantara had increased production to about 5,000 cases of pinot, mostly of it vineyard-designated, sourced from a passel of distinguished vineyards in the Santa Rita Hills, Santa Maria Valley, and Santa Lucia Highlands, and from their own custom-planted block at Bien Nacido— 10 acres of UCD 2A, plus Dijon 115, 667, and 777, set out in 1998.

WINES AND WINEMAKING NOTES

The inaugural releases, in 1997, were the aforementioned Bien Nacido bottling and a La Colline cuvée from Laetitia. Beginning in 1998, in addition to the Bien Nacido and La Colline bottlings, there was also a vineyard-designated wine from Gary Pisoni's eponymous vineyard in the Santa Lucia Highlands. In 2000 bottlings from DIERBERG VINEYARD and from Garys' Vineyard debuted, followed by a special Bien Nacido blend (from what Tantara calls the Adobe, Pentagon, Corral, and River's Edge blocks) and a Solomon Hills wine in 2002. A Rio Vista wine and another special Bien Nacido cuvée called Evelyn (sourced mostly from a 1996 planting called Block 1) were added in 2003. Since 1999, barrels of Dierberg, Solomon Hills, and Bien Nacido that were deemed "atypical of the vineyard" have been declassified into a Santa Maria Valley cuvée.

Fink says picking is "based on sampling" and usually occurs at Brix levels between 24 and 26, but is "discussed a lot," and increasingly occurs a bit less ripe that it did in the first vintages. Fruit is rigorously sorted to remove "anything funky," and 15 to 20 percent of it is retained as whole clusters. Fermentations are done in 3- and 1.5-ton tanks and half-ton fruit bins, and start with resident yeast. Whole-cluster lots are foot-trodden; destemmed fruit is hand-plunged. Water is added when necessary to compensate for high sugars at picking; occasional acid additions are also made, and the must is pressed "before the cap falls." This means there is no extended maceration by design, but sometimes extended maceration in fact.

The barrel program relies primarily on François Frères, Rousseau (Fink and Cates are "impressed with its flavor"), and Remond, with lesser use of Marsannay and Dargaud & Jaeglé; about 40 percent of barrels are new in each vintage, although the percentage of new wood varies from wine to wine. The new wines are racked once after the malolactic fermentation has completed and spend a total of fourteen to eighteen months in barrel. There is no fining or filtration, but the partners are "acutely sensitive" to brettanomyces, which is attacked when detected.

Makers who come to pinot through red Burgundy, as many do, derive different lessons from Burgundian exemplars. Cates and Fink are plainly Burgundy connoisseurs, and not unhappy occasionally to describe a Tantara wine as "Burgundian," but even the Tantara wines they are tempted to compare with Burgundies are riper picked, fleshier, and warmer than all but the most exceptional of Burgundian vintages. In the stylistic space of American pinot, however, Tantara wines are comparatively restrained and graceful.

TASTING NOTES

2002 *Pisoni Vineyard (tasted in 2006):* Transparent, dark black-red; hugely spicy nose with a floral underlay; cinnamon, clove, nuts, and cocoa power on the palate; sweet and substantial.

2002 *Bien Nacido (tasted in 2006):* Slightly lighter hued than the Pisoni; opens with an impressive whiff of signature (Bien Nacido) black pepper over cherry-plum fruit; mostly red fruit flavors on the palate, with some clove and licorice; full bodied with a bit of grip, but an almost satiny finish.

2002 *Bien Nacido Adobe Cuvée (tasted in 2006):* Red fruit aromas with very distinctive "cool" notes of mint and evergreen; earth, cedar, and exotic spice on the palate; medium in weight and very slightly chewy, but still silky and long.

1997 *Bien Nacido (tasted in 2006):* Saturated, medium-dark black-red with a hint of terra cotta; mostly secondary aromatics of evergreen, toasted cinnamon, resin, and tobacco; intense mocha with some clove in the mouth; slightly sweet, medium long, and satiny; elegant.

TAZ VINEYARDS
Templeton, California

The story of TAZ Vineyards begins with Chuck Ortman, and the story's first chapter is found in the profile for Ortman Family Wines. When Ortman sold his Meridian brand to Wine World Estates (which later became Beringer Blass Wine Estates, Foster's Wine Estates, and finally Foster's America), Robert Steinhauer, a native son of California's Central Valley and Beringer's vice president for grower relations and viticulture, assumed responsibility for acquiring, developing, and managing a collection of large Santa Barbara County vineyards to feed the thirsty Meridian label. Chief among these were Cat Canyon, near Los Olivos, North Canyon in the Cuyama River valley, and White Hills and Fiddlestix in the Santa Rita Hills.

In 2001, convinced that some parts of these sites were producing fruit that was "too good" for Meridian, Foster's created TAZ as a luxury, "reserve quality" edition of Meridian, focused on chardonnay, syrah, pinot gris, and pinot noir, and entitled to cherry-pick the best blocks from the best vineyards for its programs. The new brand's name is Steinhauer's nickname, short for Tasmanian devil, which is the image Steinhauer is said to have evoked when he sped through Central Coast vineyards, his energy and enthusiasm leaving a cloud of dust in their wake. The first winemaker was Jon Priest (see ETUDE WINES), who made the 2002 and 2003 vintages and picked the 2004. Natasha Boffman, who holds a master's degree in enology from the University of California Davis and previously worked at Meridian, succeeded Priest in time to finish the 2004 wines and make the 2005s from scratch. The first vintages were made at Central Coast Wine Services in Santa Maria, but the brand has enjoyed dedicated space in Templeton since 2006.

WINES AND WINEMAKING NOTES
TAZ's pinot program is based on fruit from 1995 through 1999 plantings of Dijon 113, 115, 667, and 777 in North Canyon, and from a combination of Dijon clones, Swan selection, and UCD 4 at Fiddlestix. (See FIDDLEHEAD CELLARS for more information about the Fiddlestix Vineyard). In 2002 a vineyard-designate was made from part of the Fiddlestix fruit, and a Santa Barbara County wine was crafted from additional Fiddlestix fruit and grapes from North Canyon. In 2003 a third pinot, called Cuyama River, which was a barrel selection of the best barrels from North Canyon, was added to the portfolio. All

three wines have continued in subsequent vintages. Generally, the fruit from North Canyon, reflecting the overall profile of the Santa Maria Valley, is red-fruit dominated and perfumed, while Fiddlestix exhibits the dark fruit, high tannin, and high acid that characterize wines from the Sta. Rita Hills.

Winemaking generally follows the typical consensus protocol for pinot, although a few lots are made in relatively large, 8- and 10-ton open-top tanks, and only the first lots in each vintage are inoculated—others finish on the strength of resident yeast. Boffman explains that some lots from Fiddlestix are pressed before they go completely dry in an effort to help manage their strong tannins, but most lots are pressed at dryness. The Santa Barbara wine is raised in about 35 percent new wood, the Cuyama River in 40 percent, and the Fiddlestix in 50 percent—all for about eleven months. The barrel stock is mostly François Fréres, Remond, and Damy, with some "in house" cooperage. All wines are filtered before bottling. These are big, fleshy, flashy, fruit-forward wines in the mainstream California style.

TASTING NOTES

2005 *Fiddlestix (tasted in 2007):*
Medium-deep black-red; huge nose of ripe fruit, fresh flowers, and tobacco; cherry dominated, very fruit-sweet, creamy, and mouth coating on the palate; considerable soft tannin from mid-palate to finish; approachable by all comers.

2004 *Cuyama River (tasted in 2007):*
Dark, barely transparent black-red; smoke and vanilla aromas, with a floral note; rich, very ripe, sweet, and almost chewy, with abundant Italian plum, dark cherry, and some infused violets; more smoke and vanilla on the palate; heady, large-framed, and fleshy.

TESTAROSSA VINEYARDS
Los Gatos, California

First, Rob and Diana Jensen planted a 25-vine mini-vineyard in the yard of their Sunnyvale home and made wine in the garage. Then they attempted to restore an overgrown vineyard in the Santa Cruz Mountains but were defeated by a combination of poison oak and hungry birds. Finally, in 1993, the two electrical engineers created Testarossa Vineyards on a shoestring. In 1994 the sale of stock in Mountain View–based Veritas Software, which was Rob Jensen's day job; a second mortgage on their primary residence; and a second mortgage on Rob's parents' house combined to generate sufficient cash to finance the purchase of a few tons of chardonnay and enough pinot noir for about 40 cases of wine—from no less a source than the CHALONE VINEYARD— plus barrels, bottles, and other essential winemaking paraphernalia. Diana retired from her Silicon Valley day job to manage Testarossa's affairs, and George Troquato was engaged to make the wines, on a custom-crush basis, at the Cinnabar Winery in Saratoga.

No pinot noir was released from the 1995 vintage, but the program recommenced in 1996, again with fruit from Chalone. In 1997 the Jensens were able to purchase pinot grapes from Robb Talbott's Sleepy Hollow Vineyard and Gary Pisoni's eponymous vineyard, both in the Santa Lucia Highlands, as well as from Bien Nacido's Block T in Santa Maria, bringing their total output of pinot noir to a commercially visible level. Since that point, vineyard sources have diversified considerably across Santa Lucia Highlands and Santa Barbara County sites, and to Sonoma County. Garys' Vineyard and Rosella's Vineyard (see ROAR WINES) joined the portfolio in 1999 and 2000, respectively; Sanford & Benedict in 2004; Brosseau (in the Chalone appellation but not owned by Chalone; see below) in 2002; the Graham Family Vineyard in the Green Valley appellation (see AUGUST WEST WINES) in 2004; and La Cruz Vineyard (see KELLER ESTATE) in 2004. At Bien Nacido, the block sources shifted from Block T to Block 1, a younger planting farther uphill where the soils belong to the Elder series of shale-y clay-loam. Michael Michaud's Chalone appellation vineyard was used briefly for vineyard designated wine, as was Clos Pepe in the Sta. Rita Hills. Other sources, never vineyard designated, came and went. The brand's heart may remain in the Santa Lucia Highlands, however, even as Jensen looks for "new hidden gems" elsewhere; Jensen argues that Santa Lucia Highlands "has the potential to be the best pinot noir growing area in the country."

In 1999 Ed Kurzman succeeded Troquato as Testarossa's winemaker. When Kurzman departed after the 2002 harvest, assistant winemaker Bill Brosseau, an enologist trained at the University of California Davis, whose family has long farmed a small vineyard in the Chalone appellation, was named to replace him. Brosseau's hands-on familiarity with grape farming, derived from experience with his family's vineyard, has been an enormous asset as Testarossa has worked to fine-tune its array of vineyard-designated offerings. He has also been responsible for cellar-based improvements, including a two-stage hand sorting of all incoming fruit, the extensive use of dry ice during the prefermentation cold soak, and reengineering of the way wine moves

through spaces in the old Novitiate Winery in Los Gatos, to which production moved after 1997.

WINES AND WINEMAKING NOTES

The raison d'être of Testarossa's pinot program is vineyard-designated wines from most of its source vineyards, although a few vineyards are sourced solely for use in its blended wine, called Palazzio, made since 2000. The single-vineyard wines may be made in lots as small as 50 cases, but lots of 200 to 500 cases are more typical. Palazzio is made largely from lots that, according to Jensen, display less site-based typicality than the barrels selected for vineyard-designation, plus the above-mentioned sites that are sourced expressly for it. Since Palazzio now accounts for more than half of Testarossa's total pinot production and stands almost alone in general distribution, the single-vineyard wines are almost entirely limited to direct sales to mailing list and Internet customers, and visitors to the downtown Los Gatos tasting room. There is also a reserve wine called Cuvée Niclaire, made from the "very best barrels" in the cellar. Lesser and lighter barrels are bottled under a second label called Novitiate, named for the facility where Testarossa has been produced since 1997. In 2007 there were nine vineyard designated wines: from Bien Nacido, Sanford & Benedict, Garys', Rosella's, Pisoni, Sleepy Hollow, Brosseau, Graham Family, and La Cruz.

Testarossa picks fruit "when it tastes ripe," which is rarely below 24.5 Brix and may be above 26. Fermentors are an assortment of 1-, 3-, 5-, 8-, and 10-ton stainless steel open-tops, with the 5-ton size a favorite. The fermentors were custom made so that only the bottom 4 feet of each is jacketed, enabling the winemakers to keep the juice cool even as the cap temperature is allowed to rise. Fruit-bins are used for overflow lots. The clusters are usually destemmed completely, and then cold-soaked with dry ice for three to five days. Pectinase is used to increase color extraction. Punchdowns are done several times daily, although Brosseau will reduce the frequency if he feels too much tannin is being extracted. The must is pressed when it goes dry.

Testarossa uses between 50 and 70 percent new barrels, but the percentage of new barrels used for any particular wine is adjusted after the first racking, based on taste. François Frères accounts for half of the barrel stock; Remond and Cadus are also used in substantial quantity. Malolactic

---

RIPE, CONCENTRATED
TEXTURE-DRIVEN WINES
RAISED IN A GENEROUS
PERCENTAGE OF NEW OAK

---

bacteria are introduced either in tank or in barrel. The first racking is done between February and April after the vintage; the second is done just prior to bottling. Testarossa's Palazzio wine (see below) is bottled after ten or eleven months in wood; the other pinots are held until after the following vintage. There is no fining or filtration.

Testarossa pinots fall firmly in the relatively late-picked, very ripe, texture-driven category, with strong barrel marking, but the fruit sources are impeccable and the wines take frequent awards in comparative tasting environments. In the 2005 vintage, I especially liked the single-vineyard wine from the La Cruz Vineyard, which seemed atypically bright and elegant.

TASTING NOTES

2005 *Palazzio (tasted in* 2007*):* Medium rosy-black-red; aromas of earth and dusty fruit; sweet, attractive attack; explosive red fruit, peppery spice, and an aftertaste of savory herbs; medium in weight, with good length and a warm finish.

2005 *Rosella's Vineyard (tasted in* 2007*):* Brilliant, medium garnet; predominantly earthy nose, with some citrus peel and herb notes; rich, sweet, and ripe fruit on the palate, wrapped with soft spice and orange peel; grippy and warm on the finish, but silky overall.

2005 *Sanford & Benedict Vineyard (tasted in* 2007*):* Brilliant, light-to-medium rosy-garnet; surprisingly evolved and leathery nose with a hint of custard; raspberries and Queen Anne cherries on the palate; sweet and ripe, but also quite lightly built; almost creamy; noticeably barrel marked.

2005 *Garys' Vineyard (tasted in* 2007*):* Very transparent, medium black-red; clean floral and ripe, red berry nose; bright and slightly resinous berry flavors in the mouth, with some wet earth underneath; a bit of pepper and soft spice; almost mouth coating, and medium in weight; fairly warm at the end.

2005 *Pisoni Vineyard (tasted in* 2007*):* Medium garnet; strong aromas of conifer, winter mint, and lavender; exotic flavors marked by infused flowers, butterscotch, and fennel, plus some earthiness; creamy at mid-palate, then mouth coating and long; tends to finish warm, but compares elegantly with some other wines from this vineyard.

2005 *La Cruz Vineyard (tasted in* 2007*):* Transparent, medium black-red; subtle, attractive evergreen and earth aromas; very intense cherry candy on the palate, followed by earth and licorice; then slightly grippy with very fine-grained tannins; remains bright through to the finish; medium long, medium in weight, and elegant.

THOMAS FOGARTY WINERY
Woodside, California

In the 1970s, Thomas J. Fogarty was a Stanford University professor, cardiovascular surgeon, tireless inventor of medical devices, and home winemaker. Late in the decade, his home winemaking turned serious. He planted grapes on a 320-acre parcel of mountainous land overlooking the Stanford campus and San Francisco Bay; hired Michael Martella, who had trained at California State University Fresno, to make his wines "professionally"; and built a commercial winery to replace the cabin he had used for his personal efforts. The Thomas Fogarty Winery was bonded in 1981.

The winery describes pinot noir as its flagship wine, although it accounts for only 20 percent of total production. In 1983 Martella and Fogarty planted 2 acres of pinot on a knoll adjacent to the winery building, at an elevation of 1,950 feet, which is now called the Sky Vineyard. Another 5-acre site, called the Rapley Trail Vineyard, was planted downhill from the winery in 1984, at about 1,750 feet. In 2006 2 acres of the estate's Razorback Vineyard, planted in 1985 to chardonnay, sangiovese, and merlot, were grafted to pinot. All these sites are cold and ripen relatively late. Early October is considered an early harvest for Sky, mid-October picks are normal, and some picks have extended into November. Rapley Trail can be picked about two weeks earlier. The soils are relatively thin, sandy loams strewn with shale and fractured sandstone; the vineyards face mostly southeast, except that Razorback, between 1,525 and 1,600 feet,

faces due east. Vines are planted 6 feet by 10 feet and minimally irrigated. (Martella does not irrigate the deeper soils toward the bottom of the vineyard at all, but the top of the hill requires some water.) After some experimentation with training and trellising configurations to deal with the sites' relatively high vigor, the property now relies on modified bilateral vertical-shoot-positioning, which has driven the yield down from 3 tons per acre to 2 tons, and improved both quality and color.

The plant material for the Sky Vineyard was sourced from DAVID BRUCE'S original vineyard nearby; its upstream source could be Mount Eden or just an unintentional field blend of UCD 4 and 13. The scion material for Rapley Trail came from the Winery Lake Vineyard in Carneros; its upstream source was probably one of Louis Martini's experimental plantings. The grafting at Razorback has been done with Swan selection and three Dijon clones.

Although the estate vineyard has been the heart of Fogarty's pinot program since it came onstream in 1989, a small amount of pinot is purchased from neighboring vineyards in the Santa Cruz Mountains appellation, and some of this is occasionally vineyard-designated. (In 2005, for example, Fogarty made 150 cases of Schultze Family Vineyard pinot; see WINDY OAKS ESTATE.) Also in 2005, a vineyard-designated pinot from the Michaud Vineyard in the Chalone appellation was added to the Fogarty portfolio, and this program is expected to continue. Before 1989, Fogarty pinots were a different beast entirely, having been sourced from the Winery Lake Vineyard in Los Carneros.

WINES AND WINEMAKING NOTES
Martella and associate winemaker Nathan Kandler tend to pick pinot noir over

an eight- to ten-day period when it has reached 24 to 25 Brix. (At lower sugars, the site has a tendency to throw fruit that tastes slightly herbaceous, so lower-Brix picks have been largely abandoned.) Ten to 20 percent of fruit is retained as whole clusters; the balance is destemmed but not crushed. A combination of 500- and 700-gallon stainless steel tanks measuring 4 feet high are used for fermentation. The fruit macerates cold for five to seven days. The must is usually inoculated to start the alcoholic fermentation, although Martella and Kandler are currently experimenting with resident-yeast fermentations. The fermentation temperatures are allowed to peak at 90°F, and cap management involves a combination of drain-and-return and punchdowns. Pressing generally occurs before the must is completely dry, or after about five to seven days of active fermentation. Lightening of the skins, as fermentation leaches the anthocyanins into the must, is one indication that the time to press has arrived, but the main indicator is the pure and simple taste of the juice. Malolactic starter is added in barrel after the wine is completely dry.

The use of new wood ranges from 25 to 85 percent depending on the lot and the vintage, and most of the barrel stock consists of *pièces* coopered from Allier stave wood that has been air dried for three years. Barrels are sourced from a wide assortment of coopers, including François Frères, Remond, Dargaud & Jaeglé, Marcel Cadet, Sirugue, Cadus, and Damy. Barrel times range from ten to eighteen months. Generally, there is no fining or filtration.

There are usually at least two finished pinots in each vintage: an estate wine and a Santa Cruz Mountains bottling, but in 2002 and 2004 a vineyard-designated wine was made from the Rapley Trail Vineyard along with a block-designated wine from

Rapley's Block B. Only a single estate wine was made in 2005, owing to a very short crop. Fogarty pinots are big, dark, structured wines that are often marked with flavors of both vanilla and chocolate. Alcohols now tend to top 14 percent, but good acidity keeps the wines in balance. Tannins are usually omnipresent and firm. The winery's long prerelease bottle aging regimen helps to soften the tannins, but consumers will be rewarded if they cellar for an additional few years. The 2004 Rapley Trail may be the most successful wine I have tasted to date from this estate.

TASTING NOTES

2004 *Rapley Trail Vineyard (tasted in 2007):* Transparent, dark ruby; aromas of roasted nuts, pencil lead, and dark fruit with minerality; more black fruit than red on the palate, intensely structured, and substantially tannic; Gevrey-like.

2004 *Rapley Trail Vineyard Block B (tasted in 2007):* Very dark ruby-magenta; sweet, slightly unctuous, creamy attack; dark fruit base with highlights of cranberry; a huge wine that is slightly peppery and borderline hot; big and ripe picked; promising; needs time.

TOLOSA WINERY
San Luis Obispo, California

In the beginning, in 1990, there was Edna Ranch Vineyards, a very large aggregation of existing vineyards and new plantings totaling about 2,600 acres of chardonnay and pinot noir, plus small blocks of syrah, merlot, and sauvignon blanc, in the heart of Edna Valley. The principals were Bob

Schiebelhut, a San Luis Obispo attorney and part-time winemaker—mentored in the 1980s by Romeo Zuech of Piedra Creek Winery—and Jim Efird, a local viticultural pioneer, who is credited with having planted or managed most of Edna Valley's vineyards. Efird is also the general manager of Pacific Vineyard Company, the vineyard services arm of Paragon Vineyard Company. Then there was Courtside Cellars, a custom-crush service company, situated on the northernmost of Edna Ranch's five vineyard sites, almost within eyeshot of San Luis Obispo's tiny airport, involving mostly the same investors.

In 1998 Tolosa Winery was born as one of Courtside's custom-crush clients, using fruit from Edna Ranch, producing tiny quantities of chardonnay and pinot noir. By 2006 Tolosa had exploded to more than 25,000 cases, of which about 11,000 were pinot noir, consuming about 10 percent of Edna Ranch's total crop. A handsome tasting room on the Courtside Cellars site gave an attractive face to the brand. (Other fruit clients of Edna Ranch include EDNA VALLEY VINEYARD, WILD HORSE WINERY, and STEPHEN ROSS WINES, and a good deal of the wine made at Courtside is bulked out.) Most of the Tolosa pinot comes from sites near Alban and Chamisal, and the scion material is mostly UCD 4; Dijon 115 and 667, with lesser amounts of Dijon 113, 114, and 777 and UCD 2A and 23. From this Tolosa makes a so-called Central Coast wine, which is all estate fruit despite its name, chosen for "prettiness" and early drinking potential; an "estate" wine with more structure; and (since 1999) a dribble of 1772, a selection of the cellar's best barrels, which is available only to Tolosa's wine club and a few California restaurants. In 2006, 1772 was joined at the top of the pyramid by Beyond, a block-designated wine (from Block 597 at Edna Ranch) based entirely on UCD 2A.

Ed Felice was Tolosa's winemaker from 1999 through 2004, when he was succeeded by Nathan Carlson, who had worked previously at LANGE in Oregon. Larry Brooks, the respected founding winemaker at ACACIA, has been involved since the beginning, and became Tolosa's "senior" winemaker in 2005. Tolosa's are attractive wines overall, with nice polish and restraint, although the 1772 was plainly selected to feature especially ripe-picked fruit.

TASTING NOTES

2006 *Beyond (tasted prerelease in 2008):* Visually brilliant and aromatically intense; bayberry and cinnamon aromas from a partial whole-cluster fermentation; intensely fruity on the plate, with savory notes, orange peel, and cigar wrapper; a very successful wine.

2005 *Central Coast (tasted in 2007):* Transparent, light-to-medium garnet; dusty, talc-ish, floral nose with some red berry fruit; full, intense, peppery-fruit palate; with some barrel marking, a silky texture, and a warm finish; attractive overall.

2005 *Edna Ranch Estate (tasted in 2007):* Transparent, medium garnet, a shade darker than the Central Coast wine; dusty, slightly minerally, and granitic on the nose; intense, inky, vinous, and grippy on the palate; core flavors are dark cherry and plum skin, with a hint of dried leaves; more mouth-weight than the Central Coast; good acid and length.

2005 *Edna Ranch 1772 (tasted in 2007):* Medium ruby; considerable very ripe fruit on the nose; rich and ripe on the palate, too, with some milk chocolate, espresso, cherries jubilee, and barrel-derived vanilla; slightly sweet; texture of rough silk; finishes warm with a bit of grip.

TORII MOR WINERY
Dundee, Oregon

In the mid 1980s, Donald R. Olson, a Stanford University–trained pediatric neurologist, purchased the Dundee Hills vineyard Jim McDaniel had planted in 1972. McDaniel's planting, a bit more than 5 acres of own-rooted UCD 2A and 5, laid out in 9-foot rows with 6 feet between vines, around the 800-foot contour, was one of the first dozen plantings in an appellation that has since mushroomed to more than 2,000 planted acres. Olson sold the grapes until 1993, when he launched Torii Mor Winery, an unlikely name he says he "invented," reportedly from a combination of Japanese and Scandinavian "roots," intended as a "way of saying *terroir.*" A decade and a half later, only 5 percent of Torii Mor's production comes from original vineyard, now called Olson Estate; the balance is purchased from two other Dundee Hills sites, Bella Vida near Maresh and La Colina overlooking Lafayette, and from almost a dozen sites located variously on the north face of the Chehalem Mountains, in the Eola Hills, in Yamhill-Carlton, and in the Umpqua Valley. Quite a few of these have been made over the years as vineyard-designated wines, but many have also fed one or more blends.

In 2005 the main release was a Willamette Valley blend, built from nearly all of the brand's vineyard sources; two "reserve" wines called Deux Verres and La Cuillière, the latter available only to members of the winery's club; and vineyard-designated wines from Anden, the lower part of the Seven Springs Vineyard in the Eola Hills; Hawks View, a Chehalem Mountains site that is used by several Oregon wineries

and SIDURI WINES; the aforementioned La Colina; Temperance Hill Vineyard just north of Bethel Heights; Shea Vineyard in Yamhill-Carlton; Olalla near the town of Winston in the Umpqua Valley; and Olson, the estate vineyard. In 2006 the Anden and Shea bottlings were discontinued, but two appellation wines were added to the portfolio, one from the Dundee Hills and the other from the Eola-Amity Hills.

Torii Mor has had a revolving-door of winemakers in its relatively short existence, including Bob McRitchie, who had previously worked at SOKOL BLOSSER; Patricia Green; Kelley Fox, who went on to EYRIE and then to SCOTT PAUL; Joe Dobbes, an ELK COVE and WILLAMETTE VALLEY VINEYARDS veteran, who subsequently founded Dobbes Family Estate; Ryan Harms, now the winemaker at REX HILL; and finally, since 2005, Jacques Tardy. Tardy is that rarity in American pinot: a true Burgundian from Nuits-Saint-Georges in the Côte d'Or, now with considerable experience in both California and Oregon, who was the winemaker at Montinore Estate near Forest Grove from 1992 to 2005.

WINEMAKING NOTES
At Torii Mor, Tardy's winemaking involves complete destemming, although some use of whole clusters is being considered for 2007; resident yeast fermentations; enzyme and tannin additions "for color stability" and acid additions "as necessary;" *saignée* if the berries are especially large; pressing at dryness unless "the tannins need to be tamed," in which case extended maceration is considered; tank stirring before the new wines are barreled so that some heavy lees go into each barrel; blends made the spring and summer after the vintage; and egg-white fining of most lots. The wines are raised in barrels sourced from "a dozen" coopers, but Tardy eschews heavy-toast barrels from any maker to avoid

strong "coffee-tar" notes. The finished wines are bottled before the following vintage.

The goal, according to Olson, is wines "with character and finesse" that avoid "overly high alcohol." These wines are nicely-made pinots, with a good balance of fruit and floral elements and attractive structures.

TASTING NOTES

2005 *Willamette Valley (tasted in* 2007*):* Transparent, light-to-medium black-red; slightly dusty, slightly smoky, strawberry-cherry nose; fruit-sweet, cherry-driven palate, with some notes of resin and hard spice that suggest sweet vermouth; bright and nicely built.

2005 *Deux Verres (tasted in* 2007*):* Medium, rosy-black-red, smoke, vanilla, and red fruit aromas; ripe and sappy on the palate, with a strong licorice flavor; considerable very fine-grained tannins; dry on the finish; serious.

2005 *Olson Estate Vineyard (tasted in* 2007*):* Intense, rosy-magenta; ripe berry fruit and dusty potpourri on the nose; strong black tea in the mouth, plus both red fruit and blackberry; emery textured from mid-palate to finish; persistently sweet, nicely made, and still very young.

TUDOR WINES
Santa Barbara, California

Dan Tudor's forefathers have a long history farming grapes and lavender on the Croatian island of Hvar. At the beginning of the last century, his cousin's grandfathers transported this vocation to California, where they grew table grapes near Delano. Dan's first brush with wine grapes occurred

in 1982, when he worked the harvest for another cousin, Louis Lucas, a Santa Maria Valley pioneer. After a detour into the world of pay-phone companies and prepaid calling cards that lasted more than a decade, Tudor returned to wine in 1997, launching Tudor Wines with his cousin Christian, and sourcing fruit from the Santa Lucia Highlands, near his new home in Carmel. The first vintage, about 1,600 cases, was made in 2000, and the second (after an unplanned two-year gap while the cousins tidied up the loose ends of Tudor's last telephone business) was made in 2003. The wines are now made in sublet space at Central Coast Wine Services in Santa Maria, and Larry Brooks (see CAMPION WINES and ACACIA WINERY) is a consultant.

Tudor Wines is devoted entirely to pinot noir, and confines its grape sources (with a single exception in 2006) to the Santa Lucia Highlands and neighboring Arroyo Grande AVAs. A second-label program, called Radog, absorbs declassified lots of pinot, some lots of pinot sourced especially for Radog, and short runs of white wine.

WINES AND WINEMAKING NOTES

Tudor reports that, in the Paraiso, Tondre, and Sarmento vineyards, where he sources most of his grapes, he is typically neither the earliest nor the latest maker to pick. He seeks to avoid "pruney" flavors and to seize "bright, cherry fruit flavors" that are produced "just when the berries begin to soften"—in the service of "wines that age better." This sweet spot typically comes between 26 and 26.5 Brix, however, so Tudor routinely uses spinning cone technology on his press juice so that finished alcohol will drop to between 13.5 and 14.2 percent when the free-run and press fractions are combined. *Cuvaisons,* which are done in 5-ton stainless steel open-tops, last from two to three weeks, of which anywhere from two to ten days may involve extended maceration. About a third of the barrel stock is new each year, and the new barrels are almost exclusively medium-plus-toast editions from François Frères, coopered from Allier forests. The wines spend ten to eleven months in barrel and are cross-flow filtered before bottling.

There were two wines in 2000: a Santa Lucia Highlands blend sourced from the Tondre and Paraiso vineyards, and a vineyard-designated wine from Tondre. In 2003 the Santa Lucia Highlands blend was made entirely from Paraiso grapes, about half of which came from that vineyard's oldest UCD 13 vines; in 2004 from a combination of old-vines Paraiso and Tondre; in 2005 entirely from Tondre; and in 2006 from old-vines Paraiso, Tondre, and Sarmento. (See CAMPION WINES for additional information about the Sarmento Vineyard.) In 2005 some vineyard-designated Tondre was also made, and in 2006 Tudor made two vineyard-designated wines, one from Sarmento and one from the Balo Vineyard (across Route 128 from GOLDENEYE) in the Anderson Valley. Tudor pinots combine fruit-forward intensity with a lean frame that creates an overall impression of elegance.

TASTING NOTES

2005 *Santa Lucia Highlands (tasted in 2007):* Transparent rosy-red; berry-driven nose of strawberry and raspberry, with a hint of spearmint; intense, fruity attack; elegant, almost austere frame; smooth and almost creamy texture, with some pepper, menthol, grip, and heat at the end.

2004 *Santa Lucia Highlands (tasted in 2007):* Transparent, dark ruby; expressive nose of pencil lead, dark red fruit, barrel char, and floral components; cherry-raspberry fruit and a silky attack; nice

acidity, a touch of sweetness, and some pepper on the mid-palate; a fairly serious, medium-weight pinot that finishes a little warm.

VARNER
Menlo Park, California

In 1980 Bob Varner, more or less fresh from graduate school in animal genetics at the University of California Berkeley, and his bother Jim, who had studied winemaking at Davis, planted wine grapes on a 230-acre ranch in Portola Valley, California. (In truth, a quarter century later, Bob is still "on leave" from Berkeley's doctoral program in gene regulation.) The ranch, farmed for decades for the hay of California red oats, is a foothills site that abuts the Windy Hill Open Space Preserve on the west side of Portola Road. The Varners' first attentions were focused on chardonnay and a bit of gewürztraminer, which they sited in parts of the hay ranch that displayed "medium productivity," on generally southeast-facing slopes. The slopes were studded with oaks, but "not a single tree" was sacrificed to plant the vines.

From 1987 Jim Varner's time was devoted increasingly to the import of wines from France (the business was done as Park Wine Company) while Bob managed the ranch. Grapes were sold to various winemakers based in the Santa Cruz Mountains. In 1996 Bob Varner began to make "Spring Ridge Vineyard" chardonnay under the Varner label, and the following year, 3 acres of pinot noir were planted on a 700-foot hillock that the brothers called Hidden Block, which had previously been all but obscured by overgrown poison oak. Vines were set out in 9-foot rows with 7 feet between vines, to optimize for the same crossbar trellising already used for the chardonnay, which can support dappled sunlight in the vines' fruiting zone without hedging. Hidden Block was planted entirely to nursery-sourced Dijon 115 grafted on 5C rootstock. In

ELEGANT, DELICATELY CRAFTED WINES WITH COMPELLING INTENSITY

2001 2 acres called Lower Oak Block were planted to Dijon 777 on 5C, and in the summer of 2006, 2 adjoining acres of own-rooted gewürztraminer were budded to 777, creating the first block of 777 outside Burgundy on mature vine roots, as far as I know. Throughout the ranch, the soil is coastal clay-loam, about 2 to 5 feet deep, over siltstone. There is no irrigation except to start young vines, nor do the Varners use fertilizers or insecticides. Yields hover around 3 tons to the acre.

WINEMAKING NOTES

Since 2000 Varner wines have been made in a tiny, very attractive, ultramodern winery on the ranch, only steps from blocks of chardonnay. Bob Varner observes that this tight proximity means he can be in the rows supervising picking at one moment and on the crushpad barely 2 minutes later to receive the same fruit. Grapes are picked (at an average of 24 Brix) in small plastic bins barely larger than a Rubbermaid dishpan. The pinot is destemmed and fermented in 5-foot by 5-foot jacketed stainless steel open-tops that have been ingeniously fitted with floating fiberglass lids. Cool mountain spring water can be used to chill the fermenters, but because Bob Varner prefers a cool soak

to an artificially cold one and because grapes are picked in the chill of early morning, the jackets are rarely used. Musts ferment dry in about 10 days at 85 to 90°F and spend twelve months in barrel after pressing. About 40 percent of barrels are new, and various cooperages are used, including Marsannay, Remond, François Frères, and Alain Fouquet. The wines are racked before bottling but are neither fined nor filtered.

Varner is a hands-on minimalist with respect to winemaking. He enjoys the manual labor of topping and racking, which he does unassisted, and without background noise or interruption, as if it were a meditative process. He is meticulous about grape health (no mold, mildew, or "bad microbes") and about in-winery sanitation, so that he can minimize sulfur treatments and other interventions. "You have to be sure," he says, "that every step is surgical and pure."

Varner pinots from Hidden Block have been made annually since 2002. The first wines from Lower Oak Block were made in 2005. In my experience these wines are elegant, delicately crafted pinots with compelling intensity, though the Oak Block wines are a bit darker than those from Hidden Block, and they privilege slightly blacker fruit flavors.

TASTING NOTES

2004 *Spring Ridge Vineyard Hidden Block (tasted in 2006):* Light-to-medium rosy-ruby color; strongly floral with some black raspberry on the nose; intense, finely-etched raspberry with licorice and a hint of slate on the palate; very silky and just slightly round; very fine indeed.

2002 *Spring Ridge Vineyard Hidden Block (tasted in 2006):* Transparent, medium-dark brick-red; earth and charcoal on the nose with hints of leather, wet fur, and orange peel; rosewater, tar, and black raspberry in the mouth; a hint of grip and just slightly chewy.

W. H. SMITH WINES
St. Helena, California

The first wine venture of Bay Area oil and gas man and real estate developer Bill Smith was the successful and much-respected La Jota project: cabernet sauvignon, cabernet franc, and petite syrah grown on Howell Mountain and made in a tiny stone winery built at the turn of the twentieth century. Early in the 1990s, however, Smith found that his personal taste was turning away from cabernet toward Burgundies, and he was seduced by a new challenge. "If you make wine," he explains, "you want to make wine out of the hard-to-do stuff." So in 1992 he bought a half-ton of pinot from the Hyde Vineyard in Los Carneros and another half-ton from a sparkling-wine vineyard in the Russian River valley, fermented the fruit in half-ton fruit bins, and concluded that pinot noir "wasn't as tough as I thought." In 1993, he discovered the wild charms of the extreme Sonoma Coast. He bought some more Russian River fruit—this time from the Quail Hill Vineyard (see LYNMAR WINERY)—and some fruit from Gard Hellenthal, a "timbering guy," who was also tending a small pinot noir vineyard on a remote, unforested ridge top northeast of Jenner. In 1994, 1995, and 1996, Smith's pinot program consisted entirely of a single, vineyard-designated Hellenthal bottling. In 1997 there were three different bottlings, all from Hellenthal grapes: the Hellenthal Vineyard, made from old vines; a Sonoma Coast bottling made from younger Hellenthal vines; and the so-called Little Billy, the lightest wine of the three. In 1998, a short-crop year, Smith reverted to the single bottling of Hellenthal Vineyard; in 1999 and 2000, both Hellenthal and Sonoma Coast were produced again, differentiated as in 1997.

In 1994 Smith purchased 360 acres adjacent to Hellenthal's property, accessible from King Ridge Road, where he planted 11 acres of his own in 1997 and 1998, in 6-foot rows with 3 feet between vines, entirely to Dijon clones, harvesting his first commercially viable crop in 2001. This estate vineyard, called Maritime Ridge, became an important part of the W. H. Smith pinot program from that point and remained so until its sale in 2005.

Meanwhile, however, Smith expanded his Sonoma Coast focus beyond Cazadero to a large array of vineyards in the hills west of Sebastopol and in the Petaluma Gap. Grape sources in these areas are not consistent from year to year. A recent snapshot includes Twin Hill Ranch, a 4-acre pinot vineyard planted to Swan selection and Dijon 777, farmed by Ben Hurst southwest of Sebastopol; Hayes, west of Sebastopol on Burnside Road; John Balletto's vineyard also on Burnside Road; Jay Morris's ranch near Petaluma, where hillside parcels were planted in 2001; the Flocchini Vineyard in the Petaluma Gap; and MARIMAR ESTATE's Doña Margarita Vineyard near Freestone.

WINES AND WINEMAKING NOTES
Fruit sourcing for W. H. Smith's Sonoma Coast bottling, made every year since 1997 except 1998, has fluctuated substantially over the life of the program. The main sources for the 2006 edition were Hellenthal, Flocchini, Twin Hill, and Morris Ranch. Vineyard-designated wines (apart from Hellenthal and

Maritime Ridge) were made from the Umimo Vineyard and from Doña Margarita Vineyard (called Marimar Torres Estate in the Smith labeling) for the first time in 2006. When the Maritime Ridge Vineyard was sold in 2005, Smith retained use of its name to designate the brand's "best" cuvée.

Smith is his own hands-on winemaker. Since 2001, all fruit has been entirely destemmed. A seven-day, very cold soak (near 35°F) is practiced. The fermentors are then warmed to about 50°F and inoculated. In early vintages, the musts were pressed at dryness, and the new wine was sent to barrel dirty; now the new wines are pressed off between 8 and 12 Brix and are allowed to finish primary fermentation in tanks before being barreled and inoculated with malolactic starter. Since 2001 all wines have been raised in 100 percent new oak barrels (sourced from a longish list of coopers that includes Tonnellerie Treuil, François Frères, Taransaud, Alain Fouquet, Radoux, and Boutes) for ten months. There is no fining or filtration. W. H. Smith pinots elicit very high marks from many reviewers. Although my experience has been less stellar and consistent than these marks would suggest, at their best these wines are aromatically interesting and richly flavored.

TASTING NOTES

2005 *Sonoma Coast (tasted in 2007):* Medium black-red; slightly funky nose suggestive of roasted vegetables and orange peel; nutty flavors on the palate with notes of barrel char and cocoa; mouth coating and long.

2005 *Maritime Vineyard (tasted in 2007):* Slightly hazy black-red; very ripe fruit and smoke on the nose; creamy and insistently sweet on the palate, with cherry, black licorice, and beetroot; dense and complex; grippy at the end; long.

WALTER HANSEL WINERY
Santa Rosa, California

Stephen Hansel is, roughly, a fourth-generation automobile dealer. His great-great-grandfather manufactured horse-drawn carriages in Stockton, California. His grandfather and father, Walter Sr. and Walter Jr., created successor businesses as automobiles gradually replaced carriages—including one of the first Ford dealerships west of the Rocky Mountains. On the side, Walter Jr. also liked to farm, initially raising both corn and kiwis in California's San Joaquin Valley. When the family moved to Santa Rosa in the 1970s, the place of the corn and kiwis was taken by 250 grapevines, which led the family into home winemaking. (Later, Walter Jr. grew quite a bit of chardonnay that was sold to DE LOACH VINEYARDS.) Stephen remembers that the homemade wine was "pretty awful."

In 1986 Stephen and his brother, attempting to solve the annual problem of a Christmas gift for their man-who-has-everything father, labeled a bottle of the homemade wine professionally. To their surprise, their father was intrigued, and one thing led to another. Walter Jr. began to putter more actively at the home brew. He appealed to his friend Tom Rochioli (see ROCHIOLI VINEYARDS AND WINERY), a customer of Hansel's Ford dealership, for advice on grape growing. He planted three rows of pinot noir with cuttings taken from Rochioli's Little Hill and East Block vineyards. Stephen watched the wine project with increasing fascination. He, too, spoke with Rochioli. When he persuaded his father that the wine project deserved better than "puttering." Walter Jr. put Stephen in charge.

In 1989 Stephen traveled to Burgundy, tasted a lot of very fine wine, and bought books about viticulture and winemaking. Confronted with the first harvest of pinot noir in 1994, he phoned Rochioli for "hotline" help, and Rochioli gamely talked Stephen through the basics of red wine fermentations. Noncommercial vintages of pinot were made that year and the next, followed by a commercial vintage in 1996. At first, the fruit came entirely from Walter Jr.'s three backyard rows. Then 1994 plantings at Stephen's house on Cahill Lane began to bear. In 1999 the Hansels bought additional nearby acreage on Hall Road, due west of downtown Santa Rosa, where they planted 65 acres equally divided between chardonnay and pinot.

By 2001 they were producing six estate grown pinot noirs made in their own basic winery on the new farm: the original "Three Rows" wine from Walter Jr.'s backyard; a Cahill Lane cuvée made from a single acre of vines in Stephen's backyard, planted to a combination of cuttings from "three rows" plus Dijon 114 and 115; and four wines from the Hall Road property. These were the North Slope Vineyard (planted to Dijon 115); the South Slope Vineyard (planted to Dijon 777); a plain "estate" wine anchored with fruit from the lowest lying blocks in between the slopes; and Cuvée Alyce, a selection of "over-the-top" barrels from the middle of the ranch. The Hall Road property was planted almost entirely in 9-foot rows with 4 feet between vines.

Walter Hansel pinots are an unapologetic homage to Stephen's father, created personally and hands-on by a man who does most of the cellar work himself but still runs the family automobile dealership as a day job. He says they are priced "under market," to be sure that as many people as possible "know my father's name." Stephen admits, however, that he does not often drink his own wine, preferring Burgundies most of the time and other American pinots "occasionally."

WINEMAKING NOTES

The fruit for Hansel pinots is picked at or above 24.5 Brix ("you want some dehydration," Hansel explains), is entirely destemmed, is cold-soaked for five to seven days, and is fermented in stainless open-tops. The fermentations rely on resident yeasts unless the harvest occurs late, in which case Hansel inoculates. The wines are lightly pressed when the must is dry, retaining just enough solid material "to protect the wine," and are barreled on their fine lees. The barrel regime consists almost exclusively of François Fréres *pièces* made of staves air-dried for three years and bought as trees. All six wines get the same percentage of new wood exposure, but the number varies from vintage to vintage: 80 percent in 2003 and 2004, but only 65 percent in 2005. After twelve months in barrel, the wines are blended and then spend three months in tank before being bottled.

TASTING NOTES

2004 *North Slope Vineyard (tasted in 2007):* Brilliant medium rosy-garnet; ripe fruit and nutmeg spice on the nose; sweet, bright cherry-raspberry flavors plus rosewater on the palate; some grip and slightly warm on the finish, but simultaneously approachable and substantial; attractive, and medium in length.

2004 *South Slope Vineyard (tasted in 2006)*: Pretty, transparent, medium-dark magenta; evergreen, fir balsam, and spiced cherry on the nose; intense and slightly sweet black cherry with more spice and barrel-marking on the palate; mouth filling; finishes warm with a hint of grip and black pepper.

WESTREY WINE COMPANY
McMinnville, Oregon

When Amy Wesselman and David Autrey graduated from Portland's Reed College in 1991 with bachelor's degrees in philosophy, they pondered what they should do "with life after college." Suggestions from local winemakers like David Adelsheim and John Paul (see CAMERON WINERY) pushed the pair toward an unconventional choice: Wesselman worked the harvest of 1991 at Domaine de l'Arlot in Nuits-Saint-Georges, while Autrey did the same not far away at Domaine Dujac in Morey-Saint-Denis. Back in Oregon the following year, both took jobs in Oregon wineries, she first at BETHEL HEIGHTS and REX HILL and then at THE EYRIE VINEYARDS, where she eventually became the assistant winemaker and general manager; he at Bethel Heights. Meanwhile, in 1993, they created Westrey Wine Company as a sidebar project, taking the opportunity to make "wine of their own."

The brand prospered, expanding from 400 cases in 1993 to more than 4,000 cases thirteen years later and moving to a dedicated, if inelegant, production facility in downtown McMinnville. By 2007 Westrey had morphed into full-time

employment for both principals, although Wesselman also functioned as the diplomatic, energetic, and much-respected executive director of the world-famous International Pinot Noir Celebration through 2008. In 2000 Wesselman and Autrey were able to purchase 50 acres on Worden Hill Road in the Dundee Hills, partially planted to old vines, and to begin the transformation of their brand from all-*négociant* to one substantially reliant on estate fruit. By 2007 12 estate acres were in production, of which 7 were pinot noir; an additional 6 were planted but are not yet bearing, and 15 more are planned. The vineyard is almost adjacent to Abbey Ridge, which has produced Westrey's flagship wine since the outset, and the soils are relatively thin instances of Jory series. Just over an acre is UCD 4 on its own roots, planted in 1977 and painstakingly restored; the balance is UCD 4 on rootstock; Dijon 115, 667, and 777 on rootstock; and a test block where the principals experiment with various combinations of scion material and rootstocks.

WINES AND WINEMAKING NOTES
A Willamette Valley blend has been made in every vintage since 1993; since 2003 this wine has been anchored with fruit from the Justice Vineyard (see below; see also the BETHEL HEIGHTS profile) and the Momtazi Vineyard in the Coast Range foothills west of McMinnville. As more fruit is produced in the estate vineyard, however, part of this is used to augment the blend. A reserve wine composed as a barrel selection that Autrey describes as a "statement of the character of the vintage" has been made since 1995, except in 2005, when a very short crop left no room for a reserve bottling. Alongside these blended wines, vineyard-designated pinots from Abbey Ridge

(see Cameron Winery) have been made since 1998, and from Justice Vineyard on the west flank of the Eola Hills since 2004. A vineyard-designated estate wine (the Oracle Vineyard) also debuted in 2004.

Westrey picks grapes "earlier than most producers" in order to retain natural acidity, and destems the majority. Prefermentation maceration "takes as long as it takes," because fermentations rely "mostly" on resident yeasts. New wines are pressed off when the must goes dry, and the wines spend eleven months in a combination of (primarily) Gillet, Cadus, and Remond barrels, of which 20 to 25 percent are new each year. The result is wines with quite intense flavors and good structure, crafted to satisfy but not specifically to impress, and wines that have the capacity to improve with a few years of bottle age.

TASTING NOTES

2005 *Willamette Valley (tasted in 2007):* Transparent, medium-dark magenta; dark plummy-cherry aromas; intense, anise-flavored, slightly resinous fruit on the mid-palate; then a substantial load of sweet, soft, fine-grained tannin; long finish that feels like crushed velvet.

2005 *Oracle Vineyard (tasted in 2007):* Medium-deep ruby; aromas of rose petal and strawberry-raspberry fruit; sweet, rich, and soft in the mouth; some flavors of infused violets; slightly primary; derives some extra structure from partial use of whole clusters; finishes with a dusty grip.

2005 *Justice Vineyard (tasted in 2007):* Medium, slightly rosy-ruby color; dusty potpourri aromas over bluish fruit; slightly sweet on the palate with earthy marionberry flavors and substantial grip from the mid-palate through the finish.

WHITCRAFT WINERY
Santa Barbara, California

Twice a year, Chris Whitcraft writes a personal, folksy, matter-of-fact, oddly under-punctuated newsletter for the people who buy his wine. It is sometimes laconic, sometimes chatty, and sometimes curmudgeonly, and it always includes a few key bits of his family's news. It reminds his customers that his is, at best, a one-, two-, or three-man show; that the other guys are mostly friends (or kids) who help out; and that he makes the wines himself, pays the bills himself, and has no office outside his home. Until recently, he didn't have much of a winery either and used rented space at Central Coast Wine Services in Santa Maria instead. (Now there is a combination winery and tasting room in an industrial-office area of Santa Barbara.)

But Whitcraft has been in the wine business for thirty years. His May Fare Wine Company on Coast Village Road in Montecito, just east of downtown Santa Barbara, operated one of the few on-premise retail tasting rooms in California in the 1970s; later, it was reinvented as a wholesale business that specialized in private labels. This second incarnation of May Fare gave Whitcraft good access to the best wine producers in California, and he forged close personal relationships with pinot-makers such as Burt Williams (WILLIAMS SELYEM), Dick Graff (CHALONE VINEYARD), and Ken Burnap (Santa Cruz Mountain Vineyard). In 1985 he turned wine producer himself, and in 1990 he produced his first pinot noir from the Miller family's Bien Nacido Vineyard on the Tepusquet Bench. Two pinots followed in 1991: a second vintage from Bien Nacido and one from Bob Pellegrini's OLIVET LANE VINEYARD in Russian River Valley. In 1992 there were two Bien Nacido wines, a blend and a block-designated wine from Block Q, plus a second vintage of Olivet Lane; in 1993 there were two block-designated Bien Nacido wines, N and Q.

WHITCRAFT MAKES WINES BY HAND, LARGELY WITHOUT ELECTRICITY, IN A CELLAR FILLED WITH SECOND-HAND EQUIPMENT

From 1994 to 2000, Whitcraft also made a vineyard-designated wine from the HIRSCH VINEYARD near Cazadero, and beginning in 2000, he made a MELVILLE VINEYARD wine from Melville's F Block. In 2004 two additional vineyards were added to the Whitcraft portfolio: Aubaine, an ocean-view site near Nipomo (see STEPHEN ROSS WINES), and Morning Dew Ranch, Burt Williams's new vineyard in the Anderson Valley.

The wines are usually highly perfumed, elegant editions of pinot noir that display considerable complexity, but a few are big, dark, and brooding. All are built to showcase the *terroirs* from which they come. Quantities are tiny. There are typically only 250 cases of each wine, totaling 1,500 cases in each vintage, plus dribs and drabs of things other than pinot, such as lagrein from the French Camp Vineyard.

WINEMAKING NOTES

Whitcraft's winemaking is mostly handwork, done largely without electricity, in a cellar filled with second-hand and rebuilt equipment. The fruit is foot-trodden as whole clusters in fruit-bins that are spread apart if the juice temperature gets too hot or moved together in the case of the reverse. There is no cold maceration, and all lots are inoculated immediately with the Williams Selyem strain of zinfandel yeast. At zero Brix, when there is still a bit of unfermented sugar in each lot, the new wine is pressed and barreled. The barrel regime, as at Williams Selyem, relies entirely on *pièces* coopered by François Fréres and on "as much wood from the Tronçais forest as I can afford," according to Whitcraft. Typically about one third of the barrel stock is new, and the new barrels are distributed evenly across all the wines. Most pinots are bottled after eleven months in wood—they are not racked or treated with sulfur dioxide until bottling unless there are problems—but a few cuvées, such as the block-designates from Bien Nacido and the Melville wine, stay in barrel for up to 18 months.

TASTING NOTES

2005 *Bien Nacido Vineyard (tasted in 2007):* Medium garnet color; lifted aromas of red fruit and wet earth; bright and earthy in the mouth; light to medium in weight; good intensity in an elegant frame; very attractive.

2005 *Bien Nacido Vineyard Q Block (tasted in 2007):* Rosy color, slightly tiling; a highly perfumed wine with bright citrus and raspberry notes and some white pepper; strong herbal properties on the palate, including bay laurel; intense and silky mouth-feel; fine. A personal favorite.

2005 *Morning Dew Ranch (tasted in 2007):* Utterly different from the Bien Nacido wines; nearly opaque black-red color; intense resinous nose marked by the whole-cluster fermentation; intense cherry fruit in the mouth; big, tough, grippy, and persistent.

2005 *Melville Vineyard Clone 115 (tasted in 2007):* Medium rosy hue, slightly closed and slightly floral; explosive on the palate with cherry, ink, wet slate, and considerable grip; minerally overall; slightly hot, with a bit of bite at the end.

WHITE ROSE VINEYARD
Dayton, Oregon

White Rose was the original high-altitude tenant on Hilltop Lane in the Dundee Hills, before there was Domaine Serene or Vista Hills—or even Domaine Drouhin, a bit lower on the hill and off to the east. The 10-acre vineyard was planted between 1980 and 1985 on a south-facing slope—in 10-foot rows with 8 feet between vines and to own-rooted UCD 4—and it provided grapes to several producers. In 2000 the vineyard was sold to Greg Sanders, a businessman from Orange County, California, who had spent much of the 1990s devouring textbooks on viticulture and winemaking, taking extension courses offered at the University of California Davis, tasting wines seriously, and almost literally *studying* his way into wine. Along the way he came to like pinot noir above all, Oregon pinots best among American efforts, and especially wines made from White Rose grapes vinted by some of Oregon's best makers, including PANTHER CREEK CELLARS and TORII MOR WINERY. Sanders retrellised the vineyard, built a tiny winery and launched White Rose Wines as a brand in 2001.

There are three pinots (each named for one of Sanders's children), two of which are made from purchased grapes and one that is from estate fruit. The non-estate wines are a Nekaia cuvée (blended from the Winter's Hill Vineyard, Durant Vineyard, and near-neighbor Vista Hills) and Mercotti's Milieu, a mid-priced wine entirely from Vista Hills. The estate wine is called Quiotee's Lair. Since 2005 White Rose fruit has been sold only to ST. INNOCENT WINERY; the balance is used to make the estate wine. Sanders says he picked his first few vintages by taste but now pays more attention to acidity, destems completely, and cold-soaks for three days before inoculation. After the new wine is pressed off, he settles it for rather a long time in tank before barreling the wines for thirteen months or more—except for the Nekaia cuvée, which is bottled before the following vintage. Sanders, saying he has decided that pinot noir does not benefit from a large load of tannin, tries to keep tannin extraction low. My experience with these wines is limited to the 2004 vintage of Quiotee's Lair, which was impressive.

TASTING NOTE
2004 *Quiotee's Lair (tasted in* 2007): Brilliant light garnet; strawberry and red currant aromas with strong floral overlay; very elegant with infused flowers and strong minerality on the palate; great length; very attractive.

WILD HORSE WINERY AND VINEYARDS
Templeton, California

Ken Volk, a third-generation Californian raised in the San Gabriel Valley, discovered wine accidentally while studying fruit science at the California State Polytechnic University in San Luis

Obispo. After some formal training in the form of extension classes offered by the University of California Davis, and after time at Napa Valley's famous Wine Lab, he and his family bought property on a mesa overlooking the Salinas River near Templeton, California, in 1981, where they began planting what eventually expanded to 40 acres of wine grapes ranging across workhorse varieties like chardonnay and merlot to outliers like malvasia bianca, dolcetto, and verdelho. Volk was among the first to plant pinot noir on the Central Coast—only Dr. Stanley Hoffman, who created Hoffman Mountain Ranch northwest of Paso Robles in the 1960s, seems to have preceded him—and pinot evolved into a flagship variety for Wild Horse, even though its estate vineyards produced only a small fraction of the fruit it used. Volk was instrumental in several non-estate plantings nearby, including the Live Oak Vineyard (farmed by Rabbit Ridge Winery in the Templeton Gap) and its neighbor, Opolo Vineyards, on Vineyard Drive. The first crush at Wild Horse, in 1983, included several tons of pinot noir sourced from the well-known Sierra Madre vineyard southeast of Santa Maria (which was made as a vineyard-designated wine) and fruit from the famous Bien Nacido Vineyard on the Tepusquet Bench, which was used to make both blended and vineyard-designated wines for many years (see below).

In 2003 Volk sold Wild Horse to Peak Wines International (now the Beam Wine Estates division of Fortune Brands Inc.), and his associate winemaker and employee since 1995, Mark Cummins, a University of California Davis graduate in fermentation science who also holds an MBA from California State Polytechnic University in San Luis Obispo, succeeded him as winemaker.

WINES AND WINEMAKING NOTES

Wild Horse's pinot noir portfolio includes a nationally distributed blend sourced from the Live Oak and Opolo vineyards in San Luis Obispo, from Edna Ranch in Edna Valley, from Bien Nacido in the Santa Maria Valley, from Ashley's in the Sta. Rita Hills, and from the dry-farmed vines of the Enz Vineyard in the Lime Kiln Valley of San Benito County. There is also a premium barrel selection called Cheval Sauvage, which could theoretically be either a blend or a single-vineyard wine, but which had been anchored with Ashley's and Bien Nacido fruit in most recent vintages. In addition, small quantities of vineyard-designated wines are made for mailing-list and tasting-room sales. In 2004 Wild Horse made pinots in this category from Ashley's and Bien Nacido vineyards.

The larger-volume wines are made in a combination of closed-top and open-top fermentors. Several days of cold-soaking precede inoculation, and the closed-top tanks are pumped over with the same frequency used for punchdowns in the open-tops. The Central Coast wine spends ten months in barrels, about 30 percent of which are new in each vintage; Cheval Sauvage is returned to wood, after the wines are racked and the blends made, for an additional four months. The barrel stock is from François Fréres, Dargaud & Jaeglé, and Cadus. Wild Horse pinots are nicely made, ripe-picked, fruit-forward, medium-weight wines that also exhibit a fair degree of complexity.

TASTING NOTES

2005 *Central Coast (tasted in 2007):* Transparent, medium black-red; exuberantly fruity and floral with dusty cherry-raspberry aromas; medium-weight on the palate, with cherry candy, rosewater, and a slightly peppery finish.

2004 *"Cheval Sauvage" (tasted in* 2007*):* Medium-dark black-red; a distinctive nose that combines flowers, berry fruits and some savory notes reminiscent of saltwater taffy; fruit-sweet attack featuring strawberry, cherry, raspberry, and rosewater; very ripe fruit flavors and extracted, with black pepper and a suede-like texture; reasonably balanced but finishes a bit warm.

WILLAKENZIE ESTATE WINERY
Yamhill, Oregon

Willakenzie Estate is the self-proclaimed "retirement" project of Bernard Lacroute, a Burgundian by birth and electronic engineer by vocation, who spent most of his career in California's Silicon Valley. Lacroute's roots are not, however, in Burgundy's Côte d'Or but in the Charollais, best known for beef cattle, on the plain east of the Saône River and south of Macon. Still, some of Lacroute's earliest memories are the glasses of red wine, sometimes Beaujolais, sometimes Burgundy, and always well diluted with water, that his parents served him as a child.

Willakenzie occupies a 420-acre ranch east of Yamhill that Lacroute acquired in 1992. It was pasture then, in somewhat deteriorated condition and overgrown with blackberries and poison oak. The soils were the well-drained, sedimentary deposits characteristic of the folded landscape on the southwest side of the Chehalem Mountains, but this hilly topography appealed to the Burgundian in Lacroute. Planting began almost immediately on rootstock (at that time unusual in

Oregon), and (even more unusually for the first time) the vineyard was entirely fitted with drip irrigation. Eventually, 104 acres were dedicated to vines—about 70 of these pinot noir. The pinot is mostly nursery-sourced Dijon selections, but Lacroute also took cuttings of various UCD 2A and UCD 4 selections from nearby vineyards like Erath and Abbey Ridge. Laurent Montalieu was the winemaker until 2002, when he left to launch a new Oregon pinot venture called Solana in partnership with his wife, Danielle Andrus. At this point the winemaking reins were passed to Thibaud Mandet, who had worked as Montalieu's assistant since 1999. Both Montalieu and Mandet were Bordeaux-trained; Lacroute believes Bordeaux offers the "strongest academic winemaking program in France."

WINES AND WINEMAKING NOTES
Willakenzie now produces a Willamette Valley wine and six block-designated wines, all from estate fruit. The Aliette and Pierre Léon cuvées debuted in 1995, followed by Kiana and Emery in 2000, and Terres Basses and Triple Black Slopes in 2001. A few clone-specific bottlings are also made

---

RICH, DEEPLY COLORED WINES WITH STURDY TANNINS THAT BENEFIT FROM BOTTLE AGE

---

for tasting-room and wine-club sales. The estate's sedimentary soils tend to make wines with big, round tannins. Pierre Léon is an especially showy wine, but the biggest, chewiest wines are the Triple Black Slopes and Terres Basses cuvées. Kiana seems to display the most symphonic aromatics.

Despite six to twelve months of bottle age before release, all benefit from cellaring.

Picked fruit is destemmed very cold so that the berries are barely crushed, and some enzymes are added. Punchdowns during the first third of the fermentation are then replaced by pumpovers "for color stability" and because Mandet believes "a little oxygen can improve pinot's aromatics." Four or five days of postfermentation maceration follow seven to ten days of primary fermentation. Typically, press juice is used only in the Willamette Valley wine and is excluded from the block-designates. Barrels are mostly François Frères, Cadus, and Saury; are mostly medium or medium-plus toast with untoasted heads; and are increasingly selected to privilege wood from the Allier and Vosges forests. The Willamette Valley wine (which sees 20 to 30 percent new oak) is bottled before the following vintage; block-designated wines (which see 40 to 60 percent new oak) go to bottle after about thirteen months in wood. Turbidity is measured with instruments before the wine is finished, and an extra racking is done about one month before bottling if it is deemed necessary to ensure clarity. These are serious, sturdy, tannin-rich wines overall that usually benefit from several years of bottle age.

TASTING NOTES

2004 *Emery (tasted in 2007):* Dense and dark, but already showing evolution toward mahogany; briary, mentholated nose; cherry and cassis fruit on the palate, ferrous (like Château Pétrus); dry from mid-palate to finish and grippy throughout.

2003 *Emery (tasted in 2006):* Dark, saturated black-red robe; *charcuterie* and licorice on the nose; crushed black currants in the mouth; fruit-sweet, and medium in weight; very fine-grained tannins create a nearly plush mouth-feel on the finish.

WILLAMETTE VALLEY VINEYARDS
Turner, Oregon

Willamette Valley Vineyards is a largely consumer-owned, publicly traded corporation based in Turner, Oregon, just southeast of Salem. It represents twenty-five years of the vision, entrepreneurship, and hands-on work of Jim Bernau, an Oregon native, "small-town boy," and former small business lobbyist at the state capitol who was largely responsible for the passage of legislation at the end of the 1970s that permitted winery construction in farm-use zones and the direct shipment of wine to consumers, and that established the winery marketing tax credit that finances today's Oregon Wine Board.

In 1983 Bernau found property in the South Salem Hills for a wine project of his own. When he discovered it, it was the remnants of a plum orchard overgrown with blackberries in red volcanic soil. He cleared land and planted vines with his own hands and a small tractor until he had 50 planted acres, of which half were the Oregon workhorse selections of pinot noir, on a west-to-southwest facing volcanic flow between the 500- and 750-foot contours. The first crops from the vineyard were sold, but in 1989, having turned hundreds of Oregon wine enthusiasts into small-scale investors and having established what is said to be the first self-underwritten public stock offering in history, Bernau built a winery and launched Willamette Valley Vineyards as a wine brand dedicated to "affordable" pinot noir, chardonnay, and pinot gris.

In 1997 Willamette Valley Vineyards acquired Tualatin Estate Vineyards in Forest Grove, a 145-acre site planted in 1973 to pinot noir and to a relatively wide array of white varieties. This was not a self-financing transaction, however. Debt was incurred to purchase Tualatin's assets, leading to several years of business losses. Since 2007 the company has also leased and farmed the well-known Elton Vineyard, established in 1983 near Hopewell, in the Eola Hills. Elton consists of 60 planted acres—of which 42 are pinot noir—in silty loam soils classified as Saum series, on an east- and southeast-facing slope. Elton has been a favored source for several well-respected Oregon labels, including FIDDLEHEAD CELLARS, KEN WRIGHT CELLARS, and (more recently) BELLE VALLÉE.

Willamette Valley Vineyards has been blessed over the years with a succession of talented winemakers and general managers, including Dean Cox, who served from 1990 until his untimely death in 1996, and Joe Dobbes (1996 to 2001). Forrest Klaffke, who worked previously at ROBERT MONDAVI WINERY and at Samuele Sebastiani, succeeded Dobbes; in 2007, with production expanding beyond the capacity of the Turner facility, Klaffke assumed the newly-created position of head winemaker, and his assistant, Don Crank III, was put in charge of "off-site" winemaking—meaning primarily the wines made at Tualatin Estate.

WINES AND WINEMAKING NOTES
Willamette Valley Vineyards's large pinot program—the state's largest until it was overtaken in 2006 by A TO Z WINEWORKS—has been built on a combination of estate and purchased fruit. The large-volume wines are a Willamette Valley blend, sourced from half a dozen vineyards that include the Tualatin and Willamette Valley Vineyards estate parcels, and a cuvée called Whole Cluster Pinot Noir, which is actually a wine made by carbonic maceration in closed tanks, like most Beaujolais. There is also an estate vineyard cuvée from Bernau's vineyard, a Tualatin Estate cuvée and, in most vintages, a "Signature Cuvée" selected from the best barrels in the cellar. A single-vineyard program based on non-estate sites was begun in 1990 with grapes from Elton Vineyard (see above), joined by Freedom Hill Vineyard and Karina Vineyard (a block in Alpine Vineyards near Monroe, Oregon) in 1992, Hoodview Vineyard (near Amity) in 1996, and Mount Hood. The Freedom Hill, Hoodview, and Karina programs were terminated in 2002, Elton continued until 2003, and the last vintage for Mount Hood was 2007.

Fruit is picked relatively early by contemporary standards, between about 22.5 and 24.5 Brix, yielding wines that typically finish at or below 14 percent alcohol. Up to 35 percent of the fruit is fermented as whole clusters (except in the Whole Cluster wine, where all fruit is fermented as whole clusters), "proprietary" strains of yeast are used, in wet years the musts are bled to compensate for dilution, and the finished wines are raised in between 20 and 50 percent new French oak barrels from a variety of coopers for between ten and eighteen months. The Signature Cuvée is generally not filtered, but most other wines are, whether with pads or, sometimes, with both pads and diatomaceous earth, producing reasonably priced and widely available pinots made with modest alcoholic concentration. Many wines display strong herbal notes, and cuvées other than the Whole Cluster wine can seem quite barrel-marked.

TASTING NOTES
2006 *Willamette Valley (tasted in 2007)*: Light-to-medium garnet; white pepper and strawberry aromas; bright, red berry

fruit on the palate with hints of espresso, menthol, and tar; medium in length.

2005 *Estate Vineyard (tasted in 2007)*: Luminous, medium garnet; rich, slightly earthy, herbal nose; almost sweet and borderline fleshy on the palate; a core of cherry and cassis fruit; smoky with a hint of black molasses; finishes long and dry.

2005 *Tualatin Estate (tasted in 2007)*: Very transparent, light-to-medium pinkish-garnet; spice-dominated nose with a hint of hazelnut; cocoa and café-au-lait on the palate; satiny attack, then grippy at mid-palate; peppery finish that also seems very slightly green.

WILLIAMS SELYEM
Healdsburg, California

Williams Selyem is an icon, and the company has had much to do with the emergence of the Russian River valley as a premier site for pinot noir. It was the first pinot-centered "cult" winery in North America, the first producer to make Joe Rochioli's grapes genuinely famous, and one of the first to sell its entire production to fanatically loyal customers by the simple and inexpensive device of a mailing list. Today there are 25,000 names on the winery's list, including restaurants, and 3,000 more on a waiting list. Allocations are small, and all customers, including restaurants, pay the same price. There is no tasting room and no name on the mailbox.

Its story is the wine-country equivalent of a Silicon Valley startup. Born as a home-winemaking project in a garage in 1979, the brand, mailing list, and two years' inventory were sold 18 years later

for $9 million. When Burt Williams and Ed Selyem, both residents of Forestville, first met in the 1970s, Williams was a pressman for the San Francisco Newspaper Agency, and Selyem was the wine buyer for a local supermarket. Enamored of French Burgundies but unable to afford the best exemplars on their salaries, they began making a few barrels of wine in Selyem's garage, beginning with zinfandel from Leno Martinelli's nearby Jackass Hill vineyard. In 1981, advised that the regulatory authorities would not ignore their home production indefinitely, they obtained a winery bond as Hacienda del Rio—named for Selyem's house on the Russian River—but the previously established (and now defunct) Hacienda Winery complained about the name, so in 1984 the partners shifted to using their own surnames. Williams, who knew a thing or two about typography from his work in the pressroom, designed a simple black-and-red label on a background of cream-colored paper, adorned with nothing more than a stock ornament of the sort known to typesetters as a dingbat. This logo has never changed.

From the beginning, Williams was the winemaker and Selyem the marketer. They owned no land and worked on a shoestring budget. They purchased grapes from growers who would grow grapes the way Williams wanted them. Their contracts were handshakes. On the two-hour bus ride between Forestville and his day job in San Francisco each morning and evening, Williams read everything he could find about wine and winemaking. Selyem came up with the then-revolutionary idea of selling wine to a mailing list: "Sign up with us, and you will get six bottles of something we make, twice a year." Faithful customers lined up to purchase everything the partners could produce. In 1987 the brand turned a corner. Judges at

California's state fair picked the partners' 1985 Rochioli Vineyard pinot noir—the winery's first vineyard-designated pinot noir—as the sweepstakes winner, and they named Williams Selyem—still operating from a two-car garage on River Road, with converted dairy tanks and an outdoor crushpad—Winery of the Year.

Friend and neighbor Howard Allen, who owned a vineyard on Westside Road adjacent to the Rochioli ranch, leased the partners some old buildings on his property in 1988, which were repurposed as a "real" winery in time for the crush in 1989. By 1992 Williams Selyem was finally self-supporting, and Williams quit his day job. The wines achieved cult status, defined Russian River pinot for many connoisseurs, and set the benchmark by which other American pinots were and are judged. Throughout its history, says Bob

---

CONSISTENT WINEMAKING
AND UNIFORM USE
OF FRANÇOIS FRÈRES
BARRELS CREATE A STRONG
IMPRESSION OF HOUSE STY_E

Cabral, Williams Selyem's current executive winemaker and general manager, "it was and is strictly about quality, not about profit. There were no great secrets. No pumps, no filters; just rigorous selection." Williams, it is said, kept meticulous winegrowing notes but was never greatly concerned if yields were low or production tiny.

Then, less than ten years after construction of the winery, in a move that made front-page news throughout the wine world, Burt Williams and Ed Selyem retired simultaneously, and Williams Selyem was sold to John Dyson, a New York–based connoisseur and investor.

No stranger to the wine business, Dyson already owned Millbrook Winery in the Hudson River Valley, Villa Pillo in Tuscany, and several hundred acres of grapes on California's Central Coast. Dyson's wife, Kathe, who had met Burt Williams at a winemaker dinner in the early 1990s, had finagled a spot on the Williams Selyem mailing list. Dyson's choice for winemaker, on Williams's recommendation, was Bob Cabral, a veteran of HARTFORD FAMILY, Alderbrook, Kunde, and DE LOACH. Cabral, too, held a spot on the Williams Selyem list (number 576!); he had signed up as a college kid who loved wine. Although the sale was greeted with skepticism in the wine press, and respected sources speculated that the brand might be on the verge of demise, subsequent vintages were mostly well reviewed, and neither business model nor winemaking protocols significantly changed—then or since.

Fruit sources have evolved, but this would probably have happened even without a change in ownership, merely in the natural course of things. ROCHIOLI's West Block was lost, owing largely to declining production, and OLIVET LANE elected to sell fruit to MERRY EDWARDS rather than continue the handshake deal it had enjoyed with Williams. Cabral compensated by contracting, over a period of several years, with several new Westside Road neighbors (including Bacigalupi, Flax, and Bucher), with the Weir Vineyard in the Yorkville Highlands, and with PEAY VINEYARD on the Sonoma Coast near Annapolis. Dyson also provided the resources to do what Williams and Selyem had never been able to afford: purchase land for estate vineyards. In 1999 32.6 acres of pinot noir (and some chardonnay) were planted 1 mile south of the Allen Ranch, on a property straddling Westside Road, called Drake Estate. A second estate vineyard, called Litton Estate, eight blocks of sandy, loamy river bottomland near Guerneville, was developed beginning in 2002. Litton Estate, which is UCD 4, Dijon 777, and 828, and the Calera, David Bruce, Swan, and Mount Eden selections, set out in 7-foot rows with 5 feet between vines, began bearing in 2005, making contributions to the Sonoma County and Sonoma Coast wines and spawning small amounts of a vineyard-designated cuvée.

Wine-wise, the main change associated with the Dyson era was the launch of wines sourced from Dyson's Vista Verde Vineyard in San Benito County (now custom-farmed for the Williams Selyem program) which are, unsurprisingly, quite different from any wines Williams Selyem sources from the north coast area. The production facility remains where it was in the Williams and Selyem era, on the Allen Ranch. Since Cabral assumed executive winemaking and general management responsibilities in 2003, Lynn Krausmann, a veteran of Freemark Abbey, Clos du Bois, and New Zealand's Cloudy Bay Winery, has handled day-to-day winemaking.

WINES AND WINEMAKING NOTES

Williams Selyem's flagship wines are its vineyard-designates, of which eight or more may be made in any single year. The so-called appellation wines command slightly lower prices and are usually the first wines made available to new names on the mailing list. The "appellation" category also includes a Sonoma *County* bottling, which combines lots from several AVAs. The concentration of the vineyard-designated wines is protected by rigorous barrel-by-barrel selection; deselected barrels of vineyard-designated wines are used as the backbone of the appellation wines. The balance of the appellation wines derives from vineyards judged to have vineyard-designation potential in due

season or (in a few cases) from vineyards sourced specifically for use in these wines. The longest-running vineyard-designate now produced is the Allen Ranch bottling (see above), made every year since 1987; it is followed by Rochioli's River Block (Williams Selyem spells this *Riverblock* on its labels) and by Hirsch Vineyard, both made since 1994. Ferrington has been made as a vineyard-designate since 1992; Coastlands since 1995, except in 2000, when an extremely meager yield did not measure up; Precious Mountain since 1996; Weir since 1999; Flax since 2001; and Bucher and Peay since 2003. The vineyard-designated wine that Williams Selyem called simply Rochioli Vineyard—actually fruit from Rochioli's West Block—was made from 1985 through 1997; vineyard-designated Olivet Lane wine was made from 1989 through 1997. Vineyard-designates were made from the Summa Vineyard in 1988, 1991, and 1993—and from the Cohn Vineyard in the Russian River Valley, near the boundary with Dry Creek, in 1993 only. A blend labeled Summa and Coastlands was also made in 1993. The Russian River and Sonoma Coast appellation wines both debuted in 1988. Thereafter the Russian River Valley wine was made from 1990 through 1995 and again since 1999, anchored with old-vines fruit from Charles Bacigalupi's Westside Road vineyard, plus declassified barrels of River Block and Allen Ranch, until Drake Estate fruit became available in 2001. A Sonoma Coast blend was made from 1988 through 1990, 1993 through 1995, and 1998 through 2000, mostly with declassified barrels of Coastlands and Hirsch, but sometimes also with deselected lots of Summa and Precious Mountain; a substantial fraction of Sonoma County has come from Drake Estate since 2002. The Sonoma County bottling, made mostly from leftovers after the vineyard-designates and appellation wines were assembled, first appeared in 1984. It was not made again until 1994, but it has been made in each vintage since, except for 1995. A blend called Westside Road Neighbors which is equal parts Allen, Bacigalupi, Bucher, Flax, and Rochioli Riverblock, debuted in 2002.

Over the years, Williams developed a "formula" for growing pinot noir, to which Cabral and Krausmann have made only minor changes since 2001. Crop thinning in the vineyard is aggressive: as much as 30 percent of the clusters are sacrificed for better concentration in the remainder. Between 10 percent and 25 percent whole clusters are used, depending on the ripeness of the stems and the history of the vineyard. A new cold room has allowed Cabral and Krausmann to hold fruit overnight before commencing crush. Three to four days of cold-soaking in open-tops precede the alcoholic fermentation, which is allowed to begin with resident yeast. At this point, when "you can smell" the resident yeast at work, the must is inoculated with a proprietary yeast made for Williams Selyem by a local laboratory, the starter for which came, during the mid-1980s, from a fermentation involving zinfandel from the Jackass Hill Vineyard. The primary fermentation then proceeds rather quickly, peaking around 88°F, and taking just five to six days (with punchdowns two to four times daily) to reach zero sugar. The must is immediately pressed, inoculated for malolactic fermentation, and transferred to barrel. The press juice, instead of being barreled separately, is used to top up each free-run barrel. New oak use, which used to run from 33 percent to 100 percent, has been slightly reduced, and now ranges from 25 percent to 80 percent, depending on the vineyard and the vintage. All barrels are François Frères medium toast from Tronçais forests.

The so-called appellation wines—Russian River Valley, Sonoma Coast, Central Coast, and sometimes also Sonoma and Mendocino County—are bottled after ten to eleven months in wood, but the vineyard-designated wines stay in barrel fourteen to nineteen months. There is no fining or filtration, and all wines get an additional eight to twelve months of bottle-aging before release. The combination of consistent winemaking and uniform use of François Frères barrels creates a strong impression of house style in all the wines, which are almost always intensely flavored and concentrated, but which remain transparent. Alcohol levels have crept up a bit in recent vintages for reasons Cabral cannot explain, but they remain relatively modest by California pinot standards.

TASTING NOTES

2005 *Allen Vineyard (tasted prerelease in 2007):* Light-to-medium garnet; whiffs of flowers, white pepper, Altoids (!), and potpourri; raspberry and strawberry on the palate, with black pepper, minerality, and some grip; soft and lactic; elegant and long.

2005 *Peay Vineyard (tasted prerelease in 2007):* Medium-dark black-red; explosive nose with all the wild aromatic superimpositions characteristic of the True Sonoma Coast; coffee and blackberry; peach pit and fresh, wild anise; potpourri and tobacco; sweet and stony with infused flowers on the palate; considerable intensity in a relatively light frame; suave, silky, impressive, and fine.

2005 *Weir Vineyard (tasted prerelease in 2007):* Medium-dark hue; aromas of ink, incense, vanilla, and Italian plum; sweet attack but then quickly minerally; intense flavors with some licorice and infused yellow flowers; tightly wound; needs time.

2002 *Sonoma Coast (tasted in 2005):* Dark, almost opaque brick-red; lifted aromatics with notes of orange peel; very rich and dense on the palate with cherry candy, forest floor, brewed black tea, and orange peel; noticeable tannin.

1999 *Rochioli Riverblock (tasted in* 2007*):* Aromas of toffee and black pepper; intense, elegant espresso and cherry flavors on the mid-palate with considerable minerality; deep, plummy cherry and kirsch in an almost chewy wrapper on the finish; quite rich but still elegant; drinks nicely.

WINDY OAKS ESTATE
Corralitos, California

Windy Oaks, 15 acres of pinot noir and one of chardonnay on a ridge overlooking Monterey Bay in the southwest corner of the Santa Cruz Mountains appellation, is the product of Jim and Judy Schultzes' three-plus decades of fascination with wine. Their passion began with trips from a home base in Chicago to various European wine lands in the 1970s and grew serious when they lived in Melbourne, Australia, in the 1980s, close to pinot-friendly vineyards in the Yarra Valley, on the Mornington Peninsula, and in Geelong.

When Jim Schultze's career in management consulting brought him to San Francisco in 1994, the couple first bought Judy's father's house near Corralitos and then adjacent land, on which they began to plant pinot noir in 1996. This land was once dry-farmed apple orchard turned to overgrown cow pasture. Most of the first crop (in 1999) was sold to DAVID BRUCE WINERY, but a small amount was saved for a debut vintage of Windy Oaks, and a tiny winery was built onsite in 2001. The site is remarkable not only for its commanding view of the

bay and a mesoclimate that features both early budbreaks and late harvests, but also for its *terroir,* where pinot seems to ripen physiologically with a relatively modest accumulation of sugar and impressive acid retention. The typical harvest at Windy Oaks picks at between 23.9 and 24.7 Brix with 8 to 9 grams of acid per liter. The plant material is mostly Dijon clones of pinot noir on various rootstocks, but Schultze also used some UCD 2A and 5, and in 2001 he planted a single block with cuttings he personally obtained from one of Burgundy's best-known vineyards. A second vineyard called Diane's Block—more accurately a separate vineyard than a separate block—about 6 miles away near Aptos, was planted entirely to pinot noir in 2002. In years when there is sufficient crop, fruit from the Corralitos vineyard is sold to THOMAS FOGARTY WINERY, Martin Alfaro, and (through 2006) TESTAROSSA VINEYARDS, which craft it into vineyard-designated (Schultze Family Vineyard) wines.

PROPRIETOR'S RESERVE IS AN ELEGANT WINE REDOLENT OF FLOWERS WITH A SILKY FINISH

WINES AND WINEMAKING NOTES
Schultze, who is his own self-taught winemaker, departs in nearly all significant respects from the consensus protocol. About a third of his fruit is fermented as whole clusters. A 50°F cold soak is followed by a hot fermentation and a long (ten to fourteen day) extended maceration. All yeasts (for both alcoholic and malolactic fermentations) are at least 50 percent resident. Beginning in 2004, some wood fermentors were used, which Schultze likes

for the flatter fermentation temperature curve they produce. The wines go to barrel without settling and are not racked barrel-to-barrel before bottling. The long barrel regime lasts nineteen to twenty-five months but emphasizes very tight-grained wood and staves that have been air-dried for three years. There is no fining or filtration.

The flagship wine, called Proprietor's Reserve, was made initially (1999–2002) from the oldest blocks (the steep Bay Block and adjacent Henry's Block) but evolved into a barrel selection as younger blocks came into production (although it is still primarily sourced from the oldest blocks). A second wine, called Estate Blend when it debuted in 2002 and Estate Cuvée since 2003, is fashioned from the fruit of younger blocks and from deselected barrels of Bay and Henry's. A block-designated Henry's was made beginning in 2003. In 2004 Windy Oaks also made a block-designated wine from the Aptos vineyard called Diane's, a block-designated wine from the 2001 planting (see above) called Estate Special Burgundy Clone, and the first of an annual "limited bottling" designed to showcase a vintage-specific experiment. In 2004 the experiment was 100 percent wild yeast. Proprietor's Reserve is an especially elegant wine redolent of flowers, orange peel, and red fruits with a long, silky finish; the Estate Cuvée usually exhibits a slightly darker, chewier, spicier, and more tannic persona.

TASTING NOTES

2003 *Proprietor's Reserve (tasted in 2007):* Brilliant light-to-medium garnet; intense sandalwood and a hint of *charcuterie* join the potpourri-dominated nose; bright attack featuring cherry-raspberry fruit and white pepper; satiny texture; extremely elegant; just a bit of bite at the end.

2002 *Proprietor's Reserve (tasted in a five-vintage vertical in 2006):* Brilliant medium

garnet; characteristic potpourri nose, but in this vintage also smoky and tarry; cherry, black fruit, resin, earth, briar, and black pepper on the palate; elegant but amply structured and almost full bodied; suede-textured and medium-long.

2001 *Proprietor's Reserve (tasted twice, in 2005 and 2006):* Brilliant, light-to-medium garnet with a pinkish rim; tangerine peel, potpourri, and exotic Indonesian spice on the nose; cherry and red berry fruit in the mouth with hints of tar, infused flowers, and mint; good acid and overall brilliance; very elegant, long, and silky.

2000 *Proprietor's Reserve (tasted in a five-vintage vertical in 2006):* Very pretty brilliant garnet color; aromas of hard spice and black pepper; cherry, raspberry, tar, and briar on the palate; intense but lithe and ethereal; simultaneously elegant and concentrated; medium in weight with a satiny finish. Very fine. A personal favorite.

1999 *Proprietor's Reserve (tasted in a five-vintage vertical in 2006):* Transparent, medium garnet; wild strawberry and potpourri dominate the expressive nose, with noticeable smokiness owing to all-new cooperage including one new half-barrel; bright cranberry fruit with hints of white pepper and mint define the palate at the outset, but blacker fruit emerges as the wine opens. Elegant, silky, and extremely attractive.

YAMHILL VALLEY VINEYARDS
McMinnville, Oregon

Yamhill Valley Vineyards is a 150-acre site in the foothills of the Coast Range southwest of McMinnville, purchased by its present owners, Denis Burger, Elaine McCall, and David Hinrichs—all with PhDs in various health science disciplines—in 1983. It is the second-oldest vineyard in what is now the McMinnville AVA, planted (and replanted) progressively in 1983, 1984, 1985, 1988, 1998, 2000, and 2006. There are now 98 acres under vine between the 200- and 600-foot contours, facing south and southeast, of which 73 acres (in eleven blocks) are dedicated to pinot noir. The soils are mostly clay-rich silt and loam overlying marine sedimentary structures. The amount of clay distinguishes this soil from most of its sedimentary neighbors, whereas its sedimentary base distinguishes it from the volcanic soils in the Dundee and Eola Hills.

The winery's first vintage was made the same year the vineyard was planted, from grapes purchased from the Hyland Vineyard, the immediate area's oldest, which had been planted in 1971. The first estate grapes were harvested in 1985, and the label has been entirely estate since 1989. Some estate fruit was sold to other makers until 2002, notably to FIDDLEHEAD CELLARS, which also made its Oregon pinots in the Yamhill Valley facility, and names its main Oregon cuvée in honor of the winery's Oldsville Road address. Since 1991 the winemaker has been Stephen Cary, who holds a master's degree in Mass Communications from Indiana University, and who worked as a wine broker and retailer before shifting his focus to wine production. Cary is also one of the founders of the well-known Steamboat Conference at which pinot-makers have gathered annually since 1981. In the last decade, he has also been a major force in the establishment of ties between North American producers pinot producers and colleagues in New Zealand and Tasmania.

WINES AND WINEMAKING NOTES

Yamhill Valley Vineyards has made an estate pinot every year since 1985. A "reserve" bottling, which is a barrel selection from four of the estate's eleven pinot blocks, was made sporadically until 1998, and annually since. In addition, a "very tight" barrel selection derived from two or three of the oldest blocks, dubbed "Tall Poppy," has been made in outstanding recent vintages: 1998, 2000, 2002, and 2005.

Observing that the estate's soils seem to produce wines that are "abnormally high in pigment and tannins," Cary has adopted winemaking protocols designed to manage extraction carefully and selectively. All grapes are destemmed. He avoids cold-soaking since "it makes the total tannin load too high," inoculates each fermenter immediately to achieve a rapid start, keeps fermentation temperatures under 88°F, and manipulates the cap by injecting air rather than by punching down. Extended macerations are avoided because "they increase the total tannin load more than they soften the present tannins." Blending is done in the late summer after the vintage, but the reserve and Tall Poppy lots are returned to barrel for a second winter. Long experience with estate-farmed grapes from a mature site has obvious advantages. It may also be that the unusual combination of high clay and sedimentary soils on a protected site in a throat through the Coast Range has created an exceptional *terroir*. But whatever is at work here, Cary is turning out some excellent wines that combine intensity of flavor and generosity of structure with seriousness and elegance.

TASTING NOTES

2005 *Estate (tasted in 2007):* Luminous, rosy-cherry color; dark fruit and earth with hints of sage; cherries, savory notes, and minerality on the palate; substantial and mouth coating with noticeable grip, but still very nicely built and finished; silky and attractive.

2003 *Reserve (tasted in 2007):* Deep, almost saturated black-red, verging on brick; lovely, unusual nose with hints of merbromin and potpourri; plainly ripe on the palate but hugely successful for a ripe vintage; wet clay and dark fruit; a beautifully sculpted mid-palate that is first satiny and then grippy; a hint of fruit-sweetness persists to the finish; tightly knit throughout and very attractive.

2002 *Tall Poppy (tasted in 2007):* Luminous medium ruby; earth and dark fruit on the nose with lively notes of lacquer and mint; fruit-sweetness wrapped in a sober, serious, and elegant package that balances fruit, grip, and minerality; some citrusy highlights; fine.

The producers listed below would have been profiled in these pages if appropriate arrangements could have been made. Unfortunately, these producers opted out, were unresponsive, or were unable to speak with me at a mutually convenient time.

AMBULLNEO VINEYARDS

AUBERT WINES

BONACCORSI WINE COMPANY

BROOKS WINERY

CARNEROS CREEK WINERY

CARTER VINEYARD

CARTLIDGE & BROWNE WINERY

DE PONTE CELLARS

J. CHRISTOPHER WINERY

FIRESTEED WINES

KALIN CELLARS

KING ESTATE

KISTLER VINEYARDS

MAGNET WINE

MARCASSIN VINEYARD

MCKINLAY VINEYARDS

RUTZ CELLARS

SOLENA CELLARS

STANGELAND WINERY

SUMMERLAND WINERY

VISION CELLARS

WHETSTONE WINE CELLARS

WITNESS TREE VINEYARD

A TO Z WINEWORKS
www.atozwineworks.com
503-538-1410

ACACIA WINERY
www.acaciawinery.com
707-226-9991
877-226-1700

ADEA WINE COMPANY
www.adeawine.com
503-662-4509

ADELAIDA CELLARS
www.adelaida.com
805-239-8980
800-676-1232

ADELSHEIM VINEYARD
www.adelsheim.com
503-538-3652

ALMA ROSA WINERY AND VINEYARDS
www.almarosawinery.com
805-688-9090

AMITY VINEYARDS
www.amityvineyards.com
503-835-2363

ANCIEN WINES
www.ancienwines.com
707-255-3908

ANDREW RICH WINES
www.andrewrichwines.com
503-284-6622

ANNE AMIE VINEYARDS
www.anneamie.com
503-864-2991

ARCADIAN WINERY
www.arcadianwinery.com
805-688-8799

ARCHERY SUMMIT ESTATE
www.archerysummit.com
503-864-4300
800-732-8822

ARGYLE WINERY
www.argylewinery.com
503-538-8520
888-427-4953

AU BON CLIMAT
www.aubonclimat.com
805-688-7111

AUGUST WEST WINES
www.augustwestwine.com

B. KOSUGE WINES
www.bkosugewines.com
707-738-8396

BABCOCK WINERY AND
VINEYARDS
www.babcockwinery.com
805-736-1455

BAILEYANA WINERY
www.baileyana.com
805-597-8200

BEAULIEU VINEYARD
www.bvwines.com
800-373-5896

BEAUX FRÈRES
www.beauxfreres.com
503-537-1137

BELLE GLOS
707-963-4204

BELLE PENTE VINEYARD AND WINERY
www.bellepente.com
503-852-9500

BELLE VALLÉE CELLARS
www.bellevallee.com
541-231-7972

BENTON-LANE WINERY
www.benton-lane.com
541-847-5792

BERAN VINEYARDS
www.beranvineyards.com
503-628-1298

BERGSTRÖM WINES
www.bergstromwines.com
503-554-0468

BETHEL HEIGHTS VINEYARD
www.bethelheights.com
503-581-2262

BOUCHAINE VINEYARDS
www.bouchaine.com
800-654-9463

BRANDBORG VINEYARD
AND WINERY
www.brandborgwine.com
541-584-2870

BREGGO CELLARS
www.breggo.com
707-895-9589

BREWER-CLIFTON
www.brewerclifton.com
805-735-9184

BRICK HOUSE WINE COMPANY
www.brickhousewines.com
503-539-5136

BROADLEY VINEYARDS AND WINERY
www.broadleyvineyards.com
541-847-5934

BROGAN CELLARS
www.brogancellars.com
707-473-0211

BUENA VISTA CARNEROS
http://buenavistacarneros.com
800-678-8504

BYRON VINEYARD AND WINERY
www.byronwines.com
805-934-4770

CALERA WINE COMPANY
www.calerawine.com
831-637-9170

CAMBRIA WINERY AND VINEYARD
www.cambriawines.com
888-339-9463
805-937-8091

CAMERON WINERY
www.cameronwines.com
503-538-0336

CAMPION WINES
www.campionwines.com
707-265-6733

CAPIAUX CELLARS
www.capiauxcellars.com
707-815-3191

CARABELLA VINEYARD
www.carabellawine.com
503-925-0972

CASA CARNEROS
www.casacarneros.com
707-257-8713

CASTLE ROCK WINERY
www.castlerockwinery.com
888-327-3777

CHALONE VINEYARD
www.chalonevineyard.com
707-299-2600

CHATEAU ST. JEAN
www.chateaustjean.com
707-833-4134

CHEHALEM WINES
www.chehalemwines.com
503-538-4700

CLOS DE LA TECH
408-943-2900

CLOS DU VAL WINE COMPANY
www.closduval.com
800-993-9463
707-261-5200

CLOS LACHANCE
www.closlachance.com
800-487-9463
408-686-1050

COBB WINES
www.cobbwines.com
707-874-1962

COOPER MOUNTAIN WINERY
www.coopermountainwine.com
503-649-0027

COPAIN WINE CELLARS
www.copainwines.com
707-836-8822

COSTA DE ORO WINERY
www.costadeorowinery.com
805-928-2727

CRISTOM VINEYARDS
www.cristomwines.com
503-375-3068

CUVAISON ESTATE WINES
www.cuvasion.com
707-942-6266

DAVID BRUCE WINERY
www.davidbrucewinery.com
800-397-9972
408-354-4214

DAVIS BYNUM WINES
www.davisbynum.com
866-442-7547

DAVIS FAMILY WINERY
www.davisfamilyvineyards.com
707-569-0171
866-338-9463

DE LOACH VINEYARDS
www.deloachvineyards.com
707-526-9111

DEHLINGER WINERY
www.delingerwinery.com
707-823-2378

DIERBERG VINEYARD AND THREE SAINTS
www.dierbergvineyard.com
www.threesaintsvineyard.com
805-693-0744

DOMAINE ALFRED
www.domainealfred.com
805-541-9463

DOMAINE CARNEROS
www.domainecarneros.com
800-716-2788

DOMAINE DROUHIN OREGON
www.domainedrouhin.com
503-864-2700

DOMAINE SERENE
www.domaineserene.com
866-864-6555

DUMOL WINE COMPANY
www.dumol.com
925-254-8922

DUNAH VINEYARD
AND WINERY
www.dunahwinery.com
707-829-9666

DUSKY GOOSE
www.duskygoose.com
503-435-7002

DUTTON-GOLDFIELD WINES
www.duttongoldfield.com
707-823-3887

EDNA VALLEY VINEYARD
www.ednavalleyvineyard.com
805-544-5855

EL MOLINO WINERY
www.elmolinowinery.com
707-963-3632

ELK COVE VINEYARDS
www.elkcove.com
503-985-7760
877-355-2683

EMERITUS VINEYARDS
www.emeritusvineyards.com
707-823-4464

ERATH VINEYARDS WINERY
www.erath.com
503-538-3318
800-539-9463

ESTERLINA VINEYARDS
www.esterlinavineyards.com
707-895-2920

ETUDE WINES
www.etudewines.com
707-257-5300

EVESHAM WOOD WINERY
www.eveshamwood.com
503-371-8478

THE EYRIE VINEYARDS
www.eyrievineyards.com
503-472-6315
888-440-4970

FAILLA WINES
www.faillawines.com
707-963-0530

FESS PARKER WINERY AND VINEYARDS
www.fessparker.com
805-688-1545
800-841-1104

FIDDLEHEAD CELLARS
www.fiddleheadcellars.com
805-742-0204

FLOWERS VINEYARD
AND WINERY
www.flowerswinery.com
707-847-3661

FLYING GOAT CELLARS
www.flyinggoatcellars.com
805-688-1814

FOLEY ESTATES VINEYARD AND
WINERY AND LINCOURT VINEYARDS
www.foleywines.com
805-737-6222
www.lincourtwines.com
805-688-8554

FORT ROSS VINEYARD
www.fortrossvineyard.com
415-701-9200

FOXEN VINEYARD AND WINERY
www.foxenvineyard.com
805-937-4251

FRANCIS TANNAHILL
www.francistannahill.com
503-554-1918

FREEMAN VINEYARD AND WINERY
www.freemanwinery.com
707-823-6937

THE GAINEY VINEYARD
www.gaineyvineyard.com
805-688-0558
888-424-6398

GARY FARRELL WINES
http://garyfarrellwines.com
707-473-2900

GLORIA FERRER CHAMPAGNE CAVES
www.gloriaferrer.com
707-996-7256

GOLDENEYE AND MIGRATION
www.goldeneyewinery.com
www.migrationwine.com
707-895-3202

GREENWOOD RIDGE VINEYARDS
www.greenwoodridge.com
707-895-2002

GUNDLACH BUNDSCHU WINERY
www.gunbun.com
707-938-5277
Tasting Room 707-939-3015

GYPSY DANCER ESTATES
www.gypsydancerestates.com
503-628-0955

HALLECK VINEYARD
www.halleckvineyard.com
707-829-8170

HAMACHER WINES
www.hamacherwines.com
503-852-7200

HAMEL WINES
707-433-9055

HANDLEY CELLARS
www.handleycellars.com
707-895-3876
800-733-3151

HANZELL VINEYARDS
www.hanzell.com
707-996-3860

HARTFORD FAMILY WINES
www.hartfordwines.com
707-887-8010

WILLIAM HATCHER WINES
www.williamhatcherwines.com
503-864-4489

HIRSCH VINEYARDS
www.hirschwineyards.com
707-847-3600

HITCHING POST WINES
www.hitchingpost2.com
805-688-0676

HUSCH VINEYARDS
www.huschvineyards.com
800-554-8724

INMAN FAMILY WINES
www.inmanfamilywines.com
707-395-0689

IRON HORSE VINEYARDS
www.ironhorsevineyards.com
707-887-1507

J. K. CARRIÈRE
www.jkcarriere.com
503-554-0721

J VINEYARDS AND WINERY
www.jwine.com
888-194-6326

JOSEPH SWAN VINEYARDS
www.swanwinery.com
707-573-3747

KAZMER & BLAISE
www.tricyclewineco.com
707-255-4929

KELLER ESTATE WINERY
www.kellerestate.com
707-765-2117

KEN BROWN WINES
www.kenbrownwines.com
805-688-4482

KEN WRIGHT CELLARS
www.kenwrightcellars.com
800-571-6825
503-852-7070

KOSTA BROWNE WINERY
www.kostabrowne.com
707-823-7430

LA CREMA WINERY
www.lacrema.com
800-314-1762

LA ROCHELLE WINERY
www.lrwine.com
925-243-6442

LACHINI VINEYARDS
www.lachinivineyards.com
503-864-4553

LAETITIA VINEYARD
AND WINERY
www.laetitiawine.com
805-481-772
888-809-8463

LANE TANNER WINES
www.lanetanner.com

LANGE ESTATE WINERY
www.langewinery.com
503-538-6476

LAZY RIVER VINEYARD
www.lazyrivervineyard.com
206-324-6708
503-852-6100

LEMELSON VINEYARDS
www.lemelsonvineyards.com
503-852-6619

LITTORAI WINES
www.littorai.com
707-823-9586

LONDER VINEYARDS
www.londervineyards.com
707-895-3900

RICHARD LONGORIA WINES
www.longoriawine.com
866-759-4637

LORING WINE COMPANY
www.loringwinecompany.com
877-592-9463

LYNMAR WINERY
www.lynmarwinery.com
707-829-3374

MACMURRAY RANCH
www.macmurrayranch.com
888-668-7729

MACPHAIL WINES
www.macphailwine.com
707-433-4780

MAHONEY VINEYARDS AND
FLEUR DE CALIFORNIA
www.mahoneyvineyards.com
www.fleurdecalifornia.com
707-265-9600
707-253-9463

MARIMAR ESTATE
www.marimarestate.com
707-823-4365

MAYSARA WINERY
www.maysara.com
503-843-1234

MELVILLE VINEYARD AND WINERY
www.melvillewinery.com
805-735-7030

MERRY EDWARDS WINES
www.merryedwards.com
707-823-7466
888-388-9050

MINER FAMILY WINERY
www.minerwines.com
800-366-9463

MIURA VINEYARDS
707-566-7739

ROBERT MONDAVI WINERY
www.robertmondaviwinery.com
888-766-6328

MORGAN WINERY
www.morganwinery.com
831-626-3700

MOUNT EDEN VINEYARDS
www.mounteden.com
888-865-9463

NALLE WINERY
www.nallewinery.com
707-433-1040

NAVARRO VINEYARDS
www.navarrowine.com
800-537-9463
707-895-3686

THE OJAI VINEYARD
www.ojaivineyard.com
805-649-1674

OLIVET LANE VINEYARD AND PELLEGRINI
FAMILY VINEYARDS
www.pellegrinisonoma.com
800-891-0244

OROGENY
www.orogenyvineyards.com
877-254-4250

ORTMAN FAMILY WINES
www.ortmanvineyards.com
805-473-9463

PANTHER CREEK CELLARS
www.panthercreekcellars.com
503-472-8080

PAPAPIETRO PERRY WINES
www.papapietro-perry.com
707-433-0422
877-467-4668

PATRICIA GREEN CELLARS
www.patriciagreencellars.com
503-554-0821

PATTON VALLEY VINEYARDS
www.pattonvalley.com
503-985-3445

PATZ & HALL WINE COMPANY
www.patzhall.com
877-265-6700
707-265-7700

PAUL HOBBS WINES
www.paulhobbs.com
707-824-9879

PAUL LATO WINES
www.paullatowines.com
805-260-3210

PEAY VINEYARDS
www.peayvineyards.com

PENNER-ASH WINES
www.pennerash.com
503-554-5545

PEY-MARIN VINEYARDS AND
PEY-LUCIA VINEYARDS
www.marinwines.com
415-455-9463

PISONI VINEYARDS AND
WINERY AND LUCIA
www.pisonivineyards.com
800-270-2525

PONZI VINEYARDS
www.ponziwines.com
503-628-1227

PORTER CREEK VINEYARDS
www.portercreekvineyards.com
707-433-6321

R. STUART & CO.
www.rstuartandco.com
866-472-6990

RADIO-COTEAU WINE CELLARS
www.radiocoteau.com
707-823-2578

RAPTOR RIDGE WINERY
www.raptoridge.com
503-887-5595

RED CAR WINES
www.red-car-wine.com
310-839-7300

REX HILL WINERY
www.rexhill.com
800-739-4455

RHYS VINEYARDS AND
ALESIA WINES
www.rhysvineyards.com
866-511-1520
650-591-1520

RIVERS-MARIE
www.riversmarie.com
707-942-2172

ROAR WINES
www.roarwines.com
831-675-1681

ROBERT SINSKEY VINEYARDS
www.robertsinskey.com
800-869-2030
707-944-9090

ROCHIOLI VINEYARD AND WINERY
www.rochiolivineyard.com
707-433-2305

RODNEY STRONG VINEYARDS
www.rodneystrong.com
707-431-1533

ROESSLER WINES
www.roesslercellars.com
707-933-4440

RR WINERY
www.ribbonridgewinery.com
503-706-9277

RUSACK VINEYARDS
www.rusack.com
805-688-1278

SAINTSBURY
www.saintsbury.com
707-252-0592

SANFORD WINERY
www.sanfordwinery.com
800-426-9463
805-735-5900

SAVANNAH-CHANELLE VINEYARD
www.savannahchanelle.com
408-741-2934

SCHERRER WINES
www.scherrerwinery.com
707-823-8980

SCHOOL HOUSE VINEYARD
www.schoolhousevineyard.com
707-963-4240

SCHUG CARNEROS ESTATE
www.schugwinery.com
707-939-9363
800-966-9365

SCOOT PAUL WINES
www.scottpaul.com
503-852-7300

SEA SMOKE CELLARS
www.seasmokecellars.com
805-737-1600

SHEA WINE CELLARS
www.sheawinecellars.com
503-241-6527

SIDURI WINES
www.siduri.com
707-578-3882

SILVAN RIDGE WINERY
www.silvanridge.com
866-574-5826

SINEANN
www.sineann.com
503-341-2698

SKEWIS WINES
www.skewis.com
707-431-2160

SOKOL BLOSSER WINERY
www.sokolblosser.com
800-582-6668
503-864-2282

SONNET WINES
www.sonnetwinecellars.com
831-685-9463

SOTER VINEYARDS
www.sotervineyards.com
503-662-5600

ST. INNOCENT WINERY
www.stinnocentwine.com
503-378-1526

STEPHEN ROSS WINES
www.stephenrosswine.com
805-594-1318

STEVENSON-BARRIE
503-550-1963

STOLLER VINEYARDS
www.stollervineyards.com
503-864-3404

T. R ELLIOTT
www.elliottfamilycellars.com
707-237-4900

TALISMAN WINES
www.talismanwine.com
707-258-5722

TALLEY VINEYARDS
www.talleyvineyards.com
805-489-0446

TANDEM WINERY
www.tandemwinery.com
707-823-2794

TANTARA WINERY
www.tantarawinery.com
805-938-5051

TAZ VINEYARDS
www.tazvineyards.com
888-544-3223

TESTAROSSA WINES
www.testarossa.com
408-354-6150

THOMAS FOGARTY WINERY
www.fogartywinery.com
650-851-6777

TOLOSA WINERY
www.tolosawinery.com
866-782-0300

TORII MOR WINERY
www.toriimorwinery.com
800-839-5004

TUDOR WINES
www.tudorwines.com
831-224-2116

VARNER
www.varnerwine.com
650-321-4894

W. H. SMITH WINES
www.whsmithwines.com
707-965-9726

WALTER HANSEL WINERY
www.walterhanselwinery.com
707-525-3614

WESTREY WINE COMPANY
www.westrey.com
503-434-6357

WHITCRAFT WINES
www.whitcraftwinery.com
805-965-0956

WHITE ROSE VINEYARD
www.whiterosewines.com
949-275-8021

WILD HORSE WINERY
AND VINEYARDS
www.wildhorsewinery.com
805-434-2541

WILLAKENZIE ESTATE WINERY
www.willakenzie.com
503-662-3280
888-953-9463

WILLAMETTE VALLEY VINEYARDS
www.willamettevalleyvineyards.com
800-344-9463
503-588-9463

WILLIAMS SELYEM
www.williamsselyem.com
707-433-6425

WINDY OAKS ESTATE
www.windyoaksestate.com
831-786-9463

YAMHILL VALLEY VINEYARDS
http://yamhill.com
503-843-3100
800-825-4845

Vintage matters. Mother Nature never behaves exactly the same way twice, anyplace, and weather is actually much more consequential than climate in winegrowing. Even in California, which has a reputation for reliably good climate year-round and especially during the growing season for wine grapes, weather can vary dramatically from year to year and place to place. Heat accumulation, defined for North American purposes as the aggregation, from April through October, of each month's excess of mean temperature over 50°F, can vary by as much as 500 degree days from one year to the next, which has a huge impact on the character of wines produced by the same vineyard in two such differing years. Even if heat accumulation is quite similar, however, the shape of the heat accumulation curve through the growing season, as well as both the total amount and the distribution of rainfall, can be decidedly different, and they can stamp even superficially similar vintages with decidedly different characters. Furthermore, the exact timing of certain weather events, such as spring frosts, hailstorms, and rain, can dictate whether those events have an important impact on the amount of fruit the vines produce during the year in question, whether they set the stage for a difficult harvest involving compromised fruit, or whether they simply pass with little effect. It is also true that weather early in the growing season substantially affects the vines' fruitfulness the following year, because buds destined for fruit production in the following season are already being produced in the preceding season and are enormously encouraged by warm, sunny weather during the period of the vines' flowering.

The volume of production in any given year is most important to producers because it affects the economics of their business, and it can ripple to consumers in the form of higher (or lower) prices and/or supply constraints. Overall, however, enlightened consumers will recognize that vintage notes are not straightforward indicators of quality, that the oft-asserted inverse correlation between quantity and quality (the bigger the crop, the less good the wine) is very often untrue, and that it is unwise to talk too loosely about "good" vintages and "poor" or "disappointing" ones based on temperature. Warm, dry years are usually well-reviewed and highly scored when the wines are first released, largely because the wines taste riper out of the gate, but the wines from cool years can be excellent and can show far better six or ten years after the vintage than do their warm vintage counterparts. And genuinely hot years, even in high-latitude locations like northern Oregon or Burgundy where heat is supposed to be a good thing, are often a mixed blessing at best, throwing a large number of ultraripe wines with raisiny or pruney flavors.

In the notes that follow, California North Coast refers generally to the coastal areas north of San Francisco, including Los Carneros; to most pinot-friendly appellations in Sonoma County; and to the Anderson Valley in Mendocino County. California Central Coast, on the other hand, applies generally to cooler appellations in the Salinas Valley and in San Luis Obispo County, and to the Santa Maria Valley and Sta. Rita Hills regions in Santa Barbara County. Willamette Valley is self-explanatory, although most of the temperature data was collected at the north end of that valley. In instances in which a single appellation within a region was affected by weather events not generally felt in the larger region, that variation is indicated.

1999

Oregon: Oregon saw a mild and very wet winter (the second wettest in a century), a late budbreak, and unusually cool temperatures in the second calendar quarter. Although the weather was then warm from mid- to late-summer, all phenological markers were pushed back chronologically, so that veraison occurred in late September, and harvest (generally) in late October, although some makers did not finish picking until mid-November. No rain fell until after the harvest, however, so growers who had the courage to wait got completely ripe fruit with excellent acidity. Very good pinots were made from this vintage, with fine structures, beautiful textures, and good potential to age brilliantly, which they have so far.

California North Coast: This region generally saw a cold, wet winter, with rainfall that persisted intermittently through much of the spring. Rainfall was about 5 inches above normal in Carneros and the True Sonoma Coast. Cool spring temperatures delayed budbreak, veraison, and harvest in many vineyards. Growers experienced widespread problems with mildew and botrytis, especially in the True Sonoma Coast. Summer temperatures were mostly moderate, followed by a few heat spikes in the early fall. The crop was generally much smaller than average, but a satisfactory combination of ripeness and acidity characterized most wines, the best of which were "bold" and "forward."

California Central Coast: This region experienced a cool, dry growing season from Monterey to San Luis Obispo, with a consequently late budbreak and poor fruit set in Monterey. A milder spring in Santa Barbara, but cool-to-mild summer temperatures throughout the area, extended the phonological calendar and pushed harvest dates into late September or early October. Exceptionally little rain fell (half the normal amount in Santa Barbara), which helped keep hanging grapes extremely healthy, and the cool season helped maintain good levels of natural acidity. Tasty, bright wines were the overall result.

2000

Willamette Valley: This area saw below average rainfall, mild weather in April and May, and warm days and cool nights for most of the summer. The conditions were perfect for good pinot overall, except for the high relative humidity during the summer months, which produced mildew in some vineyards, and about an inch of rain that occurred during harvest, which necessitated very rigorous sorting on the crushpad. Good levels of ripeness and reasonable acidity were seen in the end, although the wines are softer and lusher than the 1999s and are best suited to near-term enjoyment.

California North Coast: This region experienced a cool winter and an abnormally wet spring, especially in the Russian River Valley, but budbreak was not affected in most areas. Generally warm and sunny weather occurred from early summer through the harvest, with high diurnal temperature variation. This year was regarded as a "return to normal" by most North Coast growers, following two cool vintages. Significant rainfall occurring in October on the true Coast presented issues for growers who picked late. Well-colored, nicely proportioned, ripe wines were made in most appellations; they are neither big nor heavy and are still drinking well.

California Central Coast: Most appellations in this area saw a mild winter, but spring temperatures were erratic. A May heat spike in Monterey reduced fruit set there, while the crop size in Edna Valley was above average. Continuing drought-like conditions in Santa Barbara kept crop levels below normal. Mild to warm summer temperatures were seen throughout the region, and harvest was from mid-September through early October. Relatively big wines were the overall result.

2001

Willamette Valley: Winter rainfall was much lower than normal in this area; May and June were warm with little rain, and it was warm and dry from July through September. This vintage produced fleshy, ripe pinots that drank well early and are still holding well, but they exhibit lower-than-usual acidity. The vintage was generous, with yields considerably above average.

California North Coast: A cool-to-cold winter followed by serious frosts through-out the region between February and April characterized this region. Major loss of crop occurred in the True Sonoma Coast and in the Russian River Valley, where above average rainfall was seen as well. There was a slightly early bloom and veraison in Carneros, and quite temperate days in the last month before the harvest. Because the autumn rainy season started late in most areas, growers could choose when to pick. Ripe and nicely structured wines were the result, showing balance and finesse and a bit less alcohol than the previous vintage.

California Central Coast: There was a mild winter with above average rainfall throughout this region; especially substantial rains fell in the first calendar quarter. Temperatures were erratic but generally mild during the late spring and early summer, when the vines flowered. It was generally warm in July and August, and then dry and seasonable in September. The yield was below normal in most appellations, but the vintage produced serious wines with good structure and acidity, owing primarily to the temperate weather that prevailed from veraison through the harvest. Wines from this area are quite similar to their counterparts in the preceding vintage.

2002

Willamette Valley: This area saw another dry winter, but it was much less dry than 2001. Spring rains and frosts interfered with fruit set, reducing yields. Generally warm and dry conditions without significant heat waves prevailed for most of the summer months. Mild temperatures occurred in September and October, an inch of rain fell at the end of September, and then unusually dry weather prevailed through October. Some growers picked before the late September rain, when sugar levels were high and acid levels low, resulting in the production of some alcoholic wines; the rains revived the grapes, and growers who harvested later were blessed with a combination of good ripeness and good acidity. These are rich and relatively large wines overall, but they are generally balanced and are evolving well.

California North Coast: This area experienced a highly variable year, with above average rainfall in the Russian River Valley, but drier than average weather in Carneros, along the True Sonoma Coast, and in Anderson Valley. Spring tempera-tures bounced from warm to cool and back to warm. Warm and cool cycles contin-ued throughout the summer. It was generally warm and dry at harvest time. Yields were low overall, and about 20 percent under normal in the Russian River Valley, owing primarily to shatter caused by the cool and windy spring. Deeply-colored, serious pinots, widely regarded as some of the best in recent history, were produced from this vintage.

California Central Coast: Another drought year occurred throughout the region. Some warm temperatures were seen in February, especially in Santa Barbara, which led to early budbreak; then, the weather was erratic and often cool from March through May. A warm, dry summer, but without many significant heat spikes, occurred, followed by a cool October. The harvest was late in most appellations, extending into November for some producers in Santa Barbara. Normal crop levels were seen in Monterey, and lighter than normal in Edna Valley and Santa Barbara. The combination of small crop load, cool late-season temperatures, and late harvest produced ripe flavors with good balance and acidity.

2003

Willamette Valley: This area saw a typically wet winter, and a warmer and wetter-than-usual spring. It was consistently dry and warm from June through August and pathologically hot in September, despite some rain in late August and early September. The harvest occurred about one week earlier than usual, but many growers picked ultraripe fruit (with similarly extraripe tannins) that gave high alcohol levels and often raisiny flavors to the finished wines. The conditions were uncannily similar to Burgundy in the same vintage, although Burgundy was intensely hot as early as June.

California North Coast: An exceptionally mild, dry winter occurred in this area, but significant rain fell in April, and then it was warm in May. This combination of moisture and warm temperatures produced disease pressure and lower than normal set, and prefigured a "troublesome" vintage. The summer was generally warm and dry, although August was cool in Carneros, but another heat spell hit in September, which sent growers scurrying to harvest. Late and uneven bloom occurred in the Anderson Valley. Across Sonoma County, there were the lowest yields for pinot noir seen in the previous seven years. Rich but often acid-challenged wines with very ripe, fine-grained tannins were typical.

California Central Coast: Another mild, dry winter with above-normal temperatures in the first calendar quarter and consequential early budbreak was seen in this area. Cooler temperatures prevailed in Monterey and Santa Barbara from April through June, with some erratic spiking during May and June in Santa Barbara. Poor fruit set occurred in many vineyards, leading to low yields. Summer was warm throughout the region, and an early harvest followed in Monterey and in the Edna Valley; in Santa Barbara, the harvest began early but was subsequently very protracted owing to cool weather in September. Small berries and good concentration resulted. Most observers believe that the North Coast slightly outperformed the Central Coast, and that the north end of the Central Coast fared slightly better than did Santa Barbara.

2004

Willamette Valley: This area saw a cold, wet winter and a cool spring with a late budbreak. This combination reduced crop yields by 20 to 50 percent. It was warmer in June, hot in July, and warm again with some rain in August and September. Vineyards picked early were adversely affected by the late-season rain, but since October was dry, vineyards that were picked later gave ripe, extracted wines, minus the excessively high alcohol characteristic of the previous year.

California North Coast: The winter was mild and dry in this region; spring was early and warm; April was cool in most areas. Warm days and cool nights, which were seen throughout the summer, including September, drove both budbreak and veraison ahead of schedule. The harvest began quite early throughout the North Coast, usually before the end of August, and most pinot was entirely picked before the middle of September. Many North Coast pinots were riper and richer than normal, and some makers intervened to reduce alcohol levels. Yields were below normal, and many wines emerged concentrated and intense.

California South Coast: Near-normal rainfall occurred in all areas, thanks primarily to late winter and early spring precipitation. These rains delayed budbreak in Edna Valley, and reduced fruit set for some vineyards in Santa Barbara. Summer was generally warm and dry, but all regions experienced major and unforeseen heat spikes in September, escalating sugar levels dramatically in just a few days. Despite a rush to harvest early, much of the pinot noir on the southern Central Coast was picked ultraripe. Many wines exhibit much higher than usual concentrations of alcohol, as well as jammy flavors. For many makers, this was the vintage that "got away."

2005

Willamette Valley: This area experienced an atypically dry winter, followed by heavy rains and cool weather at the end of the first calendar quarter and the beginning of the second. Uneven set reduced yields and generated problems with mildew and rot. Warm, dry weather prevailed from July through September. The season's end was cool, and significant rain fell at the end of September, but the wines emerged nicely balanced with good acidity and supple, if not genuinely ripe, tannins, in part because the early-season set failures left a relatively light crop load to ripen.

California North Coast: Winter was wet in most areas, and it was cold until March, when most areas except Anderson Valley and Carneros warmed up significantly and experienced early budbreak. (Budbreak in Carneros was about five days later than normal.) More rain fell from March through May, after the early budbreak, resulting in very poor fruit set in some areas. Some vineyards in the "deep" end of Anderson Valley, some coastal vineyards in Sonoma, and some sites in the Santa Cruz Mountains were very badly damaged, in some cases by late frosts as well as late rain. From June onward, in most areas, temperatures were seasonable, although localized above-normal humidity created mildew and botrytis issues for some growers. Overall heat accumulation *after budbreak* coincided almost perfectly with multiyear "normal" conditions in nearly all areas. A slightly late harvest occurred on Sonoma Mountain; in the Russian River Valley, however, most growers picked by mid-September. The crop was lighter than normal almost everywhere; there was catastrophic failure in some cold, exposed sites near the coast.

California Central Coast: A warm, wet winter occurred in this area, too, with the above-normal winter temperatures leading to an early budbreak. A mild spring and summer compensated for the season's early start, bringing bloom, veraison, and harvest close to normal dates in Edna Valley and to later-than-normal dates in many vineyards in Monterey and Santa Barbara. Higher-than-normal yields were seen in most areas. Cool overnight temperatures during the warmest parts of the growing season helped maintain good acid levels in the grapes, producing ripe but elegant and refined wines in most vineyards.

2006

Willamette Valley: This area saw a much wetter than average winter (and a wetter growing season overall), but March was precociously warm, producing early budbreak. The weather was also warm and dry in the second and third calendar quarters, except that a grey and drizzly week in mid-September was sandwiched between two hot and sunny periods at the beginning and end of the month. Nights remained consistently cool, however, which worked to preserve natural acidity. Yields varied depending upon location but were higher almost everywhere than they had been in 2004 and 2005. The wines are ripe and fruit driven but also graceful and delicate; they show density and depth without weight, and have potential to age attractively.

California North Coast: This region experienced a universally cool and very wet winter, which delayed the budbreak in all areas. Warm weather was seen in July, followed by mild temperatures in August and September, which pushed the harvest into October. There was higher-than-normal rainfall in all areas, but also generally normal to above-normal yield. Tasted prerelease, many of these wines show excellent balance, full flavors, good intensity, and very modest alcoholic strength.

California Central Coast: Mild winter temperatures prevailed throughout the region, resulting in early budbreak. Considerable rain fell from March through early

May, however, slowing phonological development until the rains ceased and temperatures warmed up in late May and June. A significant heat wave affected vineyards in July; near-normal temperatures resumed in August, followed by cooler-than-normal weather in September. Monterey picked from early September to early October, but the southern Central Coast generally picked later than usual. In Edna Valley, this was the latest vintage in recent memory. Normal yields were seen in most areas, but they were lower than in 2005. As in the North Coast, many wines show an excellent equilibrium of alcoholic strength and phenological ripeness.

appellation: The geographical provenance of a wine. In the United States, the names of states, counties, and American Viticultural Areas (AVAs) can be used as wine appellations, as can Delimited Viticultural Areas (DVAs) in Canada. In France, *appellation* is usually short for *appellation d'origine contrôlée* (see *AOC*, below). Confusingly, some North American producers have begun to use the phrase *appellation wines* to designate blends made from several vineyards within a single county or AVA. In this usage, they wish to differentiate blended wines from single-vineyard (a.k.a. vineyard-designated) wines. Properly speaking, the single-vineyard wines are appellation wines, too.

AOC or *AC (Appellation d'origine contrôlée)*: The French system of controlled appellations of origin for wines and some food products debuted in the 1930s. Often described for simplicity as the French equivalent of American AVAs (see below), French appellations are much more complicated. While an AVA defines a region only by its geographic perimeter, French *AOC* regulations stipulate at least which grape varieties may be grown in the appellation and what maximum yield is permitted, and they sometimes codify other parameters of winegrowing and winemaking as well. The *AOC* delineations are especially arcane in Burgundy, where the surface area entitled to an appellation can be very small, and some appellations are nested three and four deep.

AVA (American Viticultural Area): Geographically delimited wine regions in the United States that are neither counties nor states (see *appellation,* above). They are created by petition and approved by the Alcohol and Tobacco Tax and Trade Bureau (TTB)—which was formerly the Bureau of Alcohol, Tobacco and Firearms (ATF)—in the Department of the Treasury. Some AVAs are soundly based on viticulturally relevant criteria; others are seriously heterogeneous and significant primarily as marketing mechanisms.

bleeding: To increase the concentration of a finished wine, or to produce both rosé and red wines from the same batch of grapes, winemakers sometimes elect to remove some lightly colored juice from a fermentation vessel early in the fermentation process. In principle, this has the effect of increasing the skin-to-juice ratio in what remains, enhancing color and extraction. From French *saignée.*

bloom *or* flowering: The second marker in the annual growth cycle of the vine; the point at which the vine flowers and the first small green berries are set.

brettanomyces ("brett"): A type of yeast that occurs naturally wherever wine grapes are handled. If brettanomyces is not eliminated with sulfur dioxide or through filtration, it can persist into finished wine. Controversial, it is sometimes associated with complexity in pinot noir, including the aromas and flavors described as barnyard and forest floor, but many winemakers refer to brettanomyces as a spoilage yeast that can give rise to "mousy" or dirty flavors.

Brix: A numeric value (named for Adolf Brix, a nineteenth-century German scientist) used in North America to express the concentration of dissolved compounds in grape juice. Since 90 percent of this material in ripe grapes is sugar, Brix is usually accepted as a surrogate for the sugar content at harvest and just before it. One degree Brix equates to approximately 18 grams of sugar per liter of juice.

budbreak: The first marker in the annual growth cycle of a grapevine, budbreak is the point at which small green shoots emerge from each bud on the vine. In regions with mild winters and early onset of spring, like the southern Central Coast of California, budbreak occurs early. Early budbreak can be a hazard in regions like the Finger Lakes, however, where damaging frosts can occur as late as May.

budwood: Synonymous with vine cuttings taken for the specific purpose of grafting to rootstock or to an existing vine, or for propagation as a new own-rooted vine plant (see *grafts*). Budwood is fundamental to vegetative propagation, which is the only way to generate new vine plants that are genetically identical to their parents.

canopy management: See vine farming.

cap: When red grapes are fermented, the skins and stems (if the grape clusters were not destemmed in advance) rise to the surface of the fermentation vessel, lifted by their lighter weight and by the constant formation of carbon dioxide in the must, until a raftlike "cap" forms on top of the juice. Because color, flavor, and structure in red wines come from compounds in the skins, it is essential to keep the cap in contact with the juice until the combination of juice and cap is pressed (see *pumpover; punchdown* for two illustrations of "cap management" techniques).

carbonic maceration: When grapes are held uncrushed in an anaerobic environment (i.e., carbon dioxide is used to eliminate oxygen) some sugar is converted to alcohol without the intervention of yeasts. This technique is used especially but not exclusively in Beaujolais to make light, bright, fruit-forward wines. Some American makers also use this approach for some lots of pinot noir, where they seek the same properties in the finished wine. Confusingly, however, they often call the process whole-cluster fermentation, a term usually associated with conventional, open-top fermentations of un-destemmed grapes, which has nothing to do with carbonic maceration.

chaptalize: Named for Jean-Antoine Chaptal, an early-nineteenth-century French chemist, chaptalization is the process of adding sugar to grape juice before fermentation or, more commonly, to the must during fermentation. If the concentration of sugar is increased, the finished wine will develop higher alcoholic strength. Chaptalization is common practice with pinot noir in Burgundy and is permitted in New York, Oregon, and Canada.

clones *and* clonal selection: A clone is any population of vines propagated asexually from a single mother vine. Clonal selection is the process of identifying individual, disease-free mother vines that display desirable properties, keeping the cuttings from each potential mother vine separate, and eventually propagating a large population of genetically identical clones. Clonal selection is an alternative to mass selection (*sélection massale* in French) or *field selection* (see below).

cold soak *or* prefermentation maceration: After harvested grapes, destemmed or not and crushed or not, are transferred to the vessel in which they will ferment, sometimes that vessel is kept cold for a period of time in order to delay the onset of fermentation. This first phase of winemaking is called a cold soak or a prefermentation maceration. There are many ways to keep the vessel and its contents cold: some tanks are manufactured with jackets in which cold water can be circulated; dry ice can be layered in with the fruit; or the vessel and its contents can be moved into a refrigerated room. Cold soaking favors aqueous extraction, which is generally associated with fruitier flavors in the finished wine. Maceration may also occur after the primary fermentation has finished, in which case it is called *long vatting, long skin contact, post-fermentation maceration,* or *extended maceration.* Makers who practice these techniques on pinot noir argue that tannin molecules polymerize during extended maceration, which make them seem softer in the finished wine. Recent research suggests, however, that this may not be true.

concentration; concentrator: Various techniques, processes, and equipment whose effect is to remove water from grapes or from grape must early in the fermentation process. Though controversial, concentration can be an alternative to chaptalization (see *chaptalize,* above) or a remedy for grapes that have been bloated by rain at the end of the growing season.

crushpad: Harvested grapes' first stop at the winery. The crushpad can be as simple as a bit of pavement where the winery moves the grapes, one way or another, from the bins or gondolas in which they arrive from the vineyard into the vessels in which they will be fermented. Most wineries employ destemming machines on the crushpad, or crusher-destemmers, and many also use some kind of sorting table to separate healthy grapes from rot, leaves, and other undesirable material.

custom crush: In North America, many wineries with a bit of extra space and staff agree to make wine, from scratch, for another party. In general, the other party has purchased the fruit independently, owns the wine throughout the process, and is responsible for marketing the finished product. In some instances, the client makes all winemaking decisions, instructing the winery to follow, more or less, his or her recipe. In other cases, the client relies heavily on advice from the host winery. The defining property of a custom crush, however, is that the custom-crushed lots of wine are handled separately throughout and are effectively "made to order." Many new brands of pinot noir have been launched as custom-crush operations in an existing winery.

cuvée: Derived from *cuve*, French for a tank or vat. In France, it has specialized meanings, especially in Champagne. In the Anglophone wine world, its meanings derive from the fact that one tank or vat of wine, of whatever size, is the smallest lot of wine that can be separately handled throughout the winemaking process, and thus develop and maintain a distinct identity. Thus cuvée is often used to denote a batch of wine that is somehow different from other lots made in the same winery in the same vintage. A cuvée may be distinct because it was picked from a special block of vineyard, was fermented using a different strain of yeast, followed a different barrel regime, or was left unfiltered at the end when related lots were filtered. Alternatively, in the hands of winemakers who blend, different cuvées may represent different blends from the same overall palette of raw materials.

délastage; drain-and-return: See *punchdown* and *pumpover.*

élevage: The phase of winemaking that begins when the fermented must is drained or pressed and ends when the wine is readied for bottling.

estate: In American wine parlance, wines made from grapes grown in vineyards owned by the winery or farmed by the winery under a long-term lease are called estate wines, or estate bottled wine—provided that both vineyard and winery are located within the appellation specified on the label. Grapes from winery-owned vineyards are also loosely described as estate fruit, whereas other grapes are called purchased or non-estate fruit. A winery that grows all the grapes used to make its wines is known as an estate producer.

eutypa: A destructive fungal disease that attacks the wood of grapevines, apricots, and some other plants, entering the plant through pruning wounds. Eutypa is especially prevalent in damp or windy conditions.

field selection: A process in which cuttings for propagation are deliberately taken from many mother vines in an effort to privilege and preserve genetic diversity. (By contrast, see *clones* and *clonal selection,* above.)

fining; filtration: Two principal ways to clarify wine before bottling. Fining involves the introduction into the wine of a substance like egg white, whose physical properties attach to suspended particulate matter and drag it out of the wine. Some winemakers say fining also softens aggressively astringent tannins; others believe this use of fining is futile. The other main way to clarify wine is *filtration*. Although the basic process is simple enough—the liquid is strained through some medium that interdicts the passage of particles larger than a predetermined size—there are many variations on the theme, and the suite of filtration techniques is more controversial that it deserves to be. Some winemakers are strongly opposed to filtration philosophically, especially for pinot noir, and they thus bend their winemaking practices to avoid it entirely.

FPS (Foundation Plant Services): Called FPMS (Foundation Plant Materials Service) until 2003, FPS is a self-supporting service department of the University of California Davis. It handles the import and quarantine of various plant materials including vines and cuttings of grapes, maintains a foundation vineyard of grape varieties and selections, and distributes healthy plant materials to nurseries and other customers throughout the United States. It also maintains the registry used in the United States to identify the various clones and selections of grape varieties, including pinot noir. See *UCD numbers*.

free-run juice: At the end of the primary fermentation, when the grape must is drained out of the fermentor, the free-run juice is that portion of the contents of the fermentation vessel which runs off without pressing. Free-run juice accounts for more than half of the contents of each fermentor. The balance is pressed, and the juice expelled from the press is called the *press fraction*. Free-run juice is conventionally accepted as the superior product, but many winemakers like the press fraction for the flavor and concentration it brings to the finished wine.

fruit bin: A large square bin (sometimes called a T-bin), usually about 5 feet on a side, made of plastic or plywood lined with plastic, conventionally used to store and transport fruits like apples and pears. As is or slightly modified, fruit bins are now commonly used as fermentation vessels by winemakers who work with small lots. A single-height fruit bin will generally accommodate about half a ton of grapes; double-height bins take a full ton.

grafts: Most cultivated grapevines planted since the end of the nineteenth century are grafts of wine-worthy scion material on a *rootstock* variety that is resistant to phylloxera. Resistant rootstocks are bred from nonvinifera species of the Vitis genus. If the rootstock was planted first, and the scion material joined to it in the vineyard, the vines are said to be *field grafts*. If the grafting takes place indoors and the vines are planted as prejoined units, the plants are called *bench grafts*. Ungrafted vines, which account for a tiny percentage of the total, are also called own-rooted vines. Some winegrowers believe that own-rooted vines are more vigorous than grafted vines and produce grapes with better flavors.

grand cru; premier cru: These terms are applied to a short list of Burgundy's finest vineyards, with *grand cru* theoretically reserved for just 32 vineyards regarded as the crème de la crème, and *premier cru* applying to the 476 next-best. In Burgundy, unlike Bordeaux, the terms are applied to sites, not to makers or brands. The designations are part of the *Appellation d'origine contrôlée* system (see *AOC,* above), and more stringent requirements (for sugar accumulation and yield management) apply to *grand cru* and *premier cru* wines than to village and regional wines. *Grand cru* and *premier cru* vineyards account for only a tiny fraction of Burgundy's planted surface.

green harvest: The practice of removing and discarding some of a vine's grape clusters before the end of the growing season. Green harvesting is done to reduce yield at harvest, which is thought to improve concentration and quality in the remaining fruit; to hasten ripening, especially in cool sites or unusually cool years; or to eliminate clusters that are lagging behind the overall ripening process, threatening uneven outcomes when the vineyard is finally picked.

hang time: The elapsed time from the second marker in the annual growth cycle of a grapevine (called bloom, when the first tiny green berries are set) to harvest. Most growers believe longer hang times correlate with more complete flavor development. In North America, hang times for pinot noir range from as few as thirteen weeks to as many as eighteen, depending on region and vintage.

increase block: When FPMS (see *FPS,* above) began distributing disease-free plant material in the 1950s, its small vineyards were unable to furnish enough buds to individual growers to plant entire vineyards. Agreements were therefore made with selected nurseries and wineries to take small quantities of budwood and segregate the vines propagated from those cuttings, so that cuttings taken in their turn from second-, third-, and fourth-generation vines would be as healthy and true to type as the first-generation cuttings from FPMS. The vineyard blocks set aside for this purpose are called certified increase blocks.

lees: The sediment that falls to the bottom of any vessel that is used to hold unfinished wine. Lees consist mostly of spent yeast and whatever bits of grapes survived pressing, plus insoluble tartrates. Coarse lees are usually called gross lees; finer particulate matter is usually called fine lees. Winemakers who send new wine to barrel immediately after pressing and without settling often say that their wine "goes to barrel dirty," meaning that gross lees are still present. Some winemakers also stir the lees while the wine is in barrel to eliminate reduction or encourage stabilization.

lieu-dit: In France, a *lieu-dit* is any spot in the countryside—outside the boundaries of a town or village—known by a persistent and widely accepted name. Burgundy is awash in *lieux-dits,* many of which have given their names to vineyards. Some *lieux-dits* are now used as vineyard names in their own right, particularly among *premier cru* vineyards. Other *lieux-dits* are denominated spots within the surface area set aside for various village wines, and wines from those spots are entitled to be labeled with the name of the village and the name of the *lieu-dit,* creating more granularity in Burgundy's complex naming scheme for wines.

malolactic fermentation: Usually described as a secondary fermentation, it produces no alcohol and may be more easily understood as a natural deacidification of newly made wine. Essentially, malolactic bacteria transform malic (apple) acid, which is tart, into lactic (milk) acid, which is softer. Malolactic transformation can begin during the vatting (see below) or be delayed, naturally or by intervention, until the pressed wine is settled and barreled. Most red wines, including pinot noir, are improved by malolactic fermentation.

mesoclimate; microclimate: The differences among *climate, mesoclimate,* and *microclimate* are a little fuzzy, and all three terms are frequently misused in common speech about winegrowing. Properly, *climate* applies to the temperature and weather conditions affecting a region, *mesoclimate* to an individual vineyard or cluster of vineyards that lie essentially cheek by jowl, and *microclimate* to the circumstances surrounding an individual vine.

must: The English term for the slurry of grapes, juice, yeast, and detritus, partially or completely unfermented, which is the precursor to wine. Must is the contents of each fermentor until fermentation is complete and pressing occurs.

négociant: One of many French terms for a wine merchant. In Burgundy, the *négociants* are well-established firms based primarily in Beaune and Nuits-Saint-Georges whose essential business is to buy grapes or partially made wine from multiple independent growers, and then to create blends of village and regional wines. As more growers finish and bottle their own wines, however, *négociants* have responded by acquiring vineyards of their own, and a number of grower-winemakers have begun to function as *négociants* for their immediate friends and neighbors, making it increasingly difficult to determine who is, and who is not, a *négociant.* Conventionally, about 100 firms in Burgundy are accepted as Les Maisons de négoce.

own-rooted vines: See graft.

phenology: Properly, the science of plant development. In common parlance, however, *phenology* is used interchangeably with *phenological development,* which is the timing of various benchmarks in the annual growth cycle of the vine (see *bloom; budbreak; veraison*).

pièce: the common name for the 228-liter barrel used almost universally in Burgundy, traditionally both for *élevage* and transport. A *pièce* is a tiny bit smaller and a bit squatter in shape than the standard Bordelais barrel, which is called a *barrique.*

Pierce's disease: A bacterial disease affecting grapevines, spread by small insects called sharpshooters. Epidemic in California since the end of the nineteenth century, Pierce's was first called Anaheim disease, for the part of Southern California it first affected. More recent outbreaks of Pierce's virtually eliminated viticulture in the inland areas south of Los Angeles and destroyed several vineyards in the Santa Cruz Mountains. Pinot noir, alas, seems to be particularly susceptible to Pierce's.

pigeage; pige: Pigeage is French for punchdown (see *pumpover; punchdown,* below). A *pige* is any tool used in punching down.

premier cru: See *grand cru.*

press: At the end of primary fermentation, new red wine is pressed to separate the juice from the detritus of fermentation, including stems, seeds, skins, and spent yeast. Juice that separates from detritus on its own is called *free-run juice.* The rest of the salvageable juice is called the *press fraction, press juice,* or *press lots.* Juice that can be separated with only light pressing is called a *light-press fraction*; juice that separates only with stronger pressure is called the *hard-press fraction.* Unsurprisingly, free-run juice is the most elegant fraction of the new wine, followed by the light-press fraction. The hard-press fraction is rarely used in high quality wine. Most presses in use today for fine wine are versions of the so-called basket press, used since medieval times, which operates on the same principle as a French press coffee maker except that the cylindrical container is perforated so that the juice escapes into a waiting tray; or a bladder press, which is a basket press turned on its side is fitted with an internal airbag. When the bag is inflated, the juice is squeezed through a perforated cylinder into the waiting tray.

pumpover; punchdown: Two techniques for cap management during fermentation (see *cap,* above). In a pumpover, a pump is used to withdraw juice from beneath the cap and spray it back on top, keeping the cap wet and maintaining contact between juice and skins. If this process is modified so that the entire fermentor is drained "dry" by withdrawing all the juice through a valve in the tank bottom, and the juice is then held in a separate vessel before being returned to the original tank on top of the cap, the process is called *rack and return, drain-and-return,* or *délastage.* In a punchdown, human hands or feet, a simple tamping tool, or a mechanically assisted device are used to push the cap down into the juice. Cap management by punchdowns is also called *plunging.* See *pige* and *pigeage.* Generally, pinot makers on both sides of the Atlantic believe that some form of punchdown is the gentlest and best way to work with pinot noir, but as the text makes clear, some makers dissent from this consensus.

racking: Moving wine from one container to another—barrel to tank, barrel to barrel, and so forth. Because pinot noir oxidizes easily and is easily bruised by rough handling, racking is usually minimized. Nevertheless, at least one racking is usually required before bottling, and racking is the usual remedy for barrel lots that develop funky smells because of very limited contact with air.

reserve: The antecedent terms in French, Italian, and Spanish—*réserve, reserva,* and *riserva*—have some special meanings, but the English term is unregulated and essentially meaningless. Generally, producers use it to identify some form of bottling (see *cuvée,* above) that is special or that the producer would like the consumer to construe as special. *Reserve quality* is used by some producers to describe wines superior to regular, estate, or appellation bottlings.

resident yeast: Yeasts are single-celled organisms belonging to several genera that live in vineyards, wineries, and other places where grapes or wines are handled. Contrary to popular belief, they do not cling to grape skins, but are airborne. These naturally occurring organisms are variously described as *wild yeast, native yeast, ambient yeast, natural yeast,* and *resident yeast.* Such yeasts are an alternative, in fermentations, to cultured, inoculated, or laboratory yeasts, all of which belong to the genus *Saccharomyces.*

saignée: See bleeding.

scion; scion material: The varietally significant part of a vine plant (see *grafts,* above).

second-crop fruit: After the main flowering and fruit set take place, usually around the beginning of summer, vines sometimes set additional clusters on what viticulturists call lateral shoots. Varieties differ in their propensity to set such clusters; pinot noir's propensity is high. Generally, second-crop fruit competes with first-crop for nutrients, potentially lessening the quality of the latter; it also ripens later, creating the potential for unripe fruit to find its way into picking bins at harvesttime. For these reasons, second-crop fruit is usually removed from the vines well before harvest and discarded or is carefully separated from harvested fruit on the crushpad.

settling: At the end of the vatting, the process of separating red wine from its lees often involves a period of time during which the runoff and pressed wine are held in a tank until some additional solids fall to the bottom and can be eliminated. Wines that are made with no settling step, or with only a short one, are said to go "dirty" to barrel. Winemakers disagree about the merits and demerits of settling.

spinning cone: A technology that relies on a combination of centrifugal force, a vacuum environment, and repeated evaporations and condensations to remove relatively volatile elements from wine. It has several applications in winemaking but is used most commonly to reduce the alcoholic strength of wine that has been made from very ripe grapes. Reverse osmosis is an alternative technique used to achieve the same end.

terroir: A French word with the basic meaning of "rural environment that has some form or degree of cultural impact," *terroir* is used by nearly everyone associated with wine to denote all the physical properties of a site where wine grapes are grown. Soil, slope, orientation, microclimate, and exposure are all elements of *terroir.*

tiling: A change in the color of red wine as it matures: generally, the change from the youthful hues variously described as black-red, ruby, garnet, crimson, and vermilion to colors more commonly associated with clay roof tiles and terra cotta pots. Tiling is a natural evolution in red wines and can occur anywhere between five and ten years after the vintage, but many wines evolve slowly and show no signs of tiling until they are much older.

toast: The process of forming wooden staves into barrels usually involves heating them over some kind of open fire. The fire chars the inside surface of each stave, creating "toast." In recent decades, as the taste for toast has increased, coopers have produced barrels with differing levels of toast, from light to heavy. Winemakers may specify the level of toast they desire when ordering barrels from most cooperages. Toast levels, in combination with the source of the wood and other factors, affect the flavor of the finished wine. Heavier toast levels are often associated with charred, smoky flavors.

trellis systems; trellising: Various configurations of upright posts and horizontal wires designed to support grapevines during the growing season. Trellis systems are adapted to particular vine training systems. In North America, vineyards planted before about 1980 typically involved rudimentary trellis systems, and the vines were said to "sprawl." New vineyards, at least for pinot noir, are usually trellised to support vertical vine training, especially the version known as vertical shoot positioning (VSP), which is the antithesis of sprawl. Most viticulturists believe that VSP is well adapted to pinot noir and tends to maximize the grower's control over canopy management, sunlight penetration to individual grape clusters, and related parameters.

tri; tris: A French word that denotes the result of sorting things into groups. In viticulture it is used to describe the process of picking grapes in successive passes through the vineyard, looking each time only for those grape clusters that display a predefined degree of ripeness. In French, a sorting table, used in wineries to separate grapes from leaves or to identify and discard unripe or overripe fruit, is called a *table de tri.*

TTB (Alcohol and Tobacco Tax and Trade Bureau): Successor (in 2003) to the ATF or BATF (Bureau of Alcohol, Tobacco, and Firearms). This agency, within the United States Department of the Treasury, interprets and enforces federal laws about wine. The TTB approves all wine labels and administers AVA designations, among other things. The change of name from ATF to TTB reflects the reassignment of authority for firearms to the new Department of Homeland Security.

UCD numbers: Since the 1940s, successive organizations housed at the University of California Davis have maintained a registry of grape varieties and subvarietal selections, each of which is numbered. In principle, this is an unambiguous way to identify the various clones and selections of grape varieties (e.g., UCD [Pinot Noir] 1A). UCD 1A can also be rendered as FPMS 1A (see *FPS*, above), but since the name of the unit maintaining the registry has changed over time, *UCD* is the preferred designation.

vatting: Generally, *vatting* refers to the active phase of red winemaking, beginning when the picked grapes are placed in a fermentation vessel and ending when the newly made wine is separated from its lees. In this sense, *vatting* is identical to the French *cuvaison*. However, *vatting* is sometimes also used as a synonym for *cuvée* when the latter is used to denote the contents of a single *cuve* or fermentor.

veraison: The third significant marker in the annual growth cycle of the grapevine, veraison (French *véraison*) is said to occur when the grapes change color, from green to yellow-green in the case of white varieties, and from green to some shade of red-black in the case of red varieties like pinot noir. Color change is associated with a simultaneous increase in berry size and sugar content and a decrease in acidity. At veraison, harvest is usually four to seven weeks away.

vine farming: Although many basics have not changed for centuries, no aspect of wine-growing has evolved more dramatically in the last 130 years than vineyard design and cultivation practices. Vines are now universally planted in neat rows with defined spacing between rows and vines. Each vine plant is trellised and pruned in the off-season following named protocols (e.g., cane-pruned), and both its leaves and its fruit are carefully managed during the growing season. Green harvesting (also called dropping fruit) is used to control the total weight of fruit the vineyard is permitted to produce and to help ensure that all surviving grape clusters ripen evenly and simultaneously. This is sometimes called vine-by-vine farming. Canopy management refers to the removal of some leaves that shade grape clusters to achieve more, or less, direct exposure of the grapes to sunlight. Generally, winegrowers associate too much shade with green, underripe flavors.

vineyard-designate: Denotes a wine made entirely from grapes grown in one vineyard and labeled as such. The term is generally interchangeable with single-vineyard wine, although the latter may be used for wines that are from a single vineyard de facto but do not mention the vineyard name as part of the wine's name. There are also so-called block-designates, in which all the fruit was grown in one block of one vineyard.

vinifera: The species of the genus *Vitis* to which most varieties of wine grapes belong, though wine is sometimes also made from other species of the genus. Because vinifera is not native to North America, vinifera varieties have sometimes been known here as *European varieties*. In this sense, they are differentiated from *native varieties* and from *hybrids*, which are crosses of vinifera and nonvinifera varieties.

Note: Boldfaced page numbers denote the main discussions of indexed terms. Personal names and vineyard names are indexed comprehensively throughout the book, but the names of individual vineyard blocks are usually not indexed unless they are used on wine labels. Corporate names are indexed where the reference is substantive. The proper names of grape varieties other than pinot noir are indexed, but variant names are not. When a winery's name is eponymous, references to the personal name (or names) and the winery usually are combined and listed under the personal name. Wine brands and proprietary wine names that are not also corporate or vineyard names normally are not indexed. Only the main occurrences of viticultural and winemaking terminology are indexed. Geographical names (other than vineyard names) are indexed only when they refer to pinot-producing regions in North America, and then selectively. Other geographical names, including the names of continents, countries, counties, provinces, départements, cantons, rivers, lakes, cities, and towns are not indexed—with only a few exceptions. Historical expressions (e.g., French Revolution, Middle Ages, Prohibition, and Repeal) are not indexed. Terms that occur constantly because of the book's subject matter, like pinot noir and its paranyms, Burgundy, Bourgogne, Côte d'Or, Côte de Nuits, and vinifera, are not indexed. Neither are the names of coopers, or the forests from which they source stave wood.

Karlsen, Dan, 86, 87, 116, 120
Kautzner, Don, 10
Kazmer & Blaise, **216–17**
Keefer, Marcy/Keefer Vineyard/Keefer Ranch, 153, 154, 171, 172, 287, 310, 374
Keller, Ana, 218
Keller, Arturo/Keller Estate Winery, **217–19**
Kemp, Carroll, 309
Kendall-Jackson Vineyard Estates, 74, 110
Kent Barrie Vineyard, 106
Kenwood, 1
Kickon (vineyard), 202
Kimiji, Emmanuel, 264–65
King, Anthony, 2, 4, 239
King Estate, 409
Kingston Family Vineyards, 34–35
Kiplinger, Helen, 166
Kircher (vineyard), 125, 222
Kiser (vineyard), 99
Kistler, Steve/Kistler Vineyards, 160, 409
Klaffke, Forrest, 399
Klassen, Tom, 116
Klein, Jim, 273
Klein, Tom, 326
Klindt (vineyard), 191
Klopp Ranch (vineyard), 260, 261, 262
Knight's Gambit Vineyard, 210
The Knoll (vineyard), 204, 205
Knudsen, Cal/Knudsen Vineyard, 27, 28, 103, **140–41**
Kobrand Corporation, 120–21
Koplen Vineyard, 225
Kosta Browne, 33, **224–26**
Kosta, Dan, 224–26
Kosuge, Byron/B. Kosuge Wines, **33–34**, 264, 265, 332
Krausmann, Lynn, 402
Kruse Vineyard, 358, 359
Kurtzman, Ed, 32, 33, 166, 170, 380
Kynsi Winery, 371

L

La Bête, 18
La Bohème Vineyard, 137–38
Lachini, Ron and Marianne/Lachini Vineyards, **229–30**, 352
La Colina, 20, 385
La Colline Vineyard, 38
La Crema Viñera, 226
La Crema Winery, 67, **226–27**
Lacroute, Bernard, 397–98
La Cruz (vineyard), 218, 219, 380, 381

La Encantada (vineyard), 12, 202
Laetitia Vineyard and Winery, 30, 38, 72, **230–32**, 377
La Follette, Greg, 112, 113, 129, 160, 186, 243, 373–76
Laird Estate, 374, 375, 376
Laird Family Winery, 166
Lambert Bridge, 261
Lambrix, Ginny, 112
Landmark Vineyards, 218
Lange, Don, Wendy and Jessie/Lange Estate Winery, **234–36**
La Petit Etoile (vineyard), 88
La Ribera Ranch, 203
La Rinconada (vineyard), 335
La Rocaille (vineyard), 120–21
La Rochelle Winery, **227–29**
Las Alturas (vineyard), 42
Las Amigas Vineyard, 2
Las Brisas (vineyard), 54, 252, 253, 254
Las Lomas (vineyard), 252
La Tâche, 25
Lato, Paul/Paul Lato Wines, **291–92**
Laughlin (vineyard), 227
Laumann, Eric, 134
Laurel (vineyard), 20
Laurent Perrier, 208
La Viña Vineyard, 220
Lazy Creek Vineyard, 280
Lazy River Vineyard, 188, **236–37**, 280, 300
Le Bon Climat (vineyard), 30, 31
Lee, Adam and Dianna, 316
Lee, Daniel Morgan and Donna, 265–67
Lee, Ira/Lee Vineyard, 2, 331, 333, 334
Legan Vineyard, 95
Legorreta, Ricardo, 218
Leland (vineyard), 141–42
Lemelson, Eric/Lemelson Vineyards, 5, 46, 188, **237–39**
Lemon, Ted and Heidi, 128, 218, 219, 241–43
Le Musigny, 25
Le Puits Sec (vineyard), 147–50
Leras Family Vineyard, 281
Lett, David and Jason, xxviii, 150–53
Leveque, Steven, 318
Lincourt Vineyards, 164–65
Lindleys' Knoll (vineyard), 108
Lindsay Vineyard, 58, 165, 290, 291
Lingenfelder, Mark, 65, 355
Lion Valley Vineyards, 185
Little Hill (block), 324
Litton Estate (vineyard), 401
Littorai Wines, 199, **241–43**

West, Mark, 332
Westrey Wine Company, 76, **392–93**
Wetlaufer, John, 153
Wheeler, Jeff, 272
Whetstone Wine Cellars, 409
Whistling Ridge (vineyard), 222, 283, 352
Whitcraft, Chris/Whitcraft Winery, **393–95**
White, Al, 203
Whitehall Lane Vineyards, 108
White Rose Vineyard, 362, 363, **395–96**
Whitford Cellars, 16
Whybra Vineyard, 46
Widdoes (vineyard), 80, 131, 328
Wierenga, Margi Williams, 65–66
Wildcat Mountain Vineyard, 369, 370
Wild Horse Winery and Vineyards, 68, 72, 155, **395–97**
Wildrose (vineyard), 128
Wiley Vineyard, 99
Wilkes, Jeff, 376
Willakenzie Estate Winery, **397**
Willamette Valley Vineyards, 45, 72, **398–400**
Williams, Burt, 65, 270, 276, 281, 376, 394, **400–4**
Williamson, Van, 181
Williams Selyem, xxix, 65, 96–97, 196, 199, 276, 293, 323, 400–4
William Wesley (vineyard), 139–40
Wilson, Tim, 47
Wilson Vineyard, 80
Windhill (vineyard), 137–38, 188
Wind Ridge (vineyard), 89
Windsor Gardens (vineyard), 260, 261
Windsor Oaks Vineyard, 282
Windsor Vineyards, 207
Windy Oaks Estate, **404–5**
Winery Hill (vineyard), 125
Winery Lake Vineyard, 2, 3, 226, 317, 382
The Wine Advocate (magazine), 362
Wine & Spirits (magazine): 2007 tasting, xxxiv; annual restaurant wine sales, xxx; list of pinot producers, xiv
Wine Spectator (magazine): 2005 tasting, xxxiv; award for 2003 Oregon pinot, 189; most exciting wines for 2006, 224; tasting coordinator for, 99

Wines & Vines (magazine), interview with Tim Mondavi, 317
Wine World Estates. See Foster's Wine Estates Americas
Winter's Hill Vineyard, 395
Wirtz, David, 311
Witness Tree Vineyard, 409
Wolff (vineyard), 364
Wolfspierre Vineyard, 214, 215
Wong, Vanessa, 200, 293, 298
Woodward, Philip, 37, 133–35
Wright, Joe, 45
Wright, Ken/Ken Wright Cellars, 40, 76, 124, 158, **221–24**, 280–81
Wright, Scott Paul, 343
Wyeast (vineyard), 352

Y

Yamhill Springs (vineyard), 20, 308
Yamhill Valley Vineyards, 6, 81, 158, **405–7**
Yamhill Vineyards, 235
Yost, Norman, 162–64
Youngberg Hills Vineyard, 280

Z

Zaca Mesa Winery, 29
Zarif, Nebil, 231
ZD Winery, 74
Zellerbach, James D., 192
Zeller, Scott, 42, 96, 314
Zenith Vineyards, 362
Zepaltas Wines, 218
Zilkha, Selim, 231
zinfandel, 65, 71, 105, 110, 111, 115, 193, 213, 270, 281, 306, 336, 352, 400
Zio Tony Vineyard, 310
Zotovich, 58